The PETER KROPOTKIN Collection

The PETER KROPOTKIN *Collection*

- Fields, Factories, and Workshops
- Mutual Aid • The Conquest of Bread
- The Place of Anarchism in Socialistic Evolution

ISBN: 978-1-6673-0681-0 paperback
ISBN: 978-1-6673-0682-7 hardcover

Table of Contents

Fields, Factories, and Workshops 7

Mutual Aid 227

The Conquest of Bread 533

The Place of Anarchism in Socialistic Evolution 785

Contents

Fields, Factories, and Workshops

Preface 11
CHAPTER 1: The Decentralisation of Industries 15
CHAPTER 2: The Decentralisation of Industries, Part 2 35
CHAPTER III: The Possibilities of Agriculture 52
CHAPTER IV: The Possibilities of Agriculture, Part 2 68
CHAPTER V: The Possibilities of Agriculture, Part 3 85
CHAPTER VI: Small Industries and Industrial Villages 114
CHAPTER VII: Small Industries and Industrial Villages, Part 2 168
CHAPTER VIII: Brain Work and Manual Work 190
CHAPTER IX: Conclusion 218

Mutual Aid

INTRODUCTION 229
CHAPTER I 240
CHAPTER II 269
CHAPTER III 311
CHAPTER IV 350
CHAPTER V 386
CHAPTER VI 420
CHAPTER VII 456
CHAPTER VIII 494
CONCLUSION 524

The Conquest of Bread

- THE BOOK 536
- PREFACE 538
- CHAPTER I. Our Riches 548
- CHAPTER II. Well-Being for All 558
- CHAPTER III. Anarchist Communism 570
- CHAPTER IV. Expropriation 582
- CHAPTER V. Food 597
- CHAPTER VI. Dwellings 626
- CHAPTER VII. Clothing 638
- CHAPTER VIII. Ways And Means 642
- CHAPTER IX. The Need For Luxury 650
- CHAPTER X. Agreeable Work 667
- CHAPTER XI. Free Agreement 677
- CHAPTER XII. Objections 694
- CHAPTER XIII. The Collectivist Wages System ... 714
- CHAPTER XIV. Consumption And Production ... 732
- CHAPTER XV. The Division Of Labour 740
- CHAPTER XVI. The Decentralization Of Industry ... 744
- CHAPTER XVII. Agriculture 756
- Notes 780

The Place of Anarchism in Socialistic Evolution 785

FIELDS, FACTORIES, AND WORKSHOPS

By
PETER KROPOTKIN

Contents

Preface 11

Chapter 1: The Decentralisation of Industries 15

Chapter 2: The Decentralisation of Industries, Part 2 35

Chapter III: The Possibilities of Agriculture 52

Chapter IV: The Possibilities of Agriculture, Part 2 68

Chapter V: The Possibilities of Agriculture, Part 3 85

Chapter VI: Small Industries and Industrial Villages 114

Chapter VII: Small Industries and Industrial Villages, Part 2 168

Chapter VIII: Brain Work and Manual Work 190

Chapter IX: Conclusion 218

Fields, Factories, and Workshops

Preface

FOURTEEN years have passed since the first edition of this book was published, and in revising it for this new edition I found at my disposal an immense mass of new materials, statistical and descriptive, and a great number of new works dealing with the different subjects that are treated in this book. I have thus had an excellent opportunity to verify how far the previsions that I had formulated when I first wrote this book have been confirmed by the subsequent economical evolution of the different nations.

This verification permits me to affirm that the economical tendencies that I had ventured to foreshadow then have only become more and more definite since. Everywhere we see the same decentralisation of industries going on, new nations continually entering the ranks of those which manufacture for the world market. Each of these new-comers endeavours to develop, and succeeds in developing, on its own territory the principal industries, and thus frees itself from being exploited by other nations, more advanced in their technical evolution. All nations have made a remarkable progress in this direction, as will be seen from the new data that are given in this book.

On the other hand, one sees, with all the great industrial nations, the growing tendency and need of developing at home a more intensive agricultural productivity, either by improving the now existing methods of extensive agriculture, by means of small holdings, "inner colonisation," agricultural education, and co-operative work, or by introducing different new branches of intensive agriculture. This country is especially offering us at this moment a most instructive example of a movement in the said direction. And this movement will certainly result, not only in a much-needed increase of the productive forces of the nation, which will contribute to free it from the international speculators in food produce, but also in awakening in the nation a fuller appreciation of the immense value of its soil, and the desire of repairing the error that has been committed in leaving it in the hands of great land-owners and of those who find it now more advantageous to rent the land to be turned into shooting preserves. The different steps that are being taken now for raising English agriculture and for obtaining from the land a much greater amount of produce are briefly indicated in Chapter V.

It is especially in revising the chapters dealing with the small industries that I had to incorporate the results of a great number of new researches. In so doing I was enabled to show that the growth of an infinite variety of small enterprises by the side of the very great centralised concerns is not showing any signs of abatement. On the contrary, the distribution of electrical motive power has given them a new impulse. In those places where water power was utilized for distributing electric power in the villages, and in those cities where the machinery used for producing electric light during the night hours was utilised for supplying motive power during the day, the small industries are taking a new development.

In this domain I am enabled to add to the present edition the interesting results of a work about the small industries in the United Kingdom that I made in 1900. Such a work was only possible when the British Factory Inspectors had published (in 1898, in virtue of the Factories Act of 1895) their first reports, from which I could determine the hitherto unknown numerical relations between the great and the small industries in the United Kingdom.

Until then no figures whatever as regards the distribution of operatives in the large and small factories and workshops of Great Britain were available; so that when economists spoke of the "unavoidable" death of the small industries they merely expressed hypotheses based upon a limited number of observations, which were chiefly made upon part of the textile industry and metallurgy. Only after Mr. Whitelegge had published the first figures from which reliable conclusions could be drawn was it possible to see how little such wide-reaching conclusions were confirmed by realities. In this country, as everywhere the small industries continue to exist, and new ones continue to appear as a necessary growth, in many important branches of national production, by the side of the very great factories and huge centralised works. So I add to the chapter on small industries a summary of the work that I had published in the Nineteenth Century upon this subject.

As regards France, the most interesting observations made by M. Araouin Dumazet during his many years' travels all over the country give me the possibility of showing the remarkable development of rural industries, and the advantages which were taken from them for recent developments in agriculture and horticulture. Besides, the publication of the statistical results of the French industrial census of 1896 permits me to give now, for France, most remarkable numerical data, showing the real relative importance of the great and the small industries.

And finally, the recent publication of the result of the third industrial census made in Germany in 1907 gives me the data for showing how the German small industries have been keeping their ground for the last twenty-five years a subject which I could touch only in a general way in the first editions. The results of this census, compared with the two preceding ones, as also some of the conclusions arrived at by competent German writers, are indicated in the Appendix. So also the results recently arrived at in Switzerland concerning its home industries.

As to the need, generally felt at this moment, of an education which would combine a wide scientific instruction with a sound knowledge of manual work a question which I treat in the last chapter--it can be said that this cause has already been won in this country during the last twenty years. The principle is generally recognised by this time, although most nations, impoverished as they are by their armaments, are much too slow in applying the principle in life.

BRIGHTON, October, 1912. P. KROPOTKIN.

Chapter 1 - The Decentralisation of Industries

WHO does not remember the remarkable chapter by which Adam Smith opens his inquiry into the nature and causes of the wealth of nations? Even those of our contemporary economists who seldom revert to the works of the father of political economy, and often forget the ideas which inspired them, know that chapter almost by heart, so often has it been copied and recopied since. It has become an article of faith; and the economical history of the century which has elapsed since Adam Smith wrote has been, so to speak, an actual commentary upon it.

"Division of labour" was its watchword. And the division and subdivision--the permanent subdivision--of functions has been pushed so far as to divide humanity into castes which are almost as firmly established as those of old India. We have, first, the broad division into producers and consumers: little-consuming producers on the one hand, little-producing consumers on the other hand. Then, amidst the former, a series of further subdivisions: the manual worker and the intellectual worker, sharply separated from one another to the detriment of both; the agricultural labourers and the workers in the manufacture; and, amidst the mass of the latter, numberless subdivisions again--so minute, indeed, that the modern ideal of a workman seems to be a man or a woman, or even a girl or a boy, without the knowledge of any handicraft, without any conception whatever of the industry he or she is employed in, who is only capable of making all day long and for a whole life the same infinitesimal part of something: who from the age of thirteen to that of sixty pushes the coal cart at a given spot of the mine or makes the spring of a penknife, or "the eighteenth part of a pin." Mere servants to some machine of a given description; mere flesh-and-bone parts of some immense machinery; having no idea how and why the machinery performs its rhythmical movements.

Skilled artisanship is being swept away as a survival of a past condemned to disappear. The artist who formerly found aesthetic enjoyment in the work of his hands is substituted by the human slave of an iron slave. Nay, even the agricultural labourer, who formerly used to find a relief from the hardships of his life in the home of his ancestors--the future home of his children--in his love of the field and in a keen intercourse with nature, even he has been doomed to disappear for the sake of division of labour. He is an anachronism, we are told; he must be substituted, in a Bonanza farm, by an occasional servant hired for the summer, and discharged as the autumn comes: a tramp who will never again see the field he has harvested once in his life. "An affair of a few years," the economists say, "to reform agriculture in accordance with the true principles of division of labour and modern industrial organisation."

Dazzled with the results obtained by a century of marvelous inventions, especially in England, our economists and political men went still farther in their dreams of division of labour. They proclaimed the necessity of dividing the whole of humanity into national workshops having each of them its own speciality. We were taught, for instance, that Hungary and Russia are predestined by nature to grow corn in order to feed the manufacturing countries; that Britain had to provide the worldmarket with cottons, iron goods, and coal; Belgium with woollen cloth; and so on. Nay, within each nation, each region had to have its own speciality. So it has been for some time since; so it ought to remain. Fortunes have been made in this way, and will continue to be made in the same way. It being proclaimed that the wealth of nations is measured by the amount of profits made by the few, and that the largest profits are made by means of a specialisation of labour, the question was not conceived to exist as to whether human beings would always submit to such a specialisation; whether nations could be specialised like isolated workmen. The theory was good for to-day--why should we care for to-morrow. To-morrow might bring its own theory!

And so it did. The narrow conception of life which consisted in thinking that profits are the only leading motive of human society, and the stubborn view which supposes that what has existed yesterday would last for ever, proved in disaccordance with the tendencies of human life; and life took another direction. Nobody will deny the high pitch of production which may be attained by specialisation. But, precisely in proportion as the work required from the individual in modern production becomes simpler and easier to be learned, and, therefore, also more monotonous and wearisome--the requirements of the individual for varying his work, for exercising all his capacities, become more and more prominent. Humanity perceives that there is no advantage for the community in riveting a human being for all his life to a given spot, in a workshop or a mine; no gain in depriving him of such work as would bring him into free intercourse with nature, make of him a conscious part of the grand whole, a partner in the highest enjoyments of science and art, of free work and creation.

Nations, too, refuse to be specialised. Each nation is a compound aggregate of tastes and inclinations, of wants and resources, of capacities and inventive powers. The territory occupied by each nation is in its turn a most varied texture of soils and climates, of hills and valleys, of slopes leading to a still greater variety of territories and races. Variety is the distinctive feature, both of the territory and its inhabitants; and that variety implies a variety of occupations. Agriculture calls manufactures into existence, and manufactures support agriculture. Both are inseparable: and the combination, the integration of both brings about the grandest results. In proportion as technical knowledge becomes everybody's virtual domain, in proportion as it becomes international, and can be concealed no longer, each nation acquires the possibility of applying the whole variety of her energies to the whole variety of industrial and agricultural pursuits. Knowledge ignores artificial political boundaries. So also do the industries; and the present tendency of humanity is to have the greatest possible variety of industries gathered in each country, in each separate region, side by side with agriculture. The needs of human agglomerations correspond thus to the needs of the individual; and while a temporary division of functions remains the surest guarantee of success in each separate undertaking, the permanent division is doomed to disappear, and to be substituted by a variety of pursuits--intellectual, industrial, and agricultural--corresponding to the different capacities of the individual, as well as to the variety of capacities within every human aggregate.

When we thus revert from the scholastics of our text-books, and examine human life as a whole, we soon discover that, while all the benefits of a temporary division of labour must be maintained, it is high time to claim those of the integration of labour. Political economy has hitherto insisted chiefly upon division. We proclaim integration; and we maintain that the ideal of society--that is, the state towards which society is already marching--is a society of integrated, combined labour. A society where each individual is a producer of both manual and intellectual work; where each able-bodied human being is a worker, and where each worker works both in the field and the industrial workshop; where every aggregation of individuals, large enough to dispose of a certain variety of natural resources--it may be a nation, or rather a region--produces and itself consumes most of its own agricultural and manufactured produce.

Of course, as long as society remains organised so as to permit the owners of the land and capital to appropriate for themselves, under the protection of the State and historical rights, the yearly surplus of human production, no such change can be thoroughly accomplished. But the present industrial system, based upon a permanent specialisation of functions, already bears in itself the germs of its proper ruin. The industrial crises, which grow more acute and protracted, and are rendered still worse and still more acute by the armaments and wars implied by the present system, are rendering its maintenance more and more difficult. Moreover, the workers plainly manifest their intention to support no longer patiently the misery occasioned by each crisis. And each crisis accelerates the day when the present institutions of individual property and production will be shaken to their foundations with such internal struggles as will depend upon the more or less good sense of the now privileged classes.

But we maintain also that any socialist attempt at remodeling the present relations between Capital and Labour will be a failure, if it does not take into account the above tendencies towards integration. These tendencies have not yet received, in our opinion, due attention from the different socialist schools-- but they must. A reorganised society will have to abandon the fallacy of nations specialized for the production of either agricultural or manufactured produce. It will have to rely on itself for the production of food and many, if not most, of the raw materials; it must find the best means of combining agriculture with manufacture--the work in the field with a decentralised industry; and it will have to provide for "integrated education," which education alone, by teaching both science and handicraft from earliest childhood, can give to society the men and women it really needs.

Each nation--her own agriculturist and manufacturer; each individual working in the field and in some industrial art; each individual combining scientific knowledge with the knowledge of a handicraft--such is, we affirm, the present tendency of civilised nations.

The prodigious growth of industries in Great Britain, and the simultaneous development of the international traffic which now permits the transport of raw materials and articles of food on a gigantic scale, have created the impression that a few nations of West Europe were destined to become the manufacturers of the world. They need only--it was argued--to supply the market with manufactured goods, and they will draw from all over the surface of the earth the food they cannot grow themselves, as well as the raw materials they need for their manufactures. The steadily increasing speed of trans-oceanic communications and the steadily increasing facilities of shipping have contributed to enforce the above impression. If we take the enthusiastic pictures of international traffic, drawn in such a masterly way by Neumann Spallart-- the statistician and almost the poet of the world-trade--we are inclined indeed to fall into ecstasy before the results achieved. "Why shall we grow corn, rear oxen and sheep, and cultivate orchards, go through the painful work of the labourer and the farmer, and anxiously watch the sky in fear of a bad crop, when we can get, with much less pain, mountains of corn from India, America, Hungary, or Russia, meat from New Zealand, vegetables from the Azores, apples from Canada, grapes from Malaga, and so on?" exclaim the West Europeans."Already now," they say, "our food consists, even in modest households, of produce gathered from all over the globe. Our cloth is made out of fibres grown and wool sheared in all parts of the world. The prairies of America and Australia; the mountains and steppes of Asia; the frozen wildernesses of the Arctic regions; the deserts of Africa and the depths of the oceans; the tropics and the lands of the midnight sun are our tributaries. All races of men contribute their share in supplying us with our staple food and luxuries, with plain clothing and fancy dress, while we are sending them in exchange the produce of our higher intelligence, our technical knowledge, our powerful industrial and commercial organising capacities! Is it not a grand sight, this busy and intricate exchange of produce all over the earth which has suddenly grown up within a few years?"

Grand it may be, but is it not a mere nightmare? Is it necessary? At what cost has it been obtained, and how long will it last?

Let us turn a hundred years back. France lay bleeding at the end of the Napoleonic wars. Her young industry, which had begun to grow by the end of the 18th century, was crushed down. Germany, Italy were powerless in the industrial field. The armies of the great Republic had struck a mortal blow to serfdom on the Continent; but with the return of reaction efforts were made to revive the decaying institution, and serfdom meant no industry worth speaking of. The terrible wars between France and England, which wars are often explained by merely political causes, had a much deeper meaning--an economical meaning. They were wars for the supremacy on the world market, wars against French industry and commerce, supported by a strong navy which France had begun to build--and Britain won the battle. She became supreme on the seas. Bordeaux was no more a rival to London; as to the French industries, they seemed to be killed in the bud. And, aided by the powerful impulse given to natural sciences and technology by a great era of inventions, finding no serious competitors in Europe, Britain began to develop her manufactures. To produce on a large scale in immense quantities became the watchword. The necessary human forces were at hand in the peasantry, partly driven by force from the land, partly attracted to the cities by high wages. The necessary machinery was created, and the British production of manufactured goods went on at a gigantic pace. In the course of less than seventy years--from 1810 to 1878--the output of coal grew from 10 to 133,000,000 tons; the imports of raw materials rose from 30 to 380,000,000 tons; and the exports of manufactured goods from 46 to 200,000,000 pounds. The tonnage of the commercial fleet was nearly trebled. Fifteen thousand miles of railways were built.

It is useless to repeat now at what a cost the above results were achieved. The terrible revelations of the parliamentary commissions of 1840-1842 as to the atrocious condition of the manufacturing classes, the tales of "cleared estates," and kidnapped children are still fresh in the memory. They will remain standing monuments for showing by what means the great industry was implanted in this country. But the accumulation of wealth in the hands of the privileged classes was going on at a speed never dreamed of before. The incredible riches which now astonish the foreigner in the private houses of England were accumulated during that period; the exceedingly expensive standard of life which makes a person considered rich on the Continent appear as only of modest means in Britain was introduced during that time. The taxed property alone doubled during the last thirty years of the above period, while, during the same years (1810 to 1878) no less than £1,112,000,000--nearly £2,000,000,000 by this time--was invested by English capitalists either in foreign industries or in foreign loans.1

But the monopoly of industrial production could not remain with England for ever. Neither industrial knowledge nor enterprise could be kept for ever as a privilege of these islands. Necessarily, fatally, they began to cross the Channel and spread over the Continent. The Great Revolution had created in France a numerous class of peasant proprietors, who enjoyed nearly half a century of a comparative well-being, or, at least, of a guaranteed labour. The ranks of homeless town workers increased slowly. But the middle-class revolution of 1789-1793 had already made a distinction between the peasant householders and the village proletaires, and, by favouring the former to the detriment of the latter, it compelled the labourers who had no household nor land to abandon their villages, and thus to form the first nucleus of working classes given up to the mercy of manufacturers. Moreover, the peasant-proprietors themselves, after having enjoyed a period of undeniable prosperity, began in their turn to feel the pressure of bad times, and their children were compelled to look for employment in manufactures. Wars and revolution had checked the growth of industry; but it began to grow again during the second half of our century; it developed, it improved; and now, notwithstanding the loss of Alsace, France is no longer the tributary to England for manufactured produce which she was sixty years ago. To-day her exports of manufactured goods are valued at nearly one-half of those of Great Britain, and two-thirds of them are textiles; while her imports of the same consist chiefly of the finer sorts of cotton and woollen yarn--partly reexported as stuffs--and a small quantity of woollen goods. For her own consumption France shows a decided tendency towards becoming entirely a self-supporting country, and for the sale of her manufactured goods she is tending to rely, not on her colonies, but especially on her own wealthy home market.[2]

Germany follows the same lines. During the last fifty years, and especially since the last war, her industry has undergone a thorough reorganisation. Her population having rapidly increased from forty to sixty millions, this increment went entirely to increase the urban population--without taking hands from agriculture--and in the cities it went to increase the population engaged in industry. Her industrial machinery has been thoroughly improved, and her new-born manufactures are supplied now with a machinery which mostly represents the last word of technical progress. She has plenty of workmen and technologists endowed with a superior technical and scientific education; and in an army of learned chemists, physicists and engineers her industry has a most powerful and intelligent aid, both for directly improving it and for spreading in the country serious scientific and technical knowledge. As a whole, Germany offers now the spectacle of a nation in a period of Aufschwung, of a sudden development, with all the forces of a new start in every domain of life. Fifty years ago she was a customer to England. Now she is already a competitor in the European and Asiatic markets, and at the present speedy rate of growth of her industries, her competition will soon be felt even more acutely than it is already felt.

At the same time the wave of industrial production, after having had its origin in the north-west of Europe, spreads towards the east and, south-east, always covering a wider circle. And, in proportion as it advances east, and penetrates into younger countries, it implants there all the improvements due to a century of mechanical and chemical inventions; it borrows from science all the help that science can give to industry; and it finds populations eager to grasp the last results of modern knowledge. The new manufactures of Germany begin where Manchester arrived after a century of experiments and gropings; and Russia begins where Manchester and Saxony have now reached. Russia, in her turn, tries to emancipate herself from her dependency upon Western Europe, and rapidly begins to manufacture all those goods she formerly used to import, either from Britain or from Germany.

Protective duties may, perhaps, sometimes help the birth of new industries: always at the expense of some other growing industries, and always checking the improvement of those which already exist; but the decentralisation of manufactures goes on with or without protective duties--I should even say, notwithstanding the protective duties. Austria, Hungary and Italy follow the same lines--they develop their home industries--

and even Spain and Servia are going to join the family of manufacturing nations. Nay, even India, even Brazil and Mexico, supported by English, French, and German capital and knowledge, begin to start home industries on their respective soils. Finally, a terrible competitor to all European manufacturing countries has grown up of late in the United States. In proportion as technical education spreads more and more widely, manufactures grow in the States; and they do grow at such a speed--an American speed--that in a very few years the now neutral markets will be invaded by American goods.

The monopoly of the first comers on the industrial field has ceased to exist. And it will exist no more, whatever may be the spasmodic efforts made to return to a state of things already belonging to the domain of history. New ways, new issues must be looked for: the past has lived, and it will live no more.

Before going farther, let me illustrate the march of industries towards the east by a few figures. And, to begin with, let me take the example of Russia. Not because I know it better, but because Russia is one of the latest comers on the industrial field. Fifty years ago she was considered as the ideal of an agricultural nation, doomed by nature itself to supply other nations with food, and to draw her manufactured goods from the west. So it was, indeed--but it is so no more.

In 1861--the year of the emancipation of the serfs--Russia and Poland had only 14,060 manufactories, which produced every year the value of 296,000,000 roubles (about £36,000,000). Twenty years later the number of establishments rose to 35,160, and their yearly production became nearly four times the above, i.e., 1,305,000,000 roubles (about £131,000,000); and in 1894, although the census left the smaller manufactures and all the industries which pay excise duties (sugar, spirits, matches) out of account, the aggregate production in the Empire reached already 1,759,000,000 roubles, i.e., £180,000,000. The most noteworthy feature of this increase is, that while the number of workmen employed in the manufactures has not even doubled since 1861 (it attained 1,555,000 in 1894, and 1,902,750 in 1910), the production per workman has more than trebled in the leading industries. The average was less than £70 per annum in 1861; it reaches now £219. The increase of production is thus chiefly due to the improvement of machinery.3

If we take, however, separate branches, and especially the textile industries and the machinery works, the progress appears still more striking. Thus, if we consider the eighteen years which preceded 1879 (when the import duties were increased by nearly 30 per cent. and a protective policy was definitely adopted), we find that even without protective duties the bulk of production in cottons increased three times, while the number of workers employed in that industry rose by only 26 per cent. The yearly production of each worker had thus grown from £45 to £117. During the next nine years (1880-1889) the yearly returns were more than doubled, attaining the respectable figure of £49,000,000 in money and 3,200,000 cwts. in bulk. Since that time, from 1890 to 1900, it has doubled once more, the quantity of raw cotton worked in the Russian factories having increased from 255,000 to 520,700 cwts., and the number of spindles having grown from 3,457,000 to 6,646,000 in 1900, and to 8,306,000 in 1910. It must also be remarked that, with a population of 165,000,000 inhabitants, the home market for Russian cottons is almost unlimited; while some cottons are also exported to Persia and Central Asia.4

True, that the finest sorts of yarn, as well as sewing cotton, have still to be imported. But Lancashire manufacturers will soon see to that; they now plant their mills in Russia. Two large mills for spinning the finest sorts of cotton yarn were opened in Russia in 1897, with the aid of English capital and English engineers, and a factory for making thin wire for cotton-carding has lately been opened at Moscow by a well-known Manchester manufacturer. Several more have followed since. Capital is international and, protection or no protection, it crosses the frontiers.

The same is true of woollens. In this branch Russia was for a certain time relatively backward. However, wool-combing, spinning and weaving mills, provided with the best modern plant, were built every year in Russia and Poland by English, German and Belgian millowners; so that now four-fifths of the ordinary wool, and as much of the finer sorts obtainable in Russia, are combed and spun at home--one fifth part only of each being sent abroad. The times when Russia was known as an exporter of raw wool are thus irretrievably gone.5

In machinery works no comparison can even be made between nowadays and 1861, or even 1870. Thanks to English and French engineers to begin with, and afterwards to technical progress within the country itself, Russia needs no longer to import any part of her railway plant. And as to agricultural machinery, we know, from several British Consular reports, that Russian reapers and ploughs successfully compete with the same implements of both American and English make. During the years 1880 to 1890, this branch of manufactures has largely developed in the Southern Urals (as a village industry, brought into existence by the Krasnoufimsk Technical School of the local District Council, or zemstvo), and especially on the plains sloping towards the Sea of Azov. About this last region Vice-Consul Green reported, in 1894, as follows: "Besides some eight or ten factories of importance," he wrote, "the whole of the consular district is now studded with small engineering works, engaged chiefly in the manufacture of agricultural machines and implements, most of them having their own foundries.... The town of Berdyansk," he added, "can now boast of the largest reaper manufactory in Europe, capable of turning out three thousand machines annually."6

Let me add that the above-mentioned figures, including only those manufactures which show a yearly return of more than £200, do not include the immense variety of domestic trades which also have considerably grown of late, side by side with the manufactures. The domestic industries--so characteristic of Russia, and so necessary under her climate--occupy now more than 7,500,000 peasants, and their aggregate production was estimated a few years ago at more than the aggregate production of all the manufactures. It exceeded £180,000,000 per annum. I shall have an occasion to return later on to this subject, so that I shall be sober of figures, and merely say that even in the chief manufacturing provinces of Russia round about Moscow domestic weaving--for the trade-- shows a yearly return of £4,500,000; and that even in Northern Caucasia, where the petty trades are of a recent origin, there are, in the peasants' houses, 45,000 looms showing a yearly production of £200,000.

As to the mining industries, notwithstanding over-protection, and notwithstanding the competition of fuelwood and naphtha,7 the output of the coal mines of Russia has doubled during the years 1896-1904, and in Poland it has increased fourfold.8 Nearly all steel, three-quarters of the iron, and two-thirds of the pig-iron used in Russia are home produce, and the eight Russian works for the manufacture of steel rails are strong enough to throw on the market over 10,000,000 cwts. of rails every year (10,068,000 cwts. in 1910).9

It is no wonder, therefore, that the imports of manufactured goods into Russia are so insignificant, and that since 1870--that is, nine years before the general increase of duties--the proportion of manufactured goods to the aggregate imports has been on a steady decrease. Manufactured goods make now only one-fifth of the imports, and only occasionally rise to one-third, as was the case in 1910, year of maximal imports. Besides, while the imports of Britain into Russia were valued at £16,300,000 in 1872, they were only £6,884,500 to £11,320,000 in the years 1894 to 1909. Out of them, manufactured goods were valued at a little more than £2,000,000 --the remainder being either articles of food or raw and half-manufactured goods (metals, yarn, and so on). They reached £15,300,000 in 1910-- a year of maximum, and consisted chiefly of machinery and coal. In fact, the imports of British home produce have declined in the course of ten years from £8,800,000 to £5,000,000, so as to reduce in 1910 the value of British manufactured goods imported into Russia to the following trifling items: machinery, £1,320,000; cottons and cotton yarn, £360,000; woollens and woollen yarn, £480,000; chemical produce, £476,000; and so on. But the depreciation of British goods imported into Russia is still more striking. Thus, in 1876 Russia imported 8,000,000 cwts. of British metals, and they were paid £6,000,000; but in 1884, although the same quantity was imported, the amount paid was only £3,400,000. And the same depreciation is seen for all imported goods, although not always in the same proportion.

It would be a gross error to imagine that the decline of foreign imports is mainly due to high protective duties. The decline of imports is much better explained by the growth of home industries. The protective duties have no doubt contributed (together with other causes) towards attracting German and English manufacturers to Poland and Russia. Lodz--the Manchester of Poland--is quite a German city, and the Russian trade directories are full of English and German names. English and German capitalists, English engineers and foremen, have planted within Russia the improved cotton manufactures of their mother countries; they are busy now in improving the woollen industries and the production of machinery; while Belgians have rapidly created a great iron industry in South Russia. There is now not the slightest doubt-- and this opinion is shared, not only by economists, but also by several Russian manufacturers --that a free-trade policy would not check the further growth of industries in Russia. It would only reduce the high profits of those manufacturers who do not improve their factories and chiefly rely upon cheap labour and long hours.

Moreover, as soon as Russia succeeds in obtaining more freedom, a further growth of her industries will immediately follow. Technical education--which, strange to say, was for a long time systematically suppressed by the Government--would rapidly grow and spread; and in a few years, with her natural resource and her laborious youth, which even now tries to combine workmanship with science, Russia would see her industrial powers increase tenfold. She fara da se in the industrial field. She will manufacture all she needs; and yet she will remain an agricultural nation.

At the present time only a little more than 1,500,000 men and women, out of the 112,000,000 strong population of European Russia, work in manufactures, and 7,500,000 combine agriculture with manufacturing. This figure may treble without Russia ceasing to be an agricultural nation; but if it be trebled, there will be no room for imported manufactured goods, because an agricultural country can produce them cheaper than those countries which live on imported food. Let us not forget that in the United Kingdom 1,087,200 persons, all taken, are employed in all the textile industries of England, Scotland, Ireland and Wales, and that only 300,000 out of them are males above eighteen years of age (311,000 in 1907); that these workpeople keep going 53,000,000 spindles and more than 700,000 looms in the cotton factories only; and that the yearly production of textiles during the last few years was so formidable that it represented a value of £200,000,000, and that the average value of textiles exported every year attained £136,257,500 in 1905-1910--to say nothing of the £163,400,000 reached in the extraordinary year of 1911.10

The same is still more true with regard to other European nations, much more advanced in their industrial development, and especially with regard to Germany. So much has been written about the competition which Germany offers to British trade, even in the British markets, and so much can be learned about it from a mere inspection of the London shops, that I need not enter into lengthy details. Several articles in reviews; the correspondence exchanged on the subject in The Daily Telegraph in August, 1886; numerous consular reports, regularly summed up in the leading newspapers, and still more impressive when consulted in originals; and, finally, political speeches, have familiarised the public opinion of this country with the importance and the powers of German competition.11 Moreover, the forces which German industry borrows from the technical training of her workmen, engineers and numerous scientific men, have been so often discussed by the promoters of technical education in England that the sudden growth of Germany as an industrial power can be denied no more.

Where half a century was required in olden times to develop an industry, a few years are sufficient now. In the year 1864 only 160,000 cwts. of raw cotton were imported into Germany, and only 16,000 cwts. of cotton goods were exported; cotton spinning and weaving were mostly insignificant home industries. Twenty years later the imports of raw cotton were already 3,600,000 cwts., and in another twenty years they rose to 7,400,000 cwts.; while the exports of cottons and yarn, which were valued at £3,600,000 in 1883, and £7,662,000 in 1893, attained £19,000,000 in 1905. A great industry was thus created in less than thirty years, and has been growing since. The necessary technical skill was developed, and at the present time Germany remains tributary to Lancashire for the finest sorts of yarn only. However, it is very probable that even this disadvantage will soon be equalised.12 Very fine spinning mills have lately been erected, and the emancipation from Liverpool, by means of a cotton exchange established at Bremen, is in fair progress.13

In the woollen trade we see the same rapid increase, and in 1910 the value of the exports of woollen goods attained £13,152,500 (against £8,220,300 in1894), out of which £1,799,000 worth were sent on the average to the United Kingdom during the years 1906-1910.14 The flax industry has grown at a still speedier rate, and as regards silks Germany is second only to France.

The progress realised in the German chemical trade is well known, and it is only too badly felt in Scotland and Northumberland; while the reports on the German iron and steel industries which one finds in the publications of the Iron and Steel Institute and in the inquiry which was made by the British Iron Trade Association show how formidably the production of pig-iron and of finished iron has grown in Germany since 1871. (See Appendix D.) No wonder that the imports of iron and steel into Germany were reduced by one-half during the twenty years, 1874-1894, while the exports grew nearly four times. As to the machinery works, if the Germans have committed the error of too slavishly copying English patterns, instead of taking a new departure, and of creating new patterns, as the Americans did, we must still recognise that their copies are good and that they very successfully compete in cheapness with the tools and machinery produced in this country. (See Appendix E.) I hardly need mention the superior make of German scientific apparatus. It is well known to scientific men, even in France.

In consequence of the above, the imports of manufactured goods into Germany are, as a rule, in decline. The aggregate imports of textiles (inclusive of yarn) stand so low as to be compensated by nearly equal values of exports. And there is no doubt that not only the German markets for textiles will be soon lost for other manufacturing countries, but that German competition will be felt stronger and stronger both in the neutral markets and those of Western Europe. One can easily win applause from uninformed auditories by exclaiming with more or less pathos that German produce can never equal the English! The fact is, that it competes in cheapness, and sometimes also--where it is needed--in an equally good workmanship; and this circumstance is due to many causes.

The "cheap labour" cause, so often alluded to in discussions about "German competition," which take place in this country and in France, must be dismissed by this time, since it has been well proved by so many recent investigations that low wages and long hours do not necessarily mean cheap produce. Cheap labour and protection simply mean the possibility for a number of employers to continue working with obsolete and bad machinery; but in highly developed staple industries, such as the cotton and the iron industries, the cheapest produce is obtained with high wages, short hours and the best machinery. When the number of operatives which is required for each 1000 spindles can vary from seventeen (in many Russian factories) to three (in England), and when one weaver can look either after twenty Northrop machine-looms, as we see it in the United States, or after two machine-looms only, as it is the case in backward mills, then it is evident that no reduction of wages can compensate for that immense difference. Consequently, in the best German cotton mills and ironworks the wages of the worker (we know it directly for the ironworks from the above-mentioned inquiry of the British Iron Trade Association) are not lower than they are in Great Britain. All that can be said is, that the worker in Germany gets more for his wages than he gets in this country--the paradise of the middleman--a paradise which it will remain so long as it lives chiefly on imported food produce.

The chief reason for the successes of Germany in the industrial field is the same as it is for the United States. Both countries have only lately entered the industrial phase of their development, and they have entered it with all the energy of youth. Both countries enjoy a widely spread scientifically-technical--or, at least, concrete scientific--education. In both countries manufactories are built according to the newest and best models which have been worked out elsewhere; and both countries are in a period of awakening in all branches of activity-- literature and science, industry and commerce. They enter now on the same phase in which Great Britain was in the first half of the nineteenth century, when British workers took such a large part in the invention of the wonderful modern machinery.

We have simply before us a fact of the consecutive development of nations. And instead of decrying or opposing it, it would be much better to see whether the two pioneers of the great industry--Britain and France--cannot take a new initiative and do something new again; whether an issue for the creative genius of these two nations must not be sought for in a new direction--namely, the utilisation of both the land and the industrial powers of man for securing well-being to the whole nation instead of to the few.

Chapter 2 - The Decentralisation of Industries, Part 2

THE flow of industrial growths spreads, however, not only east; it moves also southeast and south. Austria and Hungary are rapidly gaining ground in the race for industrial importance. The Triple Alliance has already been menaced by the growing tendency of Austrian manufacturers to protect themselves against German competition; and even the dual monarchy has seen its two sister nations quarreling about customs duties. Austrian industries are a modern growth, and still they already give occupation to more than 4,000,000 workpeople. Bohemia, in a few decades, has grown to be an industrial country of considerable importance; and the excellence and originality of the machinery used in the newly reformed flour-mills of Hungary show that the young industry of Hungary is on the right road, not only to become a competitor to her elder sisters, but also to add her share to our knowledge as to the use of the forces of nature. Let me add, by the way, that the same is true to some extent with regard to Finland. Figures are wanting as to the present state of the aggregate industries of Austria-Hungary; but the relatively low imports of manufactured goods, are worthy of note. For British manufacturers, Austria-Hungary is, in fact, no customer worth speaking of; but even with regard to Germany she is rapidly emancipating herself from her former dependence. (See Appendix G.)

The same industrial progress extends over the southern peninsulas. Who would have spoken in 1859 about Italian manufactures? And yet--the Turin Exhibition of 1884 has shown it--Italy ranks already among the manufacturing countries. "You see everywhere a considerable industrial and commercial effort made," wrote a French economist to the Temps. "Italy aspires to go on without foreign produce. The patriotic watchword is, Italy all by herself. It inspires the whole mass of producers. There is not a single manufacturer or tradesman who, even in the most trifling circumstances, does not do his best to emancipate himself from foreign guardianship." The best French and English patterns are imitated and improved by a touch of national genius and artistic traditions. Complete statistics are wanting, so that the statistical Annuario resorts to indirect indications. But the rapid increase of imports of coal (9,339,000 tons in 1910, as against 779,000 tons in 1871); the growth of the mining industries, which have trebled their production during the fifteen years, 1870 to 1885; the increasing production of steel and machinery (£4,800,000 in 1900), which--to use Bovio's words-- shows how a country having no fuel nor minerals of her own can have nevertheless a notable metallurgical industry; and, finally, the growth of textile industries disclosed by the net imports of raw cottons and the number of spindles -- all these show that the tendency towards becoming a manufacturing country capable of satisfying her needs by her own manufactures is not a mere dream. As to the efforts made for taking a more lively part in the trade of the world, who does not know the traditional capacities of the Italians in that direction?

I ought also to mention Spain, whose textile mining and metallurgical industries are rapidly growing; but I hasten to go over to countries which a few years ago were considered as eternal and obligatory customers to the manufacturing nations of Western Europe. Let us take, for instance, Brazil. Was it not doomed by economists to grow cotton, to export it in a raw state, and to receive cotton goods in exchange? In 1870 its nine miserable cotton mills could boast only of an aggregate of 385 spindles. But already in 1887 there were in Brazil 46 cotton mills, and five of them had already 40,000 spindles; while altogether their nearly 10,000 looms threw every year on the Brazilian markets more than 33,000,000 yards of cotton stuffs.

Twenty five years later, in 1912, there were already 161 cotton mills, with 1,500,000 spindles and 50,000 looms, employing over 100,000 operatives. Even Vera Cruz, in Mexico, under the protection of customs officers, has begun to manufacture cottons, and boasted in 1887 its 40,200 spindles, 287,700 pieces of cotton cloth, and 212,000 lb. of yarn. Since that year progress has been steady, and in 1894 Vice-Consul Chapman reported that some of the finest machines are to be found at the Orizaba spinning mills, while "cotton prints," he wrote, "are now turned out as good if not superior to the imported article." In 1910, 32,000 workpeople were already employed in 145 cotton mills, which had 703,000 spindles, and 25,000 powerlooms.

The flattest contradiction to the export theory has, however, been given by India. She was always considered as the surest customer for British cottons, and so she has been until quite lately. Out of the total of cotton goods exported from Britain she used to buy more than one-quarter, very nearly one-third (from £17,000,000 to £22,000,000, out of an aggregate of about £76,000,000 in the years 1880-1890). But things have begun to change, and in 1904-1907 the exports were only from £21,680,000 to £25,680,000 out of an aggregate of £110,440,000. The Indian cotton manufactures, which--for some causes not fully explained were so unsuccessful at their beginnings, suddenly took firm root.

In 1860 they consumed only 23,000,000 lb. of raw cotton, but the quantity was nearly four times as much in 1877, and it trebled again within the next ten years: 283,000,000 lb. of raw cotton were used in 1887-1888. The number of cotton mills grew up from 40 in 1887 to 147 in 1895; the number of spindles rose from 886,100 to 3,844,300 in the same years; and where 57,188 workers were employed in 1887, we found, seven years later, 146,240 operatives. And now, in 1909-1910, we find 237 cotton mills at work, with 6,136,000 spindles, 80,000 looms, and 231,850 workpeople. As for the quality of the mills, the blue-books praise them; the German chambers of commerce state that the best spinning mills in Bombay "do not now stand far behind the best German ones"; and two great authorities in the cotton industry, Mr. James Platt and Mr. Henry Lee, agree in saying "that in no other country of the earth except in Lancashire do the operatives possess such a natural leaning to the textile industry as in India."

The exports of cotton twist from India more than doubled in five years (1882-1887), and already in 1887 we could read in the Statement (p. 62) that "what cotton twist was imported was less and less of the coarser and even medium kind, which indicates that the Indian (spinning) mills are gradually gaining hold of the home markets." Consequently, while India continued to import nearly the same amount of British cotton goods and yarn (from £16,000,000 to £26,700,000 in 1900-1908), she threw already in 1887 on the foreign markets no less than £3,635,510 worth of her own cottons of Lancashire patterns; she exported 33,000,000 yards of gray cotton piece goods manufactured in India by Indian workmen. And the export has continued to grow since, so that in the year 1910-1911 the value of the piece-goods and yarn exported from India reached the value of £7,943,700.

The jute factories in India have grown at a still speedier rate, and the once flourishing jute trade of Dundee was brought to decay, not only by the high tariffs of continental powers, but also by Indian competition. Even woollen mills have lately been started; while the iron industry took a sudden development in India, since the means were found, after many experiments and failures, to work furnaces with local coal. In a few years, we are told by specialists, India will be self-supporting for iron. Nay, it is not without apprehension that the English manufacturers see that the imports of Indian manufactured textiles to this country are steadily growing, while in the markets of the Far East and Africa India becomes a serious competitor to the mother country.

Why should it not be so? What might prevent the growth of Indian manufactures? Is it the want of capital? But capital knows no fatherland; and if high profits can be derived from the work of Indian coolies whose wages are only one-half of those of English workmen, or even less, capital will migrate to India, as it has gone to Russia, although its migration may mean starvation for Lancashire and Dundee. Is it the want of knowledge? But longitudes and latitudes are no obstacle to its spreading; it is only the first steps that are difficult. As to the superiority of workmanship, nobody who knows the Hindoo worker will doubt about his capacities. Surely they are not below those of the 36,000 children less than fourteen years of age, or the 238,000 boys and girls less than eighteen years old, who are employed in the British textile manufactories.

Twenty years surely are not much in the life of nations. And yet within the last twenty years another powerful competitor has grown in the East. I mean Japan. In October, 1888, the Textile Recorder mentioned in a few lines that the annual production of yarns in the cotton mills of Japan had attained 9,498,500 Ib., and that fifteen more mills, which would hold 156,100 spindles, were in course of erection. Two years later, 27,000,000 lb. of yarn were spun in Japan; and while in 1887-1888 Japan imported five or six times as much yarn from abroad as was spun at home, next year two-thirds only of the total consumption of the country were imported from abroad.

From that date the production grew up regularly. From 6,435,000 lb. in 1886 it reached 91,950,000 lb. in 1893, and 153,444,000 lb. in 1895. In nine years it had thus increased twenty-four times. Since then it rose to 413,800,000 lb. in 1909; and we learn from the Financial Economical Annual for the years 1910 and 1911, published at Tokio, that there were in Japan, in 1909, no less than 3,756 textile factories, with 1,785,700 spindles and 51,185 power-looms, to which 783,155 hand-looms must be added. Japan is thus already a serious competitor of the great industrial nations for tissues altogether, and especially for cottons, in the markets of Eastern Asia; and it took it only five-and-twenty years to attain this position. The total production of tissues, valued at £1,200,000 in the year 1887, rapidly rose to £14,270,000 in 1895 and to £22,500,000 in 1909--cottons entering into this amount to the extent of nearly two-fifths. Consequently, the imports of foreign cotton goods from Europe fell from £1,640,000 in 1884 to £849,600 in 1895, and to £411,600 in 1910, while the exports of silk goods rose to nearly £3,000,000.

As to the coal and iron industries, I ventured in the first edition of this book to predict that the Japanese would not long remain a tributary to Europe for iron goods--that their ambition was also to have their own shipbuilding yards, and that the previous year 300 engineers left the Elswick works of Mr. Armstrong in order to start shipbuilding in Japan. They were engaged for five years only--the Japanese expecting to have learned enough in five years to be their own shipbuilders. This prediction has been entirely fulfilled. Japan has now 1,030 iron and machine works, and she now builds her own warships. During the last war, the progress realised in all industries connected with war was rendered fully evident.

All this shows that the much-dreaded invasion of the East upon European markets is in rapid progress. The Chinese slumber still; but I am firmly persuaded from what I saw of China that the moment they will begin to manufacture with the aid of European machinery--and the first steps have already been made--they will do it with more success, and necessarily on a far greater scale, than even the Japanese.

But what about the United States, which cannot be accused of employing cheap labour or of sending to Europe "cheap and nasty" produce? Their great industry is of yesterday's date; and yet the States already send to old Europe constantly increasing quantities of machinery. In 1890 they began even to export iron, which they obtain at a very low cost, owing to admirable new methods which they have introduced in metallurgy.

In the course of twenty years (1870-1890) the number of persons employed in the American manufactures was more than doubled, and the value of their produce was nearly trebled; and in the course of the next fifteen years, the number of persons employed increased again by nearly fifty per cent., while the value of the produce was nearly doubled. The cotton industry, supplied with excellent home-made machinery, has been rapidly developing, so that the yearly production of textiles attained in 1905 a value of 2,147,441,400 dollars, thus being twice as large as the yearly production of the United Kingdom in the same branch (which was valued at about £200,000,000); and the exports of cottons of domestic manufacture attained in 1910 the respectable figure of £8,600,000. As to the yearly output of pig-iron and steel, it is already in excess of the yearly output in Britain; and the organisation of that industry is also superior, as Mr. Berkley pointed out, already in 1891, in his address to the Institute of Civil Engineers.

But all this has grown almost entirely within the last thirty or forty years--whole industries having been created entirely since 1860. What will, then, American industry be twenty years hence, aided as it is by a wonderful development of technical skill, by excellent schools, a scientific education which goes hand in hand with technical education, and a spirit of enterprise which is unrivalled in Europe?

Volumes have been written about the crisis of 1886-1887, a crisis which, to use the words of the Parliamentary Commission, lasted since 1875, with but "a short period of prosperity enjoyed by certain branches of trade in the years 1880 to 1883," and a crisis, I shall add, which extended over all the chief manufacturing countries of the world. All possible causes of the crisis have been examined; but, whatever the cacophony of conclusions arrived at, all unanimously agreed upon one, namely, that of the Parliamentary Commission, which could be summed up as follows: "The manufacturing countries do not find such customers as would enable them to realise high profits." Profits being the basis of capitalist industry, low profits explain all ulterior consequences.

Low profits induce the employers to reduce the wages, or the number of workers, or the number of days of employment during the week, or eventually compel them to resort to the manufacture of lower kinds of goods, which, as a rule, are paid worse than the higher sorts. As Adam Smith said, low profits ultimately mean a reduction of wages, and low wages mean a reduced oonsumption by the worker. Low profits mean also a somewhat reduced consumption by the employer; and both together mean lower profits and reduced consumption with that immense class of middlemen which has grown up in manufacturing countries, and that, again, means a further reduction of profits for the employers.

A country which manufactures to a great extent for export, and therefore lives to a considerable amount on the profits derived from her foreign trade, stands very much in the same position as Switzerland, which lives to a great extent on the profits derived from the foreigners who visit her lakes and glaciers. A good "season" means an influx of from £1,000,000 to £2,000,000 of money imported by the tourists, and a bad "season" has the effects of a bad crop in an agricultural country: a general impoverishment follows. So it is also with a country which manufactures for export. If the "season" is bad, and the exported goods cannot be sold abroad for twice their value at home, the country which lives chiefly on these bargains suffers. Low profits for the innkeepers of the Alps mean narrowed circumstances in large parts of Switzerland; and low profits for the Lancashire and Scotch manufacturers, and the wholesale exporters, mean narrowed circumstances in Great Britain. The cause is the same in both cases.

For many decades past we had not seen such a cheapness of wheat and manufactured goods as we saw in 1883-1884, and yet in 1886 the country was suffering from a terrible crisis. People said, of course, that the cause of the crisis was over-production. But over-production is a word utterly devoid of sense if it does not mean that those who are in need of all kinds of produce have not the means for buying them with their low wages. Nobody would dare to affirm that there is too much furniture in the crippled cottages, too many bedsteads and bedclothes in the workmen's dwellings, too many lamps burning in the huts, and too much cloth on the shoulders, not only of those who used to sleep (in 1886) in Trafalgar Square between two newspapers, but even in those households where a silk hat makes a part of the Sunday dress. And nobody will dare to affirm that there is too much food in the homes of those agricultural labourers who earn twelve shillings a week, or of those women who earn from fivepence to sixpence a day in the clothing trade and other small industries which swarm in the outskirts of all great cities. Over-production means merely and simply a want of purchasing powers amidst the workers. And the same want of purchasing powers of the workers was felt everywhere on the Continent during the years 1885-1887.

After the bad years were over, a sudden revival of international trade took place; and, as the British exports rose in four years (1886 to 1890) by nearly 24 per cent., it began to be said that there was no reason for being alarmed by foreign competition; that the decline of exports in 1885-1887 was only temporary, and general in Europe; and that England, now as of old, fully maintained her dominant position in the international trade. It is certainly true that if we consider exclusively the money value of the exports for the years 1876 to 1895, we see no permanent decline, we notice only fluctuations. British exports, like commerce altogether, seem to show a certain periodicity. They fell from £201,000,000 sterling in 1876 to £192,000,000 in 1879, then they rose again to £241,000,000 in 1882, and fell down to £213,000,000 in 1886; again they rose to £264,000,00n in 1890, but fell again, reaching a minimum of £216,000,000 in 1894, to be followed next year by a slight movement upwards.

This periodicity being a fact, Mr. Giffen could make light in 1886 of "German competition" by showing that exports from the United Kingdom had not decreased. It can even be said that, per head of population, they had remained unchanged until 1904, undergoing only the usual ups and downs.* However, when we come to consider the quantities exported, and compare them with the money value of the exports, even Mr. Giffen had to acknowledge that the prices of 1883 were so low in comparison with those of 1873 that in order to reach the same money value the United Kingdom would have had to export four pieces of cotton instead of three, and eight or ten tons of metallic goods instead of six. " The aggregate of British foreign trade, if valued at the prices of ten years previously, would have amounted to £861,000,000 instead of £667,000,000," we were told by no less an authority than the Commission on Trade Depression.

It might, however, be said that 1873 was an exceptional year, owing to the inflated demand which took place after the Franco-German war. But the same downward movement continued for a number of years. Thus, if we take the figures given in the Statesman's Year-book, we see that while the United Kingdom exported, in 1883, 4,957,000,000 yards of piece goods (cotton, woollen and linen) and 316,000,000 lb. of yarn in order to reach an export value of £104,000,000, the same country had to export, in 1896, no less than 5,478,000,000 yards of the same stuffs and

330,000,000 lb. of yarn in order to realise £99,700,000 only. And the figures would have appeared still more unfavourable if we took the cottons alone. True, the conditions improved during the last ten years, so that in 1906 the exports were similar to those of 1873; and they were better still in 1911, which was a year of an extraordinary foreign trade, when 7,041,000,000 yards of stuffs and 307,000,000 lb. of yarn were exported--the two being valued at £163,400,000. However, it was especially the yarn which kept the high prices, because it is the finest sorts of yarn which are now exported. But the great profits of the years 1873-1880 are irretrievably gone.

We thus see that while the total value of the exports from the United Kingdom, in proportion to its growing population, remains, broadly speaking, unaltered for the last thirty years, the high prices which could be got for the exports thirty years ago, and with them the high profits, are gone. And no amount of arithmetical calculations will persuade the British manufacturers that such is not the case. They know perfectly well that the home markets grow continually overstocked; that the best foreign markets are escaping; and that in the neutral markets Britain is being undersold. This is the unavoidable consequence of the development of manufactures all over the world. (See Appendix J.)

Great hopes were laid, some time ago, in Australia as a market for British goods; but Australia will soon do what Canada already does. She will manufacture. And the colonial exhibitions, by showing to the " colonists " what they are able to do, and how they must do, are only accelerating the day when each colony fara da se in her turn. Canada and India aleady impose protective duties on British goods. As to the much-spoken-of markets en the Congo, and Mr. Stanley's calculations and promises of a trade amounting to £ 26,000,000 a year if the Lancashire people supply the Africans with loin-cloths, such promises belong to the same category of fancies as the famous nightcaps of the Chinese which were to enrich England after the first Chinese war. The Chinese prefer their own home-made nightcaps; and as to the Congo people, four countries at least are already competing for supplying them with their poor dress: Britain, Germany, the United States, and, last but not least, India.

There was a time when this country had almost the monopoly in the cotton industries; but already in 1880 she possessed only 55 per cent. of all the spindles at work in Europe, the United States and India (40,000,000 out of 72,000,000), and a little more than one-half of the looms (550,000 out of 972,000). In 1893 the proportion was further reduced to 49 per cent. of the spindles (45,300,000 out of 91,340,000), and now the United Kingdom has only 41 per cent. of all the spindles.* It was thus losing ground while the others were winning. And the fact is quite natural: it might have been foreseen. There is no reason why Britain should always be the great cotton manufactory of the world, when raw cotton has to be imported into this country as elsewhere. It was quite natural that France, Germany, Italy, Russia, India, Japan, the United States, and even Mexico and Brazil, should begin to spin their own yarns and to weave their own cotton stuffs. But the appearance of the cotton industry in a country, or, in fact, of any textile industry, unavoidably becomes the starting-point for the growth of a series of other industries; chemical and mechanical works, metallurgy and mining feel at once the impetus given by a new want. The whole of the home industries, as also technical education altogether, must improve in order to satisfy that want as soon as it has been felt.

What has happened with regard to cottons is going on also with regard to other industries. Great Britain, which stood in 1880 at the head of the list of countries producing pig-iron, came in 1904 the third in the same list, which was headed by the United States and Germany; while Russia, which occupied the seventh place in 1880, comes now fourth, after Great Britain.17 Britain and Belgium have no longer the monopoly of the woollen trade. Immense factories at Verviers are silent; the Belgian weavers are misery-stricken, while Germany yearly increases her production of woollens, and exports nine times more woollens than Belgium. Austria has her own woollens and exports them, Riga, Lodz, and Moscow supply Russia with fine woollen cloths; and the growth of the woollen industry in each of the last-named countries calls into existence hundreds of connected trades.

For many years France has had the monopoly of the silk trade. Silkworms being reared in Southern France, it was quite natural that Lyons should grow into a centre for the manufacture of silks. Spinning, domestic weaving, and dyeing works developed to a great extent. But eventually the industry took such an extension that home supplies of raw silk became insufficient, and raw silk was imported from Italy, Spain and Southern Austria, Asia Minor, the Caucasus and Japan, to the amount of from [£9,000,000 to £11,000,000 in 1875 and 1876, while France had only £800,000 worth of her own silk. Thousands of peasant boys and girls were attracted by high wages to Lyons and the neighboring district; the industry was prosperous.

However, by-and-by new centres of silk trade grew up at Basel and in the peasant houses round Zurich. French emigrants imported the trade into Switzerland, and it developed there, especially after the civil war of 1871. Then the Caucasus Administration invited French workmen and women from Lyons and Marseilles to teach the Georgians and the Russians the best means of rearing the silkworm, as well as the whole of the silk trade; and Stavropol became a new centre for silk weaving. Austria and the United States did the same; and what are now the results?

During the years 1872 to 1881 Switzerland more than doubled the produce of her silk industry; Italy and Germany increased it by one-third; and the Lyons region, which formerly manufactured to the value of 454 million francs a year, showed in 1887 a return of only 378 millions. The exports of Lyons silks, which reached an average of 425,000,000 francs in 1855-1859, and 460,000,000 in 1870-1874, fell down to 233,000,000 in 1887. And it is reckoned by French specialists that at present no less than one-third of the silk stuffs used in France are imported from Zurich, Crefeld, and Barmen. Nay, even Italy, which has now 191,000 persons engaged in the industry, sends her silks to France and competes with Lyons.,

The French manufacturers may cry as loudly as they like for protection, or resort to the production of cheaper goods of lower quality; they may sell 3,250,000 kilogrammes of silk stuffs at the same price as they sold 2,500,000 in 1855-1859--they will never again regain the position they occupied before. Italy, Switzerland, Germany, the United States and Russia have their own silk factories, and will import from Lyons only the highest qualities of stuffs. As to the lower sorts, a foulard has become a common attire with the St. Petersburg housemaids, because the North Caucasian domestic trades supply them at a price which would starve the Lyons weavers. The trade has been decentralised, and while Lyons is still a centre for the higher artistic silks, it will never be again the chief centre for the silk trade which it was thirty years ago.

Like examples could be produced by the score. Greenock no longer supplies Russia with sugar, because Russia has plenty of her own at the same price as it sells at in England. The watch trade is no more a speciality of Switzerland: watches are now made everywhere. India extracts from her ninety collieries two-thirds of her annual consumption of coal. The chemical trade which grew up on the banks of the Clyde and Tyne, owing to the special advantages offered for the import of Spanish pyrites and the agglomeration of such a variety of industries along the two estuaries, is now in decay. Spain, with the help of English capital, is beginning to utilise her own pyrites for herself; and Germany has become a great centre for the manufacture of sulphuric acid and soda--nay, she already complains about over-production.

But enough! I have before me so many figures, all telling the same tale, that examples could be multiplied at will. It is time to conclude, and, for every unprejudiced mind, the conclusion is self-evident. Industries of all kinds decentralise and are scattered all over the globe; and everywhere a variety, an integrated variety, of trades grows, instead of specialisation. Such are the prominent features of the times we live in. Each nation becomes in its turn a manufacturing nation; and the time is not far off when each nation of Europe, as well as the United States, and even the most backward nations of Asia and America, will themselves manufacture nearly everything they are in need of. Wars and several accidental causes may check for some time the scattering of industries: they will not stop it; it is unavoidable. For each new-comer the first steps only are difficult. But, as soon as any industry has taken firm root, it calls into existence hundreds of other trades; and as soon as the first steps have been made, and the first obstacles have been overcome, the industrial growth goes on at an accelerated rate.

The fact is so well felt, if not understood, that the race for colonies has become the distinctive feature of the last twenty years. Each nation will have her own colonies. But colonies will not help. There is not a second India in the world, and the old conditions will be repeated no more. Nay, some of the British colonies already threaten to become serious competitors with their mother country; others, like Australia, will not fail to follow the same lines. As to the yet neutral markets, China will never be a serious customer to Europe: she can produce much cheaper at home; and when she begins to feel a need for goods of European patterns, she will produce them herself. Woe to Europe, if on the day that the steam engine invades China she is still relying on foreign customers! As to the African half-savages, their misery is no foundation for the well-being of a civilised nation.

Progress must be looked for in another direction. It is in producing for home use. The customers for the Lancashire cottons and the Sheffield cutlery, the Lyons silks and the Hungarian flour-mills, are not in India, nor in Africa. The true consumers of the produce of our factories must be our own populations. And they can be that, once we organise our economical life so that they might issue from their present destitution. No use to send floating shops to New Guinea with British or German millinery, when there are plenty of would-be customers for British millinery in these very islands, and for German goods in Germany. Instead of worrying our brains by schemes for getting customers abroad, it would be better to try to answer the following questions: Why the British worker, whose industrial capacities are so highly praised in political speeches; why the Scotch crofter and the Irish peasant, whose obstinate labours in creating new productive soil out of peat bogs are occasionally so much spoken of, are no customers to the Lancashire weavers, the Sheffield cutlers and the Northumbrian and Welsh pitmen? Why the Lyons weavers not only do not wear silks, but sometimes have no food in their attics ? Why the Russian peasants sell their corn, and for four, six, and sometimes eight months every year are compelled to mix bark and auroch grass to a handful of flour for baking their bread ? Why famines are so common amidst the growers of wheat and rice in India?

Under the present conditions of division into capitalists and labourers, into property-holders and masses living on uncertain wages, the spreading of industries over new fields is accompanied by the very same horrible facts of pitiless oppression, massacre of children, pauperism, and insecurity of life. The Russian Fabrics Inspectors' Reports, the Reports of the Plauen Handelskammer, the Italian inquests, and the reports about the growing industries of India and Japan are full of the same revelations as the Reports of the Parliamentary Commissions of 1840 to 1842, or the modern revelations with regard to the "sweating system" at Whitechapel and Glasgow, London pauperism, and York unemployment. The Capital and Labour problem is thus universalised; but, at the same time, it is also simplified. To return to a state of affairs where corn is grown, and manufactured goods are fabricated, for the use of those very people who grow and produce them-- such will be, no doubt, the problem to be solved during the next coming years of European history. Each region will become its own producer and its own consumer of manufactured goods. But that unavoidably implies that, at the same time, it will be its own producer and consumer of agricultural produce; and that is precisely what I am going to discuss next.

Chapter III: The Possibilities of Agriculture

THE industrial and commercial history of the world during the last fifty years has been a history of decentralisation of industry. It was not a mere shifting of the centre of gravity of commerce, such as Europe witnessed in the past, when the commercial hegemony migrated from Italy to Spain, to Holland, and finally to Britain: it had a much deeper meaning, as it excluded the very possibility of commercial or industrial hegemony. It has shown the growth of quite new conditions, and new conditions require new adaptations. To endeavour to revive the past would be useless: a new departure must be taken by civilised nations.

Of course, there will be plenty of voices to argue that the former supremacy of the pioneers must be maintained at any price: all pioneers are in the habit of saying so. It will be suggested that the pioneers must attain such a superiority of technical knowledge and organisation as to enable them to beat all their younger competitors; that force must be resorted to if necessary. But force is reciprocal; and if the god of war always sides with the strongest battalions, those battalions are strongest which fight for new rights against outgrown privileges. As to the honest longing for more technical education--surely let us all have as much of it as possible: it will be a boon for humanity; for humanity, of course--not for a single nation, because knowledge cannot be cultivated for home use only. Knowledge and invention, boldness of thought and enterprise, conquests of genius and improvements of social organisation have become international growths; and no kind of progress--intellectual, industrial or social--can be kept within political boundaries; it crosses the seas, it pierces the mountains; steppes are no obstacle to it. Knowledge and inventive powers are now so thoroughly international that if a simple newspaper paragraph announces to-morrow that the problem of storing force, of printing without inking, or of aerial navigation, has received a practical solution in one country of the world, we may feel sure that within a few weeks the same problem will be solved, almost in the same way, by several inventors of different nationalities. Continually we learn that the same scientific discovery, or technical invention, has been made within a few days' distance, in countries a thousand miles apart; as if there were a kind of atmosphere which favours the germination of a given idea at a given moment. And such an atmosphere exists: steam, print and the common stock of knowledge have created it.

Those who dream of monopolising technical genius are therefore fifty years behind the times. The world--the wide, wide world--is now the true domain of knowledge; and if each nation displays some special capacities in some special branch, the various capacities of different nations compensate one another, and the advantages which could be derived from them would be only temporary. The fine British workmanship in mechanical arts, the American boldness for gigantic enterprise, the French systematic mind, and the German pedagogy, are becoming international capacities. Sir William Armstrong, in his works established in Italy and Japan, has already communicated to Italians and Japanese those capacities for managing huge iron masses which have been nurtured on the Tyne; the uproarious American spirit of enterprise pervades the Old World; the French taste for harmony becomes European taste; and German pedagogy--improved, I dare say--is at home in Russia. So, instead of trying to keep life in the old channels, it would be better to see what the new conditions are, what duties they impose on our generation.

The characters of the new conditions are plain, and their consequences are easy to understand. As the manufacturing nations of West Europe are meeting with steadily growing difficulties in selling their manufactured goods abroad, and getting food in exchange, they will be compelled to grow their food at home; they will be bound to rely on home customers for their manufactures, and on home producers for their food. And the sooner they do so the better.

Two great objections stand, however, in the way against the general acceptance of such conclusions. We have been taught, both by economists and politicians, that the territories of the West European States are so overcrowded with inhabitants that they cannot grow all the food and raw produce which are necessary for the maintenance of their steadily increasing populations. Therefore the necessity of exporting manufactured goods and of importing food. And we are told, moreover, that even if it were possible to grow in Western Europe all the food necessary for its inhabitants, there would be no advantage in doing so as long as the same food can be got cheaper from abroad. Such are the present teachings and the ideas which are current in society at large. And yet it is easy to prove that both are totally erroneous: plenty of food could be grown on the territories of Western Europe for much more than their present populations, and an immense benefit would be derived from doing so. These are the two points which I have now to discuss.

To begin by taking the most disadvantageous case: is it possible that the soil of Great Britain, which at present yields food for one-third only of its inhabitants, could provide all the necessary amount and variety of food for 41,000,000 human beings when it covers only 56,000,000 acres all told--forests and rocks, marshes and peat-bogs, cities, railways and fields--out of which only 33,000,000 acres are considered as cultivable? The current opinion is, that it by no means can; and that opinion is so inveterate that we even see men of science, who are generally cautious when dealing with current opinions, endorse that opinion without even taking the trouble of verifying it. It is accepted as an axiom. And yet, as soon as we try to find out any argument in its favour, we discover that it has not the slightest foundation, either in facts or in judgment based upon well-known facts.

Let us take, for instance, J. B. Lawes' estimates of crops which were published every year in The Times. In his estimate of the year 1887 he made the remark that during the eight harvest years 1853-1860 "nearly three-fourths of the aggregate amount of wheat consumed in the United Kingdom was of home growth, and little more than one-fourth was derived from foreign sources"; but five-and-twenty years later the figures were almost reversed--that is, "during the eight years 1879-1886, little more than one-third has been provided by home crops and nearly two-thirds by imports." But neither the increase of population by 8,000,000 nor the increase of consumption of wheat by six-tenths of a bushel per head could account for the change. In the years 1853-1860 the soil of Britain nourished one inhabitant on every two acres cultivated: why did it require three acres in order to nourish the same inhabitant in 1887? The answer is plain: merely and simply because agriculture had fallen into neglect.

In fact, the area under wheat had been reduced since 1853-1860 by full 1,590,000 acres, and therefore the average crop of the years 1883-1886 was below the average crop of 1853-1860 by more than 40,000,000 bushels; and this deficit alone represented the food of more than 7,000,000 inhabitants. At the same time the area under barley, oats, beans, and other spring crops had also been reduced by a further 560,000 acres, which, alone, at the low average of thirty bushels per acre, would have represented the cereals necessary to complete the above, for the same 7,000,000 inhabitants. It can thus be said that if the United Kingdom imported cereals for 17,000,000 inhabitants in 1887, instead of for 10,000,000 in 1860, it was simply because more than 2,000,000 acres had gone out of cultivation.

These facts are well known; but usually they are met with the remark that the character of agriculture had been altered: that instead of growing wheat, meat and milk were produced in this country. However, the figures for 1887, compared with the figures for 1860, show that the same downward movement took place under the heads of green crops and the like. The area under potatoes was reduced by 280,000 acres; under turnips by 180,000 acres; and although there was an increase under the heads of mangold, carrots, etc., still the aggregate area under all these crops was reduced by a further 330,000 acres. An increase of area was found only for permanent pasture (2,800,000 acres) and grass under rotation (1,600,000 acres); but we should look in vain for a corresponding increase of live stock. The increase of live stock which took place during those twenty-seven years was not sufficient to cover even the area reclaimed from waste land.

Since the year 1887 affairs went, however, from worse to worse. If we take Great Britain alone, we see that in 1885 the area under all corn crops was 8,392,006 acres; that is very small, indeed, in comparison to the area which could have been cultivated; but even that little was further reduced to 7,400,227 acres in 1895. The area under wheat was 2,478,318 acres in 1885 (as against 3,630,300 in 1874); but it dwindled away to 1,417,641 acres in 1895, while the area under the other cereals increased by a trifle only--from 5,198,026 acres to 5,462,184 -- the total loss on all cereals being nearly 1,000,000 acres in ten years! Another 5,000,000 people were thus compelled to get their food from abroad.

Did the area under green crops increase correspondingly, as it would have done if it were only the character of agriculture that had changed? Not in the least! This area was further reduced by nearly 500,000 acres (3,521,602 in 1885, 3,225,762 in 1895, and 3,006,000 in 1909-1911). Or was the area under clover and grasses in rotation increased in proportion to all these reductions? Alas no! It also was reduced (4,654,173 acres in 1885, 4,729,801 in 1895, and 4,164,000 acres in 1909-1911). In short, taking all the land that is under crops in rotation (17,201,490 acres in 1885, 16,166,950 acres in 1895, 14,795,570 only in 1905, and 14,682,550 in 1909-1911), we see that within the last twenty-six years another 2,500,000 acres went out of cultivation, without any compensation whatever. It went to increase that already enormous area of more than 17,000,000 acres (17,460,000 in 1909-1911) more than one-half of the cultivable area-- which goes under the head of "permanent pasture," and hardly suffices to feed one cow on each three acres!

Need I say, after that, that quite to the contrary of what we are told about the British agriculturists becoming "meat-makers "instead of "wheat-growers," no corresponding increase of live stock took place during the last twenty-five years. Far from devoting the land freed from cereals to "meat-making," the country further reduced its live stock in 1885-1895, and began to show a slight increase during the last few years only. It had 6,597,964 head of horned cattle in 1885, 6,354,336 in 1895, and 7,057,520 in 1909-1911; 26,534,600 sheep in 1885, 25,792,200 in 1895, and from 26,500,000 to 27,610,000 in 1909-1911. True, the number of horses increased; every butcher and greengrocer runs now a horse "to take orders at the gents' doors" (in Sweden and Switzerland, by the way, they do it by telephone). But if we take the numbers of horses used in agriculture, unbroken, and kept for breeding, we find only small oscillations between 1,408,790 in 1885 and 1,553,000 in 1909. But numbers of horses are imported, as also the oats and a considerable amount of the hay that is required for feeding them. And if the consumption of meat has really increased in this country, it is due to cheap imported meat, not to the meat that would be produced in these islands.

In short, agriculture has not changed its direction, as we are often told; it simply went down in all directions. Land is going out of culture at a perilous rate, while the latest improvements in market-gardening, fruit-growing and poultry-keeping are but a mere trifle if we compare them with what has been done in the same direction in France, Belgium and America.

It must be said that during the last few years there was a slight improvement. The area under all corn crops was slightly increasing, and it fluctuated about 7,000,000 acres, the increase being especially notable for wheat (1,906,000 acres in 1911 as against 1,625,450 in 1907), while the areas under barley and oats were slightly diminished. But with all that, the surface under corn crops is still nearly one-and-a-half million acres below what it was in 1885 and nearly two-and-a-half million acres below 1874. This represents, let us remember it, the bread-food of ten million people.

The cause of this general downward movement is self-evident. It is the desertion, the abandonment of the land. Each crop requiring human labour has had its area reduced; and almost one-half of the agricultural labourers have been sent away since 1861 to reinforce the ranks of the unemployed in the cities, so that far from being over-populated, the fields of Britain are starved of human labour, as James Caird used to say. The British nation does not work on her soil; she is prevented from doing so; and the would-be economists complain that the soil will not nourish its inhabitants!

I once took a knapsack and went on foot out of London, through Sussex. I had read Leonce de Lavergne's work and expected to find a soil busily cultivated; but neither round London nor still less further south did I see men in the fields. In the Weald I could walk for twenty miles without crossing anything but heath or woodlands, rented as pheasant-shooting grounds to "London gentlemen," as the labourers said. "Ungrateful soil" was my first thought; but then I would occasionally come to a farm at the crossing of two roads and see the same soil bearing a rich crop; and my next thought was tel seigneur, telle terre, as the

French peasants say. Later on I saw the rich fields of the midland counties; but even there I was struck by not perceiving the same busy human labour which I was accustomed to admire on the Belgian and French fields. But I ceased to wonder when I learnt that only 1,383,000 men and women in England and Wales work in the fields, while more than 16,000,000 belong to the "professional, domestic, indefinite, and unproductive class," as these pitiless statisticians say. One million human beings cannot productively cultivate an area of 33,000,000 acres, unless they can resort to the Bonanza farm's methods of culture.

Again, taking Harrow as the centre of my excursions, I could walk five miles towards London, or turning my back upon it, and I could see nothing east or west but meadow land on which they hardly cropped two tons of hay per acre-- scarcely enough to keep alive one milch cow on each two acres. Man is conspicuous by his abscence from those meadows; he rolls them with a heavy roller in the spring; he spreads some manure every two or three years; then he disappears until the time has come to make hay. And that--within ten miles from Charing Cross, close to a city with 5,000,000 inhabitants supplied with Flemish and Jersey potatoes, French salads and Canadian apples. In the hands of the Paris gardeners, each thousand acres situated within the same distance from the city would be cultivated by at least 2,000 human beings, who would get vegetables to the value of from £50 to £300 per acre. But here the acres which only need human hands to become an inexhaustible source of golden crops lie idle, and they say to us, "Heavy clay!" without even knowing that in the hands of man there are no unfertile soils; that the most fertile soils are not in the prairies of America, nor in the Russian steppes; that they are in the peat-bogs of Ireland, on the sand downs of the northern seacoast of France, on the craggy mountains of the Rhine, where they have been made by man's hands.

The most striking fact is, however, that in some undoubtedly fertile parts of the country things are even in a worse condition. My heart simply ached when I saw the state in which land is kept in South Devon, and when I learned to know what "permanent pasture" means. Field after field is covered with nothing but grass, three inches high, and thistles in profusion. Twenty, thirty such fields can be seen at one glance from the top of every hill; and thousands of acres are in that state, notwithstanding that the grandfathers of the present generation have devoted a formidable amount of labour to the clearing of that land from the stones, to fencing it, roughly draining it and the like. In every direction I could see abandoned cottages and orchards going to ruin. A whole population has disappeared, and even its last vestiges must disappear if things continue to go on as they have gone. And this takes place in a part of the country endowed with a most fertile soil and possessed of a climate which is certainly more congenial than the climate of Jersey in spring and early summer--a land upon which even the poorest cottagers occasionally raise potatoes as early as the first half of May. But how can that land be cultivated when there is nobody to cultivate it? "We have fields; men go by, but never go in, "an old labourer said to me; and so it is in reality.

Such were my impressions of British agriculture twenty years ago. Unfortunately, both the official statistical data and the mass of private evidence published since tend to show that but little improvement took place in the general conditions of agriculture in this country within the last twenty years. Some successful attempts in various new directions have been made in different parts of the country, and I will have the pleasure to mention them further on, the more so as they show what a quite average soil in these islands can give when it is properly treated. But over large areas, especially in the southern counties, the general conditions are even worse than they were twenty years ago.

Altogether one cannot read the mass of review and newspaper articles, and books dealing with British agriculture that have been published lately, without realising that the agricultural depression which began in the "seventies" and the "eighties" of the nineteenth century had causes much more deeply seated than the fall in the prices of wheat in consequence of American competition. However, it would lie beyond the scope of this book to enter here into such a discussion. Moreover, anyone who will read a few review articles written from the points of view of different parties, or consult such books as that of Mr. Christopher Turnor, or study the elaborate inquest made by Rider Haggard in twenty-six counties of England--paying more attention to the data accumulated in this book than to the sometimes biassed conclusions of the author--will soon see himself what are the causes which hamper the development of British agriculture.

In Scotland the conditions are equally bad. The population described as "rural" is in a steady decrease: in 1911 it was already less than 800,000; and as regards the agricultural labourers, their number has decreased by 42,370 (from 135,970 to 93,600) in the twenty years, 1881 to 1901. The land goes out, of culture, while the area under "deer forests"--that is, under hunting grounds established upon what formerly was arable land for the amusement of the rich--increases at an appalling rate. No need to say that at the same time the Scotch population is emigrating, and Scotland is depopulated at an appalling speed.

My chief purpose being to show here what can and ought to be obtained from the land under a proper and intelligent treatment, I shall only indicate one of the disadvantages of the systems of husbandry in vogue in this country. Both landlords and farmers gradually came of late to pursue other aims than that of obtaining from the land the greatest amount of produce than can be obtained; and when this problem of a maximum productivity of the land arose before the European nations, and therefore a complete modification of the methods of husbandry was rendered imperative, such a modification was not accomplished in this country. While in France, Belgium, Germany and Denmark the agriculturists did their best to meet the effects of American competition by rendering their culture more intensive in all directions, in this country the already antiquated method of reducing the area under corn crops and laying land for grass continues to prevail, although it ought to be evident that mere grazing will pay no more, and that some effort in the right direction would increase the returns of the corn crops, as also those of the roots and plants cultivated for industrial purposes. The land continues to go out of culture, while the problem of the day is to render culture more and more intensive.

Many causes have combined to produce that undesirable result. The concentration of landownership in the hands of big landowners; the high profits obtained previously; the development of a class of both landlords and farmers who rely chiefly upon other incomes than those they draw from the land, and for whom farming has thus become a sort of pleasant by-occupation or sport; the rapid development of game reserves for sportsmen, both British and foreign; the absence of men of initiative who would have shown to the nation the necessity of a new departure; the absence of a desire to win the necessary knowledge, and the absence of institutions which could widely spread practical agricultural knowledge and introduce improved seeds and seedlings, as the Experimental Farms of the United States and Canada are doing; the dislike of that spirit of agricultural cooperation to which the Danish farmers owe their successes, and so on--all these stand in the way of the unavoidable change in the methods of farming, and produce the results of which the British writers on agriculture are complaining. But it is self-evident that in order to compete with countries where machinery is largely used and new methods of farming are resorted to (including the industrial treatment of farm produce in sugar works, starch works, and the drying of vegetables, etc., connected with farming), the old methods cannot do; especially when the farmer has to pay a rent of twenty, forty, and occasionally fifty shillings per acre for wheatlands.

It may be said, of course, that this opinion strangely contrasts with the well-known superiority of British agriculture. Do we not know, indeed, that British crops average twenty-eight to thirty bushels of wheat per acre, while in France they reach only from seventeen to twenty bushels? Does it not stand in all almanacs that Britain gets every year £200,000,000 sterling worth of animal produce--milk, cheese, meat and wool--from her fields? All that is true, and there is no doubt that in many respects British agriculture is superior to that of many other nations. As regards obtaining the greatest amount of produce with the least amount of labour, Britain undoubtedly took the lead until she was superseded by America in the Bonanza farms (now disappeared or rapidly disappearing). Again, as regards the fine breeds of cattle, the splendid state of the meadows and the results obtained in separate farms, there is much to be learned from Britain. But a closer acquaintance with British agriculture as a whole discloses many features of inferiority.

However splendid, a meadow remains a meadow, much inferior in productivity to a cornfield; and the fine breeds of cattle appear to be poor creatures as long as each ox requires three acres of land to be fed upon. As regards the crops, certainly one may indulge in some admiration at the average twenty-eight or thirty bushels grown in this country; but when we learn that only 1,600,000 to 1,900,000 acres out of the cultivable 33,000,000 bear such crops, we are quite disappointed. Anyone could obtain like results if he were to put all his manure into one-twentieth part of the area which he possesses. Again, the twenty-eight to thirty bushels no longer appear to us so satisfactory when we learn that without any manuring, merely by means of a good culture, they have obtained at Rothamstead an average of 14 bushels per acre from the same plot of land for forty consecutive years; while Mr. Prout, in his farm near Sawbridgeworth (Herts), on a cold heavy clay, has obtained since 1861 crops of from thirty to thirty-eight bushels of wheat, year after year, without any farm manure at all, by good steam ploughing and artificial manure only. (R. Haggard, I. 528.) Under the allotment system the crops reach forty bushels. In some farms they occasionally attain even fifty and fifty-seven bushels per acre.

If we intend to have a correct appreciation of British agriculture, we must not base it upon what is obtained on a few selected and wellmanured plots; we must inquire what is done with the territory, taken as a whole. Now, out of each 1,000 acres of the aggregate territory of England, Wales and Scotland, 435 acres are left under wood, coppice, heath, buildings, and so on. We need not find fault with that division, because it depends very much upon natural causes. In France and Belgium one-third of the territory is in like manner also treated as uncultivable, although portions of it are continually reclaimed and brought under culture. But, leaving aside the "uncultivable" portion, let us see what is done with the 565 acres out of 1,000 of the "cultivable" part (32,145,930 acres in Great Britain in 1910). First of all, it is divided into two parts, and one of them, the largest-- 308 acres out of 1,000--is left under "permanent pasture," that is, in most cases it is entirely uncultivated. Very little hay is obtained from it, and some cattle are grazed upon it. More than one-half of the cultivable area is thus left without cultivation, and only 257 acres out of each 1,000 acres are under culture. Out of these last, 124 acres are under corn crops, twenty-one acres under potatoes, fifty-three acres under green crops, and seventy-three acres under clover fields and grasses under rotation. And finally, out of the 124 acres given to corn crops, the best thirty-three, and some years only twenty-five acres (one-fortieth part of the territory, one twenty-third of the cultivable area), are picked out and sown with wheat. They are well cultivated, well manured, and upon them an average of from twenty-eight to thirty bushels to the acre is obtained; and upon these twenty-five or thirty acres out of 1,000 the world superiority of British agriculture is based.

The net result of all that is, that on nearly 33,000,000 acres of cultivable land the food is grown for one third part only of the population (more than two-thirds of the food it consumes is imported), and we may say accordingly that, although nearly two-thirds of the territory is cultivable, British agriculture provides homegrown food for each 125 or 135 inhabitants only per square mile (out of 466). In other words, nearly three acres of the cultivable area are required to grow the food for each person. Let us then see what is done with the land in France and Belgium.

Now, if we simply compare the average thirty bushels per acre of wheat in Great Britain with the average nineteen to twenty bushels grown in France within the last ten years, the comparison is all in favour of these islands; but such averages are of little value because the two systems of agriculture are totally different in the two countries. The Frenchman also has his picked and heavily manured "twenty-five to thirty acres" in the north of France and in Ile-de France, and from these picked acres he obtains average crops ranging from thirty to thirty-three bushels. However, he sows with wheat, not only the best picked out acres, but also such fields on the Central Plateau and in Southern France as hardly yield ten, eight and even six bushels to the acre, without irrigation; and these low crops reduce the average for the whole country.

The Frenchman cultivates much that is left here under permanent pasture--and this is what is described as his "inferiority" in agriculture. In fact, although the proportion between what we have named the "cultivable area" and the total territory is very much the same in France as it is in Great Britain (624 acres out of each 1,000 acres of the territory), the area under wheat crops is nearly six times as great, in proportion, as what it is in Great Britain (182 acres instead of twenty-five or thirty, out of each 1,000 acres): the corn crops altogether cover nearly two-fifths of the cultivable area (375 acres out of 1000), and large areas are given besides to green crops, industrial crops, vine, fruit and vegetables.

Taking everything into consideration, although the Frenchman keeps less cattle, and especially grazes less sheep than the Briton, he nevertheless obtains from his soil nearly all the food that he and his cattle consume. He imports, in an average year, but one-tenth only of what the nation consumes, and he exports to this country considerable quantities of food produce (£10,000,000 worth), not only from the south, but also, and especially, from the shores of the Channel (Brittany butter and vegetables; fruit and vegetables from the suburbs of Paris, and so on).

The net result is that, although one-third part of the territory is also treated as "uncultivable," the soil of France yields the food for 170 inhabitants per square mile (out of 188), that is, for forty persons more, per square mile, than this country.

It is thus apparent that the comparison with France is not so much in favour of this country as it is said to be; and it will be still less favourable when we come, in our next chapter, to horticulture.

The comparison with Belgium is even more striking--the more so as the two systems of culture are similar in both countries. To begin with, in Belgium we also find an average crop of over thirty bushels of wheat to the acre; but the area given to wheat is five times as big as in Great Britain, in comparison to the cultivable area, and the cereals cover two-fifths of the land available for culture. The land is so well cultivated that the average crops for the years 1890-1899 (the very bad year of 1891 being left out of account) were from twenty-six and a half to twenty-eight and a half bushels per acre for winter wheat, and reached an average of thirty-three and a half bushels in 1900-1904; over fifty-four bushels for oats (thirty-five to forty-one and a half in Great Britain), and from forty to forty-three and a half bushels for winter barley (twenty-nine to thirty-five in Great Britain); while on no less than 475,000 acres catch crops of swedes (3,345,000 tons), carrots (155,000 tons), and more than 500,000 of lucerne and other grasses were obtained.

As to extraordinarily heavy crops, Mr. Seebohm Rowntree mentions, for instance, the wheat crop in the commune of Oirbeck, near Louvain, which was, in 1906, on the average, fifty-seven bushels per acre, while the average of the whole country was only thirty-four bushels, or a yield of 111.5 bushels of oats in the commune of Neuve-Eglise, while the average for Belgium was fifty-four bushels, and so on, the average crops of several communes for some cereals being seventy-three per cent. in excess of the average for Belgium, and from 106 to 153 per cent. for roots.

All taken, they grow in Belgium more than 76,000,000 bushels of cereals--that is, fifteen and seven-tenths bushels per acre of the cultivable area--while the corresponding figure for Great Britain is only eight and a half bushels; and they keep almost twice as many cattle upon each cultivable acre as is kept in Great Britain.

Chapter IV: The Possibilities of Agriculture, Part 2

FEW books have exercised so pernicious an influence upon the general development of economic thought as Malthus's Essay on the Principle of Population exercised for three consecutive generations. It appeared at the right time, like all books which have had any influence at all, and it summed up ideas already current in the minds of the wealth-possessing minority. It was precisely when the ideas of equality and liberty, awakened by the French and American revolutions, were still permeating the minds of the poor, while the richer classes had become tired of their amateur excursions into the same domains, that Malthus came to assert, in reply to Godwin, that no equality is possible; that the poverty of the many is not due to institutions, but is a natural law. Population, he wrote, grows too rapidly and the new-comers find no room at the feast of nature; and that law cannot be altered by any change of institutions. He thus gave to the rich a kind of scientific argument against the ideas of equality; and we know that though all dominion is based upon force, force itself begins to totter as soon as it is no longer supported by a firm belief in its own rightfulness. As to the poorer classes--who always feel the influence of ideas circulating at a given time amid the wealthier classes--it deprived them of the very hope of improvement; it made them sceptical as to the promises of the social reformers; and to this day the most advanced reformers entertain doubts as to the possibility of satisfying the needs of all, in case there should be a claim for their satisfaction, and a temporary welfare of the labourers resulted in a sudden increase of population.

Science, down to the present day, remains permeated with Malthus's teachings. Political economy continues to base its reasoning upon a tacit admission of the impossibility of rapidly increasing the productive powers of a nation, and of thus giving satisfaction to all wants. This postulate stands, undiscussed, in the background of whatever political economy, classical or socialist, has to say about exchange-value, wages, sale of labour force, rent, exchange, and consumption. Political economy never rises above the hypothesis of a limited and insufficient supply of the necessaries of life; it takes it for granted. And all theories connected with political economy retain the same erroneous principle. Nearly all socialists, too, admit the postulate. Nay, even in biology (so deeply interwoven now with sociology) we have recently seen the theory of variability of species borrowing a quite unexpected support from its having been connected by Darwin and Wallace with Malthus's fundamental idea, that the natural resources must inevitably fail to supply the means of existence for the rapidly multiplying animals and plants. In short, we may say that the theory of Malthus, by shaping into a pseudo-scientific form the secret desires of the wealth-possessing classes, became the foundation of a whole system of practical philosophy, which permeates the minds of both the educated and uneducated, and reacts (as practical philosophy always does) upon the theoretical philosophy of our century.

True, the formidable growth of the productive powers of man in the industrial field, since he tamed steam and electricity, has somewhat shaken Malthus's doctrine. Industrial wealth has grown at a rate which no possible increase of population could attain, and it can grow with still greater speed. But agriculture is still considered a stronghold of the Malthusian pseudo-philosophy. The recent achievements of agriculture and horticulture are not sufficiently well known; and while our gardeners defy climate and latitude, acclimatise sub-tropical plants, raise several crops a year instead of one, and themselves make the soil they want for each special culture, the economists nevertheless continue saying that the surface of the soil is limited, and still more its productive powers; they still maintain that a population which should double each thirty years would soon be confronted by a lack of the necessaries of life!

A few data to illustrate what can be obtained from the soil were given in the preceding chapter. But the deeper one goes into the subject, the more new and striking data does he discover, and the more Malthus's fears appear groundless.

To begin with an instance taken from culture in the open field--namely, that of wheat--we come upon the following interesting fact. While we are so often told that wheat-growing does not pay, and England consequently reduces from year to year the area of its wheat fields, the French peasants steadily increase the area under wheat, and the greatest increase is due to those peasant families which themselves cultivate the land they own. In the course of the nineteenth century they have nearly doubled the area under wheat, as well as the returns from each acre, so as to increase almost fourfold the amount of wheat grown in France.

At the same time the population has only increased by 41 per cent., so that the ratio of increase of the wheat crop has been six times greater than the ratio of increase of population, although agriculture has been hampered all the time by a series of serious obstacles--taxation, military service, poverty of the peasantry, and even, up to 1884, a severe prohibition of all sorts of association among the peasants. It must also be remarked that during the same hundred years, and even within the last fifty years, market-gardening, fruit-culture and culture for industrial purposes have immensely developed in France; so that there would be no exaggeration in saying that the French obtain now from their soil at least six or seven times more than they obtained a hundred years ago. The "means of existence" drawn from the soil have thus grown about fifteen times quicker than the population.

But the ratio of progress in agriculture is still better seen from the rise of the standard of requirement as regards cultivation of land. Some thirty years ago the French considered a crop very good when it yielded twenty-two bushels to the acre; but with the same soil the present requirement is at least thirty-three bushels, while in the best soils the crop is good only when it yields from forty-three to forty-eight bushels, and occasionally the produce is as much as fifty-five bushels to the acre. There are whole countries--Hesse, for example --which are satisfied only when the average crop attains thirty-seven bushels, or Denmark, where the average crop (1908-1910) is forty-one bushels per acre (forty-four bushels in 1910). As to the experimental farms of Central France, they produce from year to year, over large areas, forty-one bushels to the acre; and a number of farms in Northern France regularly yield, year after year, from fifty-five to sixty-eight bushels to the acre. Occasionally even so much as eighty bushels have been obtained upon limited areas under special care. In fact, Prof. Grandeau considers it proved that by combining a series of such operations as the selection of seeds, sowing in rows, and proper manuring, the crops can be largely increased over the best present average, while the cost of production can be reduced by 50 per cent. by the use of inexpensive machinery; to say nothing of costly machines, like the steam digger, or the pulverisers which make the soil required for each special culture. They are now occasionally resorted to here and there, and they surely will come into general use as soon as humanity feels the need of largely increasing its agricultural produce.

In fact, a considerable progress has already been realised in French agriculture by labour-saving machinery during the last twenty-five years; but there still remains an immense field for further improvement. Thus, in 1908, France had already in use 25,000 harvesting machines and 1,200 binders as against 180 only of the former and sixty of the second, which were used in 1882; but it is calculated that no less than 375,000 more harvesting machines and 300,000 mowing machines are required to satisfy the needs of French agriculture. The same must be said as regards the use of artificial manure, irrigation, pumping machinery, and so on.

When we bear in mind the very unfavourable conditions in which agriculture stands now all over the world, we must not expect to find considerable progress in its methods realised over wide regions; we must be satisfied with noting the advance accomplished in separate, especially favoured spots, where, for one cause or another, the tribute levied upon the agriculturist has not been so heavy as to stop all possibility of progress.

One such example may be seen in the district of Saffelare in East Flanders. Thirty years ago, on a territory of 37,000 acres, all taken, a population of 30,000 inhabitants, all peasants, not only used to find its food, but managed, moreover, to keep no less than 10,720 horned cattle, 3,800 sheep, 1,815 horses and 6,550 swine, to grow flax, and to export various agricultural produce. And during the last thirty years it has continued steadily to increase its exports of agricultural produce.

Another illustration of this sort may be taken from the Channel Islands, whose inhabitants have happily not known the blessings of Roman law and landlordism, as they still live under the common law of Normandy. The small island of Jersey, eight miles long and less than six miles wide, still remains a land of open-field culture; but, although it comprises only 28,707 acres, rocks included, it nourishes a population of about two inhabitants to each acre, or 1,300 inhabitants to the square mile, and there is not one writer on agriculture who, after having paid a visit to this island, did not praise the well-being of the Jersey peasants and the admirable results which they obtain in their small farms of from five to twenty acres --very often less than five acres--by means of a rational and intensive culture.

Most of my readers will probably be astonished to learn that the soil of Jersey, which consists of decomposed granite, with no organic matter in it, is not at all of astonishing fertility, and that its climate, though more sunny than the climate of these isles, offers many drawbacks on account of the small amount of sun-heat during the summer and of the cold winds in spring. But so it is in reality, and at the beginning of the nineteenth century the inhabitants of Jersey lived chiefly on imported food. (See Appendix L.) The successes accomplished lately in Jersey are entirely due to the amount of labour which a dense population is putting in the land; to a system of land-tenure, land-transference and inheritance very different from those which prevail elsewhere; to freedom from State taxation; and to the fact that communal institutions have been maintained, down to quite a recent period, while a number of communal habits and customs of mutual support, derived therefrom, are alive to the present time. As to the fertility of the soil, it is made partly by the sea-weeds gathered free on the sea-coast, but chiefly by artificial manure fabricated at Blaydon-on-Tyne, out of all sorts of refuse--inclusive of bones shipped from Plevna and mummies of cats shipped from Egypt.

It is well known that for the last thirty years the Jersey peasants and farmers have been growing early potatoes on a great scale, and that in this line they have attained most satisfactory results. Their chief aim being to have the potatoes out as early as possible, when they fetch at the Jersey Weigh-Bridge as much as £ 17 and £ 20 the ton, the digging out of potatoes begins, in the best sheltered places, as early as the first days of May, or even at the end of April. Quite a system of potato-culture, beginning with the selection of tubers, the arrangements for making them germinate, the selection of properly sheltered and well situated plots of ground, the choice of proper manure, and ending with the box in which the potatoes germinate and which has so many other useful applications, --quite a system of culture has been worked out in the island for that purpose by the collective intelligence of the peasants.

In the last weeks of May and in June, when the export is at its height, quite a fleet, of steamers runs between the small island of Jersey and various ports of England and Scotland. Every day eight to ten steamers enter the harbour of St. Hélier, and in twenty-four hours they are loaded with potatoes and steer for London, Southampton, Liverpool, Newcastle, and Scotland. From 50,000 to 60,000 tons of potatoes, valued at from £ 260,000 to £ 500,000, according to the year, are thus exported every summer; and, if the local consumption be taken into account, we have at least 60,000 to 70,000 tons that are obtained, although no more than from 6,500 to 7,500 acres are given to all potato crops, early and late--early potatoes, as is well known, never giving as heavy crops as the later ones. Ten to eleven tons per acre is thus the average, while in this country the average is only six tons per acre.

As soon as the potatoes are out, the second crop of mangold or of "three months' wheat" (a special variety of rapidly growing wheat) is sown. Not one day is lost in putting it in. The potato-field may consist of one or two acres only, but as soon as one-fourth part of it is cleared of the potatoes it is sown with the second crop. One may thus see a small field divided into four plots, three of which are sown with wheat at five or six days' distance from each other, while on the fourth plot the potatoes are being dug out.

The admirable condition of the meadows and the grazing land in the Channel Islands has often been described, and although the aggregate area which is given in Jersey to green crops, grasses under rotation, and permanent pasture --both for hay and grazing--is less than 11,000 acres, they keep in Jersey over

12,300 head of cattle and over 2,300 horses solely used for agriculture and breeding.

Moreover, about 100 bulls and 1,600 cows and heifers are exported every year, so that by this time, as was remarked in an American paper, there are more Jersey cows in America than in Jersey Island. Jersey milk and butter have a wide renown, as also the pears which are grown in the open air, but each of which is protected on the tree by a separate cap, and still more the fruit and vegetables which are grown in the hothouses. In a word, it will suffice to say that on the whole they obtain agricultural produce to the value of £ 50 to each acre of the aggregate surface of the island.

Fifty pounds' worth of agricultural produce from each acre of the land is sufficiently good. But the more we study the modern achievements of agriculture, the more we see that the limits of productivity of the soil are not attained, even in Jersey. New horizons are continually unveiled. For the last fifty years science--especially chemistry--and mechanical skill have been widening and extending the industrial powers of man upon organic and inorganic dead matter. Prodigies have been achieved in that direction. Now comes the turn of similar achievements with living plants. Human skill in the treatment of living matter, and science--in its branch dealing with living organisms--step in with the intention of doing for the art of food-growing what mechanical and chemical skill have done in the art of fashioning and shaping metals, wood and the dead fibres of plants. Almost every year brings some new, often unexpected improvement in the art of agriculture, which for so many centuries had been dormant.

We just saw that while the average potato crop in the country is six tons per acre, in Jersey it is nearly twice as big. But Mr. Knight, whose name is well known to every horticulturist in this country, has once dug out of his fields no less than 1,284 bushels of potatoes, or thirty-four tons and nine cwts. in weight, on one single acre; and at a recent competition in Minnesota 1,120 bushels, or thirty tons, could be ascertained as having been grown on one acre.

These are undoubtedly extraordinary crops, but quite recently the French Professor Aime Girard undertook a series of experiments in order to find out the best conditions for growing potatoes in his country. He did not care for show-crops obtained by means of extravagant manuring, but carefully studied all conditions: the best variety, the depth of tilling and planting, the distance between the plants. Then he entered into correspondence with some 350 growers in different parts of France, advised them by letters, and finally induced them to experiment. Strictly following his instructions, several of his correspondents made experiments on a small scale, and they obtained, --instead of the three tons which they were accustomed to grow--such crops as would correspond to twenty and thirty-six tons to the acre. Moreover, ninety growers experimented on fields more than one-quarter of an acre in size, and more than twenty growers made their experiments on larger areas of from three to twenty-eight acres. The result was that none of them obtained less than twelve tons to the acre, while some obtained twenty tons, and the average was, for the 110 growers, fourteen and a half tons per acre.

However, industry requires still heavier crops. Potatoes are largely used in Germany and Belgium for distilleries; consequently, the distillery owners try to obtain the greatest possible amounts of starch from the acre. Extensive experiments have lately been made for that purpose in Germany, and the crops were: Nine tons per acre for the poor sorts, fourteen tons for the better ones, and thirty-two and four-tenths tons for the best varieties of potatoes.

Three tons to the acre and more than thirty tons to the acre are thus the ascertained limits; and one necessarily asks oneself: Which of the two requires less labour in tilling, planting, cultivating and digging, and less expenditure in manure--thirty tons grown on ten acres, or the same thirty tons grown on one acre or two? If labour is of no consideration, while every penny spent in seeds and manure is of great importance, as is unhappily very often the case with the peasant--he will perforce choose the first method. But is it the most economic?

Again, I just mentioned that in the Saffelare district and Jersey they succeed in keeping one head of horned cattle to each acre of green crops, meadows and pasture land, while elsewhere two or three acres are required for the same purpose. But better results still can be obtained by means of irrigation, either with sewage or even with pure water. In England, farmers are contented with one and a half and two tons of hay per acre, and in the part of Flanders just mentioned, two and a half tons of hay to the acre are considered a fair crop. But on the irrigated fields of the Vosges, the Vaucluse, etc., in France, six tons of dry hay become the rule, even upon ungrateful soil; and this means considerably more than the annual food of one milch cow (which can be taken at a little less than five tons) grown on each acre. All taken, the results of irrigation have proved so satisfactory in France that during the years 1862-1882 no less than 1,355,000 acres of meadows have been irrigated, which means that the annual meat-food of at least 1,500,000 full-grown persons, or more, has been added to the yearly income of the country; home-grown, not imported. In fact, in the valley of the Seine, the value of the land was doubled by irrigation; in the Saône valley it was increased five times, and ten times in certain landes of Brittany.

The example of the Campine district, in Belgium, is classical. It was a most unproductive territory--mere sand from the sea, blown into irregular mounds which were only kept together by the roots of the heath; the acre of it used to be sold, not rented, at from 5s. to 7s. (15 to 20 francs per hectare). But now it is capable, thanks to the work of the Flemish peasants and to irrigation, to produce the food of one milch cow per acre--the dung of the cattle being utilised for further improvements.

The irrigated meadows round Milan are another well-known example. Nearly 22,000 acres are irrigated there with water derived from the sewers of the city, and they yield crops of from eight to ten tons of hay as a rule; occasionally some separate meadows will yield the fabulous amount --fabulous to-day, but no longer fabulous tomorrow--of eighteen tons of hay per acre, that is, the food of nearly four cows to the acre, and nine times the yield of good meadows in this country. However, English readers need not go so far as Milan for ascertaining the results of irrigation by sewer water. They have several such examples in this country, in the experiments of Sir John Lawes, and especially at Craigentinny, near Edinburgh, where, to use Ronna's words, "the growth of rye grass is so activated that it attains its full development in one year instead of in three to four years. Sown in August, it gives a first crop in autumn, and then, beginning with next spring, a crop of four tons to the acre is taken every month; which represents in the fourteen months more than fifty-six tons (of green fodder) to the acre." At Lodge Farm they grow forty to fifty-two tons of green crops per acre, after the cereals, without new manuring. At Aldershot they obtain excellent potato crops; and at Romford (Breton's Farm) Colonel Hope obtained, in 1871-1872, quite extravagant crops of various roots and potatoes.

It can thus be said that while at the present time we give two and three acres for keeping one head of horned cattle, and only in a few places one head of cattle is kept on each acre given to green crops, meadows and pasture, man has already in irrigation (which very soon repays when it is properly made) the possibility of keeping twice and even thrice as many head of cattle to the acre over parts of his territory. Moreover, the very heavy crops of roots which are now obtained (seventy-five to 110 tons of beetroot to the acre are not infrequent) give another powerful means for increasing the number of cattle without taking the land from what is now given to the culture of cereals.

Another new departure in agriculture, which is full of promises and probably will upset many a current notion, must be mentioned in this place. I mean the almost horticultural treatment of our corn crops, which is widely practised in the far East, and begins to claim our attention in Western Europe as well.

At the First International Exhibition, in 1851, Major Hallett, of Manor House, Brighton, had a series of very interesting exhibits which he described as "pedigree cereals." By picking out the best plants of his fields, and by submitting their descendants to a careful selection from year to year, he had succeeded in producing new prolific varieties of wheat and barley. Each grain of these cereals, instead of giving only two to four ears, as is the usual average in a cornfield, gave ten to twenty-five ears, and the best ears, instead of carrying from sixty to sixty-eight grains, had an average of nearly twice that number of grains.

In order to obtain such prolific varieties Major Hallett naturally could not sow his picked grains broadcast; he planted them, each separately, in rows, at distances of from ten to twelve inches from each other. In this way he found that each grain, having full room for what is called "tillering" (tallage in French), would produce ten, fifteen, twenty-five, and even up to ninety and 100 ears, as the case may be; and as each ear would contain from 60 to 120 grains, crops of 500 to 2,500 grains, or more, could be obtained from each separately planted grain. He even exhibited at the Exeter meeting of the British Association three plants of wheat, barley, and oats, each from a single grain, which had the following number of stems: wheat, ninety-four stems;

barley, 110 stems; oats, eighty-seven stems. The barley plant which had 110 stems thus gave something like 5,000 to 6,000 grains from one single grain. A careful drawing of that wonderful stubble was made by Major Hallett's daughter and circulated with his pamphlets. Again, in 1876, a wheat plant, with "105 heads growing on one root, on which more than 8,000 grains were growing at once," was exhibited at the Maidstone Farmers' Club.

Two different processes were thus involved in Hallett's experiments: a process of selection, in order to create new varieties of cereals, similar to the breeding of new varieties of cattle; and a method of immensely increasing the crop from each grain and from a given area, by planting each seed separately and wide apart, so as to have room for the full development of the young plant, which is usually suffocated by its neighbours in our corn-fields.

The double character of Major Hallett's method--the breeding of new prolific varieties, and the method of culture by planting the seeds wide apart-- seems, however, so far as I am entitled to judge, to have been overlooked until quite lately. The method was mostly judged upon its results; and when a farmer had experimented upon "Hallett's Wheat," and found out that it was late in ripening in his own locality, or gave a less perfect grain than some other variety, he usually did not care more about the method. However, Major Hallett's successes or non-successes in breeding such or such varieties are quite distinct from what is to be said about the method itself of selection, or the method of planting wheat seeds wide apart. Varieties which were bred, and which I saw grown still at Manor Farm, on the windy downs of Brighton may be, or may not be, suitable to this or that locality. Latest physiological researches give such an importance to evaporation in the bringing of cereals to maturity that where evaporation is not so rapid as it is on the Brighton Downs, other varieties must be resorted to and bred on purpose. I should also suggest that quite different wheats than the English ought to be experimented upon for obtaining prolific varieties; namely, the quickly-growing Norwegian wheat, the Jersey "three months' wheat," or even Yakutsk barley, which matures with an astonishing rapidity. And now that horticulturists, so experienced in "breeding" and "crossing" as Vilmorin, Carter, Sherif, W. Saunders in Canada and many others are, have taken the matter in hand, we may feel sure that future progress will be made. But breeding is one thing; and the planting wide apart of seeds of an appropriate variety of wheat is quite another thing.

This last method was lately experimented upon by M. Grandeau, Director of the Station Agronomique de l'Est, and by M. Florimond Dessprèz at the experimental station of Capelle; and in both cases the results were most remarkable. At this last station a method which is in use in France for the choice of seeds was applied. Already now some French farmers go over their wheat fields before the crop begins, choose the soundest plants which bear two or three equally strong stems, adorned with long ears, well stocked with grains, and take these ears. Then they crop off with scissors the top and the bottom of each ear and keep its middle part only, which contains the biggest seeds. With a dozen quarts of such selected grains they obtain next year the required quantity of seeds of a superior quality.

The same was done by M. Dessprèz. Then each seed was planted separately, eight inches apart in a row, by means of a specially devised tool, similar to the rayonneur which is used for planting potatoes; and the rows, also eight inches apart, were alternately given to the big and to the smaller seeds. One-fourth part of an acre having been planted in this way, with seeds obtained from both early and late ears, crops corresponding to 83.8 bushels per acre for the first series, and 90.4 bushels for the second series, were obtained; even the small grains gave in this experiment as much as 70.2 and 62 bushels respectively.

The crop was thus more than doubled by the choice of seeds and by planting them separately eight inches apart. It corresponded in Dessprèz's experiments to 600 grains obtained on the average from each grain sown; and one-tenth or one-eleventh part of an acre was sufficient in such case to grow the eight and a half bushels of wheat which are required on the average for the annual bread food per head of a population which would chiefly live on bread.

Prof. Grandeau, Director of the French Station Agronomique de l'Est, has also made, since 1886, experiments on Major Hallett's method, and he obtained similar results. "In a proper soil," he wrote, "one single grain of wheat can give as much as fifty stems (and ears), and even more, and thus cover a circle thirteen inches in diameter." But as he seems to know how difficult it often is to convince people of the plainest facts, he published the photographs of separate wheat plants grown in different soils, differently manured, including pure river sand enriched by manure. He concluded that under proper treatment 2,000 and even 4,000 grains could be easily obtained from each planted grain. The seedlings, growing from grains planted ten inches apart, cover the whole space, and the experimental plot takes the aspect of an excellent cornfield, as may be seen from a photograph given by Grandeau in his Etudes agronomiques.

In fact, the eight and a half bushels required for one man's annual food were actually grown at the Tomblaine station on a surface of 2,250 square feet, or forty-seven feet square--that is, on very nearly one-twentieth part of an acre.

Again, we may thus say, that where we require now three acres, one acre would be sufficient for growing the same amount of food, if planting wide apart were resorted to. And there is, surely, no more objection to planting wheat than there is to sowing in rows, which is now in general use, although at the time when the system was first introduced, in lieu of the formerly usual mode of sowing broadcast, it certainly was met with great distrust. While the Chinese and the Japanese used for centuries to sow wheat in rows, by means of a bamboo tube adapted to the plough, European writers objected, of course, to this method under the pretext that it would require too much labour. It is the same now with planting each seed apart. Professional writers sneer at it, although all the rice that is grown in Japan is planted and even replanted. Everyone, however, who will think of the labour which must be spent for ploughing, harrowing, fencing, and keeping free of weeds three acres instead of one, and who will calculate the corresponding expenditure in manure, will surely admit that all advantages are in favour of the one acre as against the three acres, to say nothing of the possibilities of irrigation or of the planting machine-tool, which will be devised as soon as there is a demand for it.

More than that, there is full reason to believe that even this method is liable to further improvement by means of replanting. Cereals in such cases would be treated as vegetables are treated in horticulture. Such is, at least, the idea which began to germinate since the methods of cereal culture that are resorted to in China and Japan became better known in Europe. (See Appendix O.)

The future--a near future, I hope--will show what practical importance such a method of treating cereals may have. But we need not speculate about that future. We have already, in the facts mentioned in this chapter, an experimental basis for quite a number of means of improving our present methods of culture and of largely increasing the crops. It is evident that in a book which is not intended to be a manual of agriculture, all I can do is to give only a few hints to set people thinking for themselves upon this subject. But the little that has been said is sufficient to show that we have no right to complain of over-population, and no need to fear it in the future. Our means of obtaining from the soil whatever we want, under any climate and upon any soil, have lately been improved at such a rate that we cannot foresee yet what is the limit of productivity of a few acres of land. The limit vanishes in proportion to our better study of the subject, and every year makes it vanish further and further from our sight.

Chapter V: The Possibilities of Agriculture, Part 3

ONE of the most interesting features of the present evolution of agriculture is the extension lately taken by intensive market-gardening of the same sort as has been described in the third chapter. What formerly was limited to a few hundreds of small gardens, is now spreading with an astonishing rapidity. In this country the area given to market-gardens, after having more than doubled within the years 1879 to 1894, when it attained 88,210 acres, has continued steadily to increase. But it is especially in France, Belgium, and America that this branch of culture has lately taken a great development. (See Appendix P.)

At the present time no less than 1,075,000 acres are given in France to market-gardening and intensive fruit culture, and a few years ago it was estimated that the average yield of every acre given to these cultures attains £ 33, 10s. Their character, as well as the amount of skill displayed in, and labour given to, these cultures, will best appear from the following illustrations.

About Roscoff, which is a great centre in Brittany for the export to England of such potatoes as will keep till late in summer, and of all sorts of vegetables, a territory, twenty-six miles in diameter, is entirely given to these cultures, and the rents attain and exceed £ 6 per acre. Nearly 300 steamers call at Roscoff to ship potatoes, onions and other vegetables to London and different English ports, as far north as Newcastle. Moreover, as much as 4,000 tons of vegetables are sent every year to Paris. And although the Roscoff peninsula enjoys a specially warm climate, small stone walls are erected everywhere, and rushes are grown on their tops in order to give still more protection and heat to the vegetables. The climate is improved as well as the soil.

In the neighbourhoods of Cherbourg it is upon land conquered from the sea that the best vegetables are grown--more than 800 acres of that land being given to potatoes exported to London; another 500 acres are given to cauliflower; 125 acres to Brussels sprouts; and so on. Potatoes grown under glass are also sent to the London market from the middle of April, and the total export of vegetables from Cherbourg to England attains 300,000 cwts., while from the small port of Barfleur another 100,000 cwts. are sent to this country, and about 60,000 cwts. to Paris. Nay, in a quite small commune, Surtainville, near Cherbourg, £ 2,800 are made out of 180 acres of market-gardens, three crops being taken every year: cabbage in February, early potatoes next, and various crops in the autumn--to say nothing of the catch crops.

At Ploustagel one hardly believes that he is in Brittany. Melons used to be grown at that spot, long since, in the open fields, with glass frames to protect them from the spring frost, and green peas were grown under the protection of rows of furze which sheltered them from the northern winds. Now, whole fields are covered with strawberries, roses, violets, cherries and plums, down to the very sea beach. Even the landes are reclaimed, and we are told that in five years or so there will be no more landes in that district (p. 265). Nay, the marshes of the Dol-- " The Holland of Brittany "--protected from the sea by a wall (5,050 acres), have been turned into market-gardens, covered with cauliflowers, onions, radishes, haricot beans and so on, the acre of that land being rented at from £ 2, 10s. to £ 4.

The neighbourhoods of Nantes could also be mentioned. Green peas are cultivated there on a very large scale. During the months of May and June quite an army of working people, especially women and children, are picking them. The roads leading to the great preserving factories are covered at certain hours with rows of carts, upon which the peas and onions are carted one way, while another row of carts are carrying the empty pods which are used for manure. For two months the children are missing in the schools; and in the peasant families of the neighbourhood, when the question comes about some expenditure to be made, the usual saying is, "Wait till the season of the green peas has come."

About Paris no less than 50,000 acres are given to the field culture of vegetables and 25,000 acres to the forced culture of the same. Sixty years ago the yearly rent paid by market-gardeners attained already as much as £ 18 and £ 24 per acre, and yet it has been increased since, as well as the gross receipts, which were valued by Courtois Gérard at £ 240 per acre for the larger market-gardeners, and twice as much for the smaller ones in which early vegetables are grown in frames.

The fruit culture in the neighbourhoods of Paris is equally wonderful. At Montreuil, for instance, 750 acres, belonging to 400 gardeners, are literally covered with stone walls, specially erected for growing fruit, and having an aggregate length of 400 miles. Upon these walls, peach trees, pear trees and vines are spread, and every year something like 12,000,000 peaches are gathered, as well as a considerable amount of the finest pears and grapes. The acre in such conditions brings in £ 56. This is how a "warmer climate" was made, at a time when the greenhouse was still a costly luxury. All taken, 1,250 acres are given to peaches (26,000,000 peaches every year) in the close neighbourhood of Paris. Acres and acres are also covered with pear trees which yield three to five tons of fruit per acre, such crop being sold at from £ 50 to £ 60. Nay, at Angers, on the Loire, where pears are eight days in advance of the suburbs of Paris, Baltet knows an orchard of five acres, covered with pears (pyramid trees), which brings in £ 400 every year; and at a distance of thirty-three miles from Paris one pear plantation brings in £ 24 per acre--the cost of package, transport and selling being deducted. Likewise, the plantations of plums, of which

80,000 cwts. are consumed every year at Paris alone, give an annual money income of from £ 29 to £ 48 per acre every year; and yet, pears, plums and cherries are sold at Paris, fresh and juicy, at such a price that the poor, too, can eat fresh home-grown fruit.

In the province of Anjou one may see how a heavy clay, improved with sand taken from the Loire and with manure, has been turned, in the neighbourhoods of Angers, and especially at Saint Laud, into a soil which is rented at from £ 2, 10s. to £ 5 the acre, and upon that soil fruit is grown which a few years ago was exported to America. At Bennecour, a quite small village of 850 inhabitants, near Paris, one sees what man can make out of the most unproductive soil. Quite recently the steep slopes of its hills were only mergers from which stone was extracted for the pavements of Paris Now these slopes are entirely covered with apricot and cherry trees, black-currant shrubs, and plantations of asparagus, green peas and the like. In 1881, £ 5,600 worth of apricots alone was sold out of this village, and it must be borne in mind that competition is so acute in the neighbourhoods of Paris that a delay of twenty-four hours in the sending of apricots to the market will often mean a loss of 8s.---one-seventhof the sale price on each hundredweight.

At Perpignan, green artichokes--a favourite vegetable in France--are grown, from October till June, on an area covering 2,500 acres, and the net revenue is estimated at £ 32 per acre. In Central France, artichokes are even cultivated in the open fields, and nevertheless the crops are valued (by Baltet) at from £ 48 to £ 100 per acre. In the Loiret, 1,500 gardeners, who occasionally employ 5,000 workmen, obtain from £ 400,000 to £ 480,000 worth of vegetables, and their yearly expenditure for manure is £ 60,000. This figure alone is the best answer to those who are fond of talking about the extraordinary fertility of the soil, each time they are told of some success in agriculture. At Lyons, a population of 430,000 inhabitants is entirely supplied with vegetables by the local gardeners. The same is in Amiens, which is another big industrial city. The districts surrounding Orléans form another great centre for market-gardening, and it is especially worthy of notice that the shrubberies of Orléans supply even America with large quantities of young trees.

It would take, however, a volume to describe the chief centres of market-gardening and fruit-growing in France; and I will mention only one region more, where vegetables and fruit-growing go hand in hand. It lies on the banks of the Rhône, about Vienne, where we find a narrow strip of land, partly composed of granite rocks, which has now become a garden of an incredible richness. The origin of that wealth, we are told by Ardouin Dumazet, dates from some thirty years ago, when the vineyards, ravaged by phylloxera, had to be destroyed and some new culture had to be found. The village of Ampuis became then renowned for its apricots. At the present time, for a full 100 miles along the Rhône, and in the lateral valleys of the Ardèche and the Drôme, the country is an admirable orchard, from which millions' worth of fruit is exported, and the land attains the selling price of from £ 325 to £ 400 the acre. Small plots of land are continually reclaimed for culture upon every crag. On both sides of the roads one sees the plantations of apricot and cherry trees, while between the rows of trees early beans and peas, strawberries, and all sorts of early vegetables are grown. In the spring the fine perfume of the apricot trees in bloom floats over the whole valley. Strawberries, cherries, apricots, peaches and grapes follow each other in rapid succession, and at the same time cartloads of French beans, salads, cabbages, leeks, and potatoes are sent towards the industrial cities of the region. It would be impossible to estimate the quantity and value of all that is grown in that region. Suffice it to say that a tiny commune, Saint Désirat, exported during Ardouin Dumazet's visit about 2,000 cwts. of cherries every day.

The results of this development are simply striking. Thus it appears, from an inquest made in 1906 by the French professors of agriculture, that the yearly export of fresh flowers from the département of the Alpes Maritimes attains as much as £ 400,000, and that of the flowers used for perfumes gives from £ 280,000 to £ 320,000 in addition to the just mentioned sum. From the département of the Var, 3,475 tons of flowers, valued from £ 160,000 to £ 200,000, were exported in 1902.

I must refer the reader to the work of Charles Baltet if he will know more about the extension taken by market-gardening in different countries, and will only mention Belgium and America.

The exports of vegetables from Belgium have increased twofold within the last twenty years of the nineteenth century, and whole regions, like Flanders, claim to be now the marketgarden of England, even seeds of the vegetables preferred in this country being distributed free by one horticultural society in order to increase the export. Not only the best lands are appropriated for that purpose, but even the sand deserts of the Ardennes and peat-bogs are turned into rich market-gardens, while large plains (namely at Haeren) are irrigated for the same purpose. Scores of schools, experimental farms, and small experimental stations, evening lectures, and so on, are opened by the communes, the private societies, and the State, in order to promote horticulture, and hundreds of acres of land are covered with thousands of greenhouses.

Here we see one small commune exporting 5,500 tons of potatoes and 163 4,000 worth of pears to Stratford and Scotland, and keeping for that purpose its own line of steamers. Another commune supplies the north of France and the Rhenish provinces with strawberries, and occasionally sends some of them to Covent Garden as well. Elsewhere early carrots, which are grown amidst flax, barley and white poppies, give a considerable addition to the farmer's income. In another place we learn that land is rented at £ 24 and £ 27 the acre, not for grapes or melon-growing but for the modest culture of onions; or that the gardeners have done away with such a nuisance as natural soil in their frames, and prefer to make their loam out of wood sawings, tannery refuse and hemp dust, "animalised" by various composts.

In short, Belgium, which is one of the chief manufacturing countries of Europe, is now becoming one of the chief centres of horticulture. (See Appendix R.)

The other country which must especially be recommended to the attention of horticulturists is America. When we see the mountains of fruit imported from America we are inclined to think that fruit in that country grows by itself. "Beautiful climate," "virgin soil," "immeasurable spaces"--- these words continually recur in the papers. The reality, however, is that horticulture---that is, both market-gardening and fruit culture--has been brought in America to a high degree of perfection. Prof. Baltet, a practical gardener himself, originally from the classical marais (market-gardens) of Troyes, describes the "truck farms" of Norfolk in Virginia as real "model farms." A highly complimentary appreciation from the lips of a practical maraîcher who has learned from his infancy that only in fairyland do the golden apples grow by fairies' magic wand. As to the perfection to which apple-growing has been brought in Canada, the aid which the apple-growers receive from the Canadian experimental farms, and the means which are resorted to, on a truly American scale, to spread information amongst the farmers and to supply them with new varieties of fruit trees---all this ought to be carefully studied in this country, instead of inducing Englishmen to believe that the American supremacy is due to the golden fairies' hands. If one tenth part of what is done in the States and in Canada for favouring agriculture and horticulture were done in this country, English fruit would not have been 80 shamefully driven out of the market as it was a few years ago.

The extension given to horticulture in America is immense. The "truck farms" alone--that is, the farms which work for export by rail or steam--covered in the States in 1892 no less than 400,000 acres. At the very doors of Chicago one single market-gardening farm covers 500 acres, and out of these, 150 acres are given to cucumbers, 50 acres to early peas, and so on. During the Chicago Exhibition a special "strawberry express," composed of thirty waggons, brought in every day 324,000 quarts of the freshly gathered fruit, and there are days that over 10,000 bushels of strawberries are imported in New York--three-fourths of that amount coming from the "truck farms" of Virginia by steamer.

This is what can be achieved by an intelligent combination of agriculture with industry, and undoubtedly will be applied on a still larger scale in the future.

However, a further advance is being made in order to emancipate horticulture from climate. I mean the glasshouse culture of fruit and vegetables. Formerly the greenhouse was the luxury of the rich mansion. It was kept at a high temperature, and was made use of for growing, under cold skies, the golden fruit and the bewitching flowers of the South. Now, and especially since the progress of technics allows of making cheap glass and of having all the woodwork, sashes and bars of a greenhouse made by machinery, the glasshouse becomes appropriated for growing fruit for the million, as well as for the culture of common vegetables The aristocratic hothouse, stocked with the rarest fruit trees and flowers, remains; nay, it spreads more and more for growing luxuries which become more and more accessible to the great number. But by its side we have the plebeian greenhouse, which is heated for only a couple of months in winter and the still more economically built "cool greenhouse," which is a simple glass shelter--a big "cool frame"--and is stuffed with the humble vegetables of the kitchen garden: the potatoes, the carrots, the French beans, the peas and the like. The heat of the sun, passing through the glass, but prevented by the same glass from escaping by radiation, is sufficient to keep it at a very high temperature during spring and early summer. A new system of horticulture-- the market-garden under glass--is thus rapidly gaining ground.

The greenhouse for commercial purposes essentially of British, or perhaps Scottish, origin. Already in 1851, Mr. Th. Rivers had published a book, The Orchard Houses and the Cultivation of Fruit Trees in Pots under Glass; and we were told by Mr. D. Thomson, in the Journal of Horticulture (31st January, 1889), that nearly fifty years ago grapes in February were sold at 25s. the pound by a grower in the north of England, and that part of them was sent by the buyer to Paris for Napoleon III.'s table, at 50s. the pound. " Now," Mr. Thomson added, " they are sold at the tenth or twentieth part of the above prices. Cheap coal-cheap grapes; that is the whole secret."

Large vineries and immense establishments for growing flowers under glass are of an old standing in this country, and new ones are continually built on a grand scale. Entire fields are covered with glass at Cheshunt, at Broxburn (fifty acres), at Finchley, at Bexley, at Swanley, at Whetstone, and so on, to say nothing of Scotland. Worthing is also a well known centre for growing grapes and tomatoes; while the greenhouses given to flowers and ferns at Upper Edmonton, at Chelsea, at Orpington, and so on, have a world-wide reputation. And the tendency is, on the one side, to bring grape culture to the highest, degree of perfection, and, on the other side, to cover acres and acres with glass for growing tomatoes, French beans and peas, which undoubtedly will soon be followed by the culture of still plainer vegetables. This movement, as will be seen further on, has been steadily continuing for the last twenty years.

However, the Channel Islands and Belgium still hold the lead in the development of glasshouse culture. The glory of Jersey is, of course, Mr. Bashford's establishment. When I visited it in 1890, it contained 490,000 square feet under glass-that is, nearly thirteen acres -but seven more acres under glass have been added to it since. A long row of glasshouses, interspersed with high chimneys, covers the ground-the largest of the houses being 900 feet long and forty-six feet wide; this means that about one acre of land, in one piece, is under glass. The whole is built most substantially: granite walls, great height, thick " twenty-seven oz. glass " (of the thickness of three pennies), ventilators which open upon a length of 200 and 300 feet by working one single handle; and so on. And yet the most luxurious of these greenhouses was said by the owners to have cost less than 1s. the square foot of glass (13d. the square foot of ground), while the other houses have cost much less than that, From 5d. to 9d. the square foot of glass is the habitual cost, without the heating apparatus -6d. being a current price for the ordinary glasshouses.

But it would be hardly possible to give an idea of all that is grown in such glasshouses, without producing photographs of their insides. In 1890, on the 3rd of May, exquisite grapes began to be out in Mr. Bashford's vineries, and the crop was continued till October. In other houses, cartloads of peas bad already been gathered, and tomatoes were going to take their place after a thorough cleaning of the house. The 20,000 tomato plants, which were going to be planted, had to yield no less than eighty tons of excellent fruit (eight to ten pounds per plant). In other houses melons were grown instead of the tomatoes. Thirty tons of early potatoes, six tons of early peas, and two tons of early French beans had already been sent away in April. As to the vineries, they yielded no less than twenty-five tons of grapes every year. Besides, very many other things were grown in the open air, or as catch crop, and all that amount of fruit and vegetables was the result of the labor of thirty-six men and boys only, under the supervision of one single gardener-the owner himself; true that in Jersey, and especially in Guernsey, everyone is a gardener. About 1,000 tons of coke were burnt to beat these houses. Mr. W. Bear, who had visited the same establishment in 1886, was quite right to say that from these thirteen acres they obtained money returns equivalent to what a farmer would obtain from 1,300 acres of land.

I hardly need say that Mr. Rider Haggard, who visited Jersey and Guernsey in 1901, gave of these two islands the same enthusiastic description as his predecessors. "I can only state in conclusion," he wrote, "that for my part, here (in Jersey) as in , I was amazed at the prosperity of the place. That so small an area of land can produce so much wealth is nothing short of astonishing. It is true, as I have shown, that the inquirer hears some grumblings and fears for the future; but when on the top of them he sees a little patch of twenty-three and one-third acres of land, such as I have instanced, and is informed that quite recently it sold at an auction for £ 5,760, to be used, not for building sites but for the cultivation of potatoes, he is perhaps justified in drawing his own conclusions." It need not be added that, like all his predecessors, Mr. Haggard disposes of the legend of extraordinary natural fertility of the soil, and shows at what a considerable expenditure the heavy crops of potatoes are obtained.

However, it is in the small " vineries " that one sees, perhaps, the most admirable results. As I walked through such glass-roofed kitchen gardens, I could not but admire this recent conquest of man. I saw, for instance, three-fourths of an acre heated for the first three months of the year, from which about eight tons of tomatoes and about 200 lb. of French beans had been taken as a first crop in April, to be followed by two crops more. In these houses one gardener was employed with two assistants, a small amount of coke was consumed, and there was a gas engine for watering purposes, consuming only 13s. worth of gas during the quarter. I saw again, in cool greenhouses -simple plank and glass shelters-pea plants covering the walls, for the length of one quarter of a mile, which already had yielded by the end of April 3,200 lb. of exquisite peas and were yet as full of pods as if not one had been taken off.

I saw potatoes dug from the soil in a cool greenhouse, in April, to the amount of five bushels to the twenty-one feet square. And when chance brought me, in 1896, in company with a local gardener, to a tiny, retired "vinery" of a veteran grower, I could see there, and admire, what a lover of gardening can obtain from so small a space as the two-thirds of an acre, Two small " houses " about forty feet long and twelve feet wide, and a third-formerly a pigsty, twenty feet by twelve-contained vine trees which many a professional gardener would be happy to have a look at; especially the whilom pigsty, fitted with " Muscats"! Some grapes (in June) were already in full beauty, and one fully understands that the owner could get in 1895, from a local dealer, £ 4 for three bunches of grapes (one ofthem was a "Colmar," " 13 3/4 lb. weight). The tomatoes and strawberries in the open air, as well as the fruit trees, all on tiny spaces, were equal to grapes; and when one is shown on what a space half a ton of strawberries can be gathered under proper culture, it is hardly believable.

It is especially in Guernsey that the simplification of the greenhouse must be studied. Every house in the suburbs of St. Peter has some sort of greenhouse, big or small. All over the island, especially in the north, wherever you look, you see greenhouses. They rise amid the fields and from behind the trees; they are piled upon one another on the steep crags facing the harbour of St. Peters and with them a whole generation of practical gardeners has grown up. Every farmer is more or less of a gardener, and he gives free scope to his inventive powers for devising some cheap type of greenhouses. Some of them have almost no front and back walls-the glass roofs coming low down and the two or three feet of glass in front simply reaching the ground; in some houses the, lower sheet of glass was simply plunged into a wooden trough standing on the ground and filled with sand. Many houses have only two or three planks, laid horizontally, instead of the usual stone wall, in the front of the greenhouse.

The large houses of one big company are built close to each other, and have no partitions between. /But this system cannot be recommended amended. Altogether, when I revisited Guernsey in 1903, I saw that the system of greenhouses which prevailed was that of long two-roofed glass " tents," placed by the side of each other, but separated from each other by partitions preventing the circulation of the air over the whole block. As to the extensive cool greenhouses on the Grande Maison estate, which are built by a company and are rented to gardeners for so much the 100 feet, they are simply made of thin deal board and glass. They are on the "lean" or "one roof" system, and the back wall, ten feet high, and the two side walls are in simple grooved boards, standing upright. The whole is supported by uprights inserted into cocrete pillars. They are said to cost not more than 5d. the square foot, of glass-covered ground. And yet, even such plain and cheap houses yield excellent results. The potatoe crop which had been grown in some of them was excellent, as also the green peas.

In Jersey I even saw a row of five houses, the walls of which were made of corrugated iron, for the sake of cheapness. Of course, the owner himself was not over-sanguine about his houses. "They are too cold in winter and too hot in summer". But although the five houses cover only less than one-fifth of an acre, 2,000 lb. of green peas had already been sold as a first crop; and, in the first days of June, the second crop (about 1,500 of tomatoes) was already in good progress.

It is always difficult, of course, to know that are the money returns of the growers, first of all because Thorold Rogers' complaint about modern farmers keeping no accounts holds good, even for the best gardening establishments, and next because when the returns are known to me in all details, it would not be right for me to publish them. "Don't prove too much; beware of the landlord!" a practical gardener once wrote to me. Roughly speaking, I can only confirm Mr. Bear's estimate to the effect that under proper management even a cool greenhouse, which covers 4,050 square feet, can give a gross return of £ 180.

As a rule, the Guernsey and Jersey growers have only three crops every year from their greenhouses. They will start, for instance, potatoes in December. The houses will, of course, not be heated, fires being made only when a sharp frost is expected at night; and the potato crop (from eight to ten tons per acre) will be ready in April or May before the open-air potatoes begin to be dug out. Tomatoes will be planted next and be ready by the end of the summer. Various catch crops of peas, radishes, lettuce and other small things will be taken in the meantime. Or else the house will be "started" in November with melons, which will be ready in April. They will be followed by tomatoes, either in pots, or trained as vines, and the last crop of tomatoes will be in October. Beans may follow and be ready for Christmas. I need to say that every grower has his preference method for utilising his houses, and it entirely depends upon his will and watchfulness to have all sorts of small catch crops. These last begin to have a greater and greater importance, and one can already foresee that the growers under glass will be forced to accept the methods of the French maraichers, so as to have five and six crops every year, so far as it can be done without spoiling the present high quality of the produce.

All this industry is of a relatively recent origin. One may see it still working out its methods. And yet the exports from Guernsey alone are already represented by quite extraordinary figures. It was estimated some years ago that they were as follows: Grapes, 502 tons, £ 37,500 worth at the average price of 9d. the pound; tomatoes, 1,000 tons, about £ 30,000; early potatoes (chiefly in the fields), £ 20,000; radishes and broccoli, £ 9,250; cut flowers, £ 3,000; mushrooms, £ 200; total, £ 99,950-to which total the local consumption in the houses and hotels, which have to feed nearly 30,000 tourists, must be added. Since then these figures have grown considerably. In June, 1896, 1 saw the Southampton steamers taking every day from 9,000 to 12,000, and occasionally more, baslets of fruit (grapes, tomatoes, French beans and peas), each basket representing from twelve to fourteen pounds of fruit. Taking into account what was sent by other channels, one could say that from 400 to 500 tons of tomatoes, grapes, beans and peas, worth from £ 20,000 to £ 25,000, were exported there every week in June.

When I returned to Guernsey in 1903, I found that the industry of fruit-growing under glass had grown immensely since 1896, so that the whole system of export had to be reorganised. In 1896 it was the tourists' boats which tranported the fruit and vegetables to Southampton, and the. gardeners paid one shilling for each basket taken at Guernsey and delivered at the Covent Garden market. In 1903 there was already a Guernsey Crowers' Association, which had its own boats keeping, during the summer, a regular daily service direct from Guernsey to London. The Association had its own store- houses on quay and its own cranes, which lifted immense cubic boxes containing on their shelves twenty or even a hundred baskets, and carrying them to the boats. The cost of transport was thus reduced to 4d. per basket. All this crop is sold every morning Covent Garden to the London dealers and greengrocers. The importance of this export is seen from the fact that a special steamer has to leave Guernsey every morning with its cargo of fruit and vegetables. As to the total export of fresh flowers, plants and shurbs, various fruit and vegetables (including £ 555,275 worth of potatoes), they reached £ 1,115,650 in 1910.

All this is obtained form an island whose total area, rocks and barren hill-tops included, is only 16,000 acres, of which only 9,884 acres are under culture, and 5,189 acres are given to green crops and meadows. An island, moreover, on which 1,480 horses, 7,260 he d of cattle and 900 sheep find their existence. How many inen's food is, then, grown on these 10,000 acres?

Belgium has also made, within the last few years, an immense progress in the same direction. Wile no more than 250 acres, all taken, were covered with glass some thirty years ago, more than 800 acres are under glass by this time. In the village of Hoeilaert, which is perched upon a stony hill, nearly 200 acres are under glass, given up to grape-growing. One single establishment, Baltet remarks, has 200 greenhouses and consumes 1,500 tons of coal for the vineries. "Cheap coal-cheap grapes," as the editor of the Journal of Horticulture wrote. Grapes in Brussels are certainly not dearer in the, beginning of the summer than they are in Switzerland in October, Even in March , Belgian grapes were sold in Covent Garden at from 4d. and 6d. the pound. This price alone shows sufficiently how small are the amounts of labour which are required to grow grapes in our latitudes with the aid of glass. It certainly cost less labour to grow grapes in Belgium than to grow them on the coasts of Lake Leman.

I will not conclude this chapter without casting a glance on the progress that has been made in this country since the first edition of this book was published, in 1898, by fruit and flower farming, as also by culture under glass, and on the attempts recently made to introduce in different parts of England "French Gardening," --that is, the culture maraîchère of the French gardeners.

There is not the slightest doubt that fruit-growing has notably increased--the area under fruit orchards having grown in Great Britain from 200,000 acres in 1888 to 250,000 acres in 1908; while the area under small fruit (gooseberries, currants, strawberries) has grown from acres in 1901 to 85,000 in 1908. In some counties the acreage has trebled. Large plantations of fruit have grown lately round London and all the large cities, and the counties of Kent, Devon, Hereford, Somerset, Worcester and Gloucester have now more than 20,000 acres each under fruit orchards, a great proportion of them being of a recent origin. Not only was the area of fruit-growing considerably increased, but, owing to the experiments carried on since 1894 at the Woburn Experimental Farm, where different sorts of fruit-trees and small fruit are tested, new varieties have been introduced; and the system is spreading of growing fruit trees of the pyramidal or "bush" form (instead of the old-fashioned standards)-a step the advantages of which I was enabled fully to appreciate in 1897 at the Agassiz Experimental Farm in British Columbia.

At the same time the culture of small fruit-gooseberries, raspberries, currants, and especially strawberries-took an immense development. Enormous quantities of strawberries are now grown in Mid and South Kent, where we find the culture of fruit combined with large jam factories. One of such factories is connected with great fruit farms covering 2,000 acres at Swanley, Ben its yearly output attains 3,500 tons of jam 850 tons of candied peel, and more than 100,000 bottles of bottled fruit. An extensive horticultnre has also developed of late in Cambridgeshire, wherefrom fruit is sent partly fresh to London and Manchester, and partly is transformed on the spot in the jam factory at Histon. No less than 250 workpeople were employed at his factory at the time of Rider Haggard's visit in 1900, and no less than 7,600 tons were exported; the most interesting result of this industry combined with agriculture being that quite a number of small farmers, renting from three to twenty acres each, have grown round the am factory. "Altogether," Mr. Haggard wrote, "fruit and flower culture has increased enormously; so that, in 1901, from 4,000 to 5,000 acres in the neighbourhood of Wisbeeli were devoted to this trade. Plums, apples, pears, small fruit, as also cauliflowers, asparagus, rhubarb, narcissi, pansies and other flowers were grown here on a grand scale, and as much as from 130 to 140 tons of gooseberries and from 60 to 70 tons of strawberries were despatched from Wisbech in one single day." "The result of this industry," Mr, Haggard adds, "was that the population of Wisbech and the number of houses in this little town have rapidly increased; the land has increased in value considerably in the past twenty years, and as much as £ 200 an acre had been given for choice land-holdings suitable for fruit culture." (Rural Fngland, Vol. ii., pp. 52, 54, 55.) In other words, the net result of the labour spent by the farmers and of the intelligent enterprise of the industrials was, as everywhere, immensely to increase the value of the land for the benefit of the landlords. Mr. Haggard's conclusion is worth mentioning, as he writes as follows: " Broadly, however, I may say that where the farms are large and corn is chiefly grown, there is little or no prosperity, while where they are small and assisted by pastures or fruit culture, both owners and tenants are doing fairly well." A recognition well worth mentioning, as it comes from an explorer who took at the outset of his inquest a most pessimistic view on unprotected agriculture.

I also ought to mention Essex, where fruit growing has taken of late a notable development, and Hampshire, where the acreage under fruit has trebled since 1880, according to the testimony of the author of the already mentioned Britannica article. The same must be said of Worcestershire, and especially of the Evesham district. This last is a most instructive region. Owing to certain peculiarities of its soil, which render it very profitable for growing asparagus and plum trees, and partly owing to the maintenance in this region of the old "Evesham custom" (according to which from times immemorial the ingoing tenant had to pay the outgoing tenant, not the landlord, for the agricultural improvements)-a custom raaintained till nowadays - the small holdings system and the culture of vegetables and fruit have developed to a remarkable extent. The result is that out of a rural area of 10,000 acres, 7,000 have already been taken in small holdings of under fifty acres each, and the demand for them, far from being satisfied, is still on the increase, so that in 1911 there were still nearly four hundred farmers waiting for 2,000 acres. A new town has grown at Evesham, its population of 8,340 persons being almost entirely composed of gardeners and gardeners' labourers; its markets, held twice a week, remind one of markets in the south of France; and the export traffic on the railways radiating from that little town is as lively as if it were a busy industrial spot.

One cannot read the pages given by Mr. Rider Haggard to the Bewdley and Evesham districts without being impressed by what can be obtained from the soil in England, and by what has to be done by the nation and all those who care for its well-being in obtaining from the soil what it is ready to give, if only labour be applied to it.

In the Bewdley district we see very well how the efforts of a Small Holdings Society are giving the opportunity to a number of small farmers to transform an indifferent and sometimes very poor or stony land into a fertile soil which yields rich crops of fruit, and upon which the keeping of milech-cows is combined with fruit-growing. We see also how in the big farms, as well as in the small ones, fruit-groiwing is carried on with knowledge and care-and, consequently, with a substantial profit for both the community and the farmers-which makes the author exclaim: "How different in most counties! In Norfolk, for instance (and I may add in Devonshire), the ordinary farm orchard is stocked as a rule with faggot-headed trees pruned only by the wind. Even the dead, wood is left uncut; yet it is common to hear farmers complain of the quality of the fruit, and that it will not pay to grow" (vol. i., p. 338).

Speaking of Catshill, Mr. Haggard gives also a very interesting instance of how a colony of people called " Nailers," who lived formerly by making nails by hand, and compelled to abandon this trade when machine-made nails were introduced, took to agriculture, and how they succeed with it. Some intelligent people having bought a farm of 140 acres and divided it into small farms, from 2 and a half to 8 acres, these small holdings were offered to the nailers; and at the time of Mr. Haggard's visit "every instalment which was due had been paid up." No able-bodied man out of them has gone on to the rates.

But the vale of Evesham is still more interesting. Suffice it to say, that while in most rural parishes the population is decreasing, it rose in the six parishes of the Evesham Union from 7,327 to 9,012 in the ten years, 1891 to 1901.

Although the soil of this district offers nothing extraordinary, and the conditions of sale are as bad as anywhere, owing to the importance acquired by the middlemen, we see that an extremely important industry of fruit-growing has developed; so important that in the year 1900 about 20,000 tons of fruit and vegetables were sent from the Evesham stations, in addition to large quantities exported from the small stations within a radius of ten miles round Evesham (Vol. i., p. 350). The soil, of course, is improved by digging into it large quantities of all sorts of manure-soot, fish guano, leather dust for cabbage (chamois dust being the best), and so on-and the most profitable sorts of fruit-trees and -vegetables are continually tested; all this being, of course, not the work of some scientist or of one single man, but the product of the collective experience of the district.

It must not be thought, however, that fruit-growing has been overdone. On the contrary, the imports of fruit into the United Kingdom, both for food and for jam-making, continue to be enormous, and to increase every year. Suffice it to say, that this country imports every year about £ 1,000,000 of tomatoes and £ 2,000,000 of apples, half a million worth of pears, nearly £ 730,000 worth of grapes-giving thus a total of £ 4,200,000 worth of all fruit. And at the same time we learn that immense quantities of land go every year out of culture, to be transformed into game reserves for rich Englishmen and foreigners.

Finally, I also ought to mention the recent development of fruit culture near the Broads of Norfolk, and especially in Ireland; but the examples just given will do to show what is obtained from the land in England where no obstacle is laid to the development of horticulture-are, and what amount of food can be obtained in the climate and from the soil of this country whenever it is properly cultivated. Let me only add that a similar development of fruit cult-are has taken place within the last thirty years everywhere in the civilised countries; and that in France, in Belgium, and in Germany the extension taken by horticulture during the last twenty or thirty years has been much greater than in this country. As regardsmarket--gardening, it has undoubtedly made remarkable progress in the United Kingdom within recent years. However, accurate data are failing, and those who have travelled over this country with the special purpose of studying its agriculture have not yet given sufficient attention to the recent developments of market-gardening; but it is quite certain that within the last five-and-twenty years it has taken a great development, especially in Ireland, but also in several parts of England, Scotland, and Wales.

Such are, for instance, the neighbourhoods of Penzance, in Cornwall; those of St. Neots, in Huntingdonshire; Scotter, in Lincolnshire, where the agricultural depression-we are told by Mr. Rider Haggard--was not so badly felt as elsewhere on account of market-gardening; Benington, in the same county, where the soil is a rich loam with silty subsoil, and where all sorts of vegetables, potatoes, and flower-bulbs are grown on a large scale, together with wheat. Orpington is a well-known centre for market-gardening, as well as for fruit-growing, and in this district culture under glass has also taken lately some extension.

There are many other interesting centres of market-gardening, especially in the neighbourhoods of all large cities, but I will mention only one more-namely, Potton, in Huntingdonshire. It is-we are told by Mr. Haggard- "a stronghold of small cultivators who grow vegetables upon holdings of land varying in size from one up to twenty acres, or even more." It has thus become an important centre for market-gardening, "120 trucks of produce leaving Potton daily during the season for London, in addition to fifty trucks which pass over the Great Northern line from Sandy station, together with much more from sidings and other stations." This is the more interesting as within a short distance from this animated centre "thousands of acres are quite or very nearly derelict, and the farmhouses, buildings, and cottages are slowly rotting down." The worst is that "all this land was cultivated, and grew crops up to the 'eighties."

Another oasis of market-gardening is offered by the county of Bedfordshire. "Being a county of natural small-holdings, carved out before the passing of the 1907 Act," it is rapidly becoming-we are told by Mr. F. E. Green-"a county of market-gardens." The fertility of its soil, the fact that it can easily be worked at any time of the year, and that a race of skilled gardeners has developed there long since, have contributed to that growth; but, of course, the whole is hampered by the heavy rents, which have grown up to £4 an acre for the sites near the station, where manure is received in large quantities from London.

Happily enough, the Bedfordshire County Council has been eager to acquire land for small holdings, and, after having spent £ 40,000 in the acquisition of land, they have, up to 30th June, 1911, provided one-third of the applicants with 2,759 acres-the total demand, by a thousand applicants, having already attained 12,350 acres.

And yet all this progress still appears insignificant by the side of the demand for vegetables which grows every year (and necessarily must grow, as is seen by comparing the low consumption of vegetables in this country with the consumption of home-grown vegetables in Belgium, indicated by Mr. Rowntree in his Lessons from Belgium). The result is a steadily increasing importation of vegetables to this country, which has attained now more than £8,000,000.

A branch of horticulture which has increased enormously since the first edition of this book was published, is the growing of fruit and vegetables in greenhouses, in the same way as it is done in the Channel Islands. All round London -we are told by Mr. John Weathers in the last edition of the Encyclopadia Britannica-the hothouse culture has taken a great development, and, in fact, along the railways which radiate from London in all directions the glass-houses have already become a familiar feature of the landscape. Immense quantities of grapes, tomatoes, figs, and of all sorts of early vegetables are grown at Worthing, where eighty-two acres are covered now with glass-houses, as also in the parish of Cheshunt, in Herts, where the area under hothouses is already 130 acres; while a careful estimate put in 1908 the area of individual hothouses in England at about 1,200 acres (Encyclopadia Britannica, vol. xi., p, 266). The elements of this culture having been developed by the experience of the Channel Islands growers, and by the wide extension which hothouses for the growing of flowers had taken long since in this country, it may be concluded from the various evidence we have at hand that on the whole this sort of culture is finding its reward, and is now firmly established.

The same, however, cannot yet be said of the culture maraîchère of the French market gardeners which is being introduced now into this country. Many attempts have been made in this direction in different parts of the country with varied degrees of success; but little or nothing is known about the results. An attempt on a large scale was made, as is known, by some Evesham gardeners. Having read about this sort of culture in France, and the wonderful results obtained by it, some of the Evesham gardeners wentt went to Paris with the intention of learning that culture from, the Paris mariaîchers. Finding that impossible they invited no French gardener to Evesham, gave him three-quarters of an acre, and, after, he had brought his Paris marais his glass bells, frames and lights, and, above all his knowledge, he began gardening under the eyes of his Evesham colleagues " Happily enough," he said to an interviewer I do not speak otherwise I should have had to talk all the time and give explanations, instead of working. So I show them my black trousers, and tell them in signs: Begin by making the soil as black ass these trousers, then everything will be all right.'" Of course, to be profitable, immense quantities of stable manure are required' as also immense numbers of glassbells and glass-frames, which represent a very costly outlay, and plenty of watering, to say nothing of the powers of observation required for developing a new branch of gardening in new surroundings.

What were the results obtained at Evesham it is difficult to say, the more so as the money results which, according to some papers, were obtained the first year (brutto income of £750 from three-quarters of an acre) seem to have been exaggerated for a first-year crop, and thus awakened scepticism with regard to that sort of culture altogether.

Another experiment in the same direction was made on the estate of Maryland, in Essex, which was bought by Mr. Joseph Fels in order to promote small farming in England. It must be said that, apart from the cold, damp climate of this part of England, the heavy clay of Essex represents the least appropriate soil for spade culture. In England, as everywhere, this sort of culture has always been developing in preference on a light loam, or in such places, like Jersey, where a meagre granitic soil could easily be manured-in this special case by sea-weeds.

Nevertheless, the aim of Mr. Fels having been chiefly educational, this aim has certainly been achieved, as we have now, in three different works of Mr. Thomas Smith, the manager of the farm, practical manuals teaching the would-be gardener the essentials of "French Gardening."

A French maraicher having been invited for this purpose, and 2,500 glass-bells, 1,000 lights for frames, a windmill pump, etc., having been bought at a considerable cost, the work of the French gardener on two acres of land was carefully followed by the manager of the farm, Mr. T. Smith, day by day, to be afterwards described and illustrated by photographs for the use of those who would like to try their hand at the same work.

Most of my readers will probably ask first of all: What were the money results of this venture? But it would have been foolish to expect that in this first experiment everything should have run as smoothly as it runs, let us say, in the Channel Islands, where the many years' practice of a whole population has worked out the best methods of culture.

Thus the frames were not ready in time for giving an early crop of melons; and although the melons grown at Maryland were excellent, and gave the first year as much as £ 188, they would have given much more than that had they been ready in the middle of June, which would have been possible if the frames and lights had been supplied in time.

With all that, the results obtained during the first year were really striking. All taken, Mr. Smith shows that if the gardener has a one-acre garden, and if £494 (say, £550) be spent for 1,000 glass-bells, 300 lights and 100 frames, 500 mats, the water-supply, the packing-shed, the fencing, the cart, horse and harness, etc., and £413 (say, £450) for 500 tons of manure, the rent, rates and water, and the wages and salaries (£250), the gross returns for the first year would reach £300 (making full allowance for "inexperience in this special work"). They would reach from £400 to £450 during the second year, there being greater productiveness and a lower expenditure after the loam has been made by heavy manuring, and personal experience has been won, as well t as experience for a given locality.

Taking a one-acre farm, of which only one-third is used for a French garden, the first year's expenditure for bells, lights, fencing, horse manure, water, and rent and taxes would be a little less than £300, and the returns by the end of the first year would be about £150. "Afterwards the returns ought to reach from £200 to £250 each year," Mr. Smith writes.

All that need be added to these words is, that Mr. Smith is extremely cautious in his estimates, and that, seeing the high crops obtained at Maryland, and fully dealt with in Mr. Smith's works, one is entitled to expect even better money results.

Unfortnnately, after having worked at the farm for one year, the experienced French gardener, who had obtained the just-mentioned results, left Maryland. Two young French gardeners, far less experienced, were invited instead, and they began to undo what their predecessor had done, in order to carry on the work on the lines they had learned themselves. So that it is impossible to know yet what the results of these new methods will be.

Every pioneer work has its unforeseen difficulties. But, so far as can be. judged from the facts I have at my disposal, the two ventures have proved that the climate of England is no obstacle to French gardening. Of course, the small amount of sunshine is a great obstacle for ripening the produce as early as it can be ripened in France, even in the suburbs of Paris. But home-grown fruit and vegetables have always many advantages in comparison with imported produce. Another disadvantage-the lack of horse manure-a disadvantage which will go on increasing with the spread of motor cars-is felt in France as well. This is why the French growers are eagerly experimenting with the direct heating of the soil with thermosiphons.

Let me add to these remarks that a decided awakening is to be noticed in this country for making a better use of the land than has been made for the last fifty years. There are a few counties where the County Councils, and still more so, the Parish Councils, are doing their best to break at last the land monopoly, and to permit those small farmers who intend to cultivate the soil to do so. Here and there we see a few timid attempts at imparting to the farmers and their children some knowledge of agriculture and horticulture. But all this is being made on too small a scale, and without a sincere desire to learn from other European nations, and still more so from the United States and Canada, what is being done in these countries to give to agriculture the new character of intensive culture combined with industry, which is imposed upon it by the recent progress of civilasation.

The various data which have been brought together on the

preceding pages make short work of the over-population fallacy. It is precisely in the most densely population parts of the world that agriculture has lately made such strides as hardly could have been guessed twenty years ago. A dense population, a high development of industry, and a high development of agriculture and horticulture, go hand in hand: they are inseparable. As to the future, the possibilities of agriculture are such that, in truth, we cannot yet foretell what would be the limit of the population which could live from the produce of a given area. Recent progress, already tested on a great scale, has widened the limits of agricultural prod-action to a quite unforeseen extent and recent discoveries, now tested on a small scale, promise to widen those limits still farther, to a quite unknown degree.

The present tendency of economical development in the world is-we have seen-to induce more and more every nation, or rather every region, taken in its geographical sense, to rely chiefly upon a home production of all the chief necessaries of life. Not to reduce, I mean, the world-exchange: it may still grow in bulk; but to limit it to the exchange of what really must be exchanged, and, at the same time, immensely to increase the exchange of novelties, produce of local or national art, new discoveries and inventions, knowledge and ideas. Such being the tendency of present development, there is not the slightest ground to be alarmed by it, There is not one nation in the world which, being armed with the present powers of agriculture, could not grow on its cultivable area all the food and most of the raw materials derived from agriculture which are required for its population, even if the requirements of that population were rapidly increased as they certainly ought to be. Taking the powers of man over the land and over the forces of nature-such as they are at the present day-we can maintain that two to three inhabitants to each cultivable acre of land would not yet be too much. But neither in this densely populated country nor in Belgium are we yet in such numbers. In this country we have, roughly speaking, one acre of the cultivable area per inhabitant.

Supposing, then, that each inhabitant of Great Britain were compelled to live on the produce of his own land, all he would have to do would be, first, to consider the land of this country as a common inheritance, which must be disposed of to the best advantage of each and all-this is, evidently, an absolutely necessary condition. And next, he would have to cultivate his soil, not in some extravagant way, but no better than land is already cultivated upon thousands and thousands of acres in Europe and America. He would not be bound to invent some new methods, but could simply generalise and widely apply those which have stood the test of experience. He can do it; and in so doing he would save an immense quantity of the work which is now given for buying his food abroad, and for paying all the intermediaries who live upon this trade. Under a rational culture, those necessaries and those luxuries which must be obtained from the soil, undoubtedly can be obtained with much less work than is required now for buying these commodities. I have made elsewhere (in The Conquest of Bread) approximate calculations to that effect, but with the data given in this book everyone can himself easily test the truth of this assertion. If we take, indeed, the masses of produce which are obtained under rational culture, and compare them with the amount of labour which must be spent for obtaining them under an irrational culture, for collecting them abroad, for transporting them, and for keeping armies of middlemen, we see at once how few days and hours need be given, under proper culture, for growing man's food.

Chapter VI: Small Industries and Industrial Villages

THE two sister arts of agriculture and industry were not always so estranged from one another as they are now. There was a time, and that time is not so far back, when both were thoroughly combined; the villages were then the seats of a variety of industries, and the artisans in the cities did not abandon agriculture; many towns were nothing else but industrial villages. If the medieval city was the cradle of those industries which bordered upon art and were intended to supply the wants of the richer classes, still it was the rural manufacture which supplied the wants of the million, as it does until the present day in Russia, and to a very great extent in Germany and France. But then came the water-motors, steam, the development of machinery, and they broke the link which formerly connected the farm with the workshop. Factories grew up and they abandoned the fields. They gathered where the sale of their produce was easiest, or the raw materials and fuel could be obtained with the greatest advantage. New cities rose, and the old ones rapidly enlarged; the fields were deserted. Millions of labourers, driven away by sheer force from the land, gathered in the cities in search of labour, and soon forgot the bonds which formerly attached them to the soil. And we, in our admiration of the prodigies achieved under the new factory system, overlooked the advantages of the old system under which the tiller of the soil was an industrial worker at the same time. We doomed to disappearance all those branches of industry which formerly used to prosper in the villages; we condemned in industry all that was not a big factory.

True, the results were grand as regards the increase of the productive powers of man. But they proved terrible as regards the millions of human beings who were plunged into misery and had to rely upon precarious means of living in our cities. Moreover, the system, as a whole, brought about those abnormal conditions which I have endeavoured to sketch in the two first chapters. We were thus driven into a corner; and while a thorough change in the present relations between labour and capital is becoming an imperious necessity, a thorough remodelling of the whole of our industrial organisation has also become unavoidable. The industrial nations are bound to revert to agriculture, they are compelled to find out the best means of combining it with industry, and they must do so without loss of time.

To examine the special question as to the possibility of such a combination is the aim of the following pages. Is it possible, from a technical point of view? Is it desirable? Are there, in our present industrial life, such features as might lead us to presume that a change in the above direction would find the necessary elements for its accomplishment? Such are the questions which rise before the mind. And to answer them, there is, I suppose, no better means than to study that immense but overlooked and underrated branch of industries which are described under the names of rural industries, domestic trades, and petty trades: to study them, not in the works of the economists who are too much inclined to consider them as obsolete types of industry, but in their life itself, in their struggles, their failures and achievements.

The variety of forms of organisation which is found in the small industries is hardly suspected by those who have not made them a subject of special study. There are, first, two broad categories: those industries which are carried on in the villages, in connection with agriculture; and those which are carried on in towns or in villages, with no connection with the land-the workers depending for their earnings exclusively upon their industrial work.

In Russia, in France, in Germany, in Austria, and so on, millions and millions of workers are in the first case. They are owners or occupiers of the land, they keep one or two cows, very often horses, and they cultivate their fields, or their orchards, or gardens, considering industrial work as a by-occupation. In those regions especially, where the winter is long and no work on the land is possible for several months every year, this form of small industries is widely spread. In this country, on the contrary, we find the opposite extreme. Few small industries have survived in England in connection with land-culture; but hundreds of petty trades are found in the suburbs and the slums of the great cities, and large portions of the populations of several towns, such as Sheffield and Birmingham, find their living in a variety of petty trades. Between these two extremes there is evidently a mass of intermediate forms, according to the more or less close ties which continue to exist with the land. Large villages, and even towns, are thus peopled with workers who are engaged in small trades, but most of whom have a small garden, or an orchard, or a field, or only retain some rights of pasture on the commons, while part of them live exclusively upon their industrial earnings.

With regard to the sale of the produce, the small industries offer the same variety of organisation. Here again there are two great branches. In one of them the worker sells his produce directly to the wholesale dealer; cabinetmakers, weavers, and workers in the toy trade are in this case. In the other great division the worker works for a "master" who either sells the produce to a wholesale dealer, or simply acts as a middleman who himself receives his orders from some big concern. This the "sweating system," property speaking, under which we find a mass of small trades. Part of the toy trade, the tailors who work for large clothing establishments-very often for those of the State-the women who sew and embroider the "uppers" for the boot and shoe factories, and who as often deal with the factory as with an intermediary "sweater," and so on, are in this case. All possible gradations of feudalisation and subfeudalisation of labour are evidently found in that organisation of the sale of the produce.

Again, when the industrial, or rather technical aspects of the small industries are considered, the same variety of types is soon discovered. Here also there are two great branched: those trades, on the one side, which are purely domestic -- that is, those which are carried on in the house of the worker, with the aid of his family, or of a couple of wage-workers; and those which are carried on in separate workshops -- all the just-mentioned varieties, as regards connection with land and the divers modes of disposing of the produce, being met with in both these branches. All possible trades -- weaving, workers in wood, in metals, in bone, in india-rubber, and so on -- may be found under the category of purely domestic trades, with all possible gradations between the purely domestic form of production and the workshop and the factory.

Thus, by the side of the trades which are carried on entirely at home by one or more members of the family, there are the trades in which the master keeps a small workshop attached to his house and works in it with his family, or with a few "assistants" -- that is, wage-workers. Or else the artisan has a separate workshop, supplied with wheel-power, as is the case with the Sheffield cutlers. Or several workers come together in a small factory which they maintain themselves, or hire in association, or where they are allowed to work for a certain weekly rent. And in each of these cases they work either directly for the dealer or for a small master, or for a middleman.

A further development of this system is the big factory, especially of ready-made clothes, in which hundreds of women pay so much for the sewing-machine, the gas, the gas-heated irons, and so on, and are paid themselves so much for each piece of the ready-made clothes they sew, or each part of it. Immense factories of this kind exist in England, and it appeared from testimony given before the "Sweating Committee" that women are fearfully "sweated" in such workshops -- the full price of each slightly spoiled piece of clothing being deducted from their very low piecework wages.

And, finally, there is the small workshop (often with hired wheel-power) in which a master employs three to ten workers, who are paid in wages, and sells his produce to a bigger employer or merchant -- there being all possible gradations between such a workshop and the small factory in which a few time workers (five, ten to twenty) are employed by an independent producer. In the textile trades, weaving is often done either by the family or by a master who employs one boy only, or several weavers, and after having received the yarn from a big employer, pays a skilled workman to put the yarn in the loom, invents what is necessary for weaving a given, sometimes very complicated pattern, and after having woven the cloth or the ribbons in his own loom or in a loom which he hires himself, he is paid for the piece of cloth according to a very complicated scale of wages agreed to between masters and workers. This last form, we shall see presently, is widely spread up to the present day, especially in the woolen and silk trades; it continues to exist by the side of big factories in which 50, 100, or 5,000 wage-workers, as the case may be, are working with the employers' machinery and are paid in time-wages so much the day or the week.

The small industries are thus quite a world, which, remarkable enough, continues to exist even in the most industrial countries, side by side with the big factories. Into this world we must now penetrate to cast a glimpse upon it: a glimpse only, because it would take volumes to describe its infinite variety of pursuits and organisations, and its indefinitely varied connection, with

Fields, Factories, and Workshops

agriculture as well as with other industries.

Most of the petty trades, except some of those which are connected with agriculture, are, we must admit, in a very precarious position. The earnings are very low, and the employment is often uncertain. The day of labour is by two, three, or four hours longer than it is in well-organised factories, and at certain seasons it reaches an almost incredible length. The crises are frequent and last for years. Altogether, the worker is much more at the mercy of the dealer or the employer, and the employer is at the mercy of the wholesale dealer. Both are liable to become enslaved to the latter, running into debt to him. In some of the petty trades, especially in the fabrication of the plain textiles, the workers are in dreadful misery. But those who pretend that such misery is the rule are totally wrong. Anyone who has lived among, let us say, the watch-makers in Switzerland and knows their inner family life, will recognise that the condition of these workers was out of all comparison superior, in every respect, material and moral, to the conditions of millions of factory hands. Even during such a crisis in the watch trade as was lived through in 1876-1880, their condition was preferable to the condition of factory hands during a crisis in the woollen or cotton trade; and the workers perfectly well know it themselves.

Whenever a crisis breaks out in some branch of the petty trades, there is no lack of writers to predict that that trade is going to disappear. During the crisis which I witnessed in 1877, living amidst the Swiss watchmakers, the impossibility of a recovery of the trade in the face of the competition of machine-made watches was a current topic in the press. The same was said in 1882 with regard to the silk trade of Lyons, and, in fact, wherever a crisis has broken out in the petty trades. And yet, notwithstanding the gloomy predictions, and the still gloomier prospects of the workers, that form of industry does not disappear. Even when some branch of it disappears, there always remains something of it; some portions of it continue to exist as small industries (watchmaking of a high quality, best sorts of silks, high quality velvets, etc.), or new connected branches grow up instead of the old ones, or the small industry, taking advantage of a mechanical motor, assumes a new form. We thus find it endowed with an astonishing vitality. It undergoes various modifications, it adapts itself to new conditions, it struggles without losing hope of better times to come. Anyhow, it has not the characteristics of a decaying institution. In some industries the factory is undoubtedly victorious; but there are other branches in which the petty trades hold their own position. Even in the textile industries -- especially in consequence of the wide use of the labour of children and women -- which offer so many advantages for the factory system, the hand-loom still competes with the power-loom.

As a whole, the transformation of the petty trades into great industries goes on with a slowness which cannot fail to astonish even those who are convinced of its necessity. Nay, sometimes we may even see the reverse movement going on -- occasionally, of course, and only for a time. I cannot forget my amazement when I saw at Verviers, some thirty years ago, that most of the woollen cloth factories -- immense barracks facing the streets by more than a hundred windows each -- were silent, and their costly machinery was rusting, while cloth was woven in hand-looms in the weavers' houses, for the owners of those very same factories. Here we have of course, but a temporary fact, fully explained by the spasmodic character of the trade and the heavy losses sustained by the owners of the factories when they cannot run their mills all the year round. But it illustrates the obstacles which the transformation has to comply with. As to the silk trade, it continues to spread over Europe in its rural industry state; while hundreds of new petty trades appear every year, and when they find nobody to carry them on in the villages -- as is the case in this country -- they shelter themselves in the suburbs of the great cities, as we have lately learned from the inquiry into the "sweating system."

Now, the advantages offered by a large factory in comparison with hand work are self-evident as regards the economy of labour, and especially -- this is the main point -- the facilities both for sale and for having the raw produce at a lower price. How can we then explain the persistence of the petty trades? Many causes, however, most of which cannot be valued in shillings and pence, are at work in favour of the petty trades, and these causes will be best seen from the following illustrations. I must say, however, that even a brief sketch of the countless industries which are carried on on a small scale in this country, and on the Continent, would be far beyond the scope of this chapter. When I began to study the subject some thirty years ago, I never guessed, from the little attention devoted to it by the orthodox economists, what a wide, complex, important, and interesting organisation would appear at the end of a close inquiry. So I see myself compelled to give here only a few typical illustrations, and to indicate the chief lines only of the subject.

The Small Industries in the United Kingdom

We have not for the United Kingdom such statistical data as are obtained in France and Germany by periodical censuses of all the factories and workshops, and the numbers of the workpeople, foremen and clerks, employed on a given day n each industrial and commercial establishment. Consequently, up to the present time all the statements made by economists about the so-called "concentration:" of the industry in this country, and the consequent "unavoidable" disappearance of the small industries, have been based on mere impressions of the writers, -

- not on statistical data. Up till now we cannot give, as it is done future in these pages for France and Germany, the exact numbers of factories and workshops employing, let us say, from 1,000 to 2,000 persons, from 500 to 1,000, from 50 to 500, less than 50, and so on. It is only since factory inspection has been introduced by the Factory Act of 1895 that we begin to find, in the Reports published since 1900 by the Factory Inspectors (Annual Report of the Chief Inspector of Factories and Workshops for the year 1898: London, 1900), information which permits us to get a general idea about the distribution of working men in factories of different sizes, and the extension that the petty trades have retained in this country up till now. One may see it already from the following little table for the year 1897, which I take from the just-mentioned Report. These figures are not yet complete, especially as regards the workshops, but they contain already the greater part of the English industries.

Let me remark that the Factory Inspectors consider as a workshop every industrial establishment which has no mechanical motive power, and as a factory every establishment provided with steam, gas, water, or electric power.

These figures, however, are not complete, because only those workshops are included where women and children are employed, as also all the bakeries. The others were not submitted to inspection at the time when this table was compiled. There is, nevertheless, a means to find out the approximate numbers of workpeople employed in the workshops. The number of women and female children employed in the workshops in 1897 was 356,098 and the number of men and boys was 320,678. But, as the proportion of male workers to the female in all the factories was 2,654,716 males to 1,152,308 females, we may admit that the same proportion prevails in the workshops. This would give for the latter something like 820,000 male workers and 1,176,000 persons of both sexes, employed in 147,000 workshops. At the same time, the grand total of persons employed in industry (exclusive of mining) would be 4,983,000.

We can thus say that nearly one-fourth (24 per cent.) of all the industrial workers of this country are working in workshops having less than eight to ten workers per establishment.

It must also be pointed out that out of the 4,483,800 workpeople registered in the above-mentioned tables nearly 60,000 were children who were working half-days only, 401,000 were girls less than eighteen years old, 463,000 were boy from thirteen to eighteen who were making full working days like the adults, and 1,077,115 were considered as women (more than eighteen years old). In other words, one-fifth part of all the industrial workers of this country were girls and boys, and more than two-fifths (41 per cent.) were either women or children. All the industrial production of the United Kingdom, with its immense exports, was thus giving work to less than three million adult men--2,983,000 out of a population of 42,000,000, to whom we must add 972,200 persons working in the mines. As to the textile industry, which supplies almost one-half of the English exports, there are less than 300,000 adult men who find employment in it. The remainder is the work of children, boys, girls, and women.

A fact which strikes us is that the 1,051,564 workpeople--men, women and children--who worked in 1897 in the textile industries of the United Kingdom were distributed over 10,883 factories, which gives only an average of ninety-three persons per factory in all this great industry, notwithstanding the fact that "concentration" has progressed most in this industry, and that we find in it factories employing as many as 5,000 and 6,000 persons.

It is true that the Factory Inspectors represent each separate branch of a given industry as a special establishment. Thus, if an employer or a society owns a spinning mill, a weaving factory, and a special building for dressing and finishing, the three are represented as separate factories. But this is precisely what is wanted for giving us an exact idea about the degree of concentration of a given industry. Besides, it is also known that, for instance, in the cotton industry, in the neighbourhood of Manchester, the spinning, the weaving, the dressing and so on belong very often to different employers, who send to each other the stuffs at different degrees of fabrication; those factories which combine under the same management all the three or four consecutive phases of the manufacture are an exception.

But it is especially in the division of the non-textile industries that we find an enormous development of small factories. The 2,755,460 workpeople who are employed in all the non-textile branches with the exception of mining, are scattered in 79,059 factories, each of which has only an average of thirty-five workers. Moreover, the Factory Inspectors had on their lists 676,776 workpeople employed in 88,814 workshops (without mechanical power), which makes an average of eight persons only per workshop. These last figures are, however, as we saw, below the real ones, as another sixty thousand workshops occupying half a million more workpeople were not yet tabulated.

Such averages as ninety-three and thirty-five workpeople per factory, and eight per workshop, distributed over 178,756 industrial establishments, destroy already the legend according to which the big factories have already absorbed most of the small ones. The figures show, on the contrary, what an immense number of small factories and workshops resist the absorption by the big factories, and how they multiply by the side of the great industry in various branches, especially those of recent origin.

If we had for the United Kingdom full statistics, giving lists of all the factories, with the number of workpeople employed in each of them, as we have for France and Germany (see below), it would have been easy to find the exact number of factories employing more than 1,000,000, 500, 100, and 50 workmen. But such lists are issued only for the mining industry. As to the statistics published by the Factory Inspectors, they do not contain such data, perhaps because the inspectors have no time to tabulate their figures, or have not the right to do so. Be it as it may, the Report of Mr. Whitelegge for 1897 gives the number of factories (textile and non-textile) and workshops for each of the 119 counties of the United Kingdom and for each of the nearly hundred sub-divisions of all the industries, as well as the number of workpeople in each of these more than 10,000 sub-divisions. So I was enabled to calculate the averages of persons employed in the factories and workshops for each separate branch of industry in each county. Besides, Mr Whitelegge has had the kindness to give me two very important figures-- namely, the number of factories employing more than 1,000 workpeople, and the number of those factories where less than ten workers are employed.

Let us take, first of all, the TEXTILE industries, which include cotton, wool, silk, linen, jute, and hemp, as well as machine-made lace and knitting. Many of my readers will probably be astonished to learn that even in the cotton industry a great number of quite small factories continue to exist up to the present day. Even in the West Riding district, which is second only to Lancashire for the number of its cotton mills, and where we find nearly one-third of all the workpeople employed in the cotton industry (237,444 persons), the average for all the 3,210 factories of this district is only seventy-three persons per factory. And even in Lancashire, where we find nearly one-half of all the workpeople employed in the textiles, these 434,609 men, women, and children are scattered in 3,132 factories, each of which has thus an average of only 139 workers. If we remember that in this number there are factories employing from 2,000 to 6,000 persons, one cannot but be struck by the quantity of small factories employing less than 100 persons, and which continue to exist by the side of the great cotton mills. But we shall just see that the same is true for all industries.

As to the Nottinghamshire, which is a centre for machine-made lace and knitting, its 18,434 workpeople are, most of them, working in small factories. The average for the 386 establishments of this county is only forty-eight persons per factory. The great industry is thus very far from having absorbed the small one.

The distribution of the textile factories in the other counties of the United Kingdom is even more instructive. We learn that there are nearly 2,000 textile factories in forty-nine counties, and everyone of these factories has much less than 100 workpeople; while a very considerable number of them employ only from forty to fifty, from ten to twenty, and even less than ten persons.

This could have been foreseen by everyone who has some practical knowledge of industry, but it is overlooked by the theorists, who know industry mostly from books. In every country of the world there are by the side of the large factories a great number of small ones, the success of which is due to the variety of their produce and the facilities they offer to follow the vagaries of fashion. This is especially true with regard to the woollens and the mixed stuffs made of wool and cotton.

Besides, it is well known to British manufacturers that at the time when the big cotton mills were established, the manufacturers of spinning and weaving machinery, seeing that they had no more orders coming, after they had supplied this machinery to the great factories, began to offer it at a reduced price and on credit to the small weavers. These last associated--

three, five, or more of them---to buy the machinery, and this is why we have now in Lancashire quite a region where a great number of small cotton mills continue to exist till nowadays, without there being any reason to foresee their disappearance. At times they are even quite prosperous.

On the other side, when we examine the various branches of textile industry (cotton, wool, silk jute, etc.), we see that if the great factories dominate in the spinning and weaving of cotton, worsted and flax, as well as in the spinning of silk (the result being that the average for these branches reaches 150 workers per factory for cotton, and 267 for the spinning of flax), all other textile industries belong to the domain of the middle-sized and the small industry. In other words, in the manufacture of woollens, shoddy, hemp, hair, machine-made lace, and mechanical knitting, as also in the weaving of silks, there are, of course, large factories; but the majority of these establishments belong to the domain of the small industry. Thus, for the 3,274 woollen factories, the average is only from twenty to fifty workers per factory; it is also from twenty-seven to thirty-eight for shoddy, and thirty-seven to seventy-six for the other branches. Only for knitting do the averages rise to ninety-three persons per factory; but we are just going to see that the small industry reappears in this branch in force under the name of workshops.

All these important branches of the British textile industry, which give work to more than 240,000 men and women, have thus remained up till now at the stage of a small and middle-sized industry.

If we take now the NON-TEXTILE industries, we find, on the one side, an immense number of small industries which have grown up around the great ones, and owing to them; and, on the other side, a large part of the fundamental industries have remained in the stage of small establishments. The average for all these branches, which give occupation to three-fourths of all the industrial workers of the United Kingdom--that is, 2,755,460 workers--hardly attains, we saw, thirty-five persons per factory--the workshops being not yet included in this division. However, it is especially when we go into details, and analyse the figures which I have calculated for each separate branch, that we fully realise the importance of the petty trades in England. This is what we are going to do, mentioning first what belongs here to the great industry, and studying next the small one.

Following the classification adopted by the Factory Inspectors, we see first that the gasworks belong to the domain of the fairly big establishments (seventy-eight people on the average). The india-rubber factories belong to the same category (125 workers on the average): and amidst the 456 glass-works of the United Kingdom there must be some big ones, as the average is eighty-seven workpeople.

Next come mining and metallurgy, which are carried on, as a rule, on a great scale; but already in the iron foundries we find a great number of establishments belonging to the middle-sized and small industry. Thus at Sheffield I saw myself several foundries employing only from five to six workmen, For the making of huge machinery there is, of course, a number of very large works, such as those of Armstrong, Whitworth, or those of the State at Woolwich. But it is very instructive to see how very small works prosper by the side of big ones; they are numerous enough to reduce the average to seventy workers per establishment for the 5,318 works of this category.

Shipbuilding and the manufacture of metallic tubes evidently belong to the great industry (averages, 243 and 156 persons per establisment); and the same applies to the two great metallurgical works of the State, which employ between them 23,455 workmen.

Going over to the chemical works, we find again a great industry in the fabrication of alkalies and of matches (only twenty-five works); but, on the contrary, the fabrication of soap and candles, as well as manures and all other sorts of chemical produce, which represents nearly 2,000 factories, belongs almost entirely to the domain of the small industry. The average is only twenty-nine workpeople per factory. There are, of course, half a dozen of very large soap works--one knows them only too well by their advertisements on the cliffs and in the fields; but the low average of twenty-nine workmen proves how many small factories must exist by the side of the soap kings. The 2,500 works engaged in the fabrication of furniture, both in wood and in iron, belong again chiefly to the small industry. The small and very small factories swarm by the side of a few great ones, to say nothing of the thousands of the still smaller workshops. The great storehouses of our cities are for the most part mere exhibitions of furniture made in very small factories and workshops.

In the fabrication of food produce we find several great sugar, chocolate, and preserves works; but by their side we find also a very great number of small establishments, which seem not to complain of the proximity of the big ones, as they occupy nearly two-thirds of the workers employed in this branch. I do not speak, of course, of the village windmills, but one cannot fail to be struck by the immense number of small breweries (2,076 breweries have on the average only twenty-four workmen each) and of the establishments engaged in the fabrication of aerated waters (they number 3,365, and have on the average only eleven operatives per establishment).

In calico-printing we enter once more the domain of great factories; but by their side we find a pretty large number of small ones; so that the average for all this category is 144 workpeople per factory. We find also fourteen great factories, having an average of 394 workpeople each, for dyeing in Turkey red. But we find also by their side more than 100,000 working-men employed in 2,725 small establishments of this class--bleaching, dressing, packing, and so on--and this gives us one more illustration of numerous small industries growing round the main ones.

In the making of ready-made clothing and the fabrication of hats, linen, boots and shoes, and gloves, we see the averages for the factories of this description going up to 80, 100, and 150 persons per factory. But it is here also that countless small workshops come in. It must also be noticed that most of the factories of ready-made clothing have their own special character. The factory buys the cloth and makes the cutting by means of special machinery; but the sewing is done by women, who come to work in the factory. They pay so much the sewing-machine, so much the motor power (if there is one), so much the gas, so much the iron, and so on, and they are on piece work. Very often this becomes a "sweating system" on a large scale. Round the big factories a great number of small workshops are centred.

And, finally, we find great factories for the fabrication of gunpowder and explosives (they employ less than 12,000 workpeople), stuff buttons, and umbrellas (only 6,000 employees). But we find also in the table of workshops that in these last two branches there are thousands of them by the side of a few great factories.

All taken, Mr. Whitelegge writes to me that of factories employing more than 1,000 workpeople each, he finds only sixty-five in the textile industries(102,600 workpeople) and only 128 (355,208 workpeople) in all non-textile industries.

In this brief enumeration we have gone over all that belongs to the great industry. The remainder belongs almost entirely to the domain of the small, and often the very small industry. Such are all the factories for woodwork, which have on the average only fifteen men per establishment, but represent a contingent of more than 100,000 workmen and more than 6,000 employers. The tanneries, the manufacture of all sorts of little things in ivory and bone, and even the brick-works and the potteries, representing a total of 260,000 workpeople and 11,200 employers, belong, with a very few exception, to the small industry.

Then we have the factories dealing with the burnishing and enamelling of metals, which also belong chiefly to the small industry--the average being only twenty-eight workpeople per factory. But what is especially striking is the development of the small and very small industry in the fabrication of agricultural machinery (thirty-two workers per factory), of all sorts of tools (twenty-two on the average), needles and pins (forty-three), ironmongery, sanitary apparatus, and various instruments (twenty-five), even of boilers (forty-eight per factory), chains, cables, and anchors (in many districts this work, as also the making of nails, is made by hand by women).

Needless to say that the fabrication of furniture, which occupies nearly 64,000 operatives, belongs chiefly--more than three-fourths of it--to the small industry. The average for the 1,979 factories of this branch is only twenty-one workpeople, the workshops not being included in this number. The same is true of the factories for the curing of fish, machine-made pastry, and so on, which occupy 38,030 workpeople in more than 2,700 factories, having thus an average of fourteen operatives each.

Jewelry and the manufacture of watches, photographic apparatus, and all sorts of luxury articles, again belong to the small and very small industry, and give occupation to 54,000 persons.

All that belongs to printing, lithography, bookbinding, and stationery again represents a vast field occupied by the small industry, which prospers by the side of a small number of very large establishments. More than 120,000 are employed in these branches in more than 6,000 factories (workshops not yet included).

And, finally, we find a large domain occupied by saddlery, brush-making, the making of sails, basket-making, and the fabrication of a thousand little things in leather, paper, wood, metal, and so on. This class is certainly not insignificant, as it contains more than 4,300 employers and nearly 130,000 workpeople, employed in a mass of very small factories by the side of a few very great ones, the average being only from twenty-five to thirty-five persons per factory.

In short, in the different non-textile industries, the inspectors have tabulated 32,042 factories employing, each of them, less than ten workpeople.

All taken, we find 270,000 workpeople employed in small factories having less than fifty and even twenty workers each, the result being that the very great industry (the factories employing more than 1,000 workpeople per factory) and the very small one (less than ten workers) employ nearly the same number of operatives.

The important part played by the small industry in this country fully appears from this rapid sketch. And I have not yet spoken of the workshops. The Factory Inspectors mentioned, as we saw, in their first report, 88,814 workshops, in which 676,776 workpeople (356,098 women) were employed in 1897. But, as we have already seen, these figures are incomplete. The number of workshops is about 147,000, and there must be about 1,200,000 persons employed in them (820,000 men and about 356,000 women and children).

It is evident that this class comprises a very considerable number of bakers, small carpenters, tailors, cobblers, cartwrights, village smiths, and so on. But there is also in this class an immense number of workshops belonging to industry, properly speaking-that is, workshops which manufacture for the great commercial market. Some of these workshops may of course employ fifty persons or more, but the immense majority employ only from five to twenty workpeople each.

We thus find in this class 1,348 small establishments, scattered both in the villages and the suburbs of great cities, where nearly 14,000 persons make lace, knitting, embroidery, and weaving in hand-looms; more than 100 small tanneries, more than 20,000 cartwrights, and 746 small bicycle makers. In cutlery, in the fabrication of tools and small arms, nails and screws, and even anchors and anchor chains, we find again many thousands of small work shops employing something like 60,000 workmen. All that, let us remember, without counting those workshops which employ no women or children, and therefore are not submitted to the Factory Inspectors. As to the fabrication of clothing, which gives work to more than 350,000 men and women, distributed over nearly 45,000 workshops, let it be noted that it is not small tailors that is spoken of here, but that mass of workshops which swarm in Whitechapel and the suburbs of all great cities, and where we find from five to fifty women and men making clothing for the tailor shops, big and small. In these shops the measure is taken, and sometimes the cutting is made; but the clothing is sewn in the small workshops, which are very often somewhere in the country. Even parts of the commands of linen and clothing for the army find their way to workshops in country places. As to the underclothing and mercery which are sold in the great stores, they are fabricated in small workshops, which must be counted by the thousand.

The same is true of furniture, mattresses and cushions, hats, artificial flowers, umbrellas, slippers, and even cheap jewelry. The great shops, even the largest stores, mostly keep only an assortment of samples. All is manufactured at a very low price, and day by day, in thousands of small workshops.

It can thus be said that if we exclude from the class of workshops' employees 100,000 or even 200,000 workpeople who do not work for industry properly speaking, and if we add on the other side the nearly 500,000 workers who have not yet been tabulated by the inspectors in 1897, we find a population of more than 1,000,000 men and women who belong entirely to the domain of the small industry, and so must be added to those whom we found working in the small factories. The artisans who are, working single-handed were not included in this sketch.

We thus see that even in this country, which may be considered as representing the highest development of the great industry, the number of persons employed in the small trade continues to be immense. The small industries are as much a distinctive feature of the British industry as its few immense factories and ironworks.

Going over now to what is known about the small industries of this country from direct observation, we find that the suburbs of London, Glasgow, and other great cities swarm with small workshops, and that there are regions where the petty trades are as developed as they are. in Switzerland or in Germany. Sheffield is a well known example in point. The Sheffield cutlery --one of the glories of England-is not. made by machinery: it is chiefly made by hand. There are at Sheffield a number of firms which manufacture cutlery right through from the making of steel to the finishing of tools, and employ wageworkers; and yet even these firms--I am told by Edward Carpenter, who kindly collected for me information about the Sheffield trade--let out some part of their work to the "small masters." But by far the greatest number of the cutlers work in their homes with their relatives, or in small workshops supplied with wheel-power, which they rent for a few shillings a week. Immense yards are covered with buildings, which are subdivided into numbers of small workshops. Some of these cover but a few square yards, and there I saw smiths hammering, all the day long, blades of knives on a small anvil, close by the blaze of their fires; occasionally the smith may have one helper, or two. In the upper storeys, scores of small workshops are supplied with wheel-power, and in each of them, three, four, or five workers and a "master" fabricate, with the occasional aid of a few plain machines, every description of tools: files, saws, blades of knives, razors, and so on. Grinding and glazing are done in other small workshops, and even steel is cast in a small foundry, the working staff of which consists only of five or six men.

When I walked through these workshops I easily imagined myself in a Russian cutlery village, like Pavlovo or Vorsma. The Sheffield cutlery has thus maintained its olden organisation, and the fact is the more remarkable as the earnings of the cutlers are low as a rule; but, even when they are reduced to a few shillings a week, the cutler prefers to vegetate on his small earnings than to enter as a waged labourer in a "house." The spirit of the old trade organisations, which were so much spoken of in the 'sixties of the nineteenth century, is thus still alive.

Until lately, Leeds and its environs were also the seat of extensive domestic industries. When Edward Baines wrote, in 1857, his first account of the Yorkshire industries (in Th. Baines's Yorkshire, Past and Present), most of the woollen cloth which was made in that region was woven by hand. Twice a week the hand-made cloth was brought to the Clothiers' Hall, and by noon it was sold to the merchants, who had it dressed in their factories. Joint-stock mills were run by combined clothiers in order to prepare and spin the wool, but it was woven in the hand-looms by the clothiers and the members of their families. Twelve years later the hand-loom was superseded to a great extent by the power-loom; but the clothiers, who were anxious to maintain their independence, resorted to a peculiar organisation: they rented a room, or part of a room, and sometimes also the power-looms, and they worked independently -- a characteristic organisation partly maintained until now, and well adapted to illustrate the efforts of the petty traders to keep their ground, notwithstanding the competition of the factory. And it must be said that the triumphs of the factory were too often achieved only by means of the most fraudulent adulteration and the underpaid labour of the children.

The variety of domestic industries carried on in the Lake District is much greater than might be expected,, but they still wait for careful explorers. I will only mention the hoop-makers, the basket trade, the charcoal-burners, the bobbin-makers, the small iron furnaces working with charcoal at Backbarrow, and so on.As a whole, we do not well know the petty trades of this country, and therefore we sometimes come across quite unexpected facts. Few continental writers on industrial topics would guess, indeed, that twenty-five years ago nails were made by hand by thousands of men, women, and children in the Black Country of South Staffordshire, as also in Derbyshire, The workshops, much more even than the factories, multiply wherever they find cheap labour; and the specific feature of this country is, that the cheapest labour-that is, the greatest number of destitute people-is to be found in the great. cities. The agitation raised (with no result) in connection with the "Dwellings of the Poor," the "Unemployed," and the "Sweating System," has fully disclosed that characteristic feature of the economic life of England and Scotland; and the painstaking researches made by Mr. Charles Booth have shown that one-quarter of the population of London-that is, 1,000,000 out of the

Fields, Factories, and Workshops

3,800,000 who entered within the scope of his inquest-would be happy if the heads of their families could have regular earnings of something like 91 a week all the year round. Half of them would be satisfied with even less than that. The same state of things was found by Mr. Seebohm Rowntree at York. Cheap labour is offered in such quantities in the suburbs of all the great cities of Great Britain, that the petty and domestic trades, which are scattered on the Continent in the villages, gather in this country in the cities.

Exact figures as to the small industries are wanting, but a simple walk through the suburbs of London -would do much to realise the variety of petty trades which swarm in the metropolis, and, in fact, in all chief urban agglomerations. The evidence given before the "Sweating System Committee" has shown how far the furniture and ready-made clothing palaces and the "Bonheur des Dames" bazaars of London are mere exhibitions of samples, or markets for the sale of the produce of the small industries. Thousands of sweaters, some of them having their own workshops, and others merely distributing work to sub-sweaters who distribute it again amidst the destitute, supply those palaces and bazaars with goods made in the slums or in very small workshops. The commerce is centralised in those bazaars-not the industry. The furniture palaces and bazaars are thus merely playing the part which the feudal castle formerly played in agriculture: they centralise the profits -not the production.

In reality, the extension of the petty trades, side by side with the great factories, is nothing to be wondered at. It is an economic necessity.

The absorption of the small workshops by bigger concerns is a fact which had struck the economists in the 'forties of the last century, especially in the textile trades. It is continued still in many other trades, and is especially striking in a number of very big concerns dealing with metals and war supplies for the different States. But there is another process which is going on parallel with the former, and which consists in the continuous creation of new industries, usually making their start on a small scale. Each new factory calls into existence a number of small workshops, partly to supply its own needs and partly to submit its produce to a further transformation. Thus, to quote but one instance, the cotton mills have created an immense demand for wooden bobbins and reels, and thousands of men in the Lake District set to manfuacture them-by hand first, and later on with the aid of some plain machinery. Only quite recently, after years had been spent in inventing and improving the machinery, the bobbins began to be made on a larger scale in factories. And even yet, as the machines are very costly, a great quantity of bobbins are made in small workshops, with but little aid from machines, while the factories themselves are relatively small, and seldom employ more than fifty operatives chiefly children. As to the reels of irregular shape, they are still made by hand, or partly with the aid of small machines, continually invented by the workers. New industries thus grow up to supplant the old ones; each of them passes through a preliminary stage on a small scale before reaching the great factory stage; and the more active the inventive genius of a nation is, the more it has of these budding industries. The countless small bicycle works which have lately grown up in this country, and are supplied with ready-made parts of the bicycle by the larger factories, are an instance in point. The domestic and small workshops fabrication of boxes for matches, boots, hats, confectionery, grocery and so on is another familiar instance.

Besides, the large factory stimulates the birth of now petty trades by creating new wants. The cheapness of cottons and woollens, of paper and brass, has created hundreds of new small industries. Our households are full of their produce--mostly things of quite modern invention. And while some of them already are turned out by the million in the great factory, all have passed through the small workshop stage, before the demand was great enough to require the great factory organisation, The more we may have of new inventions, the more shall we have of such small industries; and again, the more we have of them, the more shall we have of the inventive genius, the want of which is so justly complained of in this country (by W. Armstrong, amongst many others). We must not wonder, therefore, if we see so many small trades in this country; but we must regret that the great number have abandoned the villages in consequence of the bad conditions of land tenure, and that they have migrated in such numbers to the cities, to the detriment of agriculture.

In England, as everywhere, the small industries are an important factor in the industrial life of the country ; and it is chiefly in the infinite variety of the small trades, which utilise the half-fabricated produce of the great industries, that inventive genius is developed, and the rudiments of the future great industries are elaborated. The small bicycle workshops, with the hundreds of small improvements which they introduced, have been under our very eyes the primary cells out of which the great industry of the motor cars, and later on of the aeroplanes, has grown up. The small village jam-makers were the precursors and the rudiments of the great factories of preserves which now employ hundreds of workers. And soon.

Consequently, to affirm that the small industries are doomed to disappear, while we see new ones appear every day, is merely to repeat a hasty generalisation that was made in the earlier part of the nineteenth century by those who witnessed the absorption of hand-work by machinery work in the cotton industry--a generalisation which, as we saw already, and are going still better to see on the following pages, finds no confirmation from the study of industries, great and small, and is upset by the censuses of the factories and workshops. Far from showing a tendency to disappear, the small industries show, on the contrary, a tendency towards making a further development, since the municipal supply of electrical power--such as we have, for instance, in Manchester--permits the owner of a small factory to have a cheap supply of motive power, exactly in the proportion required at a given time, and to pay only for what is really consumed. and that some of this industry remains still in existence, or that the best needles are made by hand at Redditch. Chains are also made by hand at Dudley and Cradley, and although the Press is periodically moved to speak of the wretched conditions of the chain-makers, men and women, the trade still maintains itself; while nearly 7,000 men were busy in 1890 in their small workshops in making locks, even of the plainest description, at Walsall, Wolverhampton, and Willenhall. The various ironmongeries connected with horse-clothing -- bits, spurs, bridles, and so on-are also largely made by hand at Walsall.

The Birmingham gun and rifle trades, which also belong to the same domain of small industries, are well known. As to the various branches of dress, there are still important divisions of the United Kingdom where a variety of domestic trades connected with dress is carried on on a large scale. I need only mention the cottage industries of Ireland, as also some of them which have survived in the shires of Buckingham, Oxford, and Bedford; hosiery is a common occupation in the villages of the counties Of Nottingham and Derby; and several great London firms send out cloth to be made into dress in the villages of Sussex and Hampshire. Woollen hosiery is at home in the villages of Leicester, and especially in Scotland; straw-plaiting and hat-making in many parts of the country; while at Northampton, Leicester, Ipswich, and Stafford shoemaking was, till quite lately, a widely spread domestic occupation, or was carried on in small workshops; even at Norwich it remains a petty trade to some extent, notwithstanding the competition of the factories. It must also be said that the recent appearance of large boot and shoe factories has considerably increased the number of girls and women who sew the "uppers" and embroider the slippers, either in their own houses or in sweaters' workshops, while new small factories have developed of late for the making of heels, card-boxes, and so on.

The petty trades are thus an important factor of industrial life even in Great Britain, although many of them have gathered into the towns. But if we find in this country so many fewer rural, industries than on the Continent, we must -not imagine that their disappearance is due only to a keener competition of the factories. The chief cause was the compulsory exodus from the villages.

As everyone knows from Thorold Rogers' work, the growth of the factory system in England was intimately connected with that enforced exodus. Whole industries, which prospered till then, were killed downright by the forced clearing of estates.

Petty Trades in France

Small industries are met with in France in a very great variety, and they represent a most important feature of national economy. it is estimated, in fact, that while one-half of the population of France live upon agriculture, and one-third upon industry, this third part is equally distributed between the great industry and the small one. This last occupies about 1,650,000 workers and supports from 4,000,000 to 5,000,000 persons. A considerable number of peasants who resort to small industries without abandoning agriculture would have to be added to the just-mentioned items, and the additional earnings which these peasants find in industry are so important that in several parts of

France peasant proprietorship could not be maintained without the aid derived from the rural industries.

The small peasants know what they have to expect the day they become factory hands in a town; and so long as they have not been dispossessed by the money-lender of their lands and houses, and so long as the village rights in the communal grazing grounds or woods have not been lost, they cling to a combination of industry with agriculture. Having, in most cases, no horses to plough the land, they resort to an arrangement which is widely spread, if not universal, among small French landholders, even in purely rural districts (I saw it even in HauteSavoie). One of the peasants who keeps a plough and a team of horses tills all the, fields in turn. At the same time, owing to a wide maintenance of the communal spirit, which I have described elsewhere, further support is found in the communal shepherd, the communal wine-press, and various forms of "aids" amongst the peasants. And wherever the village-community spirit is maintained, the small industries persist, while no effort is spared to bring the small plots under higher culture.

Market-gardening and fruit culture often go hand in hand with small industries. And wherever well-being is found on a relatively unproductive soil, it is nearly always due to a combination of the two sister arts.

The most wonderful adaptations of the small industries to new requirements, and substantial technical progress in the methods of production, can be noted at the same time. It may even be said of France, as it has been said of Russia, that when a rural industry dies out, the cause of its decay is found much less in the competition of rival factories-in hundreds of localities the small industry undergoes a complete modification, or it changes its character in such cases-than in the decay of the population as agriculturists. Continually we see that only when the small landholders have been ruined, as such, by a group of causes-the loss of communal meadows, or abnormally high rents, or the havoc made in some locality by the marchands de biens (swindlers enticing the peasants to buy land on credit), or the bankruptcy of some shareholders' company whose shares had been eagerly taken by the peasants -only then do they abandon both the land and the rural industry and emigrate towards the towns.

Otherwise, a now industry always grows up when the competition of the factory becomes too acute -- a wonderful, hardly suspected adaptability being displayed by the small industries; or else the rural artisans resort to some form of intensive farming, gardening, etc., and in the meantime some other industry makes its appearance. A closer study of France under this aspect is instructive in a high degree.

It is evident that in most textile industries the power-loom supersedes the hand-loom, and the factory takes, or has taken already, the place of the cottage industry. Cottons, plain linen, and machine-made lace are now produced at such a low cost by machinery that hand-weaving evidently becomes an anachronism for the plainest descriptions of such goods. Consequently, though there were in France, in the year 1876, 328,300 hand-looms as against 121,340 power-looms, it may safely be taken that the number of the former has been considerably reduced within the next twenty years. However, the slowness with which this change is being accomplished is one of the most striking features of the present industrial organisation of the textile trades of France.

The causes of this power of resistance of handloom-weaving become especially apparent when one consults such works as Reybaud's Le Coton, which was written in 1863, nearly half a century ago-that is, at a time when the cottage industries were still fully alive. Though an ardent admirer himself of the great industries, Reybaud faithfully noted the striking superiority of well-being in the weavers' cottages as compared with the misery of the factory hands in the cities. Already then, the cities of St. Quentin, Lille, Roubaix and Amiens were great centres for cotton-spinning Mills and cotton-weaving factories. But, at the same time, all sorts of cottons were woven in hand-looms, in the very suburbs of St. Quentin and in a hundred villages and hamlets around it, to be sold for finishing in the city. And Reybaud remarked that the horrible dwellings in town, and the general condition of the factory hands, stood in a wonderful contrast with the relative welfare of the rural weavers. Nearly every one of these last had his own house and a small field which he continued to cultivate.

Even in such a branch as the fabrication of plain cotton velvets, in which the competition of the factories was especially keenly felt, homeweaving was widely spread, in 1863 and even in 1878, in the villages round Amiens. Although the earnings of the rural weavers were small, as a rule, the weavers preferred to keep to their own cottages, to their own crops and to their own cattle; and only repeated commercial crises, as well as several of the above-mentioned causes, hostile to the small peasant, compelled most of them to give up the struggle, and to seek employment in the factories, while part of them have, by this time, again returned to agriculture or taken to market-gardening.

Another important centre for rural industries was in the neighbourhood of Rouen, where no less than 110,000 persons were employed, in 1863, in weaving cottons for the finishing factories of that city. In the valley of the Andelle, in the department of Eure, each village was at that time an industrial bee-hive; each streamlet was utilised for setting into work a small factory. Reybaud described the condition of the peasants who combined agriculture with work at the rural factory as most satisfactory, especially in comparison with the condition of the slum-dwellers at Rouen, and he even mentioned a case or two in which the village factories belonged to the village communities.

Seventeen years later, Baudrillart depicted the same region in very much the same words; and although the rural factories bad had to yield to a great extent before the big factories, the rural industry was still valued as showing a yearly production of 85,000,000 francs (£2,400,000).

At the present time, the factories must have made further progress; but we still see from the excellent descriptions of M. Ardouin Dumazet, whose work will have in the future almost the same value as Arthur Young's Travels, that a considerable portion of the rural weavers has still survived; while at the same time one invariably meets, even nowadays, with the remark that relative well-being is prominent in the villages in which weaving is connected with agriculture.

Up to the present time, M. Ardouin Dumazet writes, "there is an industry which gives work to many hand-looms in the villages; it is the weaving of various stuffs for umbrellas and ladies' boots." Amiens is the chief centre for this weaving. In other places they are making dresses out of Amiens velvet and various stuffs woven at Roubaix. It is a new industry; it has taken the place of the old one, which was making of Amiens a second Lyons.

In the district of Le Thelle, to the south of Beauvais, there is "a multitude of petty trades, of which one hardly imagines the importance. I have seen," M. Dumazet says, "small factories of buttons made from bone, ivory, or motherof-pearl, brushes, shoe-horns, keys for pianos, dominoes, counters and dice, spectacle-cases, small articles for the writing-table, handles for tools, measures, billiard keys-what not!

There is not one single village, however small, the population of which should not have its own industry." At the same time it must not be forgotten that thousands of small articles for the writing-table and for draughtsmen are fabricated on a large scale in the small factories in the same region. Some of the workshops are situated in private houses, and in some of them artistic work is made; but most of them are located in special houses) where the necessary Power is hired by the owner of the workshop. You see here "a fantastic activity"--the word is M. Dumazet's; the division of labour is very great, and everywhere they invent new machine-tools.

Finally, in the villages of the Vermandois district (department of the Aisne), we find a considerable number of hand-looms (more than 3,000) upon which mixed stuffs made of cotton, wool and silk are Woven.

Of course, it must be recognised that, as a rule, in northern France, Where cottons are fabricated on a large scale in factory towns, hand-weaving in the villages is nearly gone. But, as is seen already from the preceding, new small industries have grown up instead, and this is also the case in many other parts of France.

Taking the region situated between Rouen in the north-east, Orleans in the south-east, Rennes in the north-west, and Nantes in the south-west--that is, the old provinces of Normandy, Perche and Maine, and partly Touraine and Anjou, as they were seen by Ardouin Dumazet in 1895--we find there quite a variety of domestic and petty industries, both in the villages and in the towns.

At Laval (to the south-east of Rennes), where drills (coutils) were formerly woven out of flax in hand-looms, and at Alencon, formerly a great centre for the cottage-weaving of linen, as well as for hand-made lace, Ardouin Dumazet found both the house and the factory linen industry in a lingering state. Cotton takes the lead. Drills are now made out of cotton in the factories, and the demand for flax goods is very small. Both domestic and factory weaving of flax goods are accordingly in a poor condition. The cottagers abandoned that branch of weaving, and the large factories, which had been erected at Alencon with the intention of creating a flax and hemp-cloth industry, had to be closed. Only one factory, occupying 250 hands, remains; while nearly 23,000 weavers, who found occupation at Mans, Fresnay and Alencon in hemp cloths and fine linen, had to abandon that industry. Those who worked in factories have emigrated to other towns, while those who had not broken with agriculture reverted to it. In this struggle of cotton versus flax and hemp, the former was victorious.

As to lace, it is made in such quantities by machinery at Calais, Caudry, St. Quentin and Tarare that only high-class artistic lace-making continues on a small scale at Alencon itself, but it still remains a by-occupation in the surrounding country. Besides, at Flers, and at Ferte Mace (a small town to the south of the former), hand-weaving is still carried on in about 5,400 hand-looms, although the whole trade, in factories and villages alike, is in a piteous state since the Spanish markets have been lost. Spain has now plenty of her own cotton mills. Twelve big spinning mills at Conde (where 4,000 tons of cotton were spun in 1883) were abandoned in 1893, and the workers were thrown into a most miserable condition.

On the contrary, in an industry which supplies the home market-namely, in the fabrication of linen handkerchiefs, which itself is of a quite recent growth-we see that cottage-weaving is, even now, in full prosperity. Cholet (in Maineet-Loire, south-west of Angers) is the centre of that trade. It has one spinning mill and one weaving mill, but both employ considerably fewer hands than domestic weaving, which is spread over no less than 200 villages of the surrounding region. Neither at Rouen nor in the industrial cities of Northern France are so many linen handkerchiefs fabricated as in this region in hand-looms, we are told by Ardouin Dumazet.

Within the curve made by the Loire as it flows past Orleans we find another prosperous centre of domestic industries connected with cottons. "From Romorantin [in Loire-et-Cher, south of Orleans] to Argenton and Le Blanc," the same writer says, "we have one immense workshop where handkerchiefs are embroidered, and shirts, cuffs, collars and all sorts of ladies' linen are sewn or embroidered. There is not one house, even in the tiniest hamlets, where the women would not be occupied in that trade . . . and if this work is a mere passe-temps in vinegrowing regions, here it has become the chief resource of the population." Even at Romorantin itself, where 400 women and girls are employed in one factory, there are more than 1,000 women who sew linen in their houses.

The same must be said of a group of industrial villages peopled with clothiers in the neighbourhood of another Normandy city, Elbaeuf. When Baudrillart visited them in 1878-1880, he was struck with the undoubted advantages offered by a combination of agriculture with industry. Clean houses, clean dresses, and a general stamp of well-being were characteristic of these villages.

Happily enough, weaving is not the only small industry of both this region and Brittany. On the contrary, scores of other small industries enliven the villages and burgs. At Fougeres (in Ille-et-Vilaine, to the north-east of Reims) one sees how the factory has contributed to the development of various small and domestic trades. In 1830 this town was a great centre for the domestic fabrication of the so-called chaussons de tresse. The competition of the prisons killed, however, this primitive industry; but it was soon substituted by the fabrication of soft socks in felt (chaussons de feutre). This last industry also went down, and then the fabrication of boots and shoes was introduced, this last giving origin, in its turn, to the boot and shoe factories, of which there are now thirty-three at Fougeres, employing 8,000 workers (yearly production about 5,000,000 pairs). But at the same time domestic industries took a new development. Thousands of women are employed now in their houses in sewing the "uppers" and in embroidering fancy shoes. Moreover, quite a number of smaller workshops grew up in the neighbourhood, for the fabrication of cardboard boxes, wooden heels, and so on, as well as a number of tanneries, big and small. And M. Ardouin Dumazet's remark is, that one is struck to find, owing to these industries, an undoubtedly higher level of well-being in the villages-quite unforeseen in the centre of this purely agricultural region.

In Brittany, in the neighbourhood of Quimperle, a great number of small workshops for the fabrication of the felt hats which are worn by the peasants is scattered in the villages; and rapidly improving agriculture goes hand in hand with that trade. Well-being is a distinctive feature of these villages. At Hennebont (on the southern coast of Brittany) 1,400 workers are employed in an immense factory in the fabrication of tins for preserves, and every year twenty-two to twenty-three tons of iron are transformed into steel, and next into tins, which are sent to Paris, Bordeaux, Nantes, and so on. But the factory has created "quite a world of tiny workshops" in this purely agricultural region: small tin-ware workshops, tanneries, potteries, and so on, while the slags are transformed in small factories into manure.

Agriculture and industry are thus going here hand in hand, the importance of not severing the union being perhaps best seen at Loudeac, a small town in the midst of Brittany (department of Cotes-du-Nord). Formerly the villages in this neighbourhood were industrial, all hamlets being peopled with weavers who fabricated the well-known Brittany linen. Now, this industry having gone down very much, the weavers have simply returned to the soil. Out of an industrial town, Loudeac has become an agricultural market town; and, what is most interesting, these populations conquer new lands for agriculture and turn the formerly quite unproductive landes into rich corn fields; while on the northern coast of Brittany, around Dol, on land which began to be conquered from the sea in the twelfth century, market-gardening is now carried on to a very great extent for export to England.

Altogether, it is striking to observe, on perusing M. Ardouin Dumazet's little volumes, how domestic industries go hand in hand with all sorts of small industries in agriculturegardening, poultry-farming, fabrication of fruit preserves, and so on-and how all sorts of associations for sale and export are easily introduced. Mans is, as known, a great centre for the export of geese and all sorts of poultry to England.

Part of Normandy (namely, the departments of Eure and Orne) is dotted with small workshops where all sorts of small brass goods and hardware are fabricated in the villages. Of course, the domestic fabrication of pins is nearly gone, and as for needles, polishing only, in a very primitive form, has been maintained in the villages. But all sorts of small hardware, including nails, lockets, etc., in great variety, are fabricated in the villages, especially round Laigle. Stays are also sewn in small workshops in many villages, notwithstanding the competition of prison work.

Tinchebrai (to the west of Flers) is a real centre for a great variety of smaller goods in iron, mother-of-pearl and horn. All sorts of hardware and locks are fabricated by the peasants during the time they can spare from agriculture, and real works of art, some of which were much admired at the exhibition of 1889, are produced by these humble peasant sculptors in horn, mother-of-pearl and iron. Farther south, the polishing of marble goods is carried on in numbers of small workshops, scattered round Solesmes and grouped round one central establishment where marble pieces are roughly shaped with the aid of steam, to be finished in the small village workshops. At Sable the workers in that branch, who all own their houses and gardens, enjoy a real well-being especially noticed by our traveler.

In the woody regions of the Perche and the Maine we find all sorts of wooden industries which evidently could only be maintained owing to the communal possession of the woods. Near the forest of Perseigne there is a small burg, Fresnaye, which is entirely peopled with workers in wood.

"There is not one house," Ardouin Dumazet writes, "in which wooden goods would not be fabricated. Some years ago there was little variety in their produce; spoons, salt-boxes, shepherds' boxes, scales, various wooden pieces for weavers, flutes and hautboys, spindles, wooden measures, funnels, and wooden bowls were only made. But Paris wanted to have a thousand things in which wood was combined with iron: mouse-traps, cloak-pegs, spoons for jam, brooms. . . . And now every house has a workshop containing either a turninglathe, or some machine-tools for chopping wood, for making lattice-work, and so on. . . . Quite a new industry was born, and the most coquettish things are now fabricated. Owing to this industry the population is happy. The earnings are not high, but each worker owns his house and garden, and occasionally a bit of field."

At Neufchatel wooden shoes are made, and the hamlet, we are told, has a most smiling aspect. To every house a garden is attached, and none of the misery of big cities is to be seen. At Jupilles and in the surrounding country other varieties of wooden goods are produced: taps, boxes of different kinds, together with wooden shoes; while at the forest of Vibraye two workshops have been erected for turning out umbrella handles by the million for all France. One of these workshops having been founded by a worker sculptor, he has invented and introduced in his workshop the most ingenious machine-tools.

About 150 men work at this factory; but it is evident that half a dozen smaller workshops, scattered in the villages, would have answered equally well.

Going now over to a quite different region, the Nievre, in the centre of France, and Haute Marne, in the east-we find that both regions are great centres for a variety of small industries, some of which are maintained by associations of workers, while others have grown up in the shadow of factories. The small iron workshops which formerly covered the country have not disappeared: they have undergone a transformation; and now the country is covered with small workshops where agricultural machinery, chemical produce, and pottery are fabricated; "one ought to go as far as Guerigny and Fourchambault to find the great industry;" while a number of small workshops for the fabrication of a variety of hardware flourish by the side of, and owing to the proximity of, the industrial centres.

Pottery makes the fortune of the valley of the Loire about Nevers. High-class art pottery is made in this town, while in the villages plain pottery is fabricated and exported by merchants who go about with their boats selling it. At Gien a large factory of china buttons (made out of felspar-powder cemented with milk) has lately been established, and employs 1,500 workmen, who produce from 3,500 to 4,500 lb. of buttons every day. And, as is often the case, part of the work is done in the villages. For many miles on both banks of the Loire, in all villages, old people, women and children sew the buttons to the cardboard pieces. Of course, that sort of work is wretchedly paid; but it is resorted to only because there is no other sort of industry in the neighbourhood to which the peasants could give their leisure time.

In the same region of the Haute Marne, especially in the neighbourhood of Nogent, we find cutlery as a by-occupation to agriculture, Landed property is very much subdivided in that

Fields, Factories, and Workshops

part of France, and great numbers of peasants own but from two to three acres per family, or even less. Consequently, in thirty villages round Nogent, about 5,000 men are engaged in cutlery, chiefly of the highest sort (artistic knives are occasionally sold at as much as £20 a piece), while the lower sorts are fabricated in the neighbourhoods of Thiers, in Puy-de-Dome (Auvergne). The Nogent industry has developed spontaneously, with no aid from without, and in its technical part it shows considerable progress. At Thiers, where the cheapest sorts of cutlery are made, the division of labour, the cheapness of rent for small workshops supplied with motive power from the Durolle river, or from small gas motors, the aid of a great variety of specially invented machine-tools, and the existing combination of machine-work with hand-work have resulted in such a perfection of the technical part of the trade that it is considered doubtful whether the factory system could further economise labour. For twelve miles round Thiers, in each direction, all the streamlets are dotted with small work-shops, in which peasants, who continue to cultivate their fields, are at work.

Basket-making is again an important cottage industry in several parts of France, namely in Aisne and in Haute Marne. In this last department, at Villaines, everyone is a basketmaker, "and all the basketmakers belong to a co-operative society," Ardouin Dumazet remarks. "There are no employers; all the produce is brought once a fortnight to the co-operative stores and there it is sold for the association. About 150 families belong to it, and each owns a house and some vineyards." At Fays-Billot, also in Haute Marne, 1,500 basket-makers belong to an association; while at Thiérache, where several thousand men are engaged in the same trade, no association has been formed, the earnings being in consequence extremely low.

Another very important centre of petty trades is the French Jura, or the French part of the Jura Mountains, where the watch trade has attained, as known, a high development. When I visited these villages between the Swiss frontier and Besançon in the year 1878, I was struck by the high degree of relative well-being which I could observe, even though I was perfectly well acquainted with the Swiss villages in the Val de Saint Imier. It is very probable that the machine-made watches have brought about a crisis in French watch-making as they have in Switzerland. But it is known that part, at least, of the Swiss watch-makers have strenuously fought against the necessity of being enrolled in the factories, and that while watch factories grew up at Geneva and elsewhere, considerable numbers of the watchmakers have taken to divers other trades which continue to be carried on as domestic or small industries. I must only add that in the French Jura great numbers of watch-makers were at the same time owners of their houses and gardens, very often of bits of fields, and especially of communal meadows, and that the communal fruitièes, or creameries, for the common sale of butter and cheese, are widely spread in that part of France.

So far as I could ascertain, the development of the machine-made watch industry has not destroyed the small industries of the Jura hills. The watch-makers have taken to new branches, and, as in Switzerland, they have created various new industries. From Ardouin Dumazet's travels we can, at anyrate, borrow an insight into the present state of the southern part of this region. In the neighbourhoods of Nantua and Cluses silks are woven in nearly all villages, the peasants giving to weaving their spare time from agriculture, while quite a number of small workshops (mostly less than twenty looms, one of 100 looms) are scattered in the little villages, on the streamlets running from the hills. Scores of small saw-mills have also been built along the streamlet Merloz, for the fabrication of all sorts of little pretty things in wood. At Oyonnax, a small town on the Ain, we have a big centre for the fabrication of combs, an industry more than

200 years old, which took a now development since the last war through the invention of celluloid. No less than 100 or 120 "masters" employ from two to fifteen workers each, while over 1,200 persons work in their houses, making combs out of Irish horn and French celluloid. Wheelpower was formerly rented in small workshops, but electricity, generated by a waterfall, has lately been introduced, and is now distributed in the houses for bringing into motion small motors of from onequarter to twelve horsepower. And it is remarkable to notice that as soon as electricity gave the possibility to return to domestic work, 300 workers left at once the small workshops and took to work in their houses. Most of these workers have their own cottages and gardens, and they show a very interesting spirit of association. They have also erected four workshops for making cardboard boxes, and their production is valued at 2,000,000 fr. every year.

At St. Claude, which is a great centre for briar pipes (sold in large quantities in London with English trade-marks, and therefore eagerly bought by those Frenchmen who visit London, as a souvenir from the other side of the Channel), both big and small workshops, supplied by motive force from the Tacon streamlet, prosper by the side of each other. Over 4,000 men and women are employed in this trade, while all sorts of small by-trades have grown by its side (amber and horn mouth-pieces, sheaths, etc.). Countless small workshops are busy besides, on the banks of the two streams, with the fabrication of all sorts of wooden things: match-boxes, beads, sheaths for spectacles, small things in horn, and so on, to say nothing of a rather large factory (200 workers) where metric measures are fabricated for the whole world. At the same time thousands of persons in St. Claude, in the neighbouring villages and in the smallest mountain hamlets, are busy in cutting diamonds (an industry only fifteen years old in this region), and other thousands are busy in cutting various less precious stones. All this is done in quite small workshops supplied by water-power.

The extraction of ice from some lakes and the gathering of oak-bark for tanneries complete the picture of these busy villages, where industry joins hands with agriculture, and modern machines and appliances are so well put in the service of the small workshops.

On the other side, at Besançon, which was, in 1878, when I visited it, a great centre for watch-making, "all taken, nothing has yet been changed in the habits of the workingclass," M. Dumazet wrote in 1901. The watchmakers continued to work in their houses or in small workshops. Only there was no complete fabrication of the watch or the clock. Many important parts-the wheels, etc.--were imported from Switzerland or from different towns of France. And, as is always the case, numerous small secondary workshops for making the watch-cases, the hands, and so on, grew up in that neighbourhood.

The same has to be said of Montbéliard--another important centre of the watch trade. By the side of the manufactures, where all the parts of the mechanism of the watch are fabricated by machinery, there is quite a number of workshops where various parts of the watch are made by skilled workmen; and this industry has already given birth to a new branch--the making of various tools for these workshops, as also for different other trades.

In other parts of the same region, such as Héricourt, a variety of small industries has grown by the side of the great ironmongery factories. The city spreads into the villages, where the population are making coffee-mills, spice-mills, machines for crushing the grain for the cattle, as well as saddlery, small ironmongery, or even watches. Elsewhere the fabrication of different small parts of the watch having been monopolised by the factories, the workshops began to manufacture the small parts of the bicycles, and later on of the motor-cars. In short, we have here quite a world of industries of modern origin, and with them of inventions made to simplify the work of the band.

Finally, omitting a mass of small trades, I will only name the hat-makers of the Loire, the stationery of the Ardèche, the fabrication of hardware in the Doubs, the glove-makers of the Isère, the broom and brush-makers of the Oise (valued at £800,000 per annum), and the house machine-knitting in the neighbourhoods of Troyes. But I must say a few words more about two important centres of small industries: the Lyons region and Paris.

At the present time the industrial region of which Lyons is the centre includes the departments of Rhône, Loire, Drôme, Saône-et-Loire, Ain, the southern part of the Jura department, and the western part of Savoy, as far as Annecy, while the silkworm is reared as far as the Alps, the Cévennes Mountains, and the neighbourhoods of Macon. It contains, besides fertile plains, large hilly tracks, also very fertile as a rule, but covered with snow during part of the winter, and the rural populations are therefore bound to resort to some industrial occupation in addition to agriculture; they find it in silk-weaving and various small industries. Altogether it may be said that the région lyonnaise is characterised as a separate centre of French civilisation and art, and that a remarkable spirit of research, discovery and invention has developed there in all directions--scientific and industrial.

The Croix Rousso at Lyons, where the silkweavers (canuts) have their chief quarters, is the centre of that industry, and in 1S95 the whole of that hill, thickly covered with houses, five, six, eight and ten storeys high, resounded with the noise of the looms which were busily going in every department of that big agglomeration. Electricity has lately been brought into the service of this domestic industry, supplying motive power to the looms.

To the south of Lyons, in the city of Vienne, hand-weaving is disappearing. "Shoddy" is now the leading produce, and twenty-eight concerns only remain out of the 120 fabriques which existed thirty years ago. Old woollen rags, rags of carpets, and all the dust from the carding and spinning in the wool and cotton factories of Northern France, with a small addition of cotton, are transformed here into cloth which flows from Vienne to all the big cities of France--20,000 yards of "shoddy" every day-to supply the ready-made clothing factories, Hand-weaving has evidently nothing to do in that industry, and in 1890 only 1,300 hand-looms were at work out of the 4,000 which were in motion in 1870. Large factories, employing a total of 1,800 workers, have taken the place of these hand-weavers, while "shoddy" has taken the place of cloth. All sorts of flannels, felt hats, tissues of horse-hair, and so on, are fabricated at the same time. But while the great factory thus conquered the city of Vienne., its suburbs and its nearest surroundings became the centre of a prosperous gardening and fruit culture, which has already been mentioned in chapter iv.

The banks of the Rhône, between Ampuis and Condrieu, are one of the wealthiest parts, of all France, owing to the shrubberies and nurseries, marketgardening, fruit-growing, vinegrowing, and cheese-making out of goats' milk. I-louse industries go there hand in hand with an intelligent culture of the soil; Condrieu, for instance, is a famous centre for embroidery, which is made partly by hand, as of old, and partly by machinery.

In the west of Lyons, at I'Arbresles, factories have grown up for making silks and velvets; but a large part of the population still continue to weave in their houses; while farther west, Panissières is the centre of quite a number of villages in which linen and silks are woven as a domestic industry. Not all these workers own their houses, but those, at least, who own or rent a small piece of land or garden, or keep a couple of cows, are said to be well off, and the land, as a rule, is said to be admirably cultivated by these weavers.

The chief industrial centre of this part of the Lyons region is certainly Tarare. At the time when Reybaud wrote his already-mentioned work, Le Coton, it was a centre for the manufacture of muslins and it occupied in this industry the same position as Leeds formerly occupied in this country in the woollen cloth trade. The spinning mills and the large finishing factories were at Tarare, while the weaving of the muslins and the embroidery of the same were made in the surrounding villages, especially in the hilly tracts of the Beaujolais and the Forez. Each peasant house, each farm and métayerie were small workshops at that time, and one could see, Reybaud wrote, the lad of twenty embroidering fine muslin after he had finished cleaning the farm stables, without the work suffering in its delicacy from a combination of two such varied pursuits. On the contrary, the delicacy of the work and the extreme variety of patterns were a distinctive feature of the Tarare muslins and a cause of their success. All testimonies agreed at the same time in recognising that, while agriculture found support in the industry, the agricultural population enjoyed a relative well-being.

By this time the industry has undergone a thorough transformation, but still no less than 60,000 persons, representing a population of about 250,000 souls, work for Tarare in the hilly tracts, weaving all sorts of muslins for all parts of the world, and they earn every year £480,000 in this way.

Amplepuis, notwithstanding its own factories of silks and blankets, remains one of the local centres for such muslins; while close by, Thizy is a centre for a variety of linings, flannels, "peruvian serges," "oxfords," and other mixed woollen-and-cotton stuffs which are woven in the mountains by the peasants.

No less than 3,000 hand-looms are thus scattered in twentytwo villages., and about £600,000 worth of various stuffs are woven every year by the rural weavers in this neighbourhood alone; while 15,000 powerlooms are at work in both Thizy and the great city of Roanne, in which two towns all varieties of cottons (linings, flannelettes, apron cloth) and. silk blankets are woven in factories by the million yards.

At Cours, 1,600 workers are employed in making "blankets," chiefly of the lowest sort (even such as are sold at 2s. and even 10d. a piece, for export to Brazil); all possible and imaginable rags and sweepings from all sorts of textile factories (jute, cotton, flax, hemp, wool and silk) are used for that industry, in which the factory is, of course, fully victorious. But even at Roanne, where the fabrication of cottons has attained a great degree of perfection and 9,000 power-looms are at work, producing every year more than 30,000,000 yards--even at Roanne one finds with astonishment that domestic industries are not dead, but yield every year the respectable amount of more than 10,000,000 yards of stuffs. At the same time, in the neighbourhood of that big city the industry of fancylinitting has taken within the last thirty years a sudden development. Only 2,000 women were employed in it in 1864, but their numbers were estimated by M. Dumazet at 20,000; and, without abandoning their rural work, they find time to knit, with the aid of small knitting-machines, all sorts of fancy articles in wool, the annual value of which attains £6360,000.

It must not be thought, however, that textiles and connected trades are the only small industries in this locality. Scores of various rural industries continue to exist besides, and in nearly all of them the methods of production are continually improved. Thus, when the rural making of plain chairs became unprofitable, articles of luxury and stylish chairs began to be fabricated in the villages, and similar transformations are found everywhere.

More details about this extremely interesting region will be found in the Appendix, but one remark must be made in this place. Notwithstanding its big industries and coal mines, this part of France has entirely maintained its rural aspect, and is now one of the best cultivated parts of the country. What most deserves admiration is-not so much the development of the great industries, which, after all, here as elsewhere, are to a great extent international in their origins-as the creative and inventive powers and capacities of adaptation which appear amongst the great mass of these industrious populations. At every step, in the field, in the garden, in the orchard, in the dairy, in the industrial arts, in the hundreds of small inventions in these arts, one sees the creative genius of the folk. In these regions one best understands why France, taking the mass of its population, is considered the richest country of Europe.

The chief centre for petty trades in France is, however, Paris. There we find, by the side of the large factories, the greatest variety of petty trades for the fabrication of goods of every description, both for the home market and for export. The petty trades at Paris so much prevail over the factories that the average number of workmen employed in the 98,000 factories and workshops of Paris is less than, six, while the number of persons employed in workshops which have less than five operatives is almost twice as big as the number of persons, employed in the larger establishments. In fact, Paris is a great bee-hive where hundreds of thousands of men and women fabricate in small workshops all possible varieties of goods which require skill, taste and invention. These small workshops, in which artistic finish and rapidity of work are so much praised, necessarily stimulate the mental powers of the producers; and we may safely admit that if the Paris workmen are generally considered, and really are, more developed intellectually than the workers of any other European capital, this is due to a great extent to the character of the work they are engaged in--a work which implies artistic taste, skill, and especially inventiveness, always wide awake in order to invent now patterns of goods and steadily to increase and to perfect the technical methods of production. It also appears very probable that if we find a highly developed working population in Vienna and Warsaw, this depends again to a very great extent upon the very considerable development of similar small industries, which stimulate invention and so much contribute to develop the worker's intelligence.

The Galerie du travail at the Paris exhibitions is always a most remarkable sight. One can appreciate in it both the variety of the small. industries which are carried on in French towns and the skill and inventing powers of the workers. And the question necessarily arises: Must all this skill, all this intelligence, be swept away by the factory, instead of becoming a new fertile source of progress under a better organisation of production? must all this independence and inventiveness of the worker disappear before the factory levelling? and, if it must, would such a transformation be a progress, as so many economists who have only studied figures and not human beings are ready to maintain?

At anyrate, it is quite certain that even if the absorption of the French petty trades by the big factories were possible-which seems extremely doubtful-the absorption would not be accomplished so soon as that. The small industry of Paris fights hard for its maintenance, and it shows its vitality by the numberless machine-tools which are continually invented by the workers for improving and cheapening the produce.

The numbers of motors which were exhibited at the last exhibitions in the Galerie du travail bear a testimony to the fact that a cheap motor, for the small industry, is one of the leading problems of the day. Motors weighing only forty-five lb., including the boiler, were exhibited in 1889 to answer that want. Small two-horsepower engines, fabricated by the engineers of the Jura (formerly watch-makers) in their small works-hops, were at that time another attempt to solve the problemto say nothing of the water, gas and. electrical motors. The transmission of steam-power to 230 small workshops which was made by the Société des Immeubles industriels was another attempt in the same direction, and the increasing efforts of the French engineers for finding out the best means of transmitting and subdividing power by means of compressed air, "toledynamic cables," and electricity are indicative of the endeavours of the small industry to retain its ground in the face of the competition of the factories. (See Appendix V.)

Such are the small industries in France, as they have been described by observers who saw them on the spot. Is is, however, most interesting to have exact statistical items concerning the extension of the small industries, and to know their importance, in comparison with the, great industry. Fortunately enough, a general census of the French industries was made in the year 1896; its results have been published in full, under the title of Résultats statistiques du recensement des industries et des professions, and in the fourth volume of this capital work we find an excellent summing up of the main results of the census, written by M. Lucien March. I give a résumé of these results in the Appendix, as otherwise I should have been compelled, in speaking of the distribution of great and small industry in France, to repeat very much what I have said in this same chapter, speaking of the United Kingdom. There is so much in common in the distribution of small and large factories in the different branches of industry in both countries that it would have been a tedious repetition. So I give here only the main items and refer the reader to Appendix W.

The general distribution of the workers' population in large, middle-sized, and *small factories in the year 1896 was as follows. First of all there was the great division of independent artisans who worked single-banded, and working men and women who were without permanent employment on the day of the census. Part of this large division belongs to agriculture but, after having deducted the agricultural establishments, M. March arrives at the figures of 483,000 establishments belonging to this category in industry, and 1,047,000 persons of both sexes working in these establishments, or temporarily attached to some industrial establishment. To these we must add 37,705 industrial establishments, where no hired workmen are employed, but the head of the establishment works with the aid of the members of his own family. We have thus, in these two divisions, about 520,700 establishments and 1,084,700 persons which I inscribe in the following table under the head of "No hired operatives." The table then appears as follows:--

	Number of Establisments.	Number of operatives and clerks.
No hired operatives	520,700	1,084,700
From 1 to 10 employees	539,449	1,134,700
From 11 to 50 "	28,626	585,000
From 51 to 100 "		268,000
From 101 to 500 "	3,865	616,000
From 501 to 1000 "	3,145	195,000
	295	
More than 1000 "		313,000
	149	
	575,529	3,111,700
Total (with first division)	1,096,229	4,196,400

These figures speak for themselves and show what an immense importance the small industry has in France. More details, showing the distribution of the great, middle-sized and small industry in different branches will be found in the Appendix, and there the reader will also see what a striking resemblance is offered under this aspect by the industry of France and that of the United Kingdom. In the next chapter it will be seen from a similar census that Germany stands in absolutely the same position.

It would have been very interesting to compare the present distribution of industries in France with what it was previously.

But M. Lucien March tells us that "no statistics previous to 1896 have given us a knowledge of that distribution." Still, an inquest made between 1840 and 1845, and which M. March considers "very complete for the more important establishments which employed more than fifty workmen," was worked out by him, and he found that such establishments numbered 3,300 in 1840; in 1896 they had already attained the number of 7,400, and they occupied more than fifty-five per cent. of all the workpeople employed in industry. As to the establishments which employed more than 500 persons and which -numbered 133 in 1840 (six per cent. of all the workpeople), they attained the number of 444 in 1896, and sixteen per cent. of all the workpeople were employed in them.

The conclusion to be drawn from these fact is thus worded by M. March: "To sum up, during the last fifty years a notable concentration of the factories took place in the big establishments; but the just-mentioned results, supported by the statistics of the patents, permit us to recognise that this concentration does not prevent the maintenance of a mass of - small enterprises, the average sizes of which increase but very slowly." This last is, in fact, what we have just seen from our brief sketch for the United Kingdom, and we can only ask ourselves whether--such being the facts--the word "concentration" is well chosen. What we see in reality is, the appearance, in some branches of industry, of a certain number of large establishments, and especially of middle-sized factories. But this does not prevent in the least that very great numbers of small factories should continue to exist, either in other branches, or in the very same branches where large factories have appeared (the textiles, work in metal), or in branches connected with the main ones, which take their origin in these main ones, as the industry of clothing takes its origin from that of the textiles.

This is the only conclusion which a serious analysis permits us to draw from the facts brought to light by the census of 1896 and subsequent observations. As to the large deductions about "concentration" made by certain economists, they are mere hypotheses--useful, of course, for stimulating research, but becoming quit obnoxious when they are represented as economical laws, when in reality they are not confirmed at all by the testimony of carefully observed facts.

Chapter VII: Small Industries and Industrial Villages, Part 2

THE various industries which still have retained in Germany the characters of petty and domestic trades have been the subject of many exhaustive explorations, especially by A. M. Thun and Prof. Issaieff, on behalf of the Russian Petty Trades Commission, Emanuel Hans Sax, Paul Voigt, and very many others. By this time the subject has a bulky literature, and such impressive and suggestive pictures have been drawn from life for different regions and trades that I felt tempted to sum up these life-true descriptions. However, as in such a summary I should have to repeat much of what has already been said and illustrated in the preceding chapter, it will probably more interest the general reader to know something about the conclusions which can be drawn from the works of the German investigators, and to know the conclusions that may be drawn from the three censuses of industries which have been made in Germany in the years 1882, 1895, and 1907. This is what I am going to do.

Unhappily, the discussion upon this important subject has often taken in Germany a passionate and even a personally aggressive character On. the one hand the ultra-conservative elements of German politics tried, and succeeded to some extent, in making of the petty trades and the domestic industries an arm for securing a return to the "olden good times." They even passed a law intended to prepare a reintroduction of the old-fashioned, closed and patriarchal corporations which could be placed under the close supervision and tutorship of the State, and they saw in such a law a weapon against social democracy. On the other hand, the social democrats, justly opposed to such measures, but themselves inclined, in their turn, to take too abstract a view of economical questions, bitterly attack all those who do not merely repeat the stereotyped phrases to the effect that "the petty trades are in decay," and "the sooner they disappear the better," as they will give room to capitalist centralisation, which, according to the social democratic creed, "will soon achieve its own ruin." In this dislike of the small industries they are, of course, at one with the economists of the orthodox school, whom they combat on nearly all other points.

Under such conditions, the polemics about the petty trades and the domestic industries are evidently doomed to remain most unproductive. However, it is pleasant to see that a considerable amount of most conscientious work has boon made for the investigation of the petty trades in Germany; and, by the side of such monographs, from which nothing can be learned but that the petty trades' workers are in a miserable condition, and nothing whatever can be gathered to explain why these workers prefer their conditions to those of factory hands-there is no lack, of very detailed monographs (such as those of Thun, Em. 14. Sax, Paul Voigt on the Berlin cabinetmakers, etc.), in which one sees the whole of the life of these classes of workers, the difficulties which they have to cope with, and the technical conditions of the trade, and finds all the elements for an independent judgment upon the matter.

It is evident that a number of petty trades are already now doomed to disappear; but. there are others, on the contrary, which are endowed with a great vitality, and all chances are in favour of their continuing to exist and to take a further development for many years to come. In the fabrication of such textiles as are woven by millions of yards, and can be best produced with the aid of a complicated machinery, the competition of the hand-loom against the power-loom is evidently nothing but a survival, which may be maintained for some time by certain local conditions, but finally must die away.

The same is true with regard to many branches of the iron industries, hardware fabrication, pottery, and so on. But wherever the direct intervention of taste and inventiveness are required, wherever new patterns of goods requiring a continual renewal of machinery and tools must continually be introduced in order to feed the demand, as is the case with all fancy textiles, even though they be fabricated to supply the millions; wherever a great variety of goods and the uninterrupted invention of new ones goes on, as is the case in the toy trade., in instrument making, watch-making, bicycle making, and so on; and finally, wherever the artistic feeling of the individual worker makes the best part of his goods, as is the case in hundreds of branches of small articles of luxury, there is a wide field for petty trades, rural workshops, domestic industries, and the like. More fresh air, more ideas, more general conceptions, and more co-operation are evidently required in those industries. But where the spirit of initiative has been awakened in one way or another, we see the petty industries taking a new development in Germany, as we have just seen that being done in France.

Now, in nearly all the petty trades in Germany, the position of the workers is unanimously described as most miserable, and the many admirers of centralisation which we find in Germany always insist upon this misery in order to predict, and to call for, the disappearance of "those mediaeval survivals" which "capitalist centralisation" must supplant for the benefit of the worker. The reality is, however, that when we compare the miserable conditions of the workers in the petty trades with the conditions of the wage workers in the factories, in the same regions and in the same trades, we see that the very same misery -prevails among the factory workers. They live upon wages of from nine to eleven shillings a week, in town slums instead of the country. They work eleven hours a day, and they also are subject to the extra misery thrown upon them during the frequently recurring crises. It is only after they have undergone all Sorts of sufferings in their struggles against their employers that some factory workers succeed, more or less, here and there, to wrest from their employers a "living wage "-and this again only in certain trades.

To welcome all these sufferings, seeing in them the action of a "natural law" and a necessary step towards the necessary concentration of industry, would be simply absurd. While to maintain that the pauperisation of all workers and the wreckage of all village industries are a necessary step towards a higher form of industrial organisation would be, not only to affirm much more than one is entitled to affirm under the present imperfect state of economical knowledge, but to show an absolute want of comprehension of the sense of both natural and economic laws. Everyone, on the contrary, who has studied the question of the growth of great industries on its own merits, will undoubtedly agree with Thorold Rogers, who considered the sufferings inflicted upon the labouring classes for that purpose as having been of no necessity whatever, and simply having been inflicted to suit the temporary interests of the few--by no means those of the nation.

Moreover, everyone knows to what extent the labour of children and girls is resorted to, even in the most prosperous factories-- even in this country which stands foremost in industrial development. Some figures relative to this subject were given in the preceding chapter. And this fact is not an accident which might be easily removed, as Maurice Block--a great admirer, of course, of the factory systemtries to represent it. The low wages paid to children and youths are now one of the necessary elements in the cheapness of the factory produced textiles, and, consequently, of the very competition of the factory with the petty trades. I have mentioned besides, whilst speaking of France, what are the effects of concentrated "industries upon village life and in Thun's work, and in many others as well, one may find enough of ghastly instances of what are the effects of accumulations of girls in the factories. To idealise the modern factory, in order to depreciate the so-called "mediaeval" forms of the small industries, is consequently to say the least-as unreasonable as to idealise the latter and try to bring mankind back to isolated homespinning and home-weaving in every peasant house.

One fact dominates all the investigations which have been made into the conditions of the small industries. We find it in Germany, as well as in France or in Russia. In an immense number of trades it is not the superiority of the technical organisation of the trade in a factory, nor the economies realised on the prime-motor, which militate against the small industry in favour of the factories, but the more advantageous conditions for selling the produce and for buying the raw produce which are at the disposal of big concerns. Wherever this difficulty has been overcome, either by means of association, or in consequence of a market being secured for the sale of the produce, it has always been found-first, that the conditions of the workers or artisans immediately improved; and next, that a rapid progress was realised in the technical aspects of the respective industries. New processes were introduced to improve the produce or to increase the rapidity of its fabrication; new machine-tools were invented; or new motors were resorted to; or the trade was reorganised so as to diminish the costs of production.

On the contrary, wherever the helpless, isolated artisans and workers continue to remain at the mercy of the wholesale buyers, who always--since Adam Smith's time--"openly or tacitly" agree to act as one man to bring down the prices almost to a starvation level-and such is the case for the immense number of the small and village industries their condition is so bad that only the longing of the workers after a certain relative independence, and their knowledge of what awaits them in the factory, prevent them from joining the ranks of the factory hands. Knowing that in most cases the advent of the factory would mean no work at all for most men, and the taking of the children and girls to the factory, they do the utmost to prevent it from appearing at all in the village.

As to combinations in the villages, cooperation and the like, one must never forget how jealously the German, the French, the Russian and the Austrian Governments have hitherto prevented the workers, and especially the village workers, from entering into any sort of combination for economical purposes. In France the peasant syndicates were permitted only by the law of 1884. To keep the peasant at the lowest possible level, by means of taxation, serfdom, and the like, has been, and is still, the policy of most continental States. It was only in 1876 that some extension of the association rights was granted in Germany, and even now a mere co-operative association for the sale of the artisans' work is soon reported as a "political association" and submitted as such to the usual limitations, such as the exclusion of women and the like. A striking example of that policy as regards a village association was given by Prof. Issaieff, who also mentioned the severe measures taken by the wholesale buyers in the toy trade to prevent the workers from entering into direct intercourse with foreign buyers.

When one examines with more than a superficial attention the life of the small industries and their struggles for life, one sees that when they perish, they perish-not because "an economy can be realised by using a hundred horsepower motor, instead of a hundred small motors "-this inconveniency never fails to be mentioned, although it is easily obviated in Sheffield, in Paris, and many other places by hiring workshops with wheel-power, supplied by a central machine, and, still more, as was so truly observed by Prof. W. Unwin, by the electric transmission of power. They do not perish because a substantial economy can be realised in the factory production-in many more cases than is usually supposed, the fact is even the reverse-but because the capitalist who establishes a factory emancipates himself from the wholesale and retail dealers in raw materials; and especially, because he emancipates himself from the buyers of his produce and can deal directly with the wholesale buyer and exporter; or else he concentrates in one concern the different stages of fabrication of a given produce. The pages which Schulze-Gäwernitz gave to the organisation of the cotton industry in England, and to the difficulties which the German cotton-mill owners had to contend with, so long as they were dependent - upon Liverpool for raw cotton, are most instructive in this direction. And what characterises the cotton trade prevails in all other industries as well.

If the Sheffield cutlers who now work in their tiny workshops, in one of the above mentioned buildings supplied with wheel-power, were incorporated in one big factory, the chief advantage which would be realised in the factory would not be an economy in the costs of production, in comparison to the quality of the produce; with a shareholders' company the costs might even increase. And yet the profits (including wages) probably would be greater than the aggregate earnings of the workers, in consequence of the reduced costs of purchase of iron and coal, and the facilities for the sale of the produce. The great concern would thus find its advantages not in such factors as are imposed by the technical necessities of the trade at the time being, but in such factors as could be eliminated by cooperative organisation. All these are elementary notions among practical men.

It hardly need be added that a further advantage which the factory owner has is, that he can find a sale even for produce of the most inferior quality, provided there is a considerable quantity of it to be sold. All those who are acquainted with commerce know, indeed, what an immense bulk of the world's trade consists of "shoddy," patraque, "Red Indians' blankets," and the like, shipped to distant countries. Whole cities-we just saw-produce nothing but "shoddy."

Altogether, it may be taken as one of the fundamental facts of the economical life of Europe that the defeat of a number of small trades, artisan work and domestic industries, came through their being incapable of organising the sale of their produce--not from the production itself. The same thing recurs at every page of economical history. The incapacity of organising the sale, without being enslaved by the merchant, was the leading feature of the Mediaeval cities, which gradually fell under the economical and political yoke of the Guild-Merchant, simply because they were not able to maintain the sale of their manufactures by the community as a whole, or to organise the sale of a new produce in the interest of the community. When the markets for such commodities came to be Asia on the one side, and the New World on the other side, such was fatally the case; since commerce had ceased to be communal, and had become individual, the cities became a prey for the rivalries of the chief merchant families.

Even nowadays, when we see the co-operative societies beginning to succeed in their productive workshops, while fifty years ago they invariably failed in their capacity of producers, we may conclude that the cause of their previous failures was not in their incapacity of properly and economically organising production, but in their inability of acting as sellers and exporters of the produce they bad fabricated. Their present successes, on the contrary, are fully accounted for by the network of distributive societies which they have at their command. The sale has been simplified, and production has been rendered possible by first organising the market.

Such are a few conclusions which may be drawn from a study of the small industries in Germany and elsewhere. And it may be safely said, with regard to Germany, that if measures are not taken for driving the peasants from the land on the same scale as they have been taken in this country; if, on the contrary, the numbers of small landholders multiply, they necessarily will turn to various small trades, in addition to agriculture, as they have done, and are doing, in France. Every step that may be taken, either for awakening intellectual life in the villages, or for assuring the peasants' or the country's rights upon the land, will necessarily further the growth of industries in the villages.

In this light it is extremely interesting to see the figures as to the distribution of the German industries into a small, middle-sized, and great industry, which are given by three industrial censuses taken during the last thirty years. But for these figures I refer the reader to the Appendix.

Petty Trades in Other Countries

If it were worth extending our inquiry to other countries, we should find a vast field for most interesting observations in Switzerland. There we should see the same vitality in a variety of petty industries, and we could mention what has been done in the different cantons for maintaining the small trades by three different sets of measures : the extension of co-operation; a wide extension of technical education in the schools and the introduction of new branches of semi-artistic production in different parts of the country; and the supply of cheap motive power in the houses by means of a hydraulic or an electric transmission of power borrowed from the waterfalls. A separate book of the greatest interest and value could be written on this subject, especially on the impulse given to a number of petty trades, old and new, by means of a cheap supply of motive power. Such a book would also offer a great interest in that it would show to what an extent that mingling together of agriculture with industry, which I described in the first edition of this book as "the factory amidst the fields," has progressed of

Fields, Factories, and Workshops

late in Switzerland. It strikes at the present time even the casual traveller. 8

Belgium would offer an equal interest. Belgium is certainly a country of centralised industry, and a country in which the productivity of the worker stands at a high level, the average annual productivity of each industrial workman--men, women, and children--attaining now the high figure of at least £250 per head. Coal mines in which more than a thousand workers are employed are numerous, and there is a fair number of textile factories in each of which from 300 to 700 workers are occupied. And yet, if we exclude from the industrial workers' population of Belgium, which numbered 823,920 persons in 1896 (1,102,240 with the clerks, travellers, supervisors and go on), the 116,300 workpeople who are employed in the coal mines, and nearly 165,000 artisans working single or with the aid of their families, we find that out of the remaining 565,200 workers very nearly one-half--that is, 270,200 persons-work in establishments in which less than fifty persons are employed, while 95,000 persons out of these last are employed in 54,500 workshops, which thus have an average of less than three workers per workshop. We may thus say that--taking the mines out of account more than one-sixth part of the Belgian industrial workers are employed in small workshops which have, on the average, less than three workers each, besides the master, and that four-tenths of all the work-people are employed in factories and workshops having on the average less than thirteen work-people each.

What is still more remarkable is, that the number of small workshops, in which from one to four aids only are employed by the master, attains the considerable figure of 1,867 (2,293 in 1880) in the textile industries, notwithstanding the high concentration of a certain portion of these industries. As to the machinery works and hardware trades, the small workshops in which the master works with from two to four assistants or journeymen are very numerous (more than 13,300), to say nothing of the gun trade which is a petty trade par excellence, and the furniture trade which has lately taken a great development. A highly concentrated industry, and a high productivity, as well as a considerable export trade, which all testify to a high industrial development of the country, thus go hand in hand with a high development of the domestic trades and small industries altogether.

It hardly need be said that in Austria, Hungary, Italy, and even the United States, the petty trades occupy a prominent position, and play in the sum total of industrial activity an even much greater part than in France, Belgium, or Germany. But it is especially in Russia that we can fully appreciate the importance of the rural industries and the terrible sufferings which will be quite uselessly inflicted on the population, if the policy of the State is going to be now the policy advocated by a number of landlords and factory-owners--namely, if the State throws its tremendous weight in favour of a pauperisation of the peasants and an artificial annihilation of the rural trades, in order to create a centralised great industry.

The most exhaustive inquiries into the present state, the growth, the technical development of the rural industries, and the difficulties they have to contend with, have been made in Russia. A house-to-house inquiry which embraces nearly 1,000,000 peasants' houses has been made in various provinces of Russia, and its results already represent 450 volumes, printed by different county councils (Zemstvos). Besides, in the fifteen volumes published by the Petty Trades Committee, and still more in the publications of the Moscow Statistical Committee, and of many provincial assemblies, we find exhaustive lists giving the name of each worker, the extent and the state of his fields, his live stock, the value of his agricultural and industrial production, his earnings from both sources, and his yearly budget; while hundreds of separate trades have been described in separate monographs from the technical, economical, and sanitary points of view.

The results obtained from these inquiries were really imposing, as it appeared that out of the 80 or 90 million population of European Russia proper, no less than 7,500,000 persons were engaged in the domestic trades, and that their production reached, at the lowest estimate, more than £150,000,000, and most probably £200,000,000 (2,000,000,000 roubles) every year. It thus exceeded the total production of the great industry. As to the relative importance of the two for the working classes suffice it to say that even in the government of Moscow, which is the chief manufacturing region of Russia (its factories yield upwards of one-fifth in value of the aggregate industrial production of European Russia), the aggregate incomes derived by the population from the domestic industries are three times larger than the aggregate wages earned in the factories.

The most striking feature of the Russian domestic trades is that the sudden start which was made by the factories in Russia did not prejudice the domestic industries. On the contrary, it gave a new impulse to their extension; they grew and developed precisely in those regions where the factories were growing up fastest.

Another most suggestive feature is the following : although the unfertile provinces of Central Russia have been from time immemorial the seat of all kinds of petty trades, several domestic industries of modern origin are developing in those provinces which are best favoured by soil and climate. Thus, the Stavropol government of North Caucasus, where the peasantry have plenty of fertile soil, has suddenly become the seat of a widely developed silkweaving industry in the peasants' houses, and now it supplies Russia with cheap silks which have completely expelled from the market the plain silks formerly imported from France. In Orenburg and on the Black Sea, the petty trades' fabrication of agricultural machinery, which has grown up lately, is another instance in point.

The capacities of the Russian domestic industrial workers for co-operative organisation would be worthy of more than a passing mention. As to the cheapness of the produce manufactured in the villages, which is really astonishing, it cannot be explained in full by the exceedingly long hours of labour and the starvation earnings, because overwork and very low wages are characteristic of the Russian factories as well. It depends also upon the circumstance that the peasant who grows his own food, but suffers from a constant want of money, sells the produce of his industrial labour at any price. Therefore, all manufactured goods used by the Russian peasantry, save the printed cottons, are the production of the rural manufacturers. But many articles of luxury, too, are made in the villages, especially around Moscow, by peasants who continue to cultivate their allotments. The silk hats which are sold in the best Moscow shops, and bear the stamp of Nonveautés Parisiennes, are made by the Moscow peasants; so also the "Vienna" furniture of the best "Vienna" shops, even if it goes to supply the palaces. And what is most to be wondered at is not the skill of the peasants -agricultural work is no obstacle to acquiring industrial skill-but the rapidity with which the fabrication of fine goods has spread in such villages as formerly manufactured only goods of the roughest description.

Much more ought to be said with regard to the rural industries of Russia, especially to "how how easily the peasants associate for buying new machinery, or for avoiding the middle man in their purchases of raw produce-as soon as misery is no obstacle to the association. Belgium, and especially Switzerland, could also be quoted for similar illustrations, but the above will be enough to give a general idea of the importance, the vital powers, and the perfectibility of the rural industries.

Conclusions

The facts which we have briefly passed in review show, to some extent, the benefits which could be derived from a combination of agriculture with industry, if the latter could come to the village, not in its present shape of a capitalist factory, but in the shape of a socially organised industrial production, with the full aid of machinery and technical knowledge. In fact, the most prominent feature of the petty trades is that a relative well-being is found only where they are combined with agriculture : where the workers have remained in possession of the soil and continue to cultivate it. Even amidst the weavers of France or Moscow, who have to reckon with the coinpetition of the factory, relative well-being prevails so long as they are not compelled to part with the soil. On the contrary, as soon as high taxation or the impoverishment during a crisis has compelled the domestic worker to abandon his last plot of land to the usurer, misery creeps into his house. The sweater becomes all-powerful, frightful overwork is resorted to, and the whole trade often falls into decay.

Such facts, as well as the pronounced tendency of the factories towards migrating to the villages, which becomes more and more apparent nowadays, and found of late its expression in the 'Garden Cities' movement, are very suggestive. Of course, it would be a great mistake to imagine that industry ought to return to its hand-work stage in order to be combined with agriculture. Whenever a saving of human labour can be obtained by means of a machine, the machine is welcome and will be resorted to; and there is hardly one single branch of industry into which machinery work could not be introduced with great advantage, at least at some of the stages of the manufacture. In the present chaotic state of industry, nails and cheap pen-knives can be made by hand, and plain cottons be woven in the hand-loom; but such an anomaly will not last. The machine will supersede handwork in the manufacture of plain goods. But at the same time, handwork very probably will extend its domain in the artistic finishing of many things which are now made entirely in the factory; and it will always remain an important factor in the growth of thousands of young and new trades.

But the question arises, Why should not the cottons, the woollen cloth, and the silks, now woven by hand in the villages, be woven by machinery in the same villages, without ceasing to remain connected with work in the fields? Why should not hundreds of domestic industries, now carried on. entirely by hand, resort to labour-saving machines, as they already do in the knitting trade and many others? There is no reason why the small motor should not be of a much more general use than it is now, wherever there is no need to have a factory; and there is no reason why the village should not have its small factory, wherever factory work is preferable, as we already see it occasionally in certain villages in France.

More than that. There is no reason why the factory, with its motive force and machinery, should not belong to the community, as is already the case for motive power in the abovementioned workshops and small factories in the French portion of the Jura hills. It is evident that now, under the capitalist system, the factory is the curse of the village, as it comes to overwork children and to make paupers out of its male inhabitants; and it is quite natural that it should be opposed by all means by the workers, if they have succeeded in maintaining their olden trades' organisations (as at Sheffield, or Solingen), or if they have not yet been reduced to sheer misery (as in the Jura). But under a more rational social organisation the factory would find no such obstacles : it would be a boon to the village. And there is already unmistakable evidence to show that a move in this direction is being made in a few village communities.

The moral and physical advantages which man would derive from dividing his work between the field and the workshop are selfevident. But the difficulty is, we are told, in the necessary centralisation of the modern industries. In industry, as well as in politics, centralisation has so many admirers! But in both spheres the ideal of the centralisers badly needs revision. In fact, if we analyse the modern industries, we soon discover that for some of them the co-operation of hundreds, or even thousands, of workers gathered at the same spot is really necessary. The great iron works and mining enterprises decidedly belong to that category; oceanic steamers cannot be built in village factories. But very many of our big factories are nothing else but agglomerations under a common management, of several distinct industries; while others are mere agglomerations of hundreds of copies of the very same machine; such are most of our gigantic spinning and weaving establishments.

The manufacture being a strictly private enterprise, its owners find it advantageous to have all the branches of a given industry under their own management; they thus cumulate the profits of the successive transformations of the raw material. And when several thousand power-looms are combined in one factory, the owner finds his advantage in being able to hold the command of the market. But from a technical point of view the advantages of such an accumulation are trifling and often doubtful. Even so centralised an industry as that of the cottons does not suffer at all from the division of production of one given sort of goods at its different stages between several separate factories : we see it at Manchester and its neighbouring towns. As to the petty trades, no inconvenience is experienced, from a still greater subdivision between the workshops in the watch trade and very many others.

We often hear that one horse-power costs so much in a small

engine, and so much less in an engine ten times more powerful; that the pound of cotton yarn costs much less when the factory doubles the number of its spindles. But, in the opinion of the best engineering authorities, such as Prof. W. Unwin, the hydraulic, and especially the electric, distribution of power from a central station sets aside the first part of the argument. As to its second part, calculations of this sort are only good for those industries which prepare the half-manufactured produce for further transformations. As to those countless descriptions of goods which derive their value chiefly from the intervention of skilled labour, they can be best fabricated in smaller factories which employ a few hundreds, or even a few scores of operatives. This is why the "concentration" so much spoken of is often nothing but an amalgamation of capitalists for the purpose of dominating the market, not for cheapening the technical process.

Even under the present conditions the leviathan factories offer great inconveniences, as they cannot rapidly reform their machinery according to the constantly varying demands of the consumers, How many failures of great concerns, too well known in this country to need to be named, were due to this cause during the crisis of 1886-1890. As for the new branches of industry which I have mentioned at the beginning of the previous chapter, they always must make a start on a small scale; and they can prosper in small towns as well as in big cities, if the smaller agglomerations are provided with institutions stimulating artistic taste and the genius of invention. The progress achieved of late in toy-making, as also the high perfection attained in the fabrication of mathematical and optical instruments, of furniture, of small luxury articles, of pottery and so on, are instances in point. Art and science are no longer the monopoly of the great cities, and further progress will be in scattering them over the country.

Fields, Factories, and Workshops

The geographical distribution of industries in a given country depends, of course, to a great extent upon a complexus of natural conditions; it is obvious that there are spots which are best suited for the development of certain industries. The banks of the Clyde and the Tyne are certainly most appropriate for ship-building yards, and shipbuilding yards must be surrounded by a variety of workshops and factories. The industries will always find some advantages in being grouped, to some extent, according to the natural features of separate regions. But we must recognise that now they are not at all grouped according to those features. Historical causeschiefly religious wars and national rivalries-have had a good deal to do with their growth and their present distribution; still more so the employers were guided by considerations as to the facilities for sale and export-that is, by considerations which are already losing their importance with the increased facilities for transport, and will lose it still more when the producers produce for themselves, and not for customers far away.

Why, in a rationally organised society, ought London to remain a great centre for the jam and preserving trade, and manufacture umbrellas for nearly the whole of the United Kingdom? Why should the countless Whitechapel petty trades remain where they are, instead of being spread all over the country? There is no reason whatever why the mantles which are worn by English ladies should be sewn at Berlin and in Whitechapel, instead of in Devonshire or Derbyshire. Why should Paris refine sugar for almost the whole of France? Why should one-half of the boots and shoes used in the United States be manufactured in the 1,500 workshops of Massachusetts? There is absolutely no reason why these and like anomalies should persist. The industries must be scattered all over the world; and the scattering of industries amidst all civilised nations will be necessarily followed by a further scattering of factories over the territories of each nation.

In the course of this evolution, the natural produce of each region and its geographical conditions certainly will be one of the factors which will determine the character of the industries going to develop in this region. But when we see that Switzerland has become a great exporter of steam-engines, railway engines, and steam-boats--although she has no iron ore and no coal for obtaining steel, and even has no seaport to import them; when we see that Belgium has succeeded in. being a great exporter of grapes, and that Manchester has managed to become a seaport--we understand that in the geographical distribution of industries, the two factors of local produces and of an advantageous position by the sea are not yet the dominant factors. We begin to understand that, all taken, it is the intellectual factor--the spirit of invention, the capacity of adaptation, political liberty, and so on-which counts for more than all others.

That all the industries find an advantage in being carried on in close contact with a great variety of other industries the reader has seen already from numerous examples. Every industry requires technical surroundings. But the same is also true of agriculture.

Agriculture cannot develop without the aid of machinery, and the use of a perfect machinery cannot be generalised without industrial surroundings : without mechanical workshops, easily accessible to the cultivator of the soil, the use of agricultural machinery is not possible. The village smith would not do. If the work of a thrashing-machine has to be stopped for a week or more, because one of the cogs in a wheel has been broken, and if to obtain a new wheel one must send a special messenger to the next province-then the use of a thrashing machine is not possible. But this is precisely what I saw in my childhood in Central Russia; and quite lately I have found the very same fact mentioned in an English autobiography in the first half of the nineteenth century. Besides, in all the northern part of the temperate zone, the cultivators of the soil must have some sort of industrial employment during the long winter months. This is what has brought about the great development of rural industries, of which we have just seen such interesting examples. But this need is also felt in the soft climate of the Channel Islands, notwithstanding the extension taken by horticulture under glass. We need such industries. Could you suggest us any?" wrote to me one of my correspondents in Guernsey.

But this is not yet all. Agriculture is so much in need of aid from those who inhabit the cities, that every summer thousands of men leave their slums in the towns and go to the country for the season of crops. The London destitutes go in thousands to Kent and Sussex as bay-makers and hop-pickers, it being estimated that Kent alone requires 80,000 additional men and women for hop-picking; whole villages in France and their cottage industries are abandoned in the summer, and the peasants wander to the more fertile parts of the country; hundreds of thousands of human beings are transported every summer to the prairies of Manitoba and Dacota. Every summer many thousands of Poles spread at harvest time over the plains of Mecklenburg, Westphalia, and even France; and in Russia there is every year an exodus of several millions of men who journey from the north to the southern prairies for harvesting the crops; while many St. Petersburg manufacturers reduce their production in the summer, because the operatives return to their native villages for the culture of their allotments.

Agriculture cannot be carried on without additional hands in the summer; but it still more needs temporary aids for improving the soil, for tenfolding its productive powers. Steam-digging, drainage, and manuring would render the heavy clays in the north-west of London a much richer soil than that of the American prairies. To become fertile, those clays want only plain, unskilled human labour, such as is necessary for digging the soil, laying in drainage tubes, pulverising phosphorites, and the like; and that labour would be gladly done by-the factory workers if it were properly organised in a free community for the benefit of the whole society. The soil claims that sort of aid, and it would have it under a proper organisation, even if it were necessary to stop many mills in the summer for that purpose. No doubt the present factory owners would consider it ruinous if they had to stop their mills for several months every year, because the capital engaged in a factory is expected to pump money every day and every, hour, if possible. But that is the capitalist's view of the matter, not the community's view.

As to the workers, who ought to be the real. managers of industries, they will find it healthy not to perform the same monotonous work all the year round, and they will abandon it for the summer, if indeed they do not find the means of keeping the factory running by relieving each other in groups.

The scattering of industries over the country ----so as to bring the factory amidst the fields, to make agriculture derive all those profits which it always finds in being combined with industry (see the Eastern States of America) and to produce a combination of industrial with agricultural work--is surely the next step to be made, as soon as a reorganisation of our present conditions is possible. It is being made already, here and there, as we saw on the preceding pages. This, step is imposed by the very necessity of producing for the producers themselves'. it is imposed by the necessity for each healthy man and woman to spend a part of their lives in manual work in the free air; and it will be rendered the more necessary when the great social movements, which have now become unavoidable, come to disturb the present international trade, and compel each nation to revert to her own resources for her own main tenance. Humanity as a whole, as well as each separate individual, will be gainers by the change, and the change will take, place.

However, such a change also implies a thorough modification of our present system of education. It implies a society composed of men and women, each of whom is able to work with his or her hands, as well as with his or her brain, and to do so in more directions than one. This "integration of capacities" and "integral education" I am now going to analyse.

Chapter VIII: Brain Work and Manual Work

IN olden times men of science, and especially those who have done most to forward the growth of natural philosophy, did not despise manual work and handicraft. Galileo made his telescopes with his own hands. Newton learned in his boyhood the art of managing tools; he exercised his young mind in contriving most ingenious machines, and when he began his researches in optics he was able himself to grind the lenses for his instruments, and himself to make the well-known telescope, which, for its time, was a fine piece of workmanship. Leibnitz was fond of inventing machines: windmills and carriages to be moved without horses preoccupied his mind as much as mathematical and philosophical speculations. Linnaeus became a botanist while helping his father-a practical gardener-in his daily work. In short, with our great geniuses handicraft was no obstacle to abstract researches -it rather favoured them. On the other hand, if the workers of old found but few opportunities for mastering science, many of them had, at least, their intelligences stimulated by the very variety of work which was performed in the then unspecialised workshops; and some of them had the benefit of familiar intercourse with men of science. Watt and Rennie were friends with Professor Robinson; Brindley, the road-maker, despite his fourteenpence-a-day wages, enjoyed intercourse with educated men, and thus developed his remarkable engineering faculties the son of a well-to-do family could "idle" at a - wheelwright's shop, so as to become later on a Smeaton or a Stephenson.

We have changed all that. Under the pretext of division of labour, we have sharply separated the brain worker from the manual worker. The masses of the workmen do not receive more scientific education than their grandfathers did; but they have been deprived of the education of even the same workshop, while their boys and girls are driven into a mine or a factory from the age of thirteen, and there they soon forget the little they may have learned at school. As to the men of science, they despise manual labour. How few of them would be able to make a telescope, or even a plainer instrument! Most of them are not capable of even designing a scientific instrument, and when they have given a vague suggestion to the instrument-maker, they leave it with him to invent the apparatus they need. Nay, they have raised the contempt of manual labour to the height of a theory. "The man of science," they say "must discover the laws of nature, the civil engineer must apply them, and the worker must execute in steel or wood, in iron or stone, the patterns devised by the engineer. He must work, with machines invented for him, not by him. No matter if he does not understand them and cannot improve them: the scientific man and the scientific engineer will take care of the progress of science and industry."

It may be objected that nevertheless there is a class of men who belong to none of the above three divisions. When young they have been manual workers, and some of them continue to be; but, owing to some happy circumstances, they have succeeded in acquiring some scientific knowledge, and thus they have combined science with handicraft. Surely there are such men; happily enough there is a nucleus of men who have escaped the so-much-advocated specialisation of labour, and it is precisely to them that industry owes its chief recent inventions. But in old Europe, at least, they are the exceptions; they are the irregulars-the Cossacks who have broken the ranks and pierced the screens so carefully erected between the classes. And they are so few, in comparison with the ever-growing requirements of industry-and of science as well, as I am about to prove-that all over the world we hear complaints about the scarcity of precisely such men.

What is the meaning, in fact, of the outcry for technical education which has been raised at one and the same time in

England, in France, in Germany, in the States, and in Russia, if it does not express a general dissatisfaction with the present division into scientists, scientific engineers, and workers? Listen to those who know industry, and you will see that the substance of their complaints is this: "The worker whose task has been specialised by the permanent division of labour has lost the intellectual interest in his labour, and it is especially so in the great industries: he has lost his inventive powers. Formerly, he invented very much. Manual workers-not men of science nor trained engineers-have invented, or brought to perfection, the prime motors arid all that mass of machinery which has revolutionised industry for the last hundred years. But since the great factory has been enthroned, the worker, depressed by the monotony of his work, invents no more. What can a weaver invent who merely supervises four looms, without knowing anything either about their complicated movements or how the machines grew to be what they are? What can a man invent who is condemned for life to bind together the ends of two threads with the greatest celerity, and knows nothing beyond making a knot?

"At the outset of modern industry, three generations of workers have invented; now they cease to do so. As to the inventions of the engineers, specially trained for devising machines, they are either devoid of genius or not practical enough. Those 'nearly to nothings,' of which Sir Frederick Bramwell spoke once at Bath, are missing in their inventions those nothings which can be learned in the workshop only, and which permitted a Murdoch and the Soho workers to make a practical engine of Watt's schemes. None but he who knows the machine-not in its drawings and models only, but in its breathing and throbbings-who unconsciously thinks of it while standing by it, can really improve it. Smeaton and Newcomen surely were excellent engineers; but in their engines a boy had to open the steam valve at each stroke of the piston; and it was one of those boys who once managed to connect the valve with the remainder of the machine, so as to make it open automatically, while he ran away to play with other boys. But in the modern machinery there is no room left for naive improvements of that kind. Scientific education on a wide scale has become necessary for further inventions, and that education is refused to the workers. So that there is no issue out of the difficulty, unless scientific education and handicraft are combined together unless integration of knowledge takes the place of the present divisions."

Such is the real substance of the present movement in favour of technical education. But, instead of bringing to public consciousness the, perhaps, unconscious motives of the present discontent, instead of widening the views of the discontented and discussing the problem to its full extent, the mouthpieces of the movement do not mostly rise above the shopkeeper's view of the question. Some of them indulge in jingo talk about crushing all foreign industries out of competition, while the others see in technical education nothing but a means of somewhat improving the flesh-machine of the factory and of transferring a few workers into the upper class of trained engineers.

Such an ideal may satisfy them, but it cannot satisfy those who keep in view the combined interests of science and industry, and consider both as a means for raising humanity to a higher level. We maintain that in the interests of both science and industry, as well as of society as a whole, every human being, without distinction of birth, ought to receive such an education as would enable him, or her, to combine a thorough knowledge of science with a thorough knowledge of handicraft. We fully recognise the necessity of specialisation of knowledge, but we maintain that specialisation must follow general education, and that general education must be given in science and handicraft alike. To the division of society into brain workers and manual workers we oppose the combination of both kinds of activities; and instead of "technical education," which means the maintenance of the present division between brain work and manual work, we advocate the education integrale, or complete education, which means the disappearance of that pernicious distinction.

Plainly stated, the aims of the school under this system ought to be the following: To give such an education that, on leaving school at the age of eighteen or twenty, each boy and each girl should be endowed with a thorough knowledge of science-such a knowledge as might enable them to be useful workers in science-and, at the same time, to give them a general knowledge of what constitutes the bases of technical training, and such a skill in some special trade as would enable each of them to take his or her place in the grand world of the manual production of wealth. I know that many will find that aim too large, or even impossible to attain, but I hope that if they have the patience to read the following pages, they will see that we require nothing beyond what can be easily attained. In fact, it has been attained; and what has been done on a small scale could be done on a wider scale, were it not for the economical and social causes which prevent any serious reform from being accomplished in our miserably organised society.

The experiment has been made at the Moscow Technical School for twenty consecutive years with many hundreds of boys; and, according to the testimonies of the most competent judges, at the exhibitions of Brussels, Philadelphia, Vienna, and Paris, the experiment has been a success. The Moscow school admitted boys not older than fifteen, and it required from boys of that age nothing but a substantial knowledge of geometry and algebra, together with the usual knowledge of their mother tongue; younger pupils were received in the preparatory classes. The school was divided into two sections-the mechanical and the chemical; but as I personally know better the former, and as it is also the more important with reference to the question before us, so I shall limit my remarks to the education given in the mechanical section.

After a five or six years' stay at the school, the students left it with a thorough knowledge of higher mathematics, physics, mechanics, and connected sciences-so thorough, indeed, that it was not second to that acquired in the best mathematical faculties of the most eminent European universities. When myself a student of the mathematical faculty of the St. Petersburg University, I had the opportunity of comparing the knowledge of the students at the Moscow Technical School with our own. I saw the courses of higher geometry some of them had compiled for the use of their comrades; I admired the facility with which they applied the integral calculus to dynamical problems, and I came to the conclusion that while we, University students, had more knowledge of a general character (for instance, in mathematical astronomy), they, the students of the Technical School, were much more advanced in higher geometry, and especially in the applications of higher mathematics to the intricate problems of dynamics, the theories of heat and elasticity. But while we, the students of the University, hardly knew the use of our hands, the students of the Technical School fabricated with their own hands, and without the help of professional workmen, fine steam-engines, from the heavy boiler to the last finely turned screw, agricultural machinery, and scientific apparatus-all for the trade-and they received the highest awards for the work of their hands at the international exhibitions. They were scientifically educated skilled workers-workers with university education-highly appreciated even by the Russian manufacturers who so much distrust science.

Now, the methods by which these wonderful results were achieved were these: In science, learning from memory was not in honour, while independent research was favoured by all means. Science was taught hand in hand with its applications, and what was learned in the schoolroom was applied in the workshop. Great attention was paid to the highest abstractions of geometry as a means for developing imagination and research.

As to the teaching of handicraft, the methods were quite different from those which proved a failure at the Cornell University, and differed, in fact, from those used in most technical schools. The student was not sent to a workshop to learn some special handicraft and to earn his existence as soon as possible; but the teaching of technical skill was prosecuted in the same systematical way as laboratory work is taught in the universities, according to a scheme elaborated by the founder of the school, M. Dellavos, and now applied at Chicago and Boston. It is evident that drawing was considered as the first step in technical education. Then the student was brought, first, to the carpenter's workshop, or rather laboratory, and there he was thoroughly taught to execute all kinds of carpentry and joinery. They did not teach the pupil to make some insignificant work of house decoration, as they do in the system of the slöjd - the Swedish method, which is taught especially at the Nääds school-but they taught him, to begin with, to make very accurately a wooden cube, a prism, a cylinder (with the planing jack), and then-all fundamental types of joining. In a word, he had to study, so to say, the philosophy of joinery by means of manual work. No efforts were spared in order to bring the pupil to a certain perfection in that branch-the real basis of all trades.

Later on, the pupil was transferred to the turner's workshop, where he was taught to make in wood the patterns of those things which he would have to make in metal in the following workshops. The foundry followed, and there he was taught to cast those parts of machines which he had prepared in wood;

and it was only after he had gone through the first three stages that lie was admitted to the smith's and engineering workshops. Such was the system which English readers will find described in full in a work by Mr. Ch. H. Ham. As for the perfection of the mechanical work of the students, I cannot do better than refer to the reports of the juries, at the above-named exhibitions.

In America the same system has been introduced, in its technical part, first, in the Chicago Manual Training School, and later on in the Boston Technical School-the best, I am told, of the sort-and finally at Tuskagee, in the excellent school for coloured young men. In this country, or rather in Scotland, I found the system applied with full success, for some years, under the direction of Dr. Ogilvie at Gordon's College in Aberdeen. It is the Moscow or Chicago system on a limited scale. While receiving substantial scientific education, the pupils are also trained in the workshops-but not for one special trade, as it unhappily too of ten is the case. They pass through the carpenter's workshop, the casting in metals, and the engineering workshop; and in each of these they learn the foundations of each of the three trades sufficiently well for supplying the school itself with a number of useful things. Besides, as far as I could ascertain from what I saw in the geographical and physical classes, as also in the chemical laboratory, the system of "through the hand to the brain," and vice versâ, is in full swing, and it is attended with the best success. The boys work with the physical instruments, and they study geography in the field, instruments in hands, as well as in the class-room. Some of their surveys filled my heart, as an old geographer, with joy.

The Moscow Technical School surely was not an ideal school. It totally neglected the humanitarian education of the young men. But we must recognise that the Moscow experiment-not to speak of hundreds of other partial experiments-has perfectly well proved the possibility of combining a scientific education of a very high standard with the education which is necessary for becoming an excellent skilled workman. It has proved, moreover, that the best means for producing really good skilled labourers is to seize the bull by the horns, and to grasp the educational problem in its great features, instead of trying to give some special skill in some handicraft, together with a few scraps of knowledge in a certain branch of some science. And it has shown also what can be obtained, without over-pressure, if a rational economy of the scholar's time is always kept in view, and theory goes hand in hand with practice. Viewed in this light, the Moscow results do not seem extraordinary at all, and still better results may be expected if the same principles are applied from the earliest years of education.

Waste of time is the leading feature of our present education. Not only are we taught a mass of rubbish, but what is not rubbish is taught so as to make us waste over it as much time as possible. Our present methods of teaching originate from a time when the accomplishments required from an educated person were extremely limited; and they have been maintained, notwithstanding the immense increase of knowledge which must be conveyed to the scholar's mind since science has so much widened its former limits. Hence the over-pressure in schools, and hence, also, the urgent necessity of totally revising both the subjects and the methods of teaching, according to the new wants and to the examples already given here and there, by separate schools and separate teachers.

It is evident that the years of childhood ought not to be spent so uselessly as they are now. German teachers have shown how the very plays of children can be made instrumental in conveying to the childish mind some concrete knowledge in both geometry and mathematics. The children who have made the squires of the theorem of Pythagoras out of pieces of coloured cardboard, will not look at the theorem, when it comes in geometry, as on a mere instrument of torture devised by the teachers; and the less so if they apply it as the carpenters do. Complicated problems of arithmetic, which so much harassed us in our boyhood, are easily solved by children seven and eight years old if they are put in the shape of interesting puzzles. And if the Kindergarten-German teachers often make of it a kind of barrack in which each movement of the child is regulated beforehand-has often become a small prison for the little ones, the idea which presided at its foundation is nevertheless true. In fact, it is almost impossible to imagine, without having tried it, how many sound notions of nature, habits of classification, and taste for natural sciences can be conveyed to the children's minds; and, if a series of concentric courses adapted to the various phases of development of the human being were generally accepted in education, the first series in all sciences, save sociology, could be taught before the age of ten or twelve, so as to give a general idea of the universe, the earth and its inhabitants, the chief physical, chemical, zoological, and botanical phenomena, leaving the discovery of the laws of those phenomena to the next series of deeper and more specialised studies.

On the other side, we all know how children like to make toys themselves, how they gladly imitate the work of full-grown people if they see them at work in the workshop or the building-yard. But the parents either stupidly paralyse that passion, or do not know how to utilise it. Most of them despise manual work and prefer sending their children to the study of Roman history, or of Franklin's teachings about saving money, to seeing them at a work which is good for the "lower classes only." They thus do their best to render subsequent learning the more difficult.

And then come the school years, and time is wasted again to an incredible extent. Take for instance, mathematics, which every one ought to know, because it is the basis of all subsequent education, and which so few really learn in our schools. In geometry, time is foolishly wasted by using a method which merely consists in committing geometry to memory. In most cases, the boy reads again and again the proof of a theorem till his memory has retained the succession of reasonings. Therefore, nine boys out of ten, if asked to prove an elementary theorem two years after having left the school will be unable to do it, unless mathematics is their speciality. They will forget which auxiliary lines to draw, and they never have been taught to discover the proofs by themselves. No wonder that later on they find such difficulties in applying geometry to physics, that their progress is despairingly sluggish, and that so few master higher mathematics.

There is, however, the other method which permits the pupil to progress, as a whole, at a much speedier rate, and under which he who once has learned geometry will know it all his life long. Under this system, each theorem is put as a problem; its solution is never given beforehand, and the pupil is induced to find it by himself. Thus, if some preliminary exercises with the rule and the compass have been made, there is not one boy or girl, out of twenty or more, who will not be able to find the means of drawing an angle which is equal to a given angle, and to prove their equality, after a few suggestions from the teacher; and if the subsequent problems are given in a systematic succession (there are excellent text-books for the purpose), and the teacher does not press his pupils to go faster than they can go at the beginning, they advance from one problem to the next with an astonishing facility, the only difficulty being to bring the pupil to solve the first problem, and thus to acquire confidence in his own reasoning.

Moreover, each abstract geometrical truth must be impressed on the mind in its concrete form as well. As soon as the pupils have solved a few problems on paper, they must solve them in the playing-ground with a few sticks and a string, and they must apply their knowledge in the workshop. Only then will the geometrical lines acquire a concrete meaning in the children's minds; only then will they see that the teacher is playing no tricks when he asks them to solve problems with the rule and the compass without resorting to the protractor; only then will they know geometry.

"Through the eyes and the hand to the brain" this is the true principle of economy of time in teaching. I remember, as if it were yesterday, how geometry suddenly acquired for me a new meaning, and how this new meaning, facilitated all ulterior studies. It was as we were mastering at school a Montgolfier balloon, and I remarked that the angles at the summits of each of the twenty strips of paper out of which we were going to make the balloon must cover less than the fifth part of a right angle each. I remember, next, how the sinuses and the tangents ceased to be mere cabalistic signs when they permitted us to calculate the length of a stick in a working profile of a fortification; and how geometry in space became plain when we began to make on a small scale a bastion with embrasures and barbettes-an occupation which obviously was soon prohibited on account of the state into which We brought our clothes. " You look like navvies," was the reproach addressed to us by our intelligent educators, while we were proud precisely of being navvies, and of discovering the use of geometry.

By compelling our children to study real things from mere graphical representations, instead of making those things themselves, we compel them to waste the most precious time; we uselessly worry their minds; we accustom them to the worst methods of learning; we kill independent thought in the bud; and very seldom we succeed in conveying a real knowledge of what we are teaching. Superficiality, parrot like repetition, slavishness and inertia of mind are the results of our method of education. We do not teach our children how to learn.

The very beginnings of science are taught on the same pernicious system. In most schools even arithmetic is taught in the abstract way, and mere rules are stuffed into the poor little heads. The idea of a unit, which is arbitrary and can be changed at will in our measurement (the match, the box of matches, the dozen of boxes, or the gross; the metre, the centimetre the kilometre, and so on), is not impressed on mind, and therefore when the children come to the decimal fractions they are at a loss to understand them. In this country, the United States and Russia, instead of accepting the decimal system, which is the system of our numeration, they still torture the children by making them learn a system of weights and measures which ought to have been abandoned long since. The pupils lose at that full two years, and when they come later on to problems in mechanics and physics, schoolboys and schoolgirls spend most of their time in endless calculations which only fatigue them and inspire in them a dislike of exact science. But even there, where the decimal measures have been introduced, much time is lost in school simply because the teachers are not accustomed to the idea that every measure is only approximate, and that it is absurd to calculate with the exactitude of one gramme, or of one metre, when the measuring itself does not give the elements of such an exactitude. Whereas in France, where the decimal system of measures and money is a matter of daily life, even those workers who have received the plainest elementary education are quite familiar with decimals. To represent twenty-five centimes, or twenty-five centimetres, they write "zero twenty-five," while most of my readers surely remember how this same zero at the 'head of a row of figures puzzled them in their boyhood. We do all that is possible to render' algebra unintelligible, and our children spend one year before they have learned what is not algebra at all, but a mere system of abbreviations, which can be learned by the way, if it is taught together with arithmetic.

The waste of time in physics is simply revolting. While young people very easily understand the principles of chemistry and its formula, as soon as they themselves make the first experiments with a few glasses and tubes, they mostly find the greatest difficulties in grasping the mechanical introduction into physics, partly because they do not know geometry, and especially because they are merely shown costly machines instead of being induced to make themselves plain apparatus for illustrating the phenomena they study.

Instead of learning the laws of force with plain instruments which a boy of fifteen can easily make, they learn them from mere drawings, in a purely abstract fashion. Instead of making themselves an Atwood's machine with a broomstick and the wheel of an old clock, or verifying the laws of falling bodies with a key gliding on an inclined string, they are shown a complicated apparatus, and in most cases the teacher himself does not know how to explain to them the principle of the apparatus, and indulges in irrelevant details. And so it goes on from 'the beginning to the end, with but a few honourable exceptions.

If waste of time is characteristic of our methods of teaching science, it is characteristic as well of the methods used for teaching handicraft. We know how years are wasted when a boy serves his apprenticeship in a workshop; but the same reproach can be addressed, to a great extent, to those technical schools which endeavour at once to teach some special handicraft, instead of resorting to the broader and surer methods of systematical teaching. Just as there are in science some notions and methods which are preparatory to the study of all sciences, so there are also some fundamental notions and methods preparatory to the special study of any handicraft.

Reuleaux has shown in that delightful book, the Theoretische Kinematik , that there is, so to say, a philosophy of all possible machinery. Each machine, however complicated, can be reduced to a few elements-plates, cylinders, discs, cones, and so on-as well as to a few tools-chisels, saws, rollers, hammers, etc.; and, however complicated its movements, they can be decomposed into a few modifications of motion, such as the transformation of circular motion into a rectilinear, and the like, with a number of intermediate links. So also each handicraft can be decomposed into a number of elements. In each trade one must know how to make a plate with parallel surfaces, a cylinder, a disc, a square, and a round hole; how to manage a limited number of tools, all tools being mere modifications of less than a dozen types; and how to transform one kind of motion into another. This is the foundation of all mechanical handicrafts; so that the knowledge of how to make in wood those primary elements, how to manage the chief tools in wood-work, and how to transform various kinds of motion ought to be considered as the very basis for the subsequent teaching of all possible kinds of mechanical handicraft. The pupil who has acquired that skill already knows one good half of all possible trades.

Besides, none can be a good worker in science unless he is in possession of good methods of scientific research; unless he has learned to observe, to describe with exactitude, to discover mutual relations between facts seemingly disconnected, to make inductive hypotheses and to verify them, to reason upon cause and effect, and so on. And none can be a good manual worker unless he has been accustomed to the good methods of handicraft altogether. He must grow accustomed to conceive the subject of his thoughts in a concrete form, to draw it, or to model, to hate badly kept tools and bad methods of work, to give to everything a fine touch of finish, to derive artistic enjoyment from the contemplation of gracious forms and combinations of colours, and dissatisfaction from what is ugly. Be it handicraft, science, or art, the chief aim of the school is not to make a specialist from a beginner, but to teach him the elements of knowledge and the good methods of work, and, above all, to give him that general inspiration which will induce him, later on, to put in whatever he does a sincere longing for truth, to like what is beautiful, both as to form and contents, to feel the necessity of being a useful unit amidst other human units, and thus to feel his heart at unison with the rest of humanity.

As for avoiding the monotony of work which would result from the pupil always mere cylinders and discs, and never making full machines or other useful things, there are thousands of means for avoiding that want of interest, and one of them, in use at Moscow, is worthy of notice. It was, not to give work for mere exercise, but to utilise everything which the pupil makes, from his very first steps. Do you remember how you were delighted, in your childhood, if your work was utilised, be it only as a part of something useful? So they did at Moscow. Each plank planed by the pupils was utilised as a part of some machine in some of the other workshops. When a pupil came to the engineering workshop, and was set to make a quadrangular block of iron with parallel and perpendicular surfaces, the block had an interest in his eyes, because, when he had finished it, verified its angles and surfaces, and corrected its defects, the block was not thrown under the bench-it was given to a more advanced pupil, who made a handle to it, painted the whole, and sent it to the shop of the school as a paper-weight. The systematical teaching thus received the necessary attractiveness.

It is evident that celerity of work is a most important factor in production. So it might be asked if, under the above system, the necessary speed of work could be obtained. But there are two kinds of celerity. There is the celerity which I saw in a Nottingham lace-factory: full-grown men, with shivering hands and heads, were feverishly binding together the ends of two threads from the remnants of cotton-yarn in the bobbins; you hardly could follow their movements. But the very fact of requiring such kind of rapid work is the condemnation of the factory system. What has remained of the human being in those shivering bodies? What will be their outcome? Why this waste of human force, when it could produce ten times the value of the odd rests of yarn? This kind of celerity is required exclusively because of the cheapness of the factory slaves; so let us hope that no school will ever aim at this kind of quickness in work.

But there is also the time-saving celerity of the well-trained worker, and this is surely achieved best by the kind of education which we advocate. However plain his work, the educated worker makes it better and quicker than the uneducated. Observe, for instance how a good worker proceeds in cutting anything-say a piece of cardboard-and compare his movements with those of an improperly trained worker. The latter seizes the cardboard, takes the tool as it is, traces a line in a haphazard way, and begins to cut; half-way he is tired, and when he has finished his work is worth nothing; whereas, the former will examine his tool and improve it if necessary; he will trace the line -with exactitude, secure both cardboard and rule, keep the tool in the right way, cut quite easily, and give you a piece of good work.

This is the true time-saving celerity, the most appropriate for economising human labour; and the best means for attaining it is an education of the most superior kind. The great masters painted with an astonishing rapidity; but their rapid work was the result of a great development of intelligence and imagination, of a keen sense of beauty, of a fine perception of colours. And that is the kind of rapid work of which humanity is in need.

Much more ought to be said as regards the duties of the school, but I hasten to say a few words more as to the desirability of the kind of education briefly sketched in the preceding pages. Certainly, I do not cherish the illusion that a thorough reform in education, or in any of the issues indicated in the preceding chapters, will be made as long as the civilised nations remain under the present narrowly egotistic system of production and consumption. All we can expect, as long as the present conditions last, is to have some microscopical attempts at reforming here and there on a small scale-attempts which necessarily will prove to be far below the expected results, because of the impossibility of reforming on a small scale when so intimate a connection exists between the manifold functions of a civilised nation. But the energy of the constructive genius of society depends chiefly upon the depths of its conception as to what ought to be done, and how; and the necessity of recasting education is one of those necessities which are most comprehensible to all, and are most appropriate for inspiring society with those ideals, without which stagnation or even-decay are unavoidable.

So let us suppose that a community-a city, or a territory which has, at least, a few millions of inhabitants-gives the above-sketched education to all its children, without distinction of birth (and we are rich enough to permit us the luxury of such an education), without asking anything in return from the children but what they will give when they have become producers of wealth. Suppose such an education is given, and analyse its probable consequences.

I will not insist upon the increase of wealth which would result from having a young army of educated and well-trained producers; nor shall I insist upon the social benefits which would be derived from erasing the present distinction between the brain workers and the manual workers, and from thus reaching the concordance of interest and harmony so much wanted in our times of social struggles. I shall not dwell upon the fulness of life which would result for each separate individual, if he were enabled to enjoy the use of both his mental and bodily powers; nor upon the advantages of raising manual labour to the place of honour it ought to occupy in society, instead of being a stamp of inferiority, as it is now. Nor shall I insist upon the disappearance of the present misery and degradation, with all their consequences-vice, crime, prisons, price of blood, denunciation, and the like-which necessarily would follow. In short, I will not touch now the great social question, upon which so much has been written and so much remains to be written yet. I merely intend to point out in these pages the benefits which science itself would derive from the change.

Some will say, of course, that to reduce men of science to therôle of manual workers would mean the decay of science and genius. But those who will take into account the following considerations probably will agree that the, result ought to be the reverse-namely, such a revival of science and art, and such a progress in industry, s we only can only faintly foresee from what we know about times of the Renaissance. It has become a commonplace to speak with emphasis about the progress of science during the nineteenth century; and it is evident that our century, if compared with centuries past, has much to be proud of. But, if we take into account that most of the problems which our century has solved already bad been indicated, and their solutions foreseen, a hundred years ago, we must admit that the progress was not so rapid as might have been expected, and that something hampered it.

The mechanical theory of heat was very well foreseen in the last century by Rumford and Humphry Davy, and even in Russia it was advocated by Lomomnosoff. However, much more than half a century elapsed before the theory appeared in science. Lamarck, and even Linnæus, Geoffroy Saint-Hilaire, Erasmus

Darwin, and several others were fully aware of the variability of species; they were opening the way for the construction of biology on the principles of variation; but here, again, half a century was wasted before the variability of species as brought again to the front; and we all remember how Darwin's ideas were carried on and forced on the attention of people, chiefly by persons who were not professional scientists themselves; and yet in Darwin's hands the theory of evolution surely was narrowed, owing to the overwhelming importance given to only one factor of evolution.

For many years past astronomy has been needing a careful revision of the Kant and Laplace's hypothesis; but no theory is yet forthcoming which would compel general acceptance. Geology surely has made, wonderful progress in the reconstitution of the paleontological record, but dynamical geology progresses at a despairingly slow rate; while all future progress in the great question as to the laws of distribution of living organisms on the surface of the earth is hampered by the want of knowledge as to the extension of glaciation during the Quaternary epoch.

In short, in each branch of science a revision of the current theories as well as new wide generalisations are wanted. And if the, revision requires some of that inspiration of genius which moved Galileo and Newton, and which depends in its appearance upon general causes of human development, it requires also an increase in the number of scientific workers. When facts contradictory to current theories become numerous, the theories must be revised (we saw it in Darwin's case), and thousands of simple intelligent workers in science are required to accumulate the necessary facts.

Immense regions of the earth still remain unexplored; the study of the geographical distribution of animals and plants meets with stumbling-blocks at every step. Travellers cross continents, and do not know even how to determine the latitude nor how to manage a barometer. Physiology, both of plants and animals, psycho-physiology, and the psychological faculties of man and animals are so many branches of knowledge requiring more data of the simplest description. History remains a fable convenue chiefly because it wants fresh ideas, but also because it wants scientifically thinking workers to reconstitute the life of past centuries in the same way as Thorold Rogers or Augustin Thierry have done it for separate epochs.

In short, there is not one, single science which does not suffer in its development from a want of men and women endowed with a philosophical conception of the universe, ready to apply their forces of investigation in a given field however limited, and having leisure for devoting themselves to scientific pursuits. In a community such as we suppose, thousands of workers would be ready to answer any appeal for exploration. Darwin spent almost thirty years in gathering and analysing facts for the elaboration of the theory of the origin of species. Had he lived in such a society as we suppose he simply would have made an appeal to volunteers for facts and partial exploration, and thousands of explorers would have answered his appeal. Scores of societies would have come to life to debate and to solve each of the partial problems involved in the theory, and in ten years the theory would have been verified; all those factors of evolution which only now begin to receive due attention would have appeared in their full light. The rate of scientific progress would have been tenfold; and if the individual would not have the same claims on posterity's gratitude as he has now, the unknown mass would have done the work with more speed and with more prospect for ulterior advance than the individual could do in his lifetime. Mr. Murray's dictionary is an illustration of that kind of work-the work of the future.

However, there is another feature of modern science which

speaks more strongly yet in favour of the change we advocate. While industry, especially by the end of the last century and during the first part of the, present, has been inventing on such a scale as to revolutionise the very face of the earth, science has been losing its inventive powers. Men of science invent no more, or very little. Is it not striking, indeed, that the steam-engine, even in its leading principles, the railway-engine, the steamboat, the telephone, the phonograph, the weaving-machine, the lace-machine, the lighthouse, the macadamised road, photography, in black and in colours, and thousands, of less, important little things, have not been invented by professional men of science, although none of them would have refused to associate his name with any of the above-named inventions? Men who hardly had received any education at school, who had merely picked up the crumbs of knowledge from the tables of the rich, and who made their experiments with the most primitive means-the attorney's clerk Smeaton, the instrument-maker Watt, the brakesman Stephenson, the jeweller's apprentice Fulton, the millwright Rennie, the mason Telford, and hundreds of others whose very names remain unknown, were, as Mr. Smiles justly says, "the real makers of modern civilisation"; while the professional men of science, provided with all means for acquiring knowledge and experimenting, have invented little, in the formidable array of implements, machines, and prime-motors which has shown to humanity how to utilise and to manage the forces of nature. The fact is striking, but its explanation is very simple: those men-the Watts and the Stephensons-knew something which the savants do not know-they knew the use of their hands; their surroundings stimulated their inventive powers; they knew machines, their leading and their work; they had breathed the atmosphere of the workshop and the building-yard.

We know how men of science will meet the reproach. They will say: "We discover the laws of nature, let others apply them; it is a simple division of labour." But such a rejoinder would be utterly untrue. The march of progress is quite the reverse, because in a hundred cases against one the mechanical invention comes before the discovery of the scientific law. It was not the dynamical theory of heat which came before the steam-engine -it followed it.

When thousands of engines already were transforming heat into motion under the eyes of hundreds of professors, and when they had done so for half a century, or more; when thousands of trains, stopped by powerful brakes, were disengaging heat and spreading sheaves of sparks on the rails at their approach to the stations; when all over the civilised world heavy hammers and perforators were rendering burning hot the masses of iron they were hammering and perforating-then, and then only, Séguin, senior, in France, and a doctor, Mayer, in Germany, ventured to bring out the mechanical theory of heat with all its consequences: and yet the men of science ignored the work of Séguin and Almost drove Mayer to madness by obstinately clinging to their mysterious caloric fluid. Worse than that, they described Joule's first determination of the mechanical equivalent of heat as "unscientific."

When thousands of engines had been illustrating for some time the impossibility of utilising all the heat disengaged by a given amount of burnt fuel, then came the second law of Clausius. When all over the world industry already was transforming motion into heat, sound, light, and electricity, and each one into each other, then only came Grove's theory of the "correlation of physical forces"; and Grove's work had the same fate before the Royal Society as Joule's. The publication of his memoir was refused till the year 1856.

It was not the theory of electricity which gave us the telegraph. When the telegraph was invented, all we knew about electricity was but a few facts more or less badly arranged in our books; the theory of electricity is not ready yet; it still waits for its Newton, notwithstanding the brilliant attempts of late years. Even the empirical knowledge of the laws of electrical currents was in its infancy when a few bold men laid a cable at the bottom of the Atlantic Ocean, despite the warnings of the authorised men of science.

The name of "applied science" is quite misleading, because, in the great majority of cases, invention, far from being an application of science, on the contrary creates a new branch of science. The American bridges were no application of the theory of elasticity; they came before the theory, and all we can say in favour of science is, that in this special branch theory and practice developed in a parallel way, helping one another. It was not the theory of the explosives which led to the discovery of gunpowder; gunpowder was in use for centuries before the action of the gases in a gun was submitted to scientific analysis. And so on. One could easily multiply the illustrations by quoting the great processes of metallurgy; the alloys and the properties they acquire from the addition of very small amounts of some metals or metalloids the recent revival of electric lighting; nay, even the weather forecasts which truly deserved the reproach of being " unscientific when they were started for the first time by that excellent observer of shooting stars, Mathieu de la Drôme and by an old Jack tar, Fitzroy-all of these could be mentioned as instances in point.

Of course, we have a number of cases in which the discovery, or the invention, was a mere application of a scientific law (cases, like the discovery of the, planet Neptune), but in the immense majority of cases the discovery, or the invention, is unscientific to begin with. It belongs much more to the domain of art-art taking the precedence over science, as Helmholtz has so well shown in one of his popular lectures--, and only after the invention has been made, science comes to interpret it. It is obvious that each invention avails itself of the previously accumulated knowledge and modes of thought; but in most cases it makes a start in advance upon what is known; it makes a leap in the unknown, and thus opens a quite new series of facts for investigation. This character of invention, which is to make a start in advance of former knowledge, instead of merely applying a law, makes it identical, as to the processes of mind, with discovery; and, therefore, people who are slow in invention are also slow in discovery.

In most cases, the inventor, however inspired by the general state of science at a given moment, starts with a very few settled facts at his disposal. The scientific facts taken' into account for inventing the steam-engine, or the telegraph. or the phonograph were strikingly elementary. So that we can affirm that what we presently know is already sufficient for resolving any of the great problems which stand in the order of the day-- prime-motors without the use of steam, the storage of energy, the transmission of force, or the flying-machine. If these problems are not yet solved, it is merely because of the want of inventive genius, the scarcity of educated men endowed with it, and the present divorce between science and industry. On the one side, we have men who are endowed with capacities for invention, but have neither the necessary scientific knowledge nor the means for experimenting during long years: and, on the other side, we have men endowed with knowledge and facilities for experimenting, but devoid of inventive genius, owing to their education, too abstract, too scholastic, too bookish, and to the surroundings they live in--not to speak of the patent system. which divides and scatters the efforts of the inventors instead of combining them.

The flight of genius which has characterised the workers at the outset of modern industry has been missing in our professional men of science. And they will not recover it as long as alley remain strangers to the world, amidst their dusty bookshelves; as long as they are not workers themselves, amidst other workers, at the blaze of the iron furnace, at the machine in the factory, at the turning-lathe in the engineering workshop; sailors amidst sailors on the sea, and fishers in the fishing-boat, woodcutters in the forest, tillers of the soil in the field.

Our teachers in art--Ruskin and his school--have repeatedly told us of late that we must not expect a revival of art as long as handicraft remains what it is; they have shown how Greek and mediaeval art were daughters of handicraft how one was feeding the other. The same is true with regard to handicraft and science; their separation is the decay of both. As to the grand inspirations which unhappily have been so much neglected in most of the recent discussions about art--and which are missing in science a well these can be expected only when humanity, breaking its present bonds, shall mate a new start in the higher principles of solidarity, doing away with the present duality of moral sense and philosophy.

It is evident, however, that all men and women cannot equally enjoy the pursuit of scientific work. The variety of inclinations is such that some will find more pleasure in science, some others in art, and others again in some of the numberless branches of the production of wealth. But, whatever the occupations preferred by everyone, everyone will be the more useful in his own branch if he is in possession of a serious scientific knowledge. And, whosoever he might be--scientist or artist physicist or surgeon, chemist or sociologist, historian or poet--he would be the gainer if he spent a part of his life in the workshop or the farm (the workshop and the farm), if he were in contact with humanity in its daily work, and had the satisfaction of knowing that he himself discharges his duties as an unprivileged producer of wealth.

How much better the historian and the sociologist would

understand humanity if they knew it, not in books only, not in a few of its representatives, but as a whole, in its daily life, daily work, and daily affairs! How much more medicine would trust to hygiene, and how much less to prescriptions, if the young doctors were the nurses of the sick and the nurses received the education of the doctors of our time! And how much the poet would gain in his feeling of the beauties of nature, how much better would he know the human heart, if he met the rising sun amidst the tillers of the soil, himself a tiller; if he fought against the storm with the sailors on board ship; if he knew the poetry of labour and rest, sorrow and joy, struggle and conquest! Greift nur hinein in's volle Menschenleben! Goethe said; Ein jeder lebt's--nicht vielen ist's bekannt. But how few poets follow his advice!

The so-called "division of labour" has grown under a system which condemned the masses to toil all the day long, and all the life long, at the same wearisome kind of labour. But if we take into account how few are the real producers of wealth in our present society, and how squandered is their labour we must recognise that Franklin was right in saying that to work five hours a day would generally do for supplying each member of a civilised nation with the comfort now accessible for the few only.

But we have made some progress since Franklin's time, and some of that progress in the hitherto most backward branch of production--agriculture --has been indicated in the preceding pages. Even in that branch the productivity of labour can be immensely increased, and work itself rendered easy and pleasant. If everyone took his share of production, and if production were socialised--as political economy, if it aimed at the satisfaction of the ever-growing needs of all, would advise us to do--then more than one half of the working day would remain to everyone for the pursuit of art, science, or any hobby he or she might prefer; and his work in those fields would be the more profitable if he spent the other half of the day in productive work--if art and science were followed from mere inclination, not for mercantile purposes. Moreover, a community organised on the principles of all being workers would be rich enough to conclude that every man and woman, after having; reached a certain age--say of forty or more--ought to be relieved from the moral obligation of taking a direct part in the performance of the necessary manual work, so as to be able entirely to devote himself or herself to whatever he or she chooses in the domain of art, or science, or any kind of work. Free pursuit in new branches of art and knowledge, free creation, and free development thus might be fully guaranteed.. And such a community would not know misery amidst wealth. It would not know the duality of conscience which permeates out life and stifles every noble effort. It would freely take its flight towards the highest regions of progress compatible with human nature.

Chapter IX: Conclusion

READERS who have had the patience to follow the facts accumulated in this book, especially those who have given them thoughtful attention, will probably feel convinced of the immense powers over the productive forces of Nature that man has acquired within the last half a century. Comparing the achievements indicated in this book with the present state of production, some will, I hope, also ask themselves the question which will be, let us hope, the main object of a scientific political economy: Are the means now in use for satisfying human needs, under the present system of permanent division of functions and production for profits, really economical? Do they really lead to economy in the expenditure of human forces? Or, are they not mere wasteful survivals from a past that wads plunged into darkness, ignorance and oppression, and never took into consideration the economical and social value of the human being?

In the domain of agriculture it may be taken as proved that if a small part only of the time that is now given in each nation or region to field culture was given to well thought out and socially carried out permanent improvements of the soil, the duration of work which would be required afterwards to grow the yearly bread-food for an average family of five would be less than a fortnight every year; and that the work required for that purpose would not be the hard toil of the ancient slave, but work which would be agreeable to the physical forces of every healthy man and woman in the country.

It has been proved that by following the methods of intensive market-gardening -- partly under glass -- vegetables and fruit can be grown in such quantities that men could be provided with food rich in vegetables and a profusion of fruit, if they simply devoted to the task of growing them the hours which everyone willingly devotes to work in the open air, after having spent most of his day in the factory, the mine, or the study. Provided, of course, that the production of food-stuffs should not be the work of the isolated individual, but the planned-out and combined action of human groups.

It has also been proved-and those who care to verify it by themselves may easily do so by calculating the real expenditure for labour which was lately made in the building of workmen's houses by both private persons and municipalities 1 -that under a proper combination of labour, twenty to twenty-four months of one man's work would be sufficient to secure for ever, for a family of five, an apartment or a house provided with all the comforts which modern hygiene and taste could require.

And it has been demonstrated by actual experiment that, by adopting methods of education, advocated long since and partially applied here and there, it is most easy to convey to children of an average intelligence, before they have reached the age of fourteen or fifteen, a broad general comprehension of Nature, as well as of human societies; to familiarise their minds with sound methods of both scientific research and technical work, and inspire their hearts with a deep feeling of human solidarity and justice; and that it is extremely easy to convey during the next four or five years a reasoned, scientific knowledge of Nature's laws, as well as a knowledge, at once reasoned and practical, of the technical methods of satisfying man's material needs. Far from being inferior to the "specialised" young persons manufactured by our universities, the complete human being, trained to use his brain and his hands, excels them, on the contrary, in all respects, especially as an initiator and an inventor in both science and technics.

All this has been proved. It is an acquisition of the times we live in-an acquisition which has been won despite the innumerable obstacles always thrown in the way of every initiative mind. It has been won by the obscure tillers of the soil, from whose hands greedy States, land lords and middlemen snatch the fruit of their labour even before it is ripe; by obscure teachers who only too often fall crushed under the weight of Church, State, commercial competition, inertia of mind and prejudice.

And now, in the presence of all these conquests - what is the reality of things?

Nine-tenths of the whole population of grain- exporting countries like Russia, one-half of it in countries like France which live on home grown food, work upon the land-most of them in the same way as the slaves of antiquity did, only to obtain a meagre crop from a soil, and with a machinery which they cannot improve, because taxation, rent and usury keep them always as near as possible to the margin of starvation. In this twentieth century, whole populations still plough with the same plough as their medaeval ancestors, live in the same incertitude of the morrow, and are as carefully denied education as their ancestors; and they have, in claiming their portion of bread, to march with their children and wives against their own sons' bayonets, as their grandfathers did hundreds of years ago.

In industrially devloped countries, a couple of months' work, or even much less than that, would be sufficient to produce for a family a rich and varied vegetable and animal food. But the researches of Engel (at Berlin) and his many followers tell us that the workman's family has to spend one full half of its yearly earnings - that is, to give six months of labour, and often more - to provide its food. And what food! Is not bread and dripping the staple food of more than one-half of English children ?

One month of work every year would be quite sufficient to provide the worker with a healthy dwelling. But it is from 25 to 40 per cent of his yearly earnings-that is, from three to five months of his working time every year-that he has to spend in order to get a dwelling, in most cases unhealthy and far too small; and this dwelling will never be his own, even though at the age of forty-five or fifty he is sure to be sent away from the factory, because the work that he used to do will by that time be accomplished by a machine and a child.

We all know that the child ought, at least, to be familiarised with the forces of Nature which some day he will have to utilise; that he ought to be prepared to keep pace in his life with the steady progress of science and technics; that he ought to study science and learn a trade. Every-one will grant thus much; but what do we do? From the age of ten or even nine we send the child to push a coal-cart in a mine, or to bind, with a little monkey's agility, the two ends of threads broken in a spinning gin. From the age of thirteen we compel the girl - a child yet - to work as a "woman" at the weaving-loom, or to stew in the poisoned, over-heated air of a cotton-dressing factory, or, perhaps, to be poisoned in the death chambers of a Staffordshire pottery. As to those who have the relatively rare luck of receiving some more education, we crush their minds by useless overtime, we consciously deprive them of all possibility of them selves becoming producers; and under an educational system of which the motive is "profits," and the means "specialisation," we simply work to death the women teachers who take their educational duties in earnest. What floods of useless sufferings deluge every so-called civilised land in the world!

When we look back on ages past, and see there the same sufferings, we may say that perhaps then they were unavoidable on account of the ignorance which prevailed. But human genius, stimulated by our modern Renaissance, has already indicated new paths to follow.

For thousands of years in succession to grow one's food was the burden, almost the curse, of mankind. But it need be so no more. If you make yourselves the soil, and partly the temperature and the moisture which each crop requires, you will see that to grow the yearly food of a family, under rational conditions of culture, requires so little labour that it might almost be done as a mere change from other pursuits. If you return to the soil, and co-operate with your neighbours instead of erecting high walls to conceal yourself from their looks; if you utilise what experiment has already taught us, and call to your aid science and technical invention, which never fail to answer to the call-look only at what they have done for warfare-you will be astonished at the facility with which you can bring a rich and varied food out of the soil. You will admire the amount of sound knowledge which your children will acquire by your side, the rapid growth of their intelligence, and the facility with which they will grasp the laws of Nature, animate and inanimate.

Have the factory and the workshop at the gates of your fields and gardens, and work in them. Not those large establishments, of course, in which huge masses of metals have to be dealt with and which are better placed at certain spots indicated by Nature, but the countless variety of workshops and factories which are required to satisfy the infinite diversity of tastes among civilised men. Not those factories in which children lose all the appearance of children in the atmosphere of an industrial hell, but those airy and hygienic, and consequently economical, factories in which human life is of more account than machinery and the making of extra profits, of which we already find a few samples here and there; factories and workshops into which men, women and children will not be driven by hunger, but will be attracted by the desire of finding an activity suited to their tastes, and where, aided by the motor and the machine, they will choose the branch of activity which best suits their inclinations.

Let those factories and workshops be erected, not for making profits by selling shoddy or use-less and noxious things to enslaved Africans, but to satisfy the unsatisfied needs of millions of Europeans. And again, you will be struck to see with what facility and in how short a time your needs of dress and of thousands of articles of luxury can be satisfied, when production is carried on for satisfying real needs rather than for satisfying shareholders by high profits or for pouring gold into the pockets of promoters and bogus directors. Very soon you will yourselves feel interested in that work, and you will have occasion to admire in your children their eager desire to become acquainted with Nature and its forces, their inquisitive inquiries as to the powers of machinery, and their rapidly developing inventive genius.

Such is the future-already possible, already realisable; such is the present-already condemned and about to disappear. And what prevents us from turning our backs to this present and from marching towards that future, or, at least, making the first steps towards it, is not the "failure of science," but first of all our crass cupidity-the cupidity of the man who killed the hen that was laying golden eggs-and then our laziness of mind-that mental cowardice so carefully nurtured in the past.

For centuries science and so-called practical wisdom have said to man: "It is good to be rich, to be able to satisfy, at least, your material needs; but the only means to be rich is to so train your mind and capacities as to be able to compel other men - slaves, serfs or wage-earners - to make these riches for you. You have no choice. Either you must stand in the ranks of the peasants and the artisans who, whatsoever economists and moralists may promise them in the future, are now periodically doomed to starve after each bad crop or during their strikes and to be shot down by their own sons the moment they lose patience. Or you must train your faculties so as to be a military commander of the masses, or to be accepted as one of the wheels of the governing machinery of the State or to become a manager of men in commerce or industry." For many centuries there was no other choice, and men followed that advice, without finding in it happiness, either for themselves and their own children, or for those whom they pretended to preserve from worse misfortunes.

But modern knowledge has another issue to offer to thinking men. It tells them that in order to be rich they need not take the bread from the mouths of others; but that the more rational outcome would be a society in which men, with the work of their own hands and intelligence, and by the aid of the machinery already invented and to be invented, should themselves create all imaginable riches. Technics and science will not be lagging behind if production takes such a direction. Guided by observation, analysis and experiment, they will answer all possible demands. They will reduce the time which is necessary for producing wealth to any desired amount, so as to leave to everyone as much leisure as he or she may ask for. They surely cannot guarantee happiness, because happiness depends as much, or even more, upon the individual himself as upon his surroundings. But they guarantee, at least, the happiness that can be found in the full and varied exercise of the different capacities of the human being, in work that need not be overwork, and in the consciousness that one is not endeavouring to base his own happiness upon the misery of others.

These are the horizons which the above inquiry opens to the unprejudiced mind.

MUTUAL AID
A FACTOR OF EVOLUTION

By
PETER KROPOTKIN

Contents

INTRODUCTION 229
CHAPTER I 240
CHAPTER II 269
CHAPTER III 311
CHAPTER IV 350
CHAPTER V 386
CHAPTER VI 420
CHAPTER VII 456
CHAPTER VIII 494
CONCLUSION 524

INTRODUCTION

Two aspects of animal life impressed me most during the journeys which I made in my youth in Eastern Siberia and Northern Manchuria. One of them was the extreme severity of the struggle for existence which most species of animals have to carry on against an inclement Nature; the enormous destruction of life which periodically results from natural agencies; and the consequent paucity of life over the vast territory which fell under my observation. And the other was, that even in those few spots where animal life teemed in abundance, I failed to find—although I was eagerly looking for it—that bitter struggle for the means of existence, among animals belonging to the same species, which was considered by most Darwinists (though not always by Darwin himself) as the dominant characteristic of struggle for life, and the main factor of evolution.

The terrible snow-storms which sweep over the northern portion of Eurasia in the later part of the winter, and the glazed frost that often follows them; the frosts and the snow-storms which return every year in the second half of May, when the trees are already in full blossom and insect life swarms everywhere; the early frosts and, occasionally, the heavy snowfalls in July and August, which suddenly destroy myriads of insects, as well as the second broods of the birds in the prairies; the torrential rains, due to the monsoons, which fall in more temperate regions in August and September—resulting in inundations on a scale which is only known in America and in Eastern Asia, and swamping, on the plateaus, areas as wide as European States; and finally, the heavy snowfalls, early in October, which eventually render a territory as large as France and Germany, absolutely impracticable for ruminants, and destroy them by the thousand—these were the conditions under which I saw animal life struggling in Northern Asia. They made me realize at an early date the overwhelming importance in Nature of what Darwin described as "the natural checks to over-multiplication," in comparison to the struggle between individuals of the same species for the means of subsistence, which may go on here and there, to some limited extent, but never attains the importance of the former. Paucity of life, under-population—not over-population—being the distinctive feature of that immense part of the globe which we name Northern Asia, I conceived since then serious doubts—which subsequent study has only confirmed—as to the reality of that fearful competition for food and life within each species, which was an article of faith with most Darwinists, and, consequently, as to the dominant part which this sort of competition was supposed to play in the evolution of new species.

On the other hand, wherever I saw animal life in abundance, as, for instance, on the lakes where scores of species and millions of individuals came together to rear their progeny; in the colonies of rodents; in the migrations of birds which took place at that time on a truly American scale along the Usuri; and especially in a migration of fallow-deer which I witnessed on the Amur, and during which scores of thousands of these intelligent animals came together from an immense territory, flying before the coming deep snow, in order to cross the Amur where it is narrowest—in all these scenes of animal life which passed before my eyes, I saw Mutual Aid and Mutual Support carried on to an extent which made me suspect in it a feature of the greatest importance for the maintenance of life, the preservation of each species, and its further evolution.

And finally, I saw among the semi-wild cattle and horses in Transbaikalia, among the wild ruminants everywhere, the squirrels, and so on, that when animals have to struggle against scarcity of food, in consequence of one of the above-mentioned causes, the whole of that portion of the species which is affected by the calamity, comes out of the ordeal so much impoverished in vigour and health, that no progressive evolution of the species can be based upon such periods of keen competition.

Consequently, when my attention was drawn, later on, to the relations between Darwinism and Sociology, I could agree with none of the works and pamphlets that had been written upon this important subject. They all endeavoured to prove that Man, owing to his higher intelligence and knowledge, may mitigate the harshness of the struggle for life between men; but they all recognized at the same time that the struggle for the means of existence, of every animal against all its congeners, and of every man against all other men, was "a law of Nature." This view, however, I could not accept, because I was persuaded that to admit a pitiless inner war for life within each species, and to see in that war a condition of progress, was to admit something which not only had not yet been proved, but also lacked confirmation from direct observation.

On the contrary, a lecture "On the Law of Mutual Aid," which was delivered at a Russian Congress of Naturalists, in January 1880, by the well-known zoologist, Professor Kessler, the then Dean of the St. Petersburg University, struck me as throwing a new light on the whole subject. Kessler's idea was, that besides the law of Mutual Struggle there is in Nature the law of Mutual Aid, which, for the success of the struggle for life, and especially for the progressive evolution of the species, is far more important than the law of mutual contest. This suggestion—which was, in reality, nothing but a further development of the ideas expressed by Darwin himself in The Descent of Man—seemed to me so correct and of so great an importance, that since I became acquainted with it (in 1883) I began to collect materials for further developing the idea, which Kessler had only cursorily sketched in his lecture, but had not lived to develop. He died in 1881.

In one point only I could not entirely endorse Kessler's views. Kessler alluded to "parental feeling" and care for progeny (see below, Chapter I) as to the source of mutual inclinations in animals. However, to determine how far these two feelings have really been at work in the evolution of sociable instincts, and how far other instincts have been at work in the same direction, seems to me a quite distinct and a very wide question, which we hardly can discuss yet. It will be only after we have well established the facts of mutual aid in different classes of animals, and their importance for evolution, that we shall be able to study what belongs in the evolution of sociable feelings, to parental feelings, and what to sociability proper—the latter having evidently its origin at the earliest stages of the evolution of the animal world, perhaps even at the "colony-stages." I consequently directed my chief attention to establishing first of all, the importance of the Mutual Aid factor of evolution, leaving to ulterior research the task of discovering the origin of the Mutual Aid instinct in Nature.

The importance of the Mutual Aid factor—"if its generality could only be demonstrated"—did not escape the naturalist's genius so manifest in Goethe. When Eckermann told once to Goethe—it was in 1827—that two little wren-fledglings, which had run away from him, were found by him next day in the nest of robin redbreasts (Rothkehlchen), which fed the little ones, together with their own youngsters, Goethe grew quite excited about this fact. He saw in it a confirmation of his pantheistic views, and said:—"If it be true that this feeding of a stranger goes through all Nature as something having the character of a general law—then many an enigma would be solved." He returned to this matter on the next day, and most earnestly entreated Eckermann (who was, as is known, a zoologist) to make a special study of the subject, adding that he would surely come "to quite invaluable treasuries of results" (Gespräche, edition of 1848, vol. iii. pp. 219, 221). Unfortunately, this study was never made, although it is very possible that Brehm, who has accumulated in his works such rich materials relative to mutual aid among animals, might have been inspired by Goethe's remark.

Several works of importance were published in the years 1872-1886, dealing with the intelligence and the mental life of animals (they are mentioned in a footnote in Chapter I of this book), and three of them dealt more especially with the subject under consideration; namely, Les Societes animales, by Espinas (Paris, 1877); La Lutte pour l'existence et l'association pout la lutte, a lecture by J.L. Lanessan (April 1881); and Louis Buchner's book, Liebe und Liebes-Leben in der Thierwelt, of which the first edition appeared in 1882 or 1883, and a second, much enlarged, in 1885. But excellent though each of these works is, they leave ample room for a work in which Mutual Aid would be considered, not only as an argument in favour of a pre-human origin of moral instincts, but also as a law of Nature and a factor of evolution. Espinas devoted his main attention to such animal societies (ants, bees) as are established upon a physiological division of labour, and though his work is full of admirable hints in all possible directions, it was written at a time when the evolution of human societies could not yet be treated with the knowledge we now possess. Lanessan's lecture has more the character of a brilliantly laid-out general plan of a work, in which mutual support would be dealt with, beginning with rocks in the sea, and then passing in review the world of plants, of animals and men. As to Buchner's work, suggestive though it is and rich in facts, I could not agree with its leading idea. The book begins with a hymn to Love, and nearly all its illustrations are intended to prove the existence of love and sympathy among animals. However, to reduce animal sociability to love and sympathy means to reduce its generality and its importance, just as human ethics based upon love and personal sympathy only have contributed to narrow the comprehension of the moral feeling as a whole. It is not love to my neighbour—whom I often do not know at all—which induces me to seize a pail of water and to rush towards his house when I see it on fire; it is a far wider, even though more vague feeling or instinct of human solidarity and sociability which moves me. So it is also with animals. It is not love, and not even sympathy (understood in its proper sense) which induces a herd of ruminants or of horses to form a ring in order to resist an attack of wolves; not love which induces wolves to form a pack for hunting; not love which induces kittens or lambs to play, or a dozen of species of young birds to spend their days together in the autumn; and it is neither love nor personal sympathy which induces many thousand fallow-deer scattered over a territory as large as France to form into a score of separate herds, all marching towards a given spot, in order to cross there a river. It is a feeling infinitely wider than love or personal sympathy—an instinct that has been slowly developed among animals and men in the course of an extremely long evolution, and which has taught animals and men alike the force they can borrow from the practice of mutual aid and support, and the joys they can find in social life.

The importance of this distinction will be easily appreciated by the student of animal psychology, and the more so by the student of human ethics. Love, sympathy and self-sacrifice certainly play an immense part in the progressive development of our moral feelings. But it is not love and not even sympathy upon which Society is based in mankind. It is the conscience—be it only at the stage of an instinct—of human solidarity. It is the unconscious recognition of the force that is borrowed by each man from the practice of mutual aid; of the close dependency of every one's happiness upon the happiness of all; and of the sense of justice, or equity, which brings the individual to consider the rights of every other individual as equal to his own. Upon this broad and necessary foundation the still higher moral feelings are developed. But this subject lies outside the scope of the present work, and I shall only indicate here a lecture, "Justice and Morality" which I delivered in reply to Huxley's Ethics, and in which the subject has been treated at some length.

Consequently I thought that a book, written on Mutual Aid as a Law of Nature and a factor of evolution, might fill an important gap. When Huxley issued, in 1888, his "Struggle-for-life" manifesto (Struggle for Existence and its Bearing upon Man), which to my appreciation was a very incorrect representation of the facts of Nature, as one sees them in the bush and in the forest, I communicated with the editor of the Nineteenth Century, asking him whether he would give the hospitality of his review to an elaborate reply to the views of one of the most prominent Darwinists; and Mr. James Knowles received the proposal with fullest sympathy. I also spoke of it to W. Bates. "Yes, certainly; that is true Darwinism," was his reply. "It is horrible what 'they' have made of Darwin. Write these articles, and when they are printed, I will write to you a letter which you may publish." Unfortunately, it took me nearly seven years to write these articles, and when the last was published, Bates was no longer living.

After having discussed the importance of mutual aid in various classes of animals, I was evidently bound to discuss the importance of the same factor in the evolution of Man. This was the more necessary as there are a number of evolutionists who may not refuse to admit the importance of mutual aid among animals, but who, like Herbert Spencer, will refuse to admit it for Man. For primitive Man—they maintain—war of each against all was the law of life. In how far this assertion, which has been too willingly repeated, without sufficient criticism, since the times of Hobbes, is supported by what we know about the early phases of human development, is discussed in the chapters given to the Savages and the Barbarians.

The number and importance of mutual-aid institutions which were developed by the creative genius of the savage and half-savage masses, during the earliest clan-period of mankind and still more during the next village-community period, and the immense influence which these early institutions have exercised upon the subsequent development of mankind, down to the present times, induced me to extend my researches to the later, historical periods as well; especially, to study that most interesting period—the free medieval city republics, of which the universality and influence upon our modern civilization have not yet been duly appreciated. And finally, I have tried to indicate in brief the immense importance which the mutual-support instincts, inherited by mankind from its extremely long evolution, play even now in our modern society, which is supposed to rest upon the principle: "every one for himself, and the State for all," but which it never has succeeded, nor will succeed in realizing.

It may be objected to this book that both animals and men are represented in it under too favourable an aspect; that their sociable qualities are insisted upon, while their anti-social and self-asserting instincts are hardly touched upon. This was, however, unavoidable. We have heard so much lately of the "harsh, pitiless struggle for life," which was said to be carried on by every animal against all other animals, every "savage" against all other "savages," and every civilized man against all his co-citizens—and these assertions have so much become an article of faith—that it was necessary, first of all, to oppose to them a wide series of facts showing animal and human life under a quite different aspect. It was necessary to indicate the overwhelming importance which sociable habits play in Nature and in the progressive evolution of both the animal species and human beings: to prove that they secure to animals a better protection from their enemies, very often facilities for getting food and (winter provisions, migrations, etc.), longevity, therefore a greater facility for the development of intellectual faculties; and that they have given to men, in addition to the same advantages, the possibility of working out those institutions which have enabled mankind to survive in its hard struggle against Nature, and to progress, notwithstanding all the vicissitudes of its history. It is a book on the law of Mutual Aid, viewed at as one of the chief factors of evolution—not on all factors of evolution and their respective values; and this first book had to be written, before the latter could become possible.

I should certainly be the last to underrate the part which the self-assertion of the individual has played in the evolution of mankind. However, this subject requires, I believe, a much deeper treatment than the one it has hitherto received. In the history of mankind, individual self-assertion has often been, and continually is, something quite different from, and far larger and deeper than, the petty, unintelligent narrow-mindedness, which, with a large class of writers, goes for "individualism" and "self-assertion." Nor have history-making individuals been limited to those whom historians have represented as heroes. My intention, consequently, is, if circumstances permit it, to discuss separately the part taken by the self-assertion of the individual in the progressive evolution of mankind. I can only make in this place the following general remark:—When the Mutual Aid institutions—the tribe, the village community, the guilds, the medieval city—began, in the course of history, to lose their primitive character, to be invaded by parasitic growths, and thus to become hindrances to progress, the revolt of individuals against these institutions took always two different aspects. Part of those who rose up strove to purify the old institutions, or to work out a higher form of commonwealth, based upon the same Mutual Aid principles; they tried, for instance, to introduce the principle of "compensation," instead of the lex talionis, and later on, the pardon of offences, or a still higher ideal of equality before the human conscience, in lieu of "compensation," according to class-value. But at the very same time, another portion of the same individual rebels endeavoured to break down the protective institutions of mutual support, with no other intention but to increase their own wealth and their own powers. In this three-cornered contest, between the two classes of revolted individuals and the supporters of what existed, lies the real tragedy of history. But to delineate that contest, and honestly to study the part played in the evolution of mankind by each one of these three forces, would require at least as many years as it took me to write this book.

Of works dealing with nearly the same subject, which have been published since the publication of my articles on Mutual Aid among Animals, I must mention The Lowell Lectures on the Ascent of Man, by Henry Drummond (London, 1894), and The Origin and Growth of the Moral Instinct, by A. Sutherland (London, 1898). Both are constructed chiefly on the lines taken in Buchner's Love, and in the second work the parental and familial feeling as the sole influence at work in the development of the moral feelings has been dealt with at some length. A third work dealing with man and written on similar lines is The Principles of Sociology, by Prof. F.A. Giddings, the first edition of which was published in 1896 at New York and London, and the leading ideas of which were sketched by the author in a pamphlet in 1894. I must leave, however, to literary critics the task of discussing the points of contact, resemblance, or divergence between these works and mine.

The different chapters of this book were published first in the Nineteenth Century ("Mutual Aid among Animals," in September and November 1890; "Mutual Aid among Savages," in April 1891; "Mutual Aid among the Barbarians," in January 1892; "Mutual Aid in the Medieval City," in August and September 1894; and "Mutual Aid amongst Modern Men," in January and June 1896). In bringing them out in a book form my first intention was to embody in an Appendix the mass of materials, as well as the discussion of several secondary points, which had to be omitted in the review articles. It appeared, however, that the Appendix would double the size of the book, and I was compelled to abandon, or, at least, to postpone its publication. The present Appendix includes the discussion of only a few points which have been the matter of scientific controversy during the last few years; and into the text I have introduced only such matter as could be introduced without altering the structure of the work.

I am glad of this opportunity for expressing to the editor of the Nineteenth Century, Mr. James Knowles, my very best thanks, both for the kind hospitality which he offered to these papers in his review, as soon as he knew their general idea, and the permission he kindly gave me to reprint them.

Bromley, Kent, 1902.

CHAPTER I

MUTUAL AID AMONG ANIMALS

Struggle for existence. Mutual Aid a law of Nature and chief factor of progressive evolution. Invertebrates. Ants and Bees. Birds, hunting and fishing associations. Sociability. Mutual protection among small birds. Cranes, parrots.

The conception of struggle for existence as a factor of evolution, introduced into science by Darwin and Wallace, has permitted us to embrace an immensely wide range of phenomena in one single generalization, which soon became the very basis of our philosophical, biological, and sociological speculations. An immense variety of facts:—adaptations of function and structure of organic beings to their surroundings; physiological and anatomical evolution; intellectual progress, and moral development itself, which we formerly used to explain by so many different causes, were embodied by Darwin in one general conception. We understood them as continued endeavours—as a struggle against adverse circumstances—for such a development of individuals, races, species and societies, as would result in the greatest possible fulness, variety, and intensity of life. It may be that at the outset Darwin himself was not fully aware of the generality of the factor which he first invoked for explaining one series only of facts relative to the accumulation of individual variations in incipient species. But he foresaw that the term which he was introducing into science would lose its philosophical and its only true meaning if it were to be used in its narrow sense only—that of a struggle between separate individuals for the sheer means of existence. And at the very beginning of his memorable work he insisted upon the term being taken in its "large and metaphorical sense including dependence of one being on another, and including (which is more important) not only the life of the individual, but success in leaving progeny."(1)

While he himself was chiefly using the term in its narrow sense for his own special purpose, he warned his followers against committing the error (which he seems once to have committed himself) of overrating its narrow meaning. In The Descent of Man he gave some powerful pages to illustrate its proper, wide sense. He pointed out how, in numberless animal societies, the struggle between separate individuals for the means of existence disappears, how struggle is replaced by co-operation, and how that substitution results in the development of intellectual and moral faculties which secure to the species the best conditions for survival. He intimated that in such cases the fittest are not the physically strongest, nor the cunningest, but those who learn to combine so as mutually to support each other, strong and weak alike, for the welfare of the community. "Those communities," he wrote, "which included the greatest number of the most sympathetic members would flourish best, and rear the greatest number of offspring" (2nd edit., p. 163). The term, which originated from the narrow Malthusian conception of competition between each and all, thus lost its narrowness in the mind of one who knew Nature.

Unhappily, these remarks, which might have become the basis of most fruitful researches, were overshadowed by the masses of facts gathered for the purpose of illustrating the consequences of a real competition for life. Besides, Darwin never attempted to submit to a closer investigation the relative importance of the two aspects under which the struggle for existence appears in the animal world, and he never wrote the work he proposed to write upon the natural checks to over-multiplication, although that work would have been the crucial test for appreciating the real purport of individual struggle. Nay, on the very pages just mentioned, amidst data disproving the narrow Malthusian conception of struggle, the old Malthusian leaven reappeared—namely, in Darwin's remarks as to the alleged inconveniences of maintaining the "weak in mind and body" in our civilized societies (ch. v). As if thousands of weak-bodied and infirm poets, scientists, inventors, and reformers, together with other thousands of so-called "fools" and "weak-minded enthusiasts," were not the most precious weapons used by humanity in its struggle for existence by intellectual and moral arms, which Darwin himself emphasized in those same chapters of Descent of Man.

It happened with Darwin's theory as it always happens with theories having any bearing upon human relations. Instead of widening it according to his own hints, his followers narrowed it still more. And while Herbert Spencer, starting on independent but closely allied lines, attempted to widen the inquiry into that great question, "Who are the fittest?" especially in the appendix to the third edition of the Data of Ethics, the numberless followers of Darwin reduced the notion of struggle for existence to its narrowest limits. They came to conceive the animal world as a world of perpetual struggle among half-starved individuals, thirsting for one another's blood. They made modern literature resound with the war-cry of woe to the vanquished, as if it were the last word of modern biology. They raised the "pitiless" struggle for personal advantages to the height of a biological principle which man must submit to as well, under the menace of otherwise succumbing in a world based upon mutual extermination. Leaving aside the economists who know of natural science but a few words borrowed from second-hand vulgarizers, we must recognize that even the most authorized exponents of Darwin's views did their best to maintain those false ideas. In fact, if we take Huxley, who certainly is considered as one of the ablest exponents of the theory of evolution, were we not taught by him, in a paper on the 'Struggle for Existence and its Bearing upon Man,' that,

> "from the point of view of the moralist, the animal world is on about the same level as a gladiators' show. The creatures are fairly well treated, and set to, fight hereby the strongest, the swiftest, and the cunningest live to fight another day. The spectator has no need to turn his thumb down, as no quarter is given."

Or, further down in the same article, did he not tell us that, as among animals, so among primitive men,

> "the weakest and stupidest went to the wall, while the toughest and shrewdest, those who were best fitted to cope with their circumstances, but not the best in another way, survived. Life was a continuous free fight, and beyond the limited and temporary relations of the family, the Hobbesian war of each against all was the normal state of existence."(2)

In how far this view of nature is supported by fact, will be seen from the evidence which will be here submitted to the reader as regards the animal world, and as regards primitive man. But it may be remarked at once that Huxley's view of nature had as little claim to be taken as a scientific deduction as the opposite view of Rousseau, who saw in nature but love, peace, and harmony destroyed by the accession of man. In fact, the first walk in the forest, the first observation upon any animal society, or even the perusal of any serious work dealing with animal life (D'Orbigny's, Audubon's, Le Vaillant's, no matter which), cannot but set the naturalist thinking about the part taken by social life in the life of animals, and prevent him from seeing in Nature nothing but a field of slaughter, just as this would prevent him from seeing in Nature nothing but harmony and peace. Rousseau had committed the error of excluding the beak-and-claw fight from his thoughts; and Huxley committed the opposite error; but neither Rousseau's optimism nor Huxley's pessimism can be accepted as an impartial interpretation of nature.

As soon as we study animals—not in laboratories and museums only, but in the forest and the prairie, in the steppe and the mountains—we at once perceive that though there is an immense amount of warfare and extermination going on amidst various species, and especially amidst various classes of animals, there is, at the same time, as much, or perhaps even more, of mutual support, mutual aid, and mutual defence amidst animals belonging to the same species or, at least, to the same society. Sociability is as much a law of nature as mutual struggle. Of course it would be extremely difficult to estimate, however roughly, the relative numerical importance of both these series of facts. But if we resort to an indirect test, and ask Nature: "Who are the fittest: those who are continually at war with each other, or those who support one another?" we at once see that those animals which acquire habits of mutual aid are undoubtedly the fittest. They have more chances to survive, and they attain, in their respective classes, the highest development of intelligence and bodily organization. If the numberless facts which can be brought forward to support this view are taken into account, we may safely say that mutual aid is as much a law of animal life as mutual struggle, but that, as a factor of evolution, it most probably has a far greater importance, inasmuch as it favours the development of such habits and characters as insure the maintenance and further development of the species, together with the greatest amount of welfare and enjoyment of life for the individual, with the least waste of energy.

Of the scientific followers of Darwin, the first, as far as I know, who understood the full purport of Mutual Aid as a law of Nature and the chief factor of evolution, was a well-known Russian zoologist, the late Dean of the St. Petersburg University, Professor Kessler. He developed his ideas in an address which he delivered in January 1880, a few months before his death, at a Congress of Russian naturalists; but, like so many good things published in the Russian tongue only, that remarkable address remains almost entirely unknown.(3)

"As a zoologist of old standing," he felt bound to protest against the abuse of a term—the struggle for existence—borrowed from zoology, or, at least, against overrating its importance. Zoology, he said, and those sciences which deal with man, continually insist upon what they call the pitiless law of struggle for existence. But they forget the existence of another law which may be described as the law of mutual aid, which law, at least for the animals, is far more essential than the former. He pointed out how the need of leaving progeny necessarily brings animals together, and, "the more the individuals keep together, the more they mutually support each other, and the more are the chances of the species for surviving, as well as for making further progress in its intellectual development." "All classes of animals," he continued, "and especially the higher ones, practise mutual aid," and he illustrated his idea by examples borrowed from the life of the burying beetles and the social life of birds and some mammalia. The examples were few, as might have been expected in a short opening address, but the chief points were clearly stated; and, after mentioning that in the evolution of mankind mutual aid played a still more prominent part, Professor Kessler concluded as follows:—

"I obviously do not deny the struggle for existence, but I maintain that the progressive development of the animal kingdom, and especially of mankind, is favoured much more by mutual support than by mutual struggle.... All organic beings have two essential needs: that of nutrition, and that of propagating the species. The former brings them to a struggle and to mutual extermination, while the needs of maintaining the species bring them to approach one another and to support one another. But I am inclined to think that in the evolution of the organic world—in the progressive modification of organic beings—mutual support among individuals plays a much more important part than their mutual struggle."(4)

The correctness of the above views struck most of the Russian zoologists present, and Syevertsoff, whose work is well known to ornithologists and geographers, supported them and illustrated them by a few more examples. He mentioned sone of the species of falcons which have "an almost ideal organization for robbery," and nevertheless are in decay, while other species of falcons, which practise mutual help, do thrive. "Take, on the other side, a sociable bird, the duck," he said; "it is poorly organized on the whole, but it practises mutual support, and it almost invades the earth, as may be judged from its numberless varieties and species."

The readiness of the Russian zoologists to accept Kessler's views seems quite natural, because nearly all of them have had opportunities of studying the animal world in the wide uninhabited regions of Northern Asia and East Russia; and it is impossible to study like regions without being brought to the same ideas. I recollect myself the impression produced upon me by the animal world of Siberia when I explored the Vitim regions in the company of so accomplished a zoologist as my friend Polyakoff was. We both were under the fresh impression of the Origin of Species, but we vainly looked for the keen competition between animals of the same species which the reading of Darwin's work had prepared us to expect, even after taking into account the remarks of the third chapter (p. 54). We saw plenty of adaptations for struggling, very often in common, against the adverse circumstances of climate, or against various enemies, and Polyakoff wrote many a good page upon the mutual dependency of carnivores, ruminants, and rodents in their geographical distribution; we witnessed numbers of facts of mutual support, especially during the migrations of birds and ruminants; but even in the Amur and Usuri regions, where animal life swarms in abundance, facts of real competition and struggle between higher animals of the same species came very seldom under my notice, though I eagerly searched for them. The same impression appears in the works of most Russian zoologists, and it probably explains why Kessler's ideas were so welcomed by the Russian Darwinists, whilst like ideas are not in vogue amidst the followers of Darwin in Western Europe.

The first thing which strikes us as soon as we begin studying the struggle for existence under both its aspects—direct and metaphorical—is the abundance of facts of mutual aid, not only for rearing progeny, as recognized by most evolutionists, but also for the safety of the individual, and for providing it with the necessary food. With many large divisions of the animal kingdom mutual aid is the rule. Mutual aid is met with even amidst the lowest animals, and we must be prepared to learn some day, from the students of microscopical pond-life, facts of unconscious mutual support, even from the life of micro-organisms. Of course, our knowledge of the life of the invertebrates, save the termites, the ants, and the bees, is extremely limited; and yet, even as regards the lower animals, we may glean a few facts of well-ascertained cooperation. The numberless associations of locusts, vanessae, cicindelae, cicadae, and so on, are practically quite unexplored; but the very fact of their existence indicates that they must be composed on about the same principles as the temporary associations of ants or bees for purposes of migration. As to the beetles, we have quite well-observed facts of mutual help amidst the burying beetles (Necrophorus). They must have some decaying organic matter to lay their eggs in, and thus to provide their larvae with food; but that matter must not decay very rapidly. So they are wont to bury in the ground the corpses of all kinds of small animals which they occasionally find in their rambles. As a rule, they live an isolated life, but when one of them has discovered the corpse of a mouse or of a bird, which it hardly could manage to bury itself, it calls four, six, or ten other beetles to perform the operation with united efforts; if necessary, they transport the corpse to a suitable soft ground; and they bury it in a very considerate way, without quarrelling as to which of them will enjoy the privilege of laying its eggs in the buried corpse. And when Gleditsch attached a dead bird to a cross made out of two sticks, or suspended a toad to a stick planted in the soil, the little beetles would in the same friendly way combine their intelligences to overcome the artifice of Man. The same combination of efforts has been noticed among the dung-beetles.

Even among animals standing at a somewhat lower stage of organization we may find like examples. Some land-crabs of the West Indies and North America combine in large swarms in order to travel to the sea and to deposit therein their spawn; and each such migration implies concert, co-operation, and mutual support. As to the big Molucca crab (Limulus), I was struck (in 1882, at the Brighton Aquarium) with the extent of mutual assistance which these clumsy animals are capable of bestowing upon a comrade in case of need. One of them had fallen upon its back in a corner of the tank, and its heavy saucepan-like carapace prevented it from returning to its natural position, the more so as there was in the corner an iron bar which rendered the task still more difficult. Its comrades came to the rescue, and for one hour's time I watched how they endeavoured to help their fellow-prisoner. They came two at once, pushed their friend from beneath, and after strenuous efforts succeeded in lifting it upright; but then the iron bar would prevent them from achieving the work of rescue, and the crab would again heavily fall upon its back. After many attempts, one of the helpers would go in the depth of the tank and bring two other crabs, which would begin with fresh forces the same pushing and lifting of their helpless comrade. We stayed in the Aquarium for more than two hours, and, when leaving, we again came to cast a glance upon the tank: the work of rescue still continued! Since I saw that, I cannot refuse credit to the observation quoted by Dr. Erasmus Darwin—namely, that "the common crab during the moulting season stations as sentinel an unmoulted or hard-shelled individual to prevent marine enemies from injuring moulted individuals in their unprotected state."(5)

Facts illustrating mutual aid amidst the termites, the ants, and the bees are so well known to the general reader, especially through the works of Romanes, L. Buchner, and Sir John Lubbock, that I may limit my remarks to a very few hints.(6) If we take an ants' nest, we not only see that every description of work-rearing of progeny, foraging, building, rearing of aphides, and so on—is performed according to the principles of voluntary mutual aid; we must also recognize, with Forel, that the chief, the fundamental feature of the life of many species of ants is the fact and the obligation for every ant of sharing its food, already swallowed and partly digested, with every member of the community which may apply for it. Two ants belonging to two different species or to two hostile nests, when they occasionally meet together, will avoid each other. But two ants belonging to the same nest or to the same colony of nests will approach each other, exchange a few movements with the antennae, and "if one of them is hungry or thirsty, and especially if the other has its crop full ... it immediately asks for food." The individual thus requested never refuses; it sets apart its mandibles, takes a proper position, and regurgitates a drop of transparent fluid which is licked up by the hungry ant. Regurgitating food for other ants is so prominent a feature in the life of ants (at liberty), and it so constantly recurs both for feeding hungry comrades and for feeding larvae, that Forel considers the digestive tube of the ants as consisting of two different parts, one of which, the posterior, is for the special use of the individual, and the other, the anterior part, is chiefly for the use of the community. If an ant which has its crop full has been selfish enough to refuse feeding a comrade, it will be treated as an enemy, or even worse. If the refusal has been made while its kinsfolk were fighting with some other species, they will fall back upon the greedy individual with greater vehemence than even upon the enemies themselves. And if an ant has not refused to feed another ant belonging to an enemy species, it will be treated by the kinsfolk of the latter as a friend. All this is confirmed by most accurate observation and decisive experiments.(7)

In that immense division of the animal kingdom which embodies more than one thousand species, and is so numerous that the Brazilians pretend that Brazil belongs to the ants, not to men, competition amidst the members of the same nest, or the colony of nests, does not exist. However terrible the wars between different species, and whatever the atrocities committed at war-time, mutual aid within the community, self-devotion grown into a habit, and very often self-sacrifice for the common welfare, are the rule. The ants and termites have renounced the "Hobbesian war," and they are the better for it. Their wonderful nests, their buildings, superior in relative size to those of man; their paved roads and overground vaulted galleries; their spacious halls and granaries; their corn-fields, harvesting and "malting" of grain;(8) their, rational methods of nursing their eggs and larvae, and of building special nests for rearing the aphides whom Linnaeus so picturesquely described as "the cows of the ants"; and, finally, their courage, pluck, and, superior intelligence—all these are the natural outcome of the mutual aid which they practise at every stage of their busy and laborious lives. That mode of life also necessarily resulted in the development of another essential feature of the life of ants: the immense development of individual initiative which, in its turn, evidently led to the development of that high and varied intelligence which cannot but strike the human observer.(9)

If we knew no other facts from animal life than what we know about the ants and the termites, we already might safely conclude that mutual aid (which leads to mutual confidence, the first condition for courage) and individual initiative (the first condition for intellectual progress) are two factors infinitely more important than mutual struggle in the evolution of the animal kingdom. In fact, the ant thrives without having any of the "protective" features which cannot be dispensed with by animals living an isolated life. Its colour renders it conspicuous to its enemies, and the lofty nests of many species are conspicuous in the meadows and forests. It is not protected by a hard carapace, and its stinging apparatus, however dangerous when hundreds of stings are plunged into the flesh of an animal, is not of a great value for individual defence; while the eggs and larvae of the ants are a dainty for a great number of the inhabitants of the forests. And yet the ants, in their thousands, are not much destroyed by the birds, not even by the ant-eaters, and they are dreaded by most stronger insects. When Forel emptied a bagful of ants in a meadow, he saw that "the crickets ran away, abandoning their holes to be sacked by the ants; the grasshoppers and the crickets fled in all directions; the spiders and the beetles abandoned their prey in order not to become prey themselves;" even the nests of the wasps were taken by the ants, after a battle during which many ants perished for the safety of the commonwealth. Even the swiftest insects cannot escape, and Forel often saw butterflies, gnats, flies, and so on, surprised and killed by the ants. Their force is in mutual support and mutual confidence. And if the ant—apart from the still higher developed termites—stands at the very top of the whole class of insects for its intellectual capacities; if its courage is only equalled by the most courageous vertebrates; and if its brain—to use Darwin's words—"is one of the most marvellous atoms of matter in the world, perhaps more so than the brain of man," is it not due to the fact that mutual aid has entirely taken the place of mutual struggle in the communities of ants?

The same is true as regards the bees. These small insects, which so easily might become the prey of so many birds, and whose honey has so many admirers in all classes of animals from the beetle to the bear, also have none of the protective features derived from mimicry or otherwise, without which an isolatedly living insect hardly could escape wholesale destruction; and yet, owing to the mutual aid they practise, they obtain the wide extension which we know and the intelligence we admire, By working in common they multiply their individual forces; by resorting to a temporary division of labour combined with the capacity of each bee to perform every kind of work when required, they attain such a degree of well-being and safety as no isolated animal can ever expect to achieve however strong or well armed it may be. In their combinations they are often more successful than man, when he neglects to take advantage of a well-planned mutual assistance. Thus, when a new swarm of bees is going to leave the hive in search of a new abode, a number of bees will make a preliminary exploration of the neighbourhood, and if they discover a convenient dwelling-place—say, an old basket, or anything of the kind—they will take possession of it, clean it, and guard it, sometimes for a whole week, till the swarm comes to settle therein. But how many human settlers will perish in new countries simply for not having understood the necessity of combining their efforts! By combining their individual intelligences they succeed in coping with adverse circumstances, even quite unforeseen and unusual, like those bees of the Paris Exhibition which fastened with their resinous propolis the shutter to a glass-plate fitted in the wall of their hive. Besides, they display none of the sanguinary proclivities and love of useless fighting with which many writers so readily endow animals. The sentries which guard the entrance to the hive pitilessly put to death the robbing bees which attempt entering the hive; but those stranger bees which come to the hive by mistake are left unmolested, especially if they come laden with pollen, or are young individuals which can easily go astray. There is no more warfare than is strictly required.

The sociability of the bees is the more instructive as predatory instincts and laziness continue to exist among the bees as well, and reappear each time that their growth is favoured by some circumstances. It is well known that there always are a number of bees which prefer a life of robbery to the laborious life of a worker; and that both periods of scarcity and periods of an unusually rich supply of food lead to an increase of the robbing class. When our crops are in and there remains but little to gather in our meadows and fields, robbing bees become of more frequent occurrence; while, on the other side, about the sugar plantations of the West Indies and the sugar refineries of Europe, robbery, laziness, and very often drunkenness become quite usual with the bees. We thus see that anti-social instincts continue to exist amidst the bees as well; but natural selection continually must eliminate them, because in the long run the practice of solidarity proves much more advantageous to the species than the development of individuals endowed with predatory inclinations. The cunningest and the shrewdest are eliminated in favour of those who understand the advantages of sociable life and mutual support.

Certainly, neither the ants, nor the bees, nor even the termites, have risen to the conception of a higher solidarity embodying the whole of the species. In that respect they evidently have not attained a degree of development which we do not find even among our political, scientific, and religious leaders. Their social instincts hardly extend beyond the limits of the hive or the nest. However, colonies of no less than two hundred nests, belonging to two different species (Formica exsecta and F. pressilabris) have been described by Forel on Mount Tendre and Mount Saleve; and Forel maintains that each member of these colonies recognizes every other member of the colony, and that they all take part in common defence; while in Pennsylvania Mr. MacCook saw a whole nation of from 1,600 to 1,700 nests of the mound-making ant, all living in perfect intelligence; and Mr. Bates has described the hillocks of the termites covering large surfaces in the "campos"—some of the nests being the refuge of two or three different species, and most of them being connected by vaulted galleries or arcades.(10) Some steps towards the amalgamation of larger divisions of the species for purposes of mutual protection are thus met with even among the invertebrate animals.

Going now over to higher animals, we find far more instances of undoubtedly conscious mutual help for all possible purposes, though we must recognize at once that our knowledge even of the life of higher animals still remains very imperfect. A large number of facts have been accumulated by first-rate observers, but there are whole divisions of the animal kingdom of which we know almost nothing. Trustworthy information as regards fishes is extremely scarce, partly owing to the difficulties of observation, and partly because no proper attention has yet been paid to the subject. As to the mammalia, Kessler already remarked how little we know about their manners of life. Many of them are nocturnal in their habits; others conceal themselves underground; and those ruminants whose social life and migrations offer the greatest interest do not let man approach their herds. It is chiefly upon birds that we have the widest range of information, and yet the social life of very many species remains but imperfectly known. Still, we need not complain about the lack of well-ascertained facts, as will be seen from the following.

I need not dwell upon the associations of male and female for rearing their offspring, for providing it with food during their first steps in life, or for hunting in common; though it may be mentioned by the way that such associations are the rule even with the least sociable carnivores and rapacious birds; and that they derive a special interest from being the field upon which tenderer feelings develop even amidst otherwise most cruel animals. It may also be added that the rarity of associations larger than that of the family among the carnivores and the birds of prey, though mostly being the result of their very modes of feeding, can also be explained to some extent as a consequence of the change produced in the animal world by the rapid increase of mankind. At any rate it is worthy of note that there are species living a quite isolated life in densely-inhabited regions, while the same species, or their nearest congeners, are gregarious in uninhabited countries. Wolves, foxes, and several birds of prey may be quoted as instances in point.

However, associations which do not extend beyond the family bonds are of relatively small importance in our case, the more so as we know numbers of associations for more general purposes, such as hunting, mutual protection, and even simple enjoyment of life. Audubon already mentioned that eagles occasionally associate for hunting, and his description of the two bald eagles, male and female, hunting on the Mississippi, is well known for its graphic powers. But one of the most conclusive observations of the kind belongs to Syevertsoff. Whilst studying the fauna of the Russian Steppes, he once saw an eagle belonging to an altogether gregarious species (the white-tailed eagle, Haliactos albicilla) rising high in the air for half an hour it was describing its wide circles in silence when at once its piercing voice was heard. Its cry was soon answered by another eagle which approached it, and was followed by a third, a fourth, and so on, till nine or ten eagles came together and soon disappeared. In the afternoon, Syevertsoff went to the place whereto he saw the eagles flying; concealed by one of the undulations of the Steppe, he approached them, and discovered that they had gathered around the corpse of a horse. The old ones, which, as a rule, begin the meal first—such are their rules of propriety-already were sitting upon the haystacks of the neighbourhood and kept watch, while the younger ones were continuing the meal, surrounded by bands of crows. From this and like observations,

Syevertsoff concluded that the white-tailed eagles combine for hunting; when they all have risen to a great height they are enabled, if they are ten, to survey an area of at least twenty-five miles square; and as soon as any one has discovered something, he warns the others.(11) Of course, it might be argued that a simple instinctive cry of the first eagle, or even its movements, would have had the same effect of bringing several eagles to the prey. But in this case there is strong evidence in favour of mutual warning, because the ten eagles came together before descending towards the prey, and Syevertsoff had later on several opportunities of ascertaining that the whitetailed eagles always assemble for devouring a corpse, and that some of them (the younger ones first) always keep watch while the others are eating. In fact, the white-tailed eagle—one of the bravest and best hunters—is a gregarious bird altogether, and Brehm says that when kept in captivity it very soon contracts an attachment to its keepers.

Sociability is a common feature with very many other birds of prey. The Brazilian kite, one of the most "impudent" robbers, is nevertheless a most sociable bird. Its hunting associations have been described by Darwin and other naturalists, and it is a fact that when it has seized upon a prey which is too big, it calls together five or six friends to carry it away. After a busy day, when these kites retire for their night-rest to a tree or to the bushes, they always gather in bands, sometimes coming together from distances of ten or more miles, and they often are joined by several other vultures, especially the percnopters, "their true friends," D'Orbigny says. In another continent, in the Transcaspian deserts, they have, according to Zarudnyi, the same habit of nesting together. The sociable vulture, one of the strongest vultures, has received its very name from its love of society. They live in numerous bands, and decidedly enjoy society; numbers of them join in their high flights for sport.

"They live in very good friendship," Le Vaillant says, "and in the same cave I sometimes found as many as three nests close together."(12) The Urubu vultures of Brazil are as, or perhaps even more, sociable than rooks.(13) The little Egyptian vultures live in close friendship. They play in bands in the air, they come together to spend the night, and in the morning they all go together to search for their food, and never does the slightest quarrel arise among them; such is the testimony of Brehm, who had plenty of opportunities of observing their life. The red-throated falcon is also met with in numerous bands in the forests of Brazil, and the kestrel (Tinnunculus cenchris), when it has left Europe, and has reached in the winter the prairies and forests of Asia, gathers in numerous societies. In the Steppes of South Russia it is (or rather was) so sociable that Nordmann saw them in numerous bands, with other falcons (Falco tinnunculus, F. oesulon, and F. subbuteo), coming together every fine afternoon about four o'clock, and enjoying their sports till late in the night. They set off flying, all at once, in a quite straight line, towards some determined point, and, having reached it, immediately returned over the same line, to repeat the same flight.(14)

To take flights in flocks for the mere pleasure of the flight, is quite common among all sorts of birds. "In the Humber district especially," Ch. Dixon writes, "vast flights of dunlins often appear upon the mud-flats towards the end of August, and remain for the winter.... The movements of these birds are most interesting, as a vast flock wheels and spreads out or closes up with as much precision as drilled troops. Scattered among them are many odd stints and sanderlings and ringed-plovers."(15)

It would be quite impossible to enumerate here the various hunting associations of birds; but the fishing associations of the pelicans are certainly worthy of notice for the remarkable order and intelligence displayed by these clumsy birds. They always go fishing in numerous bands, and after having chosen an appropriate bay, they form a wide half-circle in face of the shore, and narrow it by paddling towards the shore, catching all fish that happen to be enclosed in the circle. On narrow rivers and canals they even divide into two parties, each of which draws up on a half-circle, and both paddle to meet each other, just as if two parties of men dragging two long nets should advance to capture all fish taken between the nets when both parties come to meet. As the night comes they fly to their resting-places—always the same for each flock—and no one has ever seen them fighting for the possession of either the bay or the resting place. In South America they gather in flocks of from forty to fifty thousand individuals, part of which enjoy sleep while the others keep watch, and others again go fishing.(16) And finally, I should be doing an injustice to the much-calumniated house-sparrows if I did not mention how faithfully each of them shares any food it discovers with all members of the society to which it belongs. The fact was known to the Greeks, and it has been transmitted to posterity how a Greek orator once exclaimed (I quote from memory):—"While I am speaking to you a sparrow has come to tell to other sparrows that a slave has dropped on the floor a sack of corn, and they all go there to feed upon the grain." The more, one is pleased to find this observation of old confirmed in a recent little book by Mr. Gurney, who does not doubt that the house sparrows always inform each other as to where there is some food to steal; he says, "When a stack has been thrashed ever so far from the yard, the sparrows in the yard have always had their crops full of the grain."(17) True, the sparrows are extremely particular in keeping their domains free from the invasions of strangers; thus the sparrows of the Jardin du Luxembourg bitterly fight all other sparrows which may attempt to enjoy their turn of the garden and its visitors; but within their own communities they fully practise mutual support, though occasionally there will be of course some quarrelling even amongst the best friends.

Hunting and feeding in common is so much the habit in the feathered world that more quotations hardly would be needful: it must be considered as an established fact. As to the force derived from such associations, it is self-evident. The strongest birds of prey are powerless in face of the associations of our smallest bird pets. Even eagles—even the powerful and terrible booted eagle, and the martial eagle, which is strong enough to carry away a hare or a young antelope in its claws—are compelled to abandon their prey to bands of those beggars the kites, which give the eagle a regular chase as soon as they see it in possession of a good prey. The kites will also give chase to the swift fishing-hawk, and rob it of the fish it has captured; but no one ever saw the kites fighting together for the possession of the prey so stolen. On the Kerguelen Island, Dr. Coues saw the gulls to Buphogus—the sea-hen of the sealers—pursue make them disgorge their food, while, on the other side, the gulls and the terns combined to drive away the sea-hen as soon as it came near to their abodes, especially at nesting-time.(18) The little, but extremely swift lapwings (Vanellus cristatus) boldly attack the birds of prey. "To see them attacking a buzzard, a kite, a crow, or an eagle, is one of the most amusing spectacles. One feels that they are sure of victory, and one sees the anger of the bird of prey. In such circumstances they perfectly support one another, and their courage grows with their numbers."(19) The lapwing has well merited the name of a "good mother" which the Greeks gave to it, for it never fails to protect other aquatic birds from the attacks of their enemies. But even the little white wagtails (Motacilla alba), whom we well know in our gardens and whose whole length hardly attains eight inches, compel the sparrow-hawk to abandon its hunt. "I often admired their courage and agility," the old Brehm wrote, "and I am persuaded that the falcon alone is capable of capturing any of them.... When a band of wagtails has compelled a bird of prey to retreat, they make the air resound with their triumphant cries, and after that they separate." They thus come together for the special purpose of giving chase to their enemy, just as we see it when the whole bird-population of a forest has been raised by the news that a nocturnal bird has made its appearance during the day, and all together—birds of prey and small inoffensive singers—set to chase the stranger and make it return to its concealment.

What an immense difference between the force of a kite, a buzzard or a hawk, and such small birds as the meadow-wagtail; and yet these little birds, by their common action and courage, prove superior to the powerfully-winged and armed robbers! In Europe, the wagtails not only chase the birds of prey which might be dangerous to them, but they chase also the fishing-hawk "rather for fun than for doing it any harm;" while in India, according to Dr. Jerdon's testimony, the jackdaws chase the gowinda-kite "for simple matter of amusement." Prince Wied saw the Brazilian eagle urubitinga surrounded by numberless flocks of toucans and cassiques (a bird nearly akin to our rook), which mocked it. "The eagle," he adds, "usually supports these insults very quietly, but from time to time it will catch one of these mockers." In all such cases the little birds, though very much inferior in force to the bird of prey, prove superior to it by their common action.(20)

However, the most striking effects of common life for the security of the individual, for its enjoyment of life, and for the development of its intellectual capacities, are seen in two great families of birds, the cranes and the parrots. The cranes are extremely sociable and live in most excellent relations, not only with their congeners, but also with most aquatic birds. Their prudence is really astonishing, so also their intelligence; they grasp the new conditions in a moment, and act accordingly.

Their sentries always keep watch around a flock which is feeding or resting, and the hunters know well how difficult it is to approach them. If man has succeeded in surprising them, they will never return to the same place without having sent out one single scout first, and a party of scouts afterwards; and when the reconnoitring party returns and reports that there is no danger, a second group of scouts is sent out to verify the first report, before the whole band moves. With kindred species the cranes contract real friendship; and in captivity there is no bird, save the also sociable and highly intelligent parrot, which enters into such real friendship with man. "It sees in man, not a master, but a friend, and endeavours to manifest it," Brehm concludes from a wide personal experience. The crane is in continual activity from early in the morning till late in the night; but it gives a few hours only in the morning to the task of searching its food, chiefly vegetable. All the remainder of the day is given to society life. "It picks up small pieces of wood or small stones, throws them in the air and tries to catch them; it bends its neck, opens its wings, dances, jumps, runs about, and tries to manifest by all means its good disposition of mind, and always it remains graceful and beautiful."(21) As it lives in society it has almost no enemies, and though Brehm occasionally saw one of them captured by a crocodile, he wrote that except the crocodile he knew no enemies of the crane. It eschews all of them by its proverbial prudence; and it attains, as a rule, a very old age. No wonder that for the maintenance of the species the crane need not rear a numerous offspring; it usually hatches but two eggs. As to its superior intelligence, it is sufficient to say that all observers are unanimous in recognizing that its intellectual capacities remind one very much of those of man.

The other extremely sociable bird, the parrot, stands, as known, at the very top of the whole feathered world for the development of its intelligence. Brehm has so admirably summed up the manners of life of the parrot, that I cannot do better than translate the following sentence:—

"Except in the pairing season, they live in very numerous societies or bands. They choose a place in the forest to stay there, and thence they start every morning for their hunting expeditions. The members of each band remain faithfully attached to each other, and they share in common good or bad luck. All together they repair in the morning to a field, or to a garden, or to a tree, to feed upon fruits. They post sentries to keep watch over the safety of the whole band, and are attentive to their warnings. In case of danger, all take to flight, mutually supporting each other, and all simultaneously return to their resting-place. In a word, they always live closely united."

They enjoy society of other birds as well. In India, the jays and crows come together from many miles round, to spend the night in company with the parrots in the bamboo thickets. When the parrots start hunting, they display the most wonderful intelligence, prudence, and capacity of coping with circumstances. Take, for instance, a band of white cacadoos in Australia. Before starting to plunder a corn-field, they first send out a reconnoitring party which occupies the highest trees in the vicinity of the field, while other scouts perch upon the intermediate trees between the field and the forest and transmit the signals. If the report runs "All right," a score of cacadoos will separate from the bulk of the band, take a flight in the air, and then fly towards the trees nearest to the field. They also will scrutinize the neighbourhood for a long while, and only then will they give the signal for general advance, after which the whole band starts at once and plunders the field in no time. The Australian settlers have the greatest difficulties in beguiling the prudence of the parrots; but if man, with all his art and weapons, has succeeded in killing some of them, the cacadoos become so prudent and watchful that they henceforward baffle all stratagems.(22)

There can be no doubt that it is the practice of life in society which enables the parrots to attain that very high level of almost human intelligence and almost human feelings which we know in them. Their high intelligence has induced the best naturalists to describe some species, namely the grey parrot, as the "birdman." As to their mutual attachment it is known that when a parrot has been killed by a hunter, the others fly over the corpse of their comrade with shrieks of complaints and "themselves fall the victims of their friendship," as Audubon said; and when two captive parrots, though belonging to two different species, have contracted mutual friendship, the accidental death of one of the two friends has sometimes been followed by the death from grief and sorrow of the other friend. It is no less evident that in their societies they find infinitely more protection than they possibly might find in any ideal development of beak and claw. Very few birds of prey or mammals dare attack any but the smaller species of parrots, and Brehm is absolutely right in saying of the parrots, as he also says of the cranes and the sociable monkeys, that they hardly have any enemies besides men; and he adds: "It is most probable that the larger parrots succumb chiefly to old age rather than die from the claws of any enemies." Only man, owing to his still more superior intelligence and weapons, also derived from association, succeeds in partially destroying them. Their very longevity would thus appear as a result of their social life. Could we not say the same as regards their wonderful memory, which also must be favoured in its development by society—life and by longevity accompanied by a full enjoyment of bodily and mental faculties till a very old age?

As seen from the above, the war of each against all is not the law of nature. Mutual aid is as much a law of nature as mutual struggle, and that law will become still more apparent when we have analyzed some other associations of birds and those of the mammalia. A few hints as to the importance of the law of mutual aid for the evolution of the animal kingdom have already been given in the preceding pages; but their purport will still better appear when, after having given a few more illustrations, we shall be enabled presently to draw therefrom our conclusions.

NOTES:

1. Origin of Species, chap. iii, p. 62 of first edition.

2. Nineteenth Century, Feb. 1888, p. 165.

3. Leaving aside the pre-Darwinian writers, like Toussenel, Fee, and many others, several works containing many striking instances of mutual aid—chiefly, however, illustrating animal intelligence were issued previously to that date. I may mention those of Houzeau, Les facultes etales des animaux, 2 vols., Brussels, 1872; L. Buchner's Aus dem Geistesleben der Thiere, 2nd ed. in 1877; and Maximilian Perty's Ueber das Seelenleben der Thiere, Leipzig, 1876. Espinas published his most remarkable work, Les Societes animales, in 1877, and in that work he pointed out the importance of animal societies, and their bearing upon the preservation of species, and entered upon a most valuable discussion of the origin of societies. In fact, Espinas's book contains all that has been written since upon mutual aid, and many good things besides. If I nevertheless make a special mention of Kessler's address, it is because he raised mutual aid to the height of a law much more important in evolution than the law of mutual struggle. The same ideas were developed next year (in April 1881) by J. Lanessan in a lecture

published in 1882 under this title: La lutte pour l'existence et l'association pour la lutte. G. Romanes's capital work, Animal Intelligence, was issued in 1882, and followed next year by the Mental Evolution in Animals. About the same time (1883), Buchner published another work, Liebe und Liebes-Leben in der Thierwelt, a second edition of which was issued in 1885. The idea, as seen, was in the air.

4. Memoirs (Trudy) of the St. Petersburg Society of Naturalists, vol. xi. 1880.

5. George J. Romanes's Animal Intelligence, 1st ed. p. 233.

6. Pierre Huber's Les fourmis indigees, Geneve, 1861; Forel's Recherches sur les fourmis de la Suisse, Zurich, 1874, and J.T. Moggridge's Harvesting Ants and Trapdoor Spiders, London, 1873 and 1874, ought to be in the hands of every boy and girl. See also: Blanchard's Metamorphoses des Insectes, Paris, 1868; J.H. Fabre's Souvenirs entomologiques, Paris, 1886; Ebrard's Etudes des moeurs des fourmis, Geneve, 1864; Sir John Lubbock's Ants, Bees, and Wasps, and so on.

7. Forel's Recherches, pp. 244, 275, 278. Huber's description of the process is admirable. It also contains a hint as to the possible origin of the instinct (popular edition, pp. 158, 160). See Appendix II.

8. The agriculture of the ants is so wonderful that for a long time it has been doubted. The fact is now so well proved by Mr. Moggridge, Dr. Lincecum, Mr. MacCook, Col. Sykes, and Dr. Jerdon, that no doubt is possible. See an excellent summary of evidence in Mr. Romanes's work. See also Die Pilzgaerten einiger Sud-Amerikanischen Ameisen, by Alf. Moeller, in Schimper's Botan. Mitth. aus den Tropen, vi. 1893.

9. This second principle was not recognized at once. Former observers often spoke of kings, queens, managers, and so on; but since Huber and Forel have published their minute observations, no doubt is possible as to the free scope left for every individual's initiative in whatever the ants do, including their wars.

10. H.W. Bates, The Naturalist on the River Amazons, ii. 59 seq.

11. N. Syevertsoff, Periodical Phenomena in the Life of Mammalia, Birds, and Reptiles of Voroneje, Moscow, 1855 (in Russian).

12. A. Brehm, Life of Animals, iii. 477; all quotations after the French edition.

13. Bates, p. 151.

14. Catalogue raisonne des oiseaux de la faune pontique, in Demidoff's Voyage; abstracts in Brehm, iii. 360. During their migrations birds of prey often associate. One flock, which H. Seebohm saw crossing the Pyrenees, represented a curious assemblage of "eight kites, one crane, and a peregrine falcon" (The Birds of Siberia, 1901, p. 417).

15. Birds in the Northern Shires, p. 207.

16. Max. Perty, Ueber das Seelenleben der Thiere (Leipzig, 1876), pp. 87, 103.

17. G. H. Gurney, The House-Sparrow (London, 1885), p. 5.

18. Dr. Elliot Coues, Birds of the Kerguelen Island, in Smithsonian Miscellaneous Collections, vol. xiii. No. 2, p. 11.

19. Brehm, iv. 567.

20. As to the house-sparrows, a New Zealand observer, Mr. T.W. Kirk, described as follows the attack of these "impudent" birds upon an "unfortunate" hawk.—"He heard one day a most unusual noise, as though all the small birds of the country had joined in one grand quarrel. Looking up, he saw a large hawk (C. gouldi—a carrion feeder) being buffeted by a flock of sparrows. They kept dashing at him in scores, and from all points at once. The unfortunate hawk was quite powerless. At last, approaching some scrub, the hawk dashed into it and remained there, while the sparrows congregated in groups round the bush, keeping up a constant chattering and noise" (Paper read before the New Zealand Institute; Nature, Oct. 10, 1891).

21. Brehm, iv. 671 seq.

22. R. Lendenfeld, in Der zoologische Garten, 1889.

CHAPTER II

MUTUAL AID AMONG ANIMALS (continued)

Migrations of birds. Breeding associations. Autumn societies. Mammals: small number of unsociable species. Hunting associations of wolves, lions, etc. Societies of rodents; of ruminants; of monkeys. Mutual Aid in the struggle for life. Darwin's arguments to prove the struggle for life within the species. Natural checks to over-multiplication. Supposed extermination of intermediate links. Elimination of competition in Nature.

As soon as spring comes back to the temperate zone, myriads and myriads of birds which are scattered over the warmer regions of the South come together in numberless bands, and, full of vigour and joy, hasten northwards to rear their offspring. Each of our hedges, each grove, each ocean cliff, and each of the lakes and ponds with which Northern America, Northern Europe, and Northern Asia are dotted tell us at that time of the year the tale of what mutual aid means for the birds; what force, energy, and protection it confers to every living being, however feeble and defenceless it otherwise might be. Take, for instance, one of the numberless lakes of the Russian and Siberian Steppes. Its shores are peopled with myriads of aquatic birds, belonging to at least a score of different species, all living in perfect peace — all protecting one another.

"For several hundred yards from the shore the air is filled with gulls and terns, as with snow-flakes on a winter day. Thousands of plovers and sand-coursers run over the beach, searching their food, whistling, and simply enjoying life. Further on, on almost each wave, a duck is rocking, while higher up you notice the flocks of the Casarki ducks. Exuberant life swarms everywhere."(1)

And here are the robbers—the strongest, the most cunning ones, those "ideally organized for robbery." And you hear their hungry, angry, dismal cries as for hours in succession they watch the opportunity of snatching from this mass of living beings one single unprotected individual. But as soon as they approach, their presence is signalled by dozens of voluntary sentries, and hundreds of gulls and terns set to chase the robber. Maddened by hunger, the robber soon abandons his usual precautions: he suddenly dashes into the living mass; but, attacked from all sides, he again is compelled to retreat. From sheer despair he falls upon the wild ducks; but the intelligent, social birds rapidly gather in a flock and fly away if the robber is an erne; they plunge into the lake if it is a falcon; or they raise a cloud of water-dust and bewilder the assailant if it is a kite.(2) And while life continues to swarm on the lake, the robber flies away with cries of anger, and looks out for carrion, or for a young bird or a field-mouse not yet used to obey in time the warnings of its comrades. In the face of an exuberant life, the ideally-armed robber must be satisfied with the off-fall of that life.

Further north, in the Arctic archipelagoes,

"you may sail along the coast for many miles and see all the ledges, all the cliffs and corners of the mountain-sides, up to a height of from two to five hundred feet, literally covered with sea-birds, whose white breasts show against the dark rocks as if the rocks were closely sprinkled with chalk specks. The air, near and far, is, so to say, full with fowls."(3)

Each of such "bird-mountains" is a living illustration of mutual aid, as well as of the infinite variety of characters, individual and specific, resulting from social life. The oyster-catcher is renowned for its readiness to attack the birds of prey. The barge is known for its watchfulness, and it easily becomes the leader of more placid birds. The turnstone, when surrounded by comrades belonging to more energetic species, is a rather timorous bird; but it undertakes to keep watch for the security of the commonwealth when surrounded by smaller birds. Here you have the dominative swans; there, the extremely sociable kittiwake-gulls, among whom quarrels are rare and short; the prepossessing polar guillemots, which continually caress each other; the egoist she-goose, who has repudiated the orphans of a killed comrade; and, by her side, another female who adopts any one's orphans, and now paddles surrounded by fifty or sixty youngsters, whom she conducts and cares for as if they all were her own breed. Side by side with the penguins, which steal one another's eggs, you have the dotterels, whose family relations are so "charming and touching" that even passionate hunters recoil from shooting a female surrounded by her young ones; or the eider-ducks, among which (like the velvet-ducks, or the coroyas of the Savannahs) several females hatch together in the same nest, or the lums, which sit in turn upon a common covey. Nature is variety itself, offering all possible varieties of characters, from the basest to the highest: and that is why she cannot be depicted by any sweeping assertion. Still less can she be judged from the moralist's point of view, because the views of the moralist are themselves a result—mostly unconscious—of the observation of Nature.

Coming together at nesting-time is so common with most birds that more examples are scarcely needed. Our trees are crowned with groups of crows' nests; our hedges are full of nests of smaller birds; our farmhouses give shelter to colonies of swallows; our old towers are the refuge of hundreds of nocturnal birds; and pages might be filled with the most charming descriptions of the peace and harmony which prevail in almost all these nesting associations. As to the protection derived by the weakest birds from their unions, it is evident. That excellent observer, Dr. Coues, saw, for instance, the little cliff-swallows nesting in the immediate neighbourhood of the prairie falcon (Falco polyargus). The falcon had its nest on the top of one of the minarets of clay which are so common in the canons of Colorado, while a colony of swallows nested just beneath. The little peaceful birds had no fear of their rapacious neighbour; they never let it approach to their colony. They immediately surrounded it and chased it, so that it had to make off at once.(4)

Life in societies does not cease when the nesting period is over; it begins then in a new form. The young broods gather in societies of youngsters, generally including several species. Social life is practised at that time chiefly for its own sake—partly for security, but chiefly for the pleasures derived from it. So we see in our forests the societies formed by the young nuthatchers (Sitta caesia), together with tit-mouses, chaffinches, wrens, tree-creepers, or some wood-peckers.(5) In Spain the swallow is met with in company with kestrels, fly-catchers, and even pigeons. In the Far West of America the young horned larks live in large societies, together with another lark (Sprague's), the skylark, the Savannah sparrow, and several species of buntings and longspurs.(6) In fact, it would be much easier to describe the species which live isolated than to simply name those species which join the autumnal societies of young birds—not for hunting or nesting purposes, but simply to enjoy life in society and to spend their time in plays and sports, after having given a few hours every day to find their daily food.

And, finally, we have that immense display of mutual aid

among birds-their migrations—which I dare not even enter upon in this place. Sufficient to say that birds which have lived for months in small bands scattered over a wide territory gather in thousands; they come together at a given place, for several days in succession, before they start, and they evidently discuss the particulars of the journey. Some species will indulge every afternoon in flights preparatory to the long passage. All wait for their tardy congeners, and finally they start in a certain well chosen direction—a fruit of accumulated collective experience—the strongest flying at the head of the band, and relieving one another in that difficult task. They cross the seas in large bands consisting of both big and small birds, and when they return next spring they repair to the same spot, and, in most cases, each of them takes possession of the very same nest which it had built or repaired the previous year.(7)

This subject is so vast, and yet so imperfectly studied; it offers so many striking illustrations of mutual-aid habits, subsidiary to the main fact of migration—each of which would, however, require a special study—that I must refrain from entering here into more details. I can only cursorily refer to the numerous and animated gatherings of birds which take place, always on the same spot, before they begin their long journeys north or south, as also those which one sees in the north, after the birds have arrived at their breeding-places on the Yenisei or in the northern counties of England. For many days in succession—sometimes one month—they will come together every morning for one hour, before flying in search of food—perhaps discussing the spot where they are going to build their nests.(8) And if, during the migration, their columns are overtaken by a storm, birds of the most different species will be brought together by common misfortune. The birds which are not exactly migratory, but slowly move northwards and southwards with the seasons, also perform these peregrinations in flocks. So far from migrating isolately, in order to secure for each separate individual the advantages of better food or shelter which are to be found in another district—they always wait for each other, and gather in flocks, before they move north or south, in accordance with the season.(9)

Going now over to mammals, the first thing which strikes us is the overwhelming numerical predominance of social species over those few carnivores which do not associate. The plateaus, the Alpine tracts, and the Steppes of the Old and New World are stocked with herds of deer, antelopes, gazelles, fallow deer, buffaloes, wild goats and sheep, all of which are sociable animals. When the Europeans came to settle in America, they found it so densely peopled with buffaloes, that pioneers had to stop their advance when a column of migrating buffaloes came to cross the route they followed; the march past of the dense column lasting sometimes for two and three days. And when the Russians took possession of Siberia they found it so densely peopled with deer, antelopes, squirrels, and other sociable animals, that the very conquest of Siberia was nothing but a hunting expedition which lasted for two hundred years; while the grass plains of Eastern Africa are still covered with herds composed of zebra, the hartebeest, and other antelopes.

Not long ago the small streams of Northern America and Northern Siberia were peopled with colonies of beavers, and up to the seventeenth century like colonies swarmed in Northern Russia. The flat lands of the four great continents are still covered with countless colonies of mice, ground-squirrels, marmots, and other rodents. In the lower latitudes of Asia and Africa the forests are still the abode of numerous families of elephants, rhinoceroses, and numberless societies of monkeys. In the far north the reindeer aggregate in numberless herds; while still further north we find the herds of the musk-oxen and numberless bands of polar foxes. The coasts of the ocean are enlivened by flocks of seals and morses; its waters, by shoals of sociable cetaceans; and even in the depths of the great plateau of Central Asia we find herds of wild horses, wild donkeys, wild camels, and wild sheep. All these mammals live in societies and nations sometimes numbering hundreds of thousands of individuals, although now, after three centuries of gunpowder civilization, we find but the debris of the immense aggregations of old. How trifling, in comparison with them, are the numbers of the carnivores! And how false, therefore, is the view of those who speak of the animal world as if nothing were to be seen in it but lions and hyenas plunging their bleeding teeth into the flesh of their victims! One might as well imagine that the whole of human life is nothing but a succession of war massacres.

Association and mutual aid are the rule with mammals. We find social habits even among the carnivores, and we can only name the cat tribe (lions, tigers, leopards, etc.) as a division the members of which decidedly prefer isolation to society, and are but seldom met with even in small groups. And yet, even among lions "this is a very common practice to hunt in company."(10) The two tribes of the civets (Viverridae) and the weasels (Mustelidae) might also be characterized by their isolated life, but it is a fact that during the last century the common weasel was more sociable than it is now; it was seen then in larger groups in Scotland and in the Unterwalden canton of Switzerland. As to the great tribe of the dogs, it is eminently sociable, and association for hunting purposes may be considered as eminently characteristic of its numerous species. It is well known, in fact, that wolves gather in packs for hunting, and Tschudi left an excellent description of how they draw up in a half-circle, surround a cow which is grazing on a mountain slope, and then, suddenly appearing with a loud barking, make it roll in the abyss.(11) Audubon, in the thirties, also saw the

Labrador wolves hunting in packs, and one pack following a man to his cabin, and killing the dogs. During severe winters the packs of wolves grow so numerous as to become a danger for human settlements, as was the case in France some five-and-forty years ago. In the Russian Steppes they never attack the horses otherwise than in packs; and yet they have to sustain bitter fights, during which the horses (according to Kohl's testimony) sometimes assume offensive warfare, and in such cases, if the wolves do not retreat promptly, they run the risk of being surrounded by the horses and killed by their hoofs. The prairie-wolves (Canis latrans) are known to associate in bands of from twenty to thirty individuals when they chase a buffalo occasionally separated from its herd.(12) Jackals, which are most courageous and may be considered as one of the most intelligent representatives of the dog tribe, always hunt in packs; thus united, they have no fear of the bigger carnivores.(13) As to the wild dogs of Asia (the Kholzuns, or Dholes), Williamson saw their large packs attacking all larger animals save elephants and rhinoceroses, and overpowering bears and tigers. Hyenas always live in societies and hunt in packs, and the hunting organizations of the painted lycaons are highly praised by Cumming. Nay, even foxes, which, as a rule, live isolated in our civilized countries, have been seen combining for hunting purposes.(14) As to the polar fox, it is—or rather was in Steller's time—one of the most sociable animals; and when one reads Steller's description of the war that was waged by Behring's unfortunate crew against these intelligent small animals, one does not know what to wonder at most: the extraordinary intelligence of the foxes and the mutual aid they displayed in digging out food concealed under cairns, or stored upon a pillar (one fox would climb on its top and throw the food to its comrades beneath), or the cruelty of man, driven to despair by the numerous packs of foxes. Even some bears live in societies where they are not disturbed by man. Thus Steller saw the black bear of Kamtchatka in numerous packs, and the polar bears are occasionally found in small groups. Even the unintelligent insectivores do not always disdain association.

However, it is especially with the rodents, the ungulata, and the ruminants that we find a highly developed practice of mutual aid. The squirrels are individualist to a great extent. Each of them builds its own comfortable nest, and accumulates its own provision. Their inclinations are towards family life, and Brehm found that a family of squirrels is never so happy as when the two broods of the same year can join together with their parents in a remote corner of a forest. And yet they maintain social relations. The inhabitants of the separate nests remain in a close intercourse, and when the pine-cones become rare in the forest they inhabit, they emigrate in bands. As to the black squirrels of the Far West, they are eminently sociable. Apart from the few hours given every day to foraging, they spend their lives in playing in numerous parties. And when they multiply too rapidly in a region, they assemble in bands, almost as numerous as those of locusts, and move southwards, devastating the forests, the fields, and the gardens; while foxes, polecats, falcons, and nocturnal birds of prey follow their thick columns and live upon the individuals remaining behind. The ground-squirrel—a closely-akin genus—is still more sociable. It is given to hoarding, and stores up in its subterranean halls large amounts of edible roots and nuts, usually plundered by man in the autumn. According to some observers, it must know something of the joys of a miser. And yet it remains sociable. It always lives in large villages, and Audubon, who opened some dwellings of the hackee in the winter, found several individuals in the same apartment; they must have stored it with common efforts.

The large tribe, of the marmots, which includes the three large genuses of Arctomys, Cynomys, and Spermophilus, is still more sociable and still more intelligent. They also prefer having each one its own dwelling; but they live in big villages. That terrible enemy of the crops of South Russia—the souslik—of which some ten millions are exterminated every year by man alone, lives in numberless colonies; and while the Russian provincial assemblies gravely discuss the means of getting rid of this enemy of society, it enjoys life in its thousands in the most joyful way. Their play is so charming that no observer could refrain from paying them a tribute of praise, and from mentioning the melodious concerts arising from the sharp whistlings of the males and the melancholic whistlings of the females, before—suddenly returning to his citizen's duties—he begins inventing the most diabolic means for the extermination of the little robbers. All kinds of rapacious birds and beasts of prey having proved powerless, the last word of science in this warfare is the inoculation of cholera! The villages of the prairie-dogs in America are one of the loveliest sights. As far as the eye can embrace the prairie, it sees heaps of earth, and on each of them a prairie-dog stands, engaged in a lively conversation with its neighbours by means of short barkings. As soon as the approach of man is signalled, all plunge in a moment into their dwellings; all have disappeared as by enchantment. But if the danger is over, the little creatures soon reappear. Whole families come out of their galleries and indulge in play. The young ones scratch one another, they worry one another, and display their gracefulness while standing upright, and in the meantime the old ones keep watch. They go visiting one another, and the beaten footpaths which connect all their heaps testify to the frequency of the visitations. In short, the best naturalists have written some of their best pages in describing the associations of the prairie-dogs of America, the marmots of the Old World, and the polar marmots of the Alpine regions. And yet, I must make, as regards the marmots, the same remark as I have made when speaking of the bees. They have maintained their fighting instincts, and these instincts reappear in captivity. But in their big associations, in the face of free Nature, the unsociable instincts have no opportunity to develop, and the general result is peace and harmony.

Even such harsh animals as the rats, which continually fight in our cellars, are sufficiently intelligent not to quarrel when they plunder our larders, but to aid one another in their plundering expeditions and migrations, and even to feed their invalids. As to the beaver-rats or musk-rats of Canada, they are extremely sociable. Audubon could not but admire "their peaceful communities, which require only being left in peace to enjoy happiness." Like all sociable animals, they are lively and playful, they easily combine with other species, and they have attained a very high degree of intellectual development. In their villages, always disposed on the shores of lakes and rivers, they take into account the changing level of water; their domeshaped houses, which are built of beaten clay interwoven with reeds, have separate corners for organic refuse, and their halls are well carpeted at winter time; they are warm, and, nevertheless, well ventilated. As to the beavers, which are endowed, as known, with a most sympathetic character, their astounding dams and villages, in which generations live and die without knowing of any enemies but the otter and man, so wonderfully illustrate what mutual aid can achieve for the security of the species, the development of social habits, and the evolution of intelligence, that they are familiar to all interested in animal life. Let me only remark that with the beavers, the muskrats, and some other rodents, we already find the feature which will also be distinctive of human communities—that is, work in common.

I pass in silence the two large families which include the jerboa, the chinchilla, the biscacha, and the tushkan, or underground hare of South Russia, though all these small rodents might be taken as excellent illustrations of the pleasures derived by animals from social life.(15) Precisely, the pleasures; because it is extremely difficult to say what brings animals together—the needs of mutual protection, or simply the pleasure of feeling surrounded by their congeners. At any rate, our common hares, which do not gather in societies for life in common, and which are not even endowed with intense parental feelings, cannot live without coming together for play. Dietrich de Winckell, who is considered to be among the best acquainted with the habits of hares, describes them as passionate players, becoming so intoxicated by their play that a hare has been known to take an approaching fox for a playmate.(16) As to the rabbit, it lives in societies, and its family life is entirely built upon the image of the old patriarchal family; the young ones being kept in absolute obedience to the father and even the grandfather.(17) And here we have the example of two very closely-allied species which cannot bear each other—not because they live upon nearly the same food, as like cases are too often explained, but most probably because the passionate, eminently-individualist hare cannot make friends with that placid, quiet, and submissive creature, the rabbit. Their tempers are too widely different not to be an obstacle to friendship.

Life in societies is again the rule with the large family of horses, which includes the wild horses and donkeys of Asia, the zebras, the mustangs, the cimarrones of the Pampas, and the half-wild horses of Mongolia and Siberia. They all live in numerous associations made up of many studs, each of which consists of a number of mares under the leadership of a male. These numberless inhabitants of the Old and the New World, badly organized on the whole for resisting both their numerous enemies and the adverse conditions of climate, would soon have disappeared from the surface of the earth were it not for their sociable spirit. When a beast of prey approaches them, several studs unite at once; they repulse the beast and sometimes chase it: and neither the wolf nor the bear, not even the lion, can capture a horse or even a zebra as long as they are not detached from the herd. When a drought is burning the grass in the prairies, they gather in herds of sometimes 10,000 individuals strong, and migrate. And when a snow-storm rages in the Steppes, each stud keeps close together, and repairs to a protected ravine. But if confidence disappears, or the group has been seized by panic, and disperses, the horses perish and the survivors are found after the storm half dying from fatigue. Union is their chief arm in the struggle for life, and man is their chief enemy. Before his increasing numbers the ancestors of our domestic horse (the Equus Przewalskii, so named by Polyakoff) have preferred to retire to the wildest and least accessible plateaus on the outskirts of Thibet, where they continue to live, surrounded by carnivores, under a climate as bad as that of the Arctic regions, but in a region inaccessible to man.(18)

Many striking illustrations of social life could be taken from the life of the reindeer, and especially of that large division of ruminants which might include the roebucks, the fallow deer, the antelopes, the gazelles, the ibex, and, in fact, the whole of the three numerous families of the Antelopides, the Caprides, and the Ovides. Their watchfulness over the safety of their herds against attacks of carnivores; the anxiety displayed by all individuals in a herd of chamois as long as all of them have not cleared a difficult passage over rocky cliffs, the adoption of orphans; the despair of the gazelle whose mate, or even comrade of the same sex, has been killed; the plays of the youngsters, and many other features, could be mentioned. But perhaps the most striking illustration of mutual support is given by the occasional migrations of fallow deer, such as I saw once on the Amur. When I crossed the high plateau and its border ridge, the Great Khingan, on my way from Transbaikalia to Merghen, and further travelled over the high prairies on my way to the Amur, I could ascertain how thinly-peopled with fallow deer these mostly uninhabited regions are.(19) Two years later I was travelling up the Amur, and by the end of October reached the lower end of that picturesque gorge which the Amur pierces in the Dousse-alin (Little Khingan) before it enters the lowlands where it joins the Sungari. I found the Cossacks in the villages of that gorge in the greatest excitement, because thousands and thousands of fallow deer were crossing the Amur where it is narrowest, in order to reach the lowlands. For several days in succession, upon a length of some forty miles up the river, the Cossacks were butchering the deer as they crossed the Amur, in which already floated a good deal of ice. Thousands were killed every day, and the exodus nevertheless continued. Like migrations were never seen either before or since, and this one must have been called for by an early and heavy snow-fall in the Great Khingan, which compelled the deer to make a desperate attempt at reaching the lowlands in the east of the Dousse mountains. Indeed, a few days later the Dousse-alin was also buried under snow two or three feet deep. Now, when one imagines the immense territory (almost as big as Great Britain) from which the scattered groups of deer must have gathered for a migration which was undertaken under the pressure of exceptional circumstances, and realizes the difficulties which had to be overcome before all the deer came to the common idea of crossing the Amur further south, where it is narrowest, one cannot but deeply admire the amount of sociability displayed by these intelligent animals. The fact is not the less striking if we remember that the buffaloes of North America displayed the same powers of combination. One saw them grazing in great numbers in the plains, but these numbers were made up by an infinity of small groups which never mixed together. And yet, when necessity arose, all groups, however scattered over an immense territory, came together and made up those immense columns, numbering hundreds of thousands of individuals, which I mentioned on a preceding page.

I also ought to say a few words at least about the "compound families" of the elephants, their mutual attachment, their deliberate ways in posting sentries, and the feelings of sympathy developed by such a life of close mutual support.(20) I might mention the sociable feelings of those disreputable creatures the wild boars, and find a word of praise for their powers of association in the case of an attack by a beast of prey.(21) The hippopotamus and the rhinoceros, too, would occupy a place in a work devoted to animal sociability. Several striking pages might be given to the sociability and mutual attachment of the seals and the walruses; and finally, one might mention the most excellent feelings existing among the sociable cetaceans. But I have to say yet a few words about the societies of monkeys, which acquire an additional interest from their being the link which will bring us to the societies of primitive men.

It is hardly needful to say that those mammals, which stand at the very top of the animal world and most approach man by their structure and intelligence, are eminently sociable. Evidently we must be prepared to meet with all varieties of character and habits in so great a division of the animal kingdom which includes hundreds of species. But, all things considered, it must be said that sociability, action in common, mutual protection, and a high development of those feelings which are the necessary outcome of social life, are characteristic of most monkeys and apes. From the smallest species to the biggest ones, sociability is a rule to which we know but a few exceptions. The nocturnal apes prefer isolated life; the capuchins (Cebus capucinus), the monos, and the howling monkeys live but in small families; and the orang-outans have never been seen by A.R. Wallace otherwise than either solitary or in very small groups of three or four individuals, while the gorillas seem never to join in bands. But all the remainder of the monkey tribe—the chimpanzees, the sajous, the sakis, the mandrills, the baboons, and so on—are sociable in the highest degree. They live in great bands, and even join with other species than their own. Most of them become quite unhappy when solitary. The cries of distress of each one of the band immediately bring together the whole of the band, and they boldly repulse the attacks of most carnivores and birds of prey. Even eagles do not dare attack them. They plunder our fields always in bands—the old ones taking care for the safety of the commonwealth. The little tee-tees, whose childish sweet faces so much struck Humboldt, embrace and protect one another when it rains, rolling their tails over the necks of their shivering comrades. Several species display the greatest solicitude for their wounded, and do not abandon a wounded comrade during a retreat till they have ascertained that it is dead and that they are helpless to restore it to life. Thus James Forbes narrated in his Oriental Memoirs a fact of such resistance in reclaiming from his hunting party the dead body of a female monkey that one fully understands why "the witnesses of this extraordinary scene resolved never again to fire at one of the monkey race."(22) In some species several individuals will combine to overturn a stone in order to search for ants' eggs under it. The hamadryas not only post sentries, but have been seen making a chain for the transmission of the spoil to a safe place; and their courage is well known. Brehm's description of the regular fight which his caravan had to sustain before the hamadryas would let it resume its journey in the valley of the Mensa, in Abyssinia, has become classical.(23) The playfulness of the tailed apes and the mutual attachment which reigns in the families of chimpanzees also are familiar to the general reader. And if we find among the highest apes two species, the orang-outan and the gorilla, which are not sociable, we must remember that both—limited as they are to very small areas, the one in the heart of Africa, and the other in the two islands of Borneo and Sumatra have all the appearance of being the last remnants of formerly much more numerous species. The gorilla at least seems to have been sociable in olden times, if the apes mentioned in the Periplus really were gorillas.

We thus see, even from the above brief review, that life in societies is no exception in the animal world; it is the rule, the law of Nature, and it reaches its fullest development with the higher vertebrates. Those species which live solitary, or in small families only, are relatively few, and their numbers are limited. Nay, it appears very probable that, apart from a few exceptions, those birds and mammals which are not gregarious now, were living in societies before man multiplied on the earth and waged a permanent war against them, or destroyed the sources from which they formerly derived food. "On ne s'associe pas pour mourir," was the sound remark of Espinas; and Houzeau, who knew the animal world of some parts of America when it was not yet affected by man, wrote to the same effect.

Association is found in the animal world at all degrees of evolution; and, according to the grand idea of Herbert Spencer, so brilliantly developed in Perrier's Colonies Animales, colonies are at the very origin of evolution in the animal kingdom. But, in proportion as we ascend the scale of evolution, we see association growing more and more conscious. It loses its purely physical character, it ceases to be simply instinctive, it becomes reasoned. With the higher vertebrates it is periodical, or is resorted to for the satisfaction of a given want—propagation of the species, migration, hunting, or mutual defence. It even becomes occasional, when birds associate against a robber, or mammals combine, under the pressure of exceptional circumstances, to emigrate. In this last case, it becomes a voluntary deviation from habitual moods of life. The combination sometimes appears in two or more degrees—the family first, then the group, and finally the association of groups, habitually scattered, but uniting in case of need, as we saw it with the bisons and other ruminants. It also takes higher forms, guaranteeing more independence to the individual without depriving it of the benefits of social life. With most rodents the individual has its own dwelling, which it can retire to when it prefers being left alone; but the dwellings are laid out in villages and cities, so as to guarantee to all inhabitants the benefits and joys of social life. And finally, in several species, such as rats, marmots, hares, etc., sociable life is maintained notwithstanding the quarrelsome or otherwise egotistic inclinations of the isolated individual. Thus it is not imposed, as is the case with ants and bees, by the very physiological structure of the individuals; it is cultivated for the benefits of mutual aid, or for the sake of its pleasures. And this, of course, appears with all possible gradations and with the greatest variety of individual and specific characters—the very variety of aspects taken by social life being a consequence, and for us a further proof, of its generality.(24)

Sociability—that is, the need of the animal of associating with its like—the love of society for society's sake, combined with the "joy of life," only now begins to receive due attention from the zoologists.(25) We know at the present time that all animals, beginning with the ants, going on to the birds, and ending with the highest mammals, are fond of plays, wrestling, running after each other, trying to capture each other, teasing each other, and so on. And while many plays are, so to speak, a school for the proper behaviour of the young in mature life, there are others, which, apart from their utilitarian purposes, are, together with dancing and singing, mere manifestations of an excess of forces—"the joy of life," and a desire to communicate in some way or another with other individuals of the same or of other species—in short, a manifestation of sociability proper, which is a distinctive feature of all the animal world.(26) Whether the feeling be fear, experienced at the appearance of a bird of prey, or "a fit of gladness" which bursts out when the animals are in good health and especially when young, or merely the desire of giving play to an excess of impressions and of vital power—the necessity of communicating impressions, of playing, of chattering, or of simply feeling the proximity of other kindred living beings pervades Nature, and is, as much as any other physiological function, a distinctive feature of life and impressionability. This need takes a higher development and attains a more beautiful expression in mammals, especially amidst their young, and still more among the birds; but it pervades all Nature, and has been fully observed by the best naturalists, including Pierre Huber, even amongst the ants, and it is evidently the same instinct which brings together the big columns of butterflies which have been referred to already.

The habit of coming together for dancing and of decorating the places where the birds habitually perform their dances is, of course, well known from the pages that Darwin gave to this subject in The Descent of Man (ch. xiii). Visitors of the London Zoological Gardens also know the bower of the satin bower-bird. But this habit of dancing seems to be much more widely spread than was formerly believed, and Mr. W. Hudson gives in his master-work on La Plata the most interesting description, which must be read in the original, of complicated dances, performed by quite a number of birds: rails, jacanas, lapwings, and so on.

The habit of singing in concert, which exists in several species of birds, belongs to the same category of social instincts. It is most strikingly developed with the chakar (Chauna chavarris), to which the English have given the most unimaginative misnomer of "crested screamer." These birds sometimes assemble in immense flocks, and in such cases they frequently sing all in concert. W.H. Hudson found them once in countless numbers, ranged all round a pampas lake in well-defined flocks, of about 500 birds in each flock.

"Presently," he writes, "one flock near me began singing, and continued their powerful chant for three or four minutes; when they ceased the next flock took up the strains, and after it the next, and so on, until once more the notes of the flocks on the opposite shore came floating strong and clear across the water—then passed away, growing fainter and fainter, until once more the sound approached me travelling round to my side again."

On another occasion the same writer saw a whole plain covered with an endless flock of chakars, not in close order, but scattered in pairs and small groups. About nine o'clock in the evening, "suddenly the entire multitude of birds covering the marsh for miles around burst forth in a tremendous evening song.... It was a concert well worth riding a hundred miles to hear."(27) It may be added that like all sociable animals, the chakar easily becomes tame and grows very attached to man. "They are mild-tempered birds, and very rarely quarrel"—we are told—although they are well provided with formidable weapons. Life in societies renders these weapons useless.

That life in societies is the most powerful weapon in the struggle for life, taken in its widest sense, has been illustrated by several examples on the foregoing pages, and could be illustrated by any amount of evidence, if further evidence were required. Life in societies enables the feeblest insects, the feeblest birds, and the feeblest mammals to resist, or to protect themselves from, the most terrible birds and beasts of prey; it permits longevity; it enables the species to rear its progeny with the least waste of energy and to maintain its numbers albeit a very slow birth-rate; it enables the gregarious animals to migrate in search of new abodes. Therefore, while fully admitting that force, swiftness, protective colours, cunningness, and endurance to hunger and cold, which are mentioned by Darwin and Wallace, are so many qualities making the individual, or the species, the fittest under certain circumstances, we maintain that under any circumstances sociability is the greatest advantage in the struggle for life. Those species which willingly or unwillingly abandon it are doomed to decay; while those animals which know best how to combine, have the greatest chances of survival and of further evolution, although they may be inferior to others in each of the faculties enumerated by Darwin and Wallace, save the intellectual faculty. The highest vertebrates, and especially mankind, are the best proof of this assertion. As to the intellectual faculty, while every Darwinist will agree with Darwin that it is the most powerful arm in the struggle for life, and the most powerful factor of further evolution, he also will admit that intelligence is an eminently social faculty. Language, imitation, and accumulated experience are so many elements of growing intelligence of which the unsociable animal is deprived. Therefore we find, at the top of each class of animals, the ants, the parrots, and the monkeys, all combining the greatest sociability with the highest development of intelligence. The fittest are thus the most sociable animals, and sociability appears as the chief factor of evolution, both directly, by securing the well-being of the species while diminishing the waste of energy, and indirectly, by favouring the growth of intelligence.

Moreover, it is evident that life in societies would be utterly impossible without a corresponding development of social feelings, and, especially, of a certain collective sense of justice growing to become a habit. If every individual were constantly abusing its personal advantages without the others interfering in favour of the wronged, no society—life would be possible. And feelings of justice develop, more or less, with all gregarious animals. Whatever the distance from which the swallows or the cranes come, each one returns to the nest it has built or repaired last year. If a lazy sparrow intends appropriating the nest which a comrade is building, or even steals from it a few sprays of straw, the group interferes against the lazy comrade; and it is evident that without such interference being the rule, no nesting associations of birds could exist. Separate groups of penguins have separate resting-places and separate fishing abodes, and do not fight for them. The droves of cattle in Australia have particular spots to which each group repairs to rest, and from which it never deviates; and so on.(28) We have any numbers of direct observations of the peace that prevails in the nesting associations of birds, the villages of the rodents, and the herds of grass-eaters; while, on the other side, we know of few sociable animals which so continually quarrel as the rats in our cellars do, or as the morses, which fight for the possession of a sunny place on the shore. Sociability thus puts a limit to physical struggle, and leaves room for the development of better moral feelings. The high development of parental love in all classes of animals, even with lions and tigers, is generally known. As to the young birds and mammals whom we continually see associating, sympathy—not love—attains a further development in their associations. Leaving aside the really touching facts of mutual attachment and compassion which have been recorded as regards domesticated animals and with animals kept in captivity, we have a number of well certified facts of compassion between wild animals at liberty. Max Perty and L. Buchner have given a number of such facts.(29) J.C. Wood's narrative of a weasel which came to pick up and to carry away an injured comrade enjoys a well-merited popularity.(30) So also the observation of Captain Stansbury on his journey to Utah which is quoted by Darwin; he saw a blind pelican which was fed, and well fed, by other pelicans upon fishes which had to be brought from a distance of thirty miles.(31) And when a herd of vicunas was hotly pursued by hunters, H.A. Weddell saw more than once during his journey to Bolivia and Peru, the strong males covering the retreat of the herd and lagging behind in order to protect the retreat. As to facts of compassion with wounded comrades, they are continually mentioned by all field zoologists. Such facts are quite natural. Compassion is a necessary outcome of social life. But compassion also means a considerable advance in general intelligence and sensibility. It is the first step towards the development of higher moral sentiments. It is, in its turn, a powerful factor of further evolution.

If the views developed on the preceding pages are correct, the question necessarily arises, in how far are they consistent with the theory of struggle for life as it has been developed by Darwin, Wallace, and their followers? and I will now briefly answer this important question. First of all, no naturalist will doubt that the idea of a struggle for life carried on through organic nature is the greatest generalization of our century. Life is struggle; and in that struggle the fittest survive. But the answers to the questions, "By which arms is this struggle chiefly carried on?" and "Who are the fittest in the struggle?" will widely differ according to the importance given to the two different aspects of the struggle: the direct one, for food and safety among separate individuals, and the struggle which Darwin described as "metaphorical"—the struggle, very often collective, against adverse circumstances. No one will deny that there is, within each species, a certain amount of real competition for food—at least, at certain periods. But the question is, whether competition is carried on to the extent admitted by Darwin, or even by Wallace; and whether this competition has played, in the evolution of the animal kingdom, the part assigned to it.

The idea which permeates Darwin's work is certainly one of real competition going on within each animal group for food, safety, and possibility of leaving an offspring. He often speaks of regions being stocked with animal life to their full capacity, and from that overstocking he infers the necessity of competition. But when we look in his work for real proofs of that competition, we must confess that we do not find them sufficiently convincing. If we refer to the paragraph entitled "Struggle for Life most severe between Individuals and Varieties of the same Species," we find in it none of that wealth of proofs and illustrations which we are accustomed to find in whatever Darwin wrote. The struggle between individuals of the same species is not illustrated under that heading by even one single instance: it is taken as granted; and the competition between closely-allied animal species is illustrated by but five examples, out of which one, at least (relating to the two species of thrushes), now proves to be doubtful.(32) But when we look for more details in order to ascertain how far the decrease of one species was really occasioned by the increase of the other species, Darwin, with his usual fairness, tells us:

"We can dimly see why the competition should be most severe between allied forms which fill nearly the same place in nature; but probably in no case could we precisely say why one species has been victorious over another in the great battle of life."

As to Wallace, who quotes the same facts under a slightly-modified heading ("Struggle for Life between closely-allied Animals and Plants often most severe"), he makes the following remark (italics are mine), which gives quite another aspect to the facts above quoted. He says:

"In some cases, no doubt, there is actual war between the two, the stronger killing the weaker. But this is by no means necessary, and there may be cases in which the weaker species, physically, may prevail by its power of more rapid multiplication, its better withstanding vicissitudes of climate, or its greater cunning in escaping the attacks of common enemies."

In such cases what is described as competition may be no competition at all. One species succumbs, not because it is exterminated or starved out by the other species, but because it does not well accommodate itself to new conditions, which the other does. The term "struggle for life" is again used in its metaphorical sense, and may have no other. As to the real competition between individuals of the same species, which is illustrated in another place by the cattle of South America during a period of drought, its value is impaired by its being taken from among domesticated animals. Bisons emigrate in like circumstances in order to avoid competition. However severe the struggle between plants—and this is amply proved—we cannot but repeat Wallace's remark to the effect that "plants live where they can," while animals have, to a great extent, the power of choice of their abode. So that we again are asking ourselves, To what extent does competition really exist within each animal species? Upon what is the assumption based? The same remark must be made concerning the indirect argument in favour of a severe competition and struggle for life within each species, which may be derived from the "extermination of transitional varieties," so often mentioned by Darwin. It is known that for a long time Darwin was worried by the difficulty which he saw in the absence of a long chain of intermediate forms between closely-allied species, and that he found the solution of this difficulty in the supposed extermination of the intermediate forms.(33) However, an attentive reading of the different chapters in which Darwin and Wallace speak of this subject soon brings one to the conclusion that the word "extermination" does not mean real extermination; the same remark which Darwin made concerning his expression: "struggle for existence," evidently applies to the word "extermination" as well. It can by no means be understood in its direct sense, but must be taken "in its metaphoric sense." If we start from the supposition that a given area is stocked with animals to its fullest capacity, and that a keen competition for the sheer means of existence is consequently going on between all the inhabitants—each animal being compelled to fight against all its congeners in order to get its daily food—then the appearance of a new and successful variety would certainly mean in many cases (though not always) the appearance of individuals which are enabled to seize more than their fair share of the means of existence; and the result would be that those individuals would starve both the parental form which does not possess the new variation and the intermediate forms which do not possess it in the same degree. It may be that at the outset, Darwin understood the appearance of new varieties under this aspect; at least, the frequent use of the word "extermination" conveys such an impression. But both he and Wallace knew Nature too well not to perceive that this is by no means the only possible and necessary course of affairs.

If the physical and the biological conditions of a given area, the extension of the area occupied by a given species, and the habits of all the members of the latter remained unchanged—then the sudden appearance of a new variety might mean the starving out and the extermination of all the individuals which were not endowed in a sufficient degree with the new feature by which the new variety is characterized. But such a combination of conditions is precisely what we do not see in Nature. Each species is continually tending to enlarge its abode; migration to new abodes is the rule with the slow snail, as with the swift bird; physical changes are continually going on in every given area; and new varieties among animals consist in an immense number of cases-perhaps in the majority—not in the growth of new weapons for snatching the food from the mouth of its congeners—food is only one out of a hundred of various conditions of existence—but, as Wallace himself shows in a charming paragraph on the "divergence of characters" (Darwinism, p. 107), in forming new habits, moving to new abodes, and taking to new sorts of food. In all such cases there will be no extermination, even no competition—the new adaptation being a relief from competition, if it ever existed; and yet there will be, after a time, an absence of intermediate links, in consequence of a mere survival of those which are best fitted for the new conditions—as surely as under the hypothesis of extermination of the parental form. It hardly need be added that if we admit, with Spencer, all the Lamarckians, and Darwin himself, the modifying influence of the surroundings upon the species, there remains still less necessity for the extermination of the intermediate forms.

The importance of migration and of the consequent isolation of groups of animals, for the origin of new varieties and ultimately of new species, which was indicated by Moritz Wagner, was fully recognized by Darwin himself. Consequent researches have only accentuated the importance of this factor, and they have shown how the largeness of the area occupied by a given species—which Darwin considered with full reason so important for the appearance of new varieties—can be combined with the isolation of parts of the species, in consequence of local geological changes, or of local barriers. It would be impossible to enter here into the discussion of this wide question, but a few remarks will do to illustrate the combined action of these agencies. It is known that portions of a given species will often take to a new sort of food. The squirrels, for instance, when there is a scarcity of cones in the larch forests, remove to the fir-tree forests, and this change of food has certain well-known physiological effects on the squirrels. If this change of habits does not last—if next year the cones are again plentiful in the dark larch woods—no new variety of squirrels will evidently arise from this cause. But if part of the wide area occupied by the squirrels begins to have its physical characters altered—in consequence of, let us say, a milder climate or desiccation, which both bring about an increase of the pine forests in proportion to the larch woods—and if some other conditions concur to induce the squirrels to dwell on the outskirts of the desiccating region—we shall have then a new variety, i.e. an incipient new species of squirrels, without there having been anything that would deserve the name of extermination among the squirrels. A larger proportion of squirrels of the new, better adapted variety would survive every year, and the intermediate links would die in the course of time, without having been starved out by Malthusian competitors. This is exactly what we see going on during the great physical changes which are accomplished over large areas in Central Asia, owing to the desiccation which is going on there since the glacial period.

To take another example, it has been proved by geologists that the present wild horse (Equus Przewalski) has slowly been evolved during the later parts of the Tertiary and the Quaternary period, but that during this succession of ages its ancestors were not confined to some given, limited area of the globe. They wandered over both the Old and New World, returning, in all probability, after a time to the pastures which they had, in the course of their migrations, formerly left.(34) Consequently, if we do not find now, in Asia, all the intermediate links between the present wild horse and its Asiatic Post-Tertiary ancestors, this does not mean at all that the intermediate links have been exterminated. No such extermination has ever taken place. No exceptional mortality may even have occurred among the ancestral species: the individuals which belonged to intermediate varieties and species have died in the usual course of events—often amidst plentiful food, and their remains were buried all over the globe.

In short, if we carefully consider this matter, and, carefully re-read what Darwin himself wrote upon this subject, we see that if the word "extermination" be used at all in connection with transitional varieties, it must be used in its metaphoric sense. As to "competition," this expression, too, is continually used by Darwin (see, for instance, the paragraph "On Extinction") as an image, or as a way-of-speaking, rather than with the intention of conveying the idea of a real competition between two portions of the same species for the means of existence. At any rate, the absence of intermediate forms is no argument in favour of it.

In reality, the chief argument in favour of a keen competition for the means of existence continually going on within every animal species is—to use Professor Geddes' expression—the "arithmetical argument" borrowed from Malthus.

But this argument does not prove it at all. We might as well take a number of villages in South-East Russia, the inhabitants of which enjoy plenty of food, but have no sanitary accommodation of any kind; and seeing that for the last eighty years the birth-rate was sixty in the thousand, while the population is now what it was eighty years ago, we might conclude that there has been a terrible competition between the inhabitants. But the truth is that from year to year the population remained stationary, for the simple reason that one-third of the new-born died before reaching their sixth month of life; one-half died within the next four years, and out of each hundred born, only seventeen or so reached the age of twenty. The new-comers went away before having grown to be competitors. It is evident that if such is the case with men, it is still more the case with animals. In the feathered world the destruction of the eggs goes on on such a tremendous scale that eggs are the chief food of several species in the early summer; not to, say a word of the storms, the inundations which destroy nests by the million in America, and the sudden changes of weather which are fatal to the young mammals. Each storm, each inundation, each visit of a rat to a bird's nest, each sudden change of temperature, take away those competitors which appear so terrible in theory.

As to the facts of an extremely rapid increase of horses and cattle in America, of pigs and rabbits in New Zealand, and even of wild animals imported from Europe (where their numbers are kept down by man, not by competition), they rather seem opposed to the theory of over-population. If horses and cattle could so rapidly multiply in America, it simply proved that, however numberless the buffaloes and other ruminants were at that time in the New World, its grass-eating population was far below what the prairies could maintain. If millions of intruders have found plenty of food without starving out the former population of the prairies, we must rather conclude that the Europeans found a want of grass-eaters in America, not an excess. And we have good reasons to believe that want of animal population is the natural state of things all over the world, with but a few temporary exceptions to the rule. The actual numbers of animals in a given region are determined, not by the highest feeding capacity of the region, but by what it is every year under the most unfavourable conditions. So that, for that reason alone, competition hardly can be a normal condition. But other causes intervene as well to cut, down the animal population below even that low standard. If we take the horses and cattle which are grazing all the winter through in the Steppes of Transbaikalia, we find them very lean and exhausted at the end of the winter. But they grow exhausted not because there is not enough food for all of them—the grass buried under a thin sheet of snow is everywhere in abundance—but because of the difficulty of getting it from beneath the snow, and this difficulty is the same for all horses alike. Besides, days of glazed frost are common in early spring, and if several such days come in succession the horses grow still more exhausted. But then comes a snow-storm, which compels the already weakened animals to remain without any food for several days, and very great numbers of them die. The losses during the spring are so severe that if the season has been more inclement than usual they are even not repaired by the new breeds—the more so as all horses are exhausted, and the young foals are born in a weaker condition. The numbers of horses and cattle thus always remain beneath what they otherwise might be; all the year round there is food for five or ten times as many animals, and yet their population increases extremely slowly. But as soon as the Buriate owner makes ever so small a provision of hay in the steppe, and throws it open during days of glazed frost, or heavier snow-fall, he immediately sees the increase of his herd. Almost all free grass-eating animals and many rodents in Asia and America being in very much the same conditions, we can safely say that their numbers are not kept down by competition; that at no time of the year they can struggle for food, and that if they never reach anything approaching to over-population, the cause is in the climate, not in competition.

The importance of natural checks to over-multiplication, and especially their bearing upon the competition hypothesis, seems never to have been taken into due account. The checks, or rather some of them, are mentioned, but their action is seldom studied in detail. However, if we compare the action of the natural checks with that of competition, we must recognize at once that the latter sustains no comparison whatever with the other checks. Thus, Mr. Bates mentions the really astounding numbers of winged ants which are destroyed during their exodus. The dead or half-dead bodies of the formica de fuego (Myrmica saevissima) which had been blown into the river during a gale "were heaped in a line an inch or two in height and breadth, the line continuing without interruption for miles at the edge of the water."(35) Myriads of ants are thus destroyed amidst a nature which might support a hundred times as many ants as are actually living. Dr. Altum, a German forester, who wrote a very interesting book about animals injurious to our forests, also gives many facts showing the immense importance of natural checks. He says, that a succession of gales or cold and damp weather during the exodus of the pine-moth (Bombyx pini) destroy it to incredible amounts, and during the spring of 1871 all these moths disappeared at once, probably killed by a succession of cold nights.(36) Many like examples relative to various insects could be quoted from various parts of Europe. Dr. Altum also mentions the bird-enemies of the pine-moth, and the immense amount of its eggs destroyed by foxes; but he adds that the parasitic fungi which periodically infest it are a far more terrible enemy than any bird, because they destroy the moth over very large areas at once. As to various species of mice (Mus sylvaticus, Arvicola arvalis, and A. agrestis), the same author gives a long list of their enemies, but he remarks: "However, the most terrible enemies of mice are not other animals, but such sudden changes of weather as occur almost every year." Alternations of frost and warm weather destroy them in numberless quantities; "one single sudden change can reduce thousands of mice to the number of a few individuals." On the other side, a warm winter, or a winter which gradually steps in, make them multiply in menacing proportions, notwithstanding every enemy; such was the case in 1876 and 1877.(37) Competition, in the case of mice, thus appears a quite trifling factor when compared with weather. Other facts to the same effect are also given as regards squirrels.

As to birds, it is well known how they suffer from sudden changes of weather. Late snow-storms are as destructive of bird-life on the English moors, as they are in Siberia; and Ch. Dixon saw the red grouse so pressed during some exceptionally severe winters, that they quitted the moors in numbers, "and we have then known them actually to be taken in the streets of Sheffield. Persistent wet," he adds, "is almost as fatal to them."

On the other side, the contagious diseases which continually visit most animal species destroy them in such numbers that the losses often cannot be repaired for many years, even with the most rapidly-multiplying animals. Thus, some sixty years ago, the sousliks suddenly disappeared in the neighbourhood of Sarepta, in South-Eastern Russia, in consequence of some epidemics; and for years no sousliks were seen in that neighbourhood. It took many years before they became as numerous as they formerly were.(38)

Like facts, all tending to reduce the importance given to competition, could be produced in numbers. Of course, it might be replied, in Darwin's words, that nevertheless each organic being "at some period of its life, during some season of the year, during each generation or at intervals, has to struggle for life and to suffer great destruction," and that the fittest survive during such periods of hard struggle for life. But if the evolution of the animal world were based exclusively, or even chiefly, upon the survival of the fittest during periods of calamities; if natural selection were limited in its action to periods of exceptional drought, or sudden changes of temperature, or inundations, retrogression would be the rule in the animal world. Those who survive a famine, or a severe epidemic of cholera, or small-pox, or diphtheria, such as we see them in uncivilized countries, are neither the strongest, nor the healthiest, nor the most intelligent. No progress could be based on those survivals—the less so as all survivors usually come out of the ordeal with an impaired health, like the Transbaikalian horses just mentioned, or the Arctic crews, or the garrison of a fortress which has been compelled to live for a few months on half rations, and comes out of its experience with a broken health, and subsequently shows a quite abnormal mortality. All that natural selection can do in times of calamities is to spare the individuals endowed with the greatest endurance for privations of all kinds. So it does among the Siberian horses and cattle. They are enduring; they can feed upon the Polar birch in case of need; they resist cold and hunger. But no Siberian horse is capable of carrying half the weight which a European horse carries with ease; no Siberian cow gives half the amount of milk given by a Jersey cow, and no natives of uncivilized countries can bear a comparison with Europeans. They may better endure hunger and cold, but their physical force is very far below that of a well-fed European, and their intellectual progress is despairingly slow. "Evil cannot be productive of good," as Tchernyshevsky wrote in a remarkable essay upon Darwinism.(39)

Happily enough, competition is not the rule either in the animal world or in mankind. It is limited among animals to exceptional periods, and natural selection finds better fields for its activity. Better conditions are created by the elimination of competition by means of mutual aid and mutual Support.(40) In the great struggle for life—for the greatest possible fulness and intensity of life with the least waste of energy—natural selection continually seeks out the ways precisely for avoiding competition as much as possible. The ants combine in nests and nations; they pile up their stores, they rear their cattle—and thus avoid competition; and natural selection picks out of the ants' family the species which know best how to avoid competition, with its unavoidably deleterious consequences. Most of our birds slowly move southwards as the winter comes, or gather in numberless societies and undertake long journeys—and thus avoid competition. Many rodents fall asleep when the time comes that competition should set in; while other rodents store food for the winter, and gather in large villages for obtaining the necessary protection when at work. The reindeer, when the lichens are dry in the interior of the continent, migrate towards the sea. Buffaloes cross an immense continent in order to find plenty of food. And the beavers, when they grow numerous on a river, divide into two parties, and go, the old ones down the river, and the young ones up the river and avoid competition. And when animals can neither fall asleep, nor migrate, nor lay in stores, nor themselves grow their food like the ants, they do what the titmouse does, and what Wallace (Darwinism, ch. v) has so charmingly described: they resort to new kinds of food—and thus, again, avoid competition.

"Don't compete!—competition is always injurious to the species, and you have plenty of resources to avoid it!" That is the tendency of nature, not always realized in full, but always present. That is the watchword which comes to us from the bush, the forest, the river, the ocean. "Therefore combine—practise mutual aid! That is the surest means for giving to each and to all the greatest safety, the best guarantee of existence and progress, bodily, intellectual, and moral." That is what Nature teaches us; and that is what all those animals which have attained the highest position in their respective classes have done. That is also what man—the most primitive man—has been doing; and that is why man has reached the position upon which we stand now, as we shall see in the subsequent chapters devoted to mutual aid in human societies.

NOTES:

1. Syevettsoff's Periodical Phenomena, p. 251.

2. Seyfferlitz, quoted by Brehm, iv. 760.

3. The Arctic Voyages of A.E. Nordenskjold, London, 1879, p. 135. See also the powerful description of the St. Kilda islands by Mr. Dixon (quoted by Seebohm), and nearly all books of Arctic travel.

4. Elliot Coues, in Bulletin U.S. Geol. Survey of Territories, iv. No. 7, pp. 556, 579, etc. Among the gulls (Larus argentatus), Polyakoff saw on a marsh in Northern Russia, that the nesting grounds of a very great number of these birds were always patrolled by one male, which warned the colony of the approach of danger. All birds rose in such case and attacked the enemy with great vigour. The females, which had five or six nests together on each knoll of the marsh, kept a certain order in leaving their nests in search of food. The fledglings, which otherwise are extremely unprotected and easily become the prey of the rapacious birds, were never left alone ("Family Habits among the Aquatic Birds," in Proceedings of the Zool. Section of St. Petersburg Soc. of Nat., Dec. 17, 1874).

5. Brehm Father, quoted by A. Brehm, iv. 34 seq. See also White's Natural History of Selborne, Letter XI.

6. Dr. Coues, Birds of Dakota and Montana, in Bulletin U.S. Survey of Territories, iv. No. 7.

7. It has often been intimated that larger birds may occasionally transport some of the smaller birds when they cross together the Mediterranean, but the fact still remains doubtful. On the other side, it is certain that some smaller birds join the bigger ones for

migration. The fact has been noticed several times, and it was recently confirmed by L. Buxbaum at Raunheim. He saw several parties of cranes which had larks flying in the midst and on both sides of their migratory columns (Der zoologische Garten, 1886, p. 133).

8. H. Seebohm and Ch. Dixon both mention this habit.

9. The fact is well known to every field-naturalist, and with reference to England several examples may be found in Charles Dixon's Among the Birds in Northern Shires. The chaffinches arrive during winter in vast flocks; and about the same time, i.e. in November, come flocks of bramblings; redwings also frequent the same places "in similar large companies," and so on (pp. 165, 166).

10. S.W. Baker, Wild Beasts, etc., vol. i. p. 316.

11. Tschudi, Thierleben der Alpenwelt, p. 404.

12. Houzeau's Etudes, ii. 463.

13. For their hunting associations see Sir E. Tennant's Natural History of Ceylon, quoted in Romanes's Animal Intelligence, p. 432.

14. See Emil Huter's letter in L. Buchner's Liebe.

15. With regard to the viscacha it is very interesting to note that these highly-sociable little animals not only live peaceably together in each village, but that whole villages visit each other at nights. Sociability is thus extended to the whole species—not only to a given society, or to a nation, as we saw it with the ants. When the farmer destroys a viscacha-burrow, and buries the inhabitants under a heap of earth, other viscachas—we are told

by Hudson—"come from a distance to dig out those that are buried alive" (l.c., p. 311). This is a widely-known fact in La Plata, verified by the author.

16. Handbuch für Jäger und Jagdberechtigte, quoted by Brehm, ii. 223.

17. Buffon's Histoire Naturelle.

18. In connection with the horses it is worthy of notice that the quagga zebra, which never comes together with the dauw zebra, nevertheless lives on excellent terms, not only with ostriches, which are very good sentries, but also with gazelles, several species of antelopes, and gnus. We thus have a case of mutual dislike between the quagga and the dauw which cannot be explained by competition for food. The fact that the quagga lives together with ruminants feeding on the same grass as itself excludes that hypothesis, and we must look for some incompatibility of character, as in the case of the hare and the rabbit. Cf., among others, Clive Phillips-Wolley's Big Game Shooting (Badminton Library), which contains excellent illustrations of various species living together in East Africa.

19. Our Tungus hunter, who was going to marry, and therefore was prompted by the desire of getting as many furs as he possibly could, was beating the hill-sides all day long on horseback in search of deer. His efforts were not rewarded by even so much as one fallow deer killed every day; and he was an excellent hunter.

20. According to Samuel W. Baker, elephants combine in larger groups than the "compound family." "I have frequently observed," he wrote, "in the portion of Ceylon known as the Park Country, the tracks of elephants in great numbers which

have evidently been considerable herds that have joined together in a general retreat from a ground which they considered insecure" (Wild Beasts and their Ways, vol. i. p. 102).

21. Pigs, attacked by wolves, do the same (Hudson, l.c.).

22. Romanes's Animal Intelligence, p. 472.

23. Brehm, i. 82; Darwin's Descent of Man, ch. iii. The Kozloff expedition of 1899-1901 have also had to sustain in Northern Thibet a similar fight.

24. The more strange was it to read in the previously-mentioned article by Huxley the following paraphrase of a well-known sentence of Rousseau: "The first men who substituted mutual peace for that of mutual war—whatever the motive which impelled them to take that step—created society" (Nineteenth Century, Feb. 1888, p. 165). Society has not been created by man; it is anterior to man.

25. Such monographs as the chapter on "Music and Dancing in Nature" which we have in Hudson's Naturalist on the La Plata, and Carl Gross' Play of Animals, have already thrown a considerable light upon an instinct which is absolutely universal in Nature.

26. Not only numerous species of birds possess the habit of assembling together—in many cases always at the same spot—to indulge in antics and dancing performances, but W.H. Hudson's experience is that nearly all mammals and birds ("probably there are really no exceptions") indulge frequently in more or less regular or set performances with or without sound, or composed of sound exclusively (p. 264).

27. For the choruses of monkeys, see Brehm.

28. Haygarth, Bush Life in Australia, p. 58.

29. To quote but a few instances, a wounded badger was carried away by another badger suddenly appearing on the scene; rats have been seen feeding a blind couple (Seelenleben der Thiere, p. 64 seq.). Brehm himself saw two crows feeding in a hollow tree a third crow which was wounded; its wound was several weeks old (Hausfreund, 1874, 715; Buchner's Liebe, 203). Mr. Blyth saw Indian crows feeding two or three blind comrades; and so on.

30. Man and Beast, p. 344.

31. L.H. Morgan, The American Beaver, 1868, p. 272; Descent of Man, ch. iv.

32. One species of swallow is said to have caused the decrease of another swallow species in North America; the recent increase of the missel-thrush in Scotland has caused the decrease of the song-thrush; the brown rat has taken the place of the black rat in Europe; in Russia the small cockroach has everywhere driven before it its greater congener; and in Australia the imported hive-bee is rapidly exterminating the small stingless bee. Two other cases, but relative to domesticated animals, are mentioned in the preceding paragraph. While recalling these same facts, A.R. Wallace remarks in a footnote relative to the Scottish thrushes: "Prof. A. Newton, however, informs me that these species do not interfere in the way here stated" (Darwinism, p. 34). As to the brown rat, it is known that, owing to its amphibian habits, it usually stays in the lower parts of human dwellings (low cellars, sewers, etc.), as also on the banks of canals and rivers; it also undertakes distant migrations in numberless bands. The black rat, on the contrary, prefers staying in our dwellings themselves, under the floor, as well as in our stables

and barns. It thus is much more exposed to be exterminated by man; and we cannot maintain, with any approach to certainty, that the black rat is being either exterminated or starved out by the brown rat and not by man.

33. "But it may be urged that when several closely-allied species inhabit the same territory, we surely ought to find at the present time many transitional forms.... By my theory these allied species are descended from a common parent; and during the process of modification, each has become adapted to the conditions of life of its own region, and has supplanted and exterminated its original parent-form and all the transitional varieties between its past and present states" (Origin of Species, 6th ed. p. 134); also p. 137, 296 (all paragraph "On Extinction").

34. According to Madame Marie Pavloff, who has made a special study of this subject, they migrated from Asia to Africa, stayed there some time, and returned next to Asia. Whether this double migration be confirmed or not, the fact of a former extension of the ancestor of our horse over Asia, Africa, and America is settled beyond doubt.

35. The Naturalist on the River Amazons, ii. 85, 95.

36. Dr. B. Altum, Waldbeschadigungen durch Thiere und Gegenmittel (Berlin, 1889), pp. 207 seq.

37. Dr. B. Altum, ut supra, pp. 13 and 187.

38. A. Becker in the Bulletin de la Societe des Naturalistes de Moscou, 1889, p. 625.

39. Russkaya Mysl, Sept. 1888: "The Theory of Beneficency of Struggle for Life, being a Preface to various Treatises on Botanics, Zoology, and Human Life," by an Old Transformist.

40. "One of the most frequent modes in which Natural Selection acts is, by adapting some individuals of a species to a somewhat different mode of life, whereby they are able to seize unappropriated places in Nature" (Origin of Species, p. 145)—in other words, to avoid competition.

CHAPTER III

MUTUAL AID AMONG SAVAGES

Supposed war of each against all. Tribal origin of human society. Late appearance of the separate family. Bushmen and Hottentots. Australians, Papuas. Eskimos, Aleoutes. Features of savage life difficult to understand for the European. The Dayak's conception of justice. Common law.

The immense part played by mutual aid and mutual support in the evolution of the animal world has been briefly analyzed in the preceding chapters. We have now to cast a glance upon the part played by the same agencies in the evolution of mankind. We saw how few are the animal species which live an isolated life, and how numberless are those which live in societies, either for mutual defence, or for hunting and storing up food, or for rearing their offspring, or simply for enjoying life in common. We also saw that, though a good deal of warfare goes on between different classes of animals, or different species, or even different tribes of the same species, peace and mutual support are the rule within the tribe or the species; and that those species which best know how to combine, and to avoid competition, have the best chances of survival and of a further progressive development. They prosper, while the unsociable species decay.

It is evident that it would be quite contrary to all that we know of nature if men were an exception to so general a rule: if a creature so defenceless as man was at his beginnings should have found his protection and his way to progress, not in mutual support, like other animals, but in a reckless competition for personal advantages, with no regard to the interests of the species. To a mind accustomed to the idea of unity in nature, such a proposition appears utterly indefensible. And yet, improbable and unphilosophical as it is, it has never found a lack of supporters. There always were writers who took a pessimistic view of mankind. They knew it, more or less superficially, through their own limited experience; they knew of history what the annalists, always watchful of wars, cruelty, and oppression, told of it, and little more besides; and they concluded that mankind is nothing but a loose aggregation of beings, always ready to fight with each other, and only prevented from so doing by the intervention of some authority.

Hobbes took that position; and while some of his eighteenth-century followers endeavoured to prove that at no epoch of its existence—not even in its most primitive condition—mankind lived in a state of perpetual warfare; that men have been sociable even in "the state of nature," and that want of knowledge, rather than the natural bad inclinations of man, brought humanity to all the horrors of its early historical life,—his idea was, on the contrary, that the so-called "state of nature" was nothing but a permanent fight between individuals, accidentally huddled together by the mere caprice of their bestial existence. True, that science has made some progress since Hobbes's time, and that we have safer ground to stand upon than the speculations of Hobbes or Rousseau. But the Hobbesian philosophy has plenty of admirers still; and we have had of late quite a school of writers who, taking possession of Darwin's terminology rather than of his leading ideas, made of it an argument in favour of Hobbes's views upon primitive man, and even succeeded in giving them a scientific appearance. Huxley, as is known, took the lead of that school, and in a paper written in 1888 he represented primitive men as a sort of tigers or lions, deprived of all ethical conceptions, fighting out the struggle for existence to its bitter end, and living a life of "continual free fight"; to quote his own words—"beyond the limited and, temporary relations of the family, the Hobbesian war of each against all was the normal state of existence."(1)

It has been remarked more than once that the chief error of Hobbes, and the eighteenth-century philosophers as well, was to imagine that mankind began its life in the shape of small straggling families, something like the "limited and temporary" families of the bigger carnivores, while in reality it is now positively known that such was not the case. Of course, we have no direct evidence as to the modes of life of the first man-like beings. We are not yet settled even as to the time of their first appearance, geologists being inclined at present to see their traces in the pliocene, or even the miocene, deposits of the Tertiary period. But we have the indirect method which permits us to throw some light even upon that remote antiquity. A most careful investigation into the social institutions of the lowest races has been carried on during the last forty years, and it has revealed among the present institutions of primitive folk some traces of still older institutions which have long disappeared, but nevertheless left unmistakable traces of their previous existence. A whole science devoted to the embryology of human institutions has thus developed in the hands of Bachofen, MacLennan, Morgan, Edwin Tylor, Maine, Post, Kovalevsky, Lubbock, and many others. And that science has established beyond any doubt that mankind did not begin its life in the shape of small isolated families.

Far from being a primitive form of organization, the family is a very late product of human evolution. As far as we can go back in the palaeo-ethnology of mankind, we find men living in societies—in tribes similar to those of the highest mammals; and an extremely slow and long evolution was required to bring these societies to the gentile, or clan organization, which, in its turn, had to undergo another, also very long evolution, before the first germs of family, polygamous or monogamous, could appear. Societies, bands, or tribes—not families—were thus the primitive form of organization of mankind and its earliest ancestors. That is what ethnology has come to after its painstaking researches. And in so doing it simply came to what might have been foreseen by the zoologist. None of the higher mammals, save a few carnivores and a few undoubtedly-decaying species of apes (orang-outans and gorillas), live in small families, isolatedly straggling in the woods. All others live in societies. And Darwin so well understood that isolately-living apes never could have developed into man-like beings, that he was inclined to consider man as descended from some comparatively weak but social species, like the chimpanzee, rather than from some stronger but unsociable species, like the gorilla.(2) Zoology and palaeo-ethnology are thus agreed in considering that the band, not the family, was the earliest form of social life. The first human societies simply were a further development of those societies which constitute the very essence of life of the higher animals.(3)

If we now go over to positive evidence, we see that the earliest traces of man, dating from the glacial or the early post-glacial period, afford unmistakable proofs of man having lived even then in societies. Isolated finds of stone implements, even from the old stone age, are very rare; on the contrary, wherever one flint implement is discovered others are sure to be found, in most cases in very large quantities. At a time when men were dwelling in caves, or under occasionally protruding rocks, in company with mammals now extinct, and hardly succeeded in making the roughest sorts of flint hatchets, they already knew the advantages of life in societies. In the valleys of the tributaries of the Dordogne, the surface of the rocks is in some places entirely covered with caves which were inhabited by palaeolithic men.(4) Sometimes the cave-dwellings are superposed in storeys, and they certainly recall much more the nesting colonies of swallows than the dens of carnivores. As to the flint implements discovered in those caves, to use Lubbock's words, "one may say without exaggeration that they are numberless." The same is true of other palaeolithic stations. It also appears from Lartet's investigations that the inhabitants of the Aurignac region in the south of France partook of tribal meals at the burial of their dead. So that men lived in societies, and had germs of a tribal worship, even at that extremely remote epoch.

The same is still better proved as regards the later part of the stone age. Traces of neolithic man have been found in numberless quantities, so that we can reconstitute his manner of life to a great extent. When the ice-cap (which must have spread from the Polar regions as far south as middle France, middle Germany, and middle Russia, and covered Canada as well as a good deal of what is now the United States) began to melt away, the surfaces freed from ice were covered, first, with swamps and marshes, and later on with numberless lakes.(5) Lakes filled all depressions of the valleys before their waters dug out those permanent channels which, during a subsequent epoch, became our rivers. And wherever we explore, in Europe, Asia, or America, the shores of the literally numberless lakes of that period, whose proper name would be the Lacustrine period, we find traces of neolithic man. They are so numerous that we can only wonder at the relative density of population at that time. The "stations" of neolithic man closely follow each other on the terraces which now mark the shores of the old lakes. And at each of those stations stone implements appear in such numbers, that no doubt is possible as to the length of time during which they were inhabited by rather numerous tribes. Whole workshops of flint implements, testifying of the numbers of workers who used to come together, have been discovered by the archaeologists.

Traces of a more advanced period, already characterized by the use of some pottery, are found in the shell-heaps of Denmark. They appear, as is well known, in the shape of heaps from five to ten feet thick, from 100 to 200 feet wide, and 1,000 feet or more in length, and they are so common along some parts of the sea-coast that for a long time they were considered as natural growths. And yet they "contain nothing but what has been in some way or other subservient to the use of man," and they are so densely stuffed with products of human industry that, during a two days' stay at Milgaard, Lubbock dug out no less than 191 pieces of stone-implements and four fragments of pottery.(6) The very size and extension of the shell heaps prove that for generations and generations the coasts of Denmark were inhabited by hundreds of small tribes which certainly lived as peacefully together as the Fuegian tribes, which also accumulate like shellheaps, are living in our own times.

As to the lake-dwellings of Switzerland, which represent a still further advance in civilization, they yield still better evidence of life and work in societies. It is known that even during the stone age the shores of the Swiss lakes were dotted with a succession of villages, each of which consisted of several huts, and was built upon a platform supported by numberless pillars in the lake. No less than twenty-four, mostly stone age villages, were discovered along the shores of Lake Leman, thirty-two in the Lake of Constance, forty-six in the Lake of Neuchatel, and so on; and each of them testifies to the immense amount of labour which was spent in common by the tribe, not by the family. It has even been asserted that the life of the lake-dwellers must have been remarkably free of warfare. And so it probably was, especially if we refer to the life of those primitive folk who live until the present time in similar villages built upon pillars on the sea coasts.

It is thus seen, even from the above rapid hints, that our knowledge of primitive man is not so scanty after all, and that, so far as it goes, it is rather opposed than favourable to the Hobbesian speculations. Moreover, it may be supplemented, to a great extent, by the direct observation of such primitive tribes as now stand on the same level of civilization as the inhabitants of Europe stood in prehistoric times.

That these primitive tribes which we find now are not degenerated specimens of mankind who formerly knew a higher civilization, as it has occasionally been maintained, has sufficiently been proved by Edwin Tylor and Lubbock. However, to the arguments already opposed to the degeneration theory, the following may be added. Save a few tribes clustering in the less-accessible highlands, the "savages" represent a girdle which encircles the more or less civilized nations, and they occupy the extremities of our continents, most of which have retained still, or recently were bearing, an early post-glacial character. Such are the Eskimos and their congeners in Greenland, Arctic America, and Northern Siberia; and, in the Southern hemisphere, the Australians, the Papuas, the Fuegians, and, partly, the Bushmen; while within the civilized area, like primitive folk are only found in the Himalayas, the highlands of Australasia, and the plateaus of Brazil. Now it must be borne in mind that the glacial age did not come to an end at once over the whole surface of the earth. It still continues in Greenland. Therefore, at a time when the littoral regions of the Indian Ocean, the Mediterranean, or the Gulf of Mexico already enjoyed a warmer climate, and became the seats of higher civilizations, immense territories in middle Europe, Siberia, and Northern America, as well as in Patagonia, Southern Africa, and Southern Australasia, remained in early postglacial conditions which rendered them inaccessible to the civilized nations of the torrid and sub-torrid zones. They were at that time what the terrible urmans of North-West Siberia are now, and their population, inaccessible to and untouched by civilization, retained the characters of early post-glacial man. Later on, when desiccation rendered these territories more suitable for agriculture, they were peopled with more civilized immigrants; and while part of their previous inhabitants were assimilated by the new settlers, another part migrated further, and settled where we find them. The territories they inhabit now are still, or recently were, sub-glacial, as to their physical features; their arts and implements are those of the neolithic age; and, notwithstanding their racial differences, and the distances which separate them, their modes of life and social institutions bear a striking likeness. So we cannot but consider them as fragments of the early post-glacial population of the now civilized area.

The first thing which strikes us as soon as we begin studying primitive folk is the complexity of the organization of marriage relations under which they are living. With most of them the family, in the sense we attribute to it, is hardly found in its germs. But they are by no means loose aggregations of men and women coming in a disorderly manner together in conformity with their momentary caprices. All of them are under a certain organization, which has been described by Morgan in its general aspects as the "gentile," or clan organization.(7)

To tell the matter as briefly as possible, there is little doubt that mankind has passed at its beginnings through a stage which may be described as that of "communal marriage"; that is, the whole tribe had husbands and wives in common with but little regard to consanguinity. But it is also certain that some restrictions to that free intercourse were imposed at a very early period. Inter-marriage was soon prohibited between the sons of one mother and her sisters, granddaughters, and aunts. Later on it was prohibited between the sons and daughters of the same mother, and further limitations did not fail to follow. The idea of a gens, or clan, which embodied all presumed descendants from one stock (or rather all those who gathered in one group) was evolved, and marriage within the clan was entirely prohibited. It still remained "communal," but the wife or the husband had to be taken from another clan. And when a gens became too numerous, and subdivided into several gentes, each of them was divided into classes (usually four), and marriage was permitted only between certain well-defined classes. That is the stage which we find now among the Kamilaroi-speaking Australians. As to the family, its first germs appeared amidst the clan organization. A woman who was captured in war from some other clan, and who formerly would have belonged to the whole gens, could be kept at a later period by the capturer, under certain obligations towards the tribe. She may be taken by him to a separate hut, after she had paid a certain tribute to the clan, and thus constitute within the gens a separate family, the appearance of which evidently was opening a quite new phase of civilization.

Now, if we take into consideration that this complicated organization developed among men who stood at the lowest known degree of development, and that it maintained itself in societies knowing no kind of authority besides the authority of public opinion, we at once see how deeply inrooted social instincts must have been in human nature, even at its lowest stages. A savage who is capable of living under such an organization, and of freely submitting to rules which continually clash with his personal desires, certainly is not a beast devoid of ethical principles and knowing no rein to its passions. But the fact becomes still more striking if we consider the immense antiquity of the clan organization. It is now known that the primitive Semites, the Greeks of Homer, the prehistoric Romans, the Germans of Tacitus, the early Celts and the early Slavonians, all have had their own period of clan organization, closely analogous to that of the Australians, the Red Indians, the Eskimos, and other inhabitants of the "savage girdle."(9) So we must admit that either the evolution of marriage laws went on on the same lines among all human races, or the rudiments of the clan rules were developed among some common ancestors of the Semites, the Aryans, the Polynesians, etc., before their differentiation into separate races took place, and that these rules were maintained, until now, among races long ago separated from the common stock. Both alternatives imply, however, an equally striking tenacity of the institution—such a tenacity that no assaults of the individual could break it down through the scores of thousands of years that it was in existence. The very persistence of the clan organization shows how utterly false it is to represent primitive mankind as a disorderly agglomeration of individuals, who only obey their individual passions, and take advantage of their personal force and cunningness against all other representatives of the species. Unbridled individualism is a modern growth, but it is not characteristic of primitive mankind.(10)

Going now over to the existing savages, we may begin with the Bushmen, who stand at a very low level of development—so low indeed that they have no dwellings and sleep in holes dug in the soil, occasionally protected by some screens. It is known that when Europeans settled in their territory and destroyed deer, the Bushmen began stealing the settlers' cattle, whereupon a war of extermination, too horrible to be related here, was waged against them. Five hundred Bushmen were slaughtered in 1774, three thousand in 1808 and 1809 by the Farmers' Alliance, and so on. They were poisoned like rats, killed by hunters lying in ambush before the carcass of some animal, killed wherever met with.(11) So that our knowledge of the Bushmen, being chiefly borrowed from those same people who exterminated them, is necessarily limited. But still we know that when the Europeans came, the Bushmen lived in small tribes (or clans), sometimes federated together; that they used to hunt in common, and divided the spoil without quarrelling; that they never abandoned their wounded, and displayed strong affection to their comrades. Lichtenstein has a most touching story about a Bushman, nearly drowned in a river, who was rescued by his companions. They took off their furs to cover him, and shivered themselves; they dried him, rubbed him before the fire, and smeared his body with warm grease till they brought him back to life. And when the Bushmen found, in Johan van der Walt, a man who treated them well, they expressed their thankfulness by a most touching attachment to that man.(12) Burchell and Moffat both represent them as goodhearted, disinterested, true to their promises, and grateful,(13) all qualities which could develop only by being practised within the tribe. As to their love to children, it is sufficient to say that when a European wished to secure a Bushman woman as a slave, he stole her child: the mother was sure to come into slavery to share the fate of her child.(14)

The same social manners characterize the Hottentots, who are but a little more developed than the Bushmen. Lubbock describes them as "the filthiest animals," and filthy they really are. A fur suspended to the neck and worn till it falls to pieces is all their dress; their huts are a few sticks assembled together and covered with mats, with no kind of furniture within. And though they kept oxen and sheep, and seem to have known the use of iron before they made acquaintance with the Europeans, they still occupy one of the lowest degrees of the human scale. And yet those who knew them highly praised their sociability and readiness to aid each other. If anything is given to a Hottentot, he at once divides it among all present—a habit which, as is known, so much struck Darwin among the

Fuegians. He cannot eat alone, and, however hungry, he calls those who pass by to share his food. And when Kolben expressed his astonishment thereat, he received the answer. "That is Hottentot manner." But this is not Hottentot manner only: it is an all but universal habit among the "savages." Kolben, who knew the Hottentots well and did not pass by their defects in silence, could not praise their tribal morality highly enough.

"Their word is sacred," he wrote. They know "nothing of the corruptness and faithless arts of Europe." "They live in great tranquillity and are seldom at war with their neighbours." They are "all kindness and goodwill to one another.. One of the greatest pleasures of the Hottentots certainly lies in their gifts and good offices to one another." "The integrity of the Hottentots, their strictness and celerity in the exercise of justice, and their chastity, are things in which they excel all or most nations in the world."(15)

Tachart, Barrow, and Moodie(16) fully confirm Kolben's testimony. Let me only remark that when Kolben wrote that "they are certainly the most friendly, the most liberal and the most benevolent people to one another that ever appeared on the earth" (i. 332), he wrote a sentence which has continually appeared since in the description of savages. When first meeting with primitive races, the Europeans usually make a caricature of their life; but when an intelligent man has stayed among them for a longer time, he generally describes them as the "kindest" or "the gentlest" race on the earth. These very same words have been applied to the Ostyaks, the Samoyedes, the Eskimos, the Dayaks, the Aleoutes, the Papuas, and so on, by the highest authorities. I also remember having read them applied to the Tunguses, the Tchuktchis, the Sioux, and several others. The very frequency of that high commendation already speaks volumes in itself.

The natives of Australia do not stand on a higher level of development than their South African brothers. Their huts are of the same character: very often simple screens are the only protection against cold winds. In their food they are most indifferent: they devour horribly putrefied corpses, and cannibalism is resorted to in times of scarcity. When first discovered by Europeans, they had no implements but in stone or bone, and these were of the roughest description. Some tribes had even no canoes, and did not know barter-trade. And yet, when their manners and customs were carefully studied, they proved to be living under that elaborate clan organization which I have mentioned on a preceding page.(17)

The territory they inhabit is usually allotted between the different gentes or clans; but the hunting and fishing territories of each clan are kept in common, and the produce of fishing and hunting belongs to the whole clan; so also the fishing and hunting implements.(18) The meals are taken in common. Like many other savages, they respect certain regulations as to the seasons when certain gums and grasses may be collected.(19) As to their morality altogether, we cannot do better than transcribe the following answers given to the questions of the Paris Anthropological Society by Lumholtz, a missionary who sojourned in North Queensland:(20)—

"The feeling of friendship is known among them; it is strong. Weak people are usually supported; sick people are very well attended to; they never are abandoned or killed. These tribes are cannibals, but they very seldom eat members of their own tribe (when immolated on religious principles, I suppose); they eat strangers only. The parents love their children, play with them, and pet them. Infanticide meets with common approval. Old people are very well treated, never put to death. No religion, no idols, only a fear of death. Polygamous marriage, quarrels arising within the tribe are settled by means of duels fought with wooden swords and shields. No slaves; no culture of any kind; no pottery; no dress, save an apron sometimes worn by women. The clan consists of two hundred individuals, divided into four classes of men and four of women; marriage being only permitted within the usual classes, and never within the gens."

For the Papuas, closely akin to the above, we have the testimony of G.L. Bink, who stayed in New Guinea, chiefly in Geelwink Bay, from 1871 to 1883. Here is the essence of his answers to the same questioner:(21) —

"They are sociable and cheerful; they laugh very much. Rather timid than courageous. Friendship is relatively strong among persons belonging to different tribes, and still stronger within the tribe. A friend will often pay the debt of his friend, the stipulation being that the latter will repay it without interest to the children of the lender. They take care of the ill and the old; old people are never abandoned, and in no case are they killed — unless it be a slave who was ill for a long time. War prisoners are sometimes eaten. The children are very much petted and loved. Old and feeble war prisoners are killed, the others are sold as slaves. They have no religion, no gods, no idols, no authority of any description; the oldest man in the family is the judge. In cases of adultery a fine is paid, and part of it goes to the negoria (the community). The soil is kept in common, but the crop belongs to those who have grown it. They have pottery, and know barter-trade — the custom being that the merchant gives them the goods, whereupon they return to their houses and bring the native goods required by the merchant; if the latter cannot be obtained, the European goods are returned.(22) They are head-hunters, and in so doing they prosecute blood revenge. 'Sometimes,' Finsch says, 'the affair is referred to the Rajah of Namotott, who terminates it by imposing a fine.'"

When well treated, the Papuas are very kind. Miklukho-Maclay landed on the eastern coast of New Guinea, followed by one single man, stayed for two years among tribes reported to be cannibals, and left them with regret; he returned again to stay one year more among them, and never had he any conflict to complain of. True that his rule was never—under no pretext whatever—to say anything which was not truth, nor make any promise which he could not keep. These poor creatures, who even do not know how to obtain fire, and carefully maintain it in their huts, live under their primitive communism, without any chiefs; and within their villages they have no quarrels worth speaking of. They work in common, just enough to get the food of the day; they rear their children in common; and in the evenings they dress themselves as coquettishly as they can, and dance. Like all savages, they are fond of dancing. Each village has its barla, or balai—the "long house," "longue maison," or "grande maison"—for the unmarried men, for social gatherings, and for the discussion of common affairs—again a trait which is common to most inhabitants of the Pacific Islands, the Eskimos, the Red Indians, and so on. Whole groups of villages are on friendly terms, and visit each other en bloc.

Unhappily, feuds are not uncommon—not in consequence of "Overstocking of the area," or "keen competition," and like inventions of a mercantile century, but chiefly in consequence of superstition. As soon as any one falls ill, his friends and relatives come together, and deliberately discuss who might be the cause of the illness. All possible enemies are considered, every one confesses of his own petty quarrels, and finally the real cause is discovered. An enemy from the next village has called it down, and a raid upon that village is decided upon. Therefore, feuds are rather frequent, even between the coast villages, not to say a word of the cannibal mountaineers who are considered as real witches and enemies, though, on a closer acquaintance, they prove to be exactly the same sort of people as their neighbours on the seacoast.(23)

Many striking pages could be written about the harmony which prevails in the villages of the Polynesian inhabitants of the Pacific Islands. But they belong to a more advanced stage of civilization. So we shall now take our illustrations from the far north. I must mention, however, before leaving the Southern Hemisphere, that even the Fuegians, whose reputation has been so bad, appear under a much better light since they begin to be better known. A few French missionaries who stay among them "know of no act of malevolence to complain of." In their clans, consisting of from 120 to 150 souls, they practise the same primitive communism as the Papuas; they share everything in common, and treat their old people very well. Peace prevails among these tribes.(24) With the Eskimos and their nearest congeners, the Thlinkets, the Koloshes, and the Aleoutes, we find one of the nearest illustrations of what man may have been during the glacial age. Their implements hardly differ from those of palaeolithic man, and some of their tribes do not yet know fishing: they simply spear the fish with a kind of harpoon.(25) They know the use of iron, but they receive it from the Europeans, or find it on wrecked ships. Their social organization is of a very primitive kind, though they already have emerged from the stage of "communal marriage," even under the gentile restrictions. They live in families, but the family bonds are often broken; husbands and wives are often exchanged.(26) The families, however, remain united in clans, and how could it be otherwise? How could they sustain the hard struggle for life unless by closely combining their forces? So they do, and the tribal bonds are closest where the struggle for life is hardest, namely, in North-East Greenland. The "long house" is their usual dwelling, and several families lodge in it, separated from each other by small partitions of ragged furs, with a common passage in the front. Sometimes the house has the shape of a cross, and in such case a common fire is kept in the centre. The German Expedition which spent a winter close by one of those "long houses" could ascertain that "no quarrel disturbed the peace, no dispute arose about the use of this narrow space" throughout the long winter. "Scolding, or even unkind words, are considered as a misdemeanour, if not produced under the legal form of process, namely, the nith-song."(27) Close cohabitation and close interdependence are sufficient for maintaining century after century that deep respect for the interests of the community which is characteristic of Eskimo life. Even in the larger communities of Eskimos, "public opinion formed the real judgment-seat, the general punishment consisting in the offenders being shamed in the eyes of the people."(28)

Eskimo life is based upon communism. What is obtained by hunting and fishing belongs to the clan. But in several tribes, especially in the West, under the influence of the Danes, private property penetrates into their institutions. However, they have an original means for obviating the inconveniences arising from a personal accumulation of wealth which would soon destroy their tribal unity. When a man has grown rich, he convokes the folk of his clan to a great festival, and, after much eating, distributes among them all his fortune. On the Yukon river, Dall saw an Aleonte family distributing in this way ten guns, ten full fur dresses, 200 strings of beads, numerous blankets, ten wolf furs, 200 beavers, and 500 zibelines. After that they took off their festival dresses, gave them away, and, putting on old ragged furs, addressed a few words to their kinsfolk, saying that though they are now poorer than any one of them, they have won their friendship.(29) Like distributions of wealth appear to be a regular habit with the Eskimos, and to take place at a certain season, after an exhibition of all that has been obtained during the year.(30) In my opinion these distributions reveal a very old institution, contemporaneous with the first apparition of personal wealth; they must have been a means for re-establishing equality among the members of the clan, after it had been disturbed by the enrichment of the few. The periodical redistribution of land and the periodical abandonment of all debts which took place in historical times with so many different races (Semites, Aryans, etc.), must have been a survival of that old custom. And the habit of either burying with the dead, or destroying upon his grave, all that belonged to him personally—a habit which we find among all primitive races—must have had the same origin. In fact, while everything that belongs personally to the dead is burnt or broken upon his grave, nothing is destroyed of what belonged to him in common with the tribe, such as boats, or the communal implements of fishing. The destruction bears upon personal property alone. At a later epoch this habit becomes a religious ceremony. It receives a mystical interpretation, and is imposed by religion, when public opinion alone proves incapable of enforcing its general observance. And, finally, it is substituted by either burning simple models of the dead man's property (as in China), or by simply carrying his property to the grave and taking it back to his house after the burial ceremony is over—a habit which still prevails with the Europeans as regards swords, crosses, and other marks of public distinction.(31)

The high standard of the tribal morality of the Eskimos has often been mentioned in general literature. Nevertheless the following remarks upon the manners of the Aleoutes—nearly akin to the Eskimos—will better illustrate savage morality as a whole. They were written, after a ten years' stay among the Aleoutes, by a most remarkable man—the Russian missionary, Veniaminoff. I sum them up, mostly in his own words:—

Endurability (he wrote) is their chief feature. It is simply colossal. Not only do they bathe every morning in the frozen sea, and stand naked on the beach, inhaling the icy wind, but their endurability, even when at hard work on insufficient food, surpasses all that can be imagined. During a protracted scarcity of food, the Aleoute cares first for his children; he gives them all he has, and himself fasts. They are not inclined to stealing; that was remarked even by the first Russian immigrants. Not that they never steal; every Aleoute would confess having sometime stolen something, but it is always a trifle; the whole is so childish. The attachment of the parents to their children is touching, though it is never expressed in words or pettings. The Aleoute is with difficulty moved to make a promise, but once he has made it he will keep it whatever may happen. (An Aleoute made Veniaminoff a gift of dried fish, but it was forgotten on the beach in the hurry of the departure. He took it home. The next occasion to send it to the missionary was in January; and in November and December there was a great scarcity of food in the Aleoute encampment. But the fish was never touched by the starving people, and in January it was sent to its destination.) Their code of morality is both varied and severe. It is considered shameful to be afraid of unavoidable death; to ask pardon from an enemy; to die without ever having killed an enemy; to be convicted of stealing; to capsize a boat in the harbour; to be afraid of going to sea in stormy weather; to be the first in a party on a long journey to become an invalid in case of scarcity of food; to show greediness when spoil is divided, in which case every one gives his own part to the greedy man to shame him; to divulge a public secret to his wife; being two persons on a hunting expedition, not to offer the best game to the partner; to boast of his own deeds, especially of invented ones; to scold any one in scorn. Also to beg; to pet his wife in other people's presence, and to dance with her to bargain personally: selling must always be made through a third person, who settles the price. For a woman it is a shame not to know sewing, dancing and all kinds of woman's work; to pet her husband and children, or even to speak to her husband in the presence of a stranger.(32)

Such is Aleoute morality, which might also be further illustrated by their tales and legends. Let me also add that when Veniaminoff wrote (in 1840) one murder only had been committed since the last century in a population of 60,000 people, and that among 1,800 Aleoutes not one single common law offence had been known for forty years. This will not seem strange if we remark that scolding, scorning, and the use of rough words are absolutely unknown in Aleoute life. Even their children never fight, and never abuse each other in words. All they may say is, "Your mother does not know sewing," or "Your father is blind of one eye."(33)

Many features of savage life remain, however, a puzzle to Europeans. The high development of tribal solidarity and the good feelings with which primitive folk are animated towards each other, could be illustrated by any amount of reliable testimony. And yet it is not the less certain that those same savages practise infanticide; that in some cases they abandon their old people, and that they blindly obey the rules of blood-revenge. We must then explain the coexistence of facts which, to the European mind, seem so contradictory at the first sight. I have just mentioned how the Aleoute father starves for days and weeks, and gives everything eatable to his child; and how the Bushman mother becomes a slave to follow her child; and I might fill pages with illustrations of the really tender relations existing among the savages and their children. Travellers continually mention them incidentally. Here you read about the fond love of a mother; there you see a father wildly running through the forest and carrying upon his shoulders his child bitten by a snake; or a missionary tells you the despair of the parents at the loss of a child whom he had saved, a few years before, from being immolated at its birth, you learn that the "savage" mothers usually nurse their children till the age of four, and that, in the New Hebrides, on the loss of a specially beloved child, its mother, or aunt, will kill herself to take care of it in the other world.(34) And so on.

Like facts are met with by the score; so that, when we see that these same loving parents practise infanticide, we are bound to recognize that the habit (whatever its ulterior transformations may be) took its origin under the sheer pressure of necessity, as an obligation towards the tribe, and a means for rearing the already growing children. The savages, as a rule, do not "multiply without stint," as some English writers put it. On the contrary, they take all kinds of measures for diminishing the birth-rate. A whole series of restrictions, which Europeans certainly would find extravagant, are imposed to that effect, and they are strictly obeyed. But notwithstanding that, primitive folk cannot rear all their children. However, it has been remarked that as soon as they succeed in increasing their regular means of subsistence, they at once begin to abandon the practice of infanticide. On the whole, the parents obey that obligation reluctantly, and as soon as they can afford it they resort to all kinds of compromises to save the lives of their new-born. As has been so well pointed out by my friend Elie Reclus,(35) they invent the lucky and unlucky days of births, and spare the children born on the lucky days; they try to postpone the sentence for a few hours, and then say that if the baby has lived one day it must live all its natural life.(36) They hear the cries of the little ones coming from the forest, and maintain that, if heard, they forbode a misfortune for the tribe; and as they have no baby-farming nor creches for getting rid of the children, every one of them recoils before the necessity of performing the cruel sentence; they prefer to expose the baby in the wood rather than to take its life by violence. Ignorance, not cruelty, maintains infanticide; and, instead of moralizing the savages with sermons, the missionaries would do better to follow the example of Veniaminoff, who, every year till his old age, crossed the sea of Okhotsk in a miserable boat, or travelled on dogs among his Tchuktchis, supplying them with bread and fishing implements. He thus had really stopped infanticide.

The same is true as regards what superficial observers describe as parricide. We just now saw that the habit of abandoning old people is not so widely spread as some writers have maintained it to be. It has been extremely exaggerated, but it is occasionally met with among nearly all savages; and in such cases it has the same origin as the exposure of children. When a "savage" feels that he is a burden to his tribe; when every morning his share of food is taken from the mouths of the children—and the little ones are not so stoical as their fathers: they cry when they are hungry; when every day he has to be carried across the stony beach, or the virgin forest, on the shoulders of younger people there are no invalid carriages, nor destitutes to wheel them in savage lands—he begins to repeat what the old Russian peasants say until now-a-day. "Tchujoi vek zayedayu, Pora na pokoi!" ("I live other people's life: it is time to retire!") And he retires. He does what the soldier does in a similar case. When the salvation of his detachment depends upon its further advance, and he can move no more, and knows that he must die if left behind, the soldier implores his best friend to render him the last service before leaving the encampment. And the friend, with shivering hands, discharges his gun into the dying body. So the savages do. The old man asks himself to die; he himself insists upon this last duty towards the community, and obtains the consent of the tribe; he digs out his grave; he invites his kinsfolk to the last parting meal. His father has done so, it is now his turn; and he parts with his kinsfolk with marks of affection. The savage so much considers death as part of his duties towards his community, that he not only refuses to be rescued (as Moffat has told), but when a woman who had to be immolated on her husband's grave was rescued by missionaries, and was taken to an island, she escaped in the night, crossed a broad sea-arm, swimming and rejoined her tribe, to die on the grave.(37) It has become with them a matter of religion. But the savages, as a rule, are so reluctant to take any one's life otherwise than in fight, that none of them will take upon himself to shed human blood, and they resort to all kinds of stratagems, which have been so falsely interpreted. In most cases, they abandon the old man in the wood, after having given him more than his share of the common food. Arctic expeditions have done the same when they no more could carry their invalid comrades. "Live a few days more, maybe there will be some unexpected rescue!" West European men of science, when coming across these facts, are absolutely unable to stand them; they can not reconcile them with a high development of tribal morality, and they prefer to cast a doubt upon the exactitude of absolutely reliable observers, instead of trying to explain the parallel existence of the two sets of facts: a high tribal morality together with the abandonment of the parents and infanticide. But if these same Europeans were to tell a savage that people, extremely amiable, fond of their own children, and so impressionable that they cry when they see a misfortune simulated on the stage, are living in Europe within a stone's throw from dens in which children die from sheer want of food, the savage, too, would not understand them. I remember how vainly I tried to make some of my Tungus friends understand our civilization of individualism: they could not, and they resorted to the most fantastical suggestions. The fact is that a savage, brought up in ideas of a tribal solidarity in everything for bad and for good, is as incapable of understanding a "moral" European, who knows nothing of that solidarity, as the average European is incapable of understanding the savage. But if our scientist had lived amidst a half-starving tribe which does not possess among them all one man's food for so much as a few days to come, he probably might have understood their motives. So also the savage, if he had stayed among us, and received our education, may be, would understand our European indifference towards our neighbours, and our Royal Commissions for the prevention of "babyfarming." "Stone houses make stony hearts," the Russian peasants say. But he ought to live in a stone house first.

Similar remarks must be made as regards cannibalism. Taking into account all the facts which were brought to light during a recent controversy on this subject at the Paris Anthropological Society, and many incidental remarks scattered throughout the "savage" literature, we are bound to recognize that that practice was brought into existence by sheer necessity. But that it was further developed by superstition and religion into the proportions it attained in Fiji or in Mexico. It is a fact that until this day many savages are compelled to devour corpses in the most advanced state of putrefaction, and that in cases of absolute scarcity some of them have had to disinter and to feed upon human corpses, even during an epidemic. These are ascertained facts. But if we now transport ourselves to the conditions which man had to face during the glacial period, in a damp and cold climate, with but little vegetable food at his disposal; if we take into account the terrible ravages which scurvy still makes among underfed natives, and remember that meat and fresh blood are the only restoratives which they know, we must admit that man, who formerly was a granivorous animal, became a flesh-eater during the glacial period. He found plenty of deer at that time, but deer often migrate in the Arctic regions, and sometimes they entirely abandon a territory for a number of years. In such cases his last resources disappeared.

During like hard trials, cannibalism has been resorted to even by Europeans, and it was resorted to by the savages. Until the present time, they occasionally devour the corpses of their own dead: they must have devoured then the corpses of those who had to die. Old people died, convinced that by their death they were rendering a last service to the tribe. This is why cannibalism is represented by some savages as of divine origin, as something that has been ordered by a messenger from the sky. But later on it lost its character of necessity, and survived as a superstition. Enemies had to be eaten in order to inherit their courage; and, at a still later epoch, the enemy's eye or heart was eaten for the same purpose; while among other tribes, already having a numerous priesthood and a developed mythology, evil gods, thirsty for human blood, were invented, and human sacrifices required by the priests to appease the gods. In this religious phase of its existence, cannibalism attained its most revolting characters. Mexico is a well-known example; and in Fiji, where the king could eat any one of his subjects, we also find a mighty cast of priests, a complicated theology,(38) and a full development of autocracy. Originated by necessity, cannibalism became, at a later period, a religious institution, and in this form it survived long after it had disappeared from among tribes which certainly practised it in former times, but did not attain the theocratical stage of evolution. The same remark must be made as regards infanticide and the abandonment of parents. In some cases they also have been maintained as a survival of olden times, as a religiously-kept tradition of the past.

I will terminate my remarks by mentioning another custom which also is a source of most erroneous conclusions. I mean the practice of blood-revenge. All savages are under the impression that blood shed must be revenged by blood. If any one has been killed, the murderer must die; if any one has been wounded, the aggressor's blood must be shed. There is no exception to the rule, not even for animals; so the hunter's blood is shed on his return to the village when he has shed the blood of an animal. That is the savages' conception of justice—a conception which yet prevails in Western Europe as regards murder. Now, when both the offender and the offended belong to the same tribe, the tribe and the offended person settle the affair.(39) But when the offender belongs to another tribe, and that tribe, for one reason or another, refuses a compensation, then the offended tribe decides to take the revenge itself. Primitive folk so much consider every one's acts as a tribal affair, dependent upon tribal approval, that they easily think the clan responsible for every one's acts. Therefore, the due revenge may be taken upon any member of the offender's clan or relatives.(40) It may often happen, however, that the retaliation goes further than the offence. In trying to inflict a wound, they may kill the offender, or wound him more than they intended to do, and this becomes a cause for a new feud, so that the primitive legislators were careful in requiring the retaliation to be limited to an eye for an eye, a tooth for a tooth, and blood for blood.(41)

It is remarkable, however, that with most primitive folk like feuds are infinitely rarer than might be expected; though with some of them they may attain abnormal proportions, especially with mountaineers who have been driven to the highlands by foreign invaders, such as the mountaineers of Caucasia, and especially those of Borneo—the Dayaks. With the Dayaks—we were told lately—the feuds had gone so far that a young man could neither marry nor be proclaimed of age before he had secured the head of an enemy. This horrid practice was fully described in a modern English work.(42) It appears, however, that this affirmation was a gross exaggeration. Moreover, Dayak "head-hunting" takes quite another aspect when we learn that the supposed "headhunter" is not actuated at all by personal passion. He acts under what he considers as a moral obligation towards his tribe, just as the European judge who, in obedience to the same, evidently wrong, principle of "blood for blood," hands over the condemned murderer to the hangman. Both the Dayak and the judge would even feel remorse if sympathy moved them to spare the murderer. That is why the Dayaks, apart from the murders they commit when actuated by their conception of justice, are depicted, by all those who know them, as a most sympathetic people. Thus Carl Bock, the same author who has given such a terrible picture of head-hunting, writes:

> "As regards morality, I am bound to assign to the Dayaks a high place in the scale of civilization.... Robberies and theft are entirely unknown among them. They also are very truthful.... If I did not always get the 'whole truth,' I always got, at least, nothing but the truth from them. I wish I could say the same of the Malays" (pp. 209 and 210).

Bock's testimony is fully corroborated by that of Ida Pfeiffer. "I fully recognized," she wrote, "that I should be pleased longer to travel among them. I usually found them honest, good, and reserved ... much more so than any other nation I know."(43) Stoltze used almost the same language when speaking of them. The Dayaks usually have but one wife, and treat her well. They are very sociable, and every morning the whole clan goes out for fishing, hunting, or gardening, in large parties. Their villages consist of big huts, each of which is inhabited by a dozen families, and sometimes by several hundred persons, peacefully living together. They show great respect for their wives, and are fond of their children; and when one of them falls ill, the women nurse him in turn. As a rule they are very moderate in eating and drinking. Such is the Dayak in his real daily life.

It would be a tedious repetition if more illustrations from savage life were given. Wherever we go we find the same sociable manners, the same spirit of solidarity. And when we endeavour to penetrate into the darkness of past ages, we find the same tribal life, the same associations of men, however primitive, for mutual support. Therefore, Darwin was quite right when he saw in man's social qualities the chief factor for his further evolution, and Darwin's vulgarizers are entirely wrong when they maintain the contrary.

The small strength and speed of man (he wrote), his want of natural weapons, etc., are more than counterbalanced, firstly, by his intellectual faculties (which, he remarked on another page, have been chiefly or even exclusively gained for the benefit of the community). and secondly, by his social qualities, which led him to give and receive aid from his fellow men.(44)

In the last century the "savage" and his "life in the state of nature" were idealized. But now men of science have gone to the opposite extreme, especially since some of them, anxious to prove the animal origin of man, but not conversant with the social aspects of animal life, began to charge the savage with all imaginable "bestial" features. It is evident, however, that this exaggeration is even more unscientific than Rousseau's idealization. The savage is not an ideal of virtue, nor is he an ideal of "savagery." But the primitive man has one quality, elaborated and maintained by the very necessities of his hard struggle for life—he identifies his own existence with that of his tribe; and without that quality mankind never would have attained the level it has attained now.

Primitive folk, as has been already said, so much identify their lives with that of the tribe, that each of their acts, however insignificant, is considered as a tribal affair. Their whole behaviour is regulated by an infinite series of unwritten rules of propriety which are the fruit of their common experience as to what is good or bad—that is, beneficial or harmful for their own tribe. Of course, the reasonings upon which their rules of propriety are based sometimes are absurd in the extreme. Many of them originate in superstition; and altogether, in whatever the savage does, he sees but the immediate consequences of his acts; he cannot foresee their indirect and ulterior consequences—thus simply exaggerating a defect with which Bentham reproached civilized legislators. But, absurd or not, the savage obeys the prescriptions of the common law, however inconvenient they may be. He obeys them even more blindly than the civilized man obeys the prescriptions of the written law. His common law is his religion; it is his very habit of living. The idea of the clan is always present to his mind, and self-restriction and self-sacrifice in the interest of the clan are of daily occurrence. If the savage has infringed one of the smaller tribal rules, he is prosecuted by the mockeries of the women. If the infringement is grave, he is tortured day and night by the fear of having called a calamity upon his tribe. If he has wounded by accident any one of his own clan, and thus has committed the greatest of all crimes, he grows quite miserable: he runs away in the woods, and is ready to commit suicide, unless the tribe absolves him by inflicting upon him a physical pain and sheds some of his own blood.(45) Within the tribe everything is shared in common; every morsel of food is divided among all present; and if the savage is alone in the woods, he does not begin eating before he has loudly shouted thrice an invitation to any one who may hear his voice to share his meal.(46)

In short, within the tribe the rule of "each for all" is supreme, so long as the separate family has not yet broken up the tribal unity. But that rule is not extended to the neighbouring clans, or tribes, even when they are federated for mutual protection. Each tribe, or clan, is a separate unity. Just as among mammals and birds, the territory is roughly allotted among separate tribes, and, except in times of war, the boundaries are respected. On entering the territory of his neighbours one must show that he has no bad intentions. The louder one heralds his coming, the more confidence he wins; and if he enters a house, he must deposit his hatchet at the entrance. But no tribe is bound to share its food with the others: it may do so or it may not. Therefore the life of the savage is divided into two sets of actions, and appears under two different ethical aspects: the relations within the tribe, and the relations with the outsiders; and (like our international law) the "inter-tribal" law widely differs from the common law. Therefore, when it comes to a war the most revolting cruelties may be considered as so many claims upon the admiration of the tribe. This double conception of morality passes through the whole evolution of mankind, and maintains itself until now. We Europeans have realized some progress—not immense, at any rate—in eradicating that double conception of ethics; but it also must be said that while we have in some measure extended our ideas of solidarity—in theory, at least—over the nation, and partly over other nations as well, we have lessened the bonds of solidarity within our own nations, and even within our own families.

The appearance of a separate family amidst the clan necessarily disturbs the established unity. A separate family means separate property and accumulation of wealth. We saw how the Eskimos obviate its inconveniences; and it is one of the most interesting studies to follow in the course of ages the different institutions (village communities, guilds, and so on) by means of which the masses endeavoured to maintain the tribal unity, notwithstanding the agencies which were at work to break it down. On the other hand, the first rudiments of knowledge which appeared at an extremely remote epoch, when they confounded themselves with witchcraft, also became a power in the hands of the individual which could be used against the tribe. They were carefully kept in secrecy, and transmitted to the initiated only, in the secret societies of witches, shamans, and priests, which we find among all savages. By the same time, wars and invasions created military authority, as also castes of warriors, whose associations or clubs acquired great powers. However, at no period of man's life were wars the normal state of existence. While warriors exterminated each other, and the priests celebrated their massacres, the masses continued to live their daily life, they prosecuted their daily toil. And it is one of the most interesting studies to follow that life of the masses; to study the means by which they maintained their own social organization, which was based upon their own conceptions of equity, mutual aid, and mutual support—of common law, in a word, even when they were submitted to the most ferocious theocracy or autocracy in the State.

NOTES:

1. Nineteenth Century, February 1888, p. 165.

2. The Descent of Man, end of ch. ii. pp. 63 and 64 of the 2nd edition.

3. Anthropologists who fully endorse the above views as regards man nevertheless intimate, sometimes, that the apes live in polygamous families, under the leadership of "a strong and jealous male." I do not know how far that assertion is based upon conclusive observation. But the passage from Brehm's Life

of Animals, which is sometimes referred to, can hardly be taken as very conclusive. It occurs in his general description of monkeys; but his more detailed descriptions of separate species either contradict it or do not confirm it. Even as regards the cercopitheques, Brehm is affirmative in saying that they "nearly always live in bands, and very seldom in families" (French edition, p. 59). As to other species, the very numbers of their bands, always containing many males, render the "polygamous family" more than doubtful further observation is evidently wanted.

4. Lubbock, Prehistoric Times, fifth edition, 1890.

5. That extension of the ice-cap is admitted by most of the geologists who have specially studied the glacial age. The Russian Geological Survey already has taken this view as regards Russia, and most German specialists maintain it as regards Germany. The glaciation of most of the central plateau of France will not fail to be recognized by the French geologists, when they pay more attention to the glacial deposits altogether.

6. Prehistoric Times, pp. 232 and 242.

7. Bachofen, Das Mutterrecht, Stuttgart, 1861; Lewis H. Morgan, Ancient Society, or Researches in the Lines of Human Progress from Savagery through Barbarism to Civilization, New York, 1877; J.F. MacLennan, Studies in Ancient History, 1st series, new edition, 1886; 2nd series, 1896; L. Fison and A.W. Howitt, Kamilaroi and Kurnai, Melbourne. These four writers—as has been very truly remarked by Giraud Teulon,—starting from different facts and different general ideas, and following different methods, have come to the same conclusion. To Bachofen we owe the notion of the maternal family and the maternal succession; to Morgan—the system of kinship,

Malayan and Turanian, and a highly gifted sketch of the main phases of human evolution; to MacLennan—the law of exogeny; and to Fison and Howitt—the cuadro, or scheme, of the conjugal societies in Australia. All four end in establishing the same fact of the tribal origin of the family. When Bachofen first drew attention to the maternal family, in his epoch-making work, and Morgan described the clan-organization,—both concurring to the almost general extension of these forms and maintaining that the marriage laws lie at the very basis of the consecutive steps of human evolution, they were accused of exaggeration. However, the most careful researches prosecuted since, by a phalanx of students of ancient law, have proved that all races of mankind bear traces of having passed through similar stages of development of marriage laws, such as we now see in force among certain savages. See the works of Post, Dargun, Kovalevsky, Lubbock, and their numerous followers: Lippert, Mucke, etc.

8. None

9. For the Semites and the Aryans, see especially Prof. Maxim Kovalevsky's Primitive Law (in Russian), Moscow, 1886 and 1887. Also his Lectures delivered at Stockholm (Tableau des origines et de l'evolution de la famille et de la propriete, Stockholm, 1890), which represents an admirable review of the whole question. Cf. also A. Post, Die Geschlechtsgenossenschaft der Urzeit, Oldenburg 1875.

10. It would be impossible to enter here into a discussion of the origin of the marriage restrictions. Let me only remark that a division into groups, similar to Morgan's Hawaian, exists among birds; the young broods live together separately from their parents. A like division might probably be traced among some mammals as well. As to the prohibition of relations between

brothers and sisters, it is more likely to have arisen, not from speculations about the bad effects of consanguinity, which speculations really do not seem probable, but to avoid the too-easy precocity of like marriages. Under close cohabitation it must have become of imperious necessity. I must also remark that in discussing the origin of new customs altogether, we must keep in mind that the savages, like us, have their "thinkers" and savants-wizards, doctors, prophets, etc.—whose knowledge and ideas are in advance upon those of the masses. United as they are in their secret unions (another almost universal feature) they are certainly capable of exercising a powerful influence, and of enforcing customs the utility of which may not yet be recognized by the majority of the tribe.

11. Col. Collins, in Philips' Researches in South Africa, London, 1828. Quoted by Waitz, ii. 334.

12. Lichtenstein's Reisen im sudlichen Afrika, ii. Pp. 92, 97. Berlin, 1811.

13. Waitz, Anthropologie der Naturvölker, ii. pp. 335 seq. See also
Fritsch's Die Eingeboren Süd-Afrika's, Breslau, 1872, pp. 386 seq.; and
Drei Jahre in Süd-Afrika. Also W. Bleck, A Brief Account of Bushmen
Folklore, Capetown, 1875.

14. Elisee Reclus, Geographie Universelle, xiii. 475.

15. P. Kolben, The Present State of the Cape of Good Hope, translated from the German by Mr. Medley, London, 1731, vol. i. pp. 59, 71, 333, 336, etc.

16. Quoted in Waitz's Anthropologie, ii. 335 seq.

17. The natives living in the north of Sidney, and speaking the Kamilaroi language, are best known under this aspect, through the capital work of Lorimer Fison and A.W. Howitt, Kamilaroi and Kurnaii, Melbourne, 1880. See also A.W. Howitt's "Further Note on the Australian Class Systems," in Journal of the Anthropological Institute, 1889, vol. xviii. p. 31, showing the wide extension of the same organization in Australia.

18. The Folklore, Manners, etc., of Australian Aborigines, Adelaide, 1879, p. 11.

19. Grey's Journals of Two Expeditions of Discovery in North-West and Western Australia, London, 1841, vol. ii. pp. 237, 298.

20. Bulletin de la Societe d'Anthropologie, 1888, vol. xi. p. 652. I abridge the answers.

21. Bulletin de la Societe d'Anthropologie, 1888, vol. xi. p. 386.

22. The same is the practice with the Papuas of Kaimani Bay, who have a high reputation of honesty. "It never happens that the Papua be untrue to his promise," Finsch says in Neuguinea und seine Bewohner, Bremen, 1865, p. 829.

23. Izvestia of the Russian Geographical Society, 1880, pp. 161 seq. Few books of travel give a better insight into the petty details of the daily life of savages than these scraps from Maklay's notebooks.

24. L.F. Martial, in Mission Scientifique au Cap Horn, Paris, 1883, vol. i. pp. 183-201.

25. Captain Holm's Expedition to East Greenland.

26. In Australia whole clans have been seen exchanging all their wives, in order to conjure a calamity (Post, Studien zur Entwicklungsgeschichte des Familienrechts, 1890, p. 342). More brotherhood is their specific against calamities.

27. Dr. H. Rink, The Eskimo Tribes, p. 26 (Meddelelser om Gronland, vol. xi. 1887).

28. Dr. Rink, loc. cit. p. 24. Europeans, grown in the respect of Roman law, are seldom capable of understanding that force of tribal authority. "In fact," Dr. Rink writes, "it is not the exception, but the rule, that white men who have stayed for ten or twenty years among the Eskimo, return without any real addition to their knowledge of the traditional ideas upon which their social state is based. The white man, whether a missionary or a trader, is firm in his dogmatic opinion that the most vulgar European is better than the most distinguished native."—The Eskimo Tribes, p. 31.

29. Dall, Alaska and its Resources, Cambridge, U.S., 1870.

30. Dall saw it in Alaska, Jacobsen at Ignitok in the vicinity of the Bering Strait. Gilbert Sproat mentions it among the Vancouver indians; and Dr. Rink, who describes the periodical exhibitions just mentioned, adds: "The principal use of the accumulation of personal wealth is for periodically distributing it." He also mentions (loc. cit. p. 31) "the destruction of property for the same purpose," (of maintaining equality).

31. See Appendix VIII.

32. Veniaminoff, Memoirs relative to the District of Unalashka (Russian), 3 vols. St. Petersburg, 1840. Extracts, in English, from the above are given in Dall's Alaska. A like description of the

Australians' morality is given in Nature, xlii. p. 639.

33. It is most remarkable that several writers (Middendorff, Schrenk, O. Finsch) described the Ostyaks and Samoyedes in almost the same words. Even when drunken, their quarrels are insignificant. "For a hundred years one single murder has been committed in the tundra;" "their children never fight;" "anything may be left for years in the tundra, even food and gin, and nobody will touch it;" and so on. Gilbert Sproat "never witnessed a fight between two sober natives" of the Aht Indians of Vancouver Island. "Quarrelling is also rare among their children." (Rink, loc. cit.) And so on.

34. Gill, quoted in Gerland and Waitz's Anthropologie, v. 641. See also pp. 636-640, where many facts of parental and filial love are quoted.

35. Primitive Folk, London, 1891.

36. Gerland, loc. cit. v. 636.

37. Erskine, quoted in Gerland and Waitz's Anthropologie, v. 640.

38. W.T. Pritchard, Polynesian Reminiscences, London, 1866, p. 363.

39. It is remarkable, however, that in case of a sentence of death, nobody will take upon himself to be the executioner. Every one throws his stone, or gives his blow with the hatchet, carefully avoiding to give a mortal blow. At a later epoch, the priest will stab the victim with a sacred knife. Still later, it will be the king, until civilization invents the hired hangman. See Bastian's deep remarks upon this subject in Der Mensch in der Geschichte, iii. Die Blutrache, pp. 1-36. A remainder of this tribal habit, I am

told by Professor E. Nys, has survived in military executions till our own times. In the middle portion of the nineteenth century it was the habit to load the rifles of the twelve soldiers called out for shooting the condemned victim, with eleven ball-cartridges and one blank cartridge. As the soldiers never knew who of them had the latter, each one could console his disturbed conscience by thinking that he was not one of the murderers.

40. In Africa, and elsewhere too, it is a widely-spread habit, that if a theft has been committed, the next clan has to restore the equivalent of the stolen thing, and then look itself for the thief. A. H. Post, Afrikanische Jurisprudenz, Leipzig, 1887, vol. i. p. 77.

41. See Prof. M. Kovalevsky's Modern Customs and Ancient Law (Russian), Moscow, 1886, vol. ii., which contains many important considerations upon this subject.

42. See Carl Bock, The Head Hunters of Borneo, London, 1881. I am told, however, by Sir Hugh Law, who was for a long time Governor of Borneo, that the "head-hunting" described in this book is grossly exaggerated. Altogether, my informant speaks of the Dayaks in exactly the same sympathetic terms as Ida Pfeiffer. Let me add that Mary Kingsley speaks in her book on West Africa in the same sympathetic terms of the Fans, who had been represented formerly as the most "terrible cannibals."

43. Ida Pfeiffer, Meine zweite Weltriese, Wien, 1856, vol. i. pp. 116 seq. See also Muller and Temminch's Dutch Possessions in Archipelagic India, quoted by Elisee Reclus, in Geographie Universelle, xiii.

44. Descent of Man, second ed., pp. 63, 64.

45. See Bastian's Mensch in der Geschichte, iii. p. 7. Also Grey,

loc. cit. ii. p. 238.

46. Miklukho-Maclay, loc. cit. Same habit with the Hottentots.

CHAPTER IV

MUTUAL AID AMONG THE BARBARIANS

The great migrations. New organization rendered necessary.
The village community. Communal work. Judicial procedure.
Inter-tribal law.
Illustrations from the life of our contemporaries. Buryates.
Kabyles.
Caucasian mountaineers. African stems.

It is not possible to study primitive mankind without being deeply impressed by the sociability it has displayed since its very first steps in life. Traces of human societies are found in the relics of both the oldest and the later stone age; and, when we come to observe the savages whose manners of life are still those of neolithic man, we find them closely bound together by an extremely ancient clan organization which enables them to combine their individually weak forces, to enjoy life in common, and to progress. Man is no exception in nature. He also is subject to the great principle of Mutual Aid which grants the best chances of survival to those who best support each other in the struggle for life. These were the conclusions arrived at in the previous chapters.

However, as soon as we come to a higher stage of civilization, and refer to history which already has something to say about that stage, we are bewildered by the struggles and conflicts which it reveals. The old bonds seem entirely to be broken. Stems are seen to fight against stems, tribes against tribes, individuals against individuals; and out of this chaotic contest of hostile forces, mankind issues divided into castes, enslaved to despots, separated into States always ready to wage war against each other. And, with this history of mankind in his hands, the pessimist philosopher triumphantly concludes that warfare and oppression are the very essence of human nature; that the warlike and predatory instincts of man can only be restrained within certain limits by a strong authority which enforces peace and thus gives an opportunity to the few and nobler ones to prepare a better life for humanity in times to come.

And yet, as soon as the every-day life of man during the historical period is submitted to a closer analysis and so it has been, of late, by many patient students of very early institutions—it appears at once under quite a different aspect. Leaving aside the preconceived ideas of most historians and their pronounced predilection for the dramatic aspects of history, we see that the very documents they habitually peruse are such as to exaggerate the part of human life given to struggles and to underrate its peaceful moods. The bright and sunny days are lost sight of in the gales and storms. Even in our own time, the cumbersome records which we prepare for the future historian, in our Press, our law courts, our Government offices, and even in our fiction and poetry, suffer from the same one-sidedness. They hand down to posterity the most minute descriptions of every war, every battle and skirmish, every contest and act of violence, every kind of individual suffering; but they hardly bear any trace of the countless acts of mutual support and devotion which every one of us knows from his own experience; they hardly take notice of what makes the very essence of our daily life—our social instincts and manners. No wonder, then, if the records of the past were so imperfect. The annalists of old never failed to chronicle the petty wars and calamities which harassed their contemporaries; but they paid no attention whatever to the life of the masses, although the masses chiefly used to toil peacefully while the few indulged in fighting. The epic poems, the inscriptions on monuments, the treaties of peace—nearly all historical documents bear the same character; they deal with breaches of peace, not with peace itself. So that the best-intentioned historian unconsciously draws a distorted picture of the times he endeavours to depict; and, to restore the real proportion between conflict and union, we are now bound to enter into a minute analysis of thousands of small facts and faint indications accidentally preserved in the relics of the past; to interpret them with the aid of comparative ethnology; and, after having heard so much about what used to divide men, to reconstruct stone by stone the institutions which used to unite them.

Ere long history will have to be re-written on new lines, so as to take into account these two currents of human life and to appreciate the part played by each of them in evolution. But in the meantime we may avail ourselves of the immense preparatory work recently done towards restoring the leading features of the second current, so much neglected. From the better-known periods of history we may take some illustrations of the life of the masses, in order to indicate the part played by mutual support during those periods; and, in so doing, we may dispense (for the sake of brevity) from going as far back as the Egyptian, or even the Greek and Roman antiquity. For, in fact, the evolution of mankind has not had the character of one unbroken series. Several times civilization came to an end in one given region, with one given race, and began anew elsewhere, among other races. But at each fresh start it began again with the same clan institutions which we have seen among the savages. So that if we take the last start of our own civilization, when it began afresh in the first centuries of our era, among those whom the Romans called the "barbarians," we shall have the whole scale of evolution, beginning with the gentes and ending in the institutions of our own time. To these illustrations the following pages will be devoted.

Men of science have not yet settled upon the causes which some two thousand years ago drove whole nations from Asia into Europe and resulted in the great migrations of barbarians which put an end to the West Roman Empire. One cause, however, is naturally suggested to the geographer as he contemplates the ruins of populous cities in the deserts of Central Asia, or follows the old beds of rivers now disappeared and the wide outlines of lakes now reduced to the size of mere ponds. It is desiccation: a quite recent desiccation, continued still at a speed which we formerly were not prepared to admit.(1) Against it man was powerless. When the inhabitants of North-West Mongolia and East Turkestan saw that water was abandoning them, they had no course open to them but to move down the broad valleys leading to the lowlands, and to thrust westwards the inhabitants of the plains.(2) Stems after stems were thus thrown into Europe, compelling other stems to move and to remove for centuries in succession, westwards and eastwards, in search of new and more or less permanent abodes. Races were mixing with races during those migrations, aborigines with immigrants, Aryans with Ural-Altayans; and it would have been no wonder if the social institutions which had kept them together in their mother countries had been totally wrecked during the stratification of races which took place in Europe and Asia. But they were not wrecked; they simply underwent the modification which was required by the new conditions of life.

The Teutons, the Celts, the Scandinavians, the Slavonians, and others, when they first came in contact with the Romans, were in a transitional state of social organization. The clan unions, based upon a real or supposed common origin, had kept them together for many thousands of years in succession. But these unions could answer their purpose so long only as there were no separate families within the gens or clan itself. However, for causes already mentioned, the separate patriarchal family had slowly but steadily developed within the clans, and in the long run it evidently meant the individual accumulation of wealth and power, and the hereditary transmission of both. The frequent migrations of the barbarians and the ensuing wars only hastened the division of the gentes into separate families, while the dispersing of stems and their mingling with strangers offered singular facilities for the ultimate disintegration of those unions which were based upon kinship. The barbarians thus stood in a position of either seeing their clans dissolved into loose aggregations of families, of which the wealthiest, especially if combining sacerdotal functions or military repute with wealth, would have succeeded in imposing their authority upon the others; or of finding out some new form of organization based upon some new principle.

Many stems had no force to resist disintegration: they broke up and were lost for history. But the more vigorous ones did not disintegrate. They came out of the ordeal with a new organization—the village community—which kept them together for the next fifteen centuries or more. The conception of a common territory, appropriated or protected by common efforts, was elaborated, and it took the place of the vanishing conceptions of common descent. The common gods gradually lost their character of ancestors and were endowed with a local territorial character. They became the gods or saints of a given locality; "the land" was identified with its inhabitants. Territorial unions grew up instead of the consanguine unions of old, and this new organization evidently offered many advantages under the given circumstances. It recognized the independence of the family and even emphasized it, the village community disclaiming all rights of interference in what was going on within the family enclosure; it gave much more freedom to personal initiative; it was not hostile in principle to union between men of different descent, and it maintained at the same time the necessary cohesion of action and thought, while it was strong enough to oppose the dominative tendencies of the minorities of wizards, priests, and professional or distinguished warriors. Consequently it became the primary cell of future organization, and with many nations the village community has retained this character until now.

It is now known, and scarcely contested, that the village community was not a specific feature of the Slavonians, nor even of the ancient Teutons. It prevailed in England during both the Saxon and Norman times, and partially survived till the last century;(3) it was at the bottom of the social organization of old Scotland, old Ireland, and old Wales. In France, the communal possession and the communal allotment of arable land by the village folkmote persisted from the first centuries of our era till the times of Turgot, who found the folkmotes "too noisy" and therefore abolished them. It survived Roman rule in Italy, and revived after the fall of the Roman Empire. It was the rule with the Scandinavians, the Slavonians, the Finns (in the pittaya, as also, probably, the kihla-kunta), the Coures, and the lives. The village community in India—past and present, Aryan and non-Aryan—is well known through the epoch-making works of Sir Henry Maine; and Elphinstone has described it among the Afghans. We also find it in the Mongolian oulous, the Kabyle thaddart, the Javanese dessa, the Malayan kota or tofa, and under a variety of names in Abyssinia, the Soudan, in the interior of Africa, with natives of both Americas, with all the small and large tribes of the Pacific archipelagoes. In short, we do not know one single human race or one single nation which has not had its period of village communities. This fact alone disposes of the theory according to which the village community in Europe would have been a servile growth. It is anterior to serfdom, and even servile submission was powerless to break it. It was a universal phase of evolution, a natural outcome of the clan organization, with all those stems, at least, which have played, or play still, some part in history.(4)

It was a natural growth, and an absolute uniformity in its structure was therefore not possible. As a rule, it was a union between families considered as of common descent and owning a certain territory in common. But with some stems, and under certain circumstances, the families used to grow very numerous before they threw off new buds in the shape of new families; five, six, or seven generations continued to live under the same roof, or within the same enclosure, owning their joint household and cattle in common, and taking their meals at the common hearth. They kept in such case to what ethnology knows as the "joint family," or the "undivided household," which we still see all over China, in India, in the South Slavonian zadruga, and occasionally find in Africa, in America, in Denmark, in North Russia, and West France.(5) With other stems, or in other circumstances, not yet well specified, the families did not attain the same proportions; the grandsons, and occasionally the sons, left the household as soon as they were married, and each of them started a new cell of his own. But, joint or not, clustered together or scattered in the woods, the families remained united into village communities; several villages were grouped into tribes; and the tribes joined into confederations. Such was the social organization which developed among the so-called "barbarians," when they began to settle more or less permanently in Europe.

A very long evolution was required before the gentes, or clans, recognized the separate existence of a patriarchal family in a separate hut; but even after that had been recognized, the clan, as a rule, knew no personal inheritance of property. The few things which might have belonged personally to the individual were either destroyed on his grave or buried with him. The village community, on the contrary, fully recognized the private accumulation of wealth within the family and its hereditary transmission. But wealth was conceived exclusively in the shape of movable property, including cattle, implements, arms, and the dwelling house which—"like all things that can be destroyed by fire"—belonged to the same category(6). As to private property in land, the village community did not, and could not, recognize anything of the kind, and, as a rule, it does not recognize it now. The land was the common property of the tribe, or of the whole stem, and the village community itself owned its part of the tribal territory so long only as the tribe did not claim a re-distribution of the village allotments. The clearing of the woods and the breaking of the prairies being mostly done by the communities or, at least, by the joint work of several families—always with the consent of the community—the cleared plots were held by each family for a term of four, twelve, or twenty years, after which term they were treated as parts of the arable land owned in common. Private property, or possession "for ever" was as incompatible, with the very principles and the religious conceptions of the village community as it was with the principles of the gens; so that a long influence of the Roman law and the Christian Church, which soon accepted the Roman principles, were required to accustom the barbarians to the idea of private property in land being possible.(7) And yet, even when such property, or possession for an unlimited time, was recognized, the owner of a separate estate remained a co-proprietor in the waste lands, forests, and grazing-grounds. Moreover, we continually see, especially in the history of Russia, that when a few families, acting separately, had taken possession of some land belonging to tribes which were treated as strangers, they very soon united together, and constituted a village community which in the third or fourth generation began to profess a community of origin.

A whole series of institutions, partly inherited from the clan period, have developed from that basis of common ownership of land during the long succession of centuries which was required to bring the barbarians under the dominion of States organized upon the Roman or Byzantine pattern. The village community was not only a union for guaranteeing to each one his fair share in the common land, but also a union for common culture, for mutual support in all possible forms, for protection from violence, and for a further development of knowledge, national bonds, and moral conceptions; and every change in the judicial, military, educational, or economical manners had to be decided at the folkmotes of the village, the tribe, or the confederation. The community being a continuation of the gens, it inherited all its functions. It was the universitas, the mir—a world in itself.

Common hunting, common fishing, and common culture of the orchards or the plantations of fruit trees was the rule with the old gentes. Common agriculture became the rule in the barbarian village communities. True, that direct testimony to this effect is scarce, and in the literature of antiquity we only have the passages of Diodorus and Julius Caesar relating to the inhabitants of the Lipari Islands, one of the Celt-Iberian tribes, and the Sueves. But there is no lack of evidence to prove that common agriculture was practised among some Teuton tribes, the Franks, and the old Scotch, Irish, and Welsh.(8) As to the later survivals of the same practice, they simply are countless. Even in perfectly Romanized France, common culture was habitual some five and twenty years ago in the Morbihan (Brittany).(9) The old Welsh cyvar, or joint team, as well as the common culture of the land allotted to the use of the village sanctuary are quite common among the tribes of Caucasus the least touched by civilization,(10) and like facts are of daily occurrence among the Russian peasants. Moreover, it is well known that many tribes of Brazil, Central America, and Mexico used to cultivate their fields in common, and that the same habit is widely spread among some Malayans, in New Caledonia, with several Negro stems, and so on.(11) In short, communal culture is so habitual with many Aryan, Ural-Altayan, Mongolian, Negro, Red Indian, Malayan, and Melanesian stems that we must consider it as a universal—though not as the only possible—form of primitive agriculture.(12)

Communal cultivation does not, however, imply by necessity communal consumption. Already under the clan organization we often see that when the boats laden with fruits or fish return to the village, the food they bring in is divided among the huts and the "long houses" inhabited by either several families or the youth, and is cooked separately at each separate hearth. The habit of taking meals in a narrower circle of relatives or associates thus prevails at an early period of clan life. It became the rule in the village community. Even the food grown in common was usually divided between the households after part of it had been laid in store for communal use. However, the tradition of communal meals was piously kept alive; every available opportunity, such as the commemoration of the ancestors, the religious festivals, the beginning and the end of field work, the births, the marriages, and the funerals, being seized upon to bring the community to a common meal. Even now this habit, well known in this country as the "harvest supper," is the last to disappear. On the other hand, even when the fields had long since ceased to be tilled and sown in common, a variety of agricultural work continued, and continues still, to be performed by the community. Some part of the communal land is still cultivated in many cases in common, either for the use of the destitute, or for refilling the communal stores, or for using the produce at the religious festivals. The irrigation canals are digged and repaired in common. The communal meadows are mown by the community; and the sight of a Russian commune mowing a meadow—the men rivalling each other in their advance with the scythe, while the women turn the grass over and throw it up into heaps—is one of the most inspiring sights; it shows what human work might be and ought to be. The hay, in such case, is divided among the separate households, and it is evident that no one has the right of taking hay from a neighbour's stack without his permission; but the limitation of this last rule among the Caucasian Ossetes is most noteworthy. When the cuckoo cries and announces that spring is coming, and that the meadows will soon be clothed again with grass, every one in need has the right of taking from a neighbour's stack the hay he wants for his cattle.(13) The old communal rights are thus re-asserted, as if to prove how contrary unbridled individualism is to human nature.

When the European traveller lands in some small island of the Pacific, and, seeing at a distance a grove of palm trees, walks in that direction, he is astonished to discover that the little villages are connected by roads paved with big stones, quite comfortable for the unshod natives, and very similar to the "old roads" of the Swiss mountains. Such roads were traced by the "barbarians" all over Europe, and one must have travelled in wild, thinly-peopled countries, far away from the chief lines of communication, to realize in full the immense work that must have been performed by the barbarian communities in order to conquer the woody and marshy wilderness which Europe was some two thousand years ago. Isolated families, having no tools, and weak as they were, could not have conquered it; the wilderness would have overpowered them. Village communities alone, working in common, could master the wild forests, the sinking marshes, and the endless steppes. The rough roads, the ferries, the wooden bridges taken away in the winter and rebuilt after the spring flood was over, the fences and the palisaded walls of the villages, the earthen forts and the small towers with which the territory was dottedall these were the work of the barbarian communities. And when a community grew numerous it used to throw off a new bud. A new community arose at a distance, thus step by step bringing the woods and the steppes under the dominion of man. The whole making of European nations was such a budding of the village communities. Even now-a-days the Russian peasants, if they are not quite broken down by misery, migrate in communities, and they till the soil and build the houses in com mon when they settle on the banks of the Amur, or in Manitoba. And even the English, when they first began to colonize America, used to return to the old system; they grouped into village communities.(14)

The village community was the chief arm of the barbarians in their hard struggle against a hostile nature. It also was the bond they opposed to oppression by the cunningest and the strongest which so easily might have developed during those disturbed times. The imaginary barbarian—the man who fights and kills at his mere caprice—existed no more than the "bloodthirsty" savage. The real barbarian was living, on the contrary, under a wide series of institutions, imbued with considerations as to what may be useful or noxious to his tribe or confederation, and these institutions were piously handed down from generation to generation in verses and songs, in proverbs or triads, in sentences and instructions. The more we study them the more we recognize the narrow bonds which united men in their villages. Every quarrel arising between two individuals was treated as a communal affair—even the offensive words that might have been uttered during a quarrel being considered as an offence to the community and its ancestors. They had to be repaired by amends made both to the individual and the community;(15) and if a quarrel ended in a fight and wounds, the man who stood by and did not interpose was treated as if he himself had inflicted the wounds.(16) The judicial procedure was imbued with the same spirit. Every dispute was brought first before mediators or arbiters, and it mostly ended with them, the arbiters playing a very important part in barbarian society. But if the case was too grave to be settled in this way, it came before the folkmote, which was bound "to find the sentence," and pronounced it in a conditional form; that is, "such compensation was due, if the wrong be proved," and the wrong had to be proved or disclaimed by six or twelve persons confirming or denying the fact by oath; ordeal being resorted to in case of contradiction between the two sets of jurors. Such procedure, which remained in force for more than two thousand years in succession, speaks volumes for itself; it shows how close were the bonds between all members of the community. Moreover, there was no other authority to enforce the decisions of the folkmote besides its own moral authority. The only possible menace was that the community might declare the rebel an outlaw, but even this menace was reciprocal. A man discontented with the folkmote could declare that he would abandon the tribe and go over to another tribe—a most dreadful menace, as it was sure to bring all kinds of misfortunes upon a tribe that might have been unfair to one of its members.(17) A rebellion against a right decision of the customary law was simply "inconceivable," as Henry Maine has so well said, because "law, morality, and fact" could not be separated from each other in those times.(18) The moral authority of the commune was so great that even at a much later epoch, when the village communities fell into submission to the feudal lord, they maintained their judicial powers; they only permitted the lord, or his deputy, to "find" the above conditional sentence in accordance with the customary law he had sworn to follow, and to levy for himself the fine (the fred) due to the commune. But for a long time, the lord himself, if he remained a co-proprietor in the waste land of the commune, submitted in communal affairs to its decisions. Noble or ecclesiastic, he had to submit to the folkmote—Wer daselbst Wasser und Weid genusst, muss gehorsam sein—"Who enjoys here the right of water and pasture must obey"—was the old saying. Even when the peasants became serfs under the lord, he was bound to appear before the folkmote when they summoned him.(19)

In their conceptions of justice the barbarians evidently did not much differ from the savages. They also maintained the idea that a murder must be followed by putting the murderer to death; that wounds had to be punished by equal wounds, and that the wronged family was bound to fulfil the sentence of the customary law. This was a holy duty, a duty towards the ancestors, which had to be accomplished in broad daylight, never in secrecy, and rendered widely known. Therefore the most inspired passages of the sagas and epic poetry altogether are those which glorify what was supposed to be justice. The gods themselves joined in aiding it. However, the predominant feature of barbarian justice is, on the one hand, to limit the numbers of persons who may be involved in a feud, and, on the other hand, to extirpate the brutal idea of blood for blood and wounds for wounds, by substituting for it the system of compensation. The barbarian codes which were collections of common law rules written down for the use of judges—"first permitted, then encouraged, and at last enforced," compensation instead of revenge.(20) The compensation has, however, been totally misunderstood by those who represented it as a fine, and as a sort of carte blanche given to the rich man to do whatever he liked. The compensation money (wergeld), which was quite different from the fine or fred,(21) was habitually so high for all kinds of active offences that it certainly was no encouragement for such offences. In case of a murder it usually exceeded all the possible fortune of the murderer "Eighteen times eighteen cows" is the compensation with the Ossetes who do not know how to reckon above eighteen, while with the African tribes it attains 800 cows or 100 camels with their young, or 416 sheep in the poorer tribes.(22) In the great majority of cases, the compensation money could not be paid at all, so that the murderer had no issue but to induce the wronged family, by repentance, to adopt him. Even now, in the Caucasus, when feuds come to an end, the offender touches with his lips the breast of the oldest woman of the tribe, and becomes a "milk-brother" to all men of the wronged family.(23) With several African tribes he must give his daughter, or sister, in marriage to some one of the family; with other tribes he is bound to marry the woman whom he has made a widow; and in all cases he becomes a member of the family, whose opinion is taken in all important family matters.(24)

Far from acting with disregard to human life, the barbarians, moreover, knew nothing of the horrid punishments introduced at a later epoch by the laic and canonic laws under Roman and Byzantine influence. For, if the Saxon code admitted the death penalty rather freely even in cases of incendiarism and armed robbery, the other barbarian codes pronounced it exclusively in cases of betrayal of one's kin, and sacrilege against the community's gods, as the only means to appease the gods.

All this, as seen is very far from the supposed "moral dissoluteness" of the barbarians. On the contrary, we cannot but admire the deeply moral principles elaborated within the early village communities which found their expression in Welsh triads, in legends about King Arthur, in Brehon commentaries,(25) in old German legends and so on, or find still their expression in the sayings of the modern barbarians. In his introduction to The Story of Burnt Njal, George Dasent very justly sums up as follows the qualities of a Northman, as they appear in the sagas:—

> To do what lay before him openly and like a man, without fear of either foes, fiends, or fate; ... to be free and daring in all his deeds; to be gentle and generous to his friends and kinsmen; to be stern and grim to his foes [those who are under the lex talionis], but even towards them to fulfil all bounden duties.... To be no truce-breaker, nor tale-bearer, nor backbiter. To utter nothing against any man that he would not dare to tell him to his face. To turn no man from his door who sought food or shelter, even though he were a foe.(26)

The same or still better principles permeate the Welsh epic poetry and triads. To act "according to the nature of mildness and the principles of equity," without regard to the foes or to the friends, and "to repair the wrong," are the highest duties of man; "evil is death, good is life," exclaims the poet legislator.(27) "The World would be fool, if agreements made on lips were not honourable"—the Brehon law says. And the humble Shamanist Mordovian, after having praised the same qualities, will add, moreover, in his principles of customary law, that "among neighbours the cow and the milking-jar are in common;" that, "the cow must be milked for yourself and him who may ask milk;" that "the body of a child reddens from the stroke, but the face of him who strikes reddens from shame;"(28) and so on.

Many pages might be filled with like principles expressed and followed by the "barbarians."

One feature more of the old village communities deserves a special mention. It is the gradual extension of the circle of men embraced by the feelings of solidarity. Not only the tribes federated into stems, but the stems as well, even though of different origin, joined together in confederations. Some unions were so close that, for instance, the Vandals, after part of their confederation had left for the Rhine, and thence went over to Spain and Africa, respected for forty consecutive years the landmarks and the abandoned villages of their confederates, and did not take possession of them until they had ascertained through envoys that their confederates did not intend to return. With other barbarians, the soil was cultivated by one part of the stem, while the other part fought on or beyond the frontiers of the common territory. As to the leagues between several stems, they were quite habitual. The Sicambers united with the Cherusques and the Sueves, the Quades with the Sarmates; the Sarmates with the Alans, the Carpes, and the Huns. Later on, we also see the conception of nations gradually developing in Europe, long before anything like a State had grown in any part of the continent occupied by the barbarians. These nations—for it is impossible to refuse the name of a nation to the Merovingian France, or to the Russia of the eleventh and twelfth century—were nevertheless kept together by nothing else but a community of language, and a tacit agreement of the small republics to take their dukes from none but one special family.

Wars were certainly unavoidable; migration means war; but Sir Henry Maine has already fully proved in his remarkable study of the tribal origin of International Law, that "Man has never been so ferocious or so stupid as to submit to such an evil as war without some kind of effort to prevent it," and he has shown how exceedingly great is "the number of ancient institutions which bear the marks of a design to stand in the way of war, or to provide an alternative to it."(29) In reality, man is so far from the warlike being he is supposed to be, that when the barbarians had once settled they so rapidly lost the very habits of warfare that very soon they were compelled to keep special dukes followed by special scholae or bands of warriors, in order to protect them from possible intruders. They preferred peaceful toil to war, the very peacefulness of man being the cause of the specialization of the warrior's trade, which specialization resulted later on in serfdom and in all the wars of the "States period" of human history.

History finds great difficulties in restoring to life the institutions of the barbarians. At every step the historian meets with some faint indication which he is unable to explain with the aid of his own documents only. But a broad light is thrown on the past as soon as we refer to the institutions of the very numerous tribes which are still living under a social organization almost identical with that of our barbarian ancestors. Here we simply have the difficulty of choice, because the islands of the Pacific, the steppes of Asia, and the tablelands of Africa are real historical museums containing specimens of all possible intermediate stages which mankind has lived through, when passing from the savage gentes up to the States' organization. Let us, then, examine a few of those specimens.

If we take the village communities of the Mongol Buryates, especially those of the Kudinsk Steppe on the upper Lena which have better escaped Russian influence, we have fair representatives of barbarians in a transitional state, between cattle-breeding and agriculture.(30) These Buryates are still living in "joint families"; that is, although each son, when he is married, goes to live in a separate hut, the huts of at least three generations remain within the same enclosure, and the joint family work in common in their fields, and own in common their joint households and their cattle, as well as their "calves' grounds" (small fenced patches of soil kept under soft grass for the rearing of calves). As a rule, the meals are taken separately in each hut; but when meat is roasted, all the twenty to sixty members of the joint household feast together. Several joint households which live in a cluster, as well as several smaller families settled in the same village—mostly debris of joint households accidentally broken up—make the oulous, or the village community; several oulouses make a tribe; and the forty-six tribes, or clans, of the Kudinsk Steppe are united into one confederation. Smaller and closer confederations are entered into, as necessity arises for special wants, by several tribes. They know no private property in land—the land being held in common by the oulous, or rather by the confederation, and if it becomes necessary, the territory is re-allotted between the different oulouses at a folkmote of the tribe, and between the forty-six tribes at a folkmote of the confederation. It is worthy of note that the same organization prevails among all the 250,000 Buryates of East Siberia, although they have been for three centuries under Russian rule, and are well acquainted with Russian institutions.

With all that, inequalities of fortune rapidly develop among the Buryates, especially since the Russian Government is giving an exaggerated importance to their elected taishas (princes), whom it considers as responsible tax-collectors and representatives of the confederations in their administrative and even commercial relations with the Russians. The channels for the enrichment of the few are thus many, while the impoverishment of the great number goes hand in hand, through the appropriation of the Buryate lands by the Russians. But it is a habit with the Buryates, especially those of Kudinsk—and habit is more than law—that if a family has lost its cattle, the richer families give it some cows and horses that it may recover. As to the destitute man who has no family, he takes his meals in the huts of his congeners; he enters a hut, takes—by right, not for charity—his seat by the fire, and shares the meal which always is scrupulously divided into equal parts; he sleeps where he has taken his evening meal. Altogether, the Russian conquerors of Siberia were so much struck by the communistic practices of the Buryates, that they gave them the name of Bratskiye—"the Brotherly Ones"—and reported to Moscow. "With them everything is in common; whatever they have is shared in common." Even now, when the Lena Buryates sell their wheat, or send some of their cattle to be sold to a Russian butcher, the families of the oulous, or the tribe, put their wheat and cattle together, and sell it as a whole. Each oulous has, moreover, its grain store for loans in case of need, its communal baking oven (the four banal of the old French communities), and its blacksmith, who, like the blacksmith of the Indian communities,(31) being a member of the community, is never paid for his work within the community. He must make it for nothing, and if he utilizes his spare time for fabricating the small plates of chiselled and silvered iron which are used in Buryate land for the decoration of dress, he may occasionally sell them to a woman from another clan, but to the women of his own clan the attire is presented as a gift. Selling and buying cannot take place within the community, and the rule is so severe that when a richer family hires a labourer the labourer must be taken from another clan or from among the Russians. This habit is evidently not specific to the Buryates; it is so widely spread among the modern barbarians, Aryan and Ural-Altayan, that it must have been universal among our ancestors.

The feeling of union within the confederation is kept alive by the common interests of the tribes, their folkmotes, and the festivities which are usually kept in connection with the folkmotes. The same feeling is, however, maintained by another institution, the aba, or common hunt, which is a reminiscence of a very remote past. Every autumn, the forty-six clans of Kudinsk come together for such a hunt, the produce of which is divided among all the families. Moreover, national abas, to assert the unity of the whole Buryate nation, are convoked from time to time. In such cases, all Buryate clans which are scattered for hundreds of miles west and east of Lake Baikal, are bound to send their delegate hunters. Thousands of men come together, each one bringing provisions for a whole month. Every one's share must be equal to all the others, and therefore, before being put together, they are weighed by an elected elder (always "with the hand": scales would be a profanation of the old custom). After that the hunters divide into bands of twenty, and the parties go hunting according to a well-settled plan. In such abas the entire Buryate nation revives its epic traditions of a time when it was united in a powerful league. Let me add that such communal hunts are quite usual with the Red Indians and the Chinese on the banks of the Usuri (the kada).(32)

With the Kabyles, whose manners of life have been so well described by two French explorers,(33) we have barbarians still more advanced in agriculture. Their fields, irrigated and manured, are well attended to, and in the hilly tracts every available plot of land is cultivated by the spade. The Kabyles have known many vicissitudes in their history; they have followed for sometime the Mussulman law of inheritance, but, being adverse to it, they have returned, 150 years ago, to the tribal customary law of old. Accordingly, their land-tenure is of a mixed character, and private property in land exists side by side with communal possession. Still, the basis of their present organization is the village community, the thaddart, which usually consists of several joint families (kharoubas), claiming a community of origin, as well as of smaller families of strangers.

Several villages are grouped into clans or tribes (arch); several tribes make the confederation (thak'ebilt); and several confederations may occasionally enter into a league, chiefly for purposes of armed defence.

The Kabyles know no authority whatever besides that of the djemmaa, or folkmote of the village community. All men of age take part in it, in the open air, or in a special building provided with stone seats. And the decisions of the djemmaa are evidently taken at unanimity: that is, the discussions continue until all present agree to accept, or to submit to, some decision. There being no authority in a village community to impose a decision, this system has been practised by mankind wherever there have been village communities, and it is practised still wherever they continue to exist, i.e. by several hundred million men all over the world. The djemmaa nominates its executive—the elder, the scribe, and the treasurer; it assesses its own taxes; and it manages the repartition of the common lands, as well as all kinds of works of public utility. A great deal of work is done in common: the roads, the mosques, the fountains, the irrigation canals, the towers erected for protection from robbers, the fences, and so on, are built by the village community; while the high-roads, the larger mosques, and the great market-places are the work of the tribe. Many traces of common culture continue to exist, and the houses continue to be built by, or with the aid of, all men and women of the village. Altogether, the "aids" are of daily occurrence, and are continually called in for the cultivation of the fields, for harvesting, and so on. As to the skilled work, each community has its blacksmith, who enjoys his part of the communal land, and works for the community; when the tilling season approaches he visits every house, and repairs the tools and the ploughs, without expecting any pay, while the making of new ploughs is considered as a pious work which can by no means be recompensed in money, or by any other form of salary.

As the Kabyles already have private property, they evidently have both rich and poor among them. But like all people who closely live together, and know how poverty begins, they consider it as an accident which may visit every one. "Don't say that you will never wear the beggar's bag, nor go to prison," is a proverb of the Russian peasants; the Kabyles practise it, and no difference can be detected in the external behaviour between rich and poor; when the poor convokes an "aid," the rich man works in his field, just as the poor man does it reciprocally in his turn.(34) Moreover, the djemmaas set aside certain gardens and fields, sometimes cultivated in common, for the use of the poorest members. Many like customs continue to exist. As the poorer families would not be able to buy meat, meat is regularly bought with the money of the fines, or the gifts to the djemmaa, or the payments for the use of the communal olive-oil basins, and it is distributed in equal parts among those who cannot afford buying meat themselves. And when a sheep or a bullock is killed by a family for its own use on a day which is not a market day, the fact is announced in the streets by the village crier, in order that sick people and pregnant women may take of it what they want. Mutual support permeates the life of the Kabyles, and if one of them, during a journey abroad, meets with another Kabyle in need, he is bound to come to his aid, even at the risk of his own fortune and life; if this has not been done, the djemmaa of the man who has suffered from such neglect may lodge a complaint, and the djemmaa of the selfish man will at once make good the loss. We thus come across a custom which is familiar to the students of the mediaeval merchant guilds. Every stranger who enters a Kabyle village has right to housing in the winter, and his horses can always graze on the communal lands for twenty-four hours. But in case of need he can reckon upon an almost unlimited support. Thus, during the famine of 1867-68, the Kabyles received and fed every one who sought refuge in their villages, without distinction of origin. In the district of Dellys, no less than 12,000 people who came from all parts of Algeria, and even from Morocco, were fed in this way. While people died from starvation all over Algeria, there was not one single case of death due to this cause on Kabylian soil. The djemmaas, depriving themselves of necessaries, organized relief, without ever asking any aid from the Government, or uttering the slightest complaint; they considered it as a natural duty. And while among the European settlers all kind of police measures were taken to prevent thefts and disorder resulting from such an influx of strangers, nothing of the kind was required on the Kabyles' territory: the djemmaas needed neither aid nor protection from without.(35)

I can only cursorily mention two other most interesting features of Kabyle life; namely, the anaya, or protection granted to wells, canals, mosques, marketplaces, some roads, and so on, in case of war, and the cofs. In the anaya we have a series of institutions both for diminishing the evils of war and for preventing conflicts. Thus the market-place is anaya, especially if it stands on a frontier and brings Kabyles and strangers together; no one dares disturb peace in the market, and if a disturbance arises, it is quelled at once by the strangers who have gathered in the market town. The road upon which the women go from the village to the fountain also is anaya in case of war; and so on. As to the cof it is a widely spread form of association, having some characters of the mediaeval Burgschaften or Gegilden, as well as of societies both for mutual protection and for various purposes—intellectual, political, and emotional—which cannot be satisfied by the territorial organization of the village, the clan, and the con federation. The cof knows no territorial limits; it recruits its members in various villages, even among strangers; and it protects them in all possible eventualities of life.

Altogether, it is an attempt at supplementing the territorial grouping by an extra-territorial grouping intended to give an expression to mutual affinities of all kinds across the frontiers. The free international association of individual tastes and ideas, which we consider as one of the best features of our own life, has thus its origin in barbarian antiquity.

The mountaineers of Caucasia offer another extremely instructive field for illustrations of the same kind. In studying the present customs of the Ossetes—their joint families and communes and their judiciary conceptions—Professor Kovalevsky, in a remarkable work on Modern Custom and Ancient Law was enabled step by step to trace the similar dispositions of the old barbarian codes and even to study the origins of feudalism. With other Caucasian stems we occasionally catch a glimpse into the origin of the village community in those cases where it was not tribal but originated from a voluntary union between families of distinct origin. Such was recently the case with some Khevsoure villages, the inhabitants of which took the oath of "community and fraternity."(36) In another part of Caucasus, Daghestan, we see the growth of feudal relations between two tribes, both maintaining at the same time their village communities (and even traces of the gentile "classes"), and thus giving a living illustration of the forms taken by the conquest of Italy and Gaul by the barbarians. The victorious race, the Lezghines, who have conquered several Georgian and Tartar villages in the Zakataly district, did not bring them under the dominion of separate families; they constituted a feudal clan which now includes 12,000 households in three villages, and owns in common no less than twenty Georgian and Tartar villages. The conquerors divided their own land among their clans, and the clans divided it in equal parts among the families; but they did not interfere with the djemmaas of their tributaries which still practise the habit mentioned by Julius Caesar; namely, the djemmaa decides each year which part of the communal territory must be cultivated, and this land is divided into as many parts as there are families, and the parts are distributed by lot. It is worthy of note that although proletarians are of common occurrence among the Lezghines (who live under a system of private property in land, and common ownership of serfs(37)) they are rare among their Georgian serfs, who continue to hold their land in common. As to the customary law of the Caucasian mountaineers, it is much the same as that of the Longobards or Salic Franks, and several of its dispositions explain a good deal the judicial procedure of the barbarians of old. Being of a very impressionable character, they do their best to prevent quarrels from taking a fatal issue; so, with the Khevsoures, the swords are very soon drawn when a quarrel breaks out; but if a woman rushes out and throws among them the piece of linen which she wears on her head, the swords are at once returned to their sheaths, and the quarrel is appeased. The head-dress of the women is anaya. If a quarrel has not been stopped in time and has ended in murder, the compensation money is so considerable that the aggressor is entirely ruined for his life, unless he is adopted by the wronged family; and if he has resorted to his sword in a trifling quarrel and has inflicted wounds, he loses for ever the consideration of his kin. In all disputes, mediators take the matter in hand; they select from among the members of the clan the judges—six in smaller affairs, and from ten to fifteen in more serious matters—and Russian observers testify to the absolute incorruptibility of the judges. An oath has such a significance that men enjoying general esteem are dispensed from taking it: a simple affirmation is quite sufficient, the more so as in grave affairs the Khevsoure never hesitates to recognize his guilt (I mean, of course, the Khevsoure untouched yet by civilization). The oath is chiefly reserved for such cases, like disputes about property, which require some sort of appreciation in addition to a simple statement of facts; and in such cases the men whose affirmation will decide in the dispute, act with the greatest circumspection. Altogether it is certainly not a want of honesty or of respect to the rights of the congeners which characterizes the barbarian societies of Caucasus.

The stems of Africa offer such an immense variety of extremely interesting societies standing at all intermediate stages from the early village community to the despotic barbarian monarchies that I must abandon the idea of giving here even the chief results of a comparative study of their institutions.(38) Suffice it to say, that, even under the most horrid despotism of kings, the folkmotes of the village communities and their customary law remain sovereign in a wide circle of affairs. The law of the State allows the king to take any one's life for a simple caprice, or even for simply satisfying his gluttony; but the customary law of the people continues to maintain the same network of institutions for mutual support which exist among other barbarians or have existed among our ancestors. And with some better-favoured stems (in Bornu, Uganda, Abyssinia), and especially the Bogos, some of the dispositions of the customary law are inspired with really graceful and delicate feelings.

The village communities of the natives of both Americas have the same character. The Tupi of Brazil were found living in "long houses" occupied by whole clans which used to cultivate their corn and manioc fields in common. The Arani, much more advanced in civilization, used to cultivate their fields in common; so also the Oucagas, who had learned under their system of primitive communism and "long houses" to build good roads and to carry on a variety of domestic industries,(39) not inferior to those of the early medieval times in Europe. All of them were also living under the same customary law of which we have given specimens on the preceding pages. At another extremity of the world we find the Malayan feudalism, but this feudalism has been powerless to unroot the negaria, or village community, with its common ownership of at least part of the land, and the redistribution of land among the several negarias of the tribe.(40) With the Alfurus of Minahasa we find the communal rotation of the crops; with the Indian stem of the Wyandots we have the periodical redistribution of land within the tribe, and the clan-culture of the soil; and in all those parts of Sumatra where Moslem institutions have not yet totally destroyed the old organization we find the joint family (suka) and the village community (kota) which maintains its right upon the land, even if part of it has been cleared without its authorization.(41) But to say this, is to say that all customs for mutual protection and prevention of feuds and wars, which have been briefly indicated in the preceding pages as characteristic of the village community, exist as well. More than that: the more fully the communal possession of land has been maintained, the better and the gentler are the habits. De Stuers positively affirms that wherever the institution of the village community has been less encroached upon by the conquerors, the inequalities of fortunes are smaller, and the very prescriptions of the lex talionis are less cruel; while, on the contrary, wherever the village community has been totally broken up, "the inhabitants suffer the most unbearable oppression from their despotic rulers."(42) This is quite natural. And when Waitz made the remark that those stems which have maintained their tribal confederations stand on a higher level of development and have a richer literature than those stems which have forfeited the old bonds of union, he only pointed out what might have been foretold in advance.

More illustrations would simply involve me in tedious repetitions—so strikingly similar are the barbarian societies under all climates and amidst all races. The same process of evolution has been going on in mankind with a wonderful similarity. When the clan organization, assailed as it was from within by the separate family, and from without by the dismemberment of the migrating clans and the necessity of taking in strangers of different descent—the village community, based upon a territorial conception, came into existence. This new institution, which had naturally grown out of the preceding one—the clan—permitted the barbarians to pass through a most disturbed period of history without being broken into isolated families which would have succumbed in the struggle for life. New forms of culture developed under the new organization; agriculture attained the stage which it hardly has surpassed until now with the great number; the domestic industries reached a high degree of perfection. The wilderness was conquered, it was intersected by roads, dotted with swarms thrown off by the mother-communities. Markets and fortified centres, as well as places of public worship, were erected. The conceptions of a wider union, extended to whole stems and to several stems of various origin, were slowly elaborated. The old conceptions of justice which were conceptions of mere revenge, slowly underwent a deep modification—the idea of amends for the wrong done taking the place of revenge. The customary law which still makes the law of the daily life for two-thirds or more of mankind, was elaborated under that organization, as well as a system of habits intended to prevent the oppression of the masses by the minorities whose powers grew in proportion to the growing facilities for private accumulation of wealth. This was the new form taken by the tendencies of the masses for mutual support. And the progress—economical, intellectual, and moral—which mankind accomplished under this new popular form of organization, was so great that the States, when they were called later on into existence, simply took possession, in the interest of the minorities, of all the judicial, economical, and administrative functions which the village community already had exercised in the interest of all.

NOTES:

1. Numberless traces of post-pliocene lakes, now disappeared, are found over Central, West, and North Asia. Shells of the same species as those now found in the Caspian Sea are scattered over the surface of the soil as far East as half-way to Lake Aral, and are found in recent deposits as far north as Kazan. Traces of Caspian Gulfs, formerly taken for old beds of the Amu, intersect the Turcoman territory. Deduction must surely be made for temporary, periodical oscillations. But with all that, desiccation is evident, and it progresses at a formerly unexpected speed. Even in the relatively wet parts of South-West Siberia, the succession of reliable surveys, recently published by Yadrintseff, shows that villages have grown up on what was, eighty years ago, the bottom of one of the lakes of the Tchany group; while the other lakes of the same group, which covered hundreds of square miles some fifty years ago, are now mere ponds. In short, the desiccation of North-West Asia goes on at a rate which must be measured by centuries, instead of by the geological units of time of which we formerly used to speak.

2. Whole civilizations had thus disappeared, as is proved now by the remarkable discoveries in Mongolia on the Orkhon and in the Lukchun depression (by Dmitri Clements).

3. If I follow the opinions of (to name modern specialists only) Nasse, Kovalevsky, and Vinogradov, and not those of Mr. Seebohm (Mr. Denman Ross can only be named for the sake of completeness), it is not only because of the deep knowledge and concordance of views of these three writers, but also on account of their perfect knowledge of the village community

altogether—a knowledge the want of which is much felt in the otherwise remarkable work of Mr. Seebohm. The same remark applies, in a still higher degree, to the most elegant writings of Fustel de Coulanges, whose opinions and passionate interpretations of old texts are confined to himself.

4. The literature of the village community is so vast that but a few works can be named. Those of Sir Henry Maine, Mr. Seebohm, and Walter's Das alte Wallis (Bonn, 1859), are well-known popular sources of information about Scotland, Ireland, and Wales. For France, P. Viollet, Precis de l'histoire du droit francais. Droit prive, 1886, and several of his monographs in Bibl. de l'Ecole des Chartes; Babeau, Le Village sous l'ancien regime (the mir in the eighteenth century), third edition, 1887; Bonnemere, Doniol, etc. For Italy and Scandinavia, the chief works are named in Laveleye's Primitive Property, German version by K. Bucher. For the Finns, Rein's Forelasningar, i. 16; Koskinen, Finnische Geschichte, 1874, and various monographs. For the Lives and Coures, Prof. Lutchitzky in Severnyi Vestnil, 1891. For the Teutons, besides the well-known works of Maurer, Sohm (Altdeutsche Reichs-und Gerichts-Verfassung), also Dahn (Urzeit, Volkerwanderung, Langobardische Studien), Janssen, Wilh. Arnold, etc. For India, besides H. Maine and the works he names, Sir John Phear's Aryan Village. For Russia and South Slavonians, see Kavelin, Posnikoff, Sokolovsky, Kovalevsky, Efimenko, Ivanisheff, Klaus, etc. (copious bibliographical index up to 1880 in the Sbornik svedeniy ob obschinye of the Russ. Geog. Soc.). For general conclusions, besides Laveleye's Propriete, Morgan's Ancient Society, Lippert's Kulturgeschichte, Post, Dargun, etc., also the lectures of M. Kovalevsky (Tableau des origines et de l'evolution de la famille et de la propriete, Stockholm, 1890). Many special monographs ought to be mentioned; their titles may be found in the excellent lists given by P. Viollet in Droit prive and Droit public. For other races, see

subsequent notes.

5. Several authorities are inclined to consider the joint household as an intermediate stage between the clan and the village community; and there is no doubt that in very many cases village communities have grown up out of undivided families. Nevertheless, I consider the joint household as a fact of a different order. We find it within the gentes; on the other hand, we cannot affirm that joint families have existed at any period without belonging either to a gens or to a village community, or to a Gau. I conceive the early village communities as slowly originating directly from the gentes, and consisting, according to racial and local circumstances, either of several joint families, or of both joint and simple families, or (especially in the case of new settlements) of simple families only. If this view be correct, we should not have the right of establishing the series: gens, compound family, village community—the second member of the series having not the same ethnological value as the two others. See Appendix IX.

6. Stobbe, Beitrag zur Geschichte des deutschen Rechtes, p. 62.

7. The few traces of private property in land which are met with in the early barbarian period are found with such stems (the Batavians, the Franks in Gaul) as have been for a time under the influence of Imperial Rome. See Inama-Sternegg's Die Ausbildung der grossen Grundherrschaften in Deutschland, Bd. i. 1878. Also, Besseler, Neubruch nach dem alteren deutschen Recht, pp. 11-12, quoted by Kovalevsky, Modern Custom and Ancient Law, Moscow, 1886, i. 134.

8. Maurer's Markgenossenschaft; Lamprecht's "Wirthschaft und Recht der Franken zur Zeit der Volksrechte," in Histor. Taschenbuch, 1883; Seebohm's The English Village Community,

ch. vi, vii, and ix.

9. Letourneau, in Bulletin de la Soc. d'Anthropologie, 1888, vol. xi. p. 476.

10. Walter, Das alte Wallis, p. 323; Dm. Bakradze and N. Khoudadoff in Russian Zapiski of the Caucasian Geogr. Society, xiv. Part I.

11. Bancroft's Native Races; Waitz, Anthropologie, iii. 423; Montrozier, in Bull. Soc. d'Anthropologie, 1870; Post's Studien, etc.

12. A number of works, by Ory, Luro, Laudes, and Sylvestre, on the village community in Annam, proving that it has had there the same forms as in Germany or Russia, is mentioned in a review of these works by Jobbe-Duval, in Nouvelle Revue historique de droit francais et etranger, October and December, 1896. A good study of the village community of Peru, before the establishment of the power of the Incas, has been brought out by Heinrich Cunow (Die Soziale Verfassung des Inka-Reichs, Stuttgart, 1896.) The communal possession of land and communal culture are described in that work.

13. Kovalevsky, Modern Custom and Ancient Law, i. 115.

14. Palfrey, History of New England, ii. 13; quoted in Maine's Village Communities, New York, 1876, p. 201.

15. Konigswarter, Etudes sur le developpement des societes humaines, Paris, 1850.

16. This is, at least, the law of the Kalmucks, whose customary law bears the closest resemblance to the laws of the Teutons, the old Slavonians, etc.

17. The habit is in force still with many African and other tribes.

18. Village Communities, pp. 65-68 and 199.

19. Maurer (Gesch. der Markverfassung, sections 29, 97) is quite decisive upon this subject. He maintains that "All members of the community ... the laic and clerical lords as well, often also the partial co-possessors (Markberechtigte), and even strangers to the Mark, were submitted to its jurisdiction" (p. 312). This conception remained locally in force up to the fifteenth century.

20. Konigswarter, loc. cit. p. 50; J. Thrupp, Historical Law Tracts, London, 1843, p. 106.

21. Konigswarter has shown that the fred originated from an offering which had to be made to appease the ancestors. Later on, it was paid to the community, for the breach of peace; and still later to the judge, or king, or lord, when they had appropriated to themselves the rights of the community.

22. Post's Bausteine and Afrikanische Jurisprudenz, Oldenburg, 1887, vol. i. pp. 64 seq.; Kovalevsky, loc. cit. ii. 164-189.

23. O. Miller and M. Kovalevsky, "In the Mountaineer Communities of Kabardia," in Vestnik Evropy, April, 1884. With the Shakhsevens of the Mugan Steppe, blood feuds always end by marriage between the two hostile sides (Markoff, in appendix to the Zapiski of the Caucasian Geogr. Soc. xiv. 1, 21).

24. Post, in Afrik. Jurisprudenz, gives a series of facts illustrating the conceptions of equity inrooted among the African barbarians. The same may be said of all serious examinations into barbarian common law.

25. See the excellent chapter, "Le droit de La Vieille Irlande,"

(also "Le Haut Nord") in Etudes de droit international et de droit politique, by Prof. E. Nys, Bruxelles, 1896.

26. Introduction, p. xxxv.

27. Das alte Wallis, pp. 343-350.

28. Maynoff, "Sketches of the Judicial Practices of the Mordovians," in the ethnographical Zapiski of the Russian Geographical Society, 1885, pp. 236, 257.

29. Henry Maine, International Law, London, 1888, pp. 11-13. E. Nys, Les origines du droit international, Bruxelles, 1894.

30. A Russian historian, the Kazan Professor Schapoff, who was exiled in 1862 to Siberia, has given a good description of their institutions in the Izvestia of the East-Siberian Geographical Society, vol. v. 1874.

31. Sir Henry Maine's Village Communities, New York, 1876, pp. 193-196.

32. Nazaroff, The North Usuri Territory (Russian), St. Petersburg, 1887, p. 65.

33. Hanoteau et Letourneux, La Kabylie, 3 vols. Paris, 1883.

34. To convoke an "aid" or "bee," some kind of meal must be offered to the community. I am told by a Caucasian friend that in Georgia, when the poor man wants an "aid," he borrows from the rich man a sheep or two to prepare the meal, and the community bring, in addition to their work, so many provisions that he may repay the debt. A similar habit exists with the Mordovians.

35. Hanoteau et Letourneux, La kabylie, ii. 58. The same respect to strangers is the rule with the Mongols. The Mongol who has refused his roof to a stranger pays the full blood-compensation if the stranger has suffered therefrom (Bastian, Der Mensch in der Geschichte, iii. 231).

36. N. Khoudadoff, "Notes on the Khevsoures," in Zapiski of the Caucasian Geogr. Society, xiv. 1, Tiflis, 1890, p. 68. They also took the oath of not marrying girls from their own union, thus displaying a remarkable return to the old gentile rules.

37. Dm. Bakradze, "Notes on the Zakataly District," in same Zapiski, xiv. 1, p. 264. The "joint team" is as common among the Lezghines as it is among the Ossetes.

38. See Post, Afrikanische Jurisprudenz, Oldenburg, 1887. Munzinger, Ueber das Recht und Sitten der Bogos, Winterthur 1859; Casalis, Les Bassoutos, Paris, 1859; Maclean, Kafir Laws and Customs, Mount Coke, 1858, etc.

39. Waitz, iii. 423 seq.

40. Post's Studien zur Entwicklungsgeschichte des Familien Rechts Oldenburg, 1889, pp. 270 seq.

41. Powell, Annual Report of the Bureau of Ethnography, Washington, 1881, quoted in Post's Studien, p. 290; Bastian's Inselgruppen in Oceanien, 1883, p. 88.

42. De Stuers, quoted by Waitz, v. 141.

CHAPTER V

MUTUAL AID IN THE MEDIAEVAL CITY

Growth of authority in Barbarian Society. Serfdom in the villages. Revolt of fortified towns: their liberation; their charts. The guild. Double origin of the free medieval city. Self-jurisdiction, self-administration. Honourable position of labour. Trade by the guild and by the city.

Sociability and need of mutual aid and support are such inherent parts of human nature that at no time of history can we discover men living in small isolated families, fighting each other for the means of subsistence. On the contrary, modern research, as we saw it in the two preceding chapters, proves that since the very beginning of their prehistoric life men used to agglomerate into gentes, clans, or tribes, maintained by an idea of common descent and by worship of common ancestors. For thousands and thousands of years this organization has kept men together, even though there was no authority whatever to impose it. It has deeply impressed all subsequent development of mankind; and when the bonds of common descent had been loosened by migrations on a grand scale, while the development of the separated family within the clan itself had destroyed the old unity of the clan, a new form of union, territorial in its principle—the village community—was called into existence by the social genius of man. This institution, again, kept men together for a number of centuries, permitting them to further develop their social institutions and to pass through some of the darkest periods of history, without being dissolved into loose aggregations of families and individuals, to make a further step in their evolution, and to work out a number of secondary social institutions, several of which have survived down to the present time. We have now to follow the further developments of the same ever-living tendency for mutual aid. Taking the village communities of the so-called barbarians at a time when they were making a new start of civilization after the fall of the Roman Empire, we have to study the new aspects taken by the sociable wants of the masses in the middle ages, and especially in the medieval guilds and the medieval city.

Far from being the fighting animals they have often been compared to, the barbarians of the first centuries of our era (like so many Mongolians, Africans, Arabs, and so on, who still continue in the same barbarian stage) invariably preferred peace to war. With the exception of a few tribes which had been driven during the great migrations into unproductive deserts or highlands, and were thus compelled periodically to prey upon their better-favoured neighbours—apart from these, the great bulk of the Teutons, the Saxons, the Celts, the Slavonians, and so on, very soon after they had settled in their newly-conquered abodes, reverted to the spade or to their herds. The earliest barbarian codes already represent to us societies composed of peaceful agricultural communities, not hordes of men at war with each other. These barbarians covered the country with villages and farmhouses;(1) they cleared the forests, bridged the torrents, and colonized the formerly quite uninhabited wilderness; and they left the uncertain warlike pursuits to brotherhoods, scholae, or "trusts" of unruly men, gathered round temporary chieftains, who wandered about, offering their adventurous spirit, their arms, and their knowledge of warfare for the protection of populations, only too anxious to be left in peace. The warrior bands came and went, prosecuting their family feuds; but the great mass continued to till the soil, taking but little notice of their would-be rulers, so long as they did not interfere with the independence of their village communities.(2) The new occupiers of Europe evolved the systems of land tenure and soil culture which are still in force with hundreds of millions of men; they worked out their systems of compensation for wrongs, instead of the old tribal blood-revenge; they learned the first rudiments of industry; and while they fortified their villages with palisaded walls, or erected towers and earthen forts whereto to repair in case of a new invasion, they soon abandoned the task of defending these towers and forts to those who made of war a speciality.

The very peacefulness of the barbarians, certainly not their supposed warlike instincts, thus became the source of their subsequent subjection to the military chieftains. It is evident that the very mode of life of the armed brotherhoods offered them more facilities for enrichment than the tillers of the soil could find in their agricultural communities. Even now we see that armed men occasionally come together to shoot down Matabeles and to rob them of their droves of cattle, though the Matabeles only want peace and are ready to buy it at a high price. The scholae of old certainly were not more scrupulous than the scholae of our own time. Droves of cattle, iron (which was extremely costly at that time(3)), and slaves were appropriated in this way; and although most acquisitions were wasted on the spot in those glorious feasts of which epic poetry has so much to say—still some part of the robbed riches was used for further enrichment. There was plenty of waste land, and no lack of men ready to till it, if only they could obtain the necessary cattle and implements. Whole villages, ruined by murrains, pests, fires, or raids of new immigrants, were often abandoned by their inhabitants, who went anywhere in search of new abodes. They still do so in Russia in similar circumstances. And if one of the hirdmen of the armed brotherhoods offered the peasants some cattle for a fresh start, some iron to make a plough, if not the plough itself, his protection from further raids, and a number of years free from all obligations, before they should begin to repay the contracted debt, they settled upon the land. And when, after a hard fight with bad crops, inundations and pestilences, those pioneers began to repay their debts, they fell into servile obligations towards the protector of the territory. Wealth undoubtedly did accumulate in this way, and power always follows wealth.(4) And yet, the more we penetrate into the life of those times, the sixth and seventh centuries of our era, the more we see that another element, besides wealth and military force, was required to constitute the authority of the few. It was an element of law and tight, a desire of the masses to maintain peace, and to establish what they considered to be justice, which gave to the chieftains of the scholae—kings, dukes, knyazes, and the like—the force they acquired two or three hundred years later. That same idea of justice, conceived as an adequate revenge for the wrong done, which had grown in the tribal stage, now passed as a red thread through the history of subsequent institutions, and, much more even than military or economic causes, it became the basis upon which the authority of the kings and the feudal lords was founded.

In fact, one of the chief preoccupations of the barbarian village community always was, as it still is with our barbarian contemporaries, to put a speedy end to the feuds which arose from the then current conception of justice. When a quarrel took place, the community at once interfered, and after the folkmote had heard the case, it settled the amount of composition (wergeld) to be paid to the wronged person, or to his family, as well as the fred, or fine for breach of peace, which had to be paid to the community. Interior quarrels were easily appeased in this way. But when feuds broke out between two different tribes, or two confederations of tribes, notwithstanding all measures taken to prevent them,(5) the difficulty was to find an arbiter or sentence-finder whose decision should be accepted by both parties alike, both for his impartiality and for his knowledge of the oldest law. The difficulty was the greater as the customary laws of different tribes and confederations were at variance as to the compensation due in different cases. It therefore became habitual to take the sentence-finder from among such families, or such tribes, as were reputed for keeping the law of old in its purity; of being versed in the songs, triads, sagas, etc., by means of which law was perpetuated in memory; and to retain law in this way became a sort of art, a "mystery," carefully transmitted in certain families from generation to generation. Thus in Iceland, and in other Scandinavian lands, at every Allthing, or national folkmote, a lövsögmathr used to recite the whole law from memory for the enlightening of the assembly; and in Ireland there was, as is known, a special class of men reputed for the knowledge of the old traditions, and therefore enjoying a great authority as judges.(6) Again, when we are told by the Russian annals that some stems of North-West Russia, moved by the growing disorder which resulted from "clans rising against clans," appealed to Norman varingiar to be their judges and commanders of warrior scholae; and when we see the knyazes, or dukes, elected for the next two hundred years always from the same Norman family, we cannot but recognize that the Slavonians trusted to the Normans for a better knowledge of the law which would be equally recognized as good by different Slavonian kins. In this case the possession of runes, used for the transmission of old customs, was a decided advantage in favour of the Normans; but in other cases there are faint indications that the "eldest" branch of the stem, the supposed motherbranch, was appealed to to supply the judges, and its decisions were relied upon as just;(7) while at a later epoch we see a distinct tendency towards taking the sentence-finders from the Christian clergy, which, at that time, kept still to the fundamental, now forgotten, principle of Christianity, that retaliation is no act of justice. At that time the Christian clergy opened the churches as places of asylum for those who fled from blood revenge, and they willingly acted as arbiters in criminal cases, always opposing the old tribal principle of life for life and wound for wound. In short, the deeper we penetrate into the history of early institutions, the less we find grounds for the military theory of origin of authority. Even that power which later on became such a source of oppression seems, on the contrary, to have found its origin in the peaceful inclinations of the masses.

In all these cases the fred, which often amounted to half the compensation, went to the folkmote, and from times immemorial it used to be applied to works of common utility and defence. It has still the same destination (the erection of towers) among the Kabyles and certain Mongolian stems; and we have direct evidence that even several centuries later the judicial fines, in Pskov and several French and German cities, continued to be used for the repair of the city walls.(8) It was thus quite natural that the fines should be handed over to the sentence-finder, who was bound, in return, both to maintain the schola of armed men to whom the defence of the territory was trusted, and to execute the sentences. This became a universal custom in the eighth and ninth centuries, even when the sentence-finder was an elected bishop. The germ of a combination of what we should now call the judicial power and the executive thus made its appearance. But to these two functions the attributions of the duke or king were strictly limited. He was no ruler of the people—the supreme power still belonging to the folkmote—not even a commander of the popular militia; when the folk took to arms, it marched under a separate, also elected, commander, who was not a subordinate, but an equal to the king.(9) The king was a lord on his personal domain only. In fact, in barbarian language, the word konung, koning, or cyning synonymous with the Latin rex, had no other meaning than that of a temporary leader or chieftain of a band of men. The commander of a flotilla of boats, or even of a single pirate boat, was also a konung, and till the present day the commander of fishing in Norway is named Not-kong—"the king of the nets."(10) The veneration attached later on to the personality of a king did not yet exist, and while treason to the kin was punished by death, the slaying of a king could be recouped by the payment of compensation: a king simply was valued so much more than a freeman.(11) And when King Knu (or Canute) had killed one man of his own schola, the saga represents him convoking his comrades to a thing where he stood on his knees imploring pardon. He was pardoned, but not till he had agreed to pay nine times the regular composition, of which one-third went to himself for the loss of one of his men, one-third to the relatives of the slain man, and one-third (the fred) to the schola.(12) In reality, a complete change had to be accomplished in the current conceptions, under the double influence of the Church and the students of Roman law, before an idea of sanctity began to be attached to the personality of the king.

However, it lies beyond the scope of these essays to follow the gradual development of authority out of the elements just indicated. Historians, such as Mr. and Mrs. Green for this country, Augustin Thierry, Michelet, and Luchaire for France, Kaufmann, Janssen, W. Arnold, and even Nitzsch, for Germany, Leo and Botta for Italy, Byelaeff, Kostomaroff, and their followers for Russia, and many others, have fully told that tale. They have shown how populations, once free, and simply agreeing "to feed" a certain portion of their military defenders, gradually became the serfs of these protectors; how "commendation" to the Church, or to a lord, became a hard necessity for the freeman; how each lord's and bishop's castle became a robber's nest—how feudalism was imposed, in a word—and how the crusades, by freeing the serfs who wore the cross, gave the first impulse to popular emancipation. All this need not be retold in this place, our chief aim being to follow the constructive genius of the masses in their mutual-aid institutions.

At a time when the last vestiges of barbarian freedom seemed to disappear, and Europe, fallen under the dominion of thousands of petty rulers, was marching towards the constitution of such theocracies and despotic States as had followed the barbarian stage during the previous starts of civilization, or of barbarian monarchies, such as we see now in Africa, life in Europe took another direction. It went on on lines similar to those it had once taken in the cities of antique Greece. With a unanimity which seems almost incomprehensible, and for a long time was not understood by historians, the urban agglomerations, down to the smallest burgs, began to shake off the yoke of their worldly and clerical lords. The fortified village rose against the lord's castle, defied it first, attacked it next, and finally destroyed it. The movement spread from spot to spot, involving every town on the surface of Europe, and in less than a hundred years free cities had been called into existence on the coasts of the Mediterranean, the North Sea, the Baltic, the Atlantic Ocean, down to the fjords of Scandinavia; at the feet of the Apennines, the Alps, the Black Forest, the Grampians, and the Carpathians; in the plains of Russia, Hungary, France and Spain. Everywhere the same revolt took place, with the same features, passing through the same phases, leading to the same results. Wherever men had found, or expected to find, some protection behind their town walls, they instituted their "co-jurations," their "fraternities," their "friendships," united in one common idea, and boldly marching towards a new life of mutual support and liberty. And they succeeded so well that in three or four hundred years they had changed the very face of Europe. They had covered the country with beautiful sumptuous buildings, expressing the genius of free unions of free men, unrivalled since for their beauty and expressiveness; and they bequeathed to the following generations all the arts, all the industries, of which our present civilization, with all its achievements and promises for the future, is only a further development. And when we now look to the forces which have produced these grand results, we find them—not in the genius of individual heroes, not in the mighty organization of huge States or the political capacities of their rulers, but in the very same current of mutual aid and support which we saw at work in the village community, and which was vivified and reinforced in the Middle Ages by a new form of unions, inspired by the very same spirit but shaped on a new model—the guilds.

It is well known by this time that feudalism did not imply a dissolution of the village community. Although the lord had succeeded in imposing servile labour upon the peasants, and had appropriated for himself such rights as were formerly vested in the village community alone (taxes, mortmain, duties on inheritances and marriages), the peasants had, nevertheless, maintained the two fundamental rights of their communities: the common possession of the land, and self-jurisdiction. In olden times, when a king sent his vogt to a village, the peasants received him with flowers in one hand and arms in the other, and asked him—which law he intended to apply: the one he found in the village, or the one he brought with him? And, in the first case, they handed him the flowers and accepted him; while in the second case they fought him.(13) Now, they accepted the king's or the lord's official whom they could not refuse; but they maintained the folkmote's jurisdiction, and themselves nominated six, seven, or twelve judges, who acted with the lord's judge, in the presence of the folkmote, as arbiters and sentence-finders. In most cases the official had nothing left to him but to confirm the sentence and to levy the customary fred. This precious right of self-jurisdiction, which, at that time, meant self-administration and self-legislation, had been maintained through all the struggles; and even the lawyers by whom Karl the Great was surrounded could not abolish it; they were bound to confirm it. At the same time, in all matters concerning the community's domain, the folkmote retained its supremacy and (as shown by Maurer) often claimed submission from the lord himself in land tenure matters. No growth of feudalism could break this resistance; the village community kept its ground; and when, in the ninth and tenth centuries, the invasions of the Normans, the Arabs, and the Ugrians had demonstrated that military scholae were of little value for protecting the land, a general movement began all over Europe for fortifying the villages with stone walls and citadels. Thousands of fortified centres were then built by the energies of the village communities; and, once they had built their walls, once a common interest had been created in this new sanctuary — the town walls — they soon understood that they could henceforward resist the encroachments of the inner enemies, the lords, as well as the invasions of foreigners. A new life of freedom began to develop within the fortified enclosures. The medieval city was born.(14)

No period of history could better illustrate the constructive powers of the popular masses than the tenth and eleventh centuries, when the fortified villages and market-places, representing so many "oases amidst the feudal forest," began to free themselves from their lord's yoke, and slowly elaborated the future city organization; but, unhappily, this is a period about which historical information is especially scarce: we know the results, but little has reached us about the means by which they were achieved. Under the protection of their walls the cities' folkmotes — either quite independent, or led by the chief noble or merchant families — conquered and maintained the right of electing the military defensor and supreme judge of the town, or at least of choosing between those who pretended to occupy this position. In Italy the young communes were continually sending away their defensors or domini, fighting those who refused to go. The same went on in the East. In Bohemia, rich and poor alike (Bohemicae gentis magni et parvi, nobiles et ignobiles) took part in the election;(15) while, the vyeches (folkmotes) of the Russian cities regularly elected their dukes—always from the same Rurik family—covenanted with them, and sent the knyaz away if he had provoked discontent.(16) At the same time in most cities of Western and Southern Europe, the tendency was to take for defensor a bishop whom the city had elected itself; and so many bishops took the lead in protecting the "immunities" of the towns and in defending their liberties, that numbers of them were considered, after their death, as saints and special patrons of different cities. St. Uthelred of Winchester, St. Ulrik of Augsburg, St. Wolfgang of Ratisbon, St. Heribert of Cologne, St. Adalbert of Prague, and so on, as well as many abbots and monks, became so many cities' saints for having acted in defence of popular rights.(17) And under the new defensors, whether laic or clerical, the citizens conquered full self-jurisdiction and self-administration for their folkmotes.(18)

The whole process of liberation progressed by a series of imperceptible acts of devotion to the common cause, accomplished by men who came out of the masses—by unknown heroes whose very names have not been preserved by history. The wonderful movement of the God's peace (treuga Dei) by which the popular masses endeavoured to put a limit to the endless family feuds of the noble families, was born in the young towns, the bishops and the citizens trying to extend to the nobles the peace they had established within their town walls.(19) Already at that period, the commercial cities of Italy, and especially Amalfi (which had its elected consuls since 844, and frequently changed its doges in the tenth century)(20) worked out the customary maritime and commercial law which later on became a model for all Europe; Ravenna elaborated its craft organization, and Milan, which had made its first revolution in 980, became a great centre of commerce, its trades enjoying a full independence since the eleventh century.(21) So also Brugge and Ghent; so also several cities of France in which the Mahl or forum had become a quite independent institution.(22) And already during that period began the work of artistic decoration of the towns by works of architecture, which we still admire and which loudly testify of the intellectual movement of the times. "The basilicae were then renewed in almost all the universe," Raoul Glaber wrote in his chronicle, and some of the finest monuments of medieval architecture date from that period: the wonderful old church of Bremen was built in the ninth century, Saint Marc of Venice was finished in 1071, and the beautiful dome of Pisa in 1063. In fact, the intellectual movement which has been described as the Twelfth Century Renaissance(23) and the Twelfth Century Rationalism—the precursor of the Reform(24) date from that period, when most cities were still simple agglomerations of small village communities enclosed by walls.

However, another element, besides the village-community principle, was required to give to these growing centres of liberty and enlightenment the unity of thought and action, and the powers of initiative, which made their force in the twelfth and thirteenth centuries. With the growing diversity of occupations, crafts and arts, and with the growing commerce in distant lands, some new form of union was required, and this necessary new element was supplied by the guilds. Volumes and volumes have been written about these unions which, under the name of guilds, brotherhoods, friendships and druzhestva, minne, artels in Russia, esnaifs in Servia and Turkey, amkari in Georgia, and so on, took such a formidable development in medieval times and played such an important part in the emancipation of the cities. But it took historians more than sixty years before the universality of this institution and its true characters were understood. Only now, when hundreds of guild statutes have been published and studied, and their relationship to the Roman collegiae, and the earlier unions in Greece and in India,(25) is known, can we maintain with full confidence that these brotherhoods were but a further development of the same principles which we saw at work in the gens and the village community.

Nothing illustrates better these medieval brother hoods than those temporary guilds which were formed on board ships. When a ship of the Hansa had accomplished her first half-day passage after having left the port, the captain (Schiffer) gathered all crew and passengers on the deck, and held the following language, as reported by a contemporary: —

"'As we are now at the mercy of God and the waves,' he said, 'each one must be equal to each other. And as we are surrounded by storms, high waves, pirates and other dangers, we must keep a strict order that we may bring our voyage to a good end. That is why we shall pronounce the prayer for a good wind and good success, and, according to marine law, we shall name the occupiers of the judges' seats (Schoffenstellen).' Thereupon the crew elected a Vogt and four scabini, to act as their judges. At the end of the voyage the Vogt and the scabini abdicated their functions and addressed the crew as follows: — 'What has happened on board ship, we must pardon to each other and consider as dead (todt und ab sein lassen). What we have judged right, was for the sake of justice. This is why we beg you all, in the name of honest justice, to forget all the animosity one may nourish against another, and to swear on bread and salt that he will not think of it in a bad spirit. If any one, however, considers himself wronged, he must appeal to the land Vogt and ask justice from him before sunset.' On landing, the Stock with the fredfines was handed over to the Vogt of the sea-port for distribution among the poor."(26)

This simple narrative, perhaps better than anything else, depicts the spirit of the medieval guilds. Like organizations came into existence wherever a group of men—fishermen, hunters, travelling merchants, builders, or settled craftsmen—came together for a common pursuit. Thus, there was on board ship the naval authority of the captain; but, for the very success of the common enterprise, all men on board, rich and poor, masters and crew, captain and sailors, agreed to be equals in their mutual relations, to be simply men, bound to aid each other and to settle their possible disputes before judges elected by all of them. So also when a number of craftsmen—masons, carpenters, stone-cutters, etc.—came together for building, say, a cathedral, they all belonged to a city which had its political organization, and each of them belonged moreover to his own craft; but they were united besides by their common enterprise, which they knew better than any one else, and they joined into a body united by closer, although temporary, bonds; they founded the guild for the building of the cathedral.(27) We may see the same till now in the Kabylian. cof:(28) the Kabyles have their village community; but this union is not sufficient for all political, commercial, and personal needs of union, and the closer brotherhood of the cof is constituted.

As to the social characters of the medieval guild, any guild-statute may illustrate them. Taking, for instance, the skraa of some early Danish guild, we read in it, first, a statement of the general brotherly feelings which must reign in the guild; next come the regulations relative to self-jurisdiction in cases of quarrels arising between two brothers, or a brother and a stranger; and then, the social duties of the brethren are enumerated. If a brother's house is burned, or he has lost his ship, or has suffered on a pilgrim's voyage, all the brethren must come to his aid. If a brother falls dangerously ill, two brethren must keep watch by his bed till he is out of danger, and if he dies, the brethren must bury him—a great affair in those times of pestilences—and follow him to the church and the grave. After his death they must provide for his children, if necessary; very often the widow becomes a sister to the guild.(29)

These two leading features appeared in every brotherhood formed for any possible purpose. In each case the members treated each other as, and named each other, brother and sister;(30) all were equals before the guild. They owned some "chattel" (cattle, land, buildings, places of worship, or "stock") in common. All brothers took the oath of abandoning all feuds of old; and, without imposing upon each other the obligation of never quarrelling again, they agreed that no quarrel should degenerate into a feud, or into a law-suit before another court than the tribunal of the brothers themselves. And if a brother was involved in a quarrel with a stranger to the guild, they agreed to support him for bad and for good; that is, whether he was unjustly accused of aggression, or really was the aggressor, they had to support him, and to bring things to a peaceful end. So long as his was not a secret aggression—in which case he would have been treated as an outlaw—the brotherhood stood by him.(31) If the relatives of the wronged man wanted to revenge the offence at once by a new aggression, the brotherhood supplied him with a horse to run away, or with a boat, a pair of oars, a knife and a steel for striking light; if he remained in town, twelve brothers accompanied him to protect him; and in the meantime they arranged the composition. They went to court to support by oath the truthfulness of his statements, and if he was found guilty they did not let him go to full ruin and become a slave through not paying the due compensation: they all paid it, just as the gens did in olden times. Only when a brother had broken the faith towards his guild-brethren, or other people, he was excluded from the brotherhood "with a Nothing's name" (tha scal han maeles af brodrescap met nidings nafn).(32)

Such were the leading ideas of those brotherhoods which gradually covered the whole of medieval life. In fact, we know of guilds among all possible professions: guilds of serfs,(33) guilds of freemen, and guilds of both serfs and freemen; guilds called into life for the special purpose of hunting, fishing, or a trading expedition, and dissolved when the special purpose had been achieved; and guilds lasting for centuries in a given craft or trade. And, in proportion as life took an always greater variety of pursuits, the variety in the guilds grew in proportion. So we see not only merchants, craftsmen, hunters, and peasants united in guilds; we also see guilds of priests, painters, teachers of primary schools and universities, guilds for performing the passion play, for building a church, for developing the "mystery" of a given school of art or craft, or for a special recreation—even guilds among beggars, executioners, and lost women, all organized on the same double principle of self-jurisdiction and mutual support.(34) For Russia we have positive evidence showing that the very "making of Russia" was as much the work of its hunters', fishermen's, and traders' artels as of the budding village communities, and up to the present day the country is covered with artels.(35)

These few remarks show how incorrect was the view taken by some early explorers of the guilds when they wanted to see the essence of the institution in its yearly festival. In reality, the day of the common meal was always the day, or the morrow of the day, of election of aldermen, of discussion of alterations in the statutes, and very often the day of judgment of quarrels that had risen among the brethren,(36) or of renewed allegiance to the guild. The common meal, like the festival at the old tribal folkmote—the mahl or malum—or the Buryate aba, or the parish feast and the harvest supper, was simply an affirmation of brotherhood. It symbolized the times when everything was kept in common by the clan. This day, at least, all belonged to all; all sate at the same table and partook of the same meal. Even at a much later time the inmate of the almshouse of a London guild sat this day by the side of the rich alderman. As to the distinction which several explorers have tried to establish between the old Saxon "frith guild" and the so-called "social" or "religious" guilds—all were frith guilds in the sense above mentioned,(37) and all were religious in the sense in which a village community or a city placed under the protection of a special saint is social and religious. If the institution of the guild has taken such an immense extension in Asia, Africa, and Europe, if it has lived thousands of years, reappearing again and again when similar conditions called it into existence, it is because it was much more than an eating association, or an association for going to church on a certain day, or a burial club. It answered to a deeply inrooted want of human nature; and it embodied all the attributes which the State appropriated later on for its bureaucracy and police, and much more than that. It was an association for mutual support in all circumstances and in all accidents of life, "by deed and advise," and it was an organization for maintaining justice—with this difference from the State, that on all these occasions a humane, a brotherly element was introduced instead of the formal element which is the essential characteristic of State interference. Even when appearing before the guild tribunal, the guild-brother answered before men who knew him well and had stood by him before in their daily work, at the common meal, in the performance of their brotherly duties: men who were his equals and brethren indeed, not theorists of law nor defenders of some one else's interests.(38)

It is evident that an institution so well suited to serve the need of union, without depriving the individual of his initiative, could but spread, grow, and fortify. The difficulty was only to find such form as would permit to federate the unions of the guilds without interfering with the unions of the village communities, and to federate all these into one harmonious whole. And when this form of combination had been found, and a series of favourable circumstances permitted the cities to affirm their independence, they did so with a unity of thought which can but excite our admiration, even in our century of railways, telegraphs, and printing. Hundreds of charters in which the cities inscribed their liberation have reached us, and through all of them—notwithstanding the infinite variety of details, which depended upon the more or less greater fulness of emancipation—the same leading ideas run. The city organized itself as a federation of both small village communities and guilds.

"All those who belong to the friendship of the town"—so runs a charter given in 1188 to the burghesses of Aire by Philip, Count of Flanders—"have promised and confirmed by faith and oath that they will aid each other as brethren, in whatever is useful and honest. That if one commits against another an offence in words or in deeds, the one who has suffered there from will not take revenge, either himself or his people ... he will lodge a complaint and the offender will make good for his offence, according to what will be pronounced by twelve elected judges acting as arbiters, And if the offender or the offended, after having been warned thrice, does not submit to the decision of the arbiters, he will be excluded from the friendship as a wicked man and a perjuror.(39)

"Each one of the men of the commune will be faithful to his conjuror, and will give him aid and advice, according to what justice will dictate him"—the Amiens and Abbeville charters say. "All will aid each other, according to their powers, within the boundaries of the Commune, and will not suffer that any one takes anything from any one of them, or makes one pay contributions"—do we read in the charters of Soissons, Compiegne, Senlis, and many others of the same type.(40) And so on with countless variations on the same theme.

"The Commune," Guilbert de Nogent wrote, "is an oath of mutual aid (mutui adjutorii conjuratio) ... A new and detestable word. Through it the serfs (capite sensi) are freed from all serfdom; through it, they can only be condemned to a legally determined fine for breaches of the law; through it, they cease to be liable to payments which the serfs always used to pay."(41)

The same wave of emancipation ran, in the twelfth century, through all parts of the continent, involving both rich cities and the poorest towns. And if we may say that, as a rule, the Italian cities were the first to free themselves, we can assign no centre from which the movement would have spread. Very often a small burg in central Europe took the lead for its region, and big agglomerations accepted the little town's charter as a model for their own. Thus, the charter of a small town, Lorris, was adopted by eighty-three towns in south-west France, and that of Beaumont became the model for over five hundred towns and cities in Belgium and France. Special deputies were dispatched by the cities to their neighbours to obtain a copy from their charter, and the constitution was framed upon that model. However, they did not simply copy each other: they framed their own charters in accordance with the concessions they had obtained from their lords; and the result was that, as remarked by an historian, the charters of the medieval communes offer the same variety as the Gothic architecture of their churches and cathedrals. The same leading ideas in all of them—the cathedral symbolizing the union of parish and guild in the, city—and the same infinitely rich variety of detail.

Self-jurisdiction was the essential point, and self-jurisdiction meant self-administration. But the commune was not simply an "autonomous" part of the State—such ambiguous words had not yet been invented by that time—it was a State in itself. It had the right of war and peace, of federation and alliance with its neighbours. It was sovereign in its own affairs, and mixed with no others. The supreme political power could be vested entirely in a democratic forum, as was the case in Pskov, whose vyeche sent and received ambassadors, concluded treaties, accepted and sent away princes, or went on without them for dozens of years; or it was vested in, or usurped by, an aristocracy of merchants or even nobles, as was the case in hundreds of Italian and middle European cities. The principle, nevertheless, remained the same: the city was a State and—what was perhaps still more remarkable—when the power in the city was usurped by an aristocracy of merchants or even nobles, the inner life of the city and the democratism of its daily life did not disappear: they depended but little upon what may be called the political form of the State.

The secret of this seeming anomaly lies in the fact that a medieval city was not a centralized State. During the first centuries of its existence, the city hardly could be named a State as regards its interior organization, because the middle ages knew no more of the present centralization of functions than of the present territorial centralization. Each group had its share of sovereignty. The city was usually divided into four quarters, or into five to seven sections radiating from a centre, each quarter or section roughly corresponding to a certain trade or profession which prevailed in it, but nevertheless containing inhabitants of different social positions and occupations—nobles, merchants, artisans, or even half-serfs; and each section or quarter constituted a quite independent agglomeration. In Venice, each island was an independent political community. It had its own organized trades, its own commerce in salt, its own jurisdiction and administration, its own forum; and the nomination of a doge by the city changed nothing in the inner independence of the units.(42) In Cologne, we see the inhabitants divided into Geburschaften and Heimschaften (viciniae), i.e. neighbour guilds, which dated from the Franconian period. Each of them had its judge (Burrichter) and the usual twelve elected sentence-finders (Schoffen), its Vogt, and its greve or commander of the local militia.(43) The story of early London before the Conquest—Mr. Green says—is that "of a number of little groups scattered here and there over the area within the walls, each growing up with its own life and institutions, guilds, sokes, religious houses and the like, and only slowly drawing together into a municipal union."(44) And if we refer to the annals of the Russian cities, Novgorod and Pskov, both of which are relatively rich in local details, we find the section (konets) consisting of independent streets (ulitsa), each of which, though chiefly peopled with artisans of a certain craft, had also merchants and landowners among its inhabitants, and was a separate community. It had the communal responsibility of all members in case of crime, its own jurisdiction and administration by street aldermen (ulichanskiye starosty), its own seal and, in case of need, its own forum; its own militia, as also its self-elected priests and its, own collective life and collective enterprise.(45)

The medieval city thus appears as a double federation: of all householders united into small territorial unions—the street, the parish, the section—and of individuals united by oath into guilds according to their professions; the former being a produce of the village-community origin of the city, while the second is a subsequent growth called to life by new conditions.

To guarantee liberty, self-administration, and peace was the chief aim of the medieval city; and labour, as we shall presently see when speaking of the craft guilds, was its chief foundation. But "production" did not absorb the whole attention of the medieval economist. With his practical mind, he understood that "consumption" must be guaranteed in order to obtain production; and therefore, to provide for "the common first food and lodging of poor and rich alike" (gemeine notdurft und gemach armer und richer(46)) was the fundamental principle in each city. The purchase of food supplies and other first necessaries (coal, wood, etc.) before they had reached the market, or altogether in especially favourable conditions from which others would be excluded—the preempcio, in a word—was entirely prohibited. Everything had to go to the market and be offered there for every one's purchase, till the ringing of the bell had closed the market. Then only could the retailer buy the remainder, and even then his profit should be an "honest profit" only.(47) Moreover, when corn was bought by a baker wholesale after the close of the market, every citizen had the right to claim part of the corn (about half-a-quarter) for his own use, at wholesale price, if he did so before the final conclusion of the bargain; and reciprocally, every baker could claim the same if the citizen purchased corn for re-selling it. In the first case, the corn had only to be brought to the town mill to be ground in its proper turn for a settled price, and the bread could be baked in the four banal, or communal oven.(48) In short, if a scarcity visited the city, all had to suffer from it more or less; but apart from the calamities, so long as the free cities existed no one could die in their midst from starvation, as is unhappily too often the case in our own times.

However, all such regulations belong to later periods of the cities' life, while at an earlier period it was the city itself which used to buy all food supplies for the use of the citizens. The documents recently published by Mr. Gross are quite positive on this point and fully support his conclusion to the effect that the cargoes of subsistences "were purchased by certain civic officials in the name of the town, and then distributed in shares among the merchant burgesses, no one being allowed to buy wares landed in the port unless the municipal authorities refused to purchase them. This seem—she adds—to have been quite a common practice in England, Ireland, Wales and Scotland."(49) Even in the sixteenth century we find that common purchases of corn were made for the "comoditie and profitt in all things of this.... Citie and Chamber of London, and of all the Citizens and Inhabitants of the same as moche as in us lieth"—as the Mayor wrote in 1565.(50) In Venice, the whole of the trade in corn is well known to have been in the hands of the city; the "quarters," on receiving the cereals from the board which administrated the imports, being bound to send to every citizen's house the quantity allotted to him.(51) In France, the city of Amiens used to purchase salt and to distribute it to all citizens at cost price;(52) and even now one sees in many French towns the halles which formerly were municipal depots for corn and salt.(53) In Russia it was a regular custom in Novgorod and Pskov.

The whole matter relative to the communal purchases for the use of the citizens, and the manner in which they used to be made, seems not to have yet received proper attention from the historians of the period; but there are here and there some very interesting facts which throw a new light upon it. Thus there is, among Mr. Gross's documents, a Kilkenny ordinance of the year 1367, from which we learn how the prices of the goods were established. "The merchants and the sailors," Mr. Gross writes, "were to state on oath the first cost of the goods and the expenses of transportation. Then the mayor of the town and two discreet men were to name the price at which the wares were to be sold." The same rule held good in Thurso for merchandise coming "by sea or land." This way of "naming the price" so well answers to the very conceptions of trade which were current in medieval times that it must have been all but universal. To have the price established by a third person was a very old custom; and for all interchange within the city it certainly was a widely-spread habit to leave the establishment of prices to "discreet men"—to a third party—and not to the vendor or the buyer. But this order of things takes us still further back in the history of trade— namely, to a time when trade in staple produce was carried on by the whole city, and the merchants were only the commissioners, the trustees, of the city for selling the goods which it exported. A Waterford ordinance, published also by Mr. Gross, says "that all manere of marchandis what so ever kynde thei be of ... shal be bought by the Maire and balives which bene commene biers [common buyers, for the town] for the time being, and to distribute the same on freemen of the citie (the propre goods of free citisains and inhabitants only excepted)." This ordinance can hardly be explained otherwise than by admitting that all the exterior trade of the town was carried on by its agents. Moreover, we have direct evidence of such having been the case for Novgorod and Pskov. It was the Sovereign Novgorod and the Sovereign Pskov who sent their caravans of merchants to distant lands.

We know also that in nearly all medieval cities of Middle and Western Europe, the craft guilds used to buy, as a body, all necessary raw produce, and to sell the produce of their work through their officials, and it is hardly possible that the same should not have been done for exterior trade—the more so as it is well known that up to the thirteenth century, not only all merchants of a given city were considered abroad as responsible in a body for debts contracted by any one of them, but the whole city as well was responsible for the debts of each one of its merchants. Only in the twelfth and thirteenth century the towns on the Rhine entered into special treaties abolishing this responsibility.(54) And finally we have the remarkable Ipswich document published by Mr. Gross, from which document we learn that the merchant guild of this town was constituted by all who had the freedom of the city, and who wished to pay their contribution ("their hanse") to the guild, the whole community discussing all together how better to maintain the merchant guild, and giving it certain privileges. The merchant guild of Ipswich thus appears rather as a body of trustees of the town than as a common private guild.

In short, the more we begin to know the mediaeval city the more we see that it was not simply a political organization for the protection of certain political liberties. It was an attempt at organizing, on a much grander scale than in a village community, a close union for mutual aid and support, for consumption and production, and for social life altogether, without imposing upon men the fetters of the State, but giving full liberty of expression to the creative genius of each separate group of individuals in art, crafts, science, commerce, and political organization. How far this attempt has been successful will be best seen when we have analyzed in the next chapter the organization of labour in the medieval city and the relations of the cities with the surrounding peasant population.

NOTES:

1. W. Arnold, in his Wanderungen und Ansiedelungen der deutschen Stamme, p. 431, even maintains that one-half of the now arable area in middle Germany must have been reclaimed

from the sixth to the ninth century. Nitzsch (Geschichte des deutschen Volkes, Leipzig, 1883, vol. i.) shares the same opinion.

2. Leo and Botta, Histoire d'Italie, French edition, 1844, t. i., p. 37.

3. The composition for the stealing of a simple knife was 15 solidii and of the iron parts of a mill, 45 solidii (See on this subject Lamprecht's Wirthschaft und Recht der Franken in Raumer's Historisches Taschenbuch, 1883, p. 52.) According to the Riparian law, the sword, the spear, and the iron armour of a warrior attained the value of at least twenty-five cows, or two years of a freeman's labour. A cuirass alone was valued in the Salic law (Desmichels, quoted by Michelet) at as much as thirty-six bushels of wheat.

4. The chief wealth of the chieftains, for a long time, was in their personal domains peopled partly with prisoner slaves, but chiefly in the above way. On the origin of property see Inama Sternegg's Die Ausbildung der grossen Grundherrschaften in Deutschland, in Schmoller's Forschungen, Bd. I., 1878; F. Dahn's Urgeschichte der germanischen und romanischen Volker, Berlin, 1881; Maurer's Dorfverfassung; Guizot's Essais sur l'histoire de France; Maine's Village Community; Botta's Histoire d'Italie; Seebohm, Vinogradov, J. R. Green, etc.

5. See Sir Henry Maine's International Law, London, 1888.

6. Ancient Laws of Ireland, Introduction; E. Nys, Etudes de droit international, t. i., 1896, pp. 86 seq. Among the Ossetes the arbiters from three oldest villages enjoy a special reputation (M. Kovalevsky's Modern Custom and Old Law, Moscow, 1886, ii. 217, Russian).

7. It is permissible to think that this conception (related to the

conception of tanistry) played an important part in the life of the period; but research has not yet been directed that way.

8. It was distinctly stated in the charter of St. Quentin of the year 1002 that the ransom for houses which had to be demolished for crimes went for the city walls. The same destination was given to the Ungeld in German cities. At Pskov the cathedral was the bank for the fines, and from this fund money was taken for the wails.

9. Sohm, Frankische Rechts-und Gerichtsverfassung, p. 23; also Nitzsch, Geschichte des deutschen Volkes, i. 78.

10. See the excellent remarks on this subject in Augustin Thierry's Lettres sur l'histoire de France. 7th Letter. The barbarian translations of parts of the Bible are extremely instructive on this point.

11. Thirty-six times more than a noble, according to the Anglo-Saxon law. In the code of Rothari the slaying of a king is, however, punished by death; but (apart from Roman influence) this new disposition was introduced (in 646) in the Lombardian law—as remarked by Leo and Botta—to cover the king from blood revenge. The king being at that time the executioner of his own sentences (as the tribe formerly was of its own sentences), he had to be protected by a special disposition, the more so as several Lombardian kings before Rothari had been slain in succession (Leo and Botta, l.c., i. 66-90).

12. Kaufmann, Deutsche Geschichte, Bd. I. "Die Germanen der Urzeit," p. 133.

13. Dr. F. Dahn, Urgeschichte der germanischen und romanischen Volker, Berlin, 1881, Bd. I. 96.

14. If I thus follow the views long since advocated by Maurer (Geschichte der Stadteverfassung in Deutschland, Erlangen, 1869), it is because he has fully proved the uninterrupted evolution from the village community to the mediaeval city, and that his views alone can explain the universality of the communal movement. Savigny and Eichhorn and their followers have certainly proved that the traditions of the Roman municipia had never totally disappeared. But they took no account of the village community period which the barbarians lived through before they had any cities. The fact is, that whenever mankind made a new start in civilization, in Greece, Rome, or middle Europe, it passed through the same stages—the tribe, the village community, the free city, the state—each one naturally evolving out of the preceding stage. Of course, the experience of each preceding civilization was never lost. Greece (itself influenced by Eastern civilizations) influenced Rome, and Rome influenced our civilization; but each of them begin from the same beginning—the tribe. And just as we cannot say that our states are continuations of the Roman state, so also can we not say that the mediaeval cities of Europe (including Scandinavia and Russia) were a continuation of the Roman cities. They were a continuation of the barbarian village community, influenced to a certain extent by the traditions of the Roman towns.

15. M. Kovalevsky, Modern Customs and Ancient Laws of Russia (Ilchester Lectures, London, 1891, Lecture 4).

16. A considerable amount of research had to be done before this character of the so-called udyelnyi period was properly established by the works of Byelaeff (Tales from Russian History), Kostomaroff (The Beginnings of Autocracy in Russia), and especially Professor Sergievich (The Vyeche and the Prince). The English reader may find some information about this period

in the just-named work of M. Kovalevsky, in Rambaud's History of Russia, and, in a short summary, in the article "Russia" of the last edition of Chambers's Encyclopaedia.

17. Ferrari, Histoire des revolutions d'Italie, i. 257; Kallsen, Die deutschen Stadte im Mittelalter, Bd. I. (Halle, 1891).

18. See the excellent remarks of Mr. G.L. Gomme as regards the folkmote of London (The Literature of Local Institutions, London, 1886, p. 76). It must, however, be remarked that in royal cities the folkmote never attained the independence which it assumed elsewhere. It is even certain that Moscow and Paris were chosen by the kings and the Church as the cradles of the future royal authority in the State, because they did not possess the tradition of folkmotes accustomed to act as sovereign in all matters.

19. A. Luchaire, Les Communes francaises; also Kluckohn, Geschichte des Gottesfrieden, 1857. L. Semichon (La paix et la treve de Dieu, 2 vols., Paris, 1869) has tried to represent the communal movement as issued from that institution. In reality, the treuga Dei, like the league started under Louis le Gros for the defence against both the robberies of the nobles and the Norman invasions, was a thoroughly popular movement. The only historian who mentions this last league—that is, Vitalis—describes it as a "popular community" ("Considerations sur l'histoire de France," in vol. iv. of Aug. Thierry's OEuvres, Paris, 1868, p. 191 and note).

20. Ferrari, i. 152, 263, etc.

21. Perrens, Histoire de Florence, i. 188; Ferrari, l.c., i. 283.

22. Aug. Thierry, Essai sur l'histoire du Tiers Etat, Paris, 1875, p.

414, note.

23. F. Rocquain, "La Renaissance au XIIe siecle," in Etudes sur l'histoire de France, Paris, 1875, pp. 55-117.

24. N. Kostomaroff, "The Rationalists of the Twelfth Century," in his Monographies and Researches (Russian).

25. Very interesting facts relative to the universality of guilds will be found in "Two Thousand Years of Guild Life," by Rev. J. M. Lambert, Hull, 1891. On the Georgian amkari, see S. Eghiazarov, Gorodskiye Tsekhi ("Organization of Transcaucasian Amkari"), in Memoirs of the Caucasian Geographical Society, xiv. 2, 1891.

26. J.D. Wunderer's "Reisebericht" in Fichard's Frankfurter Archiv, ii. 245; quoted by Janssen, Geschichte des deutschen Volkes, i. 355.

27. Dr. Leonard Ennen, Der Dom zu Koln, Historische Einleitung, Koln, 1871, pp. 46, 50.

28. See previous chapter.

29. Kofod Ancher, Om gamle Danske Gilder og deres Undergang, Copenhagen, 1785. Statutes of a Knu guild.

30. Upon the position of women in guilds, see Miss Toulmin Smith's introductory remarks to the English Guilds of her father. One of the Cambridge statutes (p. 281) of the year 1503 is quite positive in the following sentence: "Thys statute is made by the comyne assent of all the bretherne and sisterne of alhallowe yelde."

31. In medieval times, only secret aggression was treated as a

murder. Blood-revenge in broad daylight was justice; and slaying in a quarrel was not murder, once the aggressor showed his willingness to repent and to repair the wrong he had done. Deep traces of this distinction still exist in modern criminal law, especially in Russia.

32. Kofod Ancher, l.c. This old booklet contains much that has been lost sight of by later explorers.

33. They played an important part in the revolts of the serfs, and were therefore prohibited several times in succession in the second half of the ninth century. Of course, the king's prohibitions remained a dead letter.

34. The medieval Italian painters were also organized in guilds, which became at a later epoch Academies of art. If the Italian art of those times is impressed with so much individuality that we distinguish, even now, between the different schools of Padua, Bassano, Treviso, Verona, and so on, although all these cities were under the sway of Venice, this was due—J. Paul Richter remarks—to the fact that the painters of each city belonged to a separate guild, friendly with the guilds of other towns, but leading a separate existence. The oldest guild-statute known is that of Verona, dating from 1303, but evidently copied from some much older statute. "Fraternal assistance in necessity of whatever kind," "hospitality towards strangers, when passing through the town, as thus information may be obtained about matters which one may like to learn," and "obligation of offering comfort in case of debility" are among the obligations of the members (Nineteenth Century, Nov. 1890, and Aug. 1892).

35. The chief works on the artels are named in the article "Russia" of the Encyclopaedia Britannica, 9th edition, p. 84.

36. See, for instance, the texts of the Cambridge guilds given by Toulmin Smith (English Guilds, London, 1870, pp. 274-276), from which it appears that the "generall and principall day" was the "eleccioun day;" or, Ch. M. Clode's The Early History of the Guild of the Merchant Taylors, London, 1888, i. 45; and so on. For the renewal of allegiance, see the Jomsviking saga, mentioned in Pappenheim's Altdanische Schutzgilden, Breslau, 1885, p. 67. It appears very probable that when the guilds began to be prosecuted, many of them inscribed in their statutes the meal day only, or their pious duties, and only alluded to the judicial function of the guild in vague words; but this function did not disappear till a very much later time. The question, "Who will be my judge?" has no meaning now, since the State has appropriated for its bureaucracy the organization of justice; but it was of primordial importance in medieval times, the more so as self-jurisdiction meant self-administration. It must also be remarked that the translation of the Saxon and Danish "guild-bretheren," or "brodre," by the Latin convivii must also have contributed to the above confusion.

37. See the excellent remarks upon the frith guild by J.R. Green and Mrs. Green in The Conquest of England, London, 1883, pp. 229-230.

38. None

39. Recueil des ordonnances des rois de France, t. xii. 562; quoted by Aug. Thierry in Considerations sur l'histoire de France, p. 196, ed. 12mo.

40. A. Luchaire, Les Communes francaises, pp, 45-46.

41. Guilbert de Nogent, De vita sua, quoted by Luchaire, l.c., p. 14.

42. Lebret, Histoire de Venise, i. 393; also Marin, quoted by Leo and Botta in Histoire de l'Italie, French edition, 1844, t. i 500.

43. Dr. W. Arnold, Verfassungsgeschichte der deutschen Freistadte, 1854, Bd. ii. 227 seq.; Ennen, Geschichte der Stadt Koeln, Bd. i. 228-229; also the documents published by Ennen and Eckert.

44. Conquest of England, 1883, p. 453.

45. Byelaeff, Russian History, vols. ii. and iii.

46. W. Gramich, Verfassungs und Verwaltungsgeschichte der Stadt Wurzburg im 13. bis zum 15. Jahrhundert, Wurzburg, 1882, p. 34.

47. When a boat brought a cargo of coal to Wurzburg, coal could only be sold in retail during the first eight days, each family being entitled to no more than fifty basketfuls. The remaining cargo could be sold wholesale, but the retailer was allowed to raise a zittlicher profit only, the unzittlicher, or dishonest profit, being strictly forbidden (Gramich, l.c.). Same in London (Liber albus, quoted by Ochenkowski, p. 161), and, in fact, everywhere.

48. See Fagniez, Etudes sur l'industrie et la classe industrielle a Paris au XIIIme et XIVme siecle, Paris, 1877, pp. 155 seq. It hardly need be added that the tax on bread, and on beer as well, was settled after careful experiments as to the quantity of bread and beer which could be obtained from a given amount of corn. The Amiens archives contain the minutes of such experiences (A. de Calonne, l.c. pp. 77, 93). Also those of London (Ochenkowski, England's wirthschaftliche Entwickelung, etc., Jena, 1879, p. 165).

49. Ch. Gross, The Guild Merchant, Oxford, 1890, i. 135. His

documents prove that this practice existed in Liverpool (ii. 148-150), Waterford in Ireland, Neath in Wales, and Linlithgow and Thurso in Scotland. Mr. Gross's texts also show that the purchases were made for distribution, not only among the merchant burgesses, but "upon all citsains and commynalte" (p. 136, note), or, as the Thurso ordinance of the seventeenth century runs, to "make offer to the merchants, craftsmen, and inhabitants of the said burgh, that they may have their proportion of the same, according to their necessitys and ability."

50. The Early History of the Guild of Merchant Taylors, by Charles M. Clode, London, 1888, i. 361, appendix 10; also the following appendix which shows that the same purchases were made in 1546.

51. Cibrario, Les conditions economiques de l'Italie au temps de Dante, Paris, 1865, p. 44.

52. A. de Calonne, La vie municipale au XVme siecle dans le Nord de la France, Paris, 1880, pp. 12-16. In 1485 the city permitted the export to Antwerp of a certain quantity of corn, "the inhabitants of Antwerp being always ready to be agreeable to the merchants and burgesses of Amiens" (ibid., pp. 75-77 and texts).

53. A. Babeau, La ville sous l'ancien regime, Paris, 1880.

54. Ennen, Geschichte der Stadt Koln, i. 491, 492, also texts.

CHAPTER VI

MUTUAL AID IN THE MEDIAEVAL CITY (continued)

Likeness and diversity among the medieval cities. The craftguilds: State-attributes in each of them. Attitude of the city towards the peasants; attempts to free them. The lords. Results achieved by the medieval city: in arts, in learning. Causes of decay.

The medieval cities were not organized upon some preconceived plan in obedience to the will of an outside legislator. Each of them was a natural growth in the full sense of the word—an always varying result of struggle between various forces which adjusted and re-adjusted themselves in conformity with their relative energies, the chances of their conflicts, and the support they found in their surroundings. Therefore, there are not two cities whose inner organization and destinies would have been identical. Each one, taken separately, varies from century to century. And yet, when we cast a broad glance upon all the cities of Europe, the local and national unlikenesses disappear, and we are struck to find among all of them a wonderful resemblance, although each has developed for itself, independently from the others, and in different conditions. A small town in the north of Scotland, with its population of coarse labourers and fishermen; a rich city of Flanders, with its world-wide commerce, luxury, love of amusement and animated life; an Italian city enriched by its intercourse with the East, and breeding within its walls a refined artistic taste and civilization; and a poor, chiefly agricultural, city in the marsh and lake district of Russia, seem to have little in common. And nevertheless, the leading lines of their organization, and the spirit which animates them, are imbued with a strong family likeness. Everywhere we see the same federations of small communities and guilds, the same "sub-towns" round the mother city, the same folkmote, and the same insigns of its independence. The defensor of the city, under different names and in different accoutrements, represents the same authority and interests; food supplies, labour and commerce, are organized on closely similar lines; inner and outer struggles are fought with like ambitions; nay, the very formulae used in the struggles, as also in the annals, the ordinances, and the rolls, are identical; and the architectural monuments, whether Gothic, Roman, or Byzantine in style, express the same aspirations and the same ideals; they are conceived and built in the same way. Many dissemblances are mere differences of age, and those disparities between sister cities which are real are repeated in different parts of Europe. The unity of the leading idea and the identity of origin make up for differences of climate, geographical situation, wealth, language and religion. This is why we can speak of the medieval city as of a well-defined phase of civilization; and while every research insisting upon local and individual differences is most welcome, we may still indicate the chief lines of development which are common to all cities.(1)

There is no doubt that the protection which used to be accorded to the market-place from the earliest barbarian times has played an important, though not an exclusive, part in the emancipation of the medieval city. The early barbarians knew no trade within their village communities; they traded with strangers only, at certain definite spots, on certain determined days. And, in order that the stranger might come to the barter-place without risk of being slain for some feud which might be running between two kins, the market was always placed under the special protection of all kins. It was inviolable, like the place of worship under the shadow of which it was held. With the Kabyles it is still annaya, like the footpath along which women carry water from the well; neither must be trodden upon in arms, even during inter-tribal wars. In medieval times the market universally enjoyed the same protection.(2) No feud could be prosecuted on the place whereto people came to trade, nor within a certain radius from it; and if a quarrel arose in the motley crowd of buyers and sellers, it had to be brought before those under whose protection the market stood—the community's tribunal, or the bishop's, the lord's, or the king's judge. A stranger who came to trade was a guest, and he went on under this very name. Even the lord who had no scruples about robbing a merchant on the high road, respected the Weichbild, that is, the pole which stood in the market-place and bore either the king's arms, or a glove, or the image of the local saint, or simply a cross, according to whether the market was under the protection of the king, the lord, the local church, or the folkmote—the vyeche.(3)

It is easy to understand how the self-jurisdiction of the city could develop out of the special jurisdiction in the market-place, when this last right was conceded, willingly or not, to the city itself. And such an origin of the city's liberties, which can be traced in very many cases, necessarily laid a special stamp upon their subsequent development. It gave a predominance to the trading part of the community. The burghers who possessed a house in the city at the time being, and were co-owners in the town-lands, constituted very often a merchant guild which held in its hands the city's trade; and although at the outset every burgher, rich and poor, could make part of the merchant guild, and the trade itself seems to have been carried on for the entire city by its trustees, the guild gradually became a sort of privileged body. It jealously prevented the outsiders who soon began to flock into the free cities from entering the guild, and kept the advantages resulting from trade for the few "families" which had been burghers at the time of the emancipation. There evidently was a danger of a merchant oligarchy being thus constituted. But already in the tenth, and still more during the two next centuries, the chief crafts, also organized in guilds, were powerful enough to check the oligarchic tendencies of the merchants.

The craft guild was then a common seller of its produce and a common buyer of the raw materials, and its members were merchants and manual workers at the same time. Therefore, the predominance taken by the old craft guilds from the very beginnings of the free city life guaranteed to manual labour the high position which it afterwards occupied in the city.(4) In fact, in a medieval city manual labour was no token of inferiority; it bore, on the contrary, traces of the high respect it had been kept in in the village community. Manual labour in a "mystery" was considered as a pious duty towards the citizens: a public function (Amt), as honourable as any other. An idea of "justice" to the community, of "right" towards both producer and consumer, which would seem so extravagant now, penetrated production and exchange. The tanner's, the cooper's, or the shoemaker's work must be "just," fair, they wrote in those times. Wood, leather or thread which are used by the artisan must be "right"; bread must be baked "in justice," and so on. Transport this language into our present life, and it would seem affected and unnatural; but it was natural and unaffected then, because the medieval artisan did not produce for an unknown buyer, or to throw his goods into an unknown market. He produced for his guild first; for a brotherhood of men who knew each other, knew the technics of the craft, and, in naming the price of each product, could appreciate the skill displayed in its fabrication or the labour bestowed upon it. Then the guild, not the separate producer, offered the goods for sale in the community, and this last, in its turn, offered to the brotherhood of allied communities those goods which were exported, and assumed responsibility for their quality. With such an organization, it was the ambition of each craft not to offer goods of inferior quality, and technical defects or adulterations became a matter concerning the whole community, because, an ordinance says, "they would destroy public confidence."(5) Production being thus a social duty, placed under the control of the whole amitas, manual labour could not fall into the degraded condition which it occupies now, so long as the free city was living.

A difference between master and apprentice, or between master and worker (compayne, Geselle), existed but in the medieval cities from their very beginnings; this was at the outset a mere difference of age and skill, not of wealth and power. After a seven years' apprenticeship, and after having proved his knowledge and capacities by a work of art, the apprentice became a master himself. And only much later, in the sixteenth century, after the royal power had destroyed the city and the craft organization, was it possible to become master in virtue of simple inheritance or wealth. But this was also the time of a general decay in medieval industries and art.

There was not much room for hired work in the early flourishing periods of the medieval cities, still less for individual hirelings. The work of the weavers, the archers, the smiths, the bakers, and so on, was performed for the craft and the city; and when craftsmen were hired in the building trades, they worked as temporary corporations (as they still do in the Russian artels), whose work was paid en bloc. Work for a master began to multiply only later on; but even in this case the worker was paid better than he is paid now, even in this country, and very much better than he used to be paid all over Europe in the first half of this century. Thorold Rogers has familiarized English readers with this idea; but the same is true for the Continent as well, as is shown by the researches of Falke and Schonberg, and by many occasional indications. Even in the fifteenth century a mason, a carpenter, or a smith worker would be paid at Amiens four sols a day, which corresponded to forty-eight pounds of bread, or to the eighth part of a small ox (bouvard). In Saxony, the salary of the Geselle in the building trade was such that, to put it in Falke's words, he could buy with his six days' wages three sheep and one pair of shoes.(6) The donations of workers (Geselle) to cathedrals also bear testimony of their relative well-being, to say nothing of the glorious donations of certain craft guilds nor of what they used to spend in festivities and pageants.(7) In fact, the more we learn about the medieval city, the more we are convinced that at no time has labour enjoyed such conditions of prosperity and such respect as when city life stood at its highest.

More than that; not only many aspirations of our modern radicals were already realized in the middle ages, but much of what is described now as Utopian was accepted then as a matter of fact. We are laughed at when we say that work must be pleasant, but—"every one must be pleased with his work," a medieval Kuttenberg ordinance says, "and no one shall, while doing nothing (mit nichts thun), appropriate for himself what others have produced by application and work, because laws must be a shield for application and work."(8) And amidst all present talk about an eight hours' day, it may be well to remember an ordinance of Ferdinand the First relative to the Imperial coal mines, which settled the miner's day at eight hours, "as it used to be of old" (wie vor Alters herkommen), and work on Saturday afternoon was prohibited. Longer hours were very rare, we are told by Janssen, while shorter hours were of common occurrence. In this country, in the fifteenth century, Rogers says, "the workmen worked only forty-eight hours a week."(9) The Saturday half-holiday, too, which we consider as a modern conquest, was in reality an old medieval institution; it was bathing-time for a great part of the community, while

Wednesday afternoon was bathing-time for the Geselle.(10) And although school meals did not exist—probably because no children went hungry to school—a distribution of bath-money to the children whose parents found difficulty in providing it was habitual in several places. As to Labour Congresses, they also were a regular Feature of the middles ages. In some parts of Germany craftsmen of the same trade, belonging to different communes, used to come together every year to discuss questions relative to their trade, the years of apprenticeship, the wandering years, the wages, and so on; and in 1572, the Hanseatic towns formally recognized the right of the crafts to come together at periodical congresses, and to take any resolutions, so long as they were not contrary to the cities' rolls, relative to the quality of goods. Such Labour Congresses, partly international like the Hansa itself, are known to have been held by bakers, founders, smiths, tanners, sword-makers and cask-makers.(11)

The craft organization required, of course, a close supervision of the craftsmen by the guild, and special jurates were always nominated for that purpose. But it is most remarkable that, so long as the cities lived their free life, no complaints were heard about the supervision; while, after the State had stepped in, confiscating the property of the guilds and destroying their independence in favour of its own bureaucracy, the complaints became simply countless.(12) On the other hand, the immensity of progress realized in all arts under the mediaeval guild system is the best proof that the system was no hindrance to individual initiative.(13) The fact is, that the medieval guild, like the medieval parish, "street," or "quarter," was not a body of citizens, placed under the control of State functionaries; it was a union of all men connected with a given trade: jurate buyers of raw produce, sellers of manufactured goods, and artisans—masters, "compaynes," and apprentices. For the inner organization of the trade its assembly was sovereign, so long as it did not hamper the other guilds, in which case the matter was brought before the guild of the guilds—the city. But there was in it something more than that. It had its own self-jurisdiction, its own military force, its own general assemblies, its own traditions of struggles, glory, and independence, its own relations with other guilds of the same trade in other cities: it had, in a word, a full organic life which could only result from the integrality of the vital functions. When the town was called to arms, the guild appeared as a separate company (Schaar), armed with its own arms (or its own guns, lovingly decorated by the guild, at a subsequent epoch), under its own self-elected commanders. It was, in a word, as independent a unit of the federation as the republic of Uri or Geneva was fifty years ago in the Swiss Confederation. So that, to compare it with a modern trade union, divested of all attributes of State sovereignty, and reduced to a couple of functions of secondary importance, is as unreasonable as to compare Florence or Brugge with a French commune vegetating under the Code Napoleon, or with a Russian town placed under Catherine the Second's municipal law. Both have elected mayors, and the latter has also its craft corporations; but the difference is—all the difference that exists between Florence and Fontenay-les-Oies or Tsarevokokshaisk, or between a Venetian doge and a modern mayor who lifts his hat before the sous-prefet's clerk.

The medieval guilds were capable of maintaining their independence; and, later on, especially in the fourteenth century, when, in consequence of several causes which shall presently be indicated, the old municipal life underwent a deep modification, the younger crafts proved strong enough to conquer their due share in the management of the city affairs. The masses, organized in "minor" arts, rose to wrest the power out of the hands of a growing oligarchy, and mostly succeeded in this task, opening again a new era of prosperity. True, that in some cities the uprising was crushed in blood, and mass decapitations of workers followed, as was the case in Paris in 1306, and in Cologne in 1371. In such cases the city's liberties rapidly fell into decay, and the city was gradually subdued by the central authority. But the majority of the towns had preserved enough of vitality to come out of the turmoil with a new life and vigour.(14) A new period of rejuvenescence was their reward. New life was infused, and it found its expression in splendid architectural monuments, in a new period of prosperity, in a sudden progress of technics and invention, and in a new intellectual movement leading to the Renaissance and to the Reformation.

The life of a mediaeval city was a succession of hard battles to conquer liberty and to maintain it. True, that a strong and tenacious race of burghers had developed during those fierce contests; true, that love and worship of the mother city had been bred by these struggles, and that the grand things achieved by the mediaeval communes were a direct outcome of that love. But the sacrifices which the communes had to sustain in the battle for freedom were, nevertheless, cruel, and left deep traces of division on their inner life as well. Very few cities had succeeded, under a concurrence of favourable circumstances, in obtaining liberty at one stroke, and these few mostly lost it equally easily; while the great number had to fight fifty or a hundred years in succession, often more, before their rights to free life had been recognized, and another hundred years to found their liberty on a firm basis—the twelfth century charters thus being but one of the stepping-stones to freedom.(15) In reality, the mediaeval city was a fortified oasis amidst a country plunged into feudal submission, and it had to make room for itself by the force of its arms. In consequence of the causes briefly alluded to in the preceding chapter, each village community had gradually fallen under the yoke of some lay or clerical lord. His house had grown to be a castle, and his brothers-in-arms were now the scum of adventurers, always ready to plunder the peasants. In addition to three days a week which the peasants had to work for the lord, they had also to bear all sorts of exactions for the right to sow and to crop, to be gay or sad, to live, to marry, or to die. And, worst of all, they were continually plundered by the armed robbers of some neighbouring lord, who chose to consider them as their master's kin, and to take upon them, and upon their cattle and crops, the revenge for a feud he was fighting against their owner. Every meadow, every field, every river, and road around the city, and every man upon the land was under some lord.

The hatred of the burghers towards the feudal barons has found a most characteristic expression in the wording of the different charters which they compelled them to sign. Heinrich V. is made to sign in the charter granted to Speier in 1111, that he frees the burghers from "the horrible and execrable law of mortmain, through which the town has been sunk into deepest poverty" (von dem scheusslichen und nichtswurdigen Gesetze, welches gemein Budel genannt wird, Kallsen, i. 307). The coutume of Bayonne, written about 1273, contains such passages as these: "The people is anterior to the lords. It is the people, more numerous than all others, who, desirous of peace, has made the lords for bridling and knocking down the powerful ones," and so on (Giry, Etablissements de Rouen, i. 117, Quoted by Luchaire, p. 24). A charter submitted for King Robert's signature is equally characteristic. He is made to say in it: "I shall rob no oxen nor other animals. I shall seize no merchants, nor take their moneys, nor impose ransom. From Lady Day to the All Saints' Day I shall seize no horse, nor mare, nor foals, in the meadows. I shall not burn the mills, nor rob the flour ... I shall offer no protection to thieves," etc. (Pfister has published that document, reproduced by Luchaire). The charter "granted" by the Besancon Archbishop Hugues, in which he has been compelled to enumerate all the mischiefs due to his mortmain rights, is equally characteristic.(16) And so on.

Freedom could not be maintained in such surroundings, and the cities were compelled to carry on the war outside their walls. The burghers sent out emissaries to lead revolt in the villages; they received villages into their corporations, and they waged direct war against the nobles. It Italy, where the land was thickly sprinkled with feudal castles, the war assumed heroic proportions, and was fought with a stern acrimony on both sides. Florence sustained for seventy-seven years a succession of bloody wars, in order to free its contado from the nobles; but when the conquest had been accomplished (in 1181) all had to begin anew. The nobles rallied; they constituted their own leagues in opposition to the leagues of the towns, and, receiving fresh support from either the Emperor or the Pope, they made the war last for another 130 years. The same took place in Rome, in Lombardy, all over Italy.

Prodigies of valour, audacity, and tenaciousness were displayed by the citizens in these wars. But the bows and the hatchets of the arts and crafts had not always the upper hand in their encounters with the armour-clad knights, and many castles withstood the ingenious siege-machinery and the perseverance of the citizens. Some cities, like Florence, Bologna, and many towns in France, Germany, and Bohemia, succeeded in emancipating the surrounding villages, and they were rewarded for their efforts by an extraordinary prosperity and tranquillity. But even here, and still more in the less strong or less impulsive towns, the merchants and artisans, exhausted by war, and misunderstanding their own interests, bargained over the peasants' heads. They compelled the lord to swear allegiance to the city; his country castle was dismantled, and he agreed to build a house and to reside in the city, of which he became a co-burgher (com-bourgeois, con-cittadino); but he maintained in return most of his rights upon the peasants, who only won a partial relief from their burdens. The burgher could not understand that equal rights of citizenship might be granted to the peasant upon whose food supplies he had to rely, and a deep rent was traced between town and village. In some cases the peasants simply changed owners, the city buying out the barons' rights and selling them in shares to her own citizens.(17) Serfdom was maintained, and only much later on, towards the end of the thirteenth century, it was the craft revolution which undertook to put an end to it, and abolished personal servitude, but dispossessed at the same time the serfs of the land.(18) It hardly need be added that the fatal results of such policy were soon felt by the cities themselves; the country became the city's enemy.

The war against the castles had another bad effect. It involved the cities in a long succession of mutual wars, which have given origin to the theory, till lately in vogue, namely, that the towns lost their independence through their own jealousies and mutual fights. The imperialist historians have especially supported this theory, which, however, is very much undermined now by modern research. It is certain that in Italy cities fought each other with a stubborn animosity, but nowhere else did such contests attain the same proportions; and in Italy itself the city wars, especially those of the earlier period, had their special causes. They were (as was already shown by Sismondi and Ferrari) a mere continuation of the war against the castles—the free municipal and federative principle unavoidably entering into a fierce contest with feudalism, imperialism, and papacy. Many towns which had but partially shaken off the yoke of the bishop, the lord, or the Emperor, were simply driven against the free cities by the nobles, the Emperor, and Church, whose policy was to divide the cities and to arm them against each other. These special circumstances (partly reflected on to Germany also) explain why the Italian towns, some of which sought support with the Emperor to combat the Pope, while the others sought support from the Church to resist the Emperor, were soon divided into a Gibelin and a Guelf camp, and why the same division appeared in each separate city.(19)

The immense economical progress realized by most italian cities just at the time when these wars were hottest,(20) and the alliances so easily concluded between towns, still better characterize those struggles and further undermine the above theory. Already in the years 1130-1150 powerful leagues came into existence; and a few years later, when Frederick Barbarossa invaded Italy and, supported by the nobles and some retardatory cities, marched against Milan, popular enthusiasm was roused in many towns by popular preachers. Crema, Piacenza, Brescia, Tortona, etc., went to the rescue; the banners of the guilds of Verona, Padua, Vicenza, and Trevisa floated side by side in the cities' camp against the banners of the Emperor and the nobles. Next year the Lombardian League came into existence, and sixty years later we see it reinforced by many other cities, and forming a lasting organization which had half of its federal war-chest in Genoa and the other half in Venice.(21) In Tuscany, Florence headed another powerful league, to which Lucca, Bologna, Pistoia, etc., belonged, and which played an important part in crushing down the nobles in middle Italy, while smaller leagues were of common occurrence. It is thus certain that although petty jealousies undoubtedly existed, and discord could be easily sown, they did not prevent the towns from uniting together for the common defence of liberty. Only later on, when separate cities became little States, wars broke out between them, as always must be the case when States struggle for supremacy or colonies.

Similar leagues were formed in Germany for the same purpose. When, under the successors of Conrad, the land was the prey of interminable feuds between the nobles, the Westphalian towns concluded a league against the knights, one of the clauses of which was never to lend money to a knight who would continue to conceal stolen goods.(22) When "the knights and the nobles lived on plunder, and murdered whom they chose to murder," as the Wormser Zorn complains, the cities on the Rhine (Mainz, Cologne, Speier, Strasburg, and Basel) took the initiative of a league which soon numbered sixty allied towns, repressed the robbers, and maintained peace. Later on, the league of the towns of Suabia, divided into three "peace districts" (Augsburg, Constance, and Ulm), had the same purpose. And even when such leagues were broken,(23) they lived long enough to show that while the supposed peacemakers—the kings, the emperors, and the Church-fomented discord, and were themselves helpless against the robber knights, it was from the cities that the impulse came for re-establishing peace and union. The cities—not the emperors—were the real makers of the national unity.(24)

Similar federations were organized for the same purpose among small villages, and now that attention has been drawn to this subject by Luchaire we may expect soon to learn much more about them. Villages joined into small federations in the contado of Florence, so also in the dependencies of Novgorod and Pskov. As to France, there is positive evidence of a federation of seventeen peasant villages which has existed in the Laonnais for nearly a hundred years (till 1256), and has fought hard for its independence. Three more peasant republics, which had sworn charters similar to those of Laon and Soissons, existed in the neighbourhood of Laon, and, their territories being contiguous, they supported each other in their liberation wars. Altogether,

Luchaire is of the opinion that many such federations must have come into existence in France in the twelfth and thirteenth centuries, but that documents relative to them are mostly lost. Of course, being unprotected by walls, they could easily be crushed down by the kings and the lords; but in certain favourable circumstances, when they found support in a league of towns and protection in their mountains, such peasant republics became independent units of the Swiss Confederation.(25)

As to unions between cities for peaceful purposes, they were of quite common occurrence. The intercourse which had been established during the period of liberation was not interrupted afterwards. Sometimes, when the scabini of a German town, having to pronounce judgment in a new or complicated case, declared that they knew not the sentence (des Urtheiles nicht weise zu sein), they sent delegates to another city to get the sentence. The same happened also in France;(26) while Forli and Ravenna are known to have mutually naturalized their citizens and granted them full rights in both cities. To submit a contest arisen between two towns, or within a city, to another commune which was invited to act as arbiter, was also in the spirit of the times.(27) As to commercial treaties between cities, they were quite habitual.(28) Unions for regulating the production and the sizes of casks which were used for the commerce in wine, "herring unions," and so on, were mere precursors of the great commercial federations of the Flemish Hansa, and, later on, of the great North German Hansa, the history of which alone might contribute pages and pages to illustrate the federation spirit which permeated men at that time. It hardly need be added, that through the Hanseatic unions the medieval cities have contributed more to the development of international intercourse, navigation, and maritime discovery than all the States of the first seventeen centuries of our era.

In a word, federations between small territorial units, as well as among men united by common pursuits within their respective guilds, and federations between cities and groups of cities constituted the very essence of life and thought during that period. The first five of the second decade of centuries of our era may thus be described as an immense attempt at securing mutual aid and support on a grand scale, by means of the principles of federation and association carried on through all manifestations of human life and to all possible degrees. This attempt was attended with success to a very great extent. It united men formerly divided; it secured them a very great deal of freedom, and it tenfolded their forces. At a time when particularism was bred by so many agencies, and the causes of discord and jealousy might have been so numerous, it is gratifying to see that cities scattered over a wide continent had so much in common, and were so ready to confederate for the prosecution of so many common aims. They succumbed in the long run before powerful enemies; not having understood the mutual-aid principle widely enough, they themselves committed fatal faults; but they did not perish through their own jealousies, and their errors were not a want of federation spirit among themselves.

The results of that new move which mankind made in the medieval city were immense. At the beginning of the eleventh century the towns of Europe were small clusters of miserable huts, adorned but with low clumsy churches, the builders of which hardly knew how to make an arch; the arts, mostly consisting of some weaving and forging, were in their infancy; learning was found in but a few monasteries. Three hundred and fifty years later, the very face of Europe had been changed. The land was dotted with rich cities, surrounded by immense thick walls which were embellished by towers and gates, each of them a work of art in itself. The cathedrals, conceived in a grand style and profusely decorated, lifted their bell-towers to the skies, displaying a purity of form and a boldness of imagination which we now vainly strive to attain. The crafts and arts had risen to a degree of perfection which we can hardly boast of having superseded in many directions, if the inventive skill of the worker and the superior finish of his work be appreciated higher than rapidity of fabrication. The navies of the free cities furrowed in all directions the Northern and the Southern Mediterranean; one effort more, and they would cross the oceans. Over large tracts of land well-being had taken the place of misery; learning had grown and spread. The methods of science had been elaborated; the basis of natural philosophy had been laid down; and the way had been paved for all the mechanical inventions of which our own times are so proud. Such were the magic changes accomplished in Europe in less than four hundred years. And the losses which Europe sustained through the loss of its free cities can only be understood when we compare the seventeenth century with the fourteenth or the thirteenth. The prosperity which formerly characterized Scotland, Germany, the plains of Italy, was gone. The roads had fallen into an abject state, the cities were depopulated, labour was brought into slavery, art had vanished, commerce itself was decaying.(29)

If the medieval cities had bequeathed to us no written documents to testify of their splendour, and left nothing behind but the monuments of building art which we see now all over Europe, from Scotland to Italy, and from Gerona in Spain to Breslau in Slavonian territory, we might yet conclude that the times of independent city life were times of the greatest development of human intellect during the Christian era down to the end of the eighteenth century. On looking, for instance, at a medieval picture representing Nuremberg with its scores of towers and lofty spires, each of which bore the stamp of free creative art, we can hardly conceive that three hundred years before the town was but a collection of miserable hovels. And our admiration grows when we go into the details of the architecture and decorations of each of the countless churches, bell-towers, gates, and communal houses which are scattered all over Europe as far east as Bohemia and the now dead towns of Polish Galicia. Not only Italy, that mother of art, but all Europe is full of such monuments. The very fact that of all arts architecture—a social art above all—had attained the highest development, is significant in itself. To be what it was, it must have originated from an eminently social life.

Medieval architecture attained its grandeur—not only because it was a natural development of handicraft; not only because each building, each architectural decoration, had been devised by men who knew through the experience of their own hands what artistic effects can be obtained from stone, iron, bronze, or even from simple logs and mortar; not only because, each monument was a result of collective experience, accumulated in each "mystery" or craft(30)—it was grand because it was born out of a grand idea. Like Greek art, it sprang out of a conception of brotherhood and unity fostered by the city. It had an audacity which could only be won by audacious struggles and victories; it had that expression of vigour, because vigour permeated all the life of the city. A cathedral or a communal house symbolized the grandeur of an organism of which every mason and stone-cutter was the builder, and a medieval building appears—not as a solitary effort to which thousands of slaves would have contributed the share assigned them by one man's imagination; all the city contributed to it. The lofty bell-tower rose upon a structure, grand in itself, in which the life of the city was throbbing—not upon a meaningless scaffold like the Paris iron tower, not as a sham structure in stone intended to conceal the ugliness of an iron frame, as has been done in the Tower Bridge.

Like the Acropolis of Athens, the cathedral of a medieval city was intended to glorify the grandeur of the victorious city, to symbolize the union of its crafts, to express the glory of each citizen in a city of his own creation. After having achieved its craft revolution, the city often began a new cathedral in order to express the new, wider, and broader union which had been called into life.

The means at hand for these grand undertakings were disproportionately small. Cologne Cathedral was begun with a yearly outlay of but 500 marks; a gift of 100 marks was inscribed as a grand donation;(31) and even when the work approached completion, and gifts poured in in proportion, the yearly outlay in money stood at about 5,000 marks, and never exceeded 14,000. The cathedral of Basel was built with equally small means. But each corporation contributed its part of stone, work, and decorative genius to their common monument. Each guild expressed in it its political conceptions, telling in stone or in bronze the history of the city, glorifying the principles of "Liberty, equality, and fraternity,"(32) praising the city's allies, and sending to eternal fire its enemies. And each guild bestowed its love upon the communal monument by richly decorating it with stained windows, paintings, "gates, worthy to be the gates of Paradise," as Michel Angelo said, or stone decorations of each minutest corner of the building.(33) Small cities, even small parishes,(34) vied with the big agglomerations in this work, and the cathedrals of Laon and St. Ouen hardly stand behind that of Rheims, or the Communal House of Bremen, or the folkmote's bell-tower of Breslau. "No works must be begun by the commune but such as are conceived in response to the grand heart of the commune, composed of the hearts of all citizens, united in one common will"—such were the words of the Council of Florence; and this spirit appears in all communal works of common utility, such as the canals, terraces, vineyards, and fruit gardens around Florence, or the irrigation canals which intersected the plains of Lombardy, or the port and aqueduct of Genoa, or, in fact, any works of the kind which were achieved by almost every city.(35)

All arts had progressed in the same way in the medieval cities, those of our own days mostly being but a continuation of what had grown at that time. The prosperity of the Flemish cities was based upon the fine woollen cloth they fabricated. Florence, at the beginning of the fourteenth century, before the black death, fabricated from 70,000 to 100,000 panni of woollen stuffs, which were valued at 1,200,000 golden florins.(36) The chiselling of precious metals, the art of casting, the fine forging of iron, were creations of the mediaeval "mysteries" which had succeeded in attaining in their own domains all that could be made by the hand, without the use of a powerful prime motor. By the hand and by invention, because, to use Whewell's words:

"Parchment and paper, printing and engraving, improved glass and steel, gunpowder, clocks, telescopes, the mariner's compass, the reformed calendar, the decimal notation; algebra, trigonometry, chemistry, counterpoint (an invention equivalent to a new creation of music); these are all possessions which we inherit from that which has so disparagingly been termed the Stationary Period" (History of Inductive Sciences, i. 252).

True that no new principle was illustrated by any of these discoveries, as Whewell said; but medieval science had done something more than the actual discovery of new principles. It had prepared the discovery of all the new principles which we know at the present time in mechanical sciences: it had accustomed the explorer to observe facts and to reason from them. It was inductive science, even though it had not yet fully grasped the importance and the powers of induction; and it laid the foundations of both mechanics and natural philosophy. Francis Bacon, Galileo, and Copernicus were the direct descendants of a Roger Bacon and a Michael Scot, as the steam engine was a direct product of the researches carried on in the Italian universities on the weight of the atmosphere, and of the mathematical and technical learning which characterized Nuremberg.

But why should one take trouble to insist upon the advance of science and art in the medieval city? Is it not enough to point to the cathedrals in the domain of skill, and to the Italian language and the poem of Dante in the domain of thought, to give at once the measure of what the medieval city created during the four centuries it lived?

The medieval cities have undoubtedly rendered an immense service to European civilization. They have prevented it from being drifted into the theocracies and despotical states of old; they have endowed it with the variety, the self-reliance, the force of initiative, and the immense intellectual and material energies it now possesses, which are the best pledge for its being able to resist any new invasion of the East. But why did these centres of civilization, which attempted to answer to deeply-seated needs of human nature, and were so full of life, not live further on? Why were they seized with senile debility in the sixteenth century? and, after having repulsed so many assaults from without, and only borrowed new vigour from their interior struggles, why did they finally succumb to both?

Various causes contributed to this effect, some of them having their roots in the remote past, while others originated in the mistakes committed by the cities themselves. Towards the end of the fifteenth century, mighty States, reconstructed on the old Roman pattern, were already coming into existence. In each country and each region some feudal lord, more cunning, more given to hoarding, and often less scrupulous than his neighbours, had succeeded in appropriating to himself richer personal domains, more peasants on his lands, more knights in his following, more treasures in his chest. He had chosen for his seat a group of happily-situated villages, not yet trained into free municipal life—Paris, Madrid, or Moscow—and with the labour of his serfs he had made of them royal fortified cities, whereto he attracted war companions by a free distribution of villages, and merchants by the protection he offered to trade. The germ of a future State, which began gradually to absorb other similar centres, was thus laid. Lawyers, versed in the study of Roman law, flocked into such centres; a tenacious and ambitious race of men issued from among the burgesses, who equally hated the naughtiness of the lords and what they called the lawlessness of the peasants. The very forms of the village community, unknown to their code, the very principles of federalism were repulsive to them as "barbarian" inheritances. Caesarism, supported by the fiction of popular consent and by the force of arms, was their ideal, and they worked hard for those who promised to realize it.(37)

The Christian Church, once a rebel against Roman law and now its ally, worked in the same direction. The attempt at constituting the theocratic Empire of Europe having proved a failure, the more intelligent and ambitious bishops now yielded support to those whom they reckoned upon for reconstituting the power of the Kings of Israel or of the Emperors of Constantinople. The Church bestowed upon the rising rulers her sanctity, she crowned them as God's representatives on earth, she brought to their service the learning and the statesmanship of her ministers, her blessings and maledictions, her riches, and the sympathies she had retained among the poor. The peasants, whom the cities had failed or refused to free, on seeing the burghers impotent to put an end to the interminable wars between the knights—which wars they had so dearly to pay for—now set their hopes upon the King, the Emperor, or the Great Prince; and while aiding them to crush down the mighty feudal owners, they aided them to constitute the centralized State. And finally, the invasions of the Mongols and the Turks, the holy war against the Maures in Spain, as well as the terrible wars which soon broke out between the growing centres of sovereignty—Ile de France and Burgundy, Scotland and England, England and France, Lithuania and Poland, Moscow and Tver, and so on—contributed to the same end. Mighty States made their appearance; and the cities had now to resist not only loose federations of lords, but strongly-organized centres, which had armies of serfs at their disposal.

The worst was, that the growing autocracies found support in the divisions which had grown within the cities themselves. The fundamental idea of the medieval city was grand, but it was not wide enough. Mutual aid and support cannot be limited to a small association; they must spread to its surroundings, or else the surroundings will absorb the association. And in this respect the medieval citizen had committed a formidable mistake at the outset. Instead of looking upon the peasants and artisans who gathered under the protection of his walls as upon so many aids who would contribute their part to the making of the city—as they really did—a sharp division was traced between the "families" of old burghers and the newcomers. For the former, all benefits from communal trade and communal lands were reserved, and nothing was left for the latter but the right of freely using the skill of their own hands. The city thus became divided into "the burghers" or "the commonalty," and "the inhabitants."(38) The trade, which was formerly communal, now became the privilege of the merchant and artisan "families," and the next step—that of becoming individual, or the privilege of oppressive trusts—was unavoidable.

The same division took place between the city proper and the surrounding villages. The commune had well tried to free the peasants, but her wars against the lords became, as already mentioned, wars for freeing the city itself from the lords, rather than for freeing the peasants. She left to the lord his rights over the villeins, on condition that he would molest the city no more and would become co-burgher. But the nobles "adopted" by the city, and now residing within its walls, simply carried on the old war within the very precincts of the city. They disliked to submit to a tribunal of simple artisans and merchants, and fought their old feuds in the streets. Each city had now its Colonnas and Orsinis, its Overstolzes and Wises. Drawing large incomes from the estates they had still retained, they surrounded themselves with numerous clients and feudalized the customs and habits of the city itself. And when discontent began to be felt in the artisan classes of the town, they offered their sword and their followers to settle the differences by a free fight, instead of letting the discontent find out the channels which it did not fail to secure itself in olden times.

The greatest and the most fatal error of most cities was to base their wealth upon commerce and industry, to the neglect of agriculture. They thus repeated the error which had once been committed by the cities of antique Greece, and they fell through it into the same crimes.(39) The estrangement of so many cities from the land necessarily drew them into a policy hostile to the land, which became more and more evident in the times of Edward the Third,(40) the French Jacqueries, the Hussite wars, and the Peasant War in Germany. On the other hand, a commercial policy involved them in distant enterprises. Colonies were founded by the Italians in the south-east, by German cities in the east, by Slavonian cities in the far northeast.

Mercenary armies began to be kept for colonial wars, and soon for local defence as well. Loans were contacted to such an extent as to totally demoralize the citizens; and internal contests grew worse and worse at each election, during which the colonial politics in the interest of a few families was at stake. The division into rich and poor grew deeper, and in the sixteenth century, in each city, the royal authority found ready allies and support among the poor.

And there is yet another cause of the decay of communal institutions, which stands higher and lies deeper than all the above. The history of the medieval cities offers one of the most striking illustrations of the power of ideas and principles upon the destinies of mankind, and of the quite opposed results which are obtained when a deep modification of leading ideas has taken place. Self-reliance and federalism, the sovereignty of each group, and the construction of the political body from the simple to the composite, were the leading ideas in the eleventh century. But since that time the conceptions had entirely changed. The students of Roman law and the prelates of the Church, closely bound together since the time of Innocent the Third, had succeeded in paralyzing the idea—the antique Greek idea—which presided at the foundation of the cities. For two or three hundred years they taught from the pulpit, the University chair, and the judges' bench, that salvation must be sought for in a strongly-centralized State, placed under a semi-divine authority;(41) that one man can and must be the saviour of society, and that in the name of public salvation he can commit any violence: burn men and women at the stake, make them perish under indescribable tortures, plunge whole provinces into the most abject misery. Nor did they fail to give object lessons to this effect on a grand scale, and with an unheard-of cruelty, wherever the king's sword and the Church's fire, or both at once, could reach. By these teachings and examples, continually repeated and enforced upon public attention, the very minds of the citizens had been shaped into a new mould. They began to find no authority too extensive, no killing by degrees too cruel, once it was "for public safety." And, with this new direction of mind and this new belief in one man's power, the old federalist principle faded away, and the very creative genius of the masses died out. The Roman idea was victorious, and in such circumstances the centralized State had in the cities a ready prey.

Florence in the fifteenth century is typical of this change. Formerly a popular revolution was the signal of a new departure. Now, when the people, brought to despair, insurged, it had constructive ideas no more; no fresh idea came out of the movement. A thousand representatives were put into the Communal Council instead of 400; 100 men entered the signoria instead of 80. But a revolution of figures could be of no avail. The people's discontent was growing up, and new revolts followed. A saviour—the "tyran"—was appealed to; he massacred the rebels, but the disintegration of the communal body continued worse than ever. And when, after a new revolt, the people of Florence appealed to their most popular man, Gieronimo Savonarola, for advice, the monk's answer was:—"Oh, people mine, thou knowest that I cannot go into State affairs ... purify thy soul, and if in such a disposition of mind thou reformest thy city, then, people of Florence, thou shalt have inaugurated the reform in all Italy!" Carnival masks and vicious books were burned, a law of charity and another against usurers were passed—and the democracy of Florence remained where it was. The old spirit had gone. By too much trusting to government, they had ceased to trust to themselves; they were unable to open new issues. The State had only to step in and to crush down their last liberties.

And yet, the current of mutual aid and support did not die out in the masses, it continued to flow even after that defeat. It rose up again with a formidable force, in answer to the communist appeals of the first propagandists of the reform, and it continued to exist even after the masses, having failed to realize the life which they hoped to inaugurate under the inspiration of a reformed religion, fell under the dominions of an autocratic power. It flows still even now, and it seeks its way to find out a new expression which would not be the State, nor the medieval city, nor the village community of the barbarians, nor the savage clan, but would proceed from all of them, and yet be superior to them in its wider and more deeply humane conceptions.

NOTES:

1. The literature of the subject is immense; but there is no work yet which treats of the medieval city as of a whole. For the French Communes, Augustin Thierry's Lettres and Considerations sur l'histoire de France still remain classical, and Luchaire's Communes francaises is an excellent addition on the same lines. For the cities of Italy, the great work of Sismondi (Histoire des republiques italiennes du moyen age, Paris, 1826, 16 vols.), Leo and Botta's History of Italy, Ferrari's Revolutions d'Italie, and Hegel's Geschichte der Stadteverfassung in Italien, are the chief sources of general information. For Germany we have Maurer's Stadteverfassung, Barthold's Geschichte der deutschen Stadte, and, of recent works, Hegel's Stadte und Gilden der germanischen Volker (2 vols. Leipzig, 1891), and Dr. Otto Kallsen's Die deutschen Stadte im Mittelalter (2 vols. Halle, 1891), as also Janssen's Geschichte des deutschen Volkes (5 vols. 1886), which, let us hope, will soon be translated into English (French translation in 1892). For Belgium, A. Wauters, Les Libertes communales (Bruxelles, 1869-78, 3 vols.). For Russia, Byelaeff's, Kostomaroff's and Sergievich's works. And finally, for

England, we posses one of the best works on cities of a wider region in Mrs. J.R. Green's Town Life in the Fifteenth Century (2 vols. London, 1894). We have, moreover, a wealth of well-known local histories, and several excellent works of general or economical history which I have so often mentioned in this and the preceding chapter. The richness of literature consists, however, chiefly in separate, sometimes admirable, researches into the history of separate cities, especially Italian and German; the guilds; the land question; the economical principles of the time; the economical importance of guilds and crafts; the leagues between, cities (the Hansa); and communal art. An incredible wealth of information is contained in works of this second category, of which only some of the more important are named in these pages.

2. Kulischer, in an excellent essay on primitive trade (Zeitschrift für Volkerpsychologie, Bd. x. 380), also points out that, according to Herodotus, the Argippaeans were considered inviolable, because the trade between the Scythians and the northern tribes took place on their territory. A fugitive was sacred on their territory, and they were often asked to act as arbiters for their neighbours. See Appendix XI.

3. Some discussion has lately taken place upon the Weichbild and the Weichbild-law, which still remain obscure (see Zopfl, Alterthumer des deutschen Reichs und Rechts, iii. 29; Kallsen, i. 316). The above explanation seems to be the more probable, but, of course, it must be tested by further research. It is also evident that, to use a Scotch expression, the "mercet cross" could be considered as an emblem of Church jurisdiction, but we find it both in bishop cities and in those in which the folkmote was sovereign.

4. For all concerning the merchant guild see Mr. Gross's

exhaustive work, The Guild Merchant (Oxford, 1890, 2 vols.); also Mrs. Green's remarks in Town Life in the Fifteenth Century, vol. ii. chaps. v. viii. x; and A. Doren's review of the subject in Schmoller's Forschungen, vol. xii. If the considerations indicated in the previous chapter (according to which trade was communal at its beginnings) prove to be correct, it will be permissible to suggest as a probable hypothesis that the guild merchant was a body entrusted with commerce in the interest of the whole city, and only gradually became a guild of merchants trading for themselves; while the merchant adventurers of this country, the Novgorod povolniki (free colonizers and merchants) and the mercati personati, would be those to whom it was left to open new markets and new branches of commerce for themselves. Altogether, it must be remarked that the origin of the mediaeval city can be ascribed to no separate agency. It was a result of many agencies in different degrees.

5. Janssen's Geschichte des deutschen Volkes, i. 315; Gramich's Wurzburg; and, in fact, any collection of ordinances.

6. Falke, Geschichtliche Statistik, i. 373-393, and ii. 66; quoted in Janssen's Geschichte, i. 339; J.D. Blavignac, in Comptes et depenses de la construction du clocher de Saint-Nicolas a Fribourg en Suisse, comes to a similar conclusion. For Amiens, De Calonne's Vie Municipale, p. 99 and Appendix. For a thorough appreciation and graphical representation of the medieval wages in England and their value in bread and meat, see G. Steffen's excellent article and curves in The Nineteenth Century for 1891, and Studier ofver lonsystemets historia i England, Stockholm, 1895.

7. To quote but one example out of many which may be found in Schonberg's and Falke's works, the sixteen shoemaker workers (Schusterknechte) of the town Xanten, on the Rhine, gave, for

erecting a screen and an altar in the church, 75 guldens of subscriptions, and 12 guldens out of their box, which money was worth, according to the best valuations, ten times its present value.

8. Quoted by Janssen, l.c. i. 343.

9. The Economical Interpretation of History, London, 1891, p. 303.

10. Janssen, l.c. See also Dr. Alwin Schultz, Deutsches Leben im XIV und XV Jahrhundert, grosse Ausgabe, Wien, 1892, pp. 67 seq. At Paris, the day of labour varied from seven to eight hours in the winter to fourteen hours in summer in certain trades, while in others it was from eight to nine hours in winter, to from ten to twelve in Summer. All work was stopped on Saturdays and on about twenty-five other days (jours de commun de vile foire) at four o'clock, while on Sundays and thirty other holidays there was no work at all. The general conclusion is, that the medieval worker worked less hours, all taken, than the present-day worker (Dr. E. Martin Saint-Leon, Histoire des corporations, p. 121).

11. W. Stieda, "Hansische Vereinbarungen uber stadtisches Gewerbe im XIV und XV Jahrhundert," in Hansische Geschichtsblatter, Jahrgang 1886, p. 121. Schonberg's Wirthschaftliche Bedeutung der Zunfte; also, partly, Roscher.

12. See Toulmin Smith's deeply-felt remarks about the royal spoliation of the guilds, in Miss Smith's Introduction to English Guilds. In France the same royal spoliation and abolition of the guilds' jurisdiction was begun from 1306, and the final blow was struck in 1382 (Fagniez, l.c. pp. 52-54).

13. Adam Smith and his contemporaries knew well what they were condemning when they wrote against the State interference in trade and the trade monopolies of State creation. Unhappily, their followers, with their hopeless superficiality, flung medieval guilds and State interference into the same sack, making no distinction between a Versailles edict and a guild ordinance. It hardly need be said that the economists who have seriously studied the subject, like Schonberg (the editor of the well-known course of Political Economy), never fell into such an error. But, till lately, diffuse discussions of the above type went on for economical "science."

14. In Florence the seven minor arts made their revolution in 1270-82, and its results are fully described by Perrens (Histoire de Florence, Paris, 1877, 3 vols.), and especially by Gino Capponi (Storia della repubblica di Firenze, 2da edizione, 1876, i. 58-80; translated into German). In Lyons, on the contrary, where the movement of the minor crafts took place in 1402, the latter were defeated and lost the right of themselves nominating their own judges. The two parties came apparently to a compromise. In Rostock the same movement took place in 1313; in Zurich in 1336; in Bern in 1363; in Braunschweig in 1374, and next year in Hamburg; in Lubeck in 1376-84; and so on. See Schmoller's Strassburg zur Zeit der Zunftkampfe and Strassburg's Bluthe; Brentano's Arbeitergilden der Gegenwart, 2 vols., Leipzig, 1871-72; Eb. Bain's Merchant and Craft Guilds, Aberdeen, 1887, pp. 26-47, 75, etc. As to Mr. Gross's opinion relative to the same struggles in England, see Mrs. Green's remarks in her Town Life in the Fifteenth Century, ii. 190-217; also the chapter on the Labour Question, and, in fact, the whole of this extremely interesting volume. Brentano's views on the crafts' struggles, expressed especially in iii. and iv. of his essay "On the History and Development of Guilds," in Toulmin Smith's English Guilds remain classical for the subject, and may be said to have been

again and again confirmed by subsequent research.

15. To give but one example—Cambrai made its first revolution in 907, and, after three or four more revolts, it obtained its charter in 1076. This charter was repealed twice (1107 and 1138), and twice obtained again (in 1127 and 1180). Total, 223 years of struggles before conquering the right to independence. Lyons—from 1195 to 1320.

16. See Tuetey, "Etude sur Le droit municipal … en Franche-Comte," in Memoires de la Societe d'emulation de Montbeliard, 2e serie, ii. 129 seq.

17. This seems to have been often the case in Italy. In Switzerland, Bern bought even the towns of Thun and Burgdorf.

18. Such was, at least, the case in the cities of Tuscany (Florence, Lucca, Sienna, Bologna, etc.), for which the relations between city and peasants are best known. (Luchitzkiy, "Slavery and Russian Slaves in Florence," in Kieff University Izvestia for 1885, who has perused Rumohr's Ursprung der Besitzlosigkeit der Colonien in Toscana, 1830.) The whole matter concerning the relations between the cities and the peasants requires much more study than has hitherto been done.

19. Ferrari's generalizations are often too theoretical to be always correct; but his views upon the part played by the nobles in the city wars are based upon a wide range of authenticated facts.

20. Only such cities as stubbornly kept to the cause of the barons, like Pisa or Verona, lost through the wars. For many towns which fought on the barons' side, the defeat was also the beginning of liberation and progress.

21. Ferrari, ii. 18, 104 seq.; Leo and Botta, i. 432.

22. Joh. Falke, Die Hansa Als Deutsche See-und Handelsmacht, Berlin, 1863, pp. 31, 55.

23. For Aachen and Cologne we have direct testimony that the bishops of these two cities—one of them bought by the enemy opened to him the gates.

24. See the facts, though not always the conclusions, of Nitzsch, iii. 133 seq.; also Kallsen, i. 458, etc.

25. On the Commune of the Laonnais, which, until Melleville's researches (Histoire de la Commune du Laonnais, Paris, 1853), was confounded with the Commune of Laon, see Luchaire, pp. 75 seq. For the early peasants' guilds and subsequent unions see R. Wilman's "Die landlichen Schutzgilden Westphaliens," in Zeitschrift für Kulturgeschichte, neue Folge, Bd. iii., quoted in Henne-am-Rhyn's Kulturgeschichte, iii. 249.

26. Luchaire, p. 149.

27. Two important cities, like Mainz and Worms, would settle a political contest by means of arbitration. After a civil war broken out in Abbeville, Amiens would act, in 1231, as arbiter (Luchaire, 149); and so on.

28. See, for instance, W. Stieda, Hansische Vereinbarungen, l.c., p. 114.

29. Cosmo Innes's Early Scottish History and Scotland in Middle Ages, quoted by Rev. Denton, l.c., pp. 68, 69; Lamprecht's Deutsches wirthschaftliche Leben im Mittelalter, review by Schmoller in his Jahrbuch, Bd. xii.; Sismondi's Tableau de l'agriculture toscane, pp. 226 seq. The dominions of Florence could be recognized at a glance through their prosperity.

30. Mr. John J. Ennett (Six Essays, London, 1891) has excellent pages on this aspect of medieval architecture. Mr. Willis, in his appendix to Whewell's History of Inductive Sciences (i. 261-262), has pointed out the beauty of the mechanical relations in medieval buildings. "A new decorative construction was matured," he writes, "not thwarting and controlling, but assisting and harmonizing with the mechanical construction. Every member, every moulding, becomes a sustainer of weight; and by the multiplicity of props assisting each other, and the consequent subdivision of weight, the eye was satisfied of the stability of the structure, notwithstanding curiously slender aspects of the separate parts." An art which sprang out of the social life of the city could not be better characterized.

31. Dr. L. Ennen, Der Dom zu Koln, seine Construction und Anstaltung, Koln, 1871.

32. The three statues are among the outer decorations of Notre Dame de Paris.

33. Mediaeval art, like Greek art, did not know those curiosity shops which we call a National Gallery or a Museum. A picture was painted, a statue was carved, a bronze decoration was cast to stand in its proper place in a monument of communal art. It lived there, it was part of a whole, and it contributed to give unity to the impression produced by the whole.

34. Cf. J. T. Ennett's "Second Essay," p. 36.

35. Sismondi, iv. 172; xvi. 356. The great canal, Naviglio Grande, which brings the water from the Tessino, was begun in 1179, i.e. after the conquest of independence, and it was ended in the thirteenth century. On the subsequent decay, see xvi. 355.

36. In 1336 it had 8,000 to 10,000 boys and girls in its primary schools, 1,000 to 1,200 boys in its seven middle schools, and from 550 to 600 students in its four universities. The thirty communal hospitals contained over 1,000 beds for a population of 90,000 inhabitants (Capponi, ii. 249 seq.). It has more than once been suggested by authoritative writers that education stood, as a rule, at a much higher level than is generally supposed. Certainly so in democratic Nuremberg.

37. Cf. L. Ranke's excellent considerations upon the essence of Roman Law in his Weltgeschichte, Bd. iv. Abth. 2, pp. 20-31. Also Sismondi's remarks upon the part played by the legistes in the constitution of royal authority, Histoire des Francais, Paris, 1826, viii. 85-99. The popular hatred against these "weise Doktoren und Beutelschneider des Volks" broke out with full force in the first years of the sixteenth century in the sermons of the early Reform movement.

38. Brentano fully understood the fatal effects of the struggle between the "old burghers" and the new-comers. Miaskowski, in his work on the village communities of Switzerland, has indicated the same for village communities.

39. The trade in slaves kidnapped in the East was never discontinued in the Italian republics till the fifteenth century. Feeble traces of it are found also in Germany and elsewhere. See Cibrario. Della schiavitu e del servaggio, 2 vols. Milan, 1868; Professor Luchitzkiy, "Slavery and Russian Slaves in Florence in the Fourteenth and Fifteenth Centuries," in Izvestia of the Kieff University, 1885.

40. J.R. Green's History of the English People, London, 1878, i. 455.

41. See the theories expressed by the Bologna lawyers, already at the Congress of Roncaglia in 1158.

CHAPTER VII

MUTUAL AID AMONGST OURSELVES

Popular revolts at the beginning of the State-period. Mutual Aid institutions of the present time. The village community; its struggles for resisting its abolition by the State. Habits derived from the village-community life, retained in our modern villages. Switzerland, France, Germany, Russia.

The mutual-aid tendency in man has so remote an origin, and is so deeply interwoven with all the past evolution of the human race, that it has been maintained by mankind up to the present time, notwithstanding all vicissitudes of history. It was chiefly evolved during periods of peace and prosperity; but when even the greatest calamities befell men—when whole countries were laid waste by wars, and whole populations were decimated by misery, or groaned under the yoke of tyranny—the same tendency continued to live in the villages and among the poorer classes in the towns; it still kept them together, and in the long run it reacted even upon those ruling, fighting, and devastating minorities which dismissed it as sentimental nonsense. And whenever mankind had to work out a new social organization, adapted to a new phasis of development, its constructive genius always drew the elements and the inspiration for the new departure from that same ever-living tendency. New economical and social institutions, in so far as they were a creation of the masses, new ethical systems, and new religions, all have originated from the same source, and the ethical progress of our race, viewed in its broad lines, appears as a gradual extension of the mutual-aid principles from the tribe to always larger and larger agglomerations, so as to finally embrace one day the whole of mankind, without respect to its divers creeds, languages, and races.

After having passed through the savage tribe, and next through the village community, the Europeans came to work out in medieval times a new form of organization, which had the advantage of allowing great latitude for individual initiative, while it largely responded at the same time to man's need of mutual support. A federation of village communities, covered by a network of guilds and fraternities, was called into existence in the medieval cities. The immense results achieved under this new form of union—in well-being for all, in industries, art, science, and commerce—were discussed at some length in two preceding chapters, and an attempt was also made to show why, towards the end of the fifteenth century, the medieval republics—surrounded by domains of hostile feudal lords, unable to free the peasants from servitude, and gradually corrupted by ideas of Roman Caesarism—were doomed to become a prey to the growing military States.

However, before submitting for three centuries to come, to the all-absorbing authority of the State, the masses of the people made a formidable attempt at reconstructing society on the old basis of mutual aid and support. It is well known by this time that the great movement of the reform was not a mere revolt against the abuses of the Catholic Church. It had its constructive ideal as well, and that ideal was life in free, brotherly communities. Those of the early writings and sermons of the period which found most response with the masses were imbued with ideas of the economical and social brotherhood of mankind. The "Twelve Articles" and similar professions of faith, which were circulated among the German and Swiss peasants and artisans, maintained not only every one's right to interpret the Bible according to his own understanding, but also included the demand of communal lands being restored to the village communities and feudal servitudes being abolished, and they always alluded to the "true" faith—a faith of brotherhood. At the same time scores of thousands of men and women joined the communist fraternities of Moravia, giving them all their fortune and living in numerous and prosperous settlements constructed upon the principles of communism.(1) Only wholesale massacres by the thousand could put a stop to this widely-spread popular movement, and it was by the sword, the fire, and the rack that the young States secured their first and decisive victory over the masses of the people.(2)

For the next three centuries the States, both on the Continent and in these islands, systematically weeded out all institutions in which the mutual-aid tendency had formerly found its expression. The village communities were bereft of their folkmotes, their courts and independent administration; their lands were confiscated. The guilds were spoliated of their possessions and liberties, and placed under the control, the fancy, and the bribery of the State's official. The cities were divested of their sovereignty, and the very springs of their inner life—the folkmote, the elected justices and administration, the sovereign parish and the sovereign guild—were annihilated; the State's functionary took possession of every link of what formerly was an organic whole. Under that fatal policy and the wars it engendered, whole regions, once populous and wealthy, were laid bare; rich cities became insignificant boroughs; the very roads which connected them with other cities became impracticable. Industry, art, and knowledge fell into decay. Political education, science, and law were rendered subservient to the idea of State centralization. It was taught in the Universities and from the pulpit that the institutions in which men formerly used to embody their needs of mutual support could not be tolerated in a properly organized State; that the State alone could represent the bonds of union between its subjects; that federalism and "particularism" were the enemies of progress, and the State was the only proper initiator of further development. By the end of the last century the kings on the Continent, the Parliament in these isles, and the revolutionary Convention in France, although they were at war with each other, agreed in asserting that no separate unions between citizens must exist within the State; that hard labour and death were the only suitable punishments to workers who dared to enter into "coalitions." "No state within the State!" The State alone, and the State's Church, must take care of matters of general interest, while the subjects must represent loose aggregations of individuals, connected by no particular bonds, bound to appeal to the Government each time that they feel a common need. Up to the middle of this century this was the theory and practice in Europe. Even commercial and industrial societies were looked at with suspicion. As to the workers, their unions were treated as unlawful almost within our own lifetime in this country and within the last twenty years on the Continent. The whole system of our State education was such that up to the present time, even in this country, a notable portion of society would treat as a revolutionary measure the concession of such rights as every one, freeman or serf, exercised five hundred years ago in the village folkmote, the guild, the parish, and the city.

The absorption of all social functions by the State necessarily favoured the development of an unbridled, narrow-minded individualism. In proportion as the obligations towards the State grew in numbers the citizens were evidently relieved from their obligations towards each other. In the guild—and in medieval times every man belonged to some guild or fraternity two "brothers" were bound to watch in turns a brother who had fallen ill; it would be sufficient now to give one's neighbour the address of the next paupers' hospital. In barbarian society, to assist at a fight between two men, arisen from a quarrel, and not to prevent it from taking a fatal issue, meant to be oneself treated as a murderer; but under the theory of the all-protecting State the bystander need not intrude: it is the policeman's business to interfere, or not. And while in a savage land, among the Hottentots, it would be scandalous to eat without having loudly called out thrice whether there is not somebody wanting to share the food, all that a respectable citizen has to do now is to pay the poor tax and to let the starving starve. The result is, that the theory which maintains that men can, and must, seek their own happiness in a disregard of other people's wants is now triumphant all round in law, in science, in religion. It is the religion of the day, and to doubt of its efficacy is to be a dangerous Utopian. Science loudly proclaims that the struggle of each against all is the leading principle of nature, and of human societies as well. To that struggle Biology ascribes the progressive evolution of the animal world. History takes the same line of argument; and political economists, in their naive ignorance, trace all progress of modern industry and machinery to the "wonderful" effects of the same principle. The very religion of the pulpit is a religion of individualism, slightly mitigated by more or less charitable relations to one's neighbours, chiefly on Sundays. "Practical" men and theorists, men of science and religious preachers, lawyers and politicians, all agree upon one thing—that individualism may be more or less softened in its harshest effects by charity, but that it is the only secure basis for the maintenance of society and its ulterior progress.

It seems, therefore, hopeless to look for mutual-aid institutions and practices in modern society. What could remain of them? And yet, as soon as we try to ascertain how the millions of human beings live, and begin to study their everyday relations, we are struck with the immense part which the mutual-aid and mutual-support principles play even now-a-days in human life. Although the destruction of mutual-aid institutions has been going on in practice and theory, for full three or four hundred years, hundreds of millions of men continue to live under such institutions; they piously maintain them and endeavour to reconstitute them where they have ceased to exist. In our mutual relations every one of us has his moments of revolt against the fashionable individualistic creed of the day, and actions in which men are guided by their mutual aid inclinations constitute so great a part of our daily intercourse that if a stop to such actions could be put all further ethical progress would be stopped at once. Human society itself could not be maintained for even so much as the lifetime of one single generation. These facts, mostly neglected by sociologists and yet of the first importance for the life and further elevation of mankind, we are now going to analyze, beginning with the standing institutions of mutual support, and passing next to those acts of mutual aid which have their origin in personal or social sympathies.

When we cast a broad glance on the present constitution of European society we are struck at once with the fact that, although so much has been done to get rid of the village community, this form of union continues to exist to the extent we shall presently see, and that many attempts are now made either to reconstitute it in some shape or another or to find some substitute for it. The current theory as regards the village community is, that in Western Europe it has died out by a natural death, because the communal possession of the soil was found inconsistent with the modern requirements of agriculture. But the truth is that nowhere did the village community disappear of its own accord; everywhere, on the contrary, it took the ruling classes several centuries of persistent but not always successful efforts to abolish it and to confiscate the communal lands.

In France, the village communities began to be deprived of their independence, and their lands began to be plundered, as early as the sixteenth century. However, it was only in the next century, when the mass of the peasants was brought, by exactions and wars, to the state of subjection and misery which is vividly depicted by all historians, that the plundering of their lands became easy and attained scandalous proportions. "Every one has taken of them according to his powers ... imaginary debts have been claimed, in order to seize upon their lands;" so we read in an edict promulgated by Louis the Fourteenth in 1667.(3) Of course the State's remedy for such evils was to render the communes still more subservient to the State, and to plunder them itself. In fact, two years later all money revenue of the communes was confiscated by the King. As to the appropriation of communal lands, it grew worse and worse, and in the next century the nobles and the clergy had already taken possession of immense tracts of land—one-half of the cultivated area, according to certain estimates—mostly to let it go out of culture.(4) But the peasants still maintained their communal institutions, and until the year 1787 the village folkmotes, composed of all householders, used to come together in the shadow of the bell-tower or a tree, to allot and re-allot what they had retained of their fields, to assess the taxes, and to elect their executive, just as the Russian mir does at the present time. This is what Babeau's researches have proved to demonstration.(5)

The Government found, however, the folkmotes "too noisy," too disobedient, and in 1787, elected councils, composed of a mayor and three to six syndics, chosen from among the wealthier peasants, were introduced instead. Two years later the Revolutionary Assemblee Constituante, which was on this point at one with the old regime, fully confirmed this law (on the 14th of December, 1789), and the bourgeois du village had now their turn for the plunder of communal lands, which continued all through the Revolutionary period. Only on the 16th of August, 1792, the Convention, under the pressure of the peasants' insurrections, decided to return the enclosed lands to the communes;(6) but it ordered at the same time that they should be divided in equal parts among the wealthier peasants only—a measure which provoked new insurrections and was abrogated next year, in 1793, when the order came to divide the communal lands among all commoners, rich and poor alike, "active" and "inactive."

These two laws, however, ran so much against the conceptions of the peasants that they were not obeyed, and wherever the peasants had retaken possession of part of their lands they kept them undivided. But then came the long years of wars, and the communal lands were simply confiscated by the State (in 1794) as a mortgage for State loans, put up for sale, and plundered as such; then returned again to the communes and confiscated again (in 1813); and only in 1816 what remained of them, i.e. about 15,000,000 acres of the least productive land, was restored to the village communities.(7) Still this was not yet the end of the troubles of the communes. Every new regime saw in the communal lands a means for gratifying its supporters, and three laws (the first in 1837 and the last under Napoleon the Third) were passed to induce the village communities to divide their estates. Three times these laws had to be repealed, in consequence of the opposition they met with in the villages; but something was snapped up each time, and Napoleon the Third, under the pretext of encouraging perfected methods of agriculture, granted large estates out of the communal lands to some of his favourites.

As to the autonomy of the village communities, what could be retained of it after so many blows? The mayor and the syndics were simply looked upon as unpaid functionaries of the State machinery. Even now, under the Third Republic, very little can be done in a village community without the huge State machinery, up to the prefet and the ministries, being set in motion. It is hardly credible, and yet it is true, that when, for instance, a peasant intends to pay in money his share in the repair of a communal road, instead of himself breaking the necessary amount of stones, no fewer than twelve different functionaries of the State must give their approval, and an aggregate of fifty-two different acts must be performed by them, and exchanged between them, before the peasant is permitted to pay that money to the communal council. All the remainder bears the same character.(8)

What took place in France took place everywhere in Western and Middle Europe. Even the chief dates of the great assaults upon the peasant lands are the same. For England the only difference is that the spoliation was accomplished by separate acts rather than by general sweeping measures—with less haste but more thoroughly than in France. The seizure of the communal lands by the lords also began in the fifteenth century, after the defeat of the peasant insurrection of 1380—as seen from Rossus's Historia and from a statute of Henry the Seventh, in which these seizures are spoken of under the heading of "enormitees and myschefes as be hurtfull ... to the common wele."(9) Later on the Great Inquest, under Henry the Eighth, was begun, as is known, in order to put a stop to the enclosure of communal lands, but it ended in a sanction of what had been done.(10) The communal lands continued to be preyed upon, and the peasants were driven from the land. But it was especially since the middle of the eighteenth century that, in England as everywhere else, it became part of a systematic policy to simply weed out all traces of communal ownership; and the wonder is not that it has disappeared, but that it could be maintained, even in England, so as to be "generally prevalent so late as the grandfathers of this generation."(11) The very object of the Enclosure Acts, as shown by Mr. Seebohm, was to remove this system,(12) and it was so well removed by the nearly four thousand Acts passed between 1760 and 1844 that only faint traces of it remain now. The land of the village communities was taken by the lords, and the appropriation was sanctioned by Parliament in each separate case.

In Germany, in Austria, in Belgium the village community was also destroyed by the State. Instances of commoners themselves dividing their lands were rare,(13) while everywhere the States coerced them to enforce the division, or simply favoured the private appropriation of their lands. The last blow to communal ownership in Middle Europe also dates from the middle of the eighteenth century. In Austria sheer force was used by the Government, in 1768, to compel the communes to divide their lands—a special commission being nominated two years later for that purpose. In Prussia Frederick the Second, in several of his ordinances (in 1752, 1763, 1765, and 1769), recommended to the Justizcollegien to enforce the division. In Silesia a special resolution was issued to serve that aim in 1771. The same took place in Belgium, and, as the communes did not obey, a law was issued in 1847 empowering the Government to buy communal meadows in order to sell them in retail, and to make a forced sale of the communal land when there was a would-be buyer for it.(14)

In short, to speak of the natural death of the village communities in virtue of economical laws is as grim a joke as to speak of the natural death of soldiers slaughtered on a battlefield. The fact was simply this: The village communities had lived for over a thousand years; and where and when the peasants were not ruined by wars and exactions they steadily improved their methods of culture. But as the value of land was increasing, in consequence of the growth of industries, and the nobility had acquired, under the State organization, a power which it never had had under the feudal system, it took possession of the best parts of the communal lands, and did its best to destroy the communal institutions.

However, the village-community institutions so well respond to the needs and conceptions of the tillers of the soil that, in spite of all, Europe is up to this date covered with living survivals of the village communities, and European country life is permeated with customs and habits dating from the community period. Even in England, notwithstanding all the drastic measures taken against the old order of things, it prevailed as late as the beginning of the nineteenth century. Mr. Gomme—one of the very few English scholars who have paid attention to the subject—shows in his work that many traces of the communal possession of the soil are found in Scotland, "runrig" tenancy having been maintained in Forfarshire up to 1813, while in certain villages of Inverness the custom was, up to 1801, to plough the land for the whole community, without leaving any boundaries, and to allot it after the ploughing was done. In Kilmorie the allotment and re-allotment of the fields was in full vigour "till the last twenty-five years," and the Crofters' Commission found it still in vigour in certain islands.(15) In Ireland the system prevailed up to the great famine; and as to England, Marshall's works, which passed unnoticed until Nasse and Sir Henry Maine drew attention to them, leave no doubt as to the village-community system having been widely spread, in nearly all English counties, at the beginning of the nineteenth century.(16) No more than twenty years ago Sir Henry Maine was "greatly surprised at the number of instances of abnormal property rights, necessarily implying the former existence of collective ownership and joint cultivation," which a comparatively brief inquiry brought under his notice.(17) And, communal institutions having persisted so late as that, a great number of mutual-aid habits and customs would undoubtedly be discovered in English villages if the writers of this country only paid attention to village life.(18)

As to the Continent, we find the communal institutions fully alive in many parts of France, Switzerland, Germany, Italy, the Scandinavian lands, and Spain, to say nothing of Eastern Europe; the village life in these countries is permeated with communal habits and customs; and almost every year the Continental literature is enriched by serious works dealing with this and connected subjects. I must, therefore, limit my illustrations to the most typical instances. Switzerland is undoubtedly one of them. Not only the five republics of Uri, Schwytz, Appenzell, Glarus, and Unterwalden hold their lands as undivided estates, and are governed by their popular folkmotes, but in all other cantons too the village communities remain in possession of a wide self-government, and own large parts of the Federal territory.(19) Two-thirds of all the Alpine meadows and two-thirds of all the forests of Switzerland are until now communal land; and a considerable number of fields, orchards, vineyards, peat bogs, quarries, and so on, are owned in common. In the Vaud, where all the householders continue to take part in the deliberations of their elected communal councils, the communal spirit is especially alive. Towards the end of the winter all the young men of each village go to stay a few days in the woods, to fell timber and to bring it down the steep slopes tobogganing way, the timber and the fuel wood being divided among all households or sold for their benefit. These excursions are real fetes of manly labour. On the banks of Lake Leman part of the work required to keep up the terraces of the vineyards is still done in common; and in the spring, when the thermometer threatens to fall below zero before sunrise, the watchman wakes up all householders, who light fires of straw and dung and protect their vine-trees from the frost by an artificial cloud. In nearly all cantons the village communities possess so-called. Burgernutzen—that is, they hold in common a number of cows, in order to supply each family with butter; or they keep communal fields or vineyards, of which the produce is divided between the burghers, or they rent their land for the benefit of the community.(20)

It may be taken as a rule that where the communes have retained a wide sphere of functions, so as to be living parts of the national organism, and where they have not been reduced to sheer misery, they never fail to take good care of their lands. Accordingly the communal estates in Switzerland strikingly contrast with the miserable state of "commons" in this country. The communal forests in the Vaud and the Valais are admirably managed, in conformity with the rules of modern forestry. Elsewhere the "strips" of communal fields, which change owners under the system of re-allotment, are very well manured, especially as there is no lack of meadows and cattle. The high level meadows are well kept as a rule, and the rural roads are excellent.(21) And when we admire the Swiss chalet, the mountain road, the peasants' cattle, the terraces of vineyards, or the school-house in Switzer land, we must keep in mind that without the timber for the chalet being taken from the communal woods and the stone from the communal quarries, without the cows being kept on the communal meadows, and the roads being made and the school-houses built by communal work, there would be little to admire.

It hardly need be said that a great number of mutual-aid habits and customs continue to persist in the Swiss villages. The evening gatherings for shelling walnuts, which take place in turns in each household; the evening parties for sewing the dowry of the girl who is going to marry; the calling of "aids" for building the houses and taking in the crops, as well as for all sorts of work which may be required by one of the commoners; the custom of exchanging children from one canton to the other, in order to make them learn two languages, French and German; and so on—all these are quite habitual;(22) while, on the other side, divers modern requirements are met in the same spirit. Thus in Glarus most of the Alpine meadows have been sold during a time of calamity; but the communes still continue to buy field land, and after the newly-bought fields have been left in the possession of separate commoners for ten, twenty, or thirty years, as the case might be, they return to the common stock, which is re-allotted according to the needs of all. A great number of small associations are formed to produce some of the necessaries for life—bread, cheese, and wine—by common work, be it only on a limited scale; and agricultural co-operation altogether spreads in Switzerland with the greatest ease. Associations formed between ten to thirty peasants, who buy meadows and fields in common, and cultivate them as co-owners, are of common occurrence; while dairy associations for the sale of milk, butter, and cheese are organized everywhere. In fact, Switzerland was the birthplace of that form of co-operation. It offers, moreover, an immense field for the study of all sorts of small and large societies, formed for the satisfaction of all sorts of modern wants. In certain parts of Switzerland one finds in almost every village a number of associations—for protection from fire, for boating, for maintaining the quays on the shores of a lake, for the supply of water, and so on; and the country is covered with societies of archers, sharpshooters, topographers, footpath explorers, and the like, originated from modern militarism.

Switzerland is, however, by no means an exception in Europe, because the same institutions and habits are found in the villages of France, of Italy, of Germany, of Denmark, and so on. We have just seen what has been done by the rulers of France in order to destroy the village community and to get hold of its lands; but notwithstanding all that one-tenth part of the whole territory available for culture, i.e. 13,500,000 acres, including one-half of all the natural meadows and nearly a fifth part of all the forests of the country, remain in communal possession. The woods supply the communers with fuel, and the timber wood is cut, mostly by communal work, with all desirable regularity; the grazing lands are free for the commoners' cattle; and what remains of communal fields is allotted and re-allotted in certain parts Ardennes—in the usual of France—namely, in the way.(23)

These additional sources of supply, which aid the poorer peasants to pass through a year of bad crops without parting with their small plots of land and without running into irredeemable debts, have certainly their importance for both the agricultural labourers and the nearly three millions of small peasant proprietors. It is even doubtful whether small peasant proprietorship could be maintained without these additional resources. But the ethical importance of the communal possessions, small as they are, is still greater than their economical value. They maintain in village life a nucleus of customs and habits of mutual aid which undoubtedly acts as a mighty check upon the development of reckless individualism and greediness, which small land-ownership is only too prone to develop. Mutual aid in all possible circumstances of village life is part of the routine life in all parts of the country. Everywhere we meet, under different names, with the charroi, i.e. the free aid of the neighbours for taking in a crop, for vintage, or for building a house; everywhere we find the same evening gatherings as have just been mentioned in Switzerland; and everywhere the commoners associate for all sorts of work. Such habits are mentioned by nearly all those who have written upon French village life. But it will perhaps be better to give in this place some abstracts from letters which I have just received from a friend of mine whom I have asked to communicate to me his observations on this subject. They come from an aged man who for years has been the mayor of his commune in South France (in Ariege); the facts he mentions are known to him from long years of personal observation, and they have the advantage of coming from one neighbourhood instead of being skimmed from a large area. Some of them may seem trifling, but as a whole they depict quite a little world of village life.

"In several communes in our neighbourhood," my friend writes, "the old custom of l'emprount is in vigour. When many hands are required in a metairie for rapidly making some work—dig out potatoes or mow the grass—the youth of the neighbourhood is convoked; young men and girls come in numbers, make it gaily and for nothing; and in the evening, after a gay meal, they dance.

"In the same communes, when a girl is going to marry, the girls of the neighbourhood come to aid in sewing the dowry. In several communes the women still continue to spin a good deal. When the winding off has to be done in a family it is done in one evening—all friends being convoked for that work. In many communes of the Ariege and other parts of the south-west the shelling of the Indian corn-sheaves is also done by all the neighbours. They are treated with chestnuts and wine, and the young people dance after the work has been done. The same custom is practised for making nut oil and crushing hemp. In the commune of L. the same is done for bringing in the corn crops. These days of hard work become fete days, as the owner stakes his honour on serving a good meal. No remuneration is given; all do it for each other.(24)

"In the commune of S. the common grazing-land is every year

increased, so that nearly the whole of the land of the commune is now kept in common. The shepherds are elected by all owners of the cattle, including women. The bulls are communal.

"In the commune of M. the forty to fifty small sheep flocks of the commoners are brought together and divided into three or four flocks before being sent to the higher meadows. Each owner goes for a week to serve as shepherd.

"In the hamlet of C. a threshing machine has been bought in common by several households; the fifteen to twenty persons required to serve the machine being supplied by all the families. Three other threshing machines have been bought and are rented out by their owners, but the work is performed by outside helpers, invited in the usual way.

"In our commune of R. we had to raise the wall of the cemetery. Half of the money which was required for buying lime and for the wages of the skilled workers was supplied by the county council, and the other half by subscription. As to the work of carrying sand and water, making mortar, and serving the masons, it was done entirely by volunteers [just as in the Kabyle djemmaa]. The rural roads were repaired in the same way, by volunteer days of work given by the commoners. Other communes have built in the same way their fountains. The wine-press and other smaller appliances are frequently kept by the commune."

Two residents of the same neighbourhood, questioned by my friend, add the following:—

"At O. a few years ago there was no mill. The commune has built one, levying a tax upon the commoners. As to the miller, they decided, in order to avoid frauds and partiality, that he should be paid two francs for each bread-eater, and the corn be ground free.

"At St. G. few peasants are insured against fire. When a conflagration has taken place—so it was lately—all give something to the family which has suffered from it—a chaldron, a bed-cloth, a chair, and so on—and a modest household is thus reconstituted. All the neighbours aid to build the house, and in the meantime the family is lodged free by the neighbours."

Such habits of mutual support—of which many more examples could be given—undoubtedly account for the easiness with which the French peasants associate for using, in turn, the plough with its team of horses, the wine-press, and the threshing machine, when they are kept in the village by one of them only, as well as for the performance of all sorts of rural work in common. Canals were maintained, forests were cleared, trees were planted, and marshes were drained by the village communities from time immemorial; and the same continues still. Quite lately, in La Borne of Lozere barren hills were turned into rich gardens by communal work. "The soil was brought on men's backs; terraces were made and planted with chestnut trees, peach trees, and orchards, and water was brought for irrigation in canals two or three miles long." Just now they have dug a new canal, eleven miles in length.(25)

To the same spirit is also due the remarkable success lately obtained by the syndicats agricoles, or peasants' and farmers' associations. It was not until 1884 that associations of more than nineteen persons were permitted in France, and I need not say that when this "dangerous experiment" was ventured upon—so it was styled in the Chambers—all due "precautions" which functionaries can invent were taken. Notwithstanding all that, France begins to be covered with syndicates. At the outset they were only formed for buying manures and seeds, falsification having attained colossal proportions in these two branches;(26) but gradually they extended their functions in various directions, including the sale of agricultural produce and permanent improvements of the land. In South France the ravages of the phylloxera have called into existence a great number of wine-growers' associations. Ten to thirty growers form a syndicate, buy a steam-engine for pumping water, and make the necessary arrangements for inundating their vineyards in turn.(27) New associations for protecting the land from inundations, for irrigation purposes, and for maintaining canals are continually formed, and the unanimity of all peasants of a neighbourhood, which is required by law, is no obstacle. Elsewhere we have the fruitieres, or dairy associations, in some of which all butter and cheese is divided in equal parts, irrespective of the yield of each cow. In the Ariege we find an association of eight separate communes for the common culture of their lands, which they have put together; syndicates for free medical aid have been formed in 172 communes out of 337 in the same department; associations of consumers arise in connection with the syndicates; and so on.(28) "Quite a revolution is going on in our villages," Alfred Baudrillart writes, "through these associations, which take in each region their own special characters."

Very much the same must be said of Germany. Wherever the peasants could resist the plunder of their lands, they have retained them in communal ownership, which largely prevails in Wurttemberg, Baden, Hohenzollern, and in the Hessian province of Starkenberg.(29) The communal forests are kept, as a rule, in an excellent state, and in thousands of communes timber and fuel wood are divided every year among all inhabitants; even the old custom of the Lesholztag is widely spread: at the ringing of the village bell all go to the forest to take as much fuel wood as they can carry.(30) In Westphalia one finds communes in which all the land is cultivated as one common estate, in accordance with all requirements of modern agronomy. As to the old communal customs and habits, they are in vigour in most parts of Germany. The calling in of aids, which are real fetes of labour, is known to be quite habitual in Westphalia, Hesse, and Nassau. In well-timbered regions the timber for a new house is usually taken from the communal forest, and all the neighbours join in building the house. Even in the suburbs of Frankfort it is a regular custom among the gardeners that in case of one of them being ill all come on Sunday to cultivate his garden.(31)

In Germany, as in France, as soon as the rulers of the people repealed their laws against the peasant associations—that was only in 1884-1888—these unions began to develop with a wonderful rapidity, notwithstanding all legal obstacles which were put in their way(32) "It is a fact," Buchenberger says, "that in thousands of village communities, in which no sort of chemical manure or rational fodder was ever known, both have become of everyday use, to a quite unforeseen extent, owing to these associations" (vol. ii. p. 507). All sorts of labour-saving implements and agricultural machinery, and better breeds of cattle, are bought through the associations, and various arrangements for improving the quality of the produce begin to be introduced. Unions for the sale of agricultural produce are also formed, as well as for permanent improvements of the land.(33)

From the point of view of social economics all these efforts of the peasants certainly are of little importance. They cannot substantially, and still less permanently, alleviate the misery to which the tillers of the soil are doomed all over Europe. But from the ethical point of view, which we are now considering, their importance cannot be overrated. They prove that even under the system of reckless individualism which now prevails the agricultural masses piously maintain their mutual-support inheritance; and as soon as the States relax the iron laws by means of which they have broken all bonds between men, these bonds are at once reconstituted, notwithstanding the difficulties, political, economical, and social, which are many, and in such forms as best answer to the modern requirements of production. They indicate in which direction and in which form further progress must be expected.

I might easily multiply such illustrations, taking them from Italy, Spain, Denmark, and so on, and pointing out some interesting features which are proper to each of these countries. The Slavonian populations of Austria and the Balkan peninsula, among whom the "compound family," or "undivided household," is found in existence, ought also to be mentioned.(34) But I hasten to pass on to Russia, where the same mutual-support tendency takes certain new and unforeseen forms. Moreover, in dealing with the village community in Russia we have the advantage: of possessing an immense mass of materials, collected during the colossal house-to-house inquest which was lately made by several zemstvos (county councils), and which embraces a population of nearly 20,000,000 peasants in different parts of the country.(35)

Two important conclusions may be drawn from the bulk of evidence collected by the Russian inquests. In Middle Russia, where fully one-third of the peasants have been brought to utter ruin (by heavy taxation, small allotments of unproductive land, rack rents, and very severe tax-collecting after total failures of crops), there was, during the first five-and-twenty years after the emancipation of the serfs, a decided tendency towards the constitution of individual property in land within the village communities. Many impoverished "horseless" peasants abandoned their allotments, and this land often became the property of those richer peasants, who borrow additional incomes from trade, or of outside traders, who buy land chiefly for exacting rack rents from the peasants. It must also be added that a flaw in the land redemption law of 1861 offered great facilities for buying peasants' lands at a very small expense,(36) and that the State officials mostly used their weighty influence in favour of individual as against communal ownership. However, for the last twenty years a strong wind of opposition to the individual appropriation of the land blows again through the Middle Russian villages, and strenuous efforts are being made by the bulk of those peasants who stand between the rich and the very poor to uphold the village community. As to the fertile steppes of the South, which are now the most populous and the richest part of European Russia, they were mostly colonized, during the present century, under the system of individual ownership or occupation, sanctioned in that form by the State. But since improved methods of agriculture with the aid of machinery have been introduced in the region, the peasant owners have gradually begun themselves to transform their individual ownership into communal possession, and one finds now, in that granary of Russia, a very great number of spontaneously formed village communities of recent origin.(37)

The Crimea and the part of the mainland which lies to the north of it (the province of Taurida), for which we have detailed data, offer an excellent illustration of that movement. This territory began to be colonized, after its annexation in 1783, by Great, Little, and White Russians—Cossacks, freemen, and runaway serfs—who came individually or in small groups from all corners of Russia. They took first to cattle-breeding, and when they began later on to till the soil, each one tilled as much as he could afford to. But when—immigration continuing, and perfected ploughs being introduced—land stood in great demand, bitter disputes arose among the settlers. They lasted for years, until these men, previously tied by no mutual bonds, gradually came to the idea that an end must be put to disputes by introducing village-community ownership. They passed decisions to the effect that the land which they owned individually should henceforward be their common property, and they began to allot and to re-allot it in accordance with the usual village-community rules. The movement gradually took a great extension, and on a small territory, the Taurida statisticians found 161 villages in which communal ownership had been introduced by the peasant proprietors themselves, chiefly in the years 1855-1885, in lieu of individual ownership. Quite a variety of village-community types has been freely worked out in this way by the settlers.(38) What adds to the interest of this transformation is that it took place, not only among the Great Russians, who are used to village-community life, but also among Little Russians, who have long since forgotten it under Polish rule, among Greeks and Bulgarians, and even among Germans, who have long since worked out in their prosperous and half-industrial Volga colonies their own type of village community.(39) It is evident that the Mussulman Tartars of Taurida hold their land under the Mussulman customary law, which is limited personal occupation; but even with them the European village community has been introduced in a few cases. As to other nationalities in Taurida, individual ownership has been abolished in six Esthonian, two Greek, two Bulgarian, one Czech, and one German village. This movement is characteristic for the whole of the fertile steppe region of the south. But separate instances of it are also found in Little Russia. Thus in a number of villages of the province of Chernigov the peasants were formerly individual owners of their plots; they had separate legal documents for their plots and used to rent and to sell their land at will. But in the fifties of the nineteenth century a movement began among them in favour of communal possession, the chief argument being the growing number of pauper families. The initiative of the reform was taken in one village, and the others followed suit, the last case on record dating from 1882. Of course there were struggles between the poor, who usually claim for communal possession, and the rich, who usually prefer individual ownership; and the struggles often lasted for years. In certain places the unanimity required then by the law being impossible to obtain, the village divided into two villages, one under individual ownership and the other under communal possession; and so they remained until the two coalesced into one community, or else they remained divided still. As to Middle Russia, its a fact that in many villages which were drifting towards individual ownership there began since 1880 a mass movement in favour of re-establishing the village community. Even peasant proprietors who had lived for years under the individualist system returned en masse to the communal institutions. Thus, there is a considerable number of ex-serfs who have received one-fourth part only of the regulation allotments, but they have received them free of redemption and in individual ownership. There was in 1890 a wide-spread movement among them (in Kursk, Ryazan, Tambov, Orel, etc.) towards putting their allotments together and introducing the village community. The "free agriculturists" (volnyie khlebopashtsy), who were liberated from serfdom under the law of 1803, and had bought their allotments—each family separately—are now nearly all under the village-community system, which they have introduced themselves. All these movements are of recent origin, and non-Russians too join them. Thus the Bulgares in the district of Tiraspol, after having remained for sixty years under the personal-property system, introduced the village community in the years 1876-1882. The German Mennonites of Berdyansk fought in 1890 for introducing the village community, and the small peasant proprietors (Kleinwirthschaftliche) among the German Baptists were agitating in their villages in the same direction. One instance more: In the province of Samara the Russian government created in the forties, by way of experiment, 103 villages on the system of individual ownership. Each household received a splendid property of 105 acres. In 1890, out of the 103 villages the peasants in 72 had already notified the desire of introducing the village community. I take all these facts from the excellent work of V.V., who simply gives, in a classified form, the facts recorded in the above-mentioned house-to-house inquest.

This movement in favour of communal possession runs badly against the current economical theories, according to which intensive culture is incompatible with the village community. But the most charitable thing that can be said of these theories is that they have never been submitted to the test of experiment: they belong to the domain of political metaphysics. The facts which we have before us show, on the contrary, that wherever the Russian peasants, owing to a concurrence of favourable circumstances, are less miserable than they are on the average, and wherever they find men of knowledge and initiative among their neighbours, the village community becomes the very means for introducing various improvements in agriculture and village life altogether. Here, as elsewhere, mutual aid is a better leader to progress than the war of each against all, as may be seen from the following facts.

Under Nicholas the First's rule many Crown officials and serf-owners used to compel the peasants to introduce the communal culture of small plots of the village lands, in order to refill the communal storehouses after loans of grain had been granted to the poorest commoners. Such cultures, connected in the peasants' minds with the worst reminiscences of serfdom, were abandoned as soon as serfdom was abolished but now the peasants begin to reintroduce them on their own account. In one district (Ostrogozhsk, in Kursk) the initiative of one person was sufficient to call them to life in four-fifths of all the villages. The same is met with in several other localities. On a given day the commoners come out, the richer ones with a plough or a cart and the poorer ones single-handed, and no attempt is made to discriminate one's share in the work. The crop is afterwards used for loans to the poorer commoners, mostly free grants, or for the orphans and widows, or for the village church, or for the school, or for repaying a communal debt.(40)

That all sorts of work which enters, so to say, in the routine of village life (repair of roads and bridges, dams, drainage, supply of water for irrigation, cutting of wood, planting of trees, etc.) are made by whole communes, and that land is rented and meadows are mown by whole communes—the work being accomplished by old and young, men and women, in the way described by Tolstoi—is only what one may expect from people living under the village-community system.(41) They are of everyday occurrence all over the country. But the village community is also by no means averse to modern agricultural improvements, when it can stand the expense, and when knowledge, hitherto kept for the rich only, finds its way into the peasant's house.

It has just been said that perfected ploughs rapidly spread in South Russia, and in many cases the village communities were instrumental in spreading their use. A plough was bought by the community, experimented upon on a portion of the communal land, and the necessary improvements were indicated to the makers, whom the communes often aided in starting the manufacture of cheap ploughs as a village industry. In the district of Moscow, where 1,560 ploughs were lately bought by the peasants during five years, the impulse came from those communes which rented lands as a body for the special purpose of improved culture.

In the north-east (Vyatka) small associations of peasants, who travel with their winnowing machines (manufactured as a village industry in one of the iron districts), have spread the use of such machines in the neighbouring governments. The very wide spread of threshing machines in Samara, Saratov, and Kherson is due to the peasant associations, which can afford to buy a costly engine, while the individual peasant cannot. And while we read in nearly all economical treatises that the village community was doomed to disappear when the three-fields system had to be substituted by the rotation of crops system, we see in Russia many village communities taking the initiative of introducing the rotation of crops. Before accepting it the peasants usually set apart a portion of the communal fields for an experiment in artificial meadows, and the commune buys the seeds.(42) If the experiment proves successful they find no difficulty whatever in re-dividing their fields, so as to suit the five or six fields system.

This system is now in use in hundreds of villages of Moscow, Tver, Smolensk, Vyatka, and Pskov.(43) And where land can be spared the communities give also a portion of their domain to allotments for fruit-growing. Finally, the sudden extension lately taken in Russia by the little model farms, orchards, kitchen gardens, and silkworm-culture grounds—which are started at the village school-houses, under the conduct of the school-master, or of a village volunteer—is also due to the support they found with the village communities.

Moreover, such permanent improvements as drainage and irrigation are of frequent occurrence. For instance, in three districts of the province of Moscow—industrial to a great extent—drainage works have been accomplished within the last ten years on a large scale in no less than 180 to 200 different villages—the commoners working themselves with the spade. At another extremity of Russia, in the dry Steppes of Novouzen, over a thousand dams for ponds were built and several hundreds of deep wells were sunk by the communes; while in a wealthy German colony of the south-east the commoners worked, men and women alike, for five weeks in succession, to erect a dam, two miles long, for irrigation purposes. What could isolated men do in that struggle against the dry climate? What could they obtain through individual effort when South Russia was struck with the marmot plague, and all people living on the land, rich and poor, commoners and individualists, had to work with their hands in order to conjure the plague? To call in the policeman would have been of no use; to associate was the only possible remedy.

And now, after having said so much about mutual aid and support which are practised by the tillers of the soil in "civilized" countries, I see that I might fill an octavo volume with illustrations taken from the life of the hundreds of millions of men who also live under the tutorship of more or less centralized States, but are out of touch with modern civilization and modern ideas. I might describe the inner life of a Turkish village and its network of admirable mutual-aid customs and habits. On turning over my leaflets covered with illustrations from peasant life in Caucasia, I come across touching facts of mutual support. I trace the same customs in the Arab djemmaa and the Afghan purra, in the villages of Persia, India, and Java, in the undivided family of the Chinese, in the encampments of the semi-nomads of Central Asia and the nomads of the far North. On consulting notes taken at random in the literature of Africa, I find them replete with similar facts—of aids convoked to take in the crops, of houses built by all inhabitants of the village—sometimes to repair the havoc done by civilized filibusters—of people aiding each other in case of accident, protecting the traveller, and so on. And when I peruse such works as Post's compendium of African customary law I understand why, notwithstanding all tyranny, oppression, robberies and raids, tribal wars, glutton kings, deceiving witches and priests, slave-hunters, and the like, these populations have not gone astray in the woods; why they have maintained a certain civilization, and have remained men, instead of dropping to the level of straggling families of decaying orang-outans. The fact is, that the slave-hunters, the ivory robbers, the fighting kings, the Matabele and the Madagascar "heroes" pass away, leaving their traces marked with blood and fire; but the nucleus of mutual-aid institutions, habits, and customs, grown up in the tribe and the village community, remains; and it keeps men united in societies, open to the progress of civilization, and ready to receive it when the day comes that they shall receive civilization instead of bullets.

The same applies to our civilized world. The natural and social calamities pass away. Whole populations are periodically reduced to misery or starvation; the very springs of life are crushed out of millions of men, reduced to city pauperism; the understanding and the feelings of the millions are vitiated by teachings worked out in the interest of the few. All this is certainly a part of our existence. But the nucleus of mutual-support institutions, habits, and customs remains alive with the millions; it keeps them together; and they prefer to cling to their customs, beliefs, and traditions rather than to accept the teachings of a war of each against all, which are offered to them under the title of science, but are no science at all.

NOTES:

1. A bulky literature, dealing with this formerly much neglected subject, is now growing in Germany. Keller's works, Ein Apostel der Wiedertaufer and Geschichte der Wiedertaufer, Cornelius's Geschichte des munsterischen Aufruhrs, and Janssen's Geschichte des deutschen Volkes may be named as the leading sources. The first attempt at familiarizing English readers with the results of the wide researches made in Germany in this direction has been made in an excellent little work by Richard Heath—"Anabaptism from its Rise at Zwickau to its Fall at Munster, 1521-1536," London, 1895 (Baptist Manuals, vol. i.)—where the leading features of the movement are well indicated, and full bibliographical information is given. Also K. Kautsky's Communism in Central Europe in the Time of the Reformation, London, 1897.

2. Few of our contemporaries realize both the extent of this movement and the means by which it was suppressed. But those who wrote immediately after the great peasant war estimated at from 100,000 to 150,000 men the number of peasants slaughtered after their defeat in Germany. See Zimmermann's Allgemeine Geschichte des grossen Bauernkrieges. For the measures taken to suppress the movement in the Netherlands see Richard Heath's Anabaptism.

3. "Chacun s'en est accommode selon sa bienseance ... on les a partages.. pour depouiller les communes, on s'est servi de dettes simulees" (Edict of Louis the Fourteenth, of 1667, quoted by several authors. Eight years before that date the communes had been taken under State management).

4. "On a great landlord's estate, even if he has millions of revenue, you are sure to find the land uncultivated" (Arthur Young). "One-fourth part of the soil went out of culture;" "for the last hundred years the land has returned to a savage state;" "the

formerly flourishing Sologne is now a big marsh;" and so on (Theron de Montauge, quoted by Taine in Origines de la France Contemporaine, tome i. p. 441).

5. A. Babeau, Le Village sous l'Ancien Regime, 3e edition. Paris, 1892.

6. In Eastern France the law only confirmed what the peasants had already done themselves. See my work, The Great French Revolution, chaps. xlvii and xlviii, London (Heinemann), 1909.

7. After the triumph of the middle-class reaction the communal lands were declared (August 24, 1794) the States domains, and, together with the lands confiscated from the nobility, were put up for sale, and pilfered by the bandes noires of the small bourgeoisie. True that a stop to this pilfering was put next year (law of 2 Prairial, An V), and the preceding law was abrogated; but then the village Communities were simply abolished, and cantonal councils were introduced instead. Only seven years later (9 Prairial, An XII), i.e. in 1801, the village communities were reintroduced, but not until after having been deprived of all their rights, the mayor and syndics being nominated by the Government in the 36,000 communes of France! This system was maintained till after the revolution of 1830, when elected communal councils were reintroduced under the law of 1787. As to the communal lands, they were again seized upon by the State in 1813, plundered as such, and only partly restored to the communes in 1816. See the classical collection of French laws, by Dalloz, Repertoire de Jurisprudence; also the works of Doniol, Dareste, Bonnemere, Babeau, and many others.

8. This procedure is so absurd that one would not believe it possible if the fifty-two different acts were not enumerated in full by a quite authoritative writer in the Journal des

Economistes (1893, April, p. 94), and several similar examples were not given by the same author.

9. Dr. Ochenkowski, Englands wirthschaftliche Entwickelung im Ausgange des Mittelalters (Jena, 1879), pp. 35 seq., where the whole question is discussed with full knowledge of the texts.

10. Nasse, Ueber die mittelalterliche Feldgemeinschaft und die Einhegungen des XVI. Jahrhunderts in England (Bonn, 1869), pp. 4, 5; Vinogradov, Villainage in England (Oxford, 1892).

11. Fr. Seebohm, The English Village Community, 3rd ed., 1884, pp. 13-15.

12. "An examination into the details of an Enclosure Act will make clear the point that the system as above described [communal ownership] is the system which it was the object of the Enclosure Act to remove" (Seebohm, l.c. p. 13). And further on, "They were generally drawn in the same form, commencing with the recital that the open and common fields lie dispersed in small pieces, intermixed with each other and inconveniently situated; that divers persons own parts of them, and are entitled to rights of common on them ... and that it is desired that they may be divided and enclosed, a specific share being let out and allowed to each owner" (p. 14). Porter's list contained 3867 such Acts, of which the greatest numbers fall upon the decades of 1770-1780 and 1800-1820, as in France.

13. In Switzerland we see a number of communes, ruined by wars, which have sold part of their lands, and now endeavour to buy them back.

14. A. Buchenberger, "Agrarwesen und Agrarpolitik," in A. Wagner's Handbuch der politischen Oekonomie, 1892, Band i.

pp. 280 seq.

15. G.L. Gomme, "The Village Community, with special reference to its Origin and Forms of Survival in Great Britain" (Contemporary Science
Series), London, 1890, pp. 141-143; also his Primitive Folkmoots (London, 1880), pp. 98 seq.

16. "In almost all parts of the country, in the Midland and Eastern counties particularly, but also in the west—in Wiltshire, for example—in the south, as in Surrey, in the north, as in Yorkshire,—there are extensive open and common fields. Out of 316 parishes of Northamptonshire 89 are in this condition; more than 100 in Oxfordshire; about 50,000 acres in Warwickshire; in Berkshire half the county; more than half of Wiltshire; in Huntingdonshire out of a total area of 240,000 acres 130,000 were commonable meadows, commons, and fields" (Marshall, quoted in Sir Henry Maine's Village Communities in the East and West, New York edition, 1876, pp. 88, 89). See also Dr. G. Slater's The English Peasantry and the Enclosure of Common Fields, London, 1907.

17. Ibid. p. 88; also Fifth Lecture.

18. In quite a number of books dealing with English country life which I have consulted I have found charming descriptions of country scenery and the like, but almost nothing about the daily life and customs of the labourers.

19. In Switzerland the peasants in the open land also fell under the dominion of lords, and large parts of their estates were appropriated by the lords in the sixteenth and seventeenth centuries. (cf. A. Miaskowski, in Schmoller's Forschungen, Bd. ii.

1879, pp. 12 seq.) But the peasant war in Switzerland did not end in such a crushing defeat of the peasants as it did in other countries, and a great deal of the communal rights and lands was retained. The self-government of the communes is, in fact, the very foundation of the Swiss liberties. (cf. K. Burtli, Der Ursprung der Eidgenossenschaft aus der Markgenossenschaft, Zurich, 1891.)

20. Dr. Reichesberg, Handworterbuch des Schweiz. Volkswirthschaft, Bern, 1903.

21. See on this subject a series of works, summed up in one of the excellent and suggestive chapters (not yet translated into English) which K. Bucher has added to the German translation of Laveleye's Primitive Ownership. Also Meitzen, "Das Agrar- und Forst-Wesen, die Allmenden und die Landgemeinden der Deutschen Schweiz," in Jahrbuch für Staatswissenschaft, 1880, iv. (analysis of Miaskowsky's works); O'Brien, "Notes in a Swiss village," in Macmillan's Magazine, October 1885.

22. The wedding gifts, which often substantially contribute in this country to the comfort of the young households, are evidently a remainder of the communal habits.

23. The communes own, 4,554,100 acres of woods out of 24,813,000 in the whole territory, and 6,936,300 acres of natural meadows out of 11,394,000 acres in France. The remaining 2,000,000 acres are fields, orchards, and so on.

24. In Caucasia they even do better among the Georgians. As the meal costs, and a poor man cannot afford to give it, a sheep is bought by those same neighbours who come to aid in the work.

25. Alfred Baudrillart, in H. Baudrillart's Les Populations

Rurales de la France, 3rd series (Paris, 1893), p. 479.

26. The Journal des Economistes (August 1892, May and August 1893) has lately given some of the results of analyses made at the agricultural laboratories at Ghent and at Paris. The extent of falsification is simply incredible; so also the devices of the "honest traders." In certain seeds of grass there was 32 per cent. of gains of sand, coloured so as to Receive even an experienced eye; other samples contained from 52 to 22 per cent. only of pure seed, the remainder being weeds. Seeds of vetch contained 11 per cent. of a poisonous grass (nielle); a flour for cattle-fattening contained 36 per cent. of sulphates; and so on ad infinitum.

27. A. Baudrillart, l.c. p. 309. Originally one grower would undertake to supply water, and several others would agee to make use of it. "What especially characterises such associations," A. Baudrillart remarks, "is that no sort of written agreement is concluded. All is arranged in words. There was, however, not one single case of difficulties having arisen between the parties."

28. A. Baudrillart, l.c. pp. 300, 341, etc. M. Terssac, president of the St. Gironnais syndicate (Ariege), wrote to my friend in substance as follows:—"For the exhibition of Toulouse our association has grouped the owners of cattle which seemed to us worth exhibiting. The society undertook to pay one-half of the travelling and exhibition expenses; one-fourth was paid by each owner, and the remaining fourth by those exhibitors who had got prizes. The result was that many took part in the exhibition who never would have done it otherwise. Those who got the highest awards (350 francs) have contributed 10 per cent. of their prizes, while those who have got no prize have only spent 6 to 7 francs each."

29. In Wurttemberg 1,629 communes out of 1,910 have

communal property. They owned in 1863 over 1,000,000 acres of land. In Baden 1,256 communes out of 1,582 have communal land; in 1884-1888 they held 121,500 acres of fields in communal culture, and 675,000 acres of forests, i.e. 46 per cent. of the total area under woods. In Saxony 39 per cent. of the total area is in communal ownership (Schmoller's Jahrbuch, 1886, p. 359). In Hohenzollern nearly two-thirds of all meadow land, and in Hohenzollern-Hechingen 41 per cent. of all landed property, are owned by the village communities (Buchenberger, Agrarwesen, vol. i. p. 300).

30. See K. Bucher, who, in a special chapter added to Laveleye's Ureigenthum, has collected all information relative to the village community in Germany.

31. K. Bucher, ibid. pp. 89, 90.

32. For this legislation and the numerous obstacles which were put in the way, in the shape of red-tapeism and supervision, see Buchenberger's Agrarwesen und Agrarpolitik, Bd. ii. pp. 342-363, and p. 506, note.

33. Buchenberger, l.c. Bd. ii. p. 510. The General Union of Agricultural Co-operation comprises an aggregate of 1,679 societies. In Silesia an aggregate of 32,000 acres of land has been lately drained by 73 associations; 454,800 acres in Prussia by 516 associations; in Bavaria there are 1,715 drainage and irrigation unions.

34. For the Balkan peninsula see Laveleye's Propriete Primitive.

35. The facts concerning the village community, contained in nearly a hundred volumes (out of 450) of these inquests, have been classified and summed up in an excellent Russian work by

"V.V." The Peasant Community (Krestianskaya Obschina), St. Petersburg, 1892, which, apart from its theoretical value, is a rich compendium of data relative to this subject. The above inquests have also given origin to an immense literature, in which the modern village-community question for the first time emerges from the domain of generalities and is put on the solid basis of reliable and sufficiently detailed facts.

36. The redemption had to be paid by annuities for forty-nine years. As years went, and the greatest part of it was paid, it became easier and easier to redeem the smaller remaining part of it, and, as each allotment could be redeemed individually, advantage was taken of this disposition by traders, who bought land for half its value from the ruined peasants. A law was consequently passed to put a stop to such sales.

37. Mr. V.V., in his Peasant Community, has grouped together all facts relative to this movement. About the rapid agricultural development of South Russia and the spread of machinery English readers will find information in the Consular Reports (Odessa, Taganrog).

38. In some instances they proceeded with great caution. In one village they began by putting together all meadow land, but only a small portion of the fields (about five acres per soul) was rendered communal; the remainder continued to be owned individually. Later on, in 1862-1864, the system was extended, but only in 1884 was communal possession introduced in full.— V.V.'s Peasant Community, pp. 1-14.

39. On the Mennonite village community see A. Klaus, Our Colonies (Nashi Kolonii), St. Petersburg, 1869.

40. Such communal cultures are known to exist in 159 villages

out of 195 in the Ostrogozhsk district; in 150 out of 187 in Slavyanoserbsk; in 107 village communities in Alexandrovsk, 93 in Nikolayevsk, 35 in Elisabethgrad. In a German colony the communal culture is made for repaying a communal debt. All join in the work, although the debt was contracted by 94 householders out of 155.

41. Lists of such works which came under the notice of the zemstvo statisticians will be found in V.V.'s Peasant Community, pp. 459-600.

42. In the government of Moscow the experiment was usually made on the field which was reserved for the above-mentioned communal culture.

43. Several instances of such and similar improvements were given in the Official Messenger, 1894, Nos. 256-258. Associations between "horseless" peasants begin to appear also in South Russia. Another extremely interesting fact is the sudden development in Southern West Siberia of very numerous co-operative creameries for making butter. Hundreds of them spread in Tobolsk and Tomsk, without any one knowing wherefrom the initiative of the movement came. It came from the Danish co-operators, who used to export their own butter of higher quality, and to buy butter of a lower quality for their own use in Siberia. After a several years' intercourse, they introduced creameries there. Now, a great export trade, carried on by a Union of the Creameries, has grown out of their endeavours and more than a thousand co-operative shops have been opened in the villages.

CHAPTER VIII

MUTUAL AID AMONGST OURSELVES (continued)

Labour-unions grown after the destruction of the guilds by the State. Their struggles. Mutual Aid in strikes. Co-operation. Free associations for various purposes. Self-sacrifice. Countless societies for combined action under all possible aspects. Mutual Aid in slum-life. Personal aid.

When we examine the every-day life of the rural populations of Europe, we find that, notwithstanding all that has been done in modern States for the destruction of the village community, the life of the peasants remains honeycombed with habits and customs of mutual aid and support; that important vestiges of the communal possession of the soil are still retained; and that, as soon as the legal obstacles to rural association were lately removed, a network of free unions for all sorts of economical purposes rapidly spread among the peasants—the tendency of this young movement being to reconstitute some sort of union similar to the village community of old. Such being the conclusions arrived at in the preceding chapter, we have now to consider, what institutions for mutual support can be found at the present time amongst the industrial populations.

For the last three hundred years, the conditions for the growth of such institutions have been as unfavourable in the towns as they have been in the villages. It is well known, indeed, that when the medieval cities were subdued in the sixteenth century by growing military States, all institutions which kept the artisans, the masters, and the merchants together in the guilds and the cities were violently destroyed. The self-government and the self-jurisdiction of both, the guild and the city were abolished;

the oath of allegiance between guild-brothers became an act of felony towards the State; the properties of the guilds were confiscated in the same way as the lands of the village communities; and the inner and technical organization of each trade was taken in hand by the State. Laws, gradually growing in severity, were passed to prevent artisans from combining in any way. For a time, some shadows of the old guilds were tolerated: merchants' guilds were allowed to exist under the condition of freely granting subsidies to the kings, and some artisan guilds were kept in existence as organs of administration. Some of them still drag on their meaningless existence. But what formerly was the vital force of medieval life and industry has long since disappeared under the crushing weight of the centralized State.

In Great Britain, which may be taken as the best illustration of the industrial policy of the modern States, we see the Parliament beginning the destruction of the guilds as early as the fifteenth century; but it was especially in the next century that decisive measures were taken. Henry the Eighth not only ruined the organization of the guilds, but also confiscated their properties, with even less excuse and manners, as Toulmin Smith wrote, than he had produced for confiscating the estates of the monasteries.(1) Edward the Sixth completed his work,(2) and already in the second part of the sixteenth century we find the Parliament settling all the disputes between craftsmen and merchants, which formerly were settled in each city separately. The Parliament and the king not only legislated in all such contests, but, keeping in view the interests of the Crown in the exports, they soon began to determine the number of apprentices in each trade and minutely to regulate the very technics of each fabrication—the weights of the stuffs, the number of threads in the yard of cloth, and the like. With little success, it must be said; because contests and technical difficulties which were arranged for centuries in succession by agreement between closely-interdependent guilds and federated cities lay entirely beyond the powers of the centralized State. The continual interference of its officials paralyzed the trades; bringing most of them to a complete decay; and the last century economists, when they rose against the State regulation of industries, only ventilated a widely-felt discontent. The abolition of that interference by the French Revolution was greeted as an act of liberation, and the example of France was soon followed elsewhere.

With the regulation of wages the State had no better success. In the medieval cities, when the distinction between masters and apprentices or journeymen became more and more apparent in the fifteenth century, unions of apprentices (Gesellenverbande), occasionally assuming an international character, were opposed to the unions of masters and merchants. Now it was the State which undertook to settle their griefs, and under the Elizabethan Statute of 1563 the Justices of Peace had to settle the wages, so as to guarantee a "convenient" livelihood to journeymen and apprentices. The Justices, however, proved helpless to conciliate the conflicting interests, and still less to compel the masters to obey their decisions. The law gradually became a dead letter, and was repealed by the end of the eighteenth century. But while the State thus abandoned the function of regulating wages, it continued severely to prohibit all combinations which were entered upon by journeymen and workers in order to raise their wages, or to keep them at a certain level. All through the eighteenth century it legislated against the workers' unions, and in 1799 it finally prohibited all sorts of combinations, under the menace of severe punishments. In fact, the British Parliament only followed in this case the example of the French Revolutionary Convention, which had issued a draconic law against coalitions of workers-coalitions between a number of citizens being considered as attempts against the sovereignty of the State, which was supposed equally to protect all its subjects. The work of destruction of the medieval unions was thus completed. Both in the town and in the village the State reigned over loose aggregations of individuals, and was ready to prevent by the most stringent measures the reconstitution of any sort of separate unions among them. These were, then, the conditions under which the mutual-aid tendency had to make its way in the nineteenth century.

Need it be said that no such measures could destroy that tendency? Throughout the eighteenth century, the workers' unions were continually reconstituted.(3) Nor were they stopped by the cruel prosecutions which took place under the laws of 1797 and 1799. Every flaw in supervision, every delay of the masters in denouncing the unions was taken advantage of. Under the cover of friendly societies, burial clubs, or secret brotherhoods, the unions spread in the textile industries, among the Sheffield cutlers, the miners, and vigorous federal organizations were formed to support the branches during strikes and prosecutions.(4) The repeal of the Combination Laws in 1825 gave a new impulse to the movement. Unions and national federations were formed in all trades.(5) and when Robert Owen started his Grand National Consolidated Trades' Union, it mustered half a million members in a few months. True that this period of relative liberty did not last long. Prosecution began anew in the thirties, and the well-known ferocious condemnations of 1832-1844 followed. The Grand National Union was disbanded, and all over the country, both the private employers and the Government in its own workshops began to compel the workers to resign all connection with unions, and to sign "the Document" to that effect. Unionists were prosecuted wholesale under the Master and Servant Act—workers being summarily arrested and condemned upon a mere complaint of misbehaviour lodged by the master.(6) Strikes were suppressed in an autocratic way, and the most astounding condemnations took place for merely having announced a strike or acted as a delegate in it—to say nothing of the military suppression of strike riots, nor of the condemnations which followed the frequent outbursts of acts of violence. To practise mutual support under such circumstances was anything but an easy task. And yet, notwithstanding all obstacles, of which our own generation hardly can have an idea, the revival of the unions began again in 1841, and the amalgamation of the workers has been steadily continued since. After a long fight, which lasted for over a hundred years, the right of combining together was conquered, and at the present time nearly one-fourth part of the regularly-employed workers, i.e. about 1,500,000, belong to trade unions.(7)

As to the other European States, sufficient to say that up to a very recent date, all sorts of unions were prosecuted as conspiracies; and that nevertheless they exist everywhere, even though they must often take the form of secret societies; while the extension and the force of labour organizations, and especially of the Knights of Labour, in the United States and in Belgium, have been sufficiently illustrated by strikes in the nineties. It must, however, be borne in mind that, prosecution apart, the mere fact of belonging to a labour union implies considerable sacrifices in money, in time, and in unpaid work, and continually implies the risk of losing employment for the mere fact of being a unionist.(8) There is, moreover, the strike, which a unionist has continually to face; and the grim reality of a strike is, that the limited credit of a worker's family at the baker's and the pawnbroker's is soon exhausted, the strike-pay goes not far even for food, and hunger is soon written on the children's faces. For one who lives in close contact with workers, a protracted strike is the most heartrending sight; while what a strike meant forty years ago in this country, and still means in all but the wealthiest parts of the continent, can easily be conceived. Continually, even now, strikes will end with the total ruin and the forced emigration of whole populations, while the shooting down of strikers on the slightest provocation, or even without any provocation,(9) is quite habitual still on the continent.

And yet, every year there are thousands of strikes and lock-outs in Europe and America—the most severe and protracted contests being, as a rule, the so-called "sympathy strikes," which are entered upon to support locked-out comrades or to maintain the rights of the unions. And while a portion of the Press is prone to explain strikes by "intimidation," those who have lived among strikers speak with admiration of the mutual aid and support which are constantly practised by them. Every one has heard of the colossal amount of work which was done by volunteer workers for organizing relief during the London dock-labourers' strike; of the miners who, after having themselves been idle for many weeks, paid a levy of four shillings a week to the strike fund when they resumed work; of the miner widow who, during the Yorkshire labour war of 1894, brought her husband's life-savings to the strike-fund; of the last loaf of bread being always shared with neighbours; of the Radstock miners, favoured with larger kitchen-gardens, who invited four hundred Bristol miners to take their share of cabbage and potatoes, and so on. All newspaper correspondents, during the great strike of miners in Yorkshire in 1894, knew heaps of such facts, although not all of them could report such "irrelevant" matters to their respective papers.(10)

Unionism is not, however, the only form in which the worker's need of mutual support finds its expression. There are, besides, the political associations, whose activity many workers consider as more conducive to general welfare than the trade-unions, limited as they are now in their purposes. Of course the mere fact of belonging to a political body cannot be taken as a manifestation of the mutual-aid tendency. We all know that politics are the field in which the purely egotistic elements of society enter into the most entangled combinations with altruistic aspirations. But every experienced politician knows that all great political movements were fought upon large and often distant issues, and that those of them were the strongest which provoked most disinterested enthusiasm. All great historical movements have had this character, and for our own generation Socialism stands in that case. "Paid agitators" is, no doubt, the favourite refrain of those who know nothing about it. The truth, however, is that—to speak only of what I know personally—if I had kept a diary for the last twenty-four years and inscribed in it all the devotion and self-sacrifice which I came across in the Socialist movement, the reader of such a diary would have had the word "heroism" constantly on his lips. But the men I would have spoken of were not heroes; they were average men, inspired by a grand idea. Every Socialist newspaper—and there are hundreds of them in Europe alone—has the same history of years of sacrifice without any hope of reward, and, in the overwhelming majority of cases, even without any personal ambition. I have seen families living without knowing what would be their food to-morrow, the husband boycotted all round in his little town for his part in the paper, and the wife supporting the family by sewing, and such a situation lasting for years, until the family would retire, without a word of reproach, simply saying: "Continue; we can hold on no more!" I have seen men, dying from consumption, and knowing it, and yet knocking about in snow and fog to prepare meetings, speaking at meetings within a few weeks from death, and only then retiring to the hospital with the words: "Now, friends, I am done; the doctors say I have but a few weeks to live. Tell the comrades that I shall be happy if they come to see me." I have seen facts which would be described as "idealization" if I told them in this place; and the very names of these men, hardly known outside a narrow circle of friends, will soon be forgotten when the friends, too, have passed away. In fact, I don't know myself which most to admire, the unbounded devotion of these few, or the sum total of petty acts of devotion of the great number. Every quire of a penny paper sold, every meeting, every hundred votes which are won at a Socialist election, represent an amount of energy and sacrifices of which no outsider has the faintest idea. And what is now done by Socialists has been done in every popular and advanced party, political and religious, in the past. All past progress has been promoted by like men and by a like devotion.

Co-operation, especially in Britain, is often described as "joint-stock individualism"; and such as it is now, it undoubtedly tends to breed a co-operative egotism, not only towards the community at large, but also among the co-operators themselves. It is, nevertheless, certain that at its origin the movement had an essentially mutual-aid character. Even now, its most ardent promoters are persuaded that co-operation leads mankind to a higher harmonic stage of economical relations, and it is not possible to stay in some of the strongholds of co-operation in the North without realizing that the great number of the rank and file hold the same opinion. Most of them would lose interest in the movement if that faith were gone; and it must be owned that within the last few years broader ideals of general welfare and of the producers' solidarity have begun to be current among the co-operators. There is undoubtedly now a tendency towards establishing better relations between the owners of the co-operative workshops and the workers.

The importance of co-operation in this country, in Holland and in Denmark is well known; while in Germany, and especially on the Rhine, the co-operative societies are already an important factor of industrial life.(11) It is, however, Russia which offers perhaps the best field for the study of cooperation under an infinite variety of aspects. In Russia, it is a natural growth, an inheritance from the middle ages; and while a formally established co-operative society would have to cope with many legal difficulties and official suspicion, the informal co-operation—the artel—makes the very substance of Russian peasant life. The history of "the making of Russia," and of the colonization of Siberia, is a history of the hunting and trading artels or guilds, followed by village communities, and at the present time we find the artel everywhere; among each group of ten to fifty peasants who come from the same village to work at a factory, in all the building trades, among fishermen and hunters, among convicts on their way to and in Siberia, among railway porters, Exchange messengers, Customs House labourers, everywhere in the village industries, which give occupation to 7,000,000 men—from top to bottom of the working world, permanent and temporary, for production and consumption under all possible aspects. Until now, many of the fishing-grounds on the tributaries of the Caspian Sea are held by immense artels, the Ural river belonging to the whole of the Ural Cossacks, who allot and re-allot the fishing-grounds—perhaps the richest in the world—among the villages, without any interference of the authorities. Fishing is always made by artels in the Ural, the Volga, and all the lakes of Northern Russia. Besides these permanent organizations, there are the simply countless temporary artels, constituted for each special purpose. When ten or twenty peasants come from some locality to a big town, to work as weavers, carpenters, masons, boat-builders, and so on, they always constitute an artel. They hire rooms, hire a cook (very often the wife of one of them acts in this capacity), elect an elder, and take their meals in common, each one paying his share for food and lodging to the artel. A party of convicts on its way to Siberia always does the same, and its elected elder is the officially-recognized intermediary between the convicts and the military chief of the party. In the hard-labour prisons they have the same organization. The railway porters, the messengers at the Exchange, the workers at the Custom House, the town messengers in the capitals, who are collectively responsible for each member, enjoy such a reputation that any amount of money or bank-notes is trusted to the artel-member by the merchants. In the building trades, artels of from 10 to 200 members are formed; and the serious builders and railway contractors always prefer to deal with an artel than with separately-hired workers. The last attempts of the Ministry of War to deal directly with productive artels, formed ad hoc in the domestic trades, and to give them orders for boots and all sorts of brass and iron goods, are described as most satisfactory; while the renting of a Crown iron work, (Votkinsk) to an artel of workers, which took place seven or eight years ago, has been a decided success.

We can thus see in Russia how the old medieval institution, having not been interfered with by the State (in its informal manifestations), has fully survived until now, and takes the greatest variety of forms in accordance with the requirements of modern industry and commerce. As to the Balkan peninsula, the Turkish Empire and Caucasia, the old guilds are maintained there in full. The esnafs of Servia have fully preserved their medieval character; they include both masters and journeymen, regulate the trades, and are institutions for mutual support in labour and sickness;(12) while the amkari of Caucasia, and especially at Tiflis, add to these functions a considerable influence in municipal life.(13)

In connection with co-operation, I ought perhaps to mention also the friendly societies, the unities of oddfellows, the village and town clubs organized for meeting the doctors' bills, the dress and burial clubs, the small clubs very common among factory girls, to which they contribute a few pence every week, and afterwards draw by lot the sum of one pound, which can at least be used for some substantial purchase, and many others. A not inconsiderable amount of sociable or jovial spirit is alive in all such societies and clubs, even though the "credit and debit" of each member are closely watched over. But there are so many associations based on the readiness to sacrifice time, health, and life if required, that we can produce numbers of illustrations of the best forms of mutual support.

The Lifeboat Association in this country, and similar institutions on the Continent, must be mentioned in the first place. The former has now over three hundred boats along the coasts of these isles, and it would have twice as many were it not for the poverty of the fisher men, who cannot afford to buy lifeboats. The crews consist, however, of volunteers, whose readiness to sacrifice their lives for the rescue of absolute strangers to them is put every year to a severe test; every winter the loss of several of the bravest among them stands on record. And if we ask these men what moves them to risk their lives, even when there is no reasonable chance of success, their answer is something on the following lines. A fearful snowstorm, blowing across the Channel, raged on the flat, sandy coast of a tiny village in Kent, and a small smack, laden with oranges, stranded on the sands near by. In these shallow waters only a flat-bottomed lifeboat of a simplified type can be kept, and to launch it during such a storm was to face an almost certain disaster. And yet the men went out, fought for hours against the wind, and the boat capsized twice. One man was drowned, the others were cast ashore. One of these last, a refined coastguard, was found next morning, badly bruised and half frozen in the snow. I asked him, how they came to make that desperate attempt? "I don't know myself," was his reply." There was the wreck; all the people from the village stood on the beach, and all said it would be foolish to go out; we never should work through the surf. We saw five or six men clinging to the mast, making desperate signals. We all felt that something must be done, but what could we do? One hour passed, two hours, and we all stood there. We all felt most uncomfortable. Then, all of a sudden, through the storm, it seemed to us as if we heard their cries—they had a boy with them. We could not stand that any longer. All at once we said, "We must go!" The women said so too; they would have treated us as cowards if we had not gone, although next day they said we had been fools to go. As one man, we rushed to the boat, and went. The boat capsized, but we took hold of it. The worst was to see poor drowning by the side of the boat, and we could do nothing to save him. Then came a fearful wave, the boat capsized again, and we were cast ashore. The men were still rescued by the D. boat, ours was caught miles away. I was found next morning in the snow."

The same feeling moved also the miners of the Rhonda Valley, when they worked for the rescue of their comrades from the inundated mine. They had pierced through thirty-two yards of coal in order to reach their entombed comrades; but when only three yards more remained to be pierced, fire-damp enveloped them. The lamps went out, and the rescue-men retired. To work in such conditions was to risk being blown up at every moment. But the raps of the entombed miners were still heard, the men were still alive and appealed for help, and several miners volunteered to work at any risk; and as they went down the mine, their wives had only silent tears to follow them—not one word to stop them.

There is the gist of human psychology. Unless men are maddened in the battlefield, they "cannot stand it" to hear appeals for help, and not to respond to them. The hero goes; and what the hero does, all feel that they ought to have done as well. The sophisms of the brain cannot resist the mutual-aid feeling, because this feeling has been nurtured by thousands of years of human social life and hundreds of thousands of years of pre-human life in societies.

"But what about those men who were drowned in the Serpentine in the presence of a crowd, out of which no one moved for their rescue?" it may be asked. "What about the child which fell into the Regent's Park Canal—also in the presence of a holiday crowd—and was only saved through the presence of mind of a maid who let out a Newfoundland dog to the rescue?" The answer is plain enough. Man is a result of both his inherited instincts and his education. Among the miners and the seamen, their common occupations and their every-day contact with one another create a feeling of solidarity, while the surrounding dangers maintain courage and pluck. In the cities, on the contrary, the absence of common interest nurtures indifference, while courage and pluck, which seldom find their opportunities, disappear, or take another direction. Moreover, the tradition of the hero of the mine and the sea lives in the miners' and fishermen's villages, adorned with a poetical halo. But what are the traditions of a motley London crowd? The only tradition they might have in common ought to be created by literature, but a literature which would correspond to the village epics hardly exists. The clergy are so anxious to prove that all that comes from human nature is sin, and that all good in man has a supernatural origin, that they mostly ignore the facts which cannot be produced as an example of higher inspiration or grace, coming from above. And as to the lay-writers, their attention is chiefly directed towards one sort of heroism, the heroism which promotes the idea of the State. Therefore, they admire the Roman hero, or the soldier in the battle, while they pass by the fisherman's heroism, hardly paying attention to it. The poet and the painter might, of course, be taken by the beauty of the human heart in itself; but both seldom know the life of the poorer classes, and while they can sing or paint the Roman or the military hero in conventional surroundings, they can neither sing nor paint impressively the hero who acts in those modest surroundings which they ignore. If they venture to do so, they produce a mere piece of rhetoric.(14)

The countless societies, clubs, and alliances, for the enjoyment of life, for study and research, for education, and so on, which have lately grown up in such numbers that it would require many years to simply tabulate them, are another manifestation of the same everworking tendency for association and mutual support. Some of them, like the broods of young birds of different species which come together in the autumn, are entirely given to share in common the joys of life. Every village in this country, in Switzerland, Germany, and so on, has its cricket, football, tennis, nine-pins, pigeon, musical or singing clubs. Other societies are much more numerous, and some of them, like the Cyclists' Alliance, have suddenly taken a formidable development. Although the members of this alliance have nothing in common but the love of cycling, there is already among them a sort of freemasonry for mutual help, especially in the remote nooks and corners which are not flooded by cyclists; they look upon the "C.A.C."—the Cyclists' Alliance Club—in a village as a sort of home; and at the yearly Cyclists' Camp many a standing friendship has been established. The Kegelbruder, the Brothers of the Nine Pins, in Germany, are a similar association; so also the Gymnasts' Societies (300,000 members in Germany), the informal brotherhood of paddlers in France, the yacht clubs, and so on. Such associations certainly do not alter the economical stratification of society, but, especially in the small towns, they contribute to smooth social distinctions, and as they all tend to join in large national and international federations, they certainly aid the growth of personal friendly intercourse between all sorts of men scattered in different parts of the globe.

The Alpine Clubs, the Jagdschutzverein in Germany, which has over 100,000 members—hunters, educated foresters, zoologists, and simple lovers of Nature—and the International Ornithological Society, which includes zoologists, breeders, and simple peasants in Germany, have the same character. Not only have they done in a few years a large amount of very useful work, which large associations alone could do properly (maps, refuge huts, mountain roads; studies of animal life, of noxious insects, of migrations of birds, and so on), but they create new bonds between men. Two Alpinists of different nationalities who meet in a refuge hut in the Caucasus, or the professor and the peasant ornithologist who stay in the same house, are no more strangers to each other; while the Uncle Toby's Society at Newcastle, which has already induced over 260,000 boys and girls never to destroy birds' nests and to be kind to all animals, has certainly done more for the development of human feelings and of taste in natural science than lots of moralists and most of our schools.

We cannot omit, even in this rapid review, the thousands of scientific, literary, artistic, and educational societies. Up till now, the scientific bodies, closely controlled and often subsidized by the State, have generally moved in a very narrow circle, and they often came to be looked upon as mere openings for getting State appointments, while the very narrowness of their circles undoubtedly bred petty jealousies. Still it is a fact that the distinctions of birth, political parties and creeds are smoothed to some extent by such associations; while in the smaller and remote towns the scientific, geographical, or musical societies, especially those of them which appeal to a larger circle of amateurs, become small centres of intellectual life, a sort of link between the little spot and the wide world, and a place where men of very different conditions meet on a footing of equality. To fully appreciate the value of such centres, one ought to know them, say, in Siberia. As to the countless educational societies which only now begin to break down the State's and the Church's monopoly in education, they are sure to become before long the leading power in that branch. To the "Froebel Unions" we already owe the Kindergarten system; and to a number of formal and informal educational associations we owe the high standard of women's education in Russia, although all the time these societies and groups had to act in strong opposition to a powerful government.(15) As to the various pedagogical societies in Germany, it is well known that they have done the best part in the working out of the modern methods of teaching science in popular schools. In such associations the teacher finds also his best support. How miserable the overworked and under-paid village teacher would have been without their aid!(16)

All these associations, societies, brotherhoods, alliances, institutes, and so on, which must now be counted by the ten thousand in Europe alone, and each of which represents an immense amount of voluntary, unambitious, and unpaid or underpaid work—what are they but so many manifestations, under an infinite variety of aspects, of the same ever-living tendency of man towards mutual aid and support? For nearly three centuries men were prevented from joining hands even for literary, artistic, and educational purposes. Societies could only be formed under the protection of the State, or the Church, or as secret brotherhoods, like free-masonry. But now that the resistance has been broken, they swarm in all directions, they extend over all multifarious branches of human activity, they become international, and they undoubtedly contribute, to an extent which cannot yet be fully appreciated, to break down the screens erected by States between different nationalities. Notwithstanding the jealousies which are bred by commercial competition, and the provocations to hatred which are sounded by the ghosts of a decaying past, there is a conscience of international solidarity which is growing both among the leading spirits of the world and the masses of the workers, since they also have conquered the right of international intercourse; and in the preventing of a European war during the last quarter of a century, this spirit has undoubtedly had its share.

The religious charitable associations, which again represent a whole world, certainly must be mentioned in this place. There is not the slightest doubt that the great bulk of their members are moved by the same mutual-aid feelings which are common to all mankind. Unhappily the religious teachers of men prefer to ascribe to such feelings a supernatural origin. Many of them pretend that man does not consciously obey the mutual-aid inspiration so long as he has not been enlightened by the teachings of the special religion which they represent, and, with St. Augustin, most of them do not recognize such feelings in the "pagan savage." Moreover, while early Christianity, like all other religions, was an appeal to the broadly human feelings of mutual aid and sympathy, the Christian Church has aided the State in wrecking all standing institutions of mutual aid and support which were anterior to it, or developed outside of it; and, instead of the mutual aid which every savage considers as due to his kinsman, it has preached charity which bears a character of inspiration from above, and, accordingly, implies a certain superiority of the giver upon the receiver. With this limitation, and without any intention to give offence to those who consider themselves as a body elect when they accomplish acts simply humane, we certainly may consider the immense numbers of religious charitable associations as an outcome of the same mutual-aid tendency.

All these facts show that a reckless prosecution of personal interests, with no regard to other people's needs, is not the only characteristic of modern life. By the side of this current which so proudly claims leadership in human affairs, we perceive a hard struggle sustained by both the rural and industrial populations in order to reintroduce standing institutions of mutual aid and support; and we discover, in all classes of society, a widely-spread movement towards the establishment of an infinite variety of more or less permanent institutions for the same purpose. But when we pass from public life to the private life of the modern individual, we discover another extremely wide world of mutual aid and support, which only passes unnoticed by most sociologists because it is limited to the narrow circle of the family and personal friendship.(17)

Under the present social system, all bonds of union among the inhabitants of the same street or neighbourhood have been dissolved. In the richer parts of the large towns, people live without knowing who are their next-door neighbours. But in the crowded lanes people know each other perfectly, and are continually brought into mutual contact. Of course, petty quarrels go their course, in the lanes as elsewhere; but groupings in accordance with personal affinities grow up, and within their circle mutual aid is practised to an extent of which the richer classes have no idea. If we take, for instance, the children of a poor neighbourhood who play in a street or a churchyard, or on a green, we notice at once that a close union exists among them, notwithstanding the temporary fights, and that that union protects them from all sorts of misfortunes. As soon as a mite bends inquisitively over the opening of a drain—"Don't stop there," another mite shouts out, "fever sits in the hole!" "Don't climb over that wall, the train will kill you if you tumble down!

Don't come near to the ditch! Don't eat those berries—poison! you will die." Such are the first teachings imparted to the urchin when he joins his mates out-doors. How many of the children whose play-grounds are the pavements around "model workers' dwellings," or the quays and bridges of the canals, would be crushed to death by the carts or drowned in the muddy waters, were it not for that sort of mutual support. And when a fair Jack has made a slip into the unprotected ditch at the back of the milkman's yard, or a cherry-cheeked Lizzie has, after all, tumbled down into the canal, the young brood raises such cries that all the neighbourhood is on the alert and rushes to the rescue.

Then comes in the alliance of the mothers. "You could not imagine" (a lady-doctor who lives in a poor neighbourhood told me lately) "how much they help each other. If a woman has prepared nothing, or could prepare nothing, for the baby which she expected—and how often that happens!—all the neighbours bring something for the new-comer. One of the neighbours always takes care of the children, and some other always drops in to take care of the household, so long as the mother is in bed." This habit is general. It is mentioned by all those who have lived among the poor. In a thousand small ways the mothers support each other and bestow their care upon children that are not their own. Some training—good or bad, let them decide it for themselves—is required in a lady of the richer classes to render her able to pass by a shivering and hungry child in the street without noticing it. But the mothers of the poorer classes have not that training. They cannot stand the sight of a hungry child; they must feed it, and so they do. "When the school children beg bread, they seldom or rather never meet with a refusal"—a lady-friend, who has worked several years in Whitechapel in connection with a workers' club, writes to me. But I may, perhaps, as well transcribe a few more passages from her letter:—

"Nursing neighbours, in cases of illness, without any shade of remuneration, is quite general among the workers. Also, when a woman has little children, and goes out for work, another mother always takes care of them.

"If, in the working classes, they would not help each other, they could not exist. I know families which continually help each other—with money, with food, with fuel, for bringing up the little children, in cases of illness, in cases of death.

"'The mine' and 'thine' is much less sharply observed among the poor than among the rich. Shoes, dress, hats, and so on,—what may be wanted on the spot—are continually borrowed from each other, also all sorts of household things.

"Last winter the members of the United Radical Club had brought together some little money, and began after Christmas to distribute free soup and bread to the children going to school. Gradually they had 1,800 children to attend to. The money came from outsiders, but all the work was done by the members of the club. Some of them, who were out of work, came at four in the morning to wash and to peel the vegetables; five women came at nine or ten (after having done their own household work) for cooking, and stayed till six or seven to wash the dishes. And at meal time, between twelve and half-past one, twenty to thirty workers came in to aid in serving the soup, each one staying what he could spare of his meal time. This lasted for two months. No one was paid."

My friend also mentions various individual cases, of which the following are typical:—

"Annie W. was given by her mother to be boarded by an old person in Wilmot Street. When her mother died, the old woman, who herself was very poor, kept the child without being paid a penny for that. When the old lady died too, the child, who was five years old, was of course neglected during her illness, and was ragged; but she was taken at once by Mrs. S., the wife of a shoemaker, who herself has six children. Lately, when the husband was ill, they had not much to eat, all of them.

"The other day, Mrs. M., mother of six children, attended Mrs. M—g throughout her illness, and took to her own rooms the elder child.... But do you need such facts? They are quite general.... I know also Mrs. D. (Oval, Hackney Road), who has a sewing machine and continually sews for others, without ever accepting any remuneration, although she has herself five children and her husband to look after.... And so on."

For every one who has any idea of the life of the labouring classes it is evident that without mutual aid being practised among them on a large scale they never could pull through all their difficulties. It is only by chance that a worker's family can live its lifetime without having to face such circumstances as the crisis described by the ribbon weaver, Joseph Gutteridge, in his autobiography.(18) And if all do not go to the ground in such cases, they owe it to mutual help. In Gutteridge's case it was an old nurse, miserably poor herself, who turned up at the moment when the family was slipping towards a final catastrophe, and brought in some bread, coal, and bedding, which she had obtained on credit. In other cases, it will be some one else, or the neighbours will take steps to save the family. But without some aid from other poor, how many more would be brought every year to irreparable ruin!(19)

Mr. Plimsoll, after he had lived for some time among the poor, on 7s. 6d. a week, was compelled to recognize that the kindly feelings he took with him when he began this life "changed into hearty respect and admiration" when he saw how the relations between the poor are permeated with mutual aid and support, and learned the simple ways in which that support is given. After a many years' experience, his conclusion was that "when you come to think of it, such as these men were, so were the vast majority of the working classes."(20) As to bringing up orphans, even by the poorest families, it is so widely-spread a habit, that it may be described as a general rule; thus among the miners it was found, after the two explosions at Warren Vale and at Lund Hill, that "nearly one-third of the men killed, as the respective committees can testify, were thus supporting relations other than wife and child." "Have you reflected," Mr. Plimsoll added, "what this is? Rich men, even comfortably-to-do men do this, I don't doubt. But consider the difference." Consider what a sum of one shilling, subscribed by each worker to help a comrade's widow, or 6d. to help a fellow-worker to defray the extra expense of a funeral, means for one who earns 16s. a week and has a wife, and in some cases five or six children to support.(21) But such subscriptions are a general practice among the workers all over the world, even in much more ordinary cases than a death in the family, while aid in work is the commonest thing in their lives.

Nor do the same practices of mutual aid and support fail among the richer classes. Of course, when one thinks of the harshness which is often shown by the richer employers towards their employees, one feels inclined to take the most pessimist view of human nature. Many must remember the indignation which was aroused during the great Yorkshire strike of 1894, when old miners who had picked coal from an abandoned pit were prosecuted by the colliery owners. And, even if we leave aside the horrors of the periods of struggle and social war, such as the extermination of thousands of workers' prisoners after the fall of the Paris Commune—who can read, for instance, revelations of the labour inquest which was made here in the forties, or what Lord Shaftesbury wrote about "the frightful waste of human life in the factories, to which the children taken from the workhouses, or simply purchased all over this country to be sold as factory slaves, were consigned"(22)—who can read that without being vividly impressed by the baseness which is possible in man when his greediness is at stake? But it must also be said that all fault for such treatment must not be thrown entirely upon the criminality of human nature. Were not the teachings of men of science, and even of a notable portion of the clergy, up to a quite recent time, teachings of distrust, despise and almost hatred towards the poorer classes? Did not science teach that since serfdom has been abolished, no one need be poor unless for his own vices? And how few in the Church had the courage to blame the children-killers, while the great numbers taught that the sufferings of the poor, and even the slavery of the negroes, were part of the Divine Plan! Was not Nonconformism itself largely a popular protest against the harsh treatment of the poor at the hand of the established Church?

With such spiritual leaders, the feelings of the richer classes necessarily became, as Mr. Pimsoll remarked, not so much blunted as "stratified." They seldom went downwards towards the poor, from whom the well-to-do-people are separated by their manner of life, and whom they do not know under their best aspects, in their every-day life. But among themselves— allowance being made for the effects of the wealth-accumulating passions and the futile expenses imposed by wealth itself— among themselves, in the circle of family and friends, the rich practise the same mutual aid and support as the poor. Dr. Ihering and L. Dargun are perfectly right in saying that if a statistical record could be taken of all the money which passes from hand to hand in the shape of friendly loans and aid, the sum total would be enormous, even in comparison with the commercial transactions of the world's trade. And if we could add to it, as we certainly ought to, what is spent in hospitality, petty mutual services, the management of other people's affairs, gifts and charities, we certainly should be struck by the importance of such transfers in national economy. Even in the world which is ruled by commercial egotism, the current expression, "We have been harshly treated by that firm," shows that there is also the friendly treatment, as opposed to the harsh, i.e. the legal treatment; while every commercial man knows how many firms are saved every year from failure by the friendly support of other firms.

As to the charities and the amounts of work for general well-being which are voluntarily done by so many well-to-do persons, as well as by workers, and especially by professional men, every one knows the part which is played by these two categories of benevolence in modern life. If the desire of acquiring notoriety, political power, or social distinction often spoils the true character of that sort of benevolence, there is no doubt possible as to the impulse coming in the majority of cases from the same mutual-aid feelings. Men who have acquired wealth very often do not find in it the expected satisfaction. Others begin to feel that, whatever economists may say about wealth being the reward of capacity, their own reward is exaggerated. The conscience of human solidarity begins to tell; and, although society life is so arranged as to stifle that feeling by thousands of artful means, it often gets the upper hand; and then they try to find an outcome for that deeply human need by giving their fortune, or their forces, to something which, in their opinion, will promote general welfare.

In short, neither the crushing powers of the centralized State nor the teachings of mutual hatred and pitiless struggle which came, adorned with the attributes of science, from obliging philosophers and sociologists, could weed out the feeling of human solidarity, deeply lodged in men's understanding and heart, because it has been nurtured by all our preceding evolution. What was the outcome of evolution since its earliest stages cannot be overpowered by one of the aspects of that same evolution. And the need of mutual aid and support which had lately taken refuge in the narrow circle of the family, or the slum neighbours, in the village, or the secret union of workers, re-asserts itself again, even in our modern society, and claims its rights to be, as it always has been, the chief leader towards further progress. Such are the conclusions which we are necessarily brought to when we carefully ponder over each of the groups of facts briefly enumerated in the last two chapters.

NOTES:

1. Toulmin Smith, English Guilds, London, 1870, Introd. p. xliii.

2. The Act of Edward the Sixth—the first of his reign—ordered to hand over to the Crown "all fraternities, brotherhoods, and guilds being within the realm of England and Wales and other of the king's dominions; and all manors, lands, tenements, and other hereditaments belonging to them or any of them" (English Guilds, Introd. p. xliii). See also Ockenkowski's Englands wirtschaftliche Entwickelung im Ausgange des Mittelalters, Jena, 1879, chaps. ii-v.

3. See Sidney and Beatrice Webb, History of Trade-Unionism, London, 1894, pp. 21-38.

4. See in Sidney Webb's work the associations which existed at that time. The London artisans are supposed to have never been

better organized than in 1810-20.

5. The National Association for the Protection of Labour included about 150 separate unions, which paid high levies, and had a membership of about 100,000. The Builders' Union and the Miners' Unions also were big organizations (Webb, l.c. p. 107).

6. I follow in this Mr. Webb's work, which is replete with documents to confirm his statements.

7. Great changes have taken place since the forties in the attitude of the richer classes towards the unions. However, even in the sixties, the employers made a formidable concerted attempt to crush them by locking out whole populations. Up to 1869 the simple agreement to strike, and the announcement of a strike by placards, to say nothing of picketing, were often punished as intimidation. Only in 1875 the Master and Servant Act was repealed, peaceful picketing was permitted, and "violence and intimidation" during strikes fell into the domain of common law. Yet, even during the dock-labourers' strike in 1887, relief money had to be spent for fighting before the Courts for the right of picketing, while the prosecutions of the last few years menace once more to render the conquered rights illusory.

8. A weekly contribution of 6d. out of an 18s. wage, or of 1s. out of 25s., means much more than 9l. out of a 300l. income: it is mostly taken upon food; and the levy is soon doubled when a strike is declared in a brother union. The graphic description of trade-union life, by a skilled craftsman, published by Mr. and Mrs. Webb (pp. 431 seq.), gives an excellent idea of the amount of work required from a unionist.

9. See the debates upon the strikes of Falkenau in Austria before the Austrian Reichstag on the 10th of May, 1894, in which

debates the fact is fully recognized by the Ministry and the owner of the colliery. Also the English Press of that time.

10. Many such facts will be found in the Daily Chronicle and partly the Daily News for October and November 1894.

11. The 31,473 productive and consumers' associations on the Middle Rhine showed, about 1890, a yearly expenditure of 18,437,500l.; 3,675,000l. were granted during the year in loans.

12. British Consular Report, April 1889.

13. A capital research on this subject has been published in Russian in the Zapiski (Memoirs) of the Caucasian Geographical Society, vol. vi. 2, Tiflis, 1891, by C. Egiazaroff.

14. Escape from a French prison is extremely difficult; nevertheless a prisoner escaped from one of the French prisons in 1884 or 1885. He even managed to conceal himself during the whole day, although the alarm was given and the peasants in the neighbourhood were on the look-out for him. Next morning found him concealed in a ditch, close by a small village. Perhaps he intended to steal some food, or some clothes in order to take off his prison uniform. As he was lying in the ditch a fire broke out in the village. He saw a woman running out of one of the burning houses, and heard her desperate appeals to rescue a child in the upper storey of the burning house. No one moved to do so. Then the escaped prisoner dashed out of his retreat, made his way through the fire, and, with a scalded face and burning clothes, brought the child safe out of the fire, and handed it to its mother. Of course he was arrested on the spot by the village gendarme, who now made his appearance. He was taken back to the prison. The fact was reported in all French papers, but none of them bestirred itself to obtain his release. If he had

shielded a warder from a comrade's blow, he would have been made a hero of. But his act was simply humane, it did not promote the State's ideal; he himself did not attribute it to a sudden inspiration of divine grace; and that was enough to let the man fall into oblivion. Perhaps, six or twelve months were added to his sentence for having stolen—"the State's property"— the prison's dress.

15. The medical Academy for Women (which has given to Russia a large portion of her 700 graduated lady doctors), the four Ladies' Universities (about 1000 pupils in 1887; closed that year, and reopened in 1895), and the High Commercial School for Women are entirely the work of such private societies. To the same societies we owe the high standard which the girls' gymnasia attained since they were opened in the sixties. The 100 gymnasia now scattered over the Empire (over 70,000 pupils), correspond to the High Schools for Girls in this country; all teachers are, however, graduates of the universities.

16. The Verein für Verbreitung gemeinnutslicher Kenntnisse, although it has only 5500 members, has already opened more than 1000 public and school libraries, organized thousands of lectures, and published most valuable books.

17. Very few writers in sociology have paid attention to it. Dr. Ihering is one of them, and his case is very instructive. When the great German writer on law began his philosophical work, Der Zweck im Rechte ("Purpose in Law"), he intended to analyze "the active forces which call forth the advance of society and maintain it," and to thus give "the theory of the sociable man." He analyzed, first, the egotistic forces at work, including the present wage-system and coercion in its variety of political and social laws; and in a carefully worked-out scheme of his work he intended to give the last paragraph to the ethical forces—the

sense of duty and mutual love—which contribute to the same aim. When he came, however, to discuss the social functions of these two factors, he had to write a second volume, twice as big as the first; and yet he treated only of the personal factors which will take in the following pages only a few lines. L. Dargun took up the same idea in Egoismus und Altruismus in der Nationalokonomie, Leipzig, 1885, adding some new facts. Buchner's Love, and the several paraphrases of it published here and in Germany, deal with the same subject.

18. Light and Shadows in the Life of an Artisan. Coventry, 1893.

19. Many rich people cannot understand how the very poor can help each other, because they do not realize upon what infinitesimal amounts of food or money often hangs the life of one of the poorest classes. Lord Shaftesbury had understood this terrible truth when he started his Flowers and Watercress Girls' Fund, out of which loans of one pound, and only occasionally two pounds, were granted, to enable the girls to buy a basket and flowers when the winter sets in and they are in dire distress. The loans were given to girls who had "not a sixpence," but never failed to find some other poor to go bail for them. "Of all the movements I have ever been connected with," Lord Shaftesbury wrote, "I look upon this Watercress Girls' movement as the most successful.... It was begun in 1872, and we have had out 800 to 1,000 loans, and have not lost 50l. during the whole period.... What has been lost—and it has been very little, under the circumstances—has been by reason of death or sickness, not by fraud" (The Life and Work of the Seventh Earl of Shaftesbury, by Edwin Hodder, vol. iii. p. 322. London, 1885-86). Several more facts in point in Ch. Booth's Life and Labour in London, vol. i; in Miss Beatrice Potter's "Pages from a Work Girl's Diary" (Nineteenth Century, September 1888, p. 310); and so on.

20. Samuel Plimsoll, Our Seamen, cheap edition, London, 1870, p. 110.

21. Our Seamen, u.s., p. 110. Mr. Plimsoll added: "I don't wish to disparage the rich, but I think it may be reasonably doubted whether these qualities are so fully developed in them; for, notwithstanding that not a few of them are not unacquainted with the claims, reasonable or unreasonable, of poor relatives, these qualities are not in such constant exercise. Riches seem in so many cases to smother the manliness of their possessors, and their sympathies become, not so much narrowed as—so to speak—stratified: they are reserved for the sufferings of their own class, and also the woes of those above them. They seldom tend downwards much, and they are far more likely to admire an act of courage ... than to admire the constantly exercised fortitude and the tenderness which are the daily characteristics of a British workman's life"—and of the workmen all over the world as well.

22. Life of the Seventh Earl of Shaftesbury, by Edwin Hodder, vol. i. pp. 137-138.

CONCLUSION

If we take now the teachings which can be borrowed from the analysis of modern society, in connection with the body of evidence relative to the importance of mutual aid in the evolution of the animal world and of mankind, we may sum up our inquiry as follows.

In the animal world we have seen that the vast majority of species live in societies, and that they find in association the best arms for the struggle for life: understood, of course, in its wide Darwinian sense—not as a struggle for the sheer means of existence, but as a struggle against all natural conditions unfavourable to the species. The animal species, in which individual struggle has been reduced to its narrowest limits, and the practice of mutual aid has attained the greatest development, are invariably the most numerous, the most prosperous, and the most open to further progress. The mutual protection which is obtained in this case, the possibility of attaining old age and of accumulating experience, the higher intellectual development, and the further growth of sociable habits, secure the maintenance of the species, its extension, and its further progressive evolution. The unsociable species, on the contrary, are doomed to decay.

Going next over to man, we found him living in clans and tribes at the very dawn of the stone age; we saw a wide series of social institutions developed already in the lower savage stage, in the clan and the tribe; and we found that the earliest tribal customs and habits gave to mankind the embryo of all the institutions which made later on the leading aspects of further progress. Out of the savage tribe grew up the barbarian village community; and a new, still wider, circle of social customs, habits, and institutions, numbers of which are still alive among ourselves, was developed under the principles of common possession of a given territory and common defence of it, under the jurisdiction of the village folkmote, and in the federation of villages belonging, or supposed to belong, to one stem. And when new requirements induced men to make a new start, they made it in the city, which represented a double network of territorial units (village communities), connected with guilds these latter arising out of the common prosecution of a given art or craft, or for mutual support and defence.

And finally, in the last two chapters facts were produced to show that although the growth of the State on the pattern of Imperial Rome had put a violent end to all medieval institutions for mutual support, this new aspect of civilization could not last. The State, based upon loose aggregations of individuals and undertaking to be their only bond of union, did not answer its purpose. The mutual-aid tendency finally broke down its iron rules; it reappeared and reasserted itself in an infinity of associations which now tend to embrace all aspects of life and to take possession of all that is required by man for life and for reproducing the waste occasioned by life.

It will probably be remarked that mutual aid, even though it may represent one of the factors of evolution, covers nevertheless one aspect only of human relations; that by the side of this current, powerful though it may be, there is, and always has been, the other current—the self-assertion of the individual, not only in its efforts to attain personal or caste superiority, economical, political, and spiritual, but also in its much more important although less evident function of breaking through the bonds, always prone to become crystallized, which the tribe, the village community, the city, and the State impose upon the individual. In other words, there is the self-assertion of the individual taken as a progressive element.

It is evident that no review of evolution can be complete, unless these two dominant currents are analyzed. However, the self-assertion of the individual or of groups of individuals, their struggles for superiority, and the conflicts which resulted therefrom, have already been analyzed, described, and glorified from time immemorial. In fact, up to the present time, this current alone has received attention from the epical poet, the annalist, the historian, and the sociologist. History, such as it has hitherto been written, is almost entirely a description of the ways and means by which theocracy, military power, autocracy, and, later on, the richer classes' rule have been promoted, established, and maintained. The struggles between these forces make, in fact, the substance of history. We may thus take the knowledge of the individual factor in human history as granted—even though there is full room for a new study of the subject on the lines just alluded to; while, on the other side, the mutual-aid factor has been hitherto totally lost sight of; it was simply denied, or even scoffed at, by the writers of the present and past generation. It was therefore necessary to show, first of all, the immense part which this factor plays in the evolution of both the animal world and human societies. Only after this has been fully recognized will it be possible to proceed to a comparison between the two factors.

To make even a rough estimate of their relative importance by any method more or less statistical, is evidently impossible. One single war—we all know—may be productive of more evil, immediate and subsequent, than hundreds of years of the unchecked action of the mutual-aid principle may be productive of good. But when we see that in the animal world, progressive development and mutual aid go hand in hand, while the inner struggle within the species is concomitant with retrogressive development; when we notice that with man, even success in struggle and war is proportionate to the development of mutual aid in each of the two conflicting nations, cities, parties, or tribes, and that in the process of evolution war itself (so far as it can go this way) has been made subservient to the ends of progress in mutual aid within the nation, the city or the clan—we already obtain a perception of the dominating influence of the mutual-aid factor as an element of progress. But we see also that the practice of mutual aid and its successive developments have created the very conditions of society life in which man was enabled to develop his arts, knowledge, and intelligence; and that the periods when institutions based on the mutual-aid tendency took their greatest development were also the periods of the greatest progress in arts, industry, and science. In fact, the study of the inner life of the medieval city and of the ancient Greek cities reveals the fact that the combination of mutual aid, as it was practised within the guild and the Greek clan, with a large initiative which was left to the individual and the group by means of the federative principle, gave to mankind the two greatest periods of its history—the ancient Greek city and the medieval city periods; while the ruin of the above institutions during the State periods of history, which followed, corresponded in both cases to a rapid decay.

As to the sudden industrial progress which has been achieved during our own century, and which is usually ascribed to the triumph of individualism and competition, it certainly has a much deeper origin than that. Once the great discoveries of the fifteenth century were made, especially that of the pressure of the atmosphere, supported by a series of advances in natural philosophy—and they were made under the medieval city organization,—once these discoveries were made, the invention of the steam-motor, and all the revolution which the conquest of a new power implied, had necessarily to follow. If the medieval cities had lived to bring their discoveries to that point, the ethical consequences of the revolution effected by steam might have been different; but the same revolution in technics and science would have inevitably taken place. It remains, indeed, an open question whether the general decay of industries which followed the ruin of the free cities, and was especially noticeable in the first part of the eighteenth century, did not considerably retard the appearance of the steam-engine as well as the consequent revolution in arts. When we consider the astounding rapidity of industrial progress from the twelfth to the fifteenth centuries—in weaving, working of metals, architecture and navigation, and ponder over the scientific discoveries which that industrial progress led to at the end of the fifteenth century—we must ask ourselves whether mankind was not delayed in its taking full advantage of these conquests when a general depression of arts and industries took place in Europe after the decay of medieval civilization. Surely it was not the disappearance of the artist-artisan, nor the ruin of large cities and the extinction of intercourse between them, which could favour the industrial revolution; and we know indeed that James Watt spent twenty or more years of his life in order to render his invention serviceable, because he could not find in the last century what he would have readily found in medieval Florence or Brugge, that is, the artisans capable of realizing his devices in metal, and of giving them the artistic finish and precision which the steam-engine requires.

To attribute, therefore, the industrial progress of our century to the war of each against all which it has proclaimed, is to reason like the man who, knowing not the causes of rain, attributes it to the victim he has immolated before his clay idol. For industrial progress, as for each other conquest over nature, mutual aid and close intercourse certainly are, as they have been, much more advantageous than mutual struggle.

However, it is especially in the domain of ethics that the dominating importance of the mutual-aid principle appears in full. That mutual aid is the real foundation of our ethical conceptions seems evident enough. But whatever the opinions as to the first origin of the mutual-aid feeling or instinct may be — whether a biological or a supernatural cause is ascribed to it — we must trace its existence as far back as to the lowest stages of the animal world; and from these stages we can follow its uninterrupted evolution, in opposition to a number of contrary agencies, through all degrees of human development, up to the present times. Even the new religions which were born from time to time — always at epochs when the mutual-aid principle was falling into decay in the theocracies and despotic States of the East, or at the decline of the Roman Empire — even the new religions have only reaffirmed that same principle. They found their first supporters among the humble, in the lowest, downtrodden layers of society, where the mutual-aid principle is the necessary foundation of every-day life; and the new forms of union which were introduced in the earliest Buddhist and Christian communities, in the Moravian brotherhoods and so on, took the character of a return to the best aspects of mutual aid in early tribal life.

Each time, however, that an attempt to return to this old principle was made, its fundamental idea itself was widened. From the clan it was extended to the stem, to the federation of stems, to the nation, and finally — in ideal, at least — to the whole of mankind. It was also refined at the same time. In primitive Buddhism, in primitive Christianity, in the writings of some of the Mussulman teachers, in the early movements of the Reform, and especially in the ethical and philosophical movements of the last century and of our own times, the total abandonment of the idea of revenge, or of "due reward" — of good for good and evil for evil — is affirmed more and more vigorously. The higher conception of "no revenge for wrongs," and of freely giving more than one expects to receive from his neighbours, is proclaimed as being the real principle of morality—a principle superior to mere equivalence, equity, or justice, and more conducive to happiness. And man is appealed to to be guided in his acts, not merely by love, which is always personal, or at the best tribal, but by the perception of his oneness with each human being. In the practice of mutual aid, which we can retrace to the earliest beginnings of evolution, we thus find the positive and undoubted origin of our ethical conceptions; and we can affirm that in the ethical progress of man, mutual support not mutual struggle—has had the leading part. In its wide extension, even at the present time, we also see the best guarantee of a still loftier evolution of our race.

THE CONQUEST OF BREAD

By
PETER KROPOTKIN

Author of "Fields, Factories, and Workshops"
"The Memoirs of a Revolutionist," Etc.

NEW YORK
VANGUARD PRESS
MCMXXVI

PRINTED IN THE UNITED STATES OF AMERICA

THE MAN (1842-1921):

Prince Peter Alexeivitch Kropotkin, revolutionary and scientist, was descended from the old Russian nobility, but decided, at the age of thirty, to throw in his lot with the social rebels not only of his own country, but of the entire world. He became the intellectual leader of Anarchist-Communism; took part in the labor movement; wrote many books and pamphlets; established *Le Révolté* in Geneva and *Freedom* in London; contributed to the *Encyclopedia Britannica*; was twice imprisoned because of his radical activities; and twice visited America. After the Bolshevist revolution he returned to Russia, kept himself apart from Soviet activities, and died true to his ideals.

THE BOOK:

The Conquest of Bread is a revolutionary idyl, a beautiful outline sketch of a future society based on liberty, equality and fraternity. It is, in Kropotkin's own words, "a study of the needs of humanity, and of the economic means to satisfy them." Read in conjunction with the same author's "Fields, Factories and Workshops," it meets all the difficulties of the social inquirer who says: "The Anarchist ideal is alluring, but how could you work it out?"

Contents

THE BOOK 536
PREFACE 538
CHAPTER I. Our Riches 548
CHAPTER II. Well-Being for All 558
CHAPTER III. Anarchist Communism 570
CHAPTER IV. Expropriation 582
CHAPTER V. Food 597
CHAPTER VI. Dwellings 626
CHAPTER VII. Clothing 638
CHAPTER VIII. Ways And Means 642
CHAPTER IX. The Need For Luxury 650
CHAPTER X. Agreeable Work 667
CHAPTER XI. Free Agreement 677
CHAPTER XII. Objections 694
CHAPTER XIII. The Collectivist Wages System 714
CHAPTER XIV. Consumption And Production 732
CHAPTER XV. The Division Of Labour 740
CHAPTER XVI. The Decentralization Of Industry 744
CHAPTER XVII. Agriculture 756
Notes 780

PREFACE

One of the current objections to Communism, and Socialism altogether, is that the idea is so old, and yet it has never been realized. Schemes of ideal States haunted the thinkers of Ancient Greece; later on, the early Christians joined in communist groups; centuries later, large communist brotherhoods came into existence during the Reform movement. Then, the same ideals were revived during the great English and French Revolutions; and finally, quite lately, in 1848, a revolution, inspired to a great extent with Socialist ideals, took place in France. "And yet, you see," we are told, "how far away is still the realization of your schemes. Don't you think that there is some fundamental error in your understanding of human nature and its needs?"

At first sight this objection seems very serious. However, the moment we consider human history more attentively, it loses its strength. We see, first, that hundreds of millions of men have succeeded in maintaining amongst themselves, in their village communities, for many hundreds of years, one of the main elements of Socialism—the common ownership of the chief instrument of production, the land, and the apportionment of the same according to the labour capacities of the different families; and we learn that if the communal possession of the land has been destroyed in Western Europe, it was not from within, but from without, by the governments which created a land monopoly in favour of the nobility and the middle classes. We learn, moreover, that the medieval cities succeeded in maintaining in their midst, for several centuries in succession, a certain socialized organization of production and trade; that these centuries were periods of a rapid intellectual, industrial, and artistic progress; while the decay of these communal institutions came mainly from the incapacity of men of combining the village with the city, the peasant with the citizen, so as jointly to oppose the growth of the military states, which destroyed the free cities.

The history of mankind, thus understood, does not offer, then, an argument against Communism. It appears, on the contrary, as a succession of endeavours to realize some sort of communist organization, endeavours which were crowned here and there with a partial success of a certain duration; and all we are authorized to conclude is, that mankind has not yet found the proper form for combining, on communistic principles, agriculture with a suddenly developed industry and a rapidly growing international trade. The latter appears especially as a disturbing element, since it is no longer individuals only, or cities, that enrich themselves by distant commerce and export; but whole nations grow rich at the cost of those nations which lag behind in their industrial development.

These conditions, which began to appear by the end of the eighteenth century, took, however, their full development in the nineteenth century only, after the Napoleonic wars came to an end. And modern Communism has to take them into account.

It is now known that the French Revolution, apart from its political significance, was an attempt made by the French people, in 1793 and 1794, in three different directions more or less akin to Socialism. It was, first, *the equalization of fortunes*, by means of an income tax and succession duties, both heavily progressive, as also by a direct confiscation of the land in order to sub-divide it, and by heavy war taxes levied upon the rich only. The second attempt was a sort of *Municipal Communism* as regards the consumption of some objects of first necessity, bought by the municipalities, and sold by them at cost price. And the third attempt was to introduce a wide *national system of rationally established prices of all commodities*, for which the real cost of production and moderate trade profits had to be taken into account. The Convention worked hard at this scheme, and had nearly completed its work, when reaction took the upper hand.

It was during this remarkable movement, which has never yet been properly studied, that modern Socialism was born — Fourierism with L'Ange, at Lyons, and authoritarian Communism with Buonarroti, Babeuf, and their comrades. And it was immediately after the Great Revolution that the three great theoretical founders of modern Socialism — Fourier, Saint Simon, and Robert Owen, as well as Godwin (the No-State Socialism) — came forward; while the secret communist societies, originated from those of Buonarroti and Babeuf, gave their stamp to militant, authoritarian Communism for the next fifty years.

To be correct, then, we must say that modern Socialism is not yet a hundred years old, and that, for the first half of these hundred years, two nations only, which stood at the head of the industrial movement, i.e., Britain and France, took part in its elaboration. Both — bleeding at that time from the terrible wounds inflicted upon them by fifteen years of Napoleonic wars, and both enveloped in the great European reaction that had come from the East.

In fact, it was only after the Revolution of July, 1830, in France, and the Reform movement of 1830-1832 in this country, had begun to shake off that terrible reaction, that the discussion of Socialism became possible for a few years before the revolution of 1848. And it was during those years that the aspirations of Fourier, St. Simon, and Robert Owen, worked out by their followers, took a definite shape, and the different schools of Socialism which exist nowadays were defined.

In Britain, Robert Owen and his followers worked out their schemes of communist villages, agricultural and industrial at the same time; immense co-operative associations were started for creating with their dividends more communist colonies; and the Great Consolidated Trades' Union was founded—the forerunner of both the Labour Parties of our days and the International Working-men's Association.

In France, the Fourierist Considérant issued his remarkable manifesto, which contains, beautifully developed, all the theoretical considerations upon the growth of Capitalism, which are now described as "Scientific Socialism." Proudhon worked out his idea of Anarchism and Mutualism, without State interference. Louis Blanc published his *Organization of Labour*, which became later on the programme of Lassalle. Vidal in France and Lorenz Stein in Germany further developed, in two remarkable works, published in 1846 and 1847 respectively, the theoretical conceptions of Considérant; and finally Vidal, and especially Pecqueur, developed in detail the system of Collectivism, which the former wanted the National Assembly of 1848 to vote in the shape of laws.

However, there is one feature, common to all Socialist schemes of that period, which must be noted. The three great founders of Socialism who wrote at the dawn of the nineteenth century were so entranced by the wide horizons which it opened before them, that they looked upon it as a new revelation, and upon themselves as upon the founders of a new religion. Socialism had to be a religion, and they had to regulate its march, as the heads of a new church. Besides, writing during the period of reaction which had followed the French Revolution, and seeing more its failures than its successes, they did not trust the masses, and they did not appeal to them for bringing about the changes which they thought necessary. They put their faith, on the contrary, into some great ruler, some Socialist Napoleon. He would understand the new revelation; he would be convinced of its desirability by the successful experiments of their phalansteries, or associations; and he would peacefully accomplish by his own authority the revolution which would bring well-being and happiness to mankind. A military genius, Napoleon, had just been ruling Europe. Why should not a social genius come forward, carry Europe with him and translate the new Gospel into life? That faith was rooted very deep, and it stood for a long time in the way of Socialism; its traces are even seen amongst us, down to the present day.

It was only during the years 1840-48, when the approach of the Revolution was felt everywhere, and the proletarians were beginning to plant the banner of Socialism on the barricades, that faith in the people began to enter once more the hearts of the social schemers: faith, on the one side, in Republican Democracy, and on the other side in *free* association, in the organizing powers of the working-men themselves.

But then came the Revolution of February, 1848, the middle-class Republic, and—with it, shattered hopes. Four months only after the proclamation of the Republic, the June insurrection of the Paris proletarians broke out, and it was crushed in blood. The wholesale shooting of the working-men, the mass deportations to New Guinea, and finally the Napoleonian *coup d'état* followed. The Socialists were prosecuted with fury, and the weeding out was so terrible and so thorough that for the next twelve or fifteen years the very traces of Socialism disappeared; its literature vanished so completely that even names, once so familiar before 1848, were entirely forgotten; ideas which were then current—the stock ideas of the Socialists before 1848—were so wiped out as to be taken, later on, by our generation, for new discoveries.

However, when a new revival began, about 1866, when Communism and Collectivism once more came forward, it appeared that the conception as to the means of their realization had undergone a deep change. The old faith in Political Democracy was dying out, and the first principles upon which the Paris working-men agreed with the British trade-unionists and Owenites, when they met in 1862 and 1864, at London, was that "the emancipation of the working-men must be accomplished by the working-men themselves." Upon another point they also were agreed. It was that the labour unions themselves would have to get hold of the instruments of production, and organize production themselves. The French idea of the Fourierist and Mutualist "Association" thus joined hands with Robert Owen's idea of "The Great Consolidated Trades' Union," which was extended now, so as to become an International Working-men's Association.

Again this new revival of Socialism lasted but a few years. Soon came the war of 1870-71, the uprising of the Paris Commune— and again the free development of Socialism was rendered impossible in France. But while Germany accepted now from the hands of its German teachers, Marx and Engels, the Socialism of the French "forty-eighters" that is, the Socialism of Considérant and Louis Blanc, and the Collectivism of Pecqueur,—France made a further step forward.

In March, 1871, Paris had proclaimed that henceforward it would not wait for the retardatory portions of France: that it intended to start within its Commune its own social development.

The movement was too short-lived to give any positive result. It remained communalist only; it merely asserted the rights of the Commune to its full autonomy. But the working-classes of the old International saw at once its historical significance. They understood that the free commune would be henceforth the medium in which the ideas of modern Socialism may come to realization. The free agro-industrial communes, of which so much was spoken in England and France before 1848, need not be small phalansteries, or small communities of 2000 persons. They must be vast agglomerations, like Paris, or, still better, small territories. These communes would federate to constitute nations in some cases, even irrespectively of the present national frontiers (like the Cinque Ports, or the Hansa). At the same time large labour associations would come into existence for the inter-communal service of the railways, the docks, and so on.

Such were the ideas which began vaguely to circulate after 1871 amongst the thinking working-men, especially in the Latin countries. In some such organization, the details of which life itself would settle, the labour circles saw the medium through which Socialist forms of life could find a much easier realization than through the seizure of all industrial property by the State, and the State organization of agriculture and industry.

These are the ideas to which I have endeavoured to give a more or less definite expression in this book.

Looking back now at the years that have passed since this book was written, I can say in full conscience that its leading ideas must have been correct. State Socialism has certainly made considerable progress. State railways, State banking, and State trade in spirits have been introduced here and there. But every step made in this direction, even though it resulted in the cheapening of a given commodity, was found to be a new obstacle in the struggle of the working-men for their emancipation. So that we find growing amongst the working-men, especially in Western Europe, the idea that even the working of such a vast national property as a railway-net could be much better handled by a Federated Union of railway employés, than by a State organization.

On the other side, we see that countless attempts have been made all over Europe and America, the leading idea of which is, on the one side, to get into the hands of the working-men themselves wide branches of production, and, on the other side, to always widen in the cities the circles of the functions which the city performs in the interest of its inhabitants. Trade-unionism, with a growing tendency towards organizing the different trades internationally, and of being not only an instrument for the improvement of the conditions of labour, but also of becoming an organization which might, at a given moment, take into its hands the management of production; Co-operation, both for production and for distribution, both in industry and agriculture, and attempts at combining both sorts of co-operation in experimental colonies; and finally, the immensely varied field of the so-called Municipal Socialism—these are the three directions in which the greatest amount of creative power has been developed lately.

Of course, none of these may, in any degree, be taken as a substitute for Communism, or even for Socialism, both of which imply the common possession of the instruments of production. But we certainly must look at all these attempts as upon *experiments*—like those which Owen, Fourier, and Saint Simon tried in their colonies—experiments which prepare human thought to conceive some of the practical forms in which a communist society might find its expression. The synthesis of all these partial experiments will have to be made some day by the constructive genius of some one of the civilized nations. But samples of the bricks out of which the great synthetic building will have to be built, and even samples of some of its rooms, are being prepared by the immense effort of the constructive genius of man.

BRIGHTON.

January, 1913.

PETER KROPOTKIN

THE CONQUEST OF BREAD

CHAPTER I
OUR RICHES

I

The human race has travelled a long way, since those remote ages when men fashioned their rude implements of flint and lived on the precarious spoils of hunting, leaving to their children for their only heritage a shelter beneath the rocks, some poor utensils—and Nature, vast, unknown, and terrific, with whom they had to fight for their wretched existence.

During the long succession of agitated ages which have elapsed since, mankind has nevertheless amassed untold treasures. It has cleared the land, dried the marshes, hewn down forests, made roads, pierced mountains; it has been building, inventing, observing, reasoning; it has created a complex machinery, wrested her secrets from Nature, and finally it pressed steam and electricity into its service. And the result is, that now the child of the civilized man finds at its birth, ready for its use, an immense capital accumulated by those who have gone before him. And this capital enables man to acquire, merely by his own labour combined with the labour of others, riches surpassing the dreams of the fairy tales of the Thousand and One Nights.

The soil is cleared to a great extent, fit for the reception of the best seeds, ready to give a rich return for the skill and labour spent upon it—a return more than sufficient for all the wants of humanity. The methods of rational cultivation are known.

On the wide prairies of America each hundred men, with the aid of powerful machinery, can produce in a few months enough wheat to maintain ten thousand people for a whole year. And where man wishes to double his produce, to treble it, to multiply it a hundred-fold, he *makes* the soil, gives to each plant the requisite care, and thus obtains enormous returns. While the hunter of old had to scour fifty or sixty square miles to find food for his family, the civilized man supports his household, with far less pains, and far more certainty, on a thousandth part of that space. Climate is no longer an obstacle. When the sun fails, man replaces it by artificial heat; and we see the coming of a time when artificial light also will be used to stimulate vegetation. Meanwhile, by the use of glass and hot water pipes, man renders a given space ten and fifty times more productive than it was in its natural state.

The prodigies accomplished in industry are still more striking. With the co-operation of those intelligent beings, modern machines—themselves the fruit of three or four generations of inventors, mostly unknown—a hundred men manufacture now the stuff to provide ten thousand persons with clothing for two years. In well-managed coal mines the labour of a hundred miners furnishes each year enough fuel to warm ten thousand families under an inclement sky. And we have lately witnessed the spectacle of wonderful cities springing up in a few months for international exhibitions, without interrupting in the slightest degree the regular work of the nations.

And if in manufactures as in agriculture, and as indeed through our whole social system, the labour, the discoveries, and the inventions of our ancestors profit chiefly the few, it is none the less certain that mankind in general, aided by the creatures of steel and iron which it already possesses, could already procure an existence of wealth and ease for every one of its members.

Truly, we are rich—far richer than we think; rich in what we already possess, richer still in the possibilities of production of our actual mechanical outfit; richest of all in what we might win from our soil, from our manufactures, from our science, from our technical knowledge, were they but applied to bringing about the well-being of all.

II

In our civilized societies we are rich. Why then are the many poor? Why this painful drudgery for the masses? Why, even to the best paid workman, this uncertainty for the morrow, in the midst of all the wealth inherited from the past, and in spite of the powerful means of production, which could ensure comfort to all, in return for a few hours of daily toil?

The Socialists have said it and repeated it unwearyingly. Daily they reiterate it, demonstrating it by arguments taken from all the sciences. It is because all that is necessary for production—the land, the mines, the highways, machinery, food, shelter, education, knowledge—all have been seized by the few in the course of that long story of robbery, enforced migration and wars, of ignorance and oppression, which has been the life of the human race before it had learned to subdue the forces of Nature. It is because, taking advantage of alleged rights acquired in the past, these few appropriate to-day two-thirds of the products of human labour, and then squander them in the most stupid and shameful way. It is because, having reduced the masses to a point at which they have not the means of subsistence for a month, or even for a week in advance, the few can allow the many to work, only on the condition of themselves receiving the lion's share. It is because these few prevent the remainder of men from producing the things they need, and force them to produce, not the necessaries of life for all, but whatever offers the greatest profits to the monopolists. In this is the substance of all Socialism.

Take, indeed, a civilized country. The forests which once covered it have been cleared, the marshes drained, the climate improved. It has been made habitable. The soil, which bore formerly only a coarse vegetation, is covered to-day with rich harvests. The rock-walls in the valleys are laid out in terraces and covered with vines. The wild plants, which yielded nought but acrid berries, or uneatable roots, have been transformed by generations of culture into succulent vegetables or trees covered with delicious fruits. Thousands of highways and railroads furrow the earth, and pierce the mountains. The shriek of the engine is heard in the wild gorges of the Alps, the Caucasus, and the Himalayas. The rivers have been made navigable; the coasts, carefully surveyed, are easy of access; artificial harbours, laboriously dug out and protected against the fury of the sea, afford shelter to the ships. Deep shafts have been sunk in the rocks; labyrinths of underground galleries have been dug out where coal may be raised or minerals extracted. At the crossings of the highways great cities have sprung up, and within their borders all the treasures of industry, science, and art have been accumulated.

Whole generations, that lived and died in misery, oppressed and ill-treated by their masters, and worn out by toil, have handed on this immense inheritance to our century.

For thousands of years millions of men have laboured to clear the forests, to drain the marshes, and to open up highways by land and water. Every rood of soil we cultivate in Europe has been watered by the sweat of several races of men. Every acre has its story of enforced labour, of intolerable toil, of the people's sufferings. Every mile of railway, every yard of tunnel, has received its share of human blood.

The shafts of the mine still bear on their rocky walls the marks made by the pick of the workman who toiled to excavate them. The space between each prop in the underground galleries might be marked as a miner's grave; and who can tell what each of these graves has cost, in tears, in privations, in unspeakable wretchedness to the family who depended on the scanty wage of the worker cut off in his prime by fire-damp, rock-fall, or flood?

The cities, bound together by railroads and waterways, are organisms which have lived through centuries. Dig beneath them and you find, one above another, the foundations of streets, of houses, of theatres, of public buildings. Search into their history and you will see how the civilization of the town, its industry, its special characteristics, have slowly grown and ripened through the co-operation of generations of its inhabitants before it could become what it is to-day. And even to-day, the value of each dwelling, factory, and warehouse, which has been created by the accumulated labour of the millions of workers, now dead and buried, is only maintained by the very presence and labour of legions of the men who now inhabit that special corner of the globe. Each of the atoms composing what we call the Wealth of Nations owes its value to the fact that it is a part of the great whole. What would a London dockyard or a great Paris warehouse be if they were not situated in these great centres of international commerce? What would become of our mines, our factories, our workshops, and our railways, without the immense quantities of merchandise transported every day by sea and land?

Millions of human beings have laboured to create this civilization on which we pride ourselves to-day. Other millions, scattered through the globe, labour to maintain it. Without them nothing would be left in fifty years but ruins.

There is not even a thought, or an invention, which is not common property, born of the past and the present. Thousands of inventors, known and unknown, who have died in poverty, have co-operated in the invention of each of these machines which embody the genius of man.

Thousands of writers, of poets, of scholars, have laboured to increase knowledge, to dissipate error, and to create that atmosphere of scientific thought, without which the marvels of our century could never have appeared. And these thousands of philosophers, of poets, of scholars, of inventors, have themselves been supported by the labour of past centuries. They have been upheld and nourished through life, both physically and mentally, by legions of workers and craftsmen of all sorts. They have drawn their motive force from the environment.

The genius of a Séguin, a Mayer, a Grove, has certainly done more to launch industry in new directions than all the capitalists in the world. But men of genius are themselves the children of industry as well as of science. Not until thousands of steam-engines had been working for years before all eyes, constantly transforming heat into dynamic force, and this force into sound, light, and electricity, could the insight of genius proclaim the mechanical origin and the unity of the physical forces. And if we, children of the nineteenth century, have at last grasped this idea, if we know now how to apply it, it is again because daily experience has prepared the way. The thinkers of the eighteenth century saw and declared it, but the idea remained undeveloped, because the eighteenth century had not grown up like ours, side by side with the steam-engine. Imagine the decades that might have passed while we remained in ignorance of this law, which has revolutionized modern industry, had

Watt not found at Soho skilled workmen to embody his ideas in metal, bringing all the parts of his engine to perfection, so that steam, pent in a complete mechanism, and rendered more docile than a horse, more manageable than water, became at last the very soul of modern industry.

Every machine has had the same history—a long record of sleepless nights and of poverty, of disillusions and of joys, of partial improvements discovered by several generations of nameless workers, who have added to the original invention these little nothings, without which the most fertile idea would remain fruitless. More than that: every new invention is a synthesis, the resultant of innumerable inventions which have preceded it in the vast field of mechanics and industry.

Science and industry, knowledge and application, discovery and practical realization leading to new discoveries, cunning of brain and of hand, toil of mind and muscle—all work together. Each discovery, each advance, each increase in the sum of human riches, owes its being to the physical and mental travail of the past and the present.

By what right then can any one whatever appropriate the least morsel of this immense whole and say—This is mine, not yours?

III

It has come about, however, in the course of the ages traversed by the human race, that all that enables man to produce and to increase his power of production has been seized by the few. Some time, perhaps, we will relate how this came to pass. For the present let it suffice to state the fact and analyze its consequences.

To-day the soil, which actually owes its value to the needs of an ever-increasing population, belongs to a minority who prevent the people from cultivating it—or do not allow them to cultivate it according to modern methods.

The mines, though they represent the labour of several generations, and derive their sole value from the requirements of the industry of a nation and the density of the population—the mines also belong to the few; and these few restrict the output of coal, or prevent it entirely, if they find more profitable investments for their capital. Machinery, too, has become the exclusive property of the few, and even when a machine incontestably represents the improvements added to the original rough invention by three or four generations of workers, it none the less belongs to a few owners. And if the descendants of the very inventor who constructed the first machine for lace-making, a century ago, were to present themselves to-day in a lace factory at Bâle or Nottingham, and claim their rights, they would be told: "Hands off! this machine is not yours," and they would be shot down if they attempted to take possession of it.

The railways, which would be useless as so much old iron without the teeming population of Europe, its industry, its commerce, and its marts, belong to a few shareholders, ignorant perhaps of the whereabouts of the lines of rails which yield them revenues greater than those of medieval kings. And if the children of those who perished by thousands while excavating the railway cuttings and tunnels were to assemble one day, crowding in their rags and hunger, to demand bread from the shareholders, they would be met with bayonets and grapeshot, to disperse them and safeguard "vested interests."

In virtue of this monstrous system, the son of the worker, on entering life, finds no field which he may till, no machine which he may tend, no mine in which he may dig, without accepting to leave a great part of what he will produce to a master. He must sell his labour for a scant and uncertain wage. His father and his grandfather have toiled to drain this field, to build this mill, to perfect this machine. They gave to the work the full measure of their strength, and what more could they give? But their heir comes into the world poorer than the lowest savage. If he obtains leave to till the fields, it is on condition of surrendering a quarter of the produce to his master, and another quarter to the government and the middlemen. And this tax, levied upon him by the State, the capitalist, the lord of the manor, and the middleman, is always increasing; it rarely leaves him the power to improve his system of culture. If he turns to industry, he is allowed to work—though not always even that—only on condition that he yield a half or two-thirds of the product to him whom the land recognizes as the owner of the machine.

We cry shame on the feudal baron who forbade the peasant to turn a clod of earth unless he surrendered to his lord a fourth of his crop. We called those the barbarous times. But if the forms have changed, the relations have remained the same, and the worker is forced, under the name of free contract, to accept feudal obligations. For, turn where he will, he can find no better conditions. Everything has become private property, and he must accept, or die of hunger.

The result of this state of things is that all our production tends in a wrong direction. Enterprise takes no thought for the needs of the community. Its only aim is to increase the gains of the speculator. Hence the constant fluctuations of trade, the periodical industrial crises, each of which throws scores of thousands of workers on the streets.

The working people cannot purchase with their wages the wealth which they have produced, and industry seeks foreign markets among the monied classes of other nations. In the East, in Africa, everywhere, in Egypt, Tonkin or the Congo, the

European is thus bound to promote the growth of serfdom. And so he does. But soon he finds that everywhere there are similar competitors. All the nations evolve on the same lines, and wars, perpetual wars, break out for the right of precedence in the market. Wars for the possession of the East, wars for the empire of the sea, wars to impose duties on imports and to dictate conditions to neighbouring states; wars against those "blacks" who revolt! The roar of the cannon never ceases in the world, whole races are massacred, the states of Europe spend a third of their budgets in armaments; and we know how heavily these taxes fall on the workers.

Education still remains the privilege of a small minority, for it is idle to talk of education when the workman's child is forced, at the age of thirteen, to go down into the mine or to help his father on the farm. It is idle to talk of studying to the worker, who comes home in the evening wearied by excessive toil, and its brutalizing atmosphere. Society is thus bound to remain divided into two hostile camps, and in such conditions freedom is a vain word. The Radical begins by demanding a greater extension of political rights, but he soon sees that the breath of liberty leads to the uplifting of the proletariat, and then he turns round, changes his opinions, and reverts to repressive legislation and government by the sword.

A vast array of courts, judges, executioners, policemen, and gaolers is needed to uphold these privileges; and this array gives rise in its turn to a whole system of espionage, of false witness, of spies, of threats and corruption.

The system under which we live checks in its turn the growth of the social sentiment. We all know that without uprightness, without self-respect, without sympathy and mutual aid, human kind must perish, as perish the few races of animals living by rapine, or the slave-keeping ants. But such ideas are not to the taste of the ruling classes, and they have elaborated a whole system of pseudo-science to teach the contrary.

Fine sermons have been preached on the text that those who have should share with those who have not, but he who would carry out this principle would be speedily informed that these beautiful sentiments are all very well in poetry, but not in practice. "To lie is to degrade and besmirch oneself," we say, and yet all civilized life becomes one huge lie. We accustom ourselves and our children to hypocrisy, to the practice of a double-faced morality. And since the brain is ill at ease among lies, we cheat ourselves with sophistry. Hypocrisy and sophistry become the second nature of the civilized man.

But a society cannot live thus; it must return to truth, or cease to exist.

Thus the consequences which spring from the original act of monopoly spread through the whole of social life. Under pain of death, human societies are forced to return to first principles: the means of production being the collective work of humanity, the product should be the collective property of the race. Individual appropriation is neither just nor serviceable. All belongs to all. All things are for all men, since all men have need of them, since all men have worked in the measure of their strength to produce them, and since it is not possible to evaluate every one's part in the production of the world's wealth.

All things for all. Here is an immense stock of tools and implements; here are all those iron slaves which we call machines, which saw and plane, spin and weave for us, unmaking and remaking, working up raw matter to produce the marvels of our time. But nobody has the right to seize a single one of these machines and say: "This is mine; if you want to use it you must pay me a tax on each of your products," any more than the feudal lord of medieval times had the right to say to the peasant: "This hill, this meadow belong to me, and you must pay me a tax on every sheaf of corn you reap, on every brick you build."

All is for all! If the man and the woman bear their fair share of work, they have a right to their fair share of all that is produced by all, and that share is enough to secure them well-being. No more of such vague formulas as "The right to work," or "To each the whole result of his labour." What we proclaim is THE RIGHT TO WELL-BEING: WELL-BEING FOR ALL!

CHAPTER II
WELL-BEING FOR ALL

I

Well-being for all is not a dream. It is possible, realizable, owing to all that our ancestors have done to increase our powers of production.

We know, indeed, that the producers, although they constitute hardly one-third of the inhabitants of civilized countries, even now produce such quantities of goods that a certain degree of comfort could be brought to every hearth. We know further that if all those who squander to-day the fruits of others' toil were forced to employ their leisure in useful work, our wealth would increase in proportion to the number of producers, and more. Finally, we know that contrary to the theory enunciated by Malthus—that Oracle of middle-class Economics—the productive powers of the human race increase at a much more rapid ratio than its powers of reproduction. The more thickly men are crowded on the soil, the more rapid is the growth of their wealth-creating power.

Thus, although the population of England has only increased from 1844 to 1890 by 62 per cent., its production has grown, even at the lowest estimate, at double that rate—to wit, by 130 per cent. In France, where the population has grown more slowly, the increase in production is nevertheless very rapid. Notwithstanding the crises through which agriculture is frequently passing, notwithstanding State interference, the blood-tax (conscription), and speculative commerce and finance, the production of wheat in France has increased four-fold, and industrial production more than tenfold, in the course of the last eighty years. In the United States this progress is still more striking. In spite of immigration, or rather precisely because of the influx of surplus European labour, the United States have multiplied their wealth tenfold.

However, these figures give but a very faint idea of what our wealth might become under better conditions. For alongside of the rapid development of our wealth-producing powers we have an overwhelming increase in the ranks of the idlers and middlemen. Instead of capital gradually concentrating itself in a few hands, so that it would only be necessary for the community to dispossess a few millionaires and enter upon its lawful heritage—instead of this Socialist forecast proving true, the exact reverse is coming to pass: the swarm of parasites is ever increasing.

In France there are not ten actual producers to every thirty inhabitants. The whole agricultural wealth of the country is the work of less than seven millions of men, and in the two great industries, mining and the textile trades, you will find that the workers number less than two and one-half millions. But the exploiters of labour, how many are they? In the United Kingdom a little over one million workers—men, women, and children, are employed in all the textile trades; less than nine hundred thousand work the mines; much less than two million till the ground, and it appeared from the last industrial census that only a little over four million men, women and children were employed in all the industries.[1] So that the statisticians have to exaggerate all the figures in order to establish a maximum of eight million producers to forty-five million inhabitants. Strictly speaking the creators of the goods exported from Britain to all the ends of the earth comprise only from six to seven million workers. And what is the number of the shareholders and middlemen who levy the first fruits of labour from far and near, and heap up unearned gains by thrusting themselves between the producer and the consumer?

Nor is this all. The owners of capital constantly reduce the output by restraining production. We need not speak of the cartloads of oysters thrown into the sea to prevent a dainty, hitherto reserved for the rich, from becoming a food for the people. We need not speak of the thousand and one luxuries—stuffs, foods, etc., etc.—treated after the same fashion as the oysters. It is enough to remember the way in which the production of the most necessary things is limited. Legions of miners are ready and willing to dig out coal every day, and send it to those who are shivering with cold; but too often a third, or even one-half, of their number are forbidden to work more than three days a week, because, forsooth, the price of coal must be kept up! Thousands of weavers are forbidden to work the looms, although their wives and children go in rags, and although three-quarters of the population of Europe have no clothing worthy the name.

Hundreds of blast-furnaces, thousands of factories periodically stand idle, others only work half-time—and in every civilized nation there is a permanent population of about two million individuals who ask only for work, but to whom work is denied.

How gladly would these millions of men set to work to reclaim waste lands, or to transform ill-cultivated land into fertile fields, rich in harvests! A year of well-directed toil would suffice to multiply fivefold the produce of those millions of acres in this country which lie idle now as "permanent pasture," or of those dry lands in the south of France which now yield only about eight bushels of wheat per acre. But men, who would be happy to become hardy pioneers in so many branches of wealth-producing activity, must remain idle because the owners of the soil, the mines and the factories prefer to invest their capital—taken in the first place from the community—in Turkish or

Egyptian bonds, or in Patagonian gold mines, and so make Egyptian fellahs, Italian emigrants, and Chinese coolies their wage-slaves.

This is the direct and deliberate limitation of production; but there is also a limitation indirect and not of set purpose, which consists in spending human toil on objects absolutely useless, or destined only to satisfy the dull vanity of the rich.

It is impossible to reckon in figures the extent to which wealth is restricted indirectly, the extent to which energy is squandered, while it might have served to produce, and above all to prepare the machinery necessary to production. It is enough to cite the immense sums spent by Europe in armaments, for the sole purpose of acquiring control of markets, and so forcing her own goods on neighbouring territories, and making exploitation easier at home; the millions paid every year to officials of all sorts, whose function it is to maintain the "rights" of minorities—the right, that is, of a few rich men—to manipulate the economic activities of the nation; the millions spent on judges, prisons, policemen, and all the paraphernalia of so-called justice—spent to no purpose, because we know that every alleviation, however slight, of the wretchedness of our great cities is always followed by a considerable diminution of crime; lastly, the millions spent on propagating pernicious doctrines by means of the press, and news "cooked" in the interest of this or that party, of this politician or of that group of speculators.

But over and above this we must take into account all the labour that goes to sheer waste,—here, in keeping up the stables, the kennels, and the retinue of the rich; there, in pandering to the caprices of society and the depraved tastes of the fashionable mob; there again, in forcing the consumer to buy what he does not need, or foisting an inferior article upon him by means of puffery, and in producing on the other hand wares which are absolutely injurious, but profitable to the manufacturer. What is squandered in this manner would be enough to double the production of useful things, or so to plenish our mills and factories with machinery that they would soon flood the shops with all that is now lacking to two-thirds of the nation. Under our present system a full quarter of the producers in every nation are forced to be idle for three or four months in the year, and the labour of another quarter, if not of the half, has no better results than the amusement of the rich or the exploitation of the public.

Thus, if we consider on the one hand the rapidity with which civilized nations augment their powers of production, and on the other hand the limits set to that production, be it directly or indirectly, by existing conditions, we cannot but conclude that an economic system a trifle more reasonable would permit them to heap up in a few years so many useful products that they would be constrained to say—"Enough! We have enough coal and bread and raiment! Let us rest and consider how best to use our powers, how best to employ our leisure."

No, plenty for all is not a dream—though it was a dream indeed in those days when man, for all his pains, could hardly win a few bushels of wheat from an acre of land, and had to fashion by hand all the implements he used in agriculture and industry. Now it is no longer a dream, because man has invented a motor which, with a little iron and a few sacks of coal, gives him the mastery of a creature strong and docile as a horse, and capable of setting the most complicated machinery in motion.

But, if plenty for all is to become a reality, this immense capital—cities, houses, pastures, arable lands, factories, highways, education—must cease to be regarded as private property, for the monopolist to dispose of at his pleasure.

This rich endowment, painfully won, builded, fashioned, or invented by our ancestors, must become common property, so that the collective interests of men may gain from it the greatest good for all.

There must be EXPROPRIATION. The well-being of all—the end; expropriation—the means.

II

Expropriation, such then is the problem which History has put before the men of the twentieth century: the return to Communism in all that ministers to the well-being of man.

But this problem cannot be solved by means of legislation. No one imagines that. The poor, as well as the rich, understand that neither the existing Governments, nor any which might arise out of possible political changes, would be capable of finding such a solution. They feel the necessity of a social revolution; and both rich and poor recognize that this revolution is imminent, that it may break out in a few years.

A great change in thought has taken place during the last half of the nineteenth century; but suppressed, as it was, by the propertied classes, and denied its natural development, this new spirit must now break its bonds by violence and realize itself in a revolution.

Whence will the revolution come? how will it announce its coming? No one can answer these questions. The future is hidden. But those who watch and think do not misinterpret the signs: workers and exploiters, Revolutionists and Conservatives, thinkers and men of action, all feel that a revolution is at our doors.

Well, then,—What are we going to do when the thunderbolt has fallen?

We have all been bent on studying the dramatic side of revolutions so much, and the practical work of revolutions so little, that we are apt to see only the stage effects, so to speak, of these great movements; the fight of the first days; the barricades. But this fight, this first skirmish, is soon ended, and it only after the breakdown of the old system that the real work of revolution can be said to begin.

Effete and powerless, attacked on all sides, the old rulers are soon swept away by the breath of insurrection. In a few days the middle-class monarchy of 1848 was no more, and while Louis Philippe was making good his escape in a cab, Paris had already forgotten her "citizen king." The government of Thiers disappeared, on the 18th of March, 1871, in a few hours, leaving Paris mistress of her destinies. Yet 1848 and 1871 were only insurrections. Before a popular revolution the masters of "the old order" disappear with a surprising rapidity. Its upholders fly the country, to plot in safety elsewhere and to devise measures for their return.

The former Government having disappeared, the army, hesitating before the tide of popular opinion, no longer obeys its commanders, who have also prudently decamped. The troops stand by without interfering, or join the rebels. The police, standing at ease, are uncertain whether to belabour the crowd, or to cry: "Long live the Commune!" while some retire to their quarters to "await the pleasure of the new Government." Wealthy citizens pack their trunks and betake themselves to places of safety. The people remain. This is how a revolution is ushered in.

In several large towns the Commune is proclaimed. In the streets wander scores of thousands of men, and in the evening they crowd into improvised clubs, asking: "What shall we do?" and ardently discuss public affairs. All take an interest in them; those who yesterday were quite indifferent are perhaps the most zealous. Everywhere there is plenty of good-will and a keen desire to make victory certain. It is a time when acts of supreme devotion are occurring. The masses of the people are full of the desire of going forward.

All this is splendid, sublime; but still, it is not a revolution. Nay, it is only now that the work of the revolutionist begins.

Doubtless there will be acts of vengeance. The Watrins and the Thomases will pay the penalty of their unpopularity; but these are mere incidents of the struggle—not the revolution.

Socialist politicians, radicals, neglected geniuses of journalism, stump orators—both middle-class people and workmen—will hurry to the Town Hall, to the Government offices, to take possession of the vacant seats. Some will decorate themselves with gold and silver lace to their hearts' content, admire themselves in ministerial mirrors, and study to give orders with an air of importance appropriate to their new position. How could they impress their comrades of the office or the workshop without having a red sash, an embroidered cap, and magisterial gestures! Others will bury themselves in official papers, trying, with the best of wills, to make head or tail of them. They will indite laws and issue high-flown worded decrees that nobody will take the trouble to carry out—because revolution has come.

To give themselves an authority which they have not they will seek the sanction of old forms of Government. They will take the names of "Provisional Government," "Committee of Public Safety," "Mayor," "Governor of the Town Hall," "Commissioner of Public Safety," and what not. Elected or acclaimed, they will assemble in Boards or in Communal Councils, where men of ten or twenty different schools will come together, representing—not as many "private chapels," as it is often said, but as many different conceptions regarding the scope, the bearing, and the goal of the revolution. Possibilists, Collectivists, Radicals, Jacobins, Blanquists, will be thrust together, and waste time in wordy warfare. Honest men will be huddled together with the ambitious ones, whose only dream is power and who spurn the crowd whence they are sprung. All coming together with diametrically opposed views, all—forced to enter into ephemeral alliances, in order to create majorities that can but last a day. Wrangling, calling each other reactionaries, authoritarians, and rascals, incapable of coming to an understanding on any serious measure, dragged into discussions about trifles, producing nothing better than bombastic proclamations; all giving themselves an awful importance while the real strength of the movement is in the streets.

All this may please those who like the stage, but it is not revolution. Nothing has been accomplished as yet.

And meanwhile the people suffer. The factories are idle, the workshops closed; trade is at a standstill. The worker does not even earn the meagre wage which was his before. Food goes up in price. With that heroic devotion which has always characterized them, and which in great crises reaches the sublime, the people will wait patiently. "We place these three months of want at the service of the Republic," they said in 1848, while "their representatives" and the gentlemen of the new Government, down to the meanest Jack-in-office received their salary regularly.

The people suffer. With the childlike faith, with the good humour of the masses who believe in their leaders, they think that "yonder," in the House, in the Town Hall, in the Committee of Public Safety, their welfare is being considered. But "yonder" they are discussing everything under the sun except the welfare of the people. In 1793, while famine ravaged France and crippled the Revolution; whilst the people were reduced to the depths of misery, although the Champs Elysées were lined with luxurious carriages where women displayed their jewels and splendour, Robespierre was urging the Jacobins to discuss his treatise on the English Constitution. While the worker was suffering in 1848 from the general stoppage of trade, the Provisional Government and the National Assembly were wrangling over military pensions and prison labour, without troubling how the people managed to live during the terrible crisis. And could one cast a reproach at the Paris Commune, which was born beneath the Prussian cannon, and lasted only seventy days, it would be for this same error—this failure to understand that the Revolution could not triumph unless those who fought on its side were fed: that on fifteen pence a day a man cannot fight on the ramparts and at the same time support a family.

The people will suffer and say: "How is a way out of these difficulties to be found?"

III

It seems to us that there is only one answer to this question: We must recognize, and loudly proclaim, that every one, whatever his grade in the old society, whether strong or weak, capable or incapable, has, before everything, THE RIGHT TO LIVE, and that society is bound to share amongst all, without exception, the means of existence it has at its disposal. We must acknowledge this, and proclaim it aloud, and act up to it.

Affairs must be managed in such a way that from the first day of the revolution the worker shall know that a new era is opening before him; that henceforward none need crouch under the bridges, while palaces are hard by, none need fast in the midst of plenty, none need perish with cold near shops full of furs; that all is for all, in practice as well as in theory, and that at last, for the first time in history, a revolution has been accomplished which considers the NEEDS of the people before schooling them in their DUTIES.

This cannot be brought about by Acts of Parliament, but only by taking immediate and effective possession of all that is necessary to ensure the well-being of all; this is the only really scientific way of going to work, the only way which can be understood and desired by the mass of the people. We must take possession, in the name of the people, of the granaries, the shops full of clothing and the dwelling houses. Nothing must be wasted. We must organize without delay a way to feed the hungry, to satisfy all wants, to meet all needs, to produce not for the special benefit of this one or that one, but so as to ensure to society as a whole its life and further development.

Enough of ambiguous words like "the right to work," with which the people were misled in 1848, and which are still resorted to with the hope of misleading them. Let us have the courage to recognise that *Well-being for all*, henceforward possible, must be realized.

When the workers claimed the right to work in 1848, national and municipal workshops were organized, and workmen were sent to drudge there at the rate of 1s. 8d. a day! When they asked the "Organization of Labour," the reply was: "Patience, friends, the Government will see to it; meantime here is your 1s. 8d. Rest now, brave toiler, after your life-long struggle for food!" And in the meantime the cannons were overhauled, the reserves called out, and the workers themselves disorganized by the many methods well known to the middle classes, till one fine day, in June, 1848, four months after the overthrow of the previous Government, they were told to go and colonize Africa, or be shot down.

Very different will be the result if the workers claim the RIGHT TO WELL-BEING! In claiming that right they claim the right to take possession of the wealth of the community—to take houses to dwell in according to the needs of each family; to socialize the stores of food and learn the meaning of plenty, after having known famine too well. They proclaim their right to all social wealth—fruit of the labour of past and present generations—and learn by its means to enjoy those higher pleasures of art and science which have too long been monopolized by the rich.

And while asserting their right to live in comfort, they assert, what is still more important, their right to decide for themselves what this comfort shall be, what must be produced to ensure it, and what discarded as no longer of value.

The "right to well-being" means the possibility of living like human beings, and of bringing up children to be members of a society better than ours, whilst the "right to work" only means the right to be always a wage-slave, a drudge, ruled over and exploited by the middle class of the future. The right to well-being is the Social Revolution, the right to work means nothing but the Treadmill of Commercialism. It is high time for the worker to assert his right to the common inheritance, and to enter into possession of it.

FOOTNOTE:

[1] 4,013,711 now employed in all the 53 branches of different industries, including the State Ordnance Works, and 241,530 workers engaged in the Construction and Maintenance of Railways, their aggregate production reaching the value of £1,041,037,000, and the net output being £406,799,000.

CHAPTER III
ANARCHIST COMMUNISM

I

Every society, on abolishing private property will be forced, we maintain, to organize itself on the lines of Communistic Anarchy. Anarchy leads to Communism, and Communism to Anarchy, both alike being expressions of the predominant tendency in modern societies, the pursuit of equality.

Time was when a peasant family could consider the corn it sowed and reaped, or the woolen garments woven in the cottage, as the products of its own soil. But even then this way of looking at things was not quite correct. There were the roads and the bridges made in common, the swamps drained by common toil, the communal pastures enclosed by hedges which were kept in repair by each and all. If the looms for weaving or the dyes for colouring fabrics were improved by somebody, all profited; and even in those days a peasant family could not live alone, but was dependent in a thousand ways on the village or the commune.

But nowadays, in the present state of industry, when everything is interdependent, when each branch of production is knit up with all the rest, the attempt to claim an Individualist origin for the products of industry is absolutely untenable. The astonishing perfection attained by the textile or mining industries in civilized countries is due to the simultaneous development of a thousand other industries, great and small, to the extension of the railroad system, to inter-oceanic navigation, to the manual skill of thousands of workers, to a certain standard of culture reached by the working class as a whole—to the labours, in short, of men in every corner of the globe.

The Italians who died of cholera while making the Suez Canal, or of anchylosis in the St. Gothard Tunnel, and the Americans mowed down by shot and shell while fighting for the abolition of slavery, have helped to develop the cotton industry of France and England, as well as the work-girls who languish in the factories of Manchester and Rouen, and the inventor who (following the suggestion of some worker) succeeds in improving the looms.

How then, shall we estimate the share of each in the riches which ALL contribute to amass?

Looking at production from this general, synthetic point of view, we cannot hold with the Collectivists that payment proportionate to the hours of labour rendered by each would be an ideal arrangement, or even a step in the right direction.

Without discussing whether exchange value of goods is really measured in existing societies by the amount of work necessary to produce it—according to the teaching of Adam Smith and Ricardo, in whose footsteps Marx has followed—suffice it to say here, leaving ourselves free to return to the subject later, that the Collectivist ideal appears to us untenable in a society which considers the instruments of labour as a common inheritance. Starting from this principle, such a society would find itself forced from the very outset to abandon all forms of wages.

The migrated individualism of the Collectivist system certainly could not maintain itself alongside a partial communism—the socialization of land and the instruments of production. A new form of property requires a new form of remuneration. A new method of production cannot exist side by side with the old forms of consumption, any more than it can adapt itself to the old forms of political organization.

The wage system arises out of the individual ownership of the land and the instruments of labour. It was the necessary condition for the development of capitalist production, and will perish with it, in spite of the attempt to disguise it as "profit-sharing." The common possession of the instruments of labour must necessarily bring with it the enjoyment in common of the fruits of common labour.

We hold further that Communism is not only desirable, but that existing societies, founded on Individualism, *are inevitably impelled in the direction of Communism*. The development of Individualism during the last three centuries is explained by the efforts of the individual to protect himself from the tyranny of Capital and of the State. For a time he imagined, and those who expressed his thought for him declared, that he could free himself entirely from the State and from society. "By means of money," he said, "I can buy all that I need." But the individual was on a wrong track, and modern history has taught him to recognize that, without the help of all, he can do nothing, although his strong-boxes are full of gold.

In fact, along this current of Individualism, we find in all modern history a tendency, on the one hand to retain all that remains of the partial Communism of antiquity, and, on the other, to establish the Communist principle in the thousand developments of modern life.

As soon as the communes of the tenth, eleventh, and twelfth centuries had succeeded in emancipating themselves from their lords, ecclesiastical or lay, their communal labour and communal consumption began to extend and develop rapidly. The township—and not private persons—freighted ships and equipped expeditions, for the export of their manufacture, and the benefit arising from the foreign trade did not accrue to individuals, but was shared by all. At the outset, the townships also bought provisions for all their citizens. Traces of these institutions have lingered on into the nineteenth century, and the people piously cherish the memory of them in their legends.

All that has disappeared. But the rural township still struggles to preserve the last traces of this Communism, and it succeeds—except when the State throws its heavy sword into the balance.

Meanwhile new organizations, based on the same principle—*to every man according to his needs*—spring up under a thousand different forms; for without a certain leaven of Communism the present societies could not exist. In spite of the narrowly egoistic turn given to men's minds by the commercial system, the tendency towards Communism is constantly appearing, and it influences our activities in a variety of ways.

The bridges, for the use of which a toll was levied in the old days, have become public property and are free to all; so are the high roads, except in the East, where a toll is still exacted from the traveller for every mile of his journey. Museums, free libraries, free schools, free meals for children; parks and gardens open to all; streets paved and lighted, free to all; water supplied to every house without measure or stint—all such arrangements are founded on the principle: "Take what you need."

The tramways and railways have already introduced monthly and annual season tickets, without limiting the number of journeys taken; and two nations, Hungary and Russia, have introduced on their railways the zone system, which permits the holder to travel five hundred or eight hundred miles for the same price. It is but a short step from that to a uniform charge, such as already prevails in the postal service. In all these innovations, and in a thousand others, the tendency is not to measure the individual consumption. One man wants to travel eight hundred miles, another five hundred. These are personal requirements. There is no sufficient reason why one should pay twice as much as the other because his need is twice as great. Such are the signs which appear even now in our individualist societies.

Moreover, there is a tendency, though still a feeble one, to consider the needs of the individual, irrespective of his past or possible services to the community. We are beginning to think of society as a whole, each part of which is so intimately bound up with the others that a service rendered to one is a service rendered to all.

When you go to a public library—not indeed the National Library of Paris, but, say, into the British Museum or the Berlin Library—the librarian does not ask what services you have rendered to society before giving you the book, or the fifty books, which you require; he even comes to your assistance if you do not know how to manage the catalogue. By means of uniform credentials—and very often a contribution of work is preferred—the scientific society opens its museums, its gardens, its library, its laboratories, and its annual conversaziones to each of its members, whether he be a Darwin, or a simple amateur.

At St. Petersburg, if you are elaborating an invention, you go into a special laboratory, where you are given a place, a carpenter's bench, a turning lathe, all the necessary tools and scientific instruments, provided only you know how to use them; and you are allowed to work there as long as you please. There are the tools; interest others in your idea; join with fellow workers skilled in various crafts, or work alone if you prefer it. Invent a flying machine, or invent nothing—that is your own affair. You are pursuing an idea—that is enough.

In the same way, those who man the lifeboat do not ask credentials from the crew of a sinking ship; they launch their boat, risk their lives in the raging waves, and sometimes perish, all to save men whom they do not even know. And what need to know them? "They are human beings, and they need our aid — that is enough, that establishes their right — — To the rescue!"

Thus we find a tendency, eminently communistic, springing up on all sides, and in various guises, in the very heart of theoretically individualist societies.

Suppose that one of our great cities, so egotistic in ordinary times, were visited to-morrow by some calamity — a siege, for instance — that same selfish city would decide that the first needs to satisfy were those of the children and the aged. Without asking what services they had rendered, or were likely to render to society, it would first of all feed them. Then the combatants would be cared for, irrespective of the courage or the intelligence which each had displayed, and thousands of men and women would outvie each other in unselfish devotion to the wounded.

This tendency exists, and is felt as soon as the most pressing needs of each are satisfied, and in proportion as the productive power of the race increases. It becomes an active force every time a great idea comes to oust the mean preoccupations of everyday life.

How can we doubt, then, that when the instruments of production are placed at the service of all, when business is conducted on Communist principles, when labour, having recovered its place of honour in society, produces much more than is necessary to all — how can we doubt that this force (already so powerful), will enlarge its sphere of action till it becomes the ruling principle of social life?

Following these indications, and considering further the

practical side of expropriation, of which we shall speak in the following chapters, we are convinced that our first obligation, when the revolution shall have broken the power upholding the present system, will be to realize Communism without delay.

But ours is neither the Communism of Fourier and the Phalansteriens, nor of the German State Socialists. It is Anarchist Communism, Communism without government—the Communism of the Free. It is the synthesis of the two ideals pursued by humanity throughout the ages—Economic and Political Liberty.

II

In taking "Anarchy" for our ideal of political organization we are only giving expression to another marked tendency of human progress. Whenever European societies have developed up to a certain point, they have shaken off the yoke of authority and substituted a system founded more or less on the principles of individual liberty. And history shows us that these periods of partial or general revolution, when the old governments were overthrown, were also periods of sudden, progress both in the economic and the intellectual field. So it was after the enfranchisement of the communes, whose monuments, produced by the free labour of the guilds, have never been surpassed; so it was after the great peasant uprising which brought about the Reformation and imperilled the papacy; and so it was again with the society, free for a brief space, which was created on the other side of the Atlantic by the malcontents from the Old world.

And, if we observe the present development of civilized nations, we see, most unmistakably, a movement ever more and more marked tending to limit the sphere of action of the Government, and to allow more and more liberty to the individual. This evolution is going on before our eyes, though cumbered by the ruins and rubbish of old institutions and old superstitions. Like all evolutions, it only waits a revolution to overthrow the old obstacles which block the way, that it may find free scope in a regenerated society.

After having striven long in vain to solve the insoluble problem—the problem of constructing a government "which will constrain the individual to obedience without itself ceasing to be the servant of society," men at last attempt to free themselves from every form of government and to satisfy their need for organization by free contacts between individuals and groups pursuing the same aim. The independence of each small territorial unit becomes a pressing need; mutual agreement replaces law in order to regulate individual interests in view of a common object—very often disregarding the frontiers of the present States.

All that was once looked on as a function of the Government is to-day called in question. Things are arranged more easily and more satisfactorily without the intervention of the State. And in studying the progress made in this direction, we are led to conclude that the tendency of the human race is to reduce Government interference to zero; in fact, to abolish the State, the personification of injustice, oppression, and monopoly.

We can already catch glimpses of a world in which the bonds which bind the individual are no longer laws, but social habits—the result of the need felt by each one of us to seek the support, the co-operation, the sympathy of his neighbours.

Assuredly the idea of a society without a State will give rise to at least as many objections as the political economy of a society without private capital. We have all been brought up from our childhood to regard the State as a sort of Providence; all our education, the Roman history we learned at school, the Byzantine code which we studied later under the name of Roman law, and the various sciences taught at the universities, accustom us to believe in Government and in the virtues of the State providential.

To maintain this superstition whole systems of philosophy have been elaborated and taught; all politics are based on this principle; and each politician, whatever his colours, comes forward and says to the people, "Give my party the power; we can and we will free you from the miseries which press so heavily upon you."

From the cradle to the grave all our actions are guided by this principle. Open any book on sociology or jurisprudence, and you will find there the Government, its organization, its acts, filling so large a place that we come to believe that there is nothing outside the Government and the world of statesmen.

The Press teaches us the same in every conceivable way. Whole columns are devoted to parliamentary debates and to political intrigues; while the vast everyday life of a nation appears only in the columns given to economic subjects, or in the pages devoted to reports of police and law cases. And when you read the newspapers, your hardly think of the incalculable number of beings—all humanity, so to say—who grow up and die, who know sorrow, who work and consume, think and create outside the few encumbering personages who have been so magnified that humanity is hidden by their shadows, enlarged by our ignorance.

And yet as soon as we pass from printed matter to life itself, as soon as we throw a glance at society, we are struck by the infinitesimal part played by the Government. Balzac already has remarked how millions of peasants spend the whole of their lives without knowing anything about the State, save the heavy taxes they are compelled to pay. Every day millions of transactions are made without Government intervention, and the greatest of them—those of commerce and of the Exchange—are carried on in such a way that the Government could not be appealed to if one of the contracting parties had the intention of not fulfilling his agreement. Should you speak to a man who understands commerce, he will tell you that the everyday business transacted by merchants would be absolutely impossible were it not based on mutual confidence. The habit of keeping his word, the desire not to lose his credit, amply suffice to maintain this relative honesty. The man who does not feel the slightest remorse when poisoning his customers with noxious drugs covered with pompous labels, thinks he is in honour bound to keep his engagements. But if this relative morality has developed under present conditions, when enrichment is the only incentive and the only aim, can we doubt its rapid progress when appropriation of the fruits of others' labour will no longer be the basis of society?

Another striking fact, which especially characterizes our generation, speaks still more in favour of our ideas. It is the continual extension of the field of enterprise due to private initiative, and the prodigious development of free organizations of all kinds. We shall discuss this more at length in the chapter devoted to *Free Agreement*. Suffice it to mention that the facts are so numerous and so customary that they are the essence of the second half of the nineteenth century, even though political and socialist writers ignore them, always preferring to talk to us about the functions of the Government.

These organizations, free and infinitely varied, are so natural an outcome of our civilization; they expand so rapidly and federate with so much ease; they are so necessary a result of the continual growth of the needs of civilized man; and lastly, they so advantageously replace governmental interference, that we must recognize in them a factor of growing importance in the life of societies. If they do not yet spread over the whole of the manifestations of life, it is that they find an insurmountable obstacle in the poverty of the worker, in the divisions of present society, in the private appropriation of capital, and in the State. Abolish these obstacles, and you will see them covering the immense field of civilized man's activity.

The history of the last fifty years furnishes a living proof that Representative Government is impotent to discharge all the functions we have sought to assign to it. In days to come the nineteenth century will be quoted as having witnessed the failure of parliamentarianism.

This impotence is becoming so evident to all; the faults of parliamentarianism, and the inherent vices of the representative principle, are so self-evident, that the few thinkers who have made a critical study of them (J. S. Mill, Leverdays), did but give literary form to the popular dissatisfaction. It is not difficult, indeed, to see the absurdity of naming a few men and saying to them, "Make laws regulating all our spheres of activity, although not one of you knows anything about them!"

We are beginning to see that government by majorities means abandoning all the affairs of the country to the tide-waiters who make up the majorities in the House and in election committees; to those, in a word, who have no opinion of their own.

Mankind is seeking and already finding new issues. The International Postal Union, the railway unions, and the learned societies give us examples of solutions based on free agreement in place and stead of law.

To-day, when groups scattered far and wide wish to organize themselves for some object or other, they no longer elect an international parliament of Jacks-of-all-trades. They proceed in a different way. Where it is not possible to meet directly or come to an agreement by correspondence, delegates versed in the question at issue are sent, and they are told: "Endeavour to come to an agreement on such or such a question, and then return, not with a law in your pocket, but with a proposition of agreement which we may or may not accept."

Such is the method of the great industrial companies, the learned societies, and numerous associations of every description, which already cover Europe and the United States. And such will be the method of a free society. A society founded on serfdom is in keeping with absolute monarchy; a society based on the wage system and the exploitation of the masses by the capitalists finds its political expression in parliamentarianism. But a free society, regaining possession of the common inheritance, must seek in free groups and free federations of groups, a new organization, in harmony with the new economic phase of history.

Every economic phase has a political phase corresponding to it, and it would be impossible to touch private property unless a new mode of political life be found at the same time.

CHAPTER IV
EXPROPRIATION

I

It is told of Rothschild that, seeing his fortune threatened by the Revolution of 1848, he hit upon the following stratagem: "I am quite willing to admit," said he, "that my fortune has been accumulated at the expense of others; but if it were divided to-morrow among the millions of Europe, the share of each would only amount to four shillings. Very well, then, I undertake to render to each his four shillings if he asks me for it."

Having given due publicity to his promise, our millionaire proceeded as usual to stroll quietly through the streets of Frankfort. Three or four passers-by asked for their four shillings, which he disbursed with a sardonic smile. His stratagem succeeded, and the family of the millionaire is still in possession of its wealth.

It is in much the same fashion that the shrewed heads among the middle classes reason when they say, "Ah, Expropriation! I know what that means. You take all the overcoats and lay them in a heap, and every one is free to help himself and fight for the best."

But such jests are irrelevant as well as flippant. What we want is not a redistribution of overcoats, although it must be said that even in such a case, the shivering folk would see advantage in it. Nor do we want to divide up the wealth of the Rothschilds. What we do want is so to arrange things that every human being born into the world shall be ensured the opportunity, in the first instance of learning some useful occupation, and of becoming skilled in it; and next, that he shall be free to work at his trade without asking leave of master or owner, and without handing over to landlord or capitalist the lion's share of what he produces. As to the wealth held by the Rothschilds or the Vanderbilts, it will serve us to organize our system of communal production.

The day when the labourer may till the ground without paying away half of what he produces, the day when the machines necessary to prepare the soil for rich harvests are at the free disposal of the cultivators, the day when the worker in the factory produces for the community and not the monopolist—that day will see the workers clothed and fed, and there will be no more Rothschilds or other exploiters.

No one will then have to sell his working power for a wage that only represents a fraction of what he produces.

"So far, so good," say our critics, "but you will have Rothschilds coming in from the outside. How are you to prevent a person from amassing millions in China, and then settling amongst you? How are you going to prevent such a one from surrounding himself with lackeys and wage-slaves—from exploiting them and enriching himself at their expense?

"You cannot bring about a revolution all over the world at the same time. Well, then—are you going to establish custom-houses on your frontiers to search all who enter your country and confiscate the money they bring with them?—Anarchist policemen firing on travellers would be a fine spectacle!"

But at the root of this argument there is a great error. Those who propound it have never paused to inquire whence come the fortunes of the rich. A little thought would, however, suffice to show them that these fortunes have their beginnings in the poverty of the poor. When there are no longer any destitute, there will no longer be any rich to exploit them.

Let us glance for a moment at the Middle Ages, when great fortunes began to spring up.

A feudal baron seizes on a fertile valley. But as long as the fertile valley is empty of folk our baron is not rich. His land brings him in nothing; he might as well possess a property in the moon.

What does our baron do to enrich himself? He looks out for peasants—for poor peasants!

If every peasant-farmer had a piece of land, free from rent and taxes, if he had in addition the tools and the stock necessary for farm labour—Who would plough the lands of the baron? Everyone would look after his own. But there are thousands of destitute persons ruined by wars, or drought, or pestilence. They have neither horse nor plough. (Iron was very costly in the Middle Ages, and a draught-horse still more so.)

All these destitute creatures are trying to better their condition. One day they see on the road at the confines of our baron's estate a notice-board indicating by certain signs adapted to their comprehension that the labourer who is willing to settle on his estate will receive the tools and materials to build his cottage and sow his fields, and a portion of land rent free for a certain number of years. The number of years is represented by so many crosses on the sign-board, and the peasant understands the meaning of these crosses.

So the poor wretches come to settle on the baron's lands. They make roads, drain the marshes, build villages. In nine or ten years the baron begins to tax them. Five years later he increases the rent. Then he doubles it, and the peasant accepts these new conditions because he cannot find better ones elsewhere. Little by little, with the aid of laws made by the barons, the poverty of the peasant becomes the source of the landlord's wealth. And it is not only the lord of the manor who preys upon him. A whole host of usurers swoop down upon the villages, multiplying as the wretchedness of the peasants increases. That is how these things happened in the Middle Ages. And to-day is it not still the same thing? If there were free lands which the peasant could cultivate if he pleased, would he pay £50 to some "shabble of a Duke"[2] for condescending to sell him a scrap? Would he burden himself with a lease which absorbed a third of the produce? Would he—on the *métayer* system—consent to give half of his harvest to the landowner?

But he has nothing. So he will accept any conditions, if only he can keep body and soul together, while he tills the soil and enriches the landlord.

So in the nineteenth century, just as in the Middle Ages, the poverty of the peasant is a source of wealth to the landed proprietor.

II

The landlord owes his riches to the poverty of the peasants, and the wealth of the capitalist comes from the same source.

Take the case of a citizen of the middle class, who somehow or other finds himself in possession of £20,000. He could, of course, spend his money at the rate of £2,000 a year, a mere bagatelle in these days of fantastic, senseless luxury. But then he would have nothing left at the end of ten years. So, being a "practical person," he prefers to keep his fortune intact, and win for himself a snug little annual income as well.

This is very easy in our society, for the good reason that the towns and villages swarm with workers who have not the wherewithal to live for a month, or even a fortnight. So our worthy citizen starts a factory. The banks hasten to lend him another £20,000, especially if he has a reputation for "business ability"; and with this round sum he can command the labour of five hundred hands.

If all the men and women in the countryside had their daily bread assured, and their daily needs already satisfied, who would work for our capitalist at a wage of half a crown a day, while the commodities one produces in a day sell in the market for a crown or more?

Unhappily—we know it all too well—the poor quarters of our towns and the neighbouring villages are full of needy wretches, whose children clamour for bread. So, before the factory is well finished, the workers hasten to offer themselves. Where a hundred are required three hundred besiege the doors, and from the time his mill is started, the owner, if he only has average business capacities, will clear £40 a year out of each mill-hand he employs.

He is thus able to lay by a snug little fortune; and if he chooses a lucrative trade, and has "business talents," he will soon increase his income by doubling the number of men he exploits.

So he becomes a personage of importance. He can afford to give dinners to other personages—to the local magnates, the civic, legal, and political dignitaries. With his money he can "marry money"; by and by he may pick and choose places for his children, and later on perhaps get something good from the Government—a contract for the army or for the police. His gold breeds gold; till at last a war, or even a rumour of war, or a speculation on the Stock Exchange, gives him his great opportunity.

Nine-tenths of the great fortunes made in the United States are (as Henry George has shown in his "Social Problems") the result of knavery on a large scale, assisted by the State. In Europe, nine-tenths of the fortunes made in our monarchies and republics have the same origin. There are not two ways of becoming a millionaire.

This is the secret of wealth: find the starving and destitute, pay them half a crown, and make them produce five shillings worth in the day, amass a fortune by these means, and then increase it by some lucky speculation, made with the help of the State.

Need we go on to speak of small fortunes attributed by the economists to forethought and frugality, when we know that mere saving in itself brings in nothing, so long as the pence saved are not used to exploit the famishing?

Take a shoemaker, for instance. Grant that his work is well paid, that he has plenty of custom, and that by dint of strict frugality he contrives to lay by from eighteen pence to two shillings a day, perhaps two pounds a month.

Grant that our shoemaker is never ill, that he does not half starve himself, in spite of his passion for economy; that he does not marry or that he has no children; that he does not die of consumption; suppose anything and everything you please!

Well, at the age of fifty he will not have scraped together £800; and he will not have enough to live on during his old age, when he is past work. Assuredly this is not how fortunes are made. But suppose our shoemaker, as soon as he has laid by a few pence, thriftily conveys them to the savings bank and that the savings bank lends them to the capitalist who is just about to "employ labour," i.e., to exploit the poor. Then our shoemaker takes an apprentice, the child of some poor wretch, who will think himself lucky if in five years' time his son has learned the trade and is able to earn his living.

Meanwhile our shoemaker does not lose by him, and if trade is brisk he soon takes a second, and then a third apprentice. By and by he will take two or three working men—poor wretches, thankful to receive half a crown a day for work that is worth five shillings, and if our shoemaker is "in luck," that is to say, if he is keen enough and mean enough, his working men and apprentices will bring him in nearly one pound a day, over and above the product of his own toil. He can then enlarge his business. He will gradually become rich, and no longer have any need to stint himself in the necessaries of life. He will leave a snug little fortune to his son.

That is what people call "being economical and having frugal, temperate habits." At bottom it is nothing more nor less than grinding the face of the poor.

Commerce seems an exception to this rule. "Such a man," we are told, "buys tea in China, brings it to France, and realizes a profit of thirty per cent. on his original outlay. He has exploited nobody."

Nevertheless the case is quite similar. If our merchant had carried his bales on his back, well and good! In early medieval times that was exactly how foreign trade was conducted, and so no one reached such giddy heights of fortune as in our days. Very few and very hardly earned were the gold coins which the medieval merchant gained from a long and dangerous voyage. It was less the love of money than the thirst of travel and adventure that inspired his undertakings.

Nowadays the method is simpler. A merchant who has some capital need not stir from his desk to become wealthy. He telegraphs to an agent telling him to buy a hundred tons of tea; he freights a ship, and in a few weeks, in three months if it is a sailing ship, the vessels brings him his cargo. He does not even take the risks of the voyage, for his tea and his vessel are insured, and if he has expended four thousand pounds he will receive more than five or six thousand; that is to say, if he has not attempted to speculate in some novel commodities, in which case he runs a chance of either doubling his fortune or losing it altogether.

Now, how could he find men willing to cross the sea, to travel to China and back, to endure hardship and slavish toil and to risk their lives for a miserable pittance? How could he find dock labourers willing to load and unload his ships for "starvation wages"? How? Because they are needy and starving. Go to the seaports, visit the cook-shops and taverns on the quays, and look at these men who have come to hire themselves, crowding round the dock-gates, which they besiege from early dawn, hoping to be allowed to work on the vessels. Look at these sailors, happy to be hired for a long voyage, after weeks and months of waiting. All their lives long they have gone to the sea in ships, and they will sail in others still, until they have perished in the waves.

Enter their homes, look at their wives and children in rags, living one knows not how till the father's return, and you will have the answer to the question.

Multiply examples, choose them where you will, consider the origin of all fortunes, large or small, whether arising out of commerce, finance, manufacturers, or the land. Everywhere you will find that the wealth of the wealthy springs from the poverty of the poor. This is why an anarchist society need not fear the advent of a Rothschild who would settle in its midst. If every member of the community knows that after a few hours of productive toil he will have a right to all the pleasures that civilization procures, and to those deeper sources of enjoyment which art and science offer to all who seek them, he will not sell his strength for a starvation wage. No one will volunteer to work for the enrichment of your Rothschild. His golden guineas will be only so many pieces of metal—useful for various purposes, but incapable of breeding more.

In answering the above objection we have at the same time indicated the scope of Expropriation. It must apply to everything that enables any man—be he financier, mill-owner, or landlord—to appropriate the product of others' toil. Our formula is simple and comprehensive.

We do not want to rob any one of his coat, but we wish to give to the workers all those things the lack of which makes them fall an easy prey to the exploiter, and we will do our utmost that none shall lack aught, that not a single man shall be forced to sell the strength of his right arm to obtain a bare subsistence for himself and his babes. This is what we mean when we talk of Expropriation; this will be our duty during the Revolution, for whose coming we look, not two hundred years hence, but soon, very soon.

III

The ideas of Anarchism in general and of Expropriation in particular find much more sympathy than we are apt to imagine among men of independent character, and those for whom idleness is not the supreme ideal. "Still," our friends often warn us, "take care you do not go too far! Humanity cannot be changed in a day, so do not be in to great a hurry with your schemes of Expropriation and Anarchy, or you will be in danger of achieving no permanent result."

Now, what we fear with regard to Expropriation is exactly the contrary. We are afraid of not going far enough, of carrying out Expropriation on too small a scale to be lasting. We would not have the revolutionary impulse arrested in mid-career, to exhaust itself in half measures, which would content no one, and while producing a tremendous confusion in society, and stopping its customary activities, would have no vital power—would merely spread general discontent and inevitably prepare the way for the triumph of reaction.

There are, in fact, in a modern State established relations which it is practically impossible to modify if one attacks them only in detail. There are wheels within wheels in our economic organization—the machinery is so complex and interdependent that no one part can be modified without disturbing the whole. This becomes clear as soon as an attempt is made to expropriate anything.

Let us suppose that in a certain country a limited form of expropriation is effected. For example, that, as it has been suggested more than once, only the property of the great landlords is socialized, whilst the factories are left untouched; or that, in a certain city, house property is taken over by the Commune, but everything else is left to private ownership; or that, in some manufacturing centre, the factories are communalized, but the land is not interfered with.

The same result would follow in each case—a terrible shattering of the industrial system, without the means of reorganizing it on new lines. Industry and finance would be at a deadlock, yet a return to the first principles of justice would not have been achieved, and society would find itself powerless to construct a harmonious whole.

If agriculture were freed from great landowners, while industry still remained the bond-slave of the capitalist, the merchant, and the banker, nothing would be accomplished. The peasant suffers to-day not only in having to pay rent to the landlord; he is oppressed on all hands by existing conditions. He is exploited by the tradesman, who makes him pay half a crown for a spade which, measured by the labour spent on it, is not worth more than sixpence. He is taxed by the State, which cannot do without its formidable hierarchy of officials, and finds it necessary to maintain an expensive army, because the traders of all nations are perpetually fighting for the markets, and any day a little quarrel arising from the exploitation of some part of Asia or Africa may result in war.

Then again the peasant suffers from the depopulation of country places: the young people are attracted to the large manufacturing towns by the bait of high wages paid temporarily by the producers of articles of luxury, or by the attractions of a more stirring life. The artificial protection of industry, the industrial exploitation of foreign countries, the prevalence of stock-jobbing, the difficulty of improving the soil and the machinery of production—all these agencies combine nowadays to work against agriculture, which is burdened not only by rent, but by the whole complex of conditions in a society based on exploitation. Thus, even if the expropriation of land were accomplished, and every one were free to till the soil and cultivate it to the best advantage, without paying rent, agriculture, even though it should enjoy—which can by no means be taken for granted—a momentary prosperity, would soon fall back into the slough in which it finds itself to-day. The whole thing would have to be begun over again, with increased difficulties.

The same holds true of industry. Take the converse case: instead of turning the agricultural labourers into peasant-proprietors, make over the factories to those who work in them. Abolish the master-manufacturers, but leave the landlord his land, the banker his money, the merchant his Exchange; maintain the swarm of idlers who live on the toil of the workmen, the thousand and one middlemen, the State with its numberless officials,—and industry would come to a standstill. Finding no purchasers in the mass of peasants who would remain poor; not possessing the raw material, and unable to export their produce, partly on account of the stoppage of trade, and still more so because industries spread all over the world, the manufacturers would feel unable to struggle, and thousands of workers would be thrown upon the streets. These starving crowds would be ready and willing to submit to the first schemer who came to exploit them; they would even consent to return to the old slavery, under promise of guaranteed work.

Or, finally, suppose you oust the landowners, and hand over the mills and factories to the worker, without interfering with the swarm of middlemen who drain the product of our manufacturers, and speculate in corn and flour, meat and groceries, in our great centres of commerce. Then, as soon as the exchange of produce is slackened; as soon as the great cities are left without bread, while the great manufacturing centres find no buyers for the articles of luxury they produce,—the counter-revolution is bound to take place, and it would come, treading upon the slain, sweeping the towns and villages with shot and shell; indulging in orgies of proscriptions and deportations, such as were seen in France in 1815, 1848, and 1871.

All is interdependent in a civilized society; it is impossible to reform any one thing without altering the whole. Therefore, on the day a nation will strike at private property, under any one of its forms, territorial or industrial, it will be obliged to attack them all. The very success of the Revolution will impose it.

Besides, even if it were desired, it would be impossible to confine the change to a partial expropriation. Once the principle of the "Divine Right of Property" is shaken, no amount of theorizing will prevent its overthrow, here by the slaves of the field, there by the slaves of the machine.

If a great town, Paris for example, were to confine itself to taking possession of the dwelling houses of the factories, it would be forced also to deny the right of the bankers to levy upon the Commune a tax amounting to £2,000,000, in the form of interest for former loans. The great city would be obliged to put itself in touch with the rural districts, and its influence would inevitably urge the peasants to free themselves from the landowner. It would be necessary to communalize the railways, that the citizens might get food and work, and lastly, to prevent the waste of supplies; and to guard against the trusts of corn-speculators, like those to whom the Paris Commune of 1793 fell a prey, it would have to place in the hands of the City the work of stocking its warehouses with commodities, and apportioning the produce.

Some Socialists still seek, however, to establish a distinction. "Of course," they say, "the soil, the mines, the mills, and manufacturers must be expropriated, these are the instruments of production, and it is right we should consider them public property. But articles of consumption—food, clothes, and dwellings—should remain private property."

Popular common sense has got the better of this subtle distinction. We are not savages who can live in the woods, without other shelter than the branches. The civilized man needs a roof, a room, a hearth, and a bed. It is true that the bed, the room, and the house is a home of idleness for the non-producer. But for the worker, a room, properly heated and lighted, is as much an instrument of production as the tool or the machine. It is the place where the nerves and sinews gather strength for the work of the morrow. The rest of the workman is the daily repairing of the machine.

The same argument applies even more obviously to food. The so-called economists, who make the just-mentioned distinction, would hardly deny that the coal burnt in a machine is as necessary to production as the raw material itself. How then can food, without which the human machine could do no work, be excluded from the list of things indispensable to the producer? Can this be a relic of religious metaphysics? The rich man's feast is indeed a matter of luxury, but the food of the worker is just as much a part of production as the fuel burnt by the steam-engine.

The same with clothing. We are not New Guinea savages. And if the dainty gowns of our ladies must rank as objects of luxury, there is nevertheless a certain quantity of linen, cotton, and woolen stuff which is a necessity of life to the producer. The shirt and trousers in which he goes to his work, the jacket he slips on after the day's toil is over, are as necessary to him as the hammer to the anvil.

Whether we like it or not, this is what the people mean by a revolution. As soon as they have made a clean sweep of the Government, they will seek first of all to ensure to themselves decent dwellings and sufficient food and clothes—free of capitalist rent.

And the people will be right. The methods of the people will be much more in accordance with science than those of the economists who draw so many distinctions between instruments of production and articles of consumption. The people understand that this is just the point where the Revolution ought to begin; and they will lay the foundations of the only economic science worthy the name—a science which might be called: "*The Study of the Needs of Humanity, and of the Economic Means to satisfy them.*"

FOOTNOTE:

[2] "Shabble of a Duke" is an expression coined by Carlyle; it is a somewhat free rendering of Kropotkine's "Monsieur le Vicomte," but I think it expresses his meaning.—*Trans.*

CHAPTER V
FOOD

I

If the coming Revolution is to be a Social Revolution, it will be distinguished from all former uprisings not only by its aim, but also by its methods. To attain a new end, new means are required.

The three great popular movements which we have seen in France during the last hundred years differ from each other in many ways, but they have one common feature.

In each case the people strove to overturn the old regime, and spent their heart's blood for the cause. Then, after having borne the brunt of the battle, they sank again into obscurity. A Government, composed of men more or less honest, was formed and undertook to organize a new regime: the Republic in 1793, Labour in 1848, the Free Commune in 1871. Imbued with Jacobin ideas, this Government occupied itself first of all with political questions, such as the reorganization of the machinery of government, the purifying of the administration, the separation of Church and State, civic liberty, and such matters. It is true the workmen's clubs kept an eye on the members of the new Government, and often imposed their ideas on them. But even in these clubs, whether the leaders belonged to the middle or the working classes, it was always middle-class ideas which prevailed. They discussed various political questions at great length, but forgot to discuss the question of bread.

Great ideas sprang up at such times, ideas that have moved the world; words were spoken which still stir our hearts, at the interval of more than a century. But the people were starving in the slums.

From the very Commencement of the Revolution industry inevitably came to a stop—the circulation of produce was checked, and capital concealed itself. The master—the employer—had nothing to fear at such times, he fattened on his dividends, if indeed he did not speculate on the wretchedness around; but the wage-earner was reduced to live from hand to mouth. Want knocked at the door.

Famine was abroad in the land—such famine as had hardly been seen under the old regime.

"The Girondists are starving us!" was the cry in the workmen's quarters in 1793, and thereupon the Girondists were guillotined, and full powers were given to "the Mountain" and to the Commune. The Commune indeed concerned itself with the question of bread, and made heroic efforts to feed Paris. At Lyons, Fouché and Collot d'Herbois established city granaries, but the sums spent on filling them were woefully insufficient. The town councils made great efforts to procure corn; the bakers who hoarded flour were hanged—and still the people lacked bread.

Then they turned on the royalist conspirators and laid the blame at their door. They guillotined a dozen or fifteen a day—servants and duchesses alike, especially servants, for the duchesses had gone to Coblentz. But if they had guillotined a hundred dukes and viscounts every day, it would have been equally hopeless.

The want only grew. For the wage-earner cannot live without his wage, and the wage was not forthcoming. What difference could a thousand corpses more or less make to him?

Then the people began to grow weary. "So much for your vaunted Revolution! You are more wretched than ever before," whispered the reactionary in the ears of the worker. And little by little the rich took courage, emerged from their hiding-places, and flaunted their luxury in the face of the starving multitude. They dressed up like scented fops and said to the workers: "Come, enough of this foolery! What have you gained by your Revolution?"

And, sick at heart, his patience at an end, the revolutionary had at last to admit to himself that the cause was lost once more. He retreated into his hovel and awaited the worst.

Then reaction proudly asserted itself, and accomplished a counter-revolutionary stroke. The Revolution dead, nothing remained but to trample its corpse under foot.

The White Terror began. Blood flowed like water, the guillotine was never idle, the prisons were crowded, while the pageant of rank and fashion resumed its old course, and went on as merrily as before.

This picture is typical of all our revolutions. In 1848 the workers of Paris placed "three months of starvation" at the service of the Republic, and then, having reached the limit of their powers, they made, in June, one last desperate effort—an effort which was drowned in blood. In 1871 the Commune perished for lack of combatants. It had taken measures for the separation of Church and State, but it neglected, alas, until too late, to take measures for providing the people with bread. And so it came to pass in Paris that *élégantes* and fine gentlemen could spurn the confederates, and bid them go sell their lives for a miserable pittance, and leave their "betters" to feast at their ease in fashionable restaurants.

At last the Commune saw its mistake, and opened communal kitchens. But it was too late. Its days were already numbered, and the troops of Versailles were on the ramparts.

"Bread, it is bread that the Revolution needs!"

Let others spend their time in issuing pompous proclamations, in decorating themselves lavishly with official gold lace, and in talking about political liberty!...

Be it ours to see, from the first day of the Revolution to the last, in all the provinces fighting for freedom, that there is not a single man who lacks bread, not a single woman compelled to stand with the wearied crowd outside the bakehouse-door, that haply a coarse loaf may be thrown to her in charity, not a single child pining for want of food.

It has always been the middle-class idea to harangue about "great principles"—great lies rather!

The idea of the people will be to provide bread for all. And while middle-class citizens, and workmen infested with middle-class ideas admire their own rhetoric in the "Talking Shops," and "practical people" are engaged in endless discussions on forms of government, we, the "Utopian dreamers"—we shall have to consider the question of daily bread.

We have the temerity to declare that all have a right to bread, that there is bread enough for all, and that with this watchword of *Bread for All* the Revolution will triumph.

II

That we are Utopians is well known. So Utopian are we that we go the length of believing that the Revolution can and ought to assure shelter, food, and clothes to all—an idea extremely displeasing to middle-class citizens, whatever their party colour, for they are quite alive to the fact that it is not easy to keep the upper hand of a people whose hunger is satisfied.

All the same, we maintain our contention: bread must be found for the people of the Revolution, and the question of bread must take precedence of all other questions. If it is settled in the interests of the people, the Revolution will be on the right road; for in solving the question of Bread we must accept the principle of equality, which will force itself upon us to the exclusion of every other solution.

It is certain that the coming Revolution—like in that respect to the Revolution of 1848—will burst upon us in the middle of a great industrial crisis. Things have been seething for half a century now, and can only go from bad to worse. Everything tends that way—new nations entering the lists of international trade and fighting for possession of the world's markets, wars, taxes ever increasing. National debts, the insecurity of the morrow, and huge colonial undertakings in every corner of the globe.

There are millions of unemployed workers in Europe at this moment. It will be still worse when Revolution has burst upon us and spread like fire laid to a train of gunpowder. The number of the out-of-works will be doubled as soon as the barricades are erected in Europe and the United States. What is to be done to provide these multitudes with bread?

We do not know whether the folk who call themselves "practical people" have ever asked themselves this question in all its nakedness. But we do know that they wish to maintain the wage system, and we must therefore expect to have "national workshops" and "public works" vaunted as a means of giving food to the unemployed.

Because national workshops were opened in 1789 and 1793; because the same means were resorted to in 1848; because

Napoleon III. succeeded in contenting the Parisian proletariat for eighteen years by giving them public works—which cost Paris to-day its debt of £80,000,000 and its municipal tax of three or four pounds a-head;[3] because this excellent method of "taming the beast" was customary in Rome, and even in Egypt four thousand years ago; and lastly, because despots, kings, and emperors have always employed the ruse of throwing a scrap of food to the people to gain time to snatch up the whip—it is natural that "practical" men should extol this method of perpetuating the wage system. What need to rack our brains when we have the time-honoured method of the Pharaohs at our disposal?

Yet should the Revolution be so misguided as to start on this path, it would be lost.

In 1848, when the national workshops were opened on February 27, the unemployed of Paris numbered only 8,000; a fortnight later they had already increased to 49,000. They would soon have been 100,000, without counting those who crowded in from the provinces.

Yet at that time trade and manufacturers in France employed half as many hands as to-day. And we know that in time of Revolution exchange and industry suffer most from the general upheaval. We have only to think, indeed, of the number of workmen whose labour depends directly or indirectly upon export trade, or of the number of hands employed in producing luxuries, whose consumers are the middle-class minority.

A revolution in Europe means, then, the unavoidable stoppage of at least half the factories and workshops. It means millions of workers and their families thrown on the streets. And our "practical men" would seek to avert this truly terrible situation by means of national relief works; that is to say, by means of new industries created on the spot to give work to the unemployed!

It is evident, as Proudhon had already pointed out more than fifty years ago, that the smallest attack upon property will bring in its train the complete disorganization of the system based upon private enterprise and wage labour. Society itself will be forced to take production in hand, in its entirety, and to reorganize it to meet the needs of the whole people. But this cannot be accomplished in a day, or even in a month; it must take a certain time to reorganize the system of production, and during this time millions of men will be deprived of the means of subsistence. What then is to be done?

There is only one really *practical* solution of the problem—boldly to face the great task which awaits us, and instead of trying to patch up a situation which we ourselves have made untenable, to proceed to reorganize production on a new basis.

Thus the really practical course of action, in our view, would be that the people should take immediate possession of all the food of the insurgent communes, keeping strict account of it all, that none might be wasted, and that by the aid of these accumulated resources every one might be able to tide over the crisis. During that time an agreement would have to be made with the factory workers, the necessary raw material given them, and the means of subsistence assured to them, while they worked to supply the needs of the agricultural population. For we must not forget that while France weaves silks and satins to deck the wives of German financiers, the Empress of Russia, and the Queen of the Sandwich Islands, and while Paris fashions wonderful trinkets and playthings for rich folk all the world over, two-thirds of the French peasantry have not proper lamps to give them light, or the implements necessary for modern agriculture. Lastly, unproductive land, of which there is plenty, would have to be turned to the best advantage, poor soils enriched, and rich soils, which yet, under the present system, do not yield a quarter, no, nor a tenth of what they might produce, would be submitted to intensive culture, and tilled with as much care as a market garden or a flower pot. It is impossible to imagine any other practical solution of the problem; and, whether we like it or not, sheer force of circumstances will bring it to pass.

III

The most prominent characteristic of our present capitalism is *the wage system*, which in brief amounts to this:—

A man, or a group of men, possessing the necessary capital, starts some industrial enterprise; he undertakes to supply the factory or workshops with raw material, to organize production, to pay the employes a fixed wage, and lastly, to pocket the surplus value or profits, under pretext of recouping himself for managing the concern, for running the risks it may involve, and for the fluctuations of price in the market value of the wares.

To preserve this system, those who now monopolize capital would be ready to make certain concessions; to share, for example, a part of the profits with the workers, or rather to establish a "sliding scale," which would oblige them to raise wages when prices were high; in brief they would consent to certain sacrifices on condition that they were still allowed to direct industry and to take its first fruits.

Collectivism, as we know, does not abolish the wage system, though it introduces considerable modifications into the existing order of things. It only substitutes the State, that is to say, some form of Representative Government, national or local, for the individual employer of labour. Under Collectivism it is the representatives of the nation, or of the Commune, and their deputies and officials who are to have the control of industry. It is they who reserve to themselves the right of employing the surplus of production—in the interests of all. Moreover, Collectivism draws a very subtle but very far-reaching distinction between the work of the labourer and of the man who has learned a craft. Unskilled labour in the eyes of the collectivist is *simple* labour, while the work of the craftsman, the mechanic, the engineer, the man of science, etc., is what Marx calls *complex* labour, and is entitled to a higher wage. But labourers and craftsmen, weavers and men of science, are all wage-servants of the State—"all officials," as was said lately, to gild the pill.

Well, then, the coming Revolution could render no greater service to humanity than by making the wage system, in all its forms, an impossibility, and by rendering Communism, which is the negation of wage-slavery, the only possible solution.

For even admitting that the Collectivist modification of the present system is possible, if introduced gradually during a period of prosperity and peace—though for my part I question its practicability even under such conditions—it would become impossible in a period of Revolution, when the need of feeding hungry millions would spring up with the first call to arms. A political revolution can be accomplished without shaking the foundations of industry, but a revolution where the people lay hands upon property will inevitably paralyse exchange and production. The millions of public money flowing into the Treasury would not suffice for paying wages to the millions of out-of-works.

This point cannot be too much insisted upon; the reorganization of industry on a new basis (and we shall presently show how tremendous this problem is) cannot be accomplished in a few days; nor, on the other hand, will the people submit to be half starved for years in order to oblige the theorists who uphold the wage system. To tide over the period of stress they will demand what they have always demanded in such cases—communization of supplies—the giving of rations.

It will be in vain to preach patience. The people will be patient no longer, and if food is not forthcoming they will plunder the bakeries.

Then, if the people are not strong enough to carry all before them, they will be shot down, to give Collectivism a fair field for experiment. To this end "*order*" must be maintained at any price—order, discipline, obedience! And as the capitalists will soon realize that when the people are shot down by those who call themselves Revolutionists, the Revolution itself will become hateful in the eyes of the masses, they will certainly lend their support to the champions of *order*—even though they are collectivists. In such a line of conduct, the capitalists will see a means of hereafter crushing the collectivists in their turn. And if "order is established" in this fashion, the consequences are easy to foresee. Not content with shooting down the "marauders," the faction of "order" will search out the "ringleaders of the mob." They will set up again the law courts and reinstate the hangman. The most ardent revolutionists will be sent to the scaffold. It will be 1793 over again.

Do not let us forget how reaction triumphed in the last century. First the "Hébertists" and "the madmen," were guillotined—those whom Mignet, with the memory of the struggle fresh upon him, still called "Anarchists." The Dantonists soon followed them; and when the party of Robespierre had guillotined these revolutionaries, they in their turn had to mount the scaffold; whereupon the people, sick of bloodshed, and seeing the revolution lost, threw up the sponge, and let the reactionaries do their worst.

If "order is restored," we say, the social democrats will hang the anarchists; the Fabians will hang the social democrats, and will in their turn be hanged by the reactionaries; and the Revolution will come to an end.

But everything confirms us in the belief that the energy of the people will carry them far enough, and that, when the Revolution takes place, the idea of anarchist Communism will have gained ground. It is not an artificial idea. The people themselves have breathed it in our ear, and the number of communists is ever increasing, as the impossibility of any other solution becomes more and more evident.

And if the impetus of the people is strong enough, affairs will take a very different turn. Instead of plundering the bakers' shops one day, and starving the next, the people of the insurgent cities will take possession of the warehouses, the cattle markets,—in fact of all the provision stores and of all the food to be had. The well-intentioned citizens, men and women both, will form themselves into bands of volunteers and address themselves to the task of making a rough general inventory of the contents of each shop and warehouse.

If such a revolution breaks out in France, namely in Paris, then in twenty-four hours the Commune will know what Paris has not found out yet, in spite of its statistical committees, and what it never did find out during the siege of 1871—the quantity of provisions it contains. In forty-eight hours millions of copies will be printed of the tables giving a sufficiently exact account of the available food, the places where it is stored, and the means of distribution.

In every block of houses, in every street, in every town ward, groups of volunteers will have been organized, and these commissariat volunteers will find it easy to work in unison and keep in touch with each other. If only the Jacobin bayonets do not get in the way; if only the self-styled "scientific" theorists do not thrust themselves in to darken counsel! Or rather let them expound their muddle-headed theories as much as they like, provided they have no authority, no power! And that admirable spirit of organization inherent in the people, above all in every social grade of the French nation, but which they have so seldom been allowed to exercise, will initiate, even in so huge a city as Paris, and in the midst of a Revolution, an immense guild of free workers, ready to furnish to each and all the necessary food.

Give the people a free hand, and in ten days the food service will be conducted with admirable regularity. Only those who have never seen the people hard at work, only those who have passed their lives buried among the documents, can doubt it. Speak of the organizing genius of the "Great Misunderstood," the people, to those who have seen it in Paris in the days of the barricades, or in London during the great dockers' strike, when half a million of starving folk had to be fed, and they will tell you how superior it is to the official ineptness of Bumbledom.

And even supposing we had to endure a certain amount of discomfort and confusion for a fortnight or a month, surely that would not matter very much. For the mass of the people it would still be an improvement on their former condition; and, besides, in times of Revolution one can dine contentedly enough on a bit of bread and cheese while eagerly discussing events.

In any case, a system which springs up spontaneously, under stress of immediate need, will be infinitely preferable to anything invented between four walls by hide-bound theorists sitting on any number of committees.

IV

The people of the great towns will be driven by force of circumstances to take possession of all the provisions, beginning with the barest necessaries, and gradually extending Communism to other things, in order to satisfy the needs of all the citizens. The sooner it is done the better; the sooner it is done the less misery there will be and the less strife.

But upon what basis must society be organized in order that all may have their due share of food produce? This is the question that meets us at the outset.

We answer that there are no two ways of it. There is only one way in which Communism can be established equitably, only one way which satisfies our instincts of justice and is at the same time practical; namely, the system already adopted by the agrarian communes of Europe.

Take for example a peasant commune, no matter where, even in France, where the Jacobins have done their best to destroy all communal usage. If the commune possesses woods and copses, then, so long as there is plenty of wood for all, every one can take as much as he wants, without other let or hindrance than the public opinion of his neighbours. As to the timber-trees, which are always scarce, they have to be carefully apportioned.

The same with the communal pasture land; while there is enough and to spare, no limit is put to what the cattle of each homestead may consume, nor to the number of beasts grazing upon the pastures. Grazing grounds are not divided, nor is fodder doled out, unless there is scarcity. All the Swiss communes, and scores of thousands in France and Germany, wherever there is communal pasture land, practise this system.

And in the countries of Eastern Europe, where there are great forests and no scarcity of land, you will find the peasants felling the trees as they need them, and cultivating as much of the soil as they require, without any thought of limiting each man's share of timber or of land. But the timber will be allowanced, and the land parcelled out, to each household according to its needs, as soon as either becomes scarce, as is already the case in Russia.

In a word, the system is this: no stint or limit to what the community possesses in abundance, but equal sharing and dividing of those commodities which are scarce or apt to run short. Of the 350 millions who inhabit Europe, 200 millions still follow this system of natural Communism.

It is a fact worth remarking that the same system prevails in the great towns in the distribution of one commodity at least, which is found in abundance, the water supplied to each house.

As long as there is no fear of the supply running short, no water company thinks of checking the consumption of water in each house. Take what you please! But during the great droughts, if there is any fear of the supply failing, the water companies know that all they have to do is to make known the fact, by means of a short advertisement in the papers, and the citizens will reduce their consumption of water and not let it run to waste.

But if water were actually scarce, what would be done? Recourse would be had to a system of rations. Such a measure is so natural, so inherent in common sense, that Paris twice asked to be put on rations during the two sieges which it underwent in 1871.

Is it necessary to go into details, to prepare tables, showing how the distribution of rations may work, to prove that it is just and equitable, infinitely more just and equitable than the existing state of things? All these tables and details will not serve to convince those of the middle classes, nor, alas, those of the workers tainted with middle-class prejudices, who regard the people as a mob of savages ready to fall upon and devour each other, as soon as the Government ceases to direct affairs. But those only who have never seen the people resolve and act on their own initiative could doubt for a moment that if the masses were masters of the situation, they would distribute rations to each and all in strictest accordance with justice and equity.

If you were to give utterance, in any gathering of people, to the opinion that delicacies—game and such-like—should be reserved for the fastidious palates of aristocratic idlers, and black bread given to the sick in the hospitals, you would be hissed. But say at the same gathering, preach at the street corners and in the market places, that the most tempting delicacies ought to be kept for the sick and feeble—especially for the sick. Say that if there are only five brace of partridge in the entire city, and only one case of sherry, they should go to sick people and convalescents. Say that after the sick come the children. For them the milk of the cows and goats should be reserved if there is not enough for all. To the children and the aged the last piece of meat, and to the strong man dry bread, if the community be reduced to that extremity.

Say, in a word, that if this or that article of consumption runs short, and has to be doled out, to those who have most need most should be given. Say that and see if you do not meet with universal agreement.

The man who is full-fed does not understand this, but the people do understand, and have always understood it; and even the child of luxury, if he is thrown on the street and comes into contact with the masses, even he will learn to understand.

The theorists—for whom the soldier's uniform and the barrack mess table are civilization's last word—would like no doubt to start a regime of National Kitchens and "Spartan Broth." They would point out the advantages thereby gained, the economy in fuel and food, if such huge kitchens were established, where every one could come for their rations of soup and bread and vegetables.

We do not question these advantages. We are well aware that important economies have already been achieved in this direction—as, for instance, when the handmill, or quern, and the baker's oven attached to each house were abandoned. We can see perfectly well that it would be more economical to cook broth for a hundred families at once, instead of lighting a hundred separate fires. We know, besides, that there are a thousand ways of preparing potatoes, but that cooked in one huge pot for a hundred families they would be just as good.

We know, in fact, that variety in cooking being a matter of the seasoning introduced by each cook or housewife, the cooking together of a hundredweight of potatoes would not prevent each cook or housewife from dressing and serving them in any way she pleased. And we know that stock made from meat can be converted into a hundred different soups to suit a hundred different tastes.

But though we are quite aware of all these facts, we still maintain that no one has a right to force a housewife to take her potatoes from the communal kitchen ready cooked if she prefers to cook them herself in her own pot on her own fire. And, above all, we should wish each one to be free to take his meals with his family, or with his friends, or even in a restaurant, if it seemed good to him.

Naturally large public kitchens will spring up to take the place of the restaurants, where people are poisoned nowadays. Already the Parisian housewife gets the stock for her soup from the butcher, and transforms it into whatever soup she likes, and London housekeepers know that they can have a joint roasted, or an apple or rhubarb tart baked at the baker's for a trifling sum, thus economizing time and fuel. And when the communal kitchen—the common bakehouse of the future—is established, and people can get their food cooked without the risk of being cheated or poisoned, the custom will no doubt become general of going to the communal kitchen for the fundamental parts of the meal, leaving the last touches to be added as individual taste shall suggest.

But to make a hard and fast rule of this, to make a duty of taking home our food ready cooked, that would be as repugnant to our modern minds as the ideas of the convent or the barrack—morbid ideas born in brains warped by tyranny or superstition.

Who will have a right to the food of the commune? will assuredly be the first question which we shall have to ask ourselves. Every township will answer for itself, and we are convinced that the answers will all be dictated by the sentiment of justice. Until labour is reorganized, as long as the disturbed period lasts, and while it is impossible to distinguish between inveterate idlers and genuine workers thrown out of work, the available food ought to be shared by all without exception. Those who have been enemies to the new order will hasten of their own accord to rid the commune of their presence. But it seems to us that the masses of the people, which have always been magnanimous, and have nothing of vindictiveness in their disposition, will be ready to share their bread with all who remain with them, conquered and conquerers alike. It will be no loss to the Revolution to be inspired by such an idea, and, when work is set agoing again, the antagonists of yesterday will stand side by side in the same workshops. A society where work is free will have nothing to fear from idlers.

"But provisions will run short in a month!" our critics at once exclaim.

"So much the better," say we. It will prove that for the first time on record the people have had enough to eat. As to the question of obtaining fresh supplies, we shall discuss the means in our next chapter.

V

By what means could a city in a state of revolution be supplied with food? We shall answer this question, but it is obvious that the means resorted to will depend on the character of the Revolution in the provinces, and in neighbouring countries. If the entire nation, or, better still, if all Europe should accomplish the Social Revolution simultaneously, and start with thoroughgoing Communism, our procedure would be simplified; but if only a few communities in Europe make the attempt, other means will have to be chosen. The circumstances will dictate the measures.

We are thus led, before we proceed further, to glance at the State of Europe, and, without pretending to prophesy, we may try to foresee what course the Revolution will take, or at least what will be its essential features.

Certainly it would be very desirable that all Europe should rise at once, that expropriation should be general, and that communistic principles should inspire all and sundry. Such a universal rising would do much to simplify the task of our century.

But all the signs lead us to believe that it will not take place. That the Revolution will embrace Europe we do not doubt. If one of the four great continental capitals—Paris, Vienna, Brussels, or Berlin—rises in revolution and overturns its Government, it is almost certain that the three others will follow its example within a few weeks' time. It is, moreover, highly probable that the Peninsulas and even London and St. Petersburg would not be long in following suit. But whether the Revolution would everywhere exhibit the same characteristics is highly doubtful.

It is more than probable that expropriation will be everywhere carried into effect on a larger scale, and that this policy carried out by any one of the great nations of Europe will influence all the rest; yet the beginnings of the Revolution will exhibit great local differences, and its course will vary in different countries. In 1789-93, the French peasantry took four years to finally rid themselves of the redemption of feudal rights, and the bourgeois to overthrow royalty. Let us keep that in mind, and therefore be prepared to see the Revolution develop itself somewhat gradually. Let us not be disheartened if here and there its steps should move less rapidly. Whether it would take an avowedly socialist character in all European nations, at any rate at the beginning, is doubtful. Germany, be it remembered, is still realizing its dream of a United Empire. Its advanced parties see visions of a Jacobin Republic like that of 1848, and of the organization of labour according to Louis Blanc; while the French people, on the other hand, want above all things a free Commune, whether it be a communist Commune or not.

There is every reason to believe that, when the coming Revolution takes place, Germany will go further than France went in 1793. The eighteenth-century Revolution in France was an advance on the English Revolution of the seventeenth, abolishing as it did at one stroke the power of the throne and the landed aristocracy, whose influence still survives in England. But, if Germany goes further and does greater things than France did in 1793, there can be no doubt that the ideas which will foster the birth of her Revolution will be those of 1848; while the ideas which will inspire the Revolution in Russia will probably be a combination of those of 1789 with those of 1848.

Without, however, attaching to these forecasts a greater importance than they merit, we may safely conclude this much: the Revolution will take a different character in each of the different European nations; the point attained in the socialization of wealth will not be everywhere the same.

Will it therefore be necessary, as is sometimes suggested, that the nations in the vanguard of the movement should adapt their pace to those who lag behind? Must we wait till the Communist Revolution is ripe in all civilized countries? Clearly not! Even if it were a thing to be desired, it is not possible. History does not wait for the laggards.

Besides, we do not believe that in any one country the Revolution will be accomplished at a stroke, in the twinkling of an eye, as some socialists dream.[4] It is highly probable that if one of the five or six large towns of France—Paris, Lyons, Marseilles, Lille, Saint-Etienne, Bordeaux—were to proclaim the Commune, the others would follow its example, and that many smaller towns would do the same. Probably also various mining districts and industrial centres would hasten to rid themselves of "owners" and "masters," and form themselves into free groups.

But many country places have not advanced to that point. Side by side with the revolutionized communes such places would remain in an expectant attitude, and would go on living on the Individualist system. Undisturbed by visits of the bailiff or the tax-collector, the peasants would not be hostile to the revolutionaries, and thus, while profiting by the new state of affairs, they would defer the settlement of accounts with the local exploiters. But with that practical enthusiasm which always characterizes agrarian uprisings (witness the passionate toil of 1792) they would throw themselves into the task of cultivating the land, which, freed from taxes and mortgages, would become so much dearer to them.

As to other countries, revolution would break out everywhere, but revolution under divers aspects; in one country State Socialism, in another Federation; everywhere more or less Socialism, not conforming to any particular rule.

VI

Let us now return to our city in revolt, and consider how its citizens can provide foodstuffs for themselves. How are the necessary provisions to be obtained if the nation as a whole has not accepted Communism? This is the question to be solved. Take, for example, one of the large French towns—take the capital itself, for that matter. Paris consumes every year thousands of tons of grain, 400,000 head of oxen, 300,000 calves, 400,000 swine, and more than two millions of sheep, besides great quantities of game. This huge city devours, besides, more than 20 million pounds of butter, 200 million eggs, and other produce in like proportion.

It imports flour and grain from the United States and from Russia, Hungary, Italy, Egypt, and the Indies; live stock from Germany, Italy, Spain—even Roumania and Russia; and as for groceries, there is not a country in the world that it does not lay under contribution.

Now, let us see how Paris or any other great town could be revictualled by home-grown produce, supplies of which could be readily and willingly sent in from the provinces.

To those who put their trust in "authority" the question will appear quite simple. They would begin by establishing a strongly centralized Government, furnished with all the machinery of coercion—the police, the army, the guillotine. This Government would draw up a statement of all the produce contained in France. It would divide the country into districts of supply, and then *command* that a prescribed quantity of some particular foodstuff be sent to such a place on such a day, and delivered at such a station, to be there received on a given day by a specified official and stored in particular warehouses.

Now, we declare with the fullest conviction, not merely that such a solution is undesirable, but that it never could by any possibility be put into practice. It is wildly Utopian!

Pen in hand, one may dream such a dream in the study, but in contact with reality it comes to nothing,—this was proved in 1793; for, like all such theories, it leaves out of account the spirit of independence that is in man. The attempt would lead to a universal uprising, to three or four *Vendées*, to the villages rising against the towns, all the country up in arms defying the city for its arrogance in attempting to impose such a system upon the country.

We have already had too much of Jacobin Utopias! Let us see if some other form of organization will meet the case.

During the great French Revolution, the provinces starved the large towns, and killed the Revolution. And yet it is a known fact that the production of grain in France during 1792-3 had not diminished; indeed, the evidence goes to show that it had increased. But after having taken possession of the manorial lands, after having reaped a harvest from them, the peasants would not part with their grain for paper-money. They withheld their produce, waiting for a rise in the price, or the introduction of gold. The most rigorous measures of the National Convention were without avail, and her executions failed to break up the ring, or force the farmers to sell their corn. For it is a matter of history that the commissaries of the Convention did not scruple to guillotine those who withheld their grain from the market, and pitilessly executed those who speculated in foodstuffs. All the same, the corn was not forthcoming, and the townsfolk suffered from famine.

But what was offered to the husbandman in exchange for his hard toil? *Assignats*, scraps of paper decreasing in value every day, promises of payment, which could not be kept. A forty-pound note would not purchase a pair of boots, and the peasant, very naturally, was not anxious to barter a year's toil for a piece of paper with which he could not even buy a shirt.

As long as worthless paper-money—whether called assignats or labour notes—is offered to the peasant-producer it will always be the same. The country will withhold its produce, and the towns will suffer want, even if the recalcitrant peasants are guillotined as before.

We must offer to the peasant in exchange for his toil not worthless paper-money, but the manufactured articles of which he stands in immediate need. He lacks the proper implements to till the land, clothes to protect him from the inclemencies of the weather, lamps and oil to replace his miserable rushlight or tallow dip, spades, rakes, ploughs. All these things, under present conditions, the peasant is forced to do without, not because he does not feel the need of them, but because, in his life of struggle and privation, a thousand useful things are beyond his reach; because he has not money to buy them.

Let the town apply itself, without loss of time, to manufacturing all that the peasant needs, instead of fashioning geegaws for the wives of rich citizens. Let the sewing machines of Paris be set to work on clothes for the country folk workaday clothes and clothes for Sunday too, instead of costly evening dresses for the English and Russian landlords and the African gold-magnates' wives. Let the factories and foundries turn out agricultural implements, spades, rakes, and such-like, instead of waiting till the English send them to France, in exchange for French wines!

Let the towns send no more inspectors to the villages, wearing red, blue, or rainbow-coloured scarves, to convey to the peasant orders to take his produce to this place or that, but let them send friendly embassies to the countryfolk and bid them in brotherly fashion: "Bring us your produce, and take from our stores and shops all the manufactured articles you please."—Then provisions would pour in on every side. The peasant would only withhold what he needed for his own use, and would send the rest into the cities, feeling *for the first time in the course of history* that these toiling townsfolk were his comrades—his brethren, and not his exploiters.

We shall be told, perhaps, that this would necessitate a complete transformation of industry. Well, yes, that is true of certain departments; but there are other branches which could be rapidly modified in such a way as to furnish the peasant with clothes, watches, furniture, and the simple implements for which the towns make him pay such exorbitant prices at the present time. Weavers, tailors, shoemakers, tinsmiths, cabinet-makers, and many other trades and crafts could easily direct their energies to the manufacture of useful and necessary articles, and abstain from producing mere luxuries. All that is needed is that the public mind should be thoroughly convinced of the necessity of this transformation, and should come to look upon it as an act of justice and of progress, and that it should no longer allow itself to be cheated by that dream, so dear to the theorists—the dream of a revolution which confines itself to taking possession of the profits of industry, and leaves production and commerce just as they are now.

This, then, is our view of the whole question. Cheat the peasant no longer with scraps of paper—be the sums inscribed upon them ever so large; but offer him in exchange for his produce the very *things* of which he, the tiller of the soil, stands in need. Then the fruits of the land will be poured into the towns. If this is not done there will be famine in our cities, and reaction and despair will follow in its train.

VII

All the great towns, we have said, buy their grain, their flour, and their meat, not only from the provinces, but also from abroad. Foreign countries send Paris not only spices, fish, and various dainties, but also immense quantities of corn and meat.

But when the Revolution comes these cities will have to depend on foreign countries as little as possible. If Russian wheat, Italian or Indian rice, and Spanish or Hungarian wines abound in the markets of western Europe, it is not that the countries which export them have a superabundance, or that such a produce grows there of itself, like the dandelion in the meadows. In Russia for instance, the peasant works sixteen hours a day, and half starves from three to six months every year, in order to export the grain with which he pays the landlord and the State. To-day the police appears in the Russian village as soon as the harvest is gathered in, and sells the peasant's last horse and last cow for arrears of taxes and rent due to the landlord, unless the victim immolates himself of his own accord by selling the grain to the exporters. Usually, rather than part with his livestock at a disadvantage, he keeps only a nine-months' supply of grain, and sells the rest. Then, in order to sustain life until the next harvest, he mixes birch-bark and tares with his flour for three months, if it has been a good year, and for six months if it has been bad, while in London they are eating biscuits made of his wheat.

But as soon as the Revolution comes, the Russian peasant will keep bread enough for himself and his children; the Italian and Hungarian peasants will do the same; the Hindoo, let us hope, will profit by these good examples; and the farmers of America will hardly be able to cover all the deficit in grain which Europe will experience. So it will not do to count on their contributions of wheat and maize satisfying all the wants.

Since all our middle-class civilization is based on the exploitation of inferior races and countries with less advanced industrial systems, the Revolution will confer a boon at the very outset, by menacing that "civilization," and allowing the so-called inferior races to free themselves.

But this great benefit will manifest itself by a steady and marked diminution of the food supplies pouring into the great cities of western Europe.

It is difficult to predict the course of affairs in the provinces. On the one hand the slave of the soil will take advantage of the Revolution to straighten his bowed back. Instead of working fourteen or fifteen hours a day, as he does at present, he will be at liberty to work only half that time, which of course would have the effect of decreasing the production of the principal articles of consumption—grain and meat.

But, on the other hand, there will be an increase of production as soon as the peasant realizes that he is no longer forced to support the idle rich by his toil. New tracts of land will be cleared, new and improved machines set a-going.

"Never was the land so energetically cultivated as in 1792, when the peasant had taken back from the landlord the soil which he had coveted so long," Michelet tells us speaking of the Great Revolution.

Of course, before long, intensive culture would be within the reach of all. Improved machinery, chemical manures, and all such matters would soon be supplied by the Commune. But everything tends to indicate that at the outset there would be a falling off in agricultural products, in France and elsewhere.

In any case it would be wisest to count upon such a falling off of contributions from the provinces as well as from abroad.—How is this falling off to be made good?

Why! by setting to work ourselves! No need to rack our brains for far-fetched panaceas when the remedy lies close at hand.

The large towns, as well as the villages, must undertake to till the soil. We must return to what biology calls "the integration of functions"—after the division of labour, the taking up of it as a whole—this is the course followed throughout Nature.

Besides, philosophy apart, the force of circumstances would bring about this result. Let Paris see that at the end of eight months it will be running short of bread, and Paris will set to work to grow wheat.

Land will not be wanting, for it is round the great towns, and round Paris especially, that the parks and pleasure grounds of the landed gentry are to be found. These thousands of acres only await the skilled labour of the husbandman to surround Paris with fields infinitely more fertile and productive than the steppes of southern Russia, where the soil is dried up by the sun. Nor will labour be lacking. To what should the two million citizens of Paris turn their attention, when they would be no longer catering for the luxurious fads and amusements of Russian princes, Roumanian grandees, and wives of Berlin financiers?

With all the mechanical inventions of the century; with all the intelligence and technical skill of the worker accustomed to deal with complicated machinery; with inventors, chemists, professors of botany, practical botanists like the market gardeners of Gennevilliers; with all the plant that they could use for multiplying and improving machinery; and, finally, with the organizing spirit of the Parisian people, their pluck and energy—with all these at its command, the agriculture of the anarchist Commune of Paris would be a very different thing from the rude husbandry of the Ardennes.

Steam, electricity, the heat of the sun, and the breath of the wind, will ere long be pressed into service. The steam plough and the steam harrow will quickly do the rough work of preparation, and the soil, thus cleaned and enriched, will only need the intelligent care of man, and of woman even more than man, to be clothed with luxuriant vegetation—not once but three or four times in the year.

Thus, learning the art of horticulture from experts, and trying experiments in different methods on small patches of soil reserved for the purpose, vying with each other to obtain the best returns, finding in physical exercise, without exhaustion or overwork, the health and strength which so often flags in cities,—men, women and children will gladly turn to the labour of the fields, when it is no longer a slavish drudgery, but has become a pleasure, a festival, a renewal of health and joy.

"There are no barren lands; the earth is worth what man is worth"—that is the last word of modern agriculture. Ask of the earth, and she will give you bread, provided that you ask aright.

A district, though it were as small as the two departments of the Seine and the Seine-et-Oise, and with so great a city as Paris to feed, would be practically sufficient to grow upon it all the food supplies, which otherwise might fail to reach it.

The combination of agriculture and industry, the husbandman and the mechanic in the same individual—this is what anarchist communism will inevitably lead us to, if it starts fair with expropriation.

Let the Revolution only get so far, and famine is not the enemy it will have to fear. No, the danger which will menace it lies in timidity, prejudice, and half-measures. The danger is where Danton saw it when he cried to France: "De l'audace, de l'audace, et encore de l'audace." The bold thought first, and the bold deed will not fail to follow.

FOOTNOTES:

[3] The municipal debt of Paris amounted in 1904 to 2,266,579,100 francs, and the charges for it were 121,000,000 francs.

[4] No fallacy more harmful has ever been spread than the fallacy of a "One-day Revolution," which is propagated in superficial Socialist pamphlets speaking of the Revolution of the 18th of March at Berlin, supposed (which is absolutely wrong) to have given Prussia its representative Government. We saw well the harm made by such fallacies in Russia in 1905-1907. The truth is that up to 1871 Prussia, like Russia of the present day, had a scrap of paper which could be described as a "Constitution," but it had no representative Government. The Ministry imposed upon the nation, up till 1870, the budget it chose to propose.

CHAPTER VI
DWELLINGS

I

Those who have closely watched the growth of Socialist ideas among the workers must have noticed that on one momentous question—the housing of the people—a definite conclusion is being imperceptibly arrived at. It is a fact that in the large towns of France, and in many of the smaller ones, the workers are coming gradually to the conclusion that dwelling-houses are in no sense the property of those whom the State recognizes as their owners.

This idea has evolved naturally in the minds of the people, and nothing will ever convince them again that the "rights of property" ought to extend to houses.

The house was not built by its owner. It was erected, decorated and furnished by innumerable workers in the timber yard, the brick field, and the workshop, toiling for dear life at a minimum wage.

The money spent by the owner was not the product of his own toil. It was amassed, like all other riches, by paying the workers two-thirds or only a half of what was their due.

Moreover—and it is here that the enormity of the whole proceeding becomes most glaring—the house owes its actual value to the profit which the owner can make out of it. Now, this profit results from the fact that his house is built in a town—that is, in an agglomeration of thousands of other houses, possessing paved streets, bridges, quays, and fine public buildings, well lighted, and affording to its inhabitants a thousand comforts and conveniences unknown in villages; a town in regular communication with other towns, and itself a centre of industry, commerce, science, and art; a town which the work of twenty or thirty generations has made habitable, healthy, and beautiful.

A house in certain parts of Paris is valued at many thousands of pounds sterling, not because thousands of pounds' worth of labour have been expended on that particular house, but because it is in Paris; because for centuries workmen, artists, thinkers, and men of learning and letters have contributed to make Paris what it is to-day—a centre of industry, commerce, politics, art, and science; because Paris has a past; because, thanks to literature, the names of its streets are household words in foreign countries as well as at home; because it is the fruit of eighteen centuries of toil, the work of fifty generations of the whole French nation.

Who, then, can appropriate to himself the tiniest plot of ground, or the meanest building in such a city, without committing a flagrant injustice? Who, then, has the right to sell to any bidder the smallest portion of the common heritage?

On that point, as we have said, the workers begin to be agreed. The idea of free dwellings showed its existence very plainly during the siege of Paris, when the cry was for an abatement pure and simple of the terms demanded by the landlords. It appeared again during the Commune of 1871, when the Paris workmen expected the Council of the Commune to decide boldly on the abolition of rent. And when the New Revolution comes, it will be the first question with which the poor will concern themselves.

Whether in time of revolution or in time of peace, the worker must be housed somehow or other; he must have some sort of roof over his head. But, however tumble-down and squalid his dwelling may be, there is always a landlord who can evict him.

True, during the Revolution the landlord cannot find bailiffs and police-sergeants to throw the workman's rags and chattels into the street, but who knows what the new Government will do tomorrow? Who can say that it will not call coercion to its aid again, and set the police pack upon the tenant to hound him out of his hovels? Have we not seen the commune of Paris proclaim the remission of rents due up to the first of April only![5] After that, rent had to be paid, though Paris was in a state of chaos, and industry at a standstill; so that the "federate" who had taken arms to defend the independence of Paris had absolutely nothing to depend upon—he and his family—but an allowance of fifteen pence a day!

Now the worker must be made to see clearly that in refusing to pay rent to a landlord or owner he is not simply profiting by the disorganization of authority. He must understand that the abolition of rent is a recognized principle, sanctioned, so to speak, by popular assent; that to be housed rent-free is a right proclaimed aloud by the people.

Are we going to wait till this measure, which is in harmony with every honest man's sense of justice, is taken up by the few socialists scattered among the middle class elements, of which the Provisionary Government will be composed? If it were so, the people should have to wait long—till the return of reaction, in fact!

This is why, refusing uniforms and badges—those outward signs of authority and servitude—and remaining people among the people, the earnest revolutionists will work side by side with the masses, that the abolition of rent, the expropriation of houses, may become an accomplished fact. They will prepare the ground and encourage ideas to grow in this direction; and when the fruit of their labours is ripe, the people will proceed to expropriate the houses without giving heed to the theories which will certainly be thrust in their way—theories about paying compensation to landlords, and finding first the necessary funds.

On the day that the expropriation of houses takes place, on that day, the exploited workers will have realized that new times have come, that Labour will no longer have to bear the yoke of the rich and powerful, that Equality has been openly proclaimed, that this Revolution is a real fact, and not a theatrical make-believe, like so many others preceding it.

II

If the idea of expropriation be adopted by the people it will be carried into effect in spite of all the "insurmountable" obstacles with which we are menaced.

Of course, the good folk in new uniforms, seated in the official arm-chairs of the Hôtel de Ville, will be sure to busy themselves in heaping up obstacles. They will talk of giving compensation to the landlords, of preparing statistics, and drawing up long reports. Yes, they would be capable of drawing up reports long enough to outlast the hopes of the people, who, after waiting and starving in enforced idleness, and seeing nothing come of all these official researches, would lose heart and faith in the Revolution and abandon the field to the reactionaries. The new bureaucracy would end by making expropriation hateful in the eyes of all.

Here, indeed, is a rock which might shipwreck our hopes. But if the people turn a deaf ear to the specious arguments used to dazzle them, and realize that new life needs new conditions, and if they undertake the task themselves, then expropriation can be effected without any great difficulty.

"But how? How can it be done?" you ask us. We shall try to reply to this question, but with a reservation. We have no intention of tracing out the plans of expropriation in their smallest details. We know beforehand that all that any man, or group of men, could suggest to-day would be far surpassed by the reality when it comes. Man will accomplish greater things, and accomplish them better and by simpler methods than those dictated to him beforehand. Thus we shall merely indicate the manner by which expropriation *might* be accomplished without the intervention of Government. We do not propose to go out of our way to answer those who declare that the thing is impossible. We confine ourselves to replying that we are not the upholders of any particular method of organization. We are only concerned to demonstrate that expropriation *could* be effected by popular initiative, and *could not* be effected by any other means whatever.

It seems very likely that, as soon as expropriation is fairly started, groups of volunteers will spring up in every district, street, and block of houses, and undertake to inquire into the number of flats and houses which are empty and of those which are overcrowded, the unwholesome slums, and the houses which are too spacious for their occupants and might well be used to house those who are stifled in swarming tenements. In a few days these volunteers would have drawn up complete lists for the street and the district of all the flats, tenements, family mansions and villa residences, all the rooms and suites of rooms, healthy and unhealthy, small and large, fœtid dens and homes of luxury.

Freely communicating with each other, these volunteers would soon have their statistics complete. False statistics can be manufactured in board rooms and offices, but true and exact statistics must begin with the individual and mount up from the simple to the complex.

Then, without waiting for anyone's leave, those citizens will probably go and find their comrades who were living in miserable garrets and hovels and will say to them simply: "It is a real Revolution this time, comrades, and no mistake about it. Come to such a place this evening; all the neighbourhood will be there; we are going to redistribute the dwelling-houses. If you are tired of your slum-garret, come and choose one of the flats of five rooms that are to be disposed of, and when you have once moved in you shall stay, never fear. The people are up in arms, and he who would venture to evict you will have to answer to them."

"But every one will want a fine house or a spacious flat!" we are told.—No, you are quite mistaken. It is not the people's way to clamour for the moon. On the contrary, every time we have seen them set about repairing a wrong we have been struck by the good sense and instinct for justice which animates the masses. Have we ever known them demand the impossible? Have we ever seen the people of Paris fighting among themselves while waiting for their rations of bread or firewood during the two sieges or during the terrible years of 1792-1794? The patience and resignation which prevailed among them in 1871 was constantly presented for admiration by the foreign Press correspondents; and yet these patient waiters knew full well that the last comers would have to pass the day without food or fire.

We do not deny that there are plenty of egotistic instincts in isolated individuals. We are quite aware of it. But we contend that the very way to revive and nourish these instincts would be to confine such questions as the housing of the people to any board or committee, in fact, to the tender mercies of officialism in any shape or form. Then indeed all the evil passions spring up, and it becomes a case of who is the most influential person on the board. The least inequality causes wranglings and recriminations. If the smallest advantage is given to any one, a tremendous hue and cry is raised—and not without reason.

But if the people themselves, organized by streets, districts, and parishes, undertake to move the inhabitants of the slums into the half-empty dwellings of the middle classes, the trifling inconveniences, the little inequalities will be easily tided over. Rarely has appeal been made to the good instincts of the masses—only as a last resort, to save the sinking ship in times of revolution—but never has such an appeal been made in vain; the heroism, the self-devotion of the toiler has never failed to respond to it. And thus it will be in the coming Revolution.

But, when all is said and done, some inequalities, some inevitable injustices, undoubtedly will remain. There are individuals in our societies whom no great crisis can lift out of the deep mire of egoism in which they are sunk. The question, however, is not whether there will be injustices or no, but rather how to limit the number of them.

Now all history, all the experience of the human race, and all social psychology, unite in showing that the best and fairest way is to trust the decision to those whom it concerns most nearly. It is they alone who can consider and allow for the hundred and one details which must necessarily be overlooked in any merely official redistribution.

III

Moreover, it is by no means necessary to make straightway an absolutely equal redistribution of all the dwellings. There will no doubt be some inconveniences at first, but matters will soon be righted in a society which has adopted expropriation.

When the masons, and carpenters, and all who are concerned in house building, know that their daily bread is secured to them, they will ask nothing better than to work at their old trades a few hours a day. They will adapt the fine houses, which absorbed the time of a whole staff of servants, for giving shelter to several families, and in a few months homes will have sprung up, infinitely healthier and more conveniently arranged than those of to-day. And to those who are not yet comfortably housed the anarchist Commune will be able to say: "Patience, comrades! Palaces fairer and finer than any the capitalists built for themselves will spring from the ground of our enfranchised city. They will belong to those who have most need of them. The anarchist Commune does not build with an eye to revenues. These monuments erected to its citizens, products of the collective spirit, will serve as models to all humanity; they will be yours."

If the people of the Revolution expropriate the houses and proclaim free lodgings—the communalizing of houses and the right of each family to a decent dwelling—then the Revolution will have assumed a communistic character from the first, and started on a course from which it will be by no means easy to turn it. It will have struck a fatal blow at individual property.

For the expropriation of dwellings contains in germ the whole social revolution. On the manner of its accomplishment depends the character of all that follows. Either we shall start on a good road leading straight to anarchist communism, or we shall remain sticking in the mud of despotic individualism.

It is easy to see the numerous objections—theoretic on the one hand, practical on the other—with which we are sure to be met. As it will be a question of maintaining iniquity at any price, our opponents will of course protest "in the name of justice." "Is it not a crying shame," they will exclaim, "that the people of Paris should take possession of all these fine houses, while the peasants in the country have only tumble-down huts to live in?" But do not let us make a mistake. These enthusiasts for justice forget, by a lapse of memory to which they are subject, the "crying shame" which they themselves are tacitly defending. They forget that in this same city the worker, with his wife and children, suffocates in a noisome garret, while from his window he sees the rich man's palace. They forget that whole generations perish in crowded slums, starving for air and sunlight, and that to redress this injustice ought to be the first task of the Revolution.

Do not let these disingenuous protests hold us back. We know that any inequality which may exist between town and country in the early days of the Revolution will be transitory and of a nature that will right itself from day to day; for the village will not fail to improve its dwellings as soon as the peasant has ceased to be the beast of burden of the farmer, the merchant, the money-lender, and the State. In order to avoid an accidental and transitory inequality, shall we stay our hand from righting an ancient wrong?

The so-called practical objections are not very formidable either. We are bidden to consider the hard case of some poor fellow who by dint of privation has contrived to buy a house just large enough to hold his family. And we are going to deprive him of his hard-earned happiness, to turn him into the street! Certainly not. If his house is only just large enough for his family, by all means let him stay there. Let him work in his little garden, too; our "boys" will not hinder him—nay, they will lend him a helping hand if need be. But suppose he lets lodgings, suppose he has empty rooms in his house; then the people will make the lodger understand that he need not pay his former landlord any more rent. Stay where you are, but rent free. No more duns and collectors; Socialism has abolished all that!

Or again, suppose that the landlord has a score of rooms all to himself, and some poor woman lives near by with five children in one room. In that case the people would see whether, with some alterations, these empty rooms could not be converted into a suitable home for the poor woman and her five children. Would not that be more just and fair than to leave the mother and her five little ones languishing in a garret, while Sir Gorgeous Midas sat at his ease in an empty mansion? Besides, good Sir Gorgeous would probably hasten to do it of his own accord; his wife will be delighted to be freed from half her big, unwieldy house when there is no longer a staff of servants to keep it in order.

"So you are going to turn everything upside down," say the defenders of law and order. "There will be no end to the evictions and removals. Would it not be better to start fresh by turning everybody out of doors and redistributing the houses by lot?" Thus our critics; but we are firmly persuaded that if no Government interferes in the matter, if all the changes are entrusted to these free groups which have sprung up to undertake the work, the evictions and removals will be less numerous than those which take place in one year under the present system, owing to the rapacity of landlords.

In the first place, there are in all large towns almost enough empty houses and flats to lodge all the inhabitants of the slums. As to the palaces and suites of fine apartments, many working people would not live in them if they could. One could not "keep up" such houses without a large staff of servants. Their occupants would soon find themselves forced to seek less luxurious dwellings. The fine ladies would find that palaces were not well adapted to self-help in the kitchen. Gradually people would shake down. There would be no need to conduct Dives to a garret at the bayonet's point, or install Lazarus in Dives's palace by the help of an armed escort. People would shake down amicably into the available dwellings with the least possible friction and disturbance. Have we not the example of the village communes redistributing fields and disturbing the owners of the allotments so little that one can only praise the intelligence and good sense of the methods they employ? Fewer fields change hands under the management of the Russian Commune than where personal property holds sway, and is for ever carrying its quarrels into courts of law. And are we to believe that the inhabitants of a great European city would be less intelligent and less capable of organization than Russian or Hindoo peasants?

Moreover, we must not blink at the fact that every revolution means a certain disturbance to everyday life, and those who expect this tremendous climb out of the old grooves to be accomplished without so much as jarring the dishes on their dinner tables will find themselves mistaken. It is true that Governments can change without disturbing worthy citizens at dinner, but the crimes of society towards those who have nourished and supported it are not to be redressed by any such political sleight of parties.

Undoubtedly there will be a disturbance, but it must not be one of pure loss; it must be minimized. And again—it is impossible to lay too much stress on this maxim—it will be by addressing ourselves to the interested parties, and not to boards and committees, that we shall best succeed in reducing the sum of inconveniences for everybody.

The people commit blunder on blunder when they have to choose by ballot some hare-brained candidate who solicits the honour of representing them, and takes upon himself to know all, to do all, and to organize all. But when they take upon themselves to organize what they know, what touches them directly, they do it better than all the "talking-shops" put together. Is not the Paris Commune an instance in point? and the great dockers' strike? and have we not constant evidence of this fact in every village commune?

FOOTNOTE:

[5] The decree of the 30 March: by this decree rents due up to the terms of October, 1870, and January and April, 1871, were annulled.

CHAPTER VII
CLOTHING

When the houses have become the common heritage of the citizens, and when each man has his daily supply of food, another forward step will have to be taken. The question of clothing will of course demand consideration next, and again the only possible solution will be to take possession, in the name of the people, of all the shops and warehouses where clothing is sold or stored, and to throw open the doors to all, so that each can take what he needs. The communalization of clothing—the right of each to take what he needs from the communal stores, or to have it made for him at the tailors and outfitters—is a necessary corollary of the communalization of houses and food.

Obviously we shall not need for that to despoil all citizens of their coats, to put all the garments in a heap and draw lots for them, as our critics, with equal wit and ingenuity, suggest. Let him who has a coat keep it still—nay, if he have ten coats it is highly improbable that any one will want to deprive him of them, for most folk would prefer a new coat to one that has already graced the shoulders of some fat bourgeois; and there will be enough new garments, and to spare, without having recourse to second-hand wardrobes.

If we were to take an inventory of all the clothes and stuff for clothing accumulated in the shops and stores of the large towns, we should find probably that in Paris, Lyons, Bordeaux, and Marseilles, there was enough to enable the commune to offer garments to all the citizens, of both sexes; and if all were not suited at once, the communal outfitters would soon make good these shortcomings. We know how rapidly our great tailoring and dressmaking establishments work nowadays, provided as they are with machinery specially adapted for production on a large scale.

"But every one will want a sable-lined coat or a velvet gown!" exclaim our adversaries.

Frankly, we do not believe it. Every woman does not dote on velvet nor does every man dream of sable linings. Even now, if we were to ask each woman to choose her gown, we should find some to prefer a simple, practical garment to all the fantastic trimmings the fashionable world affects.

Tastes change with the times, and the fashion in vogue at the time of the Revolution will certainly make for simplicity. Societies, like individuals, have their hours of cowardice, but also their heroic moments; and though the society of to-day cuts a very poor figure sunk in the pursuit of narrow personal interests and second-rate ideas, it wears a different air when great crises come. It has its moments of greatness and enthusiasm. Men of generous nature will gain the power which to-day is in the hand of jobbers. Self-devotion will spring up, and noble deeds beget their like; even the egotists will be ashamed of hanging back, and will be drawn in spite of themselves to admire, if not to imitate, the generous and brave.

The great Revolution of 1793 abounds in examples of this kind, and it is always during such times of spiritual revival—as natural to societies as to individuals—that the spring-tide of enthusiasm sweeps humanity onwards.

We do not wish to exaggerate the part played by such noble passions, nor is it upon them that we would found our ideal of society. But we are not asking too much if we expect their aid in tiding over the first and most difficult moments. We cannot hope that our daily life will be continuously inspired by such exalted enthusiasms, but we may expect their aid at the first, and that is all we need.

It is just to wash the earth clean, to sweep away the shards and refuse, accumulated by centuries of slavery and oppression, that the new anarchist society will have need of this wave of brotherly love. Later on it can exist without appealing to the spirit of self-sacrifice, because it will have eliminated oppression, and thus created a new world instinct with all the feelings of solidarity.

Besides, should the character of the Revolution be such as we have sketched here, the free initiative of individuals would find an extensive field of action in thwarting the efforts of the egotists. Groups would spring up in every street and quarter to undertake the charge of the clothing. They would make inventories of all that the city possessed, and would find out approximately what were the resources at their disposal. It is more than likely that in the matter of clothing the citizens would adopt the same principle as in the matter of provisions—that is to say, they would offer freely from the common store everything which was to be found in abundance, and dole out whatever was limited in quantity.

Not being able to offer to each man a sable-lined coat and to every woman a velvet gown, society would probably distinguish between the superfluous and the necessary, and, provisionally at least class sable and velvet among the superfluities of life, ready to let time prove whether what is a luxury to-day may not become common to all to-morrow. While the necessary clothing would be guaranteed to each inhabitant of the anarchist city, it would be left to private activity to provide for the sick and feeble those things, provisionally considered as luxuries, and to procure for the less robust such special articles, as would not enter into the daily consumption of ordinary citizens.

"But," it may be urged, "this means grey uniformity and the end of everything beautiful in life and art."

"Certainly not," we reply. And, still basing our reasonings on what already exists, we are going to show how an Anarchist society could satisfy the most artistic tastes of its citizens without allowing them to amass the fortunes of millionaires.

CHAPTER VIII
WAYS AND MEANS

I

If a society, a city or a territory were to guarantee the necessaries of life to its inhabitants (and we shall see how the conception of the necessaries of life can be so extended as to include luxuries), it would be compelled to take possession of what is absolutely needed for production; that is to say—land, machinery, factories, means of transport, etc. Capital in the hands of private owners would be expropriated, to be returned to the community.

The great harm done by bourgeois society, as we have already mentioned, is not only that capitalists seize a large share of the profits of each industrial and commercial enterprise, thus enabling themselves to live without working, but that all production has taken a wrong direction, as it is not carried on with a view to securing well-being to all. There is the reason why it must be condemned.

It is absolutely impossible that mercantile production should be carried on in the interest of all. To desire it would be to expect the capitalist to go beyond his province and to fulfil duties that he *cannot* fulfil without ceasing to be what he is—a private manufacturer seeking his own enrichment. Capitalist organization, based on the personal interest of each individual employer of labour, has given to society all that could be expected of it: it has increased the productive force of Labour. The capitalist, profiting by the revolution effected in industry by steam, by the sudden development of chemistry and machinery, and by other inventions of our century, has worked in his own interest to increase the yield of human labour, and in a great measure he has succeeded so far. But to attribute other duties to him would be unreasonable. For example, to expect that he should use this superior yield of labour in the interest of society as a whole, would be to ask philanthropy and charity of him, and a capitalist enterprise cannot be based on charity.

It now remains for society, first, to extend this greater productivity, which is limited to certain industries, and to apply it to the general good. But it is evident that to utilize this high productivity of labour, so as to guarantee well-being to all, Society must itself take possession of all means of production.

Economists, as is their wont, will not fail to remind us of the comparative well-being of a certain category of young robust workmen, skilled in certain special branches of industry which has been obtained under the present system. It is always this minority that is pointed out to us with pride. But even this well-being, which is the exclusive right of a few, is it secure? To-morrow, maybe, negligence, improvidence, or the greed of their employers, will deprive these privileged men of their work, and they will pay for the period of comfort they have enjoyed with months and years of poverty or destitution. How many important industries—the textiles, iron, sugar, etc.—without mentioning all sorts of short-lived trades, have we not seen decline or come to a standstill on account of speculations, or in consequence of natural displacement of work, or from the effects of competition amongst the capitalists themselves! If the chief textile and mechanical industries had to pass through such a crisis as they have passed through in 1886, we hardly need mention the small trades, all of which have their periods of standstill.

What, too, shall we say to the price which is paid for the relative well-being of certain categories of workmen? Unfortunately, it is paid for by the ruin of agriculture, the shameless exploitation of the peasants, the misery of the masses. In comparison with the feeble minority of workers who enjoy a certain comfort, how many millions of human beings live from hand to mouth, without a secure wage, ready to go wherever they are wanted; how many peasants work fourteen hours a day for a poor pittance! Capital depopulates the country, exploits the colonies and the countries where industries are but little developed, dooms the immense majority of workmen to remain without technical education, to remain mediocre even in their own trade.

This is not merely accidental, it is a *necessity* of the capitalist system. In order well to remunerate certain classes of workmen, peasants *must* become the beasts of burden of society; the country *must* be deserted for the town; small trades must agglomerate in the foul suburbs of large cities, and manufacture a thousand little things for next to nothing, so as to bring the goods of the greater industries within reach of buyers with small salaries. That bad cloth may be sold to ill-paid workers, garments are made by tailors who are satisfied with a starvation wage! Eastern lands in a backward state are exploited by the West, in order that, under the capitalist system, workers in a few privileged industries may obtain certain limited comforts of life.

The evil of the present system is therefore not that the "surplus-value" of production goes to the capitalist, as Rodbertus and Marx said, thus narrowing the Socialist conception and the general view of the capitalist system; the surplus-value itself is but a consequence of deeper causes. The evil lies *in the possibility of a surplus-value existing*, instead of a simple surplus not consumed by each generation; for, that a surplus-value should exist, means that men, women and children are compelled by hunger to sell their labour for a small part of what this labour produces, and still more so, of what their labour is capable of producing: But this evil will last as long as the instruments of production belong to the few. As long as men are compelled to pay a heavy tribute to property holders for the right of cultivating land or putting machinery into action, and the owners of the land and the machine are free to produce what bids fair to bring them in the largest profits—rather than the greatest amount of useful commodities—well-being can only be temporarily guaranteed to a very few; it is only to be bought by the poverty of a large section of society. It is not sufficient to distribute the profits realized by a trade in equal parts, if at the same time thousands of other workers are exploited. It is a case of PRODUCING THE GREATEST AMOUNT OF GOODS NECESSARY TO THE WELL-BEING OF ALL, WITH THE LEAST POSSIBLE WASTE OF HUMAN ENERGY.

This generalized aim cannot be the aim of a private owner; and this is why society as a whole, if it takes this view of production as its ideal, will be compelled to expropriate all that enhances well-being while producing wealth. It will have to take possession of land, factories, mines, means of communication, etc., and besides, it will have to study what products will promote general well-being, as well as the ways and means of an adequate production.

II

How many hours a day will man have to work to produce nourishing food, a comfortable home, and necessary clothing for his family? This question has often preoccupied Socialists, and they generally came to the conclusion that four or five hours a day would suffice, on condition, be it well understood, that all men work. At the end of last century, Benjamin Franklin fixed the limit at five hours; and if the need of comfort is greater now, the power of production has augmented too, and far more rapidly.

In speaking of agriculture further on, we shall see what the earth can be made to yield to man when he cultivates it in a reasonable way, instead of throwing seed haphazard in a badly ploughed soil as he mostly does to-day. In the great farms of Western America, some of which cover 30 square miles, but have a poorer soil than the manured soil of civilized countries, only 10 to 15 English bushels per English acre are obtained; that is to say, half the yield of European farms or of American farms in the Eastern States. And nevertheless, thanks to machines which enable 2 men to plough 4 English acres a day, 100 men can produce in a year all that is necessary to deliver the bread of 10,000 people at their homes during a whole year.

Thus it would suffice for a man to work under the same conditions for *30 hours, say 6 half-days of five hours each, to have bread for a whole year*; and to work 30 half-days to guarantee the same to a family of 5 people.

We shall also prove by results obtained nowadays, that if we took recourse to intensive agriculture, less than 6 half-days' work could procure bread, meat, vegetables, and even luxurious fruit for a whole family.

Again, if we study the cost of workmen's dwellings, built in large towns to-day, we can ascertain that to obtain, in a large English city, a semi-detached little house, as they are built for workmen for £250, from 1400 to 1800 half-days' work of 5 hours would be sufficient. And as a house of that kind lasts 50 years at least, it follows that 28 to 36 half-days' work a year would provide well-furnished, healthy quarters, with all necessary comfort for a family. Whereas when hiring the same apartment from an employer, a workman pays from 75 to 100 days' work per year.

Mark that these figures represent the maximum of what a house costs in England to-day, being given the defective organization of our societies. In Belgium, workmen's houses in the *cités ouvrières* have been built at a much smaller cost. So that, taking everything into consideration, we are justified in affirming that in a well-organized society 30 or 40 half-days' work a year will suffice to guarantee a perfectly comfortable home.

There now remains clothing, the exact value of which is almost impossible to fix, because the profits realized by a swarm of middlemen cannot be estimated. Let us take cloth, for example, and add up all the tribute levied on every yard of it by the landowners, the sheep owners, the wool merchants, and all their intermediate agents, then by the railway companies, mill-owners, weavers, dealers in ready-made clothes, sellers and commission agents, and we shall get then an idea of what we pay to a whole swarm of capitalists for each article of clothing. That is why it is perfectly impossible to say how many days' work an overcoat that you pay £3 or £4 for in a large London shop represents.

What is certain is that with present machinery it is possible to manufacture an incredible amount of goods both cheaply and quickly.

A few examples will suffice. Thus in the United States, in 751 cotton mills (for spinning and weaving), 175,000 men and women produce 2,033,000,000 yards of cotton goods, besides a great quantity of thread. On the average, more than 12,000 yards of cotton goods alone are obtained by a 300 days' work of nine and one-half hours each, say 40 yards of cotton in 10 hours. Admitting that a family needs 200 yards a year at most, this would be equivalent to 50 hours' work, say *10 half-days of 5 hours each*. And we should have thread besides; that is to say, cotton to sew with, and thread to weave cloth with, so as to manufacture woolen stuffs mixed with cotton.

As to the results obtained by weaving alone, the official statistics of the United States teach us that in 1870, if workmen worked 13 or 14 hours a day, they made 10,000 yards of white cotton goods in a year; sixteen years later (1886) they wove 30,000 yards by working only 55 hours a week.

Even in printed cotton goods they obtained, weaving and printing included, 32,000 yards in 2670 hours of work a year — say about 12 yards an hour. Thus to have your 200 yards of white and printed cotton goods *17 hours' work a year* would suffice. It is necessary to remark that raw material reaches these factories in about the same state as it comes from the fields, and that the transformations gone through by the piece before it is converted into goods are completed in the course of these 17 hours. But to *buy* these 200 yards from the tradesman, a well-paid workman must give *at the very least* 10 to 15 days' work of 10 hours each, say 100 to 150 hours. And as to the English peasant, he would have to toil for a month, or a little more, to obtain this luxury.

By this example we already see that by working *50 half-days per year* in a well-organized society we could dress better than the lower middle classes do to-day.

But with all this we have only required 60 half-days' work of 5 hours each to obtain the fruits of the earth, 40 for housing, and 50 for clothing, which only makes half a year's work, as the year consists of 300 working-days if we deduct holidays.

There remain still 150 half-days' work which could be made use of for other necessaries of life — wine, sugar, coffee, tea, furniture, transport, etc., etc.

It is evident that these calculations are only approximative, but they can also be proved in another way. When we take into account how many, in the so-called civilized nations, produce nothing, how many work at harmful trades, doomed to disappear, and lastly, how many are only useless middlemen, we see that in each nation the number of real producers could be doubled. And if, instead of every 10 men, 20 were occupied in producing useful commodities, and if society took the trouble to economize human energy, those 20 people would only have to work 5 hours a day without production decreasing. And it would suffice to reduce the waste of human energy which is going on in the rich families with the scores of useless servants, or in the administrations which occupy one official to every ten or even six inhabitants, and to utilize those forces, to augment immensely the productivity of a nation. In fact, work could be reduced to four or even three hours a day, to produce all the goods that are produced now.

After studying all these facts together, we may arrive, then, at the following conclusion: Imagine a society, comprising a few million inhabitants, engaged in agriculture and a great variety of industries—Paris, for example, with the Department of Seine-et-Oise. Suppose that in this society all children learn to work with their hands as well as with their brains. Admit that all adults, save women, engaged in the education of their children, bind themselves to work *5 hours a day* from the age of twenty or twenty-two to forty-five or fifty, and that they follow occupations they have chosen themselves in any one of those branches of human work which in this city are considered *necessary*. Such a society could in return guarantee well-being to all its members, a well-being more substantial than that enjoyed to-day by the middle classes. And, moreover, each worker belonging to this society would have at his disposal at least 5 hours a day which he could devote to science, art, and individual needs which do not come under the category of *necessities*, but will probably do so later on, when man's productivity will have augmented, and those objects will no longer appear luxurious or inaccessible.

CHAPTER IX
THE NEED FOR LUXURY

I

Man is not a being whose exclusive purpose in life is eating, drinking, and providing a shelter for himself. As soon as his material wants are satisfied, other needs, which, generally speaking, may be described as of an artistic character, will thrust themselves forward. These needs are of the greatest variety; they vary with each and every individual; and the more society is civilized, the more will individuality be developed, and the more will desires be varied.

Even to-day we see men and women denying themselves necessaries to acquire mere trifles, to obtain some particular gratification, or some intellectual or material enjoyment. A Christian or an ascetic may disapprove of these desires for luxury; but it is precisely these trifles that break the monotony of existence and make it agreeable. Would life, with all its inevitable drudge and sorrows, be worth living, if, besides daily work, man could never obtain a single pleasure according to his individual tastes?

If we wish for a Social Revolution, it is no doubt, first of all, to give bread to everyone; to transform this execrable society, in which we can every day see capable workmen dangling their arms for want of an employer who will exploit them; women and children wandering shelterless at night; whole families reduced to dry bread; men, women, and children dying for want of care and even for want of food. It is to put an end to these iniquities that we rebel.

But we expect more from the Revolution. We see that the

worker, compelled to struggle painfully for bare existence, is reduced to ignore the higher delights, the highest within man's reach, of science, and especially of scientific discovery; of art, and especially of artistic creation. It is in order to obtain for all of us joys that are now reserved to a few; in order to give leisure and the possibility of developing everyone's intellectual capacities, that the social revolution must guarantee daily bread to all. After bread has been secured, leisure is the supreme aim.

No doubt, nowadays, when hundreds and thousands of human beings are in need of bread, coal, clothing, and shelter, luxury is a crime; to satisfy it, the worker's child must go without bread! But in a society in which all have the necessary food and shelter, the needs which we consider luxuries to-day will be the more keenly felt. And as all men do not and cannot resemble one another (the variety of tastes and needs is the chief guarantee of human progress) there will always be, and it is desirable that there should always be, men and women whose desire will go beyond those of ordinary individuals in some particular direction.

Everybody does not need a telescope, because, even if learning were general, there are people who prefer to examine things through a microscope to studying the starry heavens. Some like statues, some like pictures. A particular individual has no other ambition than to possess a good piano, while another is pleased with an accordion. The tastes vary, but the artistic needs exist in all. In our present, poor capitalistic society, the man who has artistic needs cannot satisfy them unless he is heir to a large fortune, or by dint of hard work appropriates to himself an intellectual capital which will enable him to take up a liberal profession. Still he cherishes the *hope* of some day satisfying his tastes more or less, and for this reason he reproaches the idealist Communist societies with having the material life of each individual as their sole aim. "In your communal stores you may perhaps have bread for all," he says to us, "but you will not have beautiful pictures, optical instruments, luxurious furniture, artistic jewelry—in short, the many things that minister to the infinite variety of human tastes. And you suppress the possibility of obtaining anything besides the bread and meat which the commune can offer to all, and the drab linen in which all your lady citizens will be dressed."

These are the objections which all communist systems have to consider, and which the founders of new societies, established in American deserts, never understood. They believed that if the community could procure sufficient cloth to dress all its members, a music-room in which the "brothers" could strum a piece of music, or act a play from time to time, it was enough. They forgot that the feeling for art existed in the agriculturist as well as in the burgher, and, notwithstanding that the expression of artistic feeling varies according to the difference in culture, in the main it remains the same. In vain did the community guarantee the common necessaries of life, in vain did it suppress all education that would tend to develop individuality, in vain did it eliminate all reading save the Bible. Individual tastes broke forth, and caused general discontent; quarrels arose when somebody proposed to buy a piano or scientific instruments; and the elements of progress flagged. The society could only exist on condition that it crushed all individual feeling, all artistic tendency, and all development.

Will the anarchist Commune be impelled by the same direction?—Evidently not, if it understands that while it produces all that is necessary to material life, it must also strive to satisfy all manifestations of the human mind.

II

We frankly confess that when we think of the abyss of poverty and suffering that surrounds us, when we hear the heartrending cry of the worker walking the streets begging for work, we are loth to discuss the question: How will men act in a society, whose members are properly fed, to satisfy certain individuals desirous of possessing a piece of Sèvres china or a velvet dress?

We are tempted to answer: Let us make sure of bread to begin with, we shall see to china and velvet later on.

But as we must recognize that man has other needs besides food, and as the strength of Anarchy lies precisely in that that it understands *all* human faculties and *all* passions, and ignores none, we shall, in a few words, explain how man can contrive to satisfy all his intellectual and artistic needs.

We have already mentioned that by working 4 or 5 hours a day till the age of forty-five or fifty, man could easily produce *all* that is necessary to guarantee comfort to society.

But the day's work of a man accustomed to toil does not consist of 5 hours; it is a 10 hours' day for 300 days a year, and lasts all his life. Of course, when a man is harnessed to a machine, his health is soon undermined and his intelligence is blunted; but when man has the possibility of varying occupations, and especially of alternating manual with intellectual work, he can remain occupied without fatigue, and even with pleasure, for 10 or 12 hours a day. Consequently, the man who will have done the 4 or 5 hours of manual work that are necessary for his existence, will have before him 5 or 6 hours which he will seek to employ according to his tastes. And these 5 or 6 hours a day will fully enable him to procure for himself, if he associates with others, all he wishes for, in addition to the necessaries guaranteed to all.

He will discharge first his task in the field, the factory, and so on, which he owes to society as his contribution to the general production. And he will employ the second half of his day, his week, or his year, to satisfy his artistic or scientific needs, or his hobbies.

Thousands of societies will spring up to gratify every taste and every possible fancy.

Some, for example, will give their hours of leisure to literature. They will then form groups comprising authors, compositors, printers, engravers, draughtsmen, all pursuing a common aim — the propagation of ideas that are dear to them.

Nowadays an author knows that there is a beast of burden, the worker, to whom, for the sum of a few shillings a day, he can entrust the printing of his books; but he hardly cares to know what a printing office is like. If the compositor suffers from lead-poisoning, and if the child who sees to the machine dies of anæmia, are there not other poor wretches to replace them?

But when there will be no more starvelings ready to sell their work for a pittance, when the exploited worker of to-day will be educated, and will have his *own* ideas to put down in black and white and to communicate to others, then the authors and scientific men will be compelled to combine among themselves and with the printers, in order to bring out their prose and their poetry.

So long as men consider fustian and manual labour a mark of inferiority, it will appear amazing to them to see an author setting up his own book in type, for has he not a gymnasium or games by way of diversion? But when the opprobrium connected with manual labor has disappeared, when all will have to work with their hands, there being no one to do it for them, then the authors as well as their admirers will soon learn the art of handling composing-sticks and type; they will know the pleasure of coming together—all admirers of the work to be printed—to set up the type, to shape it into pages, to take it in its virginal purity from the press. These beautiful machines, instruments of torture to the child who attends on them from morn till night, will be a source of enjoyment for those who will make use of them in order to give voice to the thoughts of their favourite author.

Will literature lose by it? Will the poet be less a poet after having worked out of doors or helped with his hands to multiply his work? Will the novelist lose his knowledge of human nature after having rubbed shoulders with other men in the forest or the factory, in the laying out of a road or on a railway line? Can there be two answers to these questions?

Maybe some books will be less voluminous; but then, more will be said on fewer pages. Maybe fewer waste-sheets will be published; but the matter printed will be more attentively read and more appreciated. The book will appeal to a larger circle of better educated readers, who will be more competent to judge.

Moreover, the art of printing, that has so little progressed since Gutenberg, is still in its infancy. It takes two hours to compose in type what is written in ten minutes, but more expeditious methods of multiplying thought are being sought after and will be discovered.[6]

What a pity every author does not have to take his share in the printing of his works! What progress printing would have already made! We should no longer be using movable letters, as in the seventeenth century.

III

Is it a dream to conceive a society in which—all having become producers, all having received an education that enables them to cultivate science or art, and all having leisure to do so—men would combine to publish the works of their choice, by contributing each his share of manual work? We have already hundreds of learned, literary, and other societies; and these societies are nothing but voluntary groups of men, interested in certain branches of learning, and associated for the purpose of publishing their works. The authors who write for the periodicals of these societies are not paid, and the periodicals, apart from a limited number of copies, are not for sale; they are sent gratis to all quarters of the globe, to other societies, cultivating the same branches of learning. This member of the Society may insert in its review a one-page note summarizing his observations; another may publish therein an extensive work, the results of long years of study; while others will confine themselves to consulting the review as a starting-point for further research. It does not matter: all these authors and readers are associated for the production of works in which all of them take an interest.

It is true that a learned society, like the individual author, goes to a printing office where workmen are engaged to do the printing. Nowadays, those who belong to the learned societies despise manual labour which indeed is carried on under very bad conditions; but a community which would give a generous philosophic and *scientific* education to all its members, would know how to organize manual labour in such a way that it would be the pride of humanity. Its learned societies would become associations of explorers, lovers of science, and workers—all knowing a manual trade and all interested in science.

If, for example, the Society is studying geology, all will contribute to the exploration of the earth's strata; each member will take his share in research, and ten thousand observers, where we have now only a hundred, will do more in a year than we can do in twenty years. And when their works are to be published, ten thousand men and women, skilled in different trades, will be ready to draw maps, engrave designs, compose, and print the books. With gladness will they give their leisure— in summer to exploration, in winter to indoor work. And when their works appear, they will find not only a hundred, but ten thousand readers interested in their common work.

This is the direction in which progress is already moving. Even to-day, when England felt the need of a complete dictionary of the English language, the birth of a Littré, who would devote his life to this work, was not waited for. Volunteers were appealed to, and a thousand men offered their services, spontaneously and gratuitously, to ransack the libraries, to take notes, and to accomplish in a few years a work which one man could not complete in his lifetime. In all branches of human intelligence the same spirit is breaking forth, and we should have a very limited knowledge of humanity could we not guess that the future is announcing itself in such tentative co-operation, which is gradually taking the place of individual work.

For this dictionary to be a really collective work, it would have been necessary that many volunteer authors, printers, and printers' readers should have worked in common; but something in this direction is done already in the Socialist Press, which offers us examples of manual and intellectual work combined. It happens in our newspapers that a Socialist author composes in lead his own article. True, such attempts are rare, but they indicate in which direction evolution is going.

They show the road of liberty. In future, when a man will have something useful to say—a word that goes beyond the thoughts of his century, he will not have to look for an editor who might advance the necessary capital. He will look for collaborators among those who know the printing trade, and who approve the idea of his new work. Together they will publish the new book or journal.

Literature and journalism will cease to be a means of money-making and living at the cost of others. But is there any one who knows literature and journalism from within, and who does not ardently desire that literature should at last be able to free itself from those who formerly protected it, and who now exploit it, and from the multitude, which, with rare exceptions, pays for it in proportion to its mediocrity, or to the ease with which it adapts itself to the bad taste of the greater number?

Letters and science will only take their proper place in the work of human development when, freed from all mercenary bondage, they will be exclusively cultivated by those who love them, and for those who love them.

IV

Literature, science, and art must be cultivated by free men. Only on this condition will they succeed in emancipating themselves from the yoke of the State, of Capital, and of the bourgeois mediocrity which stifles them.

What means has the scientist of to-day to make researches that interest him? Should he ask help of the State, which can only be given to one candidate in a hundred, and which only he may obtain who promises ostensibly to keep to the beaten track? Let us remember how the Academy of Sciences of France repudiated Darwin, how the Academy of St. Petersburg treated Mendeléeff with contempt, and how the Royal Society of

London refused to publish Joule's paper, in which he determined the mechanical equivalent of heat, finding it "unscientific."[7]

It was why all great researches, all discoveries revolutionizing science, have been made outside academies and universities, either by men rich enough to remain independent, like Darwin and Lyell, or by men who undermined their health by working in poverty, and often in great straits, losing endless time for want of a laboratory, and unable to procure the instruments or books necessary to continue their researches, but persevering against hope, and often dying before they had reached the end in view. Their name is legion.

Altogether, the system of help granted by the State is so bad that science has always endeavoured to emancipate itself from it. For this very reason there are thousands of learned societies organized and maintained by volunteers in Europe and America,—some having developed to such a degree that all the resources of subventioned societies, and all the wealth of millionaires, would not buy their treasures. No governmental institution is as rich as the Zoological Society of London, which is supported by voluntary contributions.

It does not buy the animals which in thousands people its gardens: they are sent by other societies and by collectors of the entire world. The Zoological Society of Bombay will send an elephant as a gift; another time a hippopotamus or a rhinoceros is offered by Egyptian naturalists. And these magnificent presents are pouring in every day, arriving from all quarters of the globe—birds, reptiles, collections of insects, etc. Such consignments often comprise animals that could not be bought for all the gold in the world; thus a traveller who has captured an animal at life's peril, and now loves it as he would love a child, will give it to the Society because he is sure it will be cared for. The entrance fee paid by visitors, and they are numberless, suffices for the maintenance of that immense institution.

What is defective in the Zoological Society of London, and in other kindred societies, is that the member's fee cannot be paid in work; that the keepers and numerous employes of this large institution are not recognized as members of the Society, while many have no other incentive to joining the society than to put the cabalistic letters F.Z.S (Fellow of the Zoological Society) on their cards. In a word, what is needed is a more perfect co-operation.

We may say the same about inventors, that we have said of scientists. Who does not know what sufferings nearly all great inventions have cost? Sleepless nights, families deprived of bread, want of tools and materials for experiments, this is the history of nearly all those who have enriched industry with inventions which are the truly legitimate pride of our civilization.

But what are we to do to alter the conditions that everybody is convinced are bad? Patents have been tried, and we know with what results. The inventor sells his patent for a few pounds, and the man who has only lent the capital pockets the enormous profits often resulting from the invention. Besides, patents isolate the inventor. They compel him to keep secret his researches which therefore end in failure; whereas the simplest suggestion, coming from a brain less absorbed in the fundamental idea, sometimes suffices to fertilize the invention and make it practical. Like all State control, patents hamper the progress of industry. Thought being incapable of being patented, patents are a crying injustice in theory, and in practice they result in one of the great obstacles to the rapid development of invention.

What is needed to promote the spirit of invention is, first of all, the awakening of thought, the boldness of conception, which our entire education causes to languish; it is the spreading of a scientific education, which would increase the number of inquirers a hundredfold; it is faith that humanity is going to take a step forward, because it is enthusiasm, the hope of doing good, that has inspired all the great inventors. The Social Revolution alone can give this impulse to thought, this boldness, this knowledge, this conviction of working for all.

Then we shall have vast institutes supplied with motor-power and tools of all sorts, immense industrial laboratories open to all inquirers, where men will be able to work out their dreams, after having acquitted themselves of their duty towards society; machinery palaces where they will spend their five or six hours of leisure; where they will make their experiments; where they will find other comrades, experts in other branches of industry, likewise coming to study some difficult problem, and therefore able to help and enlighten each other,—the encounter of their ideas and experience causing the longed-for solution to be found. And yet again, this is no dream. Solanóy Gorodók, in Petersburg, has already partially realized it as regards technical matters. It is a factory well furnished with tools and free to all; tools and motor-power are supplied gratis, only metals and wood are charged for at cost price. Unfortunately workmen only go there at night when worn out by ten hours' labour in the workshop. Moreover, they carefully hide their inventions from each other, as they are hampered by patents and Capitalism—that bane of present society, that stumbling-block in the path of intellectual and moral progress.

V

And what about art? From all sides we hear lamentations about the decadence of art. We are, indeed, far behind the great masters of the Renaissance. The technicalities of art have recently made great progress; thousands of people gifted with a certain amount of talent cultivate every branch, but art seems to fly from civilization! Technicalities make headway, but inspiration frequents artists' studios less than ever.

Where, indeed, should it come from? Only a grand idea can inspire art. *Art* is in our ideal synonymous with creation, it must look ahead; but save a few rare, very rare exceptions, the professional artist remains too philistine to perceive new horizons.

Moreover, this inspiration cannot come from books; it must be drawn from life, and present society cannot arouse it.

Raphael and Murillo painted at a time when the search of a new ideal could be pursued while retaining the old religious traditions. They painted to decorate churches which themselves represented the pious work of several generations of a given city. The basilic with its mysterious aspect, its grandeur, was connected with the life itself of the city, and could inspire a painter. He worked for a popular monument; he spoke to his fellow-citizens, and in return he received inspiration; he appealed to the multitude in the same way as did the nave, the pillars, the stained windows, the statues, and the carved doors. Nowadays the greatest honour a painter can aspire to is to see his canvas, framed in gilded wood, hung in a museum, a sort of old curiosity shop, where you see, as in the Prado, Murillo's Ascension next to a beggar of Velasquez and the dogs of Philip II. Poor Velasquez and poor Murillo! Poor Greek statues which *lived* in the Acropolis of their cities, and are now stifled beneath the red cloth hangings of the Louvre!

When a Greek sculptor chiseled his marble he endeavored to express the spirit and heart of the city. All its passions, all its traditions of glory, were to live again in the work. But to-day the *united* city has ceased to exist; there is no more communion of ideas. The town is a chance agglomeration of people who do not know one another, who have no common interest, save that of enriching themselves at the expense of one another. The fatherland does not exist.... What fatherland can the international banker and the rag-picker have in common? Only when cities, territories, nations, or groups of nations, will have renewed their harmonious life, will art be able to draw its inspiration from *ideals held in common*. Then will the architect conceive the city's monument which will no longer be a temple, a prison, or a fortress; then will the painter, the sculptor, the carver, the ornament-worker know where to put their canvases, their statues, and their decoration; deriving their power of execution from the same vital source, and gloriously marching all together towards the future.

But till then art can only vegetate. The best canvases of modern artists are those that represent nature, villages, valleys, the sea with its dangers, the mountain with its splendours. But how can the painter express the poetry of work in the fields if he has only contemplated it, imagined it, if he has never delighted in it himself? If he only knows it as a bird of passage knows the country he soars over in his migrations? If, in the vigour of early youth, he has not followed the plough at dawn, and enjoyed mowing grass with a large sweep of the scythe next to hardy haymakers vying in energy with lively young girls who fill the air with their songs? The love of the soil and of what grows on it is not acquired by sketching with a paint-brush—it is only in its service; and without loving it, how paint it? This is why all that the best painters have produced in this direction is still so imperfect, not true to life, nearly always merely sentimental. There is no *strength* in it.

You must have seen a sunset when returning from work. You must have been a peasant among peasants to keep the splendour of it in your eye. You must have been at sea with fishermen at all hours of the day and night, have fished yourself, struggled with the waves, faced the storm, and after rough work experienced the joy of hauling a heavy net, or the disappointment of seeing it empty, to understand the poetry of fishing. You must have spent time in a factory, known the fatigues and the joys of creative work, forged metals by the vivid light of a blast furnace, have felt the life in a machine, to understand the power of man and to express it in a work of art. You must, in fact, be permeated with popular feelings, to describe them.

Besides, the works of future artists who will have lived the life of the people, like the great artists of the past, will not be destined for sale. They will be an integral part of a living whole that would not be complete without them, any more than they would be complete without it. Men will go to the artist's own city to gaze at his work, and the spirited and serene beauty of such creations will produce its beneficial effect on heart and mind.

Art, in order to develop, must be bound up with industry by a thousand intermediate degrees, blended, so to say, as Ruskin and the great Socialist poet Morris have proved so often and so well. Everything that surrounds man, in the street, in the interior and exterior of public monuments, must be of a pure artistic form.

But this can only be realized in a society in which all enjoy comfort and leisure. Then only shall we see art associations, of which each member will find room for his capacity; for art cannot dispense with an infinity of purely manual and technical supplementary works. These artistic associations will undertake to embellish the houses of their members, as those kind volunteers, the young painters of Edinburgh, did in decorating the walls and ceilings of the great hospital for the poor in their city.

A painter or sculptor who has produced a work of personal feeling will offer it to the woman he loves, or to a friend. Executed for love's sake,—will his work, inspired by love, be inferior to the art that to-day satisfies the vanity of the philistine, because it has cost much money?

The same will be done as regards all pleasures not comprised in the necessaries of life. He who wishes for a grand piano will enter the association of musical instrument makers. And by giving the association part of his half-days' leisure, he will soon possess the piano of his dreams. If he is fond of astronomical studies he will join the association of astronomers, with its philosophers, its observers, its calculators, with its artists in astronomical instruments, its scientists and amateurs, and he will have the telescope he desires by taking his share of the associated work, for it is especially the rough work that is needed in an astronomical observatory—bricklayer's, carpenter's, founder's, mechanic's work, the last touch being given to the instrument of precision by the artist.

In short, the five or seven hours a day which each will have at his disposal, after having consecrated several hours to the production of necessities, would amply suffice to satisfy all longings for luxury, however varied. Thousands of associations would undertake to supply them. What is now the privilege of an insignificant minority would be accessible to all. Luxury, ceasing to be a foolish and ostentatious display of the bourgeois class, would become an artistic pleasure.

Everyone would be the happier for it. In collective work, performed with a light heart to attain a desired end, a book, a work of art, or an object of luxury, each will find an incentive and the necessary relaxation that makes life pleasant.

In working to put an end to the division between master and slave, we work for the happiness of both, for the happiness of humanity.

FOOTNOTES:

[6] They *have* already been discovered since the above lines were written.

[7] We know this from Playfair, who mentioned it at Joule's death.

CHAPTER X
AGREEABLE WORK

I

When Socialists maintain that a society, freed from the rule of the capitalists, would make work agreeable, and would suppress all repugnant and unhealthy drudgery, they are laughed at. And yet even to-day we can see the striking progress that is being made in this direction; and wherever this progress has been achieved, employers congratulate themselves on the economy of energy obtained thereby.

It is evident that a factory could be made as healthy and pleasant as a scientific laboratory. And it is no less evident that it would be advantageous to make it so. In a spacious and well-ventilated factory the work is better; it is easy to introduce many small ameliorations, of which each represents an economy of time or of manual labour. And if most of the workshops we know are foul and unhealthy, it is because the workers are of no account in the organization of factories, and because the most absurd waste of human energy is the distinctive feature of the present industrial organization.

Nevertheless, now and again, we already find, even now, some factories so well managed that it would be a real pleasure to work in them, if the work, be it well understood, were not to last more than four or five hours a day, and if every one had the possibility of varying it according to his tastes.

There are immense works, which I know, in one of the Midland counties, unfortunately consecrated to engines of war. They are perfect as regards sanitary and intelligent organization. They occupy fifty English acres of land, fifteen of which are roofed with glass. The pavement of fire-proof bricks is as clean as that of a miner's cottage, and the glass roof is carefully cleaned by a gang of workmen who do nothing else. In these works are forged steel ingots or blooms weighing as much as twenty tons; and when you stand thirty feet from the immense furnace, whose flames have a temperature of more than a thousand degrees, you do not guess its presence save when its great doors open to let out a steel monster. And the monster is handled by only three or four workmen, who now here, now there, open a tap causing immense cranes to move one way or another by the pressure of water.

You enter these works expecting to hear the deafening noise of stampers, and you find that there are no stampers. The immense hundred-ton guns and the crank-shafts of transatlantic steamers are forged by hydraulic pressure, and the worker has but to turn a tap to give shape to the immense mass of steel, which makes a far more homogeneous metal, without crack or flaw, of the blooms, whatever be their thickness.

I expected an infernal grating, and I saw machines which cut blocks of steel thirty feet long with no more noise than is needed to cut cheese. And when I expressed my admiration to the engineer who showed us round, he answered—

"A mere question of economy! This machine, that planes steel, has been in use for forty-two years. It would not have lasted ten years if its parts, badly adjusted, 'interfered' and creaked at each movement of the plane!

"And the blast-furnaces? It would be a waste to let heat escape instead of utilizing it. Why roast the founders, when heat lost by radiation represents tons of coal?

"The stampers that made buildings shake five leagues off were also waste. Is it not better to forge by pressure than by impact, and it costs less—there is less loss.

"In these works, light, cleanliness, the space allotted to each bench, are but a simple question of economy. Work is better done when you can see what you do, and have elbow-room.

"It is true," he said, "we were very cramped before coming here. Land is so expensive in the vicinity of large towns—landlords are so grasping!"

It is even so in mines. We know what mines are like nowadays from Zola's descriptions and from newspaper reports. But the mine of the future will be well ventilated, with a temperature as easily regulated as that of a library; there will be no horses doomed to die below the earth: underground traction will be carried on by means of an automatic cable put into motion at the pit's mouth. Ventilators will be always working, and there will never be explosions. This is no dream, such a mine is already to be seen in England; I went down it. Here again the excellent organization is simply a question of economy. The mine of which I speak, in spite of its immense depth (466 yards), has an output of a thousand tons of coal a day, with only two hundred miners—five tons a day per each worker, whereas the average for the two thousand pits in England at the time I visited this mine in the early 'nineties, was hardly three hundred tons a year per man.

If necessary, it would be easy to multiply examples proving that as regards the material organization Fourier's dream was not a Utopia.

This question has, however, been so frequently discussed in Socialist newspapers that public opinion should already be educated on this point. Factory, forge and mine *can* be as healthy and magnificent as the finest laboratories in modern universities, and the better the organization the more will man's labour produce.

If it be so, can we doubt that work will become a pleasure and a relaxation in a society of equals, in which "hands" will not be compelled to sell themselves to toil, and to accept work under any conditions? Repugnant tasks will disappear, because it is evident that these unhealthy conditions are harmful to society as a whole. Slaves can submit to them, but free men will create new conditions, and their work will be pleasant and infinitely more productive. The exceptions of to-day will be the rule of to-morrow.

The same will come to pass as regards domestic work, which to-day society lays on the shoulders of that drudge of humanity—woman.

II

A society regenerated by the Revolution will make domestic slavery disappear—this last form of slavery, perhaps the most tenacious, because it is also the most ancient. Only it will not come about in the way dreamt of by Phalansterians, nor in the manner often imagined by authoritarian Communists.

Phalansteries are repugnant to millions of human beings. The most reserved man certainly feels the necessity of meeting his fellows for the purpose of common work, which becomes the more attractive the more he feels himself a part of an immense whole. But it is not so for the hours of leisure, reserved for rest and intimacy. The phalanstery and the familystery do not take this into account, or else they endeavour to supply this need by artificial groupings.

A phalanstery, which is in fact nothing but an immense hotel, can please some, and even all at a certain period of their life, but the great mass prefers family life (family life of the future, be it understood). They prefer isolated apartments, Anglo-Saxons even going as far as to prefer houses of from six to eight rooms, in which the family, or an agglomeration of friends, can live apart. Sometimes a phalanstery is a necessity, but it would be hateful, were it the general rule. Isolation, alternating with time spent in society, is the normal desire of human nature. This is why one of the greatest tortures in prison is the impossibility of isolation, much as solitary confinement becomes torture in its turn, when not alternated with hours of social life.

As to considerations of economy, which are sometimes laid stress on in favour of phalansteries, they are those of a petty tradesman. The most important economy, the only reasonable one, is to make life pleasant for all, because the man who is satisfied with his life produces infinitely more than the man who curses his surroundings.[8]

Other Socialists reject the phalanstery. But when you ask them how domestic work can be organized, they answer: "Each can do 'his own work.' My wife manages the house; the wives of bourgeois will do as much." And if it is a bourgeois playing at Socialism who speaks, he will add, with a gracious smile to his wife: "Is it not true, darling, that you would do without a servant in the Socialist society? You would work like the wife of our good comrade Paul or the wife of John the carpenter?"

Servant or wife, man always reckons on woman to do the housework.

But woman, too, at last claims her share in the emancipation of humanity. She no longer wants to be the beast of burden of the house. She considers it sufficient work to give many years of her life to the rearing of her children. She no longer wants to be the cook, the mender, the sweeper of the house! And, owing to

American women taking the lead in obtaining their claims, there is a general complaint of the dearth of women who will condescend to domestic work in the United States. My lady prefers art, politics, literature, or the gaming tables; as to the work-girls, they are few, those who consent to submit to apron-slavery, and servants are only found with difficulty in the States. Consequently, the solution, a very simple one, is pointed out by life itself. Machinery undertakes three-quarters of the household cares.

You black your boots, and you know how ridiculous this work is. What can be more stupid than rubbing a boot twenty or thirty times with a brush? A tenth of the European population must be compelled to sell itself in exchange for a miserable shelter and insufficient food, and woman must consider herself a slave, in order that millions of her sex should go through this performance every morning.

But hairdressers have already machines for brushing glossy or woolly heads of hair. Why should we not apply, then, the same principle to the other extremity? So it has been done, and nowadays the machine for blacking boots is in general use in big American and European hotels. Its use is spreading outside hotels. In large English schools, where the pupils are boarding in the houses of the teachers, it has been found easier to have one single establishment which undertakes to brush a thousand pairs of boots every morning.

As to washing up! Where can we find a housewife who has not a horror of this long and dirty work, that is usually done by hand, solely because the work of the domestic slave is of no account.

In America they do better. There are already a number of cities in which hot water is conveyed to the houses as cold water is in Europe. Under these conditions the problem was a simple one, and a woman—Mrs. Cochrane—solved it. Her machine washes twelve dozen plates or dishes, wipes them and dries them, in less than three minutes. A factory in Illinois manufactures these machines and sells them at a price within reach of the average middle-class purse. And why should not small households send their crockery to an establishment as well as their boots? It is even probable that the two functions, brushing and washing up, will be undertaken by the same association.

Cleaning, rubbing the skin off your hands when washing and wringing linen; sweeping floors and brushing carpets, thereby raising clouds of dust which afterwards occasion much trouble to dislodge from the places where they have settled down, all this work is still done because woman remains a slave, but it tends to disappear as it can be infinitely better done by machinery. Machines of all kinds will be introduced into households, and the distribution of motor-power in private houses will enable people to work them without muscular effort.

Such machines cost little to manufacture. If we still pay very much for them, it is because they are not in general use, and chiefly because an exorbitant tax is levied upon every machine by the gentlemen who wish to live in grand style and who have speculated on land, raw material, manufacture, sale, patents, and duties.

But emancipation from domestic toil will not be brought about by small machines only. Households are emerging from their present state of isolation; they begin to associate with other households to do in common what they did separately.

In fact, in the future we shall not have a brushing machine, a machine for washing up plates, a third for washing linen, and so on, in each house. To the future, on the contrary, belongs the common heating apparatus that sends heat into each room of a whole district and spares the lighting of fires. It is already so in a few American cities. A great central furnace supplies all houses and all rooms with hot water, which circulates in pipes; and to regulate the temperature you need only turn a tap. And should you care to have a blazing fire in any particular room you can light the gas specially supplied for heating purposes from a central reservoir. All the immense work of cleaning chimneys and keeping up fires—and woman knows what time it takes—is disappearing.

Candles, lamps, and even gas have had their day. There are entire cities in which it is sufficient to press a button for light to burst forth, and, indeed, it is a simple question of economy and of knowledge to give yourself the luxury of electric light. And lastly, also in America, they speak of forming societies for the almost complete suppression of household work. It would only be necessary to create a department for every block of houses. A cart would come to each door and take the boots to be blacked, the crockery to be washed up, the linen to be washed, the small things to be mended (if it were worth while), the carpets to be brushed, and the next morning would bring back the things entrusted to it, all well cleaned. A few hours later your hot coffee and your eggs done to a nicety would appear on your table. It is a fact that between twelve and two o'clock there are more than twenty million Americans and as many Englishmen who eat roast beef or mutton, boiled pork, potatoes and a seasonable vegetable. And at the lowest figure eight million fires burn during two or three hours to roast this meat and cook these vegetables; eight million women spend their time preparing a meal which, taking all households, represents at most a dozen different dishes.

"Fifty fires burn," wrote an American woman the other day, "where one would suffice!" Dine at home, at your own table, with your children, if you like; but only think yourself, why should these fifty women waste their whole morning to prepare a few cups of coffee and a simple meal! Why fifty fires, when two people and one single fire would suffice to cook all these pieces of meat and all these vegetables? Choose your own beef or mutton to be roasted if you are particular. Season the vegetables to your taste if you prefer a particular sauce! But have a single kitchen with a single fire and organize it as beautifully as you are able to.

Why has woman's work never been of any account? Why in every family are the mother and three or four servants obliged to spend so much time at what pertains to cooking? Because those who want to emancipate mankind have not included woman in their dream of emancipation, and consider it beneath their superior masculine dignity to think "of those kitchen arrangements," which they have put on the shoulders of that drudge—woman.

To emancipate woman, is not only to open the gates of the university, the law courts, or the parliaments to her, for the "emancipated" woman will always throw her domestic toil on to another woman. To emancipate woman is to free her from the brutalizing toil of kitchen and washhouse; it is to organize your household in such a way as to enable her to rear her children, if she be so minded, while still retaining sufficient leisure to take her share of social life.

It will come. As we have said, things are already improving. Only let us fully understand that a revolution, intoxicated with the beautiful words, Liberty, Equality, Solidarity, would not be a revolution if it maintained slavery at home. Half humanity subjected to the slavery of the hearth would still have to rebel against the other half.

FOOTNOTES:

[8] It seems that the Communists of Young Icaria had understood

the importance of a free choice in their daily relations apart from work. The ideal of religious Communists has always been to have meals in common; it is by meals in common that early Christians manifested their adhesion to Christianity. Communion is still a vestige of it. Young Icarians had given up this religious tradition. They dined in a common dining room, but at small separate tables, at which they sat according to the attractions of the moment. The Communists of Anama have each their house and dine at home, while taking their provisions at will at the communal stores.

CHAPTER XI
FREE AGREEMENT

I

Accustomed as we are by heredity prejudices and our unsound education and training to represent ourselves the beneficial hand of Government, legislation and magistracy everywhere, we have come to believe that man would tear his fellow-man to pieces like a wild beast the day the police took his eye off him; that absolute chaos would come about if authority were overthrown during a revolution. And with our eyes shut we pass by thousands and thousands of human groupings which form themselves freely, without any intervention of the law, and attain results infinitely superior to those achieved under governmental tutelage.

If you open a daily paper you find that its pages are entirely devoted to Government transactions and to political jobbery. A man from another world, reading it, would believe that, with the exception of the Stock Exchange transactions, nothing gets done in Europe save by order of some master. You find nothing in the paper about institutions that spring up, grow up, and develop without ministerial prescription! Nothing—or almost nothing! Even where there is a heading, "Sundry Events" (*Faits divers*, a favorite column in the French papers), it is because they are connected with the police. A family drama, an act of rebellion, will only be mentioned if the police have appeared on the scene.

Three hundred and fifty million Europeans love or hate one another, work, or live on their incomes; but, apart from literature, theatre, or sport, their lives remain ignored by newspapers if Governments have not intervened in it in some way or other. It is even so with history. We know the least details of the life of a king or of a parliament; all good and bad speeches pronounced by the politicians have been preserved: "speeches that have never had the least influence on the vote of a single member," as an old parliamentarian said. Royal visits, the good or bad humour of politicians, their jokes and intrigues, are all carefully recorded for posterity. But we have the greatest difficulty to reconstitute a city of the Middle Ages, to understand the mechanism of that immense commerce that was carried on between Hanseatic cities, or to know how the city of Rouen built its cathedral. If a scholar spends his life in studying these questions, his works remain unknown, and parliamentary histories—that is to say, the defective ones, as they only treat of one side of social life—multiply; they are circulated, they are taught in schools.

In this way we do not even perceive the prodigious work, accomplished every day by spontaneous groups of men, which constitutes the chief work of our century.

We therefore propose to point out some of these most striking manifestations, and to show how men, as soon as their interests do not absolutely clash, act in concert, harmoniously, and perform collective work of a very complex nature.

It is evident that in present society, based on individual property—that is to say, on plunder, and on a narrow-minded, and therefore foolish individualism—facts of this kind are necessarily limited; agreements are not always perfectly free, and often they have a mean, if not execrable aim.

But what concerns us is not to give examples which might be blindly followed, and which, moreover, present society could not possibly give us. What we have to do is to show that, in spite of the authoritarian individualism which stifles us, there remains in our life, taken as a whole, a very great part in which we only act by free agreement; and that therefore it would be much easier than is usually thought, to dispense with Government.

In support of our view we have already mentioned railways, and we will now return to them.

We know that Europe has a system of railways, over 175,000 miles long, and that on this network you can nowadays travel from north to south, from east to west, from Madrid to Petersburg, and from Calais to Constantinople, without delays, without even changing carriages (when you travel by express). More than that: a parcel deposited at a station will find its addressee anywhere, in Turkey or in Central Asia, without more formality needed for sending it than writing its destination on a bit of paper.

This result might have been obtained in two ways. A Napoleon, a Bismarck, or some potentate having conquered Europe, would from Paris, Berlin, or Rome, draw a railway map and regulate the hours of the trains. The Russian Tsar Nicholas I. dreamt of such a power. When he was shown rough drafts of railways between Moscow and Petersburg, he seized a ruler and drew on the map of Russia a straight line between these two capitals, saying, "Here is the plan." And the road was built in a straight line, filling in deep ravines, building bridges of a giddy height, which had to be abandoned a few years later, after the railway had cost about £120,000 to £150,000 per English mile.

This is one way, but happily things were managed differently. Railways were constructed piece by piece, the pieces were joined together, and the hundred different companies, to whom these pieces belonged, gradually came to an understanding concerning the arrival and departure of their trains, and the running of carriages on their rails, from all countries, without unloading merchandise as it passes from one network to another.

All this was done by free agreement, by exchange of letters and proposals, and by congresses at which delegates met to discuss well specified special points, and to come to an agreement about them, but not to make laws. After the congress was over, the delegates returned to their respective companies, not with a law, but with the draft of a contract to be accepted or rejected.

Of course difficulties were met in the way. There were obstinate men who would not be convinced. But a common interest compelled them to agree in the end, without invoking the help of armies against the refractory members.

This immense network of railways connected together, and the enormous traffic it has given rise to, no doubt constitutes the most striking trait of the nineteenth century; and it is the result of free agreement. If somebody had foretold it eighty years ago, our grandfathers would have thought him idiotic or mad. They would have said: "Never will you be able to make the shareholders of a hundred companies listen to reason! It is a Utopia, a fairy tale. A central Government, with an 'iron' dictator, can alone enforce it."

And the most interesting thing in this organization is, that there is no European Central Government of Railways! Nothing! No minister of railways, no dictator, not even a continental parliament, not even a directing committee! Everything is done by free agreement.

So we ask the believers in the State, who pretend that "we can never do without a central Government, were it only for regulating the traffic," we ask them: "But how do European railways manage without them? How do they continue to convey millions of travellers and mountains of luggage across a continent? If companies owning railways have been able to agree, why should railway workers, who would take possession of railways, not agree likewise? And if the Petersburg-Warsaw Company and that of Paris-Belfort can act in harmony, without giving themselves the luxury of a common commander, why, in the midst of our societies, consisting of groups of free workers, should we need a Government?"

II

When we endeavour to prove by examples that even to-day, in spite of the iniquitous organization of society as a whole, men, provided their interests be not diametrically opposed, agree without the intervention of authority, we do not ignore the objections that will be put forth.

All such examples have their defective side, because it is impossible to quote a single organization exempt from the exploitation of the weak by the strong, the poor by the rich. This is why the Statists will not fail to tell us with their wonted logic: "You see that the intervention of the State is necessary to put an end to this exploitation!"

Only they forget the lessons of history; they do not tell us to what extent the State itself has contributed towards the existing order by creating proletarians and delivering them up to exploiters. They forget to prove us that it is possible to put an end to exploitation while the primal causes—private capital and poverty, two-thirds of which are artificially created by the State—continue to exist.

When we speak of the accord established among the railway companies, we expect them, the worshippers of the bourgeois

State, to say to us: "Do you not see how the railway companies oppress and ill-use their employees and the travellers! The only way is, that the State should intervene to protect the workers and the public!"

But have we not said and repeated over and over again, that as long as there are capitalists, these abuses of power will be perpetuated? It is precisely the State, the would-be benefactor, that has given to the companies that monopoly and those rights upon us which they possess to-day. Has it not created concessions, guarantees? Has it not sent its soldiers against railwaymen on strike? And during the first trials (quite lately we saw it still in Russia), has it not extended the privilege of the railway magnates as far as to forbid the Press to mention railway accidents, so as not to depreciate the shares it guaranteed? Has it not favoured the monopoly which has anointed the Vanderbilts and the Polyakoffs, the directors of the P.L.M., the C.P.R., the St. Gothard, "the kings of our days"?

Therefore, if we give as an example the tacit agreement come to between railway companies, it is by no means as an ideal of economical management, nor even an ideal of technical organization. It is to show that if capitalists, without any other aim than that of augmenting their dividends at other people's expense, can exploit railways successfully without establishing an International Department,—societies of working men will be able to do it just as well, and even better, without nominating a Ministry of European railways.

Another objection is raised that is more serious at first sight. We may be told that the agreement we speak of is not perfectly *free*, that the large companies lay down the law to the small ones. It might be mentioned, for example, that a certain rich German company, supported by the State, compel travellers who go from Berlin to Bâle to pass via Cologne and Frankfort, instead of taking the Leipzig route; or that such a company carries goods a hundred and thirty miles in a roundabout way (on a long distance) to favour its influential shareholders, and thus ruins the secondary lines. In the United States travellers and goods are sometimes compelled to travel impossibly circuitous routes so that dollars may flow into the pocket of a Vanderbilt.

Our answer will be the same: As long as Capital exists, the Greater Capital will oppress the lesser. But oppression does not result from Capital only. It is also owing to the support given them by the State, to monopoly created by the State in their favour, that the large companies oppress the small ones.

The early English and French Socialists have shown long since how English legislation did all in its power to ruin the small industries, drive the peasant to poverty, and deliver over to wealthy industrial employers battalions of men, compelled to work for no matter what salary. Railway legislation did exactly the same. Strategic lines, subsidized lines, companies which received the International Mail monopoly, everything was brought into play to forward the interests of wealthy financiers. When Rothschild, creditor to all European States, puts capital in a railway, his faithful subjects, the ministers, will do their best to make him earn more.

In the United States, in the Democracy that authoritarians hold up to us as an ideal, the most scandalous fraudulency has crept into everything that concerns railroads. Thus, if a company ruins its competitors by cheap fares, it is often enabled to do so because it is reimbursed by land given to it by the State for a gratuity. Documents recently published concerning the American wheat trade have fully shown up the part played by the State in the exploitation of the weak by the strong. Here, too, the power of accumulated capital has increased tenfold and a hundredfold by means of State help. So that, when we see syndicates of railway companies (a product of free agreement) succeeding in protecting their small companies against big ones, we are astonished at the intrinsic force of free agreement that can hold its own against all-powerful Capital favoured by the State.

It is a fact that little companies exist, in spite of the State's partiality. If in France, land of centralization, we only see five or six large companies, there are more than a hundred and ten in Great Britain who agree remarkably well, and who are certainly better organized for the rapid transit of travellers and goods than the French and German companies.

Moreover, that is not the question. Large Capital, favoured by the State, can always, *if it be to its advantage,* crush the lesser one. What is of importance to us is this: The agreement between hundreds of capitalist companies to whom the railways of Europe belong, *was established without intervention of a central government* to lay down the law to the divers societies; it has subsisted by means of congresses composed of delegates, who discuss among themselves, and submit *proposals,* not *laws,* to their constituents. It is a new principle that differs completely from all governmental principle, monarchical or republican, absolute or parliamentarian. It is an innovation that has been timidly introduced into the customs of Europe, but has come to stay.

III

How often have we not read in the writings of State-loving Socialists: "Who, then, will undertake the regulation of canal traffic in the future society? Should it enter the mind of one of your Anarchist 'comrades' to put his barge across a canal and obstruct thousands of boats, who will force him to reason?"

Let us confess the supposition to be somewhat fanciful. Still, it might be said, for instance: "Should a certain commune, or a group of communes, want to make their barges pass before others, they might perhaps block the canal in order to carry stones, while wheat, needed in another commune, would have to stand by. Who, then, would regulate the traffic if not the Government?"

But real life has again demonstrated that Government can be very well dispensed with here as elsewhere. Free agreement, free organization, replace that noxious and costly system, and do better.

We know what canals mean to Holland. They are its highways. We also know how much traffic there is on the canals. What is carried along our highroads and railroads is transported on canal-boats in Holland. There you could find cause to fight, in order to make your boats pass before others. There the Government might really interfere to keep the traffic in order.

Yet it is not so. The Dutch settled matters in a more practical way, long ago, by founding guilds, or syndicates of boatmen. These were free associations sprung from the very needs of navigation. The right of way for the boats was adjusted by the order of inscription in a navigation register; they had to follow one another in turn. Nobody was allowed to get ahead of the others under pain of being excluded from the guild. None could station more than a certain number of days along the quay; and if the owner found no goods to carry during that time, so much the worse for him; he had to depart with his empty barge to leave room for newcomers. Obstruction was thus avoided, even though the competition between the private owners of the boats continued to exist. Were the latter suppressed, the agreement would have been only the more cordial.

It is unnecessary to add that the shipowners could adhere or not to the syndicate. That was their business, but most of them elected to join it. Moreover, these syndicates offered such great advantages that they spread also along the Rhine, the Weser, the Oder, and as far as Berlin. The boatmen did not wait for a great Bismarck to annex Holland to Germany, and to appoint an Ober Haupt General Staats Canal Navigation's Rath (Supreme Head Councillor of the General States Canal Navigation), with a number of gold stripes on his sleeves, corresponding to the length of the title. They preferred coming to an international understanding. Besides, a number of shipowners, whose sailing-vessels ply between Germany and Scandinavia, as well as Russia, have also joined these syndicates, in order to regulate traffic in the Baltic, and to bring about a certain harmony in the *chassé-croisé* of vessels. These associations have sprung up freely, recruiting volunteer adherents, and have nought in common with governments.

It is, however, more than probable that here too greater capital oppresses lesser. Maybe the syndicate has also a tendency to become a monopoly, especially where it receives the precious patronage of the State that surely did not fail to interfere with it. Let us not forget either, that these syndicates represent associations whose members have only private interests at stake, and that if at the same time each shipowner were compelled—by the socializing of production, consumption, and exchange—to belong to federated Communes, or to a hundred other associations for the satisfying of his needs, things would have a different aspect. A group of shipowners, powerful on sea, would feel weak on land, and they would be obliged to lessen their claims in order to come to terms with railways, factories, and other groups.

At any rate, without discussing the future, here is another spontaneous association that has dispensed with Government.

Let us quote more examples.

As we are talking of ships and boats, let us mention one of the most splendid organizations that the nineteenth century has brought forth, one of those we may with right be proud of—the English Lifeboat Association.

It is known that every year more than a thousand ships are wrecked on the shores of England. At sea a good ship seldom fears a storm. It is near the coasts that danger threatens—rough seas that shatter her stern-post, squalls that carry off her masts and sails, currents that render her unmanageable, reefs and sand banks on which she runs aground.

Even in olden times, when it was a custom among inhabitants of the coasts to light fires in order to attract vessels on to reefs, in order to plunder their cargoes, they always strove to save the crew. Seeing a ship in distress, they launched their boats and went to the rescue of shipwrecked sailors, only too often finding a watery grave themselves. Every hamlet along the sea shore has its legends of heroism, displayed by woman as well as by man, to save crews in distress.

No doubt the State and men of science have done something to diminish the number of casualties. Lighthouses, signals, charts, meteorological warnings have diminished them greatly, but there remains a thousand ships and several thousand human lives to be saved every year.

To this end a few men of goodwill put their shoulders to the wheel. Being good sailors and navigators themselves, they invented a lifeboat that could weather a storm without being torn to pieces or capsizing, and they set to work to interest the public in their venture, to collect the necessary funds for constructing boats, and for stationing them along the coasts, wherever they could be of use.

These men, not being Jacobins, did not turn to the Government. They understood that to bring their enterprise to a successful issue they must have the co-operation, the enthusiasm, the local knowledge, and especially the self-sacrifice of the local sailors. They also understood that to find men who at the first signal would launch their boat at night, in a chaos of waves, not suffering themselves to be deterred by darkness or breakers, and struggling five, six, ten hours against the tide before reaching a vessel in distress—men ready to risk their lives to save those of others—there must be a feeling of solidarity, a spirit of sacrifice not to be bought with galloon. It was therefore a perfectly spontaneous movement, sprung from agreement and individual initiative. Hundreds of local groups arose along the coasts. The initiators had the common senses not to pose as masters. They looked for sagacity in the fishermen's hamlets, and when a rich man sent £1,000 to a village on the coast to erect a lifeboat station, and his offer was accepted, he left the choice of a site to the local fishermen and sailors.

Models of new boats were not submitted to the Admiralty. We read in a Report of the Association: "As it is of importance that life-boatmen should have full confidence in the vessel they man, the Committee will make a point of constructing and equipping the boats according to the life-boatmen's expressed wish." In consequence every year brings with it new improvements.

The work is wholly conducted by volunteers organizing in committees and local groups; by mutual aid and agreement!—Oh, Anarchists! Moreover, they ask nothing of the ratepayers, and in a year they may receive £40,000 in spontaneous subscriptions.

As to the results, here they are: In 1891 the Association possessed 293 lifeboats. The same year it saved 601 shipwrecked sailors and 33 vessels. Since its foundation it has saved 32,671 human beings.

In 1886, three lifeboats with all their men having perished at sea, hundreds of new volunteers entered their names, organized themselves into local groups, and the agitation resulted in the construction of twenty additional boats. As we proceed, let us note that every year the Association sends to the fishermen and sailors excellent barometers at a price three times less than their sale price in private shops. It propagates meteorological knowledge, and warns the parties concerned of the sudden changes of weather predicted by men of science.

Let us repeat that these hundreds of committees and local groups are not organized hierarchically, and are composed exclusively of volunteers, lifeboatmen, and people interested in the work. The Central Committee, which is more of a centre for correspondence, in no wise interferes.

It is true that when a voting on some question of education or local taxation takes place in a district, these committees of the National Lifeboat Association do not, as such, take part in the deliberations—a modesty, which unfortunately the members of elected bodies do not imitate. But, on the other hand, these brave men do not allow those who have never faced a storm to legislate for them about saving life. At the first signal of distress they rush to their boats, and go ahead. There are no embroidered uniforms, but much goodwill.

Let us take another society of the same kind, that of the Red Cross. The name matters little; let us examine it.

Imagine somebody saying fifty years ago: "The State, capable as it is of massacring twenty thousand men in a day, and of wounding fifty thousand more, is incapable of helping its own victims; consequently, as long as war exists private initiative must intervene, and men of goodwill must organize internationally for this humane work!" What mockery would not have met the man who would have dared to speak thus! To begin with, he would have been called a Utopian, and if that did not silence him he would have been told: "What nonsense! Your volunteers will be found wanting precisely where they are most needed, your volunteer hospitals will be centralized in a safe place, while everything will be wanting in the ambulances. Utopians like you forget the national rivalries which will cause the poor soldiers to die without any help." Such disheartening remarks would have only been equalled by the number of speakers. Who of us has not heard men hold forth in this strain?

Now we know what happened. Red Cross societies organized themselves freely, everywhere, in all countries, in thousands of localities; and when the war of 1870-1 broke out, the volunteers set to work. Men and women offered their services. Thousands of hospitals and ambulances were organized; trains were started carrying ambulances, provisions, linen, and medicaments for the wounded. The English committees sent entire convoys of food, clothing, tools, grain to sow, beasts of draught, even steam-ploughs with their attendants to help in the tillage of departments devastated by the war! Only consult *La Croix Rouge,* by Gustave Moynier, and you will be really struck by the immensity of the work performed.

As to the prophets ever ready to deny other men's courage, good sense, and intelligence, and believing themselves to be the only ones capable of ruling the world with a rod, none of their predictions were realized. The devotion of the Red Cross volunteers was beyond all praise. They were only too eager to occupy the most dangerous posts; and whereas the salaried doctors of the Napoleonic State fled with their staff when the Prussians approached, the Red Cross volunteers continued their work under fire, enduring the brutalities of Bismarck's and Napoleon's officers, lavishing their care on the wounded of all nationalities. Dutch, Italians, Swedes, Belgians, even Japanese and Chinese agreed remarkably well. They distributed their hospitals and their ambulances according to the needs of the occasion. They vied with one another especially in the hygiene of their hospitals. And there is many a Frenchman who still speaks with deep gratitude of the tender care he received from the Dutch or German volunteers in the Red Cross ambulances. But what is this to an authoritarian? His ideal is the regiment doctor, salaried by the State. What does he care for the Red Cross and its hygienic hospitals, if the nurses be not functionaries!

Here is then an organization, sprung up but yesterday, and which reckons its members by hundreds of thousands; possesses ambulances, hospital trains, elaborates new processes for treating wounds, and so on, and is due to the spontaneous initiative of a few devoted men.

Perhaps we shall be told that the State has something to do with this organization. Yes, States have laid hands on it to seize it. The directing committees are presided over by those whom flunkeys call princes of the blood. Emperors and queens lavishly patronize the national committees. But it is not to this patronage that the success of the organization is due. It is to the thousand local committees of each nation; to the activity of individuals, to the devotion of all those who try to help the victims of war. And this devotion would be far greater if the State did not meddle with it.

In any case, it was not by the order of an International Directing Committee that Englishmen and Japanese, Swedes and Chinamen, bestirred themselves to send help to the wounded in 1871. It was not by order of an international ministry that hospitals rose on the invaded territory and that ambulances were carried on to the battlefield. It was by the initiative of volunteers from each country. Once on the spot, they did not get hold of one another by the hair as was foreseen by the Jacobinists of all nations; they all set to work without distinction of nationality.

We may regret that such great efforts should be put to the service of so bad a cause, and we may ask ourselves like the poet's child: "Why inflict wounds if you are to heal them afterwards?" In striving to destroy the power of capitalist and middle-class authority, we work to put an end to the massacres called wars, and we would far rather see the Red Cross volunteers put forth their activity to bring about (with us) the suppression of war; but we had to mention this immense organization as another illustration of results produced by free agreement and free aid.

If we wished to multiply examples taken from the art of exterminating men we should never end. Suffice to quote the numerous societies to which the German army owes its force, that does not only depend on discipline, as is generally believed. I mean the societies whose aim is to propagate military knowledge.

At one of the last congresses of the Military Alliance (Kriegerbund), delegates from 2,452 federated societies, comprising 151,712 members, were present. But there are besides very numerous Shooting, Military Games, Strategical Games, Topographical Studies Societies—these are the workshops in which the technical knowledge of the German army is developed, not in regimental schools. It is a formidable network of all kinds of societies, including military men and civilians, geographers and gymnasts, sportsmen and technologists, which rise up spontaneously, organize, federate, discuss, and explore the country. It is these voluntary and free associations that go to make the real backbone of the German army.

Their aim is execrable. It is the maintenance of the Empire. But what concerns us, is to point out that, in spite of military organization being the "Great Mission of the State," success in this branch is the more certain the more it is left to the free agreement of groups and to the free initiative of individuals.

Even in matters pertaining to war, free agreement is thus appealed to; and to further prove our assertion let us mention the Volunteer Topographers' Corps of Switzerland who study in detail the mountain passages, the Aeroplane Corps of France, the three hundred thousand British volunteers, the British National Artillery Association, and the Society, now in course of organization, for the defence of England's coasts, as well as the appeals made to the commercial fleet, the Bicyclists' Corps, and the new organizations of private motorcars and steam launches.

Everywhere the State is abdicating and abandoning its holy functions to private individuals. Everywhere free organization trespasses on its domain. And yet, the facts we have quoted give us only a glimpse of what free government has in store for us in the future when there will be no more State.

CHAPTER XII
OBJECTIONS

I

Let us now examine the principal objections put forth against Communism. Most of them are evidently caused by a simple misunderstanding, yet they raise important questions and merit our attention.

It is not for us to answer the objections raised by authoritarian Communism—we ourselves hold with them. Civilized nations have suffered too much in the long, hard struggle for the emancipation of the individual, to disown their past work and to tolerate a Government that would make itself felt in the smallest details of a citizen's life, even if that Government had no other aim than the good of the community. Should an authoritarian Socialist society ever succeed in establishing itself, it could not last; general discontent would soon force it to break up, or to reorganize itself on principles of liberty.

It is of an Anarchist-Communist society we are about to speak, a society that recognizes the absolute liberty of the individual, that does not admit of any authority, and makes use of no compulsion to drive men to work. Limiting our studies to the economic side of the question, let us see if such a society, composed of men as they are to-day, neither better nor worse, neither more nor less industrious, would have a chance of successful development.

The objection is known. "If the existence of each is guaranteed, and if the necessity of earning wages does not compel men to work, nobody will work. Every man will lay the burden of his work on another if he is not forced to do it himself." Let us first note the incredible levity with which this objection is raised, without even realizing that the real question raised by this objection is merely to know, on the one hand, whether you effectively obtain by wage-work, the results that are said to be obtained, and, on the other hand, whether voluntary work is not already now more productive than work stimulated by wages. A question which, to be dealt with properly, would require a serious study. But whereas in exact sciences men give their opinion on subjects infinitely less important and less complicated after serious research, after carefully collecting and analyzing facts—on this question they will pronounce judgment without appeal, resting satisfied with any one particular event, such as, for example, the want of success of some communist association in America. They act like the barrister who does not see in the counsel for the opposite side a representative of a cause, or an opinion contrary to his own, but a simple nuisance,—an adversary in an oratorical debate; and if he be lucky enough to find a repartee, does not otherwise care to justify his cause. Therefore the study of this essential basis of all Political Economy, *the study of the most favourable conditions for giving society the greatest amount of useful products with the least waste of human energy*, does not advance. People either limit themselves to repeating commonplace assertions, or else they pretend ignorance of our assertions.

What is most striking in this levity is that even in capitalist Political Economy you already find a few writers compelled by facts to doubt the axiom put forth by the founders of their science, that the threat of hunger is man's best stimulant for productive work. They begin to perceive that in production a certain *collective element* is introduced, which has been too much neglected up till now, and which might be more important than personal gain. The inferior quality of wage-work, the terrible waste of human energy in modern agricultural and industrial labour, the ever-growing quantity of pleasure-seekers, who shift their burden on to others' shoulders, the absence of a certain animation in production that is becoming more and more apparent; all this is beginning to preoccupy the economists of the "classical" school. Some of them ask themselves if they have not got on the wrong track: if the imaginary evil being, that was supposed to be tempted exclusively by a bait of lucre or wages, really exists. This heresy penetrates even into universities; it is found in books of orthodox economy.

But this does not prevent a great many Socialist reformers from remaining partisans of individual remuneration, and defending the old citadel of wagedom, notwithstanding that it is being delivered over stone by stone to the assailants by its former defenders.

They fear that without compulsion the masses will not work.

But during our own lifetime, have we not heard the same fears expressed twice? Once, by the anti-abolitionists in America before the emancipation of the Negroes, and, for a second time, by the Russian nobility before the liberation of the serfs? "Without the whip the Negro will not work," said the anti-abolitionist. "Free from their master's supervision the serfs will leave the fields uncultivated," said the Russian serf-owners. It was the refrain of the French noblemen in 1789, the refrain of the Middle Ages, a refrain as old as the world, and we shall hear it every time there is a question of sweeping away an injustice. And each time actual facts give it the lie. The liberated peasant of 1792 ploughed with an eager energy, unknown to his ancestors; the emancipated Negro works more than his fathers; and the Russian peasant, after having honoured the honeymoon of his emancipation by celebrating Fridays as well as Sundays, has taken up work with an eagerness proportionate to the completeness of his liberation. There, where the soil is his, he works desperately; that is the exact word for it. The anti-abolitionist refrain can be of value to slave-owners; as to the slaves themselves, they know what it is worth, as they know its motive.

Moreover, who but the economists themselves taught us that while a wage-earner's work is very often indifferent, an intense and productive work is only obtained from a man who sees his wealth increase in proportion to his efforts? All hymns sung in honour of private property can be reduced to this axiom.

For it is remarkable that when economists, wishing to celebrate the blessings of property, show us how an unproductive, marshy, or stony soil is clothed with rich harvests when cultivated by the peasant proprietor, they in nowise prove their thesis in favour of private property. By admitting that the only guarantee not to be robbed of the fruits of your labour is to possess the instruments of labour—which is true—the economists only prove that man really produces most when he works in freedom, when he has a certain choice in his occupations, when he has no overseer to impede him, and lastly, when he sees his work bringing in a profit to him and to others who work like him, but bringing in little to idlers. Nothing else can be deducted from their argumentation, and this is what we maintain ourselves.

As to the form of possession of the instruments of labour, the economists only mention it *indirectly* in their demonstration, as a guarantee to the cultivator that he shall not be robbed of the profits of his yield nor of his improvements. Besides, in support of their thesis in favour of *private property* against all other forms of *possession*, should not the economists demonstrate that under the form of communal property land never produces such rich harvests as when the possession is private? But this they could not prove; in fact, it is the contrary that has been observed.

Take for example a commune in the canton of Vaud, in the winter time, when all the men of the village go to fell wood in the forest, which belongs to them all. It is precisely during these festivals of labour that the greatest ardour for work and the most considerable display of human energy are apparent. No salaried labour, no effort of a private owner can bear comparison with it.

Or let us take a Russian village, when all its inhabitants mow a field belonging to the commune, or farmed by it. There you will see what man *can* produce when he works in common for communal production. Comrades vie with one another in cutting the widest swathe, women bestir themselves in their wake so as not to be distanced by the mowers. It is a festival of labour, in which a hundred people accomplish in a few hours a work that would not have been finished in a few days had they worked separately. What a miserable contrast compared to them is offered by the work of the isolated owner!

In fact, we might quote scores of examples among the pioneers of America, in Swiss, German, Russian, and in certain French villages; or the work done in Russia by gangs (*artels*) of masons, carpenters, boatmen, fishermen, etc., who undertake a task and divide the produce or the remuneration among themselves without it passing through an intermediary of middlemen; or else the amount of work I saw performed in English ship-yards when the remuneration was paid on the same principle. We could also mention the great communal hunts of nomadic tribes, and an infinite number of successful collective enterprises. And in every case we could show the unquestionable superiority of communal work compared to that of the wage-earner or the isolated private owner.

Well-being—that is to say, the satisfaction of physical, artistic, and moral needs, has always been the most powerful stimulant to work. And where a hireling hardly succeeds to produce the bare necessities with difficulty, a free worker, who sees ease and luxury increasing for him and for others in proportion to his efforts, spends infinitely far more energy and intelligence, and obtains products in a far greater abundance. The one feels riveted to misery, the other hopes for ease and luxury in the future. In this lies the whole secret. Therefore a society aiming at the well-being of all, and at the possibility of all enjoying life in all its manifestations, will give voluntary work, which will be infinitely superior and yield far more than work has produced up till now under the goad of slavery, serfdom, or wagedom.

II

Nowadays, whoever can load on others his share of labour indispensable to existence does so, and it is believed that it will always be so.

Now, work indispensable to existence is essentially manual. We may be artists or scientists; but none of us can do without things obtained by manual work—bread, clothes, roads, ships, light, heat, etc. And, moreover, however highly artistic or however subtly metaphysical are our pleasures, they all depend on manual labour. And it is precisely this labour—the basis of life—that everyone tries to avoid.

We understand perfectly well that it must be so nowadays.

Because, to do manual work now, means in reality to shut yourself up for ten or twelve hours a day in an unhealthy workshop, and to remain chained to the same task for twenty or thirty years, and maybe for your whole life.

It means to be doomed to a paltry wage, to the uncertainty of the morrow, to want of work, often to destitution, more often than not to death in a hospital, after having worked forty years to feed, clothe, amuse, and instruct others than yourself and your children.

It means to bear the stamp of inferiority all your life; because, whatever the politicians tell us, the manual worker is always considered inferior to the brain worker, and the one who has toiled ten hours in a workshop has not the time, and still less the means, to give himself the high delights of science and art, nor even to prepare himself to appreciate them; he must be content with the crumbs from the table of privileged persons.

We understand that under these conditions manual labour is considered a curse of fate.

We understand that all men have but one dream—that of emerging from, or enabling their children to emerge from this inferior state; to create for themselves an "independent" position, which means what?—To also live by other men's work!

As long as there will be a class of manual workers and a class of "brain" workers, black hands and white hands, it will be thus.

What interest, in fact, can this depressing work have for the worker, when he knows that the fate awaiting him from the cradle to the grave will be to live in mediocrity, poverty, and insecurity of the morrow? Therefore, when we see the immense majority of men take up their wretched task every morning, we feel surprised at their perseverance, at their zeal for work, at the habit that enables them, like machines blindly obeying an impetus given, to lead this life of misery without hope for the morrow; without foreseeing ever so vaguely that some day they, or at least their children, will be part of a humanity rich in all the treasures of a bountiful nature, in all the enjoyments of knowledge, scientific and artistic creation, reserved to-day to a few privileged favourites.

It is precisely to put an end to this separation between manual and brain work that we want to abolish wagedom, that we want the Social Revolution. Then work will no longer appear a curse of fate: it will become what it should be—the free exercise of *all* the faculties of man.

Moreover, it is time to submit to a serious analysis this legend about superior work, supposed to be obtained under the lash of wagedom.

It would be sufficient to visit, not the model factory and workshop that we find now and again, but a number of the ordinary factories, to conceive the immense waste of human energy that characterizes modern industry. For one factory more or less rationally organized, there are a hundred or more which waste man's labour, without any more substantial motive than that of perhaps bringing in a few pounds more per day to the employer.

Here you see youths from twenty to twenty-five years of age, sitting all day long on a bench, their chests sunken in, feverishly shaking their heads and bodies, to tie, with the speed of conjurers, the two ends of worthless scraps of cotton, the refuse of the lace-looms. What progeny will these trembling and rickety bodies bequeath to their country? "But they occupy so little room in the factory, and each of them brings me in sixpence net every day," will say the employer.

In an immense London factory we saw girls, bald at seventeen from carrying trays of matches on their heads from one room to another, when the simplest machine could wheel the matches to their tables. But "It costs so little, the work of women who have no special trade! Why should we use a machine? When these can do no more, they will be easily replaced, there are so many of them in the street!"

On the steps of a mansion on an icy night you will find a bare-footed child asleep, with its bundle of papers in its arms ... child-labour costs so little that it may be well employed, every evening, to sell tenpenny-worth of papers, of which the poor boy will receive a penny, or a penny halfpenny. And continually in all big cities you may see robust men tramping about who have been out of work for months, while their daughters grow pale in the overheated vapours of the workshops for dressing stuffs, and their sons are filling blacking-pots by hand, or spend those years during which they ought to have learned a trade, in carrying about baskets for a greengrocer, and at the age of eighteen or twenty become regular unemployed.

And so it is everywhere, from San Francisco to Moscow, and from Naples to Stockholm. The waste of human energy is the distinguishing and predominant trait of our industry, not to mention trade where it attains still more colossal proportions.

What a sad satire is that name, Political *Economy*, given to the science of waste and energy under the system of wagedom!

This is not all. If you speak to the director of a well-organized factory, he will naively explain to you that it is difficult nowadays to find a skilful, vigorous, and energetic workman, who works with a will. "Should such a man present himself among the twenty or thirty who call every Monday asking us for work, he is sure to be received, even if we are reducing the number of our hands. We recognize him at the first glance, and he is always accepted, even though we have to get rid of an older and less active worker the next day." And the one who has just received notice to quit, and all those who will receive it to-morrow, go to reinforce that immense reserve-army of capital—workmen out of work—who are only called to the loom or the bench when there is pressure of work, or to oppose strikers. And those others—the average workers who are sent away by the better-class factories as soon as business is slackened? They also join the formidable army of aged and indifferent workers who continually circulate among the second-class factories—those which barely cover their expenses and make their way in the world by trickery and snares laid for the buyer, and especially for the consumer in distant countries.

And if you talk to the workmen themselves, you will soon learn that the rule in such factories is—never to do your best. "Shoddy pay—shoddy work!" this is the advice which the working man receives from his comrades upon entering such a factory.

For the workers know that if in a moment of generosity they give way to the entreaties of an employer and consent to intensify the work in order to carry out a pressing order, this nervous work will be exacted in the future as a rule in the scale of wages. Therefore in all such factories they prefer never to produce as much as they can. In certain industries production is limited so as to keep up high prices, and sometimes the password, "Go-canny," is given, which signifies, "Bad work for bad pay!"

Wage-work is serf-work; it cannot, it must not, produce all that it could produce. And it is high time to disbelieve the legend which represents wagedom as the best incentive to productive work. If industry nowadays brings in a hundred times more than it did in the days of our grandfathers, it is due to the sudden awakening of physical and chemical sciences towards the end of last century; not to the capitalist organization of wagedom, but *in spite* of that organization.

III

Those who have seriously studied the question do not deny any of the advantages of Communism, on condition, be it well understood, that Communism be perfectly free, that is to say, Anarchist. They recognize that work paid with money, even disguised under the name of "labour cheques," to Workers' associations governed by the State, would keep up the characteristics of wagedom and would retain its disadvantages. They agree that the whole system would soon suffer from it, even if Society came into possession of the instruments of production. And they admit that, thanks to an "integral" complete education given to all children, to the laborious habits of civilized societies, with the liberty of choosing and varying their occupations and the attractions of work done by equals for the well-being of all, a Communist society would not be wanting in producers who would soon make the fertility of the soil triple and tenfold, and give a new impulse to industry.

This our opponents agree to. "But the danger," they say, "will come from that minority of loafers who will not work, and will not have regular habits, in spite of the excellent conditions that would make work pleasant. To-day the prospect of hunger compels the most refractory to move along with the others. The one who does not arrive in time is dismissed. But one black sheep suffices to contaminate the whole flock, and two or three sluggish or refractory workmen would lead the others astray and bring a spirit of disorder and rebellion into the workshop that would make work impossible; so that in the end we should have to return to a system of compulsion that would force such ringleaders back into the ranks. And then,—Is not the system of wages, paid in proportion to work performed, the only one that enables compulsion to be employed, without hurting the feelings of independence of the worker? All other means would imply the continual intervention of an authority that would be repugnant to free men." This, we believe, is the objection fairly stated.

To begin with, such an objection belongs to the category of arguments which try to justify the State, the Penal Law, the Judge, and the Gaoler.

"As there are people, a feeble minority, who will not submit to social customs," the authoritarians say, "we must maintain magistrates, tribunals and prisons, although these institutions become a source of new evils of all kinds."

Therefore we can only repeat what we have so often said concerning authority in general: "To avoid a possible evil you have recourse to means which in themselves are a greater evil, and become the source of those same abuses that you wish to remedy. For, do not forget that it is wagedom, the impossibility of living otherwise than by selling your labour, which has created the present Capitalist system, whose vices you begin to recognize." Besides, this way of reasoning is merely a sophistical justification of the evils of the present system. Wagedom was *not* instituted to remove the disadvantages of Communism; its origin, like that of the State and private ownership, is to be found elsewhere. It is born of slavery and serfdom imposed by force, and only wears a more modern garb. Thus the argument in favour of wagedom is as valueless as those by which they seek to apologize for private property and the State.

We are, nevertheless, going to examine the objection, and see if there is any truth in it.

First of all,—Is it not evident that if a society, founded on the principle of free work, were really menaced by loafers, it could protect itself without the authoritarian organization we have nowadays, and without having recourse to wagedom?

Let us take a group of volunteers, combining for some particular enterprise. Having its success at heart, they all work with a will, save one of the associates, who is frequently absent from his post. Must they on his account dissolve the group, elect a president to impose fines, and work out a code of penalties? It is evident that neither the one nor the other will be done, but that some day the comrade who imperils their enterprise will be told: "Friend, we should like to work with you; but as you are often absent from your post, and you do your work negligently, we must part. Go and find other comrades who will put up with your indifference!"

This way is so natural that it is practiced everywhere, even nowadays, in all industries, in competition with all possible systems of fines, docking of wages, supervision, etc.; a workman may enter the factory at the appointed time, but if he does his work badly, if he hinders his comrades by his laziness or other defects, if he is quarrelsome, there is an end of it; he is compelled to leave the workshop.

Authoritarians pretend that it is the almighty employer and his overseers who maintain regularity and quality of work in factories. In reality, in every somewhat complicated enterprise, in which the goods produced pass through many hands before being finished, it is the factory itself, the workmen as a unity, who see to the good quality of the work. Therefore the best factories of British private industry have few overseers, far less on an average than the French factories, and less than the British State factories.

A certain standard of public morals is maintained in the same way. Authoritarians say it is due to rural guards, judges, and policemen, whereas in reality it is maintained *in spite* of judges, policemen, and rural guards. "Many are the laws producing criminals!" was said long ago.

Not only in industrial workshops do things go on in this way; it happens everywhere, every day, on a scale that only bookworms have as yet no notion of. When a railway company, federated with other companies, fails to fulfil its engagements, when its trains are late and goods lie neglected at the stations, the other companies threaten to cancel the contract, and that threat usually suffices.

It is generally believed, at any rate it is taught in State-approved schools, that commerce only keeps to its engagements from fear of lawsuits. Nothing of the sort; nine times in ten the trader who has not kept his word will not appear before a judge. There, where trade is very active, as in London, the sole fact of having driven a creditor to bring a lawsuit suffices for the immense majority of merchants to refuse for good to have any dealings with a man who has compelled one of them to go to law.

This being so, why should means that are used to-day among workers in the workshop, traders in the trade, and railway companies in the organization of transport, not be made use of in a society based on voluntary work?

Take, for example, an association stipulating that each of its members should carry out the following contract: "We undertake to give you the use of our houses, stores, streets, means of transport, schools, museums, etc., on condition that, from twenty to forty-five or fifty years of age, you consecrate four or five hours a day to some work recognized as necessary to existence. Choose yourself the producing groups which you wish to join, or organize a new group, provided that it will undertake to produce necessaries. And as for the remainder of your time, combine together with whomsoever you like, for recreation, art, or science, according to the bent of your taste.

"Twelve or fifteen hundred hours of work a year, in one of the groups producing food, clothes, or houses, or employed in public sanitation, transport, and so on, is all we ask of you. For this amount of work we guarantee to you the free use of all that these groups produce, or will produce. But if not one, of the thousands of groups of our federation, will receive you, whatever be their motive; if you are absolutely incapable of producing anything useful, or if you refuse to do it, then live like an isolated man or like an invalid. If we are rich enough to give you the necessaries of life we shall be delighted to give them to you. You are a man, and you have the right to live. But as you wish to live under special conditions, and leave the ranks, it is more than probable that you will suffer for it in your daily relations with other citizens. You will be looked upon as a ghost of bourgeois society, unless some friends of yours, discovering you to be a talent, kindly free you from all moral obligation towards society by doing all the necessary work for you.

"And finally, if it does not please you, go and look for other conditions elsewhere in the wide world, or else seek adherents and organize with them on novel principles. We prefer our own."

This is what could be done in a communal society in order to turn away sluggards if they became too numerous.

IV

We very much doubt that we need fear this contingency in a society really based on the entire freedom of the individual.

In fact, in spite of the premium on idleness offered by the private ownership of capital, the really lazy man is comparatively rare, unless his laziness be due to illness.

Among workmen it is often said that the bourgeois are idlers. There are certainly enough of them, but they, too, are the exception. On the contrary, in every industrial enterprise, you are sure to find one or more bourgeois who work very hard. It is true that the majority of bourgeois profit by their privileged position to award themselves the least unpleasant tasks, and that they work under hygienic conditions of air, food, etc., which permits them to do their business without too much fatigue. But these are precisely the conditions which we claim for all workers, without exception.

It must also be said that if, thanks to their privileged position, rich people often perform absolutely useless or even harmful work in society, nevertheless the Ministers, Heads of Departments, factory owners, traders, bankers, etc., subject themselves for a number of hours every day to work which they find more or less tiresome, all preferring their hours of leisure to this obligatory work. And if in nine cases out of ten this work is a harmful work, they find it none the less tiring for that. But it is precisely because the middle class put forth a great energy, even in doing harm (knowingly or not) and defending their privileged position, that they have succeeded in defeating the landed nobility, and that they continue to rule the masses. If they were idlers, they would long since have ceased to exist, and would have disappeared like the aristocracy. In a society that would expect only four or five hours a day of useful, pleasant, and hygienic work, these same middle-class people would perform their task perfectly well, and they certainly would not put up with the horrible conditions in which men toil nowadays without reforming them. If a Huxley spent only five hours in the sewers of London, rest assured that he would have found the means of making them as sanitary as his physiological laboratory.

As to the laziness of the great majority of workers, only philistine economists and philanthropists can utter such nonsense.

If you ask an intelligent manufacturer, he will tell you that if workmen only put it into their heads to be lazy, all factories would have to be closed, for no measure of severity, no system of spying would be of any use. You should have seen the terror caused in 1887 among British employers when a few agitators started preaching the "*go-canny*" theory—"Bad pay, bad work"; "Take it easy, do not overwork yourselves, and waste all you can."—"They demoralize the worker, they want to kill our industry!" cried those same people who the day before inveighed against the immorality of the worker and the bad quality of his work. But if the workers were what they are represented to be—namely, the idler whom the employer is supposed continually to threaten with dismissal from the workshop—what would the word "demoralization" signify?

So when we speak of possible idlers, we must well understand that it is a question of a small minority in society; and before legislating for that minority, would it not be wise to study the origin of that idleness? Whoever observes with an intelligent eye, sees well enough that the child reputed lazy at school is often the one which simply does not understand, because he is being badly taught. Very often, too, it is suffering from cerebral anæmia, caused by poverty and an anti-hygienic education. A boy who is lazy at Greek or Latin would work admirably were he taught science, especially if he were taught with the aid of manual labour. A girl who is stupid at mathematics becomes the first mathematician of her class if she by chance meets somebody who can explain to her the elements of arithmetic which she did not understand. And a workman, lazy in the workshop, cultivates his garden at dawn, while gazing at the rising sun, and will be at work again at nightfall, when all nature goes to its rest.

Somebody has said that dust is matter in the wrong place. The same definition applies to nine-tenths of those called lazy. They are people gone astray in a direction that does not answer to their temperament nor to their capacities. In reading the biography of great men, we are struck with the number of "idlers" among them. They were lazy so long as they had not found the right path; afterwards they became laborious to excess. Darwin, Stephenson, and many others belonged to this category of idlers.

Very often the idler is but a man to whom it is repugnant to spend all his life making the eighteenth part of a pin, or the hundredth part of a watch, while he feels he has exuberant energy which he would like to expend elsewhere. Often, too, he is a rebel who cannot submit to being fixed all his life to a workbench in order to procure a thousand pleasures for his employer, while knowing himself to be far the less stupid of the two, and knowing his only fault to be that of having been born in a hovel instead of coming into the world in a castle.

Lastly, an immense number of "idlers" are idlers because they do not know well enough the trade by which they are compelled to earn their living. Seeing the imperfect thing they make with their own hands, striving vainly to do better, and perceiving that they never will succeed on account of the bad habits of work already acquired, they begin to hate their trade, and, not knowing any other, hate work in general. Thousands of workmen and artists who are failures suffer from this cause.

On the other hand, he who since his youth has learned to play the piano *well*, to handle the plane *well*, the chisel, the brush, or the file, so that he feels that what he does is *beautiful*, will never give up the piano, the chisel, or the file. He will find pleasure in his work which does not tire him, so long as he is not overdriven.

Under the one name, *idleness*, a series of results due to different causes have been grouped, of which each one could be a source of good, instead of being a source of evil to society. Like all questions concerning criminality and related to human faculties, facts have been collected having nothing in common with one another. People speak of laziness or crime, without giving themselves the trouble to analyze the cause. They are in a hurry to punish these faults without inquiring if the punishment itself does not contain a premium on "laziness" or "crime."[9]

This is why a free society, if it saw the number of idlers increasing in its midst, would no doubt think of looking first for the *cause* of laziness, in order to suppress it, before having recourse to punishment. When it is a case, as we have already mentioned, of simple bloodlessness, then before stuffing the brain of a child with science, nourish his system so as to produce blood, strengthen him, and, that he shall not waste his time, take him to the country or to the seaside; there, teach him in the open air, not in books—geometry, by measuring the distance to a spire, or the height of a tree; natural sciences, while picking flowers and fishing in the sea; physical science, while building the boat he will go to fish in. But for mercy's sake do not fill his brain with classical sentences and dead languages. Do not make an idler of him!...

Or, here is a child which has neither order nor regular habits. Let the children first inculcate order among themselves, and later on, the laboratory, the workshop, the work that will have to be done in a limited space, with many tools about, under the guidance of an intelligent teacher, will teach them method. But do not make disorderly beings out of them by your school, whose only order is the symmetry of its benches, and which—true image of the chaos in its teachings—will never inspire anybody with the love of harmony, of consistency, and method in work.

Do not you see that by your methods of teaching, framed by a

Ministry for eight million scholars, who represent eight million different capacities, you only impose a system good for mediocrities, conceived by an average of mediocrities? Your school becomes a University of laziness, as your prison is a University of crime. Make the school free, abolish your University grades, appeal to the volunteers of teaching; begin that way, instead of making laws against laziness which only serve to increase it.

Give the workman who cannot condemn himself to make all his life a minute particle of some object, who is stifled at his little tapping machine, which he ends by loathing, give him the chance of tilling the soil, of felling trees in the forest, sailing the seas in the teeth of a storm, dashing through space on an engine, but do not make an idler of him by forcing him all his life to attend to a small machine, to plough the head of a screw, or to drill the eye of a needle.

Suppress the cause of idleness, and you may take it for granted that few individuals will really hate work, especially voluntary work, and that there will be no need to manufacture a code of laws on their account.

FOOTNOTE:

[9] *Kropotkin: In Russian and French Prisons.* London, 1887.

CHAPTER XIII
THE COLLECTIVIST WAGES SYSTEM

I

In their plans for the reconstruction of society the collectivists commit, in our opinion, a twofold error. While speaking of abolishing capitalist rule, they intend nevertheless to retain two institutions which are the very basis of this rule—Representative Government and the Wages' System.

As regards so-called representative government, we have often spoken about it. It is absolutely incomprehensible to us that intelligent men—and such are not wanting in the collectivist party—can remain partisans of national or municipal parliaments after all the lessons history has given them—in France, in England, in Germany, or in the United States.

While we see parliamentary rule breaking up, and from all sides criticism of this rule growing louder—not only of its results, but also of *its principles*—how is it that the revolutionary socialists defend a system already condemned to die?

Built up by the middle classes to hold their own against royalty, sanctioning, and, at the same time strengthening, their sway over the workers, parliamentary rule is pre-eminently a middle-class rule. The upholders of this system have never seriously maintained that a parliament or a municipal council represent a nation or a city. The most intelligent among them know that this is impossible. The middle classes have simply used the parliamentary system to raise a protecting barrier against the pretensions of royalty, without giving the people liberty. But gradually, as the people become conscious of their real interests, and the variety of their interests is growing, the system can no longer work. Therefore democrats of all countries vainly imagine various palliatives. The *Referendum* is tried and found to be a failure; proportional representation is spoken of, the representation of minorities, and other parliamentary Utopias. In a word, they strive to find what is not to be found, and after each new experiment they are bound to recognize that it was a failure; so that confidence in Representative Government vanishes more and more.

It is the same with the Wages' system; because, once the abolition of private property is proclaimed, and the possession in common of all means of production is introduced,—how can the wages' system be maintained in any form? This is, nevertheless, what collectivists are doing when they recommend the use of the *labour-cheques* as a mode of remuneration for labour accomplished for the great Collectivist employer—the State.

It is easy to understand why the early English socialists, since the time of Robert Owen, came to the system of labour-cheques. They simply tried to make Capital and Labour agree. They repudiated the idea of laying hands on capitalist property by means of revolutionary measures.

It is also easy to understand why Proudhon took up later on the same idea. In his Mutualist system he tried to make Capital less offensive, notwithstanding the retaining of private property, which he detested from the bottom of his heart, but which he believed to be necessary to guarantee individuals against the State.

Neither is it astonishing that certain economists, more or less bourgeois, admit labour-cheques. They care little whether the worker is paid in labour-notes or in coin stamped with the effigy of the Republic or the Empire. They only care to save from destruction the individual ownership of dwelling-houses, of land, of factories; in any case—that, at least, of dwelling-houses and the capital that is necessary for manufacturing. And labour-notes would just answer the purpose of upholding this private property.

As long as labour-notes can be exchanged for jewels or carriages, the owner of the house will willingly accept them for rent. And as long as dwelling houses, fields, and factories belong to isolated owners, men will have to pay these owners, in one way or another, for being allowed to work in the fields or factories, or for living in the houses. The owners will agree to be paid by the workers in gold, in paper-money, or in cheques exchangeable for all sorts of commodities, once that toll upon labour is maintained, and the right to levy it is left with them. But how can we defend labour-notes, this new form of wagedom, when we admit that the houses, the fields, and the factories will no longer be private property,—that they will belong to the commune or the nation?

II

Let us closely examine this system of remuneration for work done, preached by the French, German, English, and Italian collectivists (the Spanish anarchists, who still call themselves collectivists, imply by Collectivism the possession in common of all instruments of production, and the "liberty of each group to divide the produce, as they think fit, according to communist or any other principles").

It amounts to this: Everybody works in field, factory, school, hospital, etc. The working-day is fixed by the State, which owns the land, the factories, the roads, etc. Every work-day is paid for with a *labour-note*, which is inscribed with these words: *Eight hours' work*. With this cheque the worker can procure all sorts of merchandise in the stores owned by the State or by divers corporations. The cheque is divisible, so that you can buy an hour's-work worth of meat, ten minutes' worth of matches, or half an hour of tobacco. After the Collectivist Revolution, instead of saying "twopence worth of soap," we shall say "five minutes' worth of soap."

Most collectivists, true to the distinction laid down by middle-class economists (and by Marx as well) between *qualified* work and *simple* work, tell us, moreover, that *qualified* or professional work must be paid a certain quantity more than *simple* work. Thus one hour's work of a doctor will have to be considered as equivalent to two or three hours' work of a hospital nurse, or to three or five hours' work of a navvy. "Professional, or qualified work, will be a multiple of simple work," says the collectivist Grönlund, "because this kind of work needs a more or less long apprenticeship."

Some other collectivists, such as the French Marxist, Guesde, do not make this distinction. They proclaim the "Equality of Wages." The doctor, the schoolmaster, and the professor will be paid (in labour-cheques) at the same rate as the navvy. Eight hours visiting the sick in a hospital will be worth the same as eight hours spent in earthworks or else in mines or factories.

Some make a greater concession; they admit that disagreeable or unhealthy work—such as sewerage—could be paid for at a higher rate than agreeable work. One hour's work of a sewerman would be worth, they say, two hours of a professor's work.

Let us add that certain collectivists admit of corporations being paid a lump sum for work done. Thus a corporation would say: "Here are a hundred tons of steel. A hundred workmen were required to produce them, and it took them ten days. Their work-day being an eight-hours day, it has taken them eight thousand working hours to produce a hundred tons of steel—eight hours a ton." For this the State would pay them eight thousand labour-notes of one hour each, and these eight thousand cheques would be divided among the members of the iron-works as they themselves thought proper.

On the other hand, a hundred miners having taken twenty days to extract eight thousand tons of coal, coal would be worth two hours a ton, and the sixteen thousand cheques of one hour each, received by the Guild of Miners, would be divided among their members according to their own appreciation.

If the miners protested and said that a ton of steel should only cost six hours' work instead of eight; if the professor wished to have his day paid four times more than the nurse, then the State would interfere and would settle their differences.

Such is, in a few words, the organization the collectivists wish to see arise out of the Social Revolution. As we see, their principles are: Collective property of the instruments of production, and remuneration to each according to the time spent in producing, while taking into account the productivity of his labour. As to the political system, it would be the Parliamentary system, modified by *positive instructions* given to those elected, and by the *Referendum*—a vote, taken by *noes* or *ayes* by the nation.

Let us own that this system appears to us simply unrealizable.

Collectivists begin by proclaiming a revolutionary principle—the abolition of private property—and then they deny it, no sooner than proclaimed, by upholding an organization of production and consumption which originated in private property.

They proclaim a revolutionary principle, and ignore the consequences that this principle will inevitably bring about.

They forget that the very fact of abolishing individual property in the instruments of work—land, factories, road, capital—must launch society into absolutely new channels; must completely overthrow the present system of production, both in its aim as well as in its means; must modify daily relations between individuals, as soon as land, machinery, and all other instruments of production are considered common property.

They say, "No private property," and immediately after strive to maintain private property in its daily manifestations. "You shall be a Commune as far as regards production: fields, tools, machinery, all that has been invented up till now—factories, railways, harbours, mines, etc., all are yours. Not the slightest distinction will be made concerning the share of each in this collective property.

"But from to-morrow you will minutely debate the share you are going to take in the creation of new machinery, in the digging of new mines. You will carefully weigh what part of the new produce belongs to you. You will count your minutes of work, and you will take care that a minute of your neighbours should not buy more than yours.

"And as an hour measures nothing, as in some factories a worker can see to six power-looms at a time, while in another he only tends two, you will weigh the muscular force, the brain energy, and the nervous energy you have expended. You will accurately calculate the years of apprenticeship in order to appraise the amount each will contribute to future production. And this—after having declared that you do not take into account his share in *past* production."

Well, for us it is evident that a society cannot be based on two absolutely opposed principles, two principles that contradict one another continually. And a nation or a commune which would have such an organization would be compelled to revert to private property in the instruments of production, or to transform itself into a communist society.

III

We have said that certain collectivist writers desire that a distinction should be made between *qualified* or professional work and *simple* work. They pretend that an hour's work of an engineer, an architect, or a doctor, must be considered as two or three hours' work of a blacksmith, a mason, or a hospital nurse. And the same distinction must be made between all sorts of trades necessitating apprenticeship, and the simple toil of day labourers.

Well, to establish this distinction would be to maintain all the inequalities of present society. It would mean fixing a dividing line, from the beginning, between the workers and those who pretend to govern them. It would mean dividing society into two very distinct classes—the aristocracy of knowledge placed above the horny-handed lower orders—the one doomed to serve the other; the one working with its hands to feed and clothe those who, profiting by their leisure, study how to govern their fosterers.

It would mean reviving one of the distinct peculiarities of present society and giving it the sanction of the Social Revolution. It would mean setting up as a principle an abuse already condemned in our ancient crumbling society.

We know the answer we shall get. They will speak of "Scientific Socialism"; they will quote bourgeois economists, and Marx too, to prove that a scale of wages has its *raison d'être*, as "the labour force" of the engineer will have cost more to society than the "labour-force" of the navvy. In fact—have not economists tried to prove to us that if an engineer is paid twenty times more than a navvy it is *because* the "necessary" outlay to make an engineer is greater than that necessary to make a navvy? And has not Marx asserted that the same distinction is equally logical between two branches of manual labour? He could not conclude otherwise, having taken up on his own account Ricardo's theory of value, and upheld that goods *are* exchanged in proportion to the quantity of work socially necessary for their production.

But we know what to think of this. We know that if engineers, scientists, or doctors are paid ten or a hundred times more than a labourer, and if a weaver earns three times more than an agricultural labourer, and ten times more than a girl in a match factory, it is not by reason of their "cost of production," but by reason of a monopoly of education, or a monopoly of industry. Engineers, scientists, and doctors merely exploit their capital—their diplomas—as middle-class employers exploit a factory, or as nobles used to exploit their titles of nobility.

As to the employer who pays an engineer twenty times more than a labourer, it is simply due to personal interest; if the engineer can economize £4,000 a year on the cost of production, the employer pays him £800. And if the employer has a foreman who saves £400 on the work by cleverly sweating workmen, he gladly gives him £80 or £120 a year. He parts with an extra £40 when he expects to gain £400 by it; and this is the essence of the Capitalist system. The same differences obtain among different manual trades.

Let them, therefore, not talk to us of "the cost of production" which raises the cost of skilled labour, and tell us that a student who has gaily spent his youth in a university has a *right* to a wage ten times greater than the son of a miner who has grown pale in a mine since the age of eleven; or that a weaver has a *right* to a wage three or four times greater than that of an agricultural labourer. The cost of teaching a weaver his work is not four times greater than the cost of teaching a peasant his. The weaver simply benefits by the advantages his industry reaps in international trade, from countries that have as yet no industries, and in consequence of the privileges accorded by all States to industries in preference to the tilling of the soil.

Nobody has ever calculated the *cost of production* of a producer; and if a noble loafer costs far more to society than a worker, it remains to be seen whether a robust day-labourer does not cost more to society than a skilled artisan, when we have taken into account infant-mortality among the poor, the ravages of anæmia, and premature deaths.

Could they, for example, make us believe that the 1s. 3d. paid to a Paris workwoman, the 3d. paid to an Auvergne peasant girl who grows blind at lace-making, or the 1s. 8d. paid to the peasant represent their "cost of production." We know full well that people work for less, but we also know that they do so exclusively because, thanks to our wonderful organization, they would die of hunger did they not accept these mock wages.

For us the scale of remuneration is a complex result of taxes, of governmental tutelage, of Capitalist monopoly. In a word, of State and Capital. Therefore, we say that all wages' theories have been invented after the event to justify injustices at present existing, and that we need not take them into consideration.

Neither will they fail to tell us that the Collectivist scale of wages would be an improvement. "It would be better," so they say, "to see certain artisans receiving a wage two or three times higher than common labourers, than to see a minister receiving in a day what a workman cannot earn in a year. It would be a great step towards equality."

For us this step would be the reverse of progress. To make a distinction between simple and professional work in a new society would result in the Revolution sanctioning and recognizing as a principle a brutal fact we submit to nowadays, but that we nevertheless find unjust. It would mean imitating those gentlemen of the French Assembly who proclaimed on August 4th, 1789, the abolition of feudal rights, but who on August 8th sanctioned these same rights by imposing dues on the peasants to compensate the noblemen, placing these dues under the protection of the Revolution. It would mean imitating the Russian Government, which proclaimed, at the time of the emancipation of the serfs, that certain lands should henceforth belong to the nobility, while formerly these lands were considered as belonging to the serfs.

Or else, to take a better known example, when the Commune of 1871 decided to pay members of the Commune Council 12s. 6d. a day, while the Federates on the ramparts received only 1s. 3d., this decision was hailed as an act of superior democratic equality. In reality, the Commune only ratified the former inequality between functionary and soldier, Government and governed. Coming from an Opportunist Chamber of Deputies, such a decision would have appeared admirable, but the Commune doomed her own revolutionary principles when she failed to put them into practice.

Under our existing social system, when a minister gets paid £4,000 a year, while a workman must content himself with £40 or less; when a foreman is paid two or three times more than a workman, and among workmen there is every gradation, from 8s. a day down to the peasant girl's 3d., we disapprove of the high salary of the minister as well as of the difference between the 8s. of the workman and the 3d. of the poor woman. And we say, "'Down with the privileges of education, as well as with those of birth!" We are anarchists precisely because these privileges revolt us.

They revolt us already in this authoritarian society. Could we endure them in a society that began by proclaiming equality?

This is why some collectivists, understanding the impossibility of maintaining a scale of wages in a society inspired by the breath of the Revolution, hasten to proclaim equality of wage. But they meet with new difficulties, and their equality of wages becomes the same unrealizable Utopia as the scale of wages of other collectivists.

A society having taken possession of all social wealth, having boldly proclaimed the right of all to this wealth—whatever share they may have taken in producing it—will be compelled to abandon any system of wages, whether in currency or labour-notes.

IV

The collectivists say, "To each according to his deeds"; or, in other terms, according to his share of services rendered to society. They think it expedient to put this principle into practice, as soon as the Social Revolution will have made all instruments of production common property. But we think that if the Social Revolution had the misfortune of proclaiming such a principle, it would mean its necessary failure; it would mean leaving the social problem, which past centuries have burdened us with, unsolved.

Of course, in a society like ours, in which the more a man works the less he is remunerated, this principle, at first sight, may appear to be a yearning for justice. But in reality it is only the perpetuation of injustice. It was by proclaiming this principle that wagedom began, to end in the glaring inequalities and all the abominations of present society; because, from the moment work done began to be appraised in currency, or in any other form of wage, the day it was agreed upon that man would only receive the wage he should be able to secure to himself, the whole history of a State-aided Capitalist Society was as good as written; it was contained in germ in this principle.

Shall we, then, return to our starting-point, and go through the same evolution again? Our theorists desire it, but fortunately it is impossible. The Revolution, we maintain, must be communist; if not, it will be drowned in blood, and have to be begun over again.

Services rendered to society, be they work in factory or field, or mental services, *cannot be* valued in money. There can be no exact measure of value (of what has been wrongly termed exchange value), nor of use value, in terms of production. If two individuals work for the community five hours a day, year in year out, at different work which is equally agreeable to them, we may say that on the whole their labour is approximately equivalent. But we cannot divide their work, and say that the result of any particular day, hour, or minute of work of the one is worth the result of one day, one hour, or one minute of the other.

We may roughly say that the man, who during his lifetime has deprived himself of leisure during ten hours a day has given far more to society than the one who has only deprived himself of leisure during five hours a day, or who has not deprived himself at all. But we cannot take what he has done during two hours, and say that the yield of his two hours' work is worth twice as much as the yield of another individual, who has worked only one hour, and remunerate the two in proportion. It would be disregarding all that is complex in industry, in agriculture, in the whole life of present society; it would be ignoring to what extent all individual work is the result of the past and the present labour of society as a whole. It would mean believing ourselves to be living in the Stone Age, whereas we are living in an age of steel.

If you enter a modern coal-mine you will see a man in charge of a huge machine that raises and lowers a cage. In his hand he holds a lever that stops and reverses the course of the machine; he lowers it and the cage reverses its course in the twinkling of an eye; he sends it upwards or downwards into the depths of the shaft with a giddy swiftness. All attention, he follows with his eyes fixed on an indicator which shows him, on a small scale, at which point of the shaft the cage is at each second of its progress; and as soon as the indicator has reached a certain level, he suddenly stops the course of the cage, not a yard higher nor lower than the required spot. And no sooner have the colliers unloaded their coal-wagonettes, and pushed empty ones instead, than he reverses the lever and again sends the cage back into space.

During eight or ten consecutive hours every day he must keep the same strain of attention. Should his brain relax for a moment, the cage would inevitably strike against the gear, break its wheels, snap the rope, crush men, and put a stop to all work in the mine. Should he waste three seconds at each touch of the lever,—the extraction, in our modern, perfected mines, would be reduced from twenty to fifty tons a day.

Is it he who is the most necessary man in the mine? Or, is it perhaps the boy who signals to him from below to raise the cage? Is it the miner at the bottom of the shaft, who risks his life every instant, and who will some day be killed by fire-damp? Or is it the engineer, who would lose the layer of coal, and would cause the miners to dig on rock by a simple mistake in his calculations? Or is it the mine owner who has put his capital into the mine, and who has perhaps, contrary to expert advice, asserted that excellent coal would be found there?

All those who are engaged in the mine contribute to the extraction of coal in proportion to their strength, their energy, their knowledge, their intelligence, and their skill. And we may say that all have the right to *live*, to satisfy their needs, and even their whims, when the necessaries of life have been secured for all. But how can we appraise the work of each one of them?

And, moreover, Is the coal they have extracted entirely *their* work? Is it not also the work of the men who have built the railway leading to the mine and the roads that radiate from all the railway stations? Is it not also the work of those that have tilled and sown the fields, extracted iron, cut wood in the forests, built the machines that burn coal, slowly developed the mining industry altogether, and so on?

It is utterly impossible to draw a distinction between the work of each of those men. To measure the work by its results leads us to an absurdity; to divide the total work, and to measure its fractions by the number of hours spent on the work also leads us to absurdity. One thing remains: to put the *needs* above the *works*, and first of all to recognize *the right to live*, and later on *the right to well-being* for all those who took their share in production.

But take any other branch of human activity—take the manifestations of life as a whole. Which one of us can claim the higher remuneration for his work? Is it the doctor who has found out the illness, or the nurse who has brought about recovery by her hygienic care? Is it the inventor of the first steam-engine, or the boy, who, one day getting tired of pulling the rope that formerly opened the valve to let steam under the piston, tied the rope to the lever of the machine, without suspecting that he had invented the essential mechanical part of all modern machinery—the automatic valve?

Is it the inventor of the locomotive, or the workman of

Newcastle, who suggested replacing the stones formerly laid under the rails by wooden sleepers, as the stones, for want of elasticity, caused the trains to derail? Is it the engineer on the locomotive? The signalman who stops the trains, or lets them pass by? The switchman who transfers a train from one line to another?

Again, to whom do we owe the transatlantic cable? Is it to the electrical engineer who obstinately affirmed that the cable would transmit messages while learned men of science declared it to be impossible? Is it to Maury, the learned physical geographer, who advised that thick cables should be set aside for others as thin as a walking cane? Or else to those volunteers, come from nobody knows where, who spent their days and nights on deck minutely examining every yard of the cable, and removed the nails that the shareholders of steamship companies stupidly caused to be driven into the non-conducting wrapper of the cable, so as to make it unserviceable?

And in a wider sphere, the true sphere of life, with its joys, its sufferings, and its accidents, cannot each one of us recall someone who has rendered him so great a service that we should be indignant if its equivalent in coin were mentioned? The service may have been but a word, nothing but a word spoken at the right time, or else it may have been months and years of devotion, and we are going to appraise these "incalculable" services in "labour-notes"?

"The works of each!" But human society would not exist for more than two consecutive generations if everyone did not give infinitely more than that for which he is paid in coin, in "cheques," or in civic rewards. The race would soon become extinct if mothers did not sacrifice their lives to take care of their children, if men did not give continually, without demanding an equivalent reward, if men did not give most precisely when they expect no reward.

If middle-class society is decaying, if we have got into a blind alley from which we cannot emerge without attacking past institutions with torch and hatchet, it is precisely because we have given too much to counting. It is because we have let ourselves be influenced into *giving* only to *receive*. It is because we have aimed at turning society into a commercial company based on *debit* and *credit*.

After all, the Collectivists know this themselves. They vaguely understand that a society could not exist if it carried out the principle of "Each according to his deeds." They have a notion that *necessaries*—we do not speak of whims—the needs of the individual, do not always correspond to his *works*. Thus De Paepe tells us: "The principle—the eminently Individualist principle—would, however, be *tempered* by social intervention for the education of children and young persons (including maintenance and lodging), and by the social organization for assisting the infirm and the sick, for retreats for aged workers, etc." They understand that a man of forty, father of three children, has other needs than a young man of twenty. They know that the woman who suckles her infant and spends sleepless nights at its bedside, cannot do as much *work* as the man who has slept peacefully. They seem to take in that men and women, worn out maybe by dint of overwork for society, may be incapable of doing as much *work* as those who have spent their time leisurely and pocketed their "labour-notes" in the privileged career of State functionaries.

They are eager to temper their principle. They say: "Society will not fail to maintain and bring up its children; to help both aged and infirm. Without doubt *needs* will be the measure of the cost that society will burden itself with, to temper the principle of deeds."

Charity, charity, always Christian charity, organized by the State this time. They believe in improving the asylums for foundlings, in effecting old-age and sick insurances—so as to *temper* their principle. But they cannot yet throw aside the idea of "wounding first and healing afterwards"!

Thus, after having denied Communism, after having laughed at their ease at the formula—"To each according to his needs"—these great economists discover that they have forgotten something, the needs of the producers, which they now admit. Only it is for the State to estimate them, for the State to verify if the needs are not disproportionate to the work.

The State will dole out charity. Thence to the English poor-law and the workhouse is but a step.

There is but a slight difference, because even this stepmother of a society against whom we are in revolt has also been compelled to *temper* her individualist principles; she, too, has had to make concessions in a communist direction and under the same form of charity.

She, too, distributes halfpenny dinners to prevent the pillaging of her shops; builds hospitals—often very bad ones, but sometimes splendid ones—to prevent the ravages of contagious diseases. She, too, after having paid the hours of labour, shelters the children of those she has wrecked. She takes their needs into consideration and doles out charity.

Poverty, we have said elsewhere, was the primary cause of wealth. It was poverty that created the first capitalist; because, before accumulating "surplus value," of which we hear so much, men had to be sufficiently destitute to consent to sell their labour, so as not to die of hunger. It was poverty that made capitalists. And if the number of the poor increased so rapidly during the Middle Ages, it was due to the invasions and wars that followed the founding of States, and to the increase of riches resulting from the exploitation of the East. These two causes tore asunder the bonds that kept men together in the agrarian and urban communities, and taught them to proclaim the principle of *wages*, so dear to the exploiters, instead of the solidarity they formerly practiced in their tribal life.

And it is this principle that is to spring from a revolution which men dare to call by the name of Social Revolution,—a name so dear to the starved, the oppressed, and the sufferers!

It can never be. For the day on which old institutions will fall under the proletarian axe, voices will cry out: "Bread, shelter, ease for all!" And those voices will be listened to; the people will say: "Let us begin by allaying our thirst for life, for happiness, for liberty, that we have never quenched. And when we shall have tasted of this joy, we will set to work to demolish the last vestiges of middle-class rule: its morality drawn from account books, its 'debit and credit' philosophy, its 'mine and yours' institutions. 'In demolishing we shall build,' as Proudhon said; and we shall build in the name of Communism and Anarchy."

CHAPTER XIV
CONSUMPTION AND PRODUCTION

I

Looking at society and its political organization from a different standpoint than that of all the authoritarian schools—for we start from a free individual to reach a free society, instead of beginning by the State to come down to the individual—we follow the same method in economic questions. We study the needs of the individuals, and the means by which they satisfy them, before discussing Production, Exchange, Taxation, Government, and so on. At first sight the difference may appear trifling, but in reality it upsets all the canons of official Political Economy.

If you open the works of any economist you will find that he begins with PRODUCTION, *i. e.*, by the analysis of the means employed nowadays for the creation of wealth: division of labour, the factory, its machinery, the accumulation of capital. From Adam Smith to Marx, all have proceeded along these lines. Only in the latter parts of their books do they treat of CONSUMPTION, that is to say, of the means resorted to in our present Society to satisfy the needs of the individuals; and even there they confine themselves to explaining how riches *are* divided among those who vie with one another for their possession.

Perhaps you will say this is logical. Before satisfying needs you must create the wherewithal to satisfy them. But, before producing anything, must you not feel the need of it? Was it not necessity that first drove man to hunt, to raise cattle, to cultivate land, to make implements, and later on to invent machinery? Is it not the study of the needs that should govern production? To say the least, it would therefore be quite as logical to begin by considering the needs, and afterwards to discuss how production is, and ought to be, organized, in order to satisfy these needs.

This is precisely what we mean to do.

But as soon as we look at Political Economy from this point of view, it entirely changes its aspect. It ceases to be a simple description of facts, and becomes a *science*, and we may define this science as: "*The study of the needs of mankind, and the means of satisfying them with the least possible waste of human energy*". Its true name should be, *Physiology of Society*. It constitutes a parallel science to the physiology of plants and animals, which is the study of the needs of plants and animals, and of the most advantageous ways of satisfying them. In the series of sociological sciences, the economy of human societies takes the place, occupied in the series of biological sciences by the physiology of organic bodies.

We say, here are human beings, united in a society. All of them feel the need of living in healthy houses. The savage's hut no longer satisfies them; they require a more or less comfortable solid shelter. The question is, then: whether, taking the present capacity of men for production, every man can have a house of his own? and what is hindering him from having it?

And as soon as we ask *this* question, we see that every family in Europe could perfectly well have a comfortable house, such as are built in England, in Belgium, or in Pullman City, or else an equivalent set of rooms. A certain number of days' work would suffice to build a pretty little airy house, well fitted up and lighted by electricity.

But nine-tenths of Europeans have never possessed a healthy

house, because at all times common people have had to work day after day to satisfy the needs of their rulers, and have never had the necessary leisure or money to build, or to have built, the home of their dreams. And they can have no houses, and will inhabit hovels as long as present conditions remain unchanged.

It is thus seen that our method is quite contrary to that of the economists, who immortalize the so-called *laws* of production, and, reckoning up the number of houses built every year, demonstrate by statistics, that as the number of the new-built houses *is* too small to meet all demands, nine-tenths of Europeans *must* live in hovels.

Let us pass on to food. After having enumerated the benefits accruing from the division of labour, economists tell us the division of labour requires that some men should work at agriculture and others at manufacture. Farmers producing so much, factories so much, exchange being carried on in such a way, they analyze the sale, the profit, the net gain or the surplus value, the wages, the taxes, banking, and so on.

But after having followed them so far, we are none the wiser, and if we ask them: "How is it that millions of human beings are in want of bread, when every family could grow sufficient wheat to feed ten, twenty, and even a hundred people annually?" they answer us by droning the same anthem—division of labour, wages, surplus value, capital, etc.—arriving at the same conclusion, that production is insufficient to satisfy all needs; a conclusion which, if true, does not answer the question: "Can or cannot man by his labour produce the bread he needs? And if he cannot, what is it that hinders him?"

Here are 350 million Europeans. They need so much bread, so much meat, wine, milk, eggs, and butter every year. They need so many houses, so much clothing. This is the minimum of their needs. Can they produce all this? and if they can, will sufficient leisure be left them for art, science, and amusement?—in a word, for everything that is not comprised in the category of absolute necessities? If the answer is in the affirmative,—What hinders them going ahead? What must they do to remove the obstacles? Is it time that is needed to achieve such a result? Let them take it! But let us not lose sight of the aim of production—the satisfaction of the needs of all.

If the most imperious needs of man remain unsatisfied now,— What must we do to increase the productivity of our work? But is there no other cause? Might it not be that production, having lost sight of the *needs* of man, has strayed in an absolutely wrong direction, and that its organization is at fault? And as we can prove that such is the case, let us see how to reorganize production so as to really satisfy all needs.

This seems to us the only right way of facing things. The only way that would allow of Political Economy becoming a science—the Science of Social Physiology.

It is evident that so long as science treats of production, as *it is* carried on at present by civilized nations, by Hindoo communes, or by savages, it can hardly state facts otherwise than the economists state them now; that is to say, as a simple *descriptive* chapter, analogous to the descriptive chapters of Zoology and Botany. But if this chapter were written so as to throw some light on the economy of the energy that is necessary to satisfy human needs, the chapter would gain in precision, as well as in descriptive value. It would clearly show the frightful waste of human energy under the present system, and it would prove that as long as this system exists, the needs of humanity will never be satisfied.

The point of view, we see, would be entirely changed. Behind the loom that weaves so many yards of cloth, behind the steel-plate perforator, and behind the safe in which dividends are hoarded, we should see man, the artisan of production, more often than not excluded from the feast he has prepared for others. We should also understand that the standpoint being wrong, the so-called "laws" of value and exchange are but a very false explanation of events, as they happen nowadays; and that things will come to pass very differently when production is organized in such a manner as to meet all needs of society.

II

There is not one single principle of Political Economy that does not change its aspect if you look at it from our point of view.

Take, for instance, over-production, a word which every day re-echoes in our ears. Is there a single economist, academician, or candidate for academical honours, who has not supported arguments, proving that economic crises are due to over-production—that at a given moment more cotton, more cloth, more watches are produced than are needed! Have we not, all of us, thundered against the rapacity of the capitalists who are obstinately bent on producing more than can possibly be consumed!

However, on careful examination all these reasonings prove unsound. In fact, Is there one single commodity among those in universal use which is produced in greater quantity than need be. Examine one by one all commodities sent out by countries exporting on a large scale, and you will see that nearly all are produced in *insufficient* quantities for the inhabitants of the countries exporting them.

It is not a surplus of wheat that the Russian peasant sends to Europe. The most plentiful harvests of wheat and rye in

European Russia only yield *enough* for the population. And as a rule, the peasant deprives himself of what he actually needs when he sells his wheat or rye to pay rent and taxes.

It is not a surplus of coal that England sends to the four corners of the globe, because only three-quarters of a ton, per head of population, annually, remains for home domestic consumption, and millions of Englishmen are deprived of fire in the winter, or have only just enough to boil a few vegetables. In fact, setting aside useless luxuries, there is in England, which exports more than any other country, one single commodity in universal use—cottons—whose production is sufficiently great to *perhaps* exceed the needs of the community. Yet when we look upon the rags that pass for wearing apparel worn by over a third of the inhabitants of the United Kingdom, we are led to ask ourselves whether the cottons exported would not, on the whole, suit the *real* needs of the population?

As a rule it is not a surplus that is exported, though it may have been so originally. The fable of the barefooted shoemaker is as true of nations as it was formerly of individual artisans. We export the *necessary* commodities. And we do so, because the workmen cannot buy with their wages what they have produced, *and pay besides the rent and interest to the capitalist and the banker*.

Not only does the ever-growing need of comfort remain unsatisfied, but the strict necessities of life are often wanting. Therefore, "surplus production" does *not* exist, at least not in the sense given to it by the theorists of Political Economy.

Taking another point—all economists tell us that there is a well-proved law: "Man produces more than he consumes." After he has lived on the proceeds of his toil, there remains a surplus. Thus, a family of cultivators produces enough to feed several families, and so forth.

For us, this oft-repeated sentence has no sense. If it meant that each generation leaves something to future generations, it would be true; thus, for example, a farmer plants a tree that will live, maybe, for thirty, forty, or a hundred years, and whose fruits will still be gathered by the farmer's grandchildren. Or he clears a few acres of virgin soil, and we say that the heritage of future generations has been increased by that much. Roads, bridges, canals, his house and his furniture are so much wealth bequeathed to succeeding generations.

But this is not what is meant. We are told that the cultivator produces more than he *need* consume. Rather should they say that, the State having always taken from him a large share of his produce for taxes, the priest for tithe, and the landlord for rent, a whole class of men has been created, who formerly consumed what they produced—save what was set aside for unforeseen accidents, or expenses incurred in afforestation, roads, etc.—but who to-day are compelled to live very poorly, from hand to mouth, the remainder having been taken from them by the State, the landlord, the priest, and the usurer.

Therefore we prefer to say: The agricultural labourer, the industrial worker and so on *consume less than they produce,*—because they are *compelled* to sell most of the produce of their labour and to be satisfied with but a small portion of it.

Let us also observe that if the needs of the individual are taken as the starting-point of our political economy, we cannot fail to reach Communism, an organization which enables us to satisfy all needs in the most thorough and economical way. While if we start from our present method of production, and aim at gain and surplus value, without asking whether our production corresponds to the satisfaction of needs, we necessarily arrive at Capitalism, or at most at Collectivism—both being but two different forms of the present wages' system.

In fact, when we consider the needs of the individual and of society, and the means which man has resorted to in order to satisfy them during his varied phases of development, we see at once the necessity of systematizing our efforts, instead of producing haphazard as we do nowadays. It becomes evident that the appropriation by a few of all riches not consumed, and transmitted from one generation to another, is not in the general interest. And we see as a fact that owing to these methods the needs of three-quarters of society are *not* satisfied, so that the present waste of human strength in useless things is only the more criminal.

We discover, moreover, that the most advantageous use of all commodities would be, for each of them, to go, first, for satisfying those needs which are the most pressing: that, in other words, the so-called "value in use" of a commodity does not depend on a simple whim, as has often been affirmed, but on the satisfaction it brings to *real* needs.

Communism—that is to say, an organization which would correspond to a view of Consumption, Production, and Exchange, taken as a whole—therefore becomes the logical consequence of such a comprehension of things—the only one, in our opinion, that is really scientific.

A society that will satisfy the needs of all, and which will know how to organize production to answer to this aim will also have to make a clean sweep of several prejudices concerning industry, and first of all the theory often preached by economists—*The Division of Labour* theory—which we are going to discuss in the next chapter.

CHAPTER XV
THE DIVISION OF LABOUR

Political Economy has always confined itself to stating facts occurring in society, and justifying them in the interest of the dominant class. Therefore, it pronounces itself in favour of the division of labour in industry. Having found it profitable to capitalists, it has set it up as a *principle*.

Look at the village smith, said Adam Smith, the father of modern Political Economy. If he has never been accustomed to making nails he will only succeed by hard toil in forging two or three hundred a day, and even then they will be bad. But if this same smith has never made anything but nails, he will easily supply as many as two thousand three hundred in the course of a day. And Smith hastened to the conclusion—"Divide labour, specialize, go on specializing; let us have smiths who only know how to make heads or points of nails, and by this means we shall produce more. We shall grow rich."

That a smith condemned for life to make the heads of nails would lose all interest in his work, that he would be entirely at the mercy of his employer with his limited handicraft, that he would be out of work four months out of twelve, and that his wages would fall very low down, when it would be easy to replace him by an apprentice, Smith did not think of all this when he exclaimed—"Long live the division of labour. This is the real gold-mine that will enrich the nation!" And all joined him in this cry.

And later on, when a Sismondi or a J. B. Say began to understand that the division of labour, instead of enriching the whole nation, only enriches the rich, and that the worker, who is doomed for life to making the eighteenth part of a pin, grows stupid and sinks into poverty—what did official economists propose? Nothing! They did not say to themselves that by a lifelong grind at one and the same mechanical toil the worker would lose his intelligence and his spirit of invention, and that, on the contrary, a variety of occupations would result in considerably augmenting the productivity of a nation. But this is the very issue we have now to consider.

If, however, learned economists were the only ones to preach the permanent and often hereditary division of labour, we might allow them to preach it as much as they pleased. But the ideas taught by doctors of science filter into men's minds and pervert them; and from repeatedly hearing the division of labour, profits, interest, credit, etc., spoken of as problems long since solved, all middle-class people, and workers too, end by arguing like economists; they venerate the same fetishes.

Thus we see most socialists, even those who have not feared to point out the mistakes of economical science, justifying the division of labour. Talk to them about the organization of work during the Revolution, and they answer that the division of labour must be maintained; that if you sharpened pins before the Revolution you must go on sharpening them after. True, you will not have to work more than five hours a day, but you will have to sharpen pins all your life, while others will make designs for machines that will enable you to sharpen hundreds of millions of pins during your life-time; and others again will be specialists in the higher branches of literature, science, and art, etc. You were born to sharpen pins while Pasteur was born to invent the inoculation against anthrax, and the Revolution will leave you both to your respective employments. Well, it is this horrible principle, so noxious to society, so brutalizing to the individual, source of so much harm, that we propose to discuss in its divers manifestations.

We know the consequences of the division of labour full well. It is evident that, first of all, we are divided into two classes: on the one hand, producers, who consume very little and are exempt from thinking because they only do physical work, and who work badly because their brains remain inactive; and on the other hand, the consumers, who, producing little or hardly anything, have the privilege of thinking for the others, and who think badly because the whole world of those who toil with their hands is unknown to them. Then, we have the labourers of the soil who know nothing of machinery, while those who work at machinery ignore everything about agriculture. The idea of modern industry is a child *tending* a machine that he cannot and must not understand, and a foreman who fines him if his attention flags for a moment. The ideal of industrial agriculture is to do away with the agricultural labourer altogether and to set a man who does odd jobs to tend a steam-plough or a threshing-machine. The division of labour means labelling and stamping men for life—some to splice ropes in factories, some to be foremen in a business, others to shove huge coal-baskets in a particular part of a mine; but none of them to have any idea of machinery as a whole, nor of business, nor of mines. And thereby they destroy the love of work and the capacity for invention that, at the beginning of modern industry, created the machinery on which we pride ourselves so much.

What they have done for individuals, they also wanted to do for nations. Humanity was to be divided into national workshops, having each its speciality. Russia, we were taught, was destined by nature to grow corn; England to spin cotton; Belgium to weave cloth; while Switzerland was to train nurses and governesses. Moreover, each separate city was to establish a specialty. Lyons was to weave silk, Auvergne to make lace, and Paris fancy articles. In this way, economists said, an immense field was opened for production and consumption, and in this way an era of limitless wealth for mankind was at hand.

However, these great hopes vanished as fast as technical knowledge spread abroad. As long as England stood alone as a weaver of cotton and as a metal-worker on a large scale; as long as only Paris made artistic fancy articles, etc., all went well, economists could preach the so-called division of labour without being refuted.

But a new current of thought induced bye and bye all civilized nations to manufacture for themselves. They found it advantageous to produce what they formerly received from other countries, or from their colonies, which in their turn aimed at emancipating themselves from the mother-country. Scientific discoveries universalized the methods of production, and henceforth it was useless to pay an exorbitant price abroad for what could easily be produced at home. And now we see already that this industrial revolution strikes a crushing blow at the theory of the division of labour which for a long time was supposed to be so sound.

CHAPTER XVI
THE DECENTRALIZATION OF INDUSTRY[10]

I

After the Napoleonic wars Britain had nearly succeeded in ruining the main industries which had sprung up in France at the end of the preceding century. She also became mistress of the seas and had no rivals of importance. She took in the situation, and knew how to turn its privileges and advantages to account. She established an industrial monopoly, and, imposing upon her neighbours her prices for the goods she alone could manufacture, accumulated riches upon riches.

But as the middle-class Revolution of the eighteenth century had abolished serfdom and created a proletariat in France, French industry, hampered for a time in its flight, soared again, and from the second half of the nineteenth century France ceased to be a tributary of England for manufactured goods. To-day she too has grown into a nation with an export trade. She sells far more than sixty million pounds' worth of manufactured goods, and two-thirds of these goods are fabrics. The number of Frenchmen working for export or living by their foreign trade, is estimated at three millions.

France is therefore no longer England's tributary. In her turn she has striven to monopolize certain branches of foreign industry, such as silks and ready-made clothes, and has reaped immense profits therefrom; but she is on the point of losing this monopoly for ever, just as England is on the point of losing the monopoly of cotton goods.

Travelling eastwards, industry has reached Germany. Fifty years ago Germany was a tributary of England and France for most manufactured commodities in the higher branches of industry. It is no longer so. In the course of the last fifty years, and especially since the Franco-German war, Germany has completely reorganized her industry. The new factories are stocked with the best machinery; the latest creations of industrial art in cotton goods from Manchester, or in silks from Lyons, etc., are now realized in new German factories. It took two or three generations of workers, at Lyons and Manchester, to construct the modern machinery; but Germany adopted it in its perfected state. Technical schools, adapted to the needs of industry, supply the factories with an army of intelligent workmen—practical engineers, who can work with both hand and brain. German industry starts at the point which was only reached by Manchester and Lyons after fifty years of groping in the dark, of exertion and experiments.

It follows that since Germany manufactures so well at home, she diminishes her imports from France and England year by year. She has not only become their rival in manufactured goods in Asia and in Africa, but also in London and in Paris. Shortsighted people in France may cry out against the Frankfort Treaty; English manufacturers may explain German competition by little differences in railway tariffs; they may linger on the petty side of questions, and neglect great historical facts. But it is none the less certain that the main industries, formerly in the hands of England and France, have progressed eastward, and in Germany they have found a country, young, full of energy, possessing an intelligent middle class, and eager in its turn to enrich itself by foreign trade.

While Germany has freed herself from subjection to France and England, has manufactured her own cotton-cloth, and constructed her own machines—in fact, manufactured all commodities—the main industries have also taken root in Russia, where the development of manufacture is the more instructive as it sprang up but yesterday.

At the time of the abolition of serfdom in 1861, Russia had hardly any factories. Everything needed in the way of machines, rails, railway-engines, fine dress materials, came from the West. Twenty years later she possessed already 85,000 factories, and the value of the goods manufactured in Russia had increased fourfold.

The old machinery was superseded, and now nearly all the steel in use in Russia, three-quarters of the iron, two-thirds of the coal, all railway-engines, railway-carriages, rails, nearly all steamers, are made in Russia.

Russia, destined—so wrote economists—to remain an agricultural territory, has rapidly developed into a manufacturing country. She orders hardly anything from England, and very little from Germany.

Economists hold the customs responsible for these facts, and yet cottons manufactured in Russia are sold at the same price as in London. Capital taking no cognizance of father-lands, German and English capitalists, accompanied by engineers and foremen of their own nationalities, have introduced in Russia and in Poland manufactories whose goods compete in excellence with the best from England. If customs were abolished to-morrow, manufacture would only gain by it. Not long ago the British manufacturers delivered another hard blow to the import of cloth and woolens from the West. They set up in southern and middle Russia immense wool factories, stocked with the most perfect machinery from Bradford, and already now Russia imports only the highest sorts of cloth and woolen fabrics from England, France and Austria. The remainder is fabricated at home, both in factories and as domestic industries.

The main industries not only move eastward, they are spreading also to the southern peninsulas. The Turin Exhibition of 1884 already demonstrated the progress made in Italian manufactured produce; and, let us not make any mistake about it, the mutual hatred of the French and Italian middle classes has no other origin than their industrial rivalry. Spain is also becoming an industrial country; while in the East, Bohemia has suddenly sprung into importance as a new centre of manufactures, provided with perfected machinery and applying the best scientific methods.

We might also mention Hungary's rapid progress in the main industries, but let us rather take Brazil as an example. Economists sentenced Brazil to cultivate cotton forever, to export it in its raw state, and to receive cotton-cloth from Europe in exchange. In fact, forty years ago Brazil had only nine wretched little cotton factories with 385 spindles. To-day there are 160 cotton-mills, possessing 1,500,000 spindles and 50,000 looms, which throw 500 million yards of textiles on the market annually.

Even Mexico is now very successful in manufacturing cotton-cloth, instead of importing it from Europe. As to the United States they have quite freed themselves from European tutelage, and have triumphantly developed their manufacturing powers to an enormous extent.

But it was India which gave the most striking proof against the specialization of national industry.

We all know the theory: the great European nations need colonies, for colonies send raw material—cotton fibre, unwashed wool, spices, etc., to the mother-land. And the mother-land, under pretense of sending them manufactured wares, gets rid of her damaged stuffs, her machine scrap-iron and everything which she no longer has any use for. It costs her little or nothing, and none the less the articles are sold at exorbitant prices.

Such was the theory—such was the practice for a long time. In London and Manchester fortunes were made, while India was being ruined. In the India Museum in London unheard of riches, collected in Calcutta and Bombay by English merchants, are to be seen.

But other English merchants and capitalists conceived the very simple idea that it would be more expedient to exploit the natives of India by making cotton-cloth in India itself, than to import from twenty to twenty-four million pounds' worth of goods annually.

At first a series of experiments ended in failure. Indian weavers—artists and experts in their own craft—could not inure themselves to factory life; the machinery sent from Liverpool was bad; the climate had to be taken into account; and merchants had to adapt themselves to new conditions, now fully mastered, before British India could become the menacing rival of the Mother-land she is to-day.

She now possesses more than 200 cotton-mills which employ about 230,000 workmen, and contain more than 6,000,000 spindles and 80,000 looms, and 40 jute-mills, with 400,000 spindles. She exports annually to China, to the Dutch Indies, and to Africa, nearly eight million pounds' worth of the same white cotton-cloth, said to be England's specialty. And while English workmen are often unemployed and in great want, Indian women weave cotton by machinery, for the Far East at wages of six-pence a day. In short, the intelligent manufacturers are fully aware that the day is not far off when they will not know what to do with the "factory hands" who formerly wove cotton-cloth for export from England. Besides which it is becoming more and more evident that India will no import a single ton of iron from England. The initial difficulties in using the coal and the iron-ore obtained in India have been overcome; and foundries, rivalling those in England, have been built on the shores of the Indian Ocean.

Colonies competing with the mother-land in its production of manufactured goods, such is the factor which will regulate economy in the twentieth century.

And why should India not manufacture? What should be the hindrance? Capital?—But capital goes wherever there are men, poor enough to be exploited. Knowledge? But knowledge recognizes no national barriers. Technical skill of the worker?—No. Are, then, Hindoo workmen inferior to the hundreds of thousands of boys and girls, not eighteen years old, at present working in the English textile factories?

II

After having glanced at national industries it would be very interesting to turn to some special branches.

Let us take silk, for example, an eminently French produce in the first half of the nineteenth century. We all know how Lyons became the emporium of the silk trade. At first raw silk was gathered in southern France, till little by little they ordered it from Italy, from Spain, from Austria, from the Caucasus, and from Japan, for the manufacture of their silk fabrics. In 1875, out of five million kilos of raw silk converted into stuffs in the vicinity of Lyons, there were only four hundred thousand kilos of French silk. But if Lyons manufactured imported silk, why should not Switzerland, Germany, Russia, do as much? Consequently, silk-weaving began to develop in the villages round Zurich. Bâle became a great centre of the silk trade. The

Caucasian Administration engaged women from Marseilles and workmen from Lyons to teach Georgians the perfected rearing of silk-worms, and the art of converting silk into fabrics to the Caucasian peasants. Austria followed. Then Germany, with the help of Lyons workmen, built great silk factories. The United States did likewise at Paterson.

And to-day the silk trade is no longer a French monopoly. Silks are made in Germany, in Austria, in the United States, and in England, and it is now reckoned that one-third of the silk stuffs used in France are imported. In winter, Caucasian peasants weave silk handkerchiefs at a wage that would mean starvation to the silk-weavers of Lyons. Italy and Germany send silks to France; and Lyons, which in 1870-4 exported 460 million francs' worth of silk fabrics, exports now only one-half of that amount. In fact, the time is not far off when Lyons will only send higher class goods and a few novelties as patterns to Germany, Russia and Japan.

And so it is in all industries. Belgium has no longer the cloth monopoly; cloth is made in Germany, in Russia, in Austria, in the United States. Switzerland and the French Jura have no longer a clockwork monopoly; watches are made everywhere. Scotland no longer refines sugar for Russia: refined Russian sugar is imported into England. Italy, although neither possessing coal nor iron, makes her own iron-clads and engines for her steamers. Chemical industry is no longer an English monopoly; sulphuric acid and soda are made even in the Urals. Steam-engines, made at Winterthur, have acquired everywhere a wide reputation, and at the present moment, Switzerland, which has neither coal nor iron, and no sea-ports to import them—nothing but excellent technical schools—makes machinery better and cheaper than England. So ends the theory of Exchange.

The tendency of trade, as for all else, is toward decentralization.

Every nation finds it advantageous to combine agriculture with the greatest possible variety of factories. The specialization, of which economists spoke so highly, certainly has enriched a number of capitalists, but is now no longer of any use. On the contrary, it is to the advantage of every region, every nation, to grow their own wheat, their own vegetables, and to manufacture at home most of the produce they consume. This diversity is the surest pledge of the complete development of production by mutual co-operation, and the moving cause of progress, while specialization is now a hindrance to progress.

Agriculture can only prosper in proximity to factories. And no sooner does a single factory appear than an infinite variety of other factories *must* spring up around, so that, mutually supporting and stimulating one another by their inventions, they increase their productivity.

III

It is foolish indeed to export wheat and to import flour, to export wool and import cloth, to export iron and import machinery; not only because transportation is a waste of time and money, but, above all, because a country with no developed industry inevitably remains behind the times in agriculture; because a country with no large factories to bring steel to a finished condition is doomed to be backward in all other industries; and lastly, because the industrial and technical capacities of the nation remain undeveloped, if they are not exercised in a variety of industries.

Nowadays everything holds together in the world of production. Cultivation of the soil is no longer possible without machinery, without great irrigation works, without railways, without manure factories. And to adapt this machinery, these railways, these irrigation engines, etc., to local conditions, a certain spirit of invention, and a certain amount of technical skill must be developed, while they necessarily lie dormant so long as spades and ploughshares are the only implements of cultivation.

If fields are to be properly cultivated, if they are to yield the abundant harvests that man has the right to expect, it is essential that workshops, foundries, and factories develop within the reach of the fields. A variety of occupations, and a variety of skill arising therefrom, both working together for a common aim—these are the true forces of progress.

And now let us imagine the inhabitants of a city or a territory—whether vast or small—stepping for the first time on to the path of the Social Revolution.

We are sometimes told that "nothing will have changed": that the mines, the factories, etc., will be expropriated, and proclaimed national or communal property, that every man will go back to his usual work, and that the Revolution will then be accomplished.

But this is a mere dream: the Social Revolution cannot take place so simply.

We have already mentioned that should the Revolution break out to-morrow in Paris, Lyons, or any other city—should the workers lay hands on factories, houses, and banks, present production would be completely revolutionized by this simple fact.

International commerce will come to a standstill; so also will the importation of foreign bread-stuffs; the circulation of commodities and of provisions will be paralyzed. And then, the city or territory in revolt will be compelled to provide for itself, and to reorganize its production, so as to satisfy its own needs. If it fails to do so, it is death. If it succeeds, it will revolutionize the economic life of the country.

The quantity of imported provisions having decreased, consumption having increased, one million Parisians working for exportation purposes having been thrown out of work, a great number of things imported to-day from distant or neighbouring countries not reaching their destination, fancy-trade being temporarily at a standstill,—What will the inhabitants have to eat six months after the Revolution?

We think that when the stores containing food-stuffs are empty, the masses will seek to obtain their food from the land. They will see the necessity of cultivating the soil, of combining agricultural production with industrial production in the suburbs of Paris itself and its environs. They will have to abandon the merely ornamental trades and consider their most urgent need—bread.

A great number of the inhabitants of the cities will have to become agriculturists. Not in the same manner as the present peasants who wear themselves out, ploughing for a wage that barely provides them with sufficient food for the year, but by following the principles of the intensive agriculture, of the market gardeners, applied on a large scale by means of the best machinery that man has invented or can invent. They will till the land—not, however, like the country beast of burden: a Paris jeweller would object to that. They will organize cultivation on better principles; and not in the future, but at once, during the revolutionary struggles, from fear of being worsted by the enemy.

Agriculture will have to be carried out on intelligent lines, by men and women availing themselves of the experience of the present time, organizing themselves in joyous gangs for pleasant work, like those who, a hundred years ago, worked in the Champ de Mars for the Feast of the Federation—a work of delight, when not carried to excess, when scientifically organized, when man invents and improves his tools and is conscious of being a useful member of the community.

Of course, they will not only cultivate wheat and oats—they will also produce those things which they formerly used to order from foreign parts. And let us not forget that for the inhabitants of a revolted territory, "foreign parts" may include all districts that have not joined in the revolutionary movement. During the Revolutions of 1793 and 1871 Paris was made to feel that "foreign parts" meant even the country district at her very gates. The speculator in grains at Troyes starved in 1793 and 1794 the sansculottes of Paris as badly, and even worse, than the German armies brought on to French soil by the Versailles conspirators. The revolted city will be compelled to do without these "foreigners," and why not? France invented beet-root sugar when sugar-cane ran short during the continental blockade. Parisians discovered saltpetre in their cellars when they no longer received any from abroad. Shall we be inferior to our grandfathers, who hardly lisped the first words of science?

A revolution is more than a mere change of the prevailing political system. It implies the awakening of human intelligence, the increasing of the inventive spirit tenfold, a hundredfold; it is the dawn of a new science—the science of men like Laplace, Lamarck, Lavoisier. It is a revolution in the minds of men, as deep, and deeper still, than in their institutions.

And there are still economists, who tell us that once the "revolution is made," everyone will return to his workshop, as if passing through a revolution were going home after a walk in the Epping forest!

To begin with, the sole fact of having laid hands on middle-class property will imply the necessity of completely reorganizing the whole of economic life in the workshops, the dockyards, the factories.

And the revolution surely will not fail to act in this direction. Should Paris, during the social revolution, be cut off from the world for a year or two by the supporters of middle-class rule, its millions of intellects, not yet depressed by factory life—that City of little trades which stimulate the spirit of invention—will show the world what man's brain can accomplish without asking for help from without, but the motor force of the sun that gives light, the power of the wind that sweeps away impurities, and the silent life-forces at work in the earth we tread on.

We shall see then what a variety of trades, mutually cooperating on a spot of the globe and animated by a revolution, can do to feed, clothe, house, and supply with all manner of luxuries millions of intelligent men.

We need write no fiction to prove this. What we are sure of, what has already been experimented upon, and recognized as practical, would suffice to carry it into effect, if the attempt were fertilized, vivified by the daring inspiration of the Revolution and the spontaneous impulse of the masses.

FOOTNOTE:

[10] A fuller development of these ideas will be found in my book, *Fields, Factories, and Workshops*, published by Messrs. Thomas Nelson and Sons in their popular series in 1912.

CHAPTER XVII
AGRICULTURE

I

Political Economy has often been reproached with drawing all its deductions from the decidedly false principle, that the only incentive capable of forcing a man to augment his power of production is personal interest in its narrowest sense.

The reproach is perfectly true; so true that epochs of great industrial discoveries and true progress in industry are precisely those in which the happiness of all was inspiring men, and in which personal enrichment was least thought of. The great investigators in science and the great inventors aimed, above all, at giving greater freedom of mankind. And if Watt, Stephenson, Jacquard, etc., could have only foreseen what a state of misery their sleepless nights would bring to the workers, they certainly would have burned their designs and broken their models.

Another principle that pervades Political Economy is just as false. It is the tacit admission, common to all economists, that if there is often over-production in certain branches, a society will nevertheless never have sufficient products to satisfy the wants of all, and that consequently the day will never come when nobody will be forced to sell his labour in exchange for wages. This tacit admission is found at the basis of all theories and all the so-called "laws" taught by economists.

And yet it is certain that the day when any civilized association of individuals would ask itself, *what are the needs of all, and the means of satisfying them*, it would see that, in industry, as in agriculture, it already possesses sufficient to provide abundantly for all needs, on condition that it knows how to apply these means to satisfy real needs.

That this is true as regards industry no one can contest. Indeed, it suffices to study the processes already in use to extract coals and ore, to obtain steel and work it, to manufacture on a great scale what is used for clothing, etc., in order to perceive that we could already increase our production fourfold or more, and yet use for that *less* work than we are using now.

We go further. We assert that agriculture is in the same position: those who cultivate the soil, like the manufacturers, already could increase their production, not only fourfold but tenfold, and they can put it into practice as soon as they feel the need of it,—as soon as a socialist organization of work will be established instead of the present capitalistic one.

Each time agriculture is spoken of, men imagine a peasant bending over the plough, throwing badly assorted corn haphazard into the ground and waiting anxiously for what the good or bad season will bring forth; they think of a family working from morn to night and reaping as reward a rude bed, dry bread, and coarse beverage. In a word, they picture "the savages" of La Bruyère.

And for these men, ground down to such a misery, the utmost relief that society proposes, is to reduce their taxes or their rent. But even most social reformers do not care to imagine a cultivator standing erect, taking leisure, and producing by a few hours' work per day sufficient food to nourish, not only his own family, but a hundred men more at the least. In their most glowing dreams of the future Socialists do not go beyond American extensive culture, which, after all, is but the infancy of agricultural art.

But the thinking agriculturist has broader ideas to-day—his conceptions are on a far grander scale. He only asks for a fraction of an acre in order to produce sufficient vegetables for a family; and to feed twenty-five horned beasts he needs no more space than he formerly required to feed one; his aim is to make his own soil, to defy seasons and climate, to warm both air and earth around the young plant; to produce, in a word, on one acre what he used to gather from fifty acres, and that without any excessive fatigue—by greatly reducing, on the contrary, the total of former labour. He knows that we will be able to feed everybody by giving to the culture of the fields no more time than what each can give with pleasure and joy.

This is the present tendency of agriculture.

While scientific men, led by Liebig, the creator of the chemical theory of agriculture, often got on the wrong tack in their love of mere theories, unlettered agriculturists opened up new roads to prosperity. Market-gardeners of Paris, Troyes, Rouen, Scotch and English gardeners, Flemish and Lombardian farmers, peasants of Jersey, Guernsey, and farmers on the Scilly Isles have opened up such large horizons that the mind hesitates to grasp them. While up till lately a family of peasants needed at least seventeen to twenty acres to live on the produce of the soil—and we know how peasants live—we can now no longer say what is the minimum area on which all that is necessary to a family can be grown, even including articles of luxury, if the soil is worked by means of intensive culture.

Twenty years ago it could already be asserted that a population of thirty million individuals could live very well, without importing anything, on what could be grown in Great Britain. But now, when we see the progress recently made in France, in Germany, in England, and when we contemplate the new horizons which open before us, we can say that in cultivating the earth as it is already cultivated in many places, even on poor soils, fifty or sixty million inhabitants to the territory of Great

Britain would still be a very feeble proportion to what man could extract from the soil.

In any case (as we are about to demonstrate) we may consider it as absolutely proved that if to-morrow Paris and the two departments of Seine and of Seine-et-Oise organized themselves as an Anarchist commune, in which all worked with their hands, and if the entire universe refused to send them a single bushel of wheat, a single head of cattle, a single basket of fruit, and left them only the territory of the two departments, they could not only produce all the corn, meat, and vegetables necessary for themselves, but also vegetables and fruit which are now articles of luxury, in sufficient quantities for all.

And, in addition, we affirm that the sum total of this labour would be far less than that expended at present to feed these people with corn harvested in Auvergne and Russia, with vegetables produced a little everywhere by extensive agriculture, and with fruit grown in the South.

It is self-evident that we in nowise desire all exchange to be suppressed, nor that each region should strive to produce that which will only grow in its climate by a more or less artificial culture. But we care to draw attention to the fact that the theory of exchange, such as is understood to-day, is strangely exaggerated—that exchange is often useless and even harmful. We assert, moreover, that people have never had a right conception of the immense labour of Southern wine growers, nor that of Russian and Hungarian corn growers, whose excessive labour could also be very much reduced if they adopted intensive culture, instead of their present system of extensive agriculture.

II

It would be impossible to quote here the mass of facts on which we base our assertions. We are therefore obliged to refer our readers who want further information to another book, "Fields, Factories, and Workshops."[11] Above all we earnestly invite those who are interested in the question to read several excellent works published in France and elsewhere, and of which we give a list at the close of this book[12]. As to the inhabitants of large towns, who have as yet no real notion of what agriculture can be, we advise them to explore the surrounding market-gardens. They need but observe and question the market-gardeners, and a new world will be open to them. They will then be able to see what European agriculture may be in the twentieth century; and they will understand with what force the social revolution will be armed when we know the secret of taking everything we need from the soil.

A few facts will suffice to show that our assertions are in no way exaggerated. We only wish them to be preceded by a few general remarks.

We know in what a wretched condition European agriculture is. If the cultivator of the soil is not plundered by the landowner, he is robbed by the State. If the State taxes him moderately, the money-lender enslaves him by means of promissory notes, and soon turns him into the simple tenant of soil belonging in reality to a financial company. The landlord, the State, and the banker thus plunders the cultivator by means of rent, taxes, and interest. The sum varies in each country, but it never falls below the quarter, very often the half of the raw produce. In France and in Italy agriculturists paid the State quite recently as much as 44 per cent. of the gross produce.

Moreover, the share of the owner and of State always goes on increasing. As soon as the cultivator has obtained more plentiful crops by prodigies of labour, invention, or initiative, the tribute he will owe to the landowner, the State, and the banker will augment in proportion. If he doubles the number of bushels reaped per acre, rent will be doubled, and taxes too, and the State will take care to raise them still more if the prices go up. And so on. In short, everywhere the cultivator of the soil works twelve to sixteen hours a day; these three vultures take from him everything he might lay by; they rob him everywhere of what would enable him to improve his culture. This is why agriculture progresses so slowly.

The cultivator can only occasionally make some progress, in some exceptional regions, under quite exceptional circumstances, following upon a quarrel between the three vampires. And yet we have said nothing about the tribute every cultivator pays to the manufacturer. Every machine, every spade, every barrel of chemical manure, is sold to him at three or four times its real cost. Nor let us forget the middleman, who levies the lion's share of the earth's produce.

This is why, during all this century of invention and progress, agriculture has only improved from time to time on very limited areas.

Happily there have always been small oases, neglected for some time by the vulture; and here we learn what intensive agriculture can produce for mankind. Let us mention a few examples.

In the American prairies (which, however, only yield meagre spring wheat crops, from 7 to 15 bushels acre, and even these are often marred by periodical droughts), 500 men, working only during eight months, produce the annual food of 50,000 people. With all the improvements of the last three years, one man's yearly labour (300 days) yields, delivered in Chicago as flour, the yearly food of 250 men. Here the result is obtained by a great economy in manual labour: on those vast plains, ploughing, harvesting, thrashing, are organized in almost military fashion. There is no useless running to and fro, no loss of time—all is done with parade-like precision.

This is agriculture on a large scale—extensive agriculture, which takes the soil from nature without seeking to improve it. When the earth has yielded all it can, they leave it; they seek elsewhere for a virgin soil, to be exhausted in its turn. But here is also "intensive" agriculture, which is already worked, and will be more and more so, by machinery. Its object is to cultivate a limited space well, to manure, to improve, to concentrate work, and to obtain the largest crop possible. This kind of culture spreads every year, and whereas agriculturists in the south of France and on the fertile plains of western America are content with an average crop of 11 to 15 bushels per acre by extensive culture, they reap regularly 39, even 55, and sometimes 60 bushels per acre in the north of France. The annual consumption of a man is thus obtained from less than a quarter of an acre.

And the more intense the culture is, the less work is expended to obtain a bushel of wheat. Machinery replaces man at the preliminary work and for the improvements needed by the land—such as draining, clearing of stones—which will double the crops in future, once and for ever. Sometimes nothing but keeping the soil free of weeds, without manuring, allows an average soil to yield excellent crops from year to year. It has been done for forty years in succession at Rothamstead, in Hertfordshire.

However, let us not write an agricultural romance, but be satisfied with a crop of 44 bushels per acre. That needs no exceptional soil, but merely a rational culture; and let us see what it means.

The 3,600,000 individuals who inhabit the two departments of Seine and Seine-et-Oise consume yearly for their food a little less than 22 million bushels of cereals, chiefly wheat; and in our hypothesis they would have to cultivate, in order to obtain this crop, 494,200 acres out of the 1,507,300 acres which they possess. It is evident they would not cultivate them with spades. That would need too much time—96 work-days of 5 hours per acre. It would be preferable to improve the soil once for all—to drain what needed draining, to level what needed levelling, to clear the soil of stones, were it even necessary to spend 5 million days of 5 hours in this preparatory work—an average of 10 work-days to each acre.

Then they would plough with the steam-digger, which would take one and three-fifths of a day per acre, and they would give another one and three-fifths of a day for working with the double plough. Seeds would be sorted by steam instead of taken haphazard, and they would be carefully sown in rows instead of being thrown to the four winds. Now all this work would not take 10 days of 5 hours per acre if the work were done under good conditions. But if 10 million work-days are given to good culture during 3 or 4 years, the result will be that later on crops of 44 to 55 bushels per acre will be obtained by only working half the time.

Fifteen million work-days will thus have been spent to give bread to a population of 3,600,000 inhabitants. And the work would be such that everyone could do it without having muscles of steel, or without having even worked the ground before. The initiative and the general distribution of work would come from those who know the soil. As to the work itself, there is no townsman of either sex so enfeebled as to be incapable of looking after machines and of contributing his share to agrarian work after a few hours' apprenticeship.

Well, when we consider that in the present chaos there are, in a city like Paris, without counting the unemployed of the upper classes, there are always about 100,000 workmen out of work in their several trades, we see that the power lost in our present organization would alone suffice to give, with a rational culture, all the bread that is necessary for the three or four million inhabitants of the two departments.

We repeat, this is no fancy dream, and we have not yet spoken of the truly intensive agriculture. We have not depended upon the wheat (obtained in three years by Mr. Hallett) of which one grain, replanted, produced 5,000 or 6,000, and occasionally 10,000 grains, which would give the wheat necessary for a family of five individuals on an area of 120 square yards. On the contrary, we have only mentioned what is being already achieved by numerous farmers in France, England, Belgium, etc., and what might be done to-morrow with the experience and knowledge acquired already by practice on a large scale.

But without a revolution, neither to-morrow, nor after to-morrow will see it done, because it is not to the interest of landowners and capitalists; and because peasants who would find their profit in it have neither the knowledge nor the money, nor the time to obtain what is necessary to go ahead.

The society of to-day has not yet reached this stage. But let Parisians proclaim an Anarchist Commune, and they will of necessity come to it, because they will not be foolish enough to continue making luxurious toys (which Vienna, Warsaw, and Berlin make as well already), and to run the risk of being left without bread.

Moreover, agricultural work, by the help of machinery, would soon become the most attractive and the most joyful of all occupations.

"We have had enough jewelery and enough dolls' clothes," they would say; "it is high time for the workers to recruit their strength in agriculture, to go in search of vigour, of impressions of nature, of the joy of life, that they have forgotten in the dark factories of the suburbs."

In the Middle Ages it was Alpine pasture lands, rather than guns, which allowed the Swiss to shake off lords and kings. Modern agriculture will allow a city in revolt to free itself from the combined bourgeois forces.

III

We have seen how the three and one-half million inhabitants of the two departments round Paris could find ample bread by cultivating only a third of their territory. Let us now pass on to cattle.

Englishmen, who eat much meat, consume on an average a little less than 220 pounds a year per adult. Supposing all meats consumed were oxen, that makes a little less than the third of an ox. An ox a year for five individuals (including children) is already a sufficient ration. For three and one-half million inhabitants this would make an annual consumption of 700,000 head of cattle.

To-day, with the pasture system, we need at least five million acres to nourish 660,000 head of cattle. This makes nine acres per each head of horned cattle. Nevertheless, with prairies moderately watered by spring water (as recently done on thousands of acres in the southwest of France), one and one-fourth million acres already suffice. But if intensive culture is practiced, and beet-root is grown for fodder, you only need a quarter of that area, that is to say, about 310,000 acres. And if we have recourse to maize and practice ensilage (the compression of fodder while green) like Arabs, we obtain fodder on an area of 217,500 acres.

In the environs of Milan, where sewer water is used to irrigate the fields, fodder for two to three horned cattle per each acre is obtained on an area of 22,000 acres; and on a few favoured fields, up to 177 tons of hay to the 10 acres have been cropped, the yearly provender of 36 milch cows. Nearly nine acres per head of cattle are needed under the pasture system, and only two and one-half acres for nine oxen or cows under the new system. These are the opposite extremes in modern agriculture.

In Guernsey, on a total of 9,884 acres utilized, nearly half (4,695 acres) are covered with cereals and kitchen-gardens; only 5,189 acres remain as meadows. On these 5,189 acres, 1,480 horses, 7,260 head of cattle, 900 sheep, and 4,200 pigs are fed, which makes more than three head of cattle per two acres, without reckoning the sheep or the pigs. It is needless to add that the fertility of the soil is made by seaweed and chemical manures.

Returning to our three and one-half million inhabitants belonging to Paris and its environs, we see that the land necessary for the rearing of cattle comes down from five million acres to 197,000. Well, then, let us not stop at the lowest figures, let us take those of ordinary intensive culture; let us liberally add to the land necessary for smaller cattle which must replace some of the horned beasts and allow 395,000 acres for the rearing of cattle—494,000 if you like, on the 1,013,000 acres remaining after bread has been provided for the people.

Let us be generous and give five million work-days to put this land into a productive state.

After having therefore employed in the course of a year twenty million work-days, half of which are for permanent improvements, we shall have bread and meat assured to us, without including all the extra meat obtainable in the shape of fowls, pigs, rabbits, etc.; without taking into consideration that a population provided with excellent vegetables and fruit consumes less meat than Englishmen, who supplement their poor supply of vegetables by animal food. Now, how much do twenty million work-days of five hours make per inhabitant? Very little indeed. A population of three and one-half millions must have at least 1,200,000 adult men, and as many women capable of work. Well, then, to give bread and meat to all, it would need only seventeen half-days of work a year per man. Add three million work-days, or double that number if you like, in order to obtain milk. That will make twenty-five work-days of five hours in all—nothing more than a little pleasureable country exercise—to obtain the three principal products: bread, meat, and milk. The three products which, after housing, cause daily anxiety to nine-tenths of mankind.

And yet—let us not tire of repeating—these are not fancy dreams. We have only told what is, what been, obtained by experience on a large scale. Agriculture could be reorganized in this way to-morrow if property laws and general ignorance did not offer opposition.

The day Paris has understood that to know what you eat and how it is produced, is a question of public interest; the day when everybody will have understood that this question is infinitely more important than all the parliamentary debates of the present times—on that day the Revolution will be an accomplished fact. Paris will take possession of the two departments and cultivate them. And then the Parisian worker, after having laboured a third of his existence in order to buy bad and insufficient food, will produce it himself, under his walls, within the enclosure of his forts (if they still exist), and in a few hours of healthy and attractive work.

And now we pass on to fruit and vegetables. Let us go outside Paris and visit the establishment of a market-gardener who accomplishes wonders (ignored by learned economists) at a few miles from the academies.

Let us visit, suppose, M. Ponce, the author of a work on market-gardening, who makes no secret of what the earth yields him, and who has published it all along.

M. Ponce, and especially his workmen, work like niggers. It takes eight men to cultivate a plot a little less than three acres (2.7). They work twelve and even fifteen hours a day, that is to say, three times more than is needed. Twenty-four of them would not be too many. To which M. Ponce will probably answer that as he pays the terrible sum of £100 rent a year for his 2.7 acres of land, and £100 for manure bought in the barracks, he is obliged to exploit. He would no doubt answer, "Being exploited, I exploit in my turn." His installation has also cost him £1,200, of which certainly more than half went as tribute to the idle barons of industry. In reality, this establishment represents at most 3,000 work-days, probably much less.

But let us examine his crops: nearly ten tons of carrots, nearly ten tons of onions, radishes, and small vegetables, 6,000 heads of cabbage, 3,000 heads of cauliflower, 5,000 baskets of tomatoes, 5,000 dozen of choice fruit, 154,000 salads; in short, a total of 123 tons of vegetables and fruit to 2.7 acres—120 yards long by 109 yards broad, which makes more than forty-four tons of vegetables to the acre.

But a man does not eat more than 660 pounds of vegetables and fruit a year, and two and one-half acres of a market-garden yield enough vegetables and fruit to richly supply the table of 350 adults during the year. Thus twenty-four persons employed a whole year in cultivating 2.7 acres of land, and only five working hours a day, would produce sufficient vegetables and fruit for 350 adults, which is equivalent at least to 500 individuals.

To put it another way: in cultivating like M. Ponce—and his results have already been surpassed—350 adults should each give a little more than 100 hours a year (103) to produce vegetables and fruit necessary for 500 people.

Let us mention that such a production is not the exception. It takes place, under the walls of Paris, on an area of 2,220 acres, by 5,000 market-gardeners. Only these market-gardeners are reduced nowadays to a state of beasts of burden, in order to pay an average rent of £32 per acre.

But do not these facts, which can be verified by every one, prove that 17,300 acres (of the 519,000 remaining to us) would suffice to give all necessary vegetables, as well as a liberal amount of fruit to the three and one-half million inhabitants of our two departments?

As to the quantity of work necessary to produce these fruits and vegetables, it would amount to fifty million work-days of five hours (50 days per adult male), if we measure by the market-gardeners' standard of work. But we could reduce this quantity if we had recourse to the process in vogue in Jersey and Guernsey. We must also remember that the Paris market-gardener is forced to work so hard because he mostly produces early season fruits, the high prices of which have to pay for fabulous rents, and that this system of culture entails more work than is necessary for growing the ordinary staple-food vegetables and fruit. Besides, the market-gardeners of Paris, not having the means to make a great outlay on their gardens, and being obliged to pay heavily for glass, wood, iron, and coal, obtain their artificial heat out of manure, while it can be had at much less cost in hothouses.

IV

The market-gardeners, we say, are forced to become machines and to renounce all joys of life in order to obtain their marvellous crops. But these hard grinders have rendered a great service to humanity in teaching us that the soil can be "made." They *make* it with old hot-beds of manure, which have already served to give the necessary warmth to young plants and to early fruit; and they make it in such great quantity that they are compelled to sell it in part, otherwise it would raise the level of their gardens by one inch every year. They do it so well (so Barral teaches us, in his "Dictionary of Agriculture," in an article on market-gardeners) that in recent contracts, the market-gardener stipulates that he will carry away his soil with him when he leaves the bit of ground he is cultivating. Loam carried away on carts, with furniture and glass frames—that is the answer of practical cultivators to the learned treatises of a Ricardo, who represented rent as a means of equalizing the natural advantages of the soil. "The soil is worth what the man is worth," that is the gardeners' motto.

And yet the market-gardeners of Paris and Rouen labour three times as hard to obtain the same results as their fellow-workers in Guernsey or in England. Applying industry to agriculture, these last make their climate in addition to their soil, by means of the greenhouse.

Fifty years ago the greenhouse was the luxury of the rich. It was kept to grow exotic plants for pleasure. But nowadays its use begins to be generalized. A tremendous industry has grown up lately in Guernsey and Jersey, where hundreds of acres are already covered with glass—to say nothing of the countless small greenhouses kept in every little farm garden. Acres and acres of greenhouses have lately been built also at Worthing (103 acres in 1912), in the suburbs of London, and in several other parts of England and Scotland.

They are built of all qualities, beginning with those which have granite walls, down to those which represent mere shelters made in planks and glass frames, which cost, even now, with all the tribute paid to capitalists and middlemen, less than 3s. 6d. per square yard under glass. Most of them are heated for at least three of four months every year; but even the cool greenhouses, which are not heated at all, give excellent results—of course, not for growing grapes and tropical plants, but for potatoes, carrots, peas, tomatoes, and so on.

In this way man emancipates himself from climate, and at the same time he avoids also the heavy work with the hot-beds, and he saves both in buying much less manure and in work. Three men to the acre, each of them working less than sixty hours a week, produce on very small spaces what formerly required acres and acres of land.

The result of all these recent conquests of culture is, that if one-half only of the adults of a city gave each about fifty half-days for the culture of the finest fruit and vegetables *out of season*, they would have all the year round an unlimited supply of that sort of fruit and vegetables for the whole population.

But there is a still more important fact to notice. The greenhouse has nowadays a tendency to become a mere *kitchen garden under glass*. And when it is used to such a purpose, the simplest plank-and-glass unheated shelters already give fabulous crops—such as, for instance, 500 bushels of potatoes per acre as a first crop, ready by the end of April; after which a second and a third crop are obtained in the extremely high temperature which prevails in the summer under glass.

I gave in my "Fields, Factories, and Workshops," most striking facts in this direction. Sufficient to say here, that at Jersey, thirty-four men, with one trained gardener only, cultivate thirteen acres under glass, from which they obtain 143 tons of fruit and early vegetables, using for this extraordinary culture less than 1,000 tons of coal.

And this is done now in Guernsey and Jersey on a very large scale, quite a number of steamers constantly plying between Guernsey and London, only to export the crops of the greenhouses.

Nowadays, in order to obtain that same crop of 500 bushels of potatoes, we must plough every year a surface of four acres, plant it, cultivate it, weed, it, and so on; whereas with the glass, even if we shall have to give perhaps, to start with, half a day's work per square yard in order to build the greenhouse—we shall save afterwards at least one-half, and probably three-quarters of the yearly labour required formerly.

These are *facts*, results which every one can verify himself. And these facts are already a hint as to what man could obtain from the earth if he treated it with intelligence.

V

In all the above we have reasoned upon what already withstood the test of experience. Intensive culture of the fields, irrigated meadows, the hot-house, and finally the kitchen garden under glass are realities. Moreover, the tendency is to extend and to generalize these methods of culture, because they allow of obtaining more produce with less work and with more certainty.

In fact, after having studied the most simple glass shelters of Guernsey, we affirm that, taking all in all, far less work is expended for obtaining potatoes under glass in April, than in growing them in the open air, which requires digging a space four times as large, watering it, weeding it, etc. Work is likewise economized in employing a perfected tool or machine, even when an initial expense had to be incurred to buy the tool.

Complete figures concerning the culture of common vegetables under glass are still wanting. This culture is of recent origin, and is only carried out on small areas. But we have already figures concerning the fifty years old culture of early season grapes, and these figures are conclusive.

In the north of England, on the Scotch frontier, where coal only costs 3s. a ton at the pit's mouth, they have long since taken to growing hot-house grapes. Thirty years ago these grapes, ripe in January, were sold by the grower at 20s. per pound and resold at 40s. per pound for Napoleon III.'s table. To-day the same grower sells them at only 2s. 6d. per pound. He tells us so himself in a horticultural journal. The fall in the prices is caused by the tons and tons of grapes arriving in January to London and Paris.

Thanks to the cheapness of coal and an intelligent culture, grapes from the north travel now southwards, in a contrary direction to ordinary fruit. They cost so little that in May, English and Jersey grapes are sold at 1s. 8d. per pound by the gardeners, and yet this price, like that of 40s. thirty years ago, is only kept up by slack production.

In March, Belgium grapes are sold at from 6d. to 8d., while in October, grapes cultivated in immense quantities—under glass, and with a little artificial heating in the environs of London—are sold at the same price as grapes bought by the pound in the vineyards of Switzerland and the Rhine, that is to say, for a few halfpence. Yet they still cost two-thirds too much, by reason of the excessive rent of the soil and the cost of installation and heating, on which the gardener pays a formidable tribute to the manufacturer and the middleman. This being understood, we may say that it costs "next to nothing" to have delicious grapes under the latitude of, and in our misty London in autumn. In one of the suburbs, for instance, a wretched glass and plaster shelter, nine feet ten inches long by six and one-half feet wide, resting against our cottage, gave us about fifty pounds of grapes of an exquisite flavour in October, for nine consecutive years. The crop came from a Hamburg vine-stalk, six year old. And the shelter was so bad that the rain came through. At night the temperature was always that of outside. It was evidently not heated, for it would have been as useless as heating the street! And the care which was given was: pruning the vine, half an hour every year; and bringing a wheel-barrowful of manure, which was thrown over the stalk of the vine, planted in red clay outside the shelter.

On the other hand, if we estimate the amount of care given to the vine on the borders of the Rhine of Lake Leman, the terraces constructed stone upon stone on the slopes of the hills, the transport of manure and also of earth to a height of two or three hundred feet, we come to the conclusion that on the whole the expenditure of work necessary to cultivate vines is more considerable in Switzerland or on the banks of the Rhine than it is under glass in London suburbs.

This may seem paradoxical, because it is generally believed that vines grow of themselves in the south of Europe, and that the vine-grower's work costs nothing. But gardeners and horticulturists, far from contradicting us, confirm our assertions.

"The most advantageous culture in England is vine culture," wrote a practical gardener, editor of the "English Journal of Horticulture" in the *Nineteenth Century*. Prices speak eloquently for themselves, as we know.

Translating these facts into communist language, we may assert that the man or woman who takes twenty hours a year from his leisure time to give some little care—very pleasant in the main—to two or three vine-stalks sheltered by simple glass under any European climate, will gather as many grapes as their family and friends can eat. And that applies not only to vines, but to all fruit trees.

The Commune that will put the processes of intensive culture into practice on a large scale will have all possible vegetables, indigenous or exotic, and all desirable fruits, without employing more than about ten hours a year per inhabitant.

In fact, nothing would be easier than to verify the above statements by direct experiment. Suppose 100 acres of a light loam (such as we have at Worthing) are transformed into a number of market gardens, each one with its glass houses for the rearing of the seedlings and young plants. Suppose also that fifty more acres are covered with glass houses, and the organization of the whole is left to practical experienced French *maraîchers*, and Guernsey or Worthing greenhouse gardeners.

In basing the maintenance of these 150 acres on the Jersey average, requiring the work of three men per acre under glass—which makes less than 8,600 hours of work a year—it would need about 1,300,000 hours for the 150 acres. Fifty competent gardeners could give five hours a day to this work, and the rest would be simply done by people who, without being gardeners by profession, would soon learn how to use a spade, and to handle the plants. But this work would yield at least—we have seen it in a preceding chapter—all necessaries and articles of luxury in the way of fruit and vegetables for at least 40,000 or 50,000 people. Let us admit that among this number there are 13,500 adults, willing to work at the kitchen garden; then, each one would have to give 100 hours a year distributed over the whole year. These hours of work would become hours of recreation spent among friends and children in beautiful gardens, more beautiful probably than those of the legendary Semiramis.

This is the balance sheet of the labour to be spent in order to be able to eat to satiety fruit which we are deprived of to-day, and to have vegetables in abundance, now so scrupulously rationed out by the housewife, when she has to reckon each half-penny which must go to enrich capitalists and landowners[13].

If only humanity had the consciousness of what it CAN, and if that consciousness only gave it the power to WILL!

If it only knew that cowardice of the spirit is the rock on which all revolutions have stranded until now.

VI

We can easily perceive the new horizons opening before the social revolution.

Each time we speak of revolution, the face of the worker who has seen children wanting food darkens and he asks—"What of bread? Will there be sufficient, if everyone eats according to his appetite? What if the peasants, ignorant tools of reaction, starve our towns as the black bands did in France in 1793—what shall we do?"

Let them do their worst. The large cities will have to do without them.

At what, then, should the hundreds of thousands of workers, who are asphyxiated to-day in small workshops and factories, be employed on the day they regain their liberty? Will they continue to shut themselves up in factories after the Revolution? Will they continue to make luxurious toys for export when they see their stock or corn getting exhausted, meat becoming scarce, and vegetables disappearing without being replaced?

Evidently not! They will leave the town and go into the fields! Aided by a machinery which will enable the weakest of us to put a shoulder to the wheel, they will carry revolution into previously enslaved culture as they will have carried it into institutions and ideas.

Hundreds of acres will be covered with glass, and men, and women with delicate fingers, will foster the growth of young plants. Hundreds of other acres will be ploughed by steam, improved by manures, or enriched by artificial soil obtained by the pulverization of rocks. Happy crowds of occasional labourers will cover these acres with crops, guided in the work and experiments partly by those who know agriculture, but especially by the great and practical spirit of a people roused from long slumber and illumined by that bright beacon—the happiness of all.

And in two or three months the early crops will receive the most pressing wants, and provide food for a people who, after so many centuries of expectation, will at least be able to appease their hunger and eat according to their appetite.

In the meanwhile, popular genius, the genius of a nation which revolts and knows its wants, will work at experimenting with new processes of culture that we already catch a glimpse of, and that only need the baptism of experience to become universal. Light will be experimented with—that unknown agent of culture which makes barley ripen in forty-five days under the latitude of Yakutsk; light, concentrated or artificial, will rival heat in hastening the growth of plants. A Mouchot of the future will invent a machine to guide the rays of the sun and make them work, so that we shall no longer seek sun-heat stored in coal in the depths of the earth. They will experiment the watering of the soil with cultures of micro-organisms—a rational idea, conceived but yesterday, which will permit us to give to the soil those little living beings, necessary to feed the rootlets, to decompose and assimilate the component parts of the soil.

They will experiment.... But let us stop here, or we shall enter into the realm of fancy. Let us remain in the reality of acquired facts. With the processes of culture in use, applied on a large scale, and already victorious in the struggle against industrial competition, we can give ourselves ease and luxury in return for agreeable work. The near future will show what is practical in the processes that recent scientific discoveries give us a glimpse of. Let us limit ourselves at present to opening up the new path that consists in *the study of the needs of man, and the means of satisfying them.*

The only thing that may be wanting to the Revolution is the boldness of initiative.

With our minds already narrowed in our youth and enslaved by the past in our mature age, we hardly dare to think. If a new idea is mentioned—before venturing on an opinion of our own, we consult musty books a hundred years old, to know what ancient masters thought on the subject.

It is not food that will fail, if boldness of thought and initiative are not wanting to the revolution.

Of all the great days of the French Revolution, the most beautiful, the greatest, was the one on which delegates who had come from all parts of France to Paris, worked all with the spade to plane the ground of the Champ de Mars, preparing it for the fête of the Federation.

That day France was united: animated by the new spirit, she had a vision of the future in the working in common of the soil.

And it will again be by the working in common of the soil that the enfranchised societies will find their unity and will obliterate the hatred and oppression which has hitherto divided them.

Henceforth, able to conceive solidarity—that immense power which increases man's energy and creative forces a hundredfold—the new society will march to the conquest of the future with all the vigour of youth.

Ceasing to produce for unknown buyers, and looking in its midst for needs and tastes to be satisfied, society will liberally assure the life and ease of each of its members, as well as that moral satisfaction which work give when freely chosen and freely accomplished, and the joy of living without encroaching on the life of others.

Inspired by a new daring—born of the feeling of solidarity—all will march together to the conquest of the high joys of knowledge and artistic creation.

A society thus inspired will fear neither dissensions within nor enemies without. To the coalitions of the past it will oppose a new harmony, the initiative of each and all, the daring which springs from the awakening of a people's genius.

Before such an irresistible force "conspiring kings" will be powerless. Nothing will remain for them but to bow before it, and to harness themselves to the chariot of humanity, rolling towards new horizons opened up by the Social Revolution.

FOOTNOTE:

[11] A new enlarged edition of it has been published by Thomas Nelson and Sons in their "Shilling Library."

NOTES

[12] Consult "La Répartition métrique des impôts," by A. Toubeau, two vols., published by Guillaumin in 1880. (We do not in the least agree with Toubeau's conclusions, but it is a real encyclopædia, indicating the sources which prove what can be obtained from the soil.) "La Culture maraîchere," by M. Ponce, Paris, 1869. "Le Potager Gressent," Paris, 1885, an excellent practical work. "Physiologie et culture du blé," by Risler, Paris, 1881. "Le blé, sa culture intensive et extensive," by Lecouteux, Paris, 1883. "La Cité Chinoise," by Eugène Simon. "Le dictionnaire d'agriculture," by Barral (Hachette, editor). "The Rothamstead Experiments," by Wm. Fream, London, 1888—culture without manure, etc. (the "Field" office, editor). "Fields, Factories, and Workshops," by the author. (Thomas Nelson & Sons.)

[13] Summing up the figures given on agriculture, figures proving that the inhabitants of the two departments of Seine and Seine-et-Oise can live perfectly well on their own territory by employing very little time annually to obtain food, we have:—

DEPARTMENTS OF SEINE AND SEINE-ET-OISE

Number of inhabitants in 1889	3,900,000
Area in acres	1,507,300
Average number of inhabitants per acre	2.6
Areas to be cultivated to feed the inhabitants (in acres):—	
Corn and Cereals	494,000
Natural and artificial meadows	494,000
Vegetables and fruit	from 17,300 to 25,000
Leaving a balance for houses, roads, parks, forests	494,000
Quantity of annual work necessary to improve and cultivate the above surfaces in five-hour workdays:—	
Cereals (culture and crop)	15,000,000
Meadows, milk, rearing of cattle	10,000,000
Market-gardening culture, high-class fruit	33,000,000
Extras	12,000,000
Total	70,000,000

If we suppose that only half of the able-bodied adults (men and women) are willing to work at agriculture, we see that 70 million work-days must be divided among 1,200,000 individuals, which gives us fifty-eight work-days of 5 hours for each of these workers. With that the population of the two departments would have all necessary bread, meat, milk, vegetables, and fruit, both for ordinary and even luxurious consumption. To-day a workman spends for the necessary food of his family (generally less than what is necessary) at least one-third of his 300 work-days a year, about 1,000 hours be it, instead of 290. That is, he thus gives about 700 hours too much to fatten the idle and the would-be administrators, because he does not produce his own food, but buys it of middlemen, who in their turn buy it of peasants who exhaust themselves by working with bad tools, because, being robbed by the landowners and the State, they cannot procure better ones.

New Edition (enlarged) TWO PENCE

THE PLACE OF ANARCHISM IN SOCIALISTIC EVOLUTION

By
PETER KROPOTKIN

**An Address delivered in Paris
BY PETER KROPOTKIN**

Translated by HENRY GLASSE

AN APPEAL TO THE YOUNG
By Petter Kropotkin
PRICE - - - 2d.

WILLIAM REEVES 83 CHARING CROSS ROAD,
BOOKSELLER LIMITED. —LONDON, W.C.2.—

PART I.

You must often have asked yourselves what is the cause of Anarchism, and why, since there are already so many Socialist schools, it is necessary to found an additional one—that of Anarchism. In order to answer this question I will go back to the close of last century.

You all know the characteristics which marked that epoch: there was an expansion of intelligence, a prodigious development of the natural sciences, a pitiless examination of accepted prejudices, the formation of a theory of Nature based on a truly scientific foundation, observation and reasoning. In addition to these there was criticism of the political institutions bequeathed to Humanity by preceding ages, and a movement towards that ideal of Liberty, Equality, and Fraternity which has in all times been the ideal of the popular masses. Fettered in its free development by despotism and by the narrow selfishness of the privileged classes, this movement, being at the same time favoured by an explosion of popular indignation, engendered the Great Revolution which had to force its way through the midst of a thousand obstacles both without and within.

The Revolution was vanquished, but its ideas remained. Though at first persecuted and derided, they became the watchword for a whole century of slow evolution. The history of the nineteenth century is summed up in an effort to put in practice the principles elaborated at the end of last century: this is the lot of revolutions: though vanquished they establish the course of the evolution which follows them. In the domain of politics these ideas are abolition of aristocratic privileges, abolition of personal government, and equality before the law. In the economic order the Revolution proclaimed freedom of business transactions; it said—"Sell and buy freely. Sell, all of you, your products, if you can produce, and if you do not possess the implements necessary for that purpose but have only your arms to sell, sell them, sell your labour to the highest bidder, the State will not interfere! Compete among yourselves, contractors! No favour shall be shown, the law of natural selection will take upon itself the function of killing off those who do not keep pace with the progress of industry, and will reward those who take the lead."

The above is at least the *theory* of the Revolution of 1789, and if the State intervenes in the struggle to favour some to the detriment of others, as we have lately seen when the monopolies of mining and railway companies have been under discussion, such action is regarded by the liberal school as a lamentable deviation from the grand principles of the Revolution.

What has been the result? You know only too well, both women and men, idle opulence for a few and uncertainty for the morrow and misery for the greater number; crisis and wars for the conquest of markets, and a lavish expenditure of public money to find openings for industrial speculators. All this is because in proclaiming liberty of contract an essential point was neglected by our fathers. Not but what some of them caught sight of it, the best of them earnestly desired but did not dare to realise it. While liberty of transactions, that is to say a conflict between the members of society, was proclaimed, the contending parties were not equally matched, and the powerful, armed for the contest by the means inherited from their fathers, have gained the upper hand over the weak. Under such conditions the millions of poor ranged against a few rich could not do otherwise than give in.

Comrades! you have often asked yourselves —"Whence comes the wealth of the rich? Is it from their labour?" It would be a mockery to say that it was so. Let us suppose that M. Rothschild has worked all his life: well, you also, every one of you working men have also laboured: then why should the fortune of M. Rothschild be measured by hundreds of millions while your possessions are so small? The reason is simple: you have exerted yourselves to produce by your own labour, while M. Rothschild has devoted himself to accumulating the product of the labour of others—the whole matter lies in that.

But some one may say to me;—"How comes it that millions of men thus allow the Rothschilds and the Mackays to appropriate the fruit of their labour?" Alas, they cannot help themselves under the existing social system! But let us picture to our minds a city all of whose inhabitants find their lodging, clothing, food and occupation secured to them, on condition of producing things useful to the community, and let us suppose a Rothschild to enter this city bringing with him a cask full of gold. If he spends his gold it will diminish rapidly; if he locks it up it will not increase, because gold does not grow like seed, and after the lapse of a twelvemonth he will not find £110 in his drawer if he only put £100 into it. If he sets up a factory and proposes to the inhabitants of the town that they should work in it for four shillings a day while producing to the value of eight shillings a day they reply—"Among us you'll find no one willing to work on those terms. Go elsewhere and settle in some town where the unfortunate people have neither clothing, bread, nor work assured to them, and where they will consent to give up to you the lion's share of the result of their labour in return for the barest necessaries of life. Go where men starve! there you will make your fortune!"

The origin of the wealth of the rich is your misery. Let there be no poor, then we shall have no millionaires.

The facts I have just stated were such as the Revolution of last century did not comprehend or else could not act upon. That Revolution placed face to face two opposing ranks, the one consisting of a hungry, ill-clad army of former serfs, the other of men well provided with means. It then said to these two arrays—"Fight

The Place of Anarchism in Socialistic Evolution

out your battle." The unfortunate were vanquished. They possessed no fortunes, but they had something more precious than all the gold in the world—their arms; and these arms, the source of all wealth, were monopolised by the wealthy. Thus we have seen those immense fortunes which are the characteristic feature of our age spring up on all sides. A king of the last century, "the great Louis the Fourteenth" of mercenary historians, would never have dreamed of possessing a fortune such as are held by those kings of the nineteenth century, the Vanderbilts and the Mackays.

On the other hand we have seen the poor reduced still more and more to toil for others, and while those who produced on their own account have rapidly disappeared, we find ourselves compelled under an ever increasing pressure to labour more and more to enrich the rich. Attempts have been made to remove these evils. Some have said—"Let us give equal instruction to all," and forthwith education has been spread abroad. Better human machines have been turned out, but these educated machines still labour to enrich others. This illustrious scientist, that renowned novelist, despite their education are still beasts of burden to the capitalist. Instruction improves the cattle to be exploited but the exploitation remains. Next, there was great talk about association, but the workers soon learned that they could not get the better of capital by associating their miseries, and those who cherished this illusion most earnestly were compelled to turn to Socialism.

Timid, at the outset, Socialism spoke at first in the name of Christian sentiment and morality: men profoundly imbued with the moral principles of Christianity—principles which it possesses in common with all other religions—came forward and said—"A Christian has no right to exploit his brethren!" But the ruling classes laughed in their faces with the reply—"Teach the people Christian resignation, tell them in the name of Christ that they should offer their left cheek to whosoever smites them on the right, then you will be welcome; as for the dreams of equality which you find in Christianity, go and meditate on your discoveries in prison."

Later on Socialism spoke in the name of Governmentalism; it said—"Since it is the special mission of the State to protect the weak against the strong, it is its duty to aid working men's associations; the State alone can enable working men to fight against capital and to oppose to capitalistic exploitation the free workshop of workers pocketing the entire value of the produce of their labour." To this the Bourgeoisie replied with grapeshot in 1848.

It was not until between twenty to thirty years later, at a time when the popular masses were invited to express their mind in the International Working Men's Association, that Socialism spoke in the name of the people, and formulating itself little by little in the Congresses of the great Association and later on among its successors, arrived at some such conclusion as the following:

All accumulated wealth is the product of the labour of all—of the present and of all preceding generations. This hall in which we are now assembled derives its value from the fact that it is situated in Paris—this magnificent city built by the labours of twenty successive generations. If this same hall were conveyed amid the snows of Siberia its value would be next to nothing. The machinery which you have invented and patented bears within itself the intelligence of five or six generations and is only possessed of value because it forms part of that immense whole that we call the progress of the nineteenth century. If you send your lace-making machine among the natives of New Guinea it will become valueless. We defy any man of genius of our times to tell us what share his intellect has had in the magnificent deductions of the book, the work of talent which he has produced! Generations have toiled to accumulate facts for him, his ideas have perhaps been suggested to him by a locomotive crossing the plains, as for elegance of design he has grasped it while admiring the Venus of Milo or the work of Murillo, and finally, if his book exercises any influence over us, it does so, thanks to all the circumstances of our civilisation.

Everything belongs to all! We defy anyone soever to tell us what share of the general wealth is due to each individual. See the enormous mass of appliances which the nineteenth century has created; behold those millions of iron slaves which we call machines, and which plane and saw, weave and spin for us, separate and combine the raw materials, and work the miracles of our times. No one has the right to monopolise any one of these machines and to say to others—"This is mine, if you wish to make use of it you must pay me a tax on each article you produce," any more than the feudal lord of the middle ages had the right to say to the cultivator—"This hill and this meadow are mine and you must pay me tribute for every sheaf of barley you bind, and on each haycock you heap up."

All belongs to everyone! And provided each man and woman contributes his and her share of labour for the production of necessary objects, they have a right to share in all that is produced by everybody.

PART II.

ALL things belong to all, and provided that men and women contribute their share of labour for the production of necessary objects, they are entitled to their share of all that is produced by the community at large. «But this is Communism,» you may say. Yes, it is Communism, but it is the Communism which no longer speaks in the name of religion or of the state, but in the name of the people. During the past fifty years a great awakening of the working-class has taken place! the prejudice in favour of private property is passing away. The worker grows more and more accustomed to regard the factory, the railway, or the mine, not as a feudal castle belonging to a lord, but as an institution of public utility which the public has the right to control. The idea of possession in common has not been worked out from the slow deductions of some thinker buried in his private study, it is a thought which is germinating in the brains of the working masses, and when the revolution, which the close of this century has in store for us, shall have hurled confusion into the camp of our exploiters, you will see that the mass of the people will demand Expropriation, and will proclaim its right to the factory, the locomotive, and the steamship.

Just as the sentiment of the inviolability of the home has developed during the latter half of our century, so also the sentiment of collective right to all that serves for the production of wealth has developed among the masses. It is a fact, and he who, like ourselves, wishes to share the popular life and follow its development, must acknowledge that this affirmation is a faithful summary of the people's aspirations. The tendency of this closing century is towards Communism, not the monastic or barrack-room Communism formerly advocated, but the free Communism which places the products reaped or manufactured in common at the disposal of all, leaving to each the liberty to consume them as he pleases in his own home.

This is the solution of which the mass of the people can most readily take hold, and it is the solution which the people demands at the most solemn epochs. In 1848 the formula "From each according to his abilities, to each according to his needs" was the one which went straight to the heart of the masses, and if they acclaimed the Republic and universal suffrage, it was because they hoped to attain to Communism through them. In 1871, also, when the people besieged in Paris desired to make a supreme effort to resist the invader, what was their demand?—That free rations should be served out to everyone. Let all articles be put into one common stock and let them be distributed according to the requirements of each. Let each one take freely of all that is abundant and let those objects which are less plentiful be distributed more sparingly and in due proportions—this is the solution which the mass of the workers understand best. This is also the system which is commonly practised in the rural districts (of France). So long as the common lands afford abundant

The Place of Anarchism in Socialistic Evolution

pasture, what Commune seeks to restrict their use? When brush-wood and chestnuts are plentiful, what Commune forbids its members to take as much as they want? And when the larger wood begins to grow scarce, what course does the peasant adopt?—The allowancing of individuals.

Let us take from the common stock the articles which are abundant, and let those objects whose production is more restricted be served out in allowances according to requirements, giving preference to children and old persons, that is to say, to the weak. And, moreover, let all be consumed, not in public, but at home, according to individual tastes and in company with one's family and friends. This is the ideal of the masses.

But it is not enough to argue about, "Communism" and "Expropriation;" it is furthermore necessary to know who should have the management of the common patrimony, and it is especially on this question that different schools of Socialists are opposed to one another, some desiring authoritarian Communism, and others, like ourselves, declaring unreservedly in favour of anarchist Communism. In order to judge between these two, let us return once again to our starting point, the Revolution of last century.

In overturning royalty the Revolution proclaimed the sovereignty of the people; but, by an inconsistency which was very natural at that time, it proclaimed, not a permanent sovereignty, but an intermittent one, to be exercised at certain intervals only, for the nomination of deputies supposed to represent the people. In reality it copied its institutions from the representative government of England. The Revolution was drowned in blood, and, nevertheless, representative government became the watchword of Europe. All Europe, with the exception of Russia, has tried it, under all possible forms, from government based on a property qualification to the direct government of the little Swiss republics. But, strange to say, just in proportion as we have approached nearer to the ideal of a representative government, elected by a perfectly free universal suffrage, in that same proportion have its essential vices become manifest to us, till we have clearly seen that this mode of government is radically defective. Is it not indeed absurd to take a certain number of men from out the mass, and to entrust them with the management of *all* public affairs, saying to them, «Attend to these matters, we exonerate ourselves from the task by laying it upon you: it is for you to make laws on all manner of subjects—armaments and mad dogs, observatories and chimneys, instruction and street-sweeping: arrange these things as you please and make laws about them, since you are the chosen ones whom the people has voted capable of doing everything!» It appears to me that if a thoughtful and honest man were offered such a post, he would answer somewhat in this fashion:—

"You entrust me with a task which I am unable to fulfil. I am unacquainted with most of the questions

The Place of Anarchism in Socialistic Evolution

upon which I shall be called on to legislate. I shall either have to work to some extent in the dark, which will not be to your advantage, or I shall appeal to you and summon meetings in which you will yourselves seek to come to an understanding on the questions at issue, in which case my office will be unnecessary. If you have formed an opinion and have formulated it, and if you are anxious to come to an understanding with others who have also formed an opinion on the same subject, then all you need do is to communicate with your neighbours and send a delegate to come to an understanding with other delegates on this specific question; but you will certainly reserve to yourselves the right of taking an ultimate decision; you will not entrust your delegate with the making of laws for you. This is how scientists and business men act each time that they have to come to an agreement."

But the above reply would be a repudiation of the representative system, and nevertheless it is a faithful expression of the idea which is growing everywhere since the vices of representative government have been exposed in all their nakedness. Our age, however, has gone still further, for it has begun to discuss the rights of the State and of Society in relation to the individual; people now ask to what point the interference of the State is necessary in the multitudinous functions of society.

Do we require a government to educate our children? Only let the worker have leisure to instruct himself, and you will see that, through the free initiative of parents and of persons fond of tuition, thousands of educational societies and schools of all kinds will spring up, rivalling one another in the excellence of their teaching. If we were not crushed by taxation and exploited by employers, as we now are, could we not ourselves do much better than is now done for us? The great centres would initiate progress and set the example, and you may be sure that the progress realised would be incomparably superior to what we now attain through our ministeries.—Is the State even necessary for the defence of a territory? If armed brigands attack a people, is not that same people, armed with good weapons, the surest rampart to oppose to the foreign aggressor? Standing armies are always beaten by invaders, and history teaches that the latter are to be repulsed by a popular rising alone.—While Government is an excellent machine to protect monopoly, has it ever been able to protect us against ill-disposed persons? Does it not, by creating misery, increase the number of crimes instead of diminishing them? In establishing prisons into which multitudes of men, women, and children are thrown for a time in order to come forth infinitely worse than when they went in, does not the State maintain nurseries of vice at the expense of the tax-payers? In obliging us to commit to others the care of our affairs, does it not create the most terrible vice of societies—indifference to public matters?

On the other hand, if we analyse all the great advances made in this century—our international traffic, our industrial discoveries, our means of communication—do we find that we owe them to the State or to private enterprise? Look at the network of railways which cover Europe. At Madrid, for example, you take a ticket for St. Petersburg direct. You travel along railroads which have been constructed by millions of workers, set in motion by dozens of companies; your carriage is attached in turn to Spanish, French, Bavarian, and Russian locomotives: you travel without losing twenty minutes anywhere, and the two hundred francs which you paid in Madrid will be divided to a nicety among the companies which have combined to forward you to your destination. This line from Madrid to St. Petersburg has been constructed in small isolated branches which have been gradually connected, and direct trains are the result of an understanding which has been arrived at between twenty different companies. Of course there has been considerable friction at the outset, and at times some companies, influenced by an unenlightened egotism have been unwilling to come to terms with the others; but, I ask, was it better to put up with this occasional friction, or to wait until some Bismarck, Napoleon, or Zengis Khan should have conquered Europe, traced the lines with a pair of compasses, and regulated the despatch of the trains? If the latter course had been adopted, we should still be in the days of stage-coaches.

The network of railways is the work of the human mind proceeding from the simple to the complex by the spontaneous efforts of the parties interested, and it is thus that all the great enterprises of our age have been undertaken. It is quite true, indeed, that we pay too much to the managers of these enterprises; this is an additional reason for suppressing their incomes, but not for confiding the management of European railways to a central European government.

What thousands of examples one could cite in support of his same idea! Take all great enterprises such as the Suez Canal, the lines of Atlantic steamers, the telegraph which connects us with North and South America. Consider also that commercial organisation which enables you on rising in the morning to find bread at the baker's—that is, if you have the money to pay for it, which is not always the case now-a-days—meat at the butcher's, and all other things that you want at other shops. Is this the work of the State? It is true that we pay abominably dearly for middlemen; this is, however, an additional reason for suppressing them, but not for believing that we must entrust government with the care of providing for our feeding and clothing. If we closely scan the development of the human mind in our times we are struck by the number of associations which spring up to meet the varied requirement of the individual of our age—societies for study, for commerce, for pleasure and recreation; some of them, very small, for the propagation of a universal language or a certain method of short-hand writing; others with large arms, such as that which has recently been established for the defence of the English coast, or for the avoidance of lawsuits, and so on. To make a list of the associations which exist in Europe, volumes would be necessary, and it would be seen that there is not a single branch of human activity with which one or other does not concern itself. The State itself appeals to them in the discharge of its most important function—war; it says, "We undertake to slaughter, but we cannot take care of our victims; form a Red Cross Society to gather up the wounded on the battle-field and to take care of them."

Let others, if they will, advocate industrial barracks or the monastery of Authoritarian Communism, we declare that the tendency of society is in an opposite direction. We foresee millions and millions of groups freely constituting themselves for the satisfaction of all the varied needs of human beings—some of these groups organised by quarter, street, and house; others extending hands across the walls of cities, over frontiers and oceans. All of these will be composed of human beings who will combine freely, and after having performed their share of productive labour will meet together, either for the purpose of consumption, or to produce objects of art or luxury, or to advance science in a new direction. This is the tendency of the nineteenth century, and we follow it; we only ask to develop it freely, without any governmental interference. Individual liberty! "Take pebbles," said Fourrier, "put them into a box and shake them, and they will arrange themselves in a mosaic that you could never get by entrusting to anyone the work of arranging them harmoniously."

PART III.

NOW let me pass to the third part of my subject—the most important with respect to the future.

There is no more room for doubting that religions are going; the nineteenth century has given them their death blow. But religions—all religions—have a double composition. They contain in the first place a primitive cosmogony, a rude attempt at explaining nature, and they furthermore contain a statement of the public morality born and developed within the mass of the people. But when we throw religions overboard or store them among our public records as historical curiosities, shall we also relegate to museums the moral principles which they contain? This has sometimes been done, and we have seen people declare that as they no longer believed in the various religions so they despised morality and boldly proclaimed the maxim of bourgeois selfishness, "Everyone for himself." But a Society, human or animal, cannot exist without certain rules and moral habits springing up within it; religion may go, morality remains. If we were to come to consider that a man did well in lying, deceiving his neighbours, or plundering them when possible (this is the middle-class business morality), we should come to such a pass that we could no longer live together. You might assure me of your friendship, but perhaps you might only do so in order to rob me more easily; you might promise to do a certain thing for me, only to deceive me; you might promise to forward a letter for me, and you might steal it just like an ordinary governor of a jail. Under such conditions society would become impossible, and this is so generally understood that the repudiation of religions in no way prevents public morality from being maintained, developed, and raised to a higher and ever higher standard. This fact is so striking that philosophers seek to explain it by the principles of utilitarianism, and recently Spencer sought to base the morality which exists among us upon physiological causes and the needs connected with the preservation of the race.

Let me give you an example in order to explain to you what *we* think on the matter.

A child is drowning, and four men who stand upon the bank see it struggling in the water. One of them does not stir, he is a partisan of "Each one for himself," the maxim of the commercial middle-class; this one is a brute and we need not speak of him further. The next one reasons thus: "If I save the child, a good report of my action will be made to the ruler of heaven, and the Creator will reward me by increasing my flocks and my serfs," and thereupon he plunges into the water. Is he therefore a moral man? Clearly not! He is a shrewd calculator, that is all. The third, who is an utilitarian, reflects thus (or at least utilitarian philosophers represent him as so reasoning): "Pleasures can be classed in two categories, inferior pleasures and higher ones. To save the life of anyone is a superior pleasure infinitely more intense and more durable than others; therefore I will save the child." Admitting that any man ever reasoned thus, would he not be a terrible egotist? and, moreover, could we ever be sure that his sophistical brain would not at some given moment cause his will to incline toward an inferior pleasure, that is to say, towards refraining from troubling himself? There remains the fourth individual. This man has been brought up from his childhood to feel himself *one* with the rest of humanity: from his childhood he has always regarded men as possessing interests in common: he has accustomed himself to suffer when his neighbours suffer, and to feel happy when everyone around him is happy. Directly he hears the heart-rending cry of the mother, he leaps into the water, not through reflection but by instinct, and when she thanks him for saving her child, he says, «What have I done to deserve thanks, my good woman? I am happy to see you happy; I have acted from natural impulse and could not do otherwise!»

You recognise in this case the truly moral man, and feel that the others are only egotists in comparison with him. The whole anarchist morality is represented in this example. It is the morality of a people which does not look for the sun at midnight—a morality without compulsion or authority, a morality of habit. Let us create circumstances in which man shall not be led to deceive nor exploit others, and then by the very force of things the moral level of humanity will rise to a height hitherto unknown. Men are certainly not to be moralised by teaching them a moral catechism: tribunals and prisons do not diminish vice; they pour it over society in floods. Men are to be moralised only by placing them in a position which shall contribute to develop in them those habits which are social, and to weaken those which are not so. A morality which has become instinctive is the true morality, the only morality which endures while religions and systems of philosophy pass away.

Let us now combine the three preceding elements, and we shall have Anarchy and its place in Socialistic Evolution.

Emancipation of the producer from the yoke of capital; production in common and free consumption of all the products of the common labour.

Emancipation from the governmental yoke; free development of individuals in groups and federations; free organisation ascending from the simple to the complex, according to mutual needs and tendencies.

Emancipation from religious morality; free morality, without compulsion or authority, developing itself from social life and becoming habitual.

The above is no dream of students, it is a conclusion which results from an analysis of the tendencies of modern society: Anarchist Communism is the union of the two fundamental tendencies of our society—a tendency towards economic equality, and a tendency towards political liberty. So long as Communism presented itself under an authoritarian form, which necessarily implies government, armed with much greater power than that which it possesses to-day, inasmuch as it implies economic in addition to political power—so long as this was the case, Communism met with no sufficient response. Before 1848 it could, indeed, sometimes excite for a moment the enthusiasm of the worker who was prepared to submit to any all-powerful government, provided it would release him from the terrible situation in which he was placed, but it left the true friends of liberty indifferent.

Anarchist Communism maintains that most valuable of all conquests—individual liberty—and moreover extends it and gives it a solid basis—economic liberty—without which political liberty in delusive; it does not ask the individual who has rejected god, the universal tyrant, god the king, and god the parliament, to give unto himself a god more terrible than any of the preceding—god the Community, or to abdicate upon its altar his independence, his will, his tastes, and to renew the vow of asceticism which he formerly made before the crucified god. It says to him, on the contrary, "No society is free so long as the individual is not so! Do not seek to modify society by imposing upon it an authority which shall make everything right; if you do, you will fail as popes and emperors have failed. Modify society so that your fellows may not be any longer your enemies by the force of circumstances: abolish the conditions which allow some to monopolise the fruit of the labour of others; and instead of attempting to

The Place of Anarchism in Socialistic Evolution

construct society from top to bottom, or from the centre to the circumference, let it develop itself freely from the simple to the composite, by the free union of free groups. This course, which is so much obstructed at present, is the true forward march of society: do not seek to hinder it, do not turn your back on progress, but march along with it! Then the sentiment of sociability which is common to human beings, as it is to all animals living in society, will be able to develop itself freely, because our fellows will no longer be our enemies, and we shall thus arrive at a state of things in which each individual will be able to give free rein to his inclinations, and even to his passions, without any other restraint than the love and respect of those who surround him."

This is our ideal, and it is the ideal which lies deep in the hearts of peoples—of all peoples. We know full well that this ideal will not be attained without violent shocks; the close of this century has a formidable revolution in store for us: whether it begins in France, Germany, Spain, or Russia, it will be an European one, and spreading with the same rapidity as that of our fathers, the heroes of 1848, it will set all Europe in a blaze. This coming Revolution will not aim at a mere change of government, but will have a social character; the work of expropriation will commence, and exploiters will be driven out. Whether we like it or not, this will be done independently of the will of individuals, and when hands are laid on private property we shall arrive at Communism, because we shall be forced to do so. Communism, however, cannot be either authoritarian or parliamentary, it must either be anarchist or non-existent; the mass of the people does not desire to trust itself again to any saviour, but will seek to organise itself by itself.

We do not advocate Communism and Anarchy because we imagine men to be better than they really are; if we had angels among us we might be tempted to entrust to them the task of organising us, though doubtless even *they* would show the cloven foot very soon. But it is just because we take men as they are that we say: «Do not entrust them with the governing of you. This or that despicable minister might have been an excellent man if power had not been given to him. The only way of arriving at harmony of interests is by a society without exploiters and without rulers.» It is precisely because men are not angels that we say, «Let us arrange matters so that each man may see his interest bound up with the interests of others, then you will no longer have to fear his evil passions.»

Anarchist Communism being the inevitable result of existing tendencies, it is towards this ideal that we must direct our steps, instead of saying, "Yes, Anarchy is an excellent ideal," and then turning our backs upon it. Should the approaching revolution not succeed in realising the whole of this ideal, still all that shall have been effected in the direction of it will remain; but all that shall have been done in a contrary direction will be doomed to disappear. It is a general rule that a popular revolution may be vanquished, but that, nevertheless, it furnishes a motto for the evolution of the succeeding century. France expired under the heel of the allies in 1815, and yet the action of France had rendered serfdom impossible of continuance, all over Europe, and representative government inevitable; universal suffrage was drowned in blood, and yet universal suffrage is the watchword of the century. In 1871 the Commune expired under volleys of grapeshot, and yet the watchword in France to-day is "the Free Commune." And if Anarchist Communism is vanquished in the coming revolution, after having asserted itself in the light of day, not only will it leave behind it the abolition of private property, not only will the working man have learned his true place in society, not only will the landed and mercantile aristocracy have received a mortal blow, but Communist Anarchism will be the goal of the evolution of the twentieth century.

Anarchist Communism sums up all that is most beautiful and most durable in the progress of humanity; the sentiment of justice, the sentiment of liberty, and solidarity or community of interest. It guarantees the free evolution, both of the individual and of society. Therefore, it will triumph.

Printed by THE NEW TEMPLE PRESS,
Norbury, London, Great Britain.